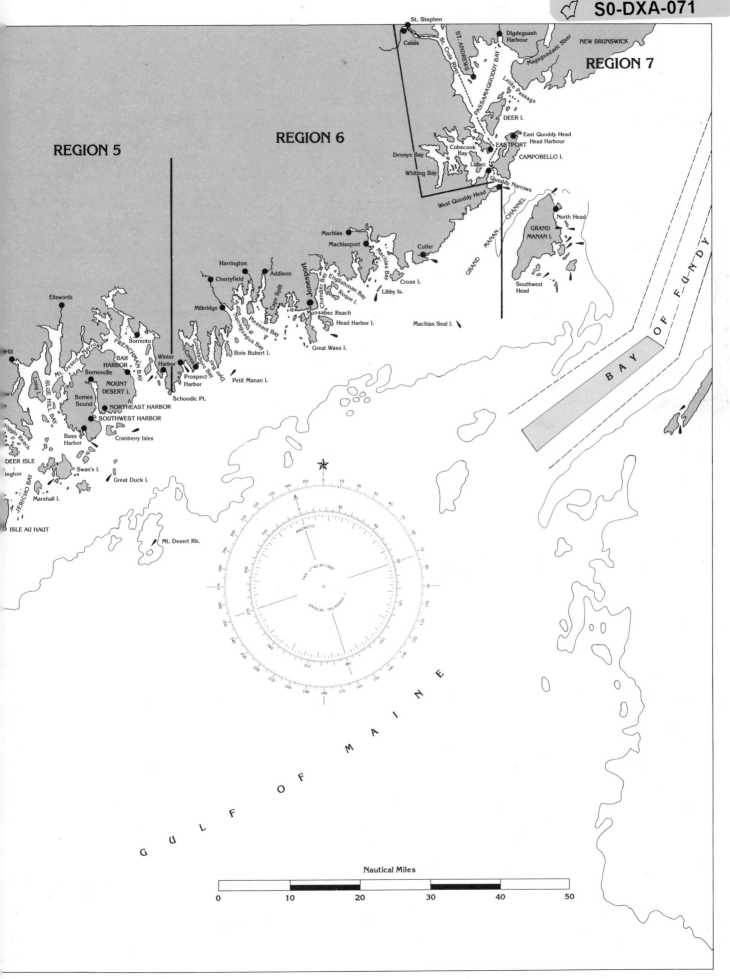

A Cruising Guide to the

M·A·I·N·E C·O·A·S·T

A Cruising Guide to the
M·A·I·N·E

Hank and Jan Taft

C·O·A·S·T

 International Marine Publishing
Camden, Maine

Published by International Marine Publishing

10   9   8   7   6   5   4   3   2   1

Copyright © 1988, 1991 by Henry W. Taft and Jan B.
Taft. Published by International Marine Publishing, an
imprint of TAB BOOKS. TAB BOOKS is a division of
McGraw-Hill, Inc.

TAB BOOKS offers software for sale. For information
and a catalog, please contact TAB Software
Department, Blue Ridge Summit, PA 17294-0850.

Questions regarding the content of this book should be
addressed to:

International Marine Publishing
P.O. Box 220
Camden, ME 04843

Library of Congress Cataloging-in-Publication Data

Taft, Hank.
    A cruising guide to the Maine coast / Hank and Jan
Taft.—2nd ed.
        p.   cm.
    Includes index.
    ISBN 0-87742-282-6
    1. Boats and boating—Maine—Guide-books.
2. Marinas—Maine.   3. Maine—Description and
travel—1981—Guide-books. I. Taft, Jan.   II. Title.
III. Title: Maine coast.
GV776.M2T34   1991   90-25831
797.1'09741—dc20   CIP

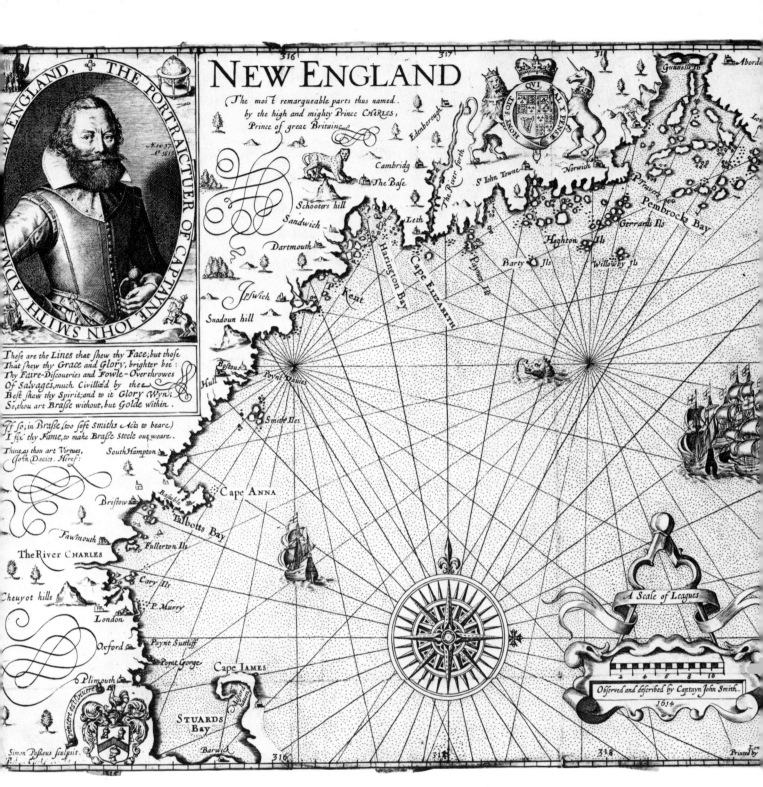

NEW ENGLAND

The moſt remarqueable parts thus named.
by the high and mighty Prince CHARLES,
Prince of great Britaine

HONI SOIT QVI MAL Y PENSE

THE PORTRAICTURE OF CAPTAINE IOHN SMITH ADMIRALL OF NEW ENGLAND

Æ. tat 37. A° 1616

Theſe are the Lines that ſhew thy Face; but thoſe
That ſhew thy Grace and Glory, brighter bee:
Thy Faire-Diſcoueries and Fowle-Overthrowes
Of Salvages, much Civilliz'd by thee
Beſt ſhew thy Spirit; and to it Glory Wyn;
So, thou art Braſſe without, but Golde within.

If ſo; in Braſſe (too ſoft Smiths Acts to beare.)
I fix thy Fame, to make Braſſe Steele out weare.
Thine, as thou art Virtues.
{John Daues. Heref:

A Scale of Leagues

Obſerved and deſcribed by Captayn John Smith. 1614

Simon Paſſæus ſculpſit.

It was Captain John Smith's lyric descriptions of the beauty, lushness, and potential of New England which fired the English imagination and spurred the growth of the new colonies. And it was Smith who realized that the real treasure of Maine was not gold or silver, but codfish. (Library of Congress)

It may be it was not my chance to see the best; but least others may be deceived as I was, or through dangerous ignorance hazard themselves as I did, I have drawn a Map from Point to Point, Ile to Ile, and Harbour to Harbour, with the Soundings, Sands, Rocks, and Landmarks as I passed close aboard the Shore in a little Boat. . . .

Captain John Smith,
The Description of New England, 1616

Contents

Acknowledgments

We are particularly indebted to Philip Conkling, founding Director of Island Institute, for sharing his broad knowledge of the natural world, the Maine coast, and islands. And to Roger Taylor, former Publisher of International Marine, who encouraged this ambitious project, and his dynamic successor, Bob Martin.

Thanks to Kathy Brandes, who pruned the manuscript with a firm sense of style, and to Cynthia Bourgeault, islander, sailor, advisor, and Editor-in-charge, for her unfailing enthusiasm, energy, and literary taste. Thanks to Molly Mulhern, Director of Production, who supervised the art and layout to create a beautiful book, and to Editor-in-Chief Jon Eaton who guided the project to completion.

Many people gave us the benefit of their experience. Thanks to old sailing friends Phil and Fran Snyder, John and Barbara Staples, Jean and Harvey Picker, Bill and Barbara Hadlock, Dick and Ginny Walters, Vern and Alan Sinclair, Throop and Trink Wilder, and Barbara and Will Turner, who reviewed and commented on large sections of the coast. Thanks to dauntless sailing companions Peter and Betty Heimann.

Mike deLesseps, Brooks Thomas, Clark Staples, and Lance Lee made invaluable comments. So did George and Marie Underwood, Sarah and Andy Rheault, Paul and Marty Rogers, Judy Payne and her sons Jim and Bill, Stuart Gillespie, Phil Burling, Dan Amory, Bob Weiler, Chief Al Smith, Bill and Caroline Zuber, Henry Scheel, Jack Sanford, and Ken Black.

Thanks to Charlie Foote, Tom Cabot, Dave Thomas, Ann and Dave Montgomery, Molly Scheu, John Carter, John Burke, Pete Bixler, Priscilla Taylor, and George and Louise Bates for their helpful suggestions. Thanks also to Rick Perry, Dave Jackson, Hank and Marion White, Steve Bailey, Bob and Mary Eddy, Gratian and Barbara Yatsevitch, Bobby Edwards, Jack and Ann Williams, Tom Judge, Ray Leonard, and Dave Getchell.

We appreciated the help of Andrew Anderson-Bell, Frank Snyder, Lev Davis, Bob and Susan St. John Rheault, Bill Page, Nancy and Rudy Talbot, Ann Bresnahan, Sharon Lawrence, George Putz, Vicky Dyer, and Sims McGrath. Thanks also to George Armstrong, Chip Bauer, Ed Dietrich, David Schick, Bill Caldwell, Tom Motley, Willard Wight, Stuart Farnum, Sis and Lyt Gould, Dick Crossman, Chip Porter, and Missy Hatch.

Thanks to George and Jack Gardner, Ellen Higgins, and Ken Rich, who reviewed the material on Roque Island; to Page and Betsy Burr and Caitlin Bunker Owen who commented on Matinicus; to Steven Kress for his knowledge of the Audubon Camp at Hog Island; and to Steve and Jeanne Rollins for their thoughts on Monhegan.

It was a pleasure to have our children, Josh and Jennifer, aboard from time to time, not to mention our constant companion Luke, our golden retriever, who provided love and dog hair in equal parts.

We were fortunate to have the expert advice of Steven Katona, who reviewed the section on whales, of Leslie Cowperthwaite on seals, of Richard Podolsky on birds, of Frank Simon on mussels, and of Jim Mays, who commented on currents, wind and weather. Thanks to many others who reviewed our material on particular islands or harbors and added their accumulated knowledge.

Thanks as well to the many people who contributed to the artwork for this book: to photographers Christopher Ayres, Red Boutilier, Dick Durrance II, Robert Hylander, Neal A. Parent, and Peter Ralston; to designer-illustrator-mapmaker Bob Rose; to Doug Alvord for his bird sketches and Dorothy Lee for her silhouettes. Special thanks to Frank Claes and to the Maine Historical Society for their valuable and fascinating historical photographs.

Acknowledgments, Second Edition

Since the book was published, we have received dozens of wonderfully encouraging and useful letters. Especially helpful were Emmett Holt, who explained the chart errors in Seal Cove, and Andy Nixon, who clarified a confusing buoy in Quahog Bay. Richard Hill was informative about the Cranberry Islands, Philip Crossman about Vinalhaven, and Cynthia Bourgeault about Swan's Island. Lucy Bell Sellers described a shortcut from Mackerel Cove to Minturn, and David Shipler alerted us to an uncharted rock off Roderick Head.

Thanks to Ed Myers, who corrected our description of Allen Island, Bill Thorndike, who updated buoys in the New Meadows River, and Dick Taylor, who told us of changes on Peaks Island. John Armitage sang the praises of radar in the fog, and passed along information on half a dozen places.

Many cruising friends, including Jim and Nancy Payne, Bob and Karen Rooks, Bob and Cynthia Carter, Jane and Joel Leighton, and Jim Hawkins and Ellie Adams shared their observations with us. Howie and Bunnie Hodgson were wonderful hosts in St. Andrews. We were guided and encouraged by editor Tom McCarthy, and again by Molly Mulhern. Thanks to you all.

To our old friends Peter and Betty Willauer—sailors,
founders of the Hurricane Island Outward Bound School,
strong, kind, and wise.

The coast of Maine is a magnificent cruising ground—one of the best in the world—with spruce-dark headlands, good winds, thousands of islands, and a seemingly inexhaustible variety of harbors, remote coves, and snug anchorages. The lobsterboats go about their work, the seagulls wheel and cry, seals bask lazily on their rocks, and in the distance are the tall masts and tanbark sails of a schooner tacking up the bay. There is so much that is beautiful in Maine, so much unchanged.

To be sure, there are more yachts here than 10 years ago, just as there are more transatlantic crossings and circumnavigations. But the coast of Maine remains relatively uncrowded compared with the cruising grounds of New England, Chesapeake Bay, Florida, and the Caribbean.

Perhaps it will always be so. Population has a lot to do with it; the whole state of Maine has fewer than a million people, and it takes time to reach the coast of Maine from elsewhere. But time is not the whole explanation. Maine is neither easy nor forgiving as a cruising area. Except for the southern coast, the shoreline is granite hard, the water is cold; you must deal with fog, currents, and a wide tidal range. And so perhaps only certain kinds of people cruise in Maine.

Our purpose in writing this cruising guide is to provide a new look at the coast as it is today, in greater depth than has been done before. We offer guidance both for the sailor coming new to Maine and for the sailor who knows many of the familiar harbors. If you are in the latter category, we hope to pique your interest in areas you have never before explored.

In the four years it took to prepare this book, we have cruised the coast of Maine aboard our 43-foot ketch *Outward Bound* from the Isles of Shoals to the Canadian border, and beyond to Grand Manan Island and Passamaquoddy Bay. We have visited the outlying islands, ventured up almost all the rivers, and spent time in every significant harbor and in the interesting coves and tickles—more than 500 anchorages altogether.

"Don't tell them about *our* cove," is a frequent plea, one with which we sympathize, and which has caused us some anguish. If the request refers to an anchorage already well known to cruising folk, you will find it listed here. But there are some coves that are clearly a private domain—just room enough for the owner's mooring—and a visiting yacht is an intrusion. These we have omitted.

Preparing this guide has not only been a fascinating adventure in cruising, but also a college course on the coast of Maine. Knowing the history of a harbor we visit adds a great deal to our enjoyment of it, and there's a lot of history here, on this oldest coast of North America. We have spent as much time in libraries and museums as on the water.

Outward Bound, the authors' 43-foot Hans Christian cruising ketch, on a passage Down East.

We don't claim to be dispassionate; in fact, we feel that would be a mistake. This book is full of subjective opinion. You ask, "What did you think of such-and-such a harbor?" If we loved it, we will tell you so; if we hated it, likewise. In matters of safety and protection, of course, greater objectivity is possible. We have evaluated harbors ourselves under as many different conditions as possible, as well as relying on the experience of others.

We accept no advertising and have no commercial interest in any restaurants, marinas, or stores. Those mentioned are ones we found to be unique, or particularly inviting, or convenient for yachtsmen.

While the information here is as accurate and up-to-date as we can make it, some things will have changed by the time you arrive—especially buoys, boatyards, stores, and restaurants. There will be areas you feel deserve more attention, and things we have missed. Help us to improve this guide by sending us your comments (Box 724, Camden, Maine 04843).

Enjoy your cruise!

Preface to the Second Edition

The reception to our cruising guide has been heartwarming, and we have met so many delightful cruising families since the book was published three years ago.

This second edition was undertaken partly in response to your helpful comments, and partly, of course, to update the information. Though rocks and shoals remain the same, everything else seems to change—boatyards, restaurants, stores, and phone numbers; even buoys. We have added a dozen new anchorages, and written about salmon aquaculture, lighthouses, Liberty ships, and sea urchins. Information on currents in Casco Bay and Penobscot Bay is presented graphically here for the first time.

What's new on the coast? More moorings mean less room to anchor in some of the popular harbors. New marinas have been built in Portland and Damariscotta, and more are proposed in Southwest Harbor and Bass Harbor. Major marinas these days are equipped with fax machines, and some have pumpout stations. Facilities for yachts have improved in some places, such as Eastport and Bangor and Matinicus; in other places they have disappeared, Burnt Coat Harbor, for one. Hydraulic trailers are common now, and there are more inland storage areas. Bright shoals of kayaks have come to Maine, paddles flashing.

As traditional fisheries continue to decline, fish plants have closed in several Maine towns, some commercial yards are converting to pleasure craft, and Russian factory ships have appeared offshore. There are promising new fisheries—sea urchins for Japan, and salmon aquaculture. Fish pens, once seen only in Canada, are now moored in a growing number of Maine harbors.

Meanwhile, seals and ospreys are doing very well, and bald eagles are coming back, too. Thanks to the efforts of groups such as The Nature Conservancy, Maine Coast Heritage Trust, and Island Institute, the water is cleaner and some of the most beautiful parts of the coast have been preserved from development. With the establishment of the Maine Island Trail there is better access to the islands now for small boaters.

As people are attracted to Maine, we must all be more sensitive to preserving the environment, and to the privacy and property rights of island owners. Even with increasing popularity, the coast of Maine remains relatively little used, and surpassingly beautiful. We are very privileged.

January 1991
Camden, Maine

Hank and Jan Taft

Preface

General Information

A lot of general information about the coast of Maine is covered in the Introduction, including sections on fog, wind, communications, supplies, and services. We suggest you read this section first.

Regions

This book divides the coast of Maine into seven regions. The regions are shown on the chart inside the front cover and pictured again on the upper corner of each left-hand page. You will also find them listed in the Table of Contents. In most cases these regions are subdivided into still smaller geographical units, also listed in the Table of Contents.

Harbors

Harbors are listed in geographical order from west to east, starting at the Isles of Shoals. To find a particular harbor, check the Index, or use the running heads printed on the upper corner of each right-hand page. These will lead you to the immediate geographical vicinity and in many cases to the harbor itself.

Harbor Ratings

Harbors suitable for overnight stops are rated in three ways:

- Beauty and Interest
- Protection
- Facilities

The code used for the harbor ratings is shown below, and also inside the front cover.

Beauty/Interest

★★★★★ Both beautiful and interesting. Not to be missed.

★★★★ Very attractive or interesting. Worth going out of your way.

★★★ Attractive or interesting.

★★ Nothing special by Maine standards, but still pleasant.

★ Not very attractive.

Protection

☐5 Best protection available; hurricane hole.

☐4 Well protected under most conditions; good anchorage.

☐3 Well protected for prevailing southwest summer winds.

☐2 Reasonably protected for prevailing winds; some exposure.

☐1 Exposed in 2 or more directions; OK as temporary anchorage.

⊠ No protection.

Facilities
All facilities

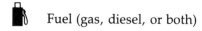 Fuel (gas, diesel, or both)

Water

Repairs

Moorings and/or slips

Groceries (within 1/2 mile)

Laundromat

Shower

Restaurant and/or takeout

No facilities

4- and 5-Star (Flag) Harbors

At the beginning of each region is an overall chart showing all harbors rated at 4 and 5 stars for beauty and interest, or at 4 and 5 flags for protection.

Region head

Bold type shows preferred chart

Sketch map

Running head

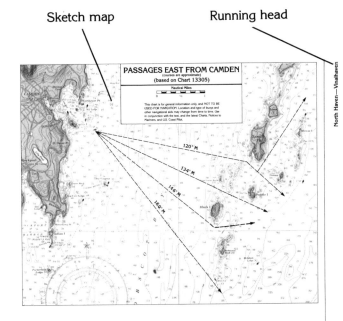

Blacksmith Shop, and Museum. At the end of Conway Road is Merryspring Nature Park, with 66 acres of fields and woods, an arboretum, and marked trails.

A lovely walk that takes in one of the town's quieter residential districts goes out Bay View or Chestnut Street, past Aldermere Farm, home of the intriguing Belted Galloway cattle. If you go beyond the farm, all the way to Rockport, it is about three miles each way.

Windjammers have operated out of Camden for more than half a century. Not only do they offer a wonderful experience for their guests, but their tall sails provide a glorious sight on the horizon. Even

their names are evocative: the *Mary Day*, *Adventure*, *Mattie*, *Mercantile*, *Mistress*, *Angelique*, *Roseway*, and *Stephen Taber*. Some are a century old and converted from the coastal trade, some brand new and built for the purpose. Monday mornings, you will see a procession of these magnificent vessels departing Camden Harbor, their decks colorful with passengers. Some proceed under their own power, but many are pushed by yawlboats until they reach open waters and can hoist sail. After leaving Camden, the schooners spread to all points of the compass to spend the week exploring the remote harbors, small villages, and deserted islands of Penobscot Bay and beyond.

PASSAGES EAST FROM CAMDEN
Charts: 13302, **13305**

Going east from Camden, you will have to pass through the chain of islands that splits Penobscot Bay—Mark, Saddle, Lasell, Lime, and Islesboro. If you are heading for the Fox Islands Thorofare, the easiest route is south of the whole chain, picking up red whistle "8" at the end of Robinson Rock and leaving it to port.

However, if you are bound for Pulpit Harbor on North Haven, or points north, there are several slots through the islands. The cleanest and safest route is between Mark Island and Robinson Rock, leaving the daybeacon south of Mark Island 100 yards or so to port.

The next choice, a bit more direct but not quite as easy, is to pass between Mark and Saddle islands. Be sure to identify East Goose Rock (always visible) and leave it to port. To avoid the ledge east of East Goose Rock, stay south of a line between East Goose and the southern tip of Saddle Island. Give Mark Island a fair berth to starboard, noting the outlying rocks on the chart.

Next north is the passage between Saddle and

Lasell islands—less comfortable because of the ledge (usually invisible) northeast of East Goose Rock. (At least one schooner has fetched up on this ledge.) The safest route is to stay within 100 or 200 yards of Lasell Island. The rocks running out like a breakwater at the southwestern tip of Lasell are visible, and there is a privately maintained marker off the end of the cove formed by these rocks. Leave it to port. Once past the tip of Lasell, continue southeast, leaving Goose Island to port. Or turn northeast between Lasell and Mouse islands, emerging north of can "3" and Mouse, on which there often are seals basking.

Do not try going between Lasell and Lime islands. North of Lime is a treeless islet known locally as "Little Bermuda." The chart shows five feet just north of Little Bermuda, and you can cross this bar with caution on a rising tide.

All of these routes are shown on the accompanying sketch map, with approximate magnetic courses from red bell "2" at the entrance to Camden Harbor.

NORTH HAVEN, VINALHAVEN
and Fox Islands Thorofare
Charts: 13302, **13305**, **13308**

Known collectively as The Fox Islands, North Haven and Vinalhaven are a paradise for cruising sailors. Fox Islands Thorofare provides a convenient and fascinating passage from west to east, and there are enough harbors and coves, passages and bays in the deeply indented shores of these large islands to keep you well occupied for a week. Pulpit Harbor on North Haven is one of the finest harbors in Maine, and one of the most beautiful.

The Fox Islands were named by Martin Pring, in command of *Discoverer* and *Speedwell*, who saw foxes on the islands during his voyage of exploration in 1603. Separated by only a few hundred feet of water, North Haven and Vinalhaven are worlds apart.

North Haven and the Thorofare are home to summer people from Boston, Philadelphia, and New York: Saltonstalls and Lamonts, Cabots and

Watsons. Splendid summer cottages and docks line both sides of Fox Islands Thorofare, and a working lobsterboat here seems like a quaint anachronism.

Vinalhaven is entirely different. Although the population swells in summer, this island never has become fashionable, and the year-round residents are still in charge. The people of Vinalhaven are fishermen and lobstermen from generations back.

Here the names are Dyer and Carver, Arey and Vinal, Calderwood and Coombs. The Reach, the entry to Carvers Harbor, is a working man's thoroughfare, bordered with modest homes. A Hinckley yawl here seems out of place.

As if to emphasize the difference, each island has its own separate ferry departing from the same terminal in Rockland.

PULPIT HARBOR ★★★★★ /
Charts: 13302, 13305 **13308**

On the northwest coast of North Haven Island, Pulpit is only a two-hour sail from Camden, or less than an hour from the Fox Islands Thorofare. It is a marvelous harbor, the favorite of many skippers, with a hidden entrance that reveals itself at the last moment, an osprey nest guarding the mouth, and

excellent protection under any conditions for a fleet of a hundred boats. Once inside, there are plenty of choices for an anchorage, and through the entrance the sun sets over Penobscot Bay and the Camden Hills.

It is customary for several windjammers to an-

184

185

Subregion head

Individual harbor entry

Harbor ratings: Beauty/Interest; Protection; Facilities

Sketch Maps

Sketch maps are included where appropriate to help you navigate a tricky channel or passage, identify anchorage and moorings areas, or locate shoreside services.

Caveat Yachtsman

In preparing this book every effort has been made to provide information which is accurate and up-to-date, but it is impossible to guarantee complete accuracy, and there is no substitute for experience and prudent seamanship. This guide should be used as a supplement to official U.S. and Canadian charts and other publications. The authors and publisher disclaim any liability for loss or damage to persons or property which may occur as a result of the use or interpretation of any information in this book.

How to Use This Book

Introduction

Many harbors in Maine shelter yachts and fishing boats
side by side. (Neal A. Parent photo)

ENJOYING MAINE

WHEN TO COME

July 1 to Labor Day is typically the cruising season in Maine. The days are warm, the nights are cool, and the prevailing southwest winds are light to moderate. Because the short season is well known, there are more boats in Maine during July and August. Don't worry. It still won't be too crowded.

May and early June have some wonderful days of spring sailing, but you are likely to encounter rain and cold as well. The last half of June is often delightful. It may still be chilly, and many facilities will not have opened for the season, but you will own the whole coast.

If life allows it, consider coming in September. In the first half of the month, Maine truly comes into its own. Loons and lobstermen are out in full force, but in many a cove you'll be the only sail. Toward the end of the month, it gets cold in the mornings, with occasional winds from the north.

October has wonderful bright sailing days as well, but then you start to press your luck.

WHERE TO GO

Only 250 miles long as the crow flies, Maine's convoluted coastline measures more than 3,500 miles. There's enough here for a lifetime of cruising. Some people like to come back to the old familiar harbors, others like the adventure of new places, and some like a bit of each.

The best cruising grounds, in our opinion, are Penobscot Bay, Blue Hill and Frenchman bays, Mount Desert and the offshore islands. These waters are dotted with islands and offer an enormous variety of fishing villages, resort towns, and remote coves framed against the spectacular backdrop of Mount Desert and the Camden Hills.

But that doesn't mean you must go way down east to see the real Maine. There is wonderful sailing in the western part of the state, from Kittery to the Kennebec River. Casco Bay has most of the natural features of Penobscot Bay, although, being closer to population centers, it also has more boats. The mid-coast and Muscongus Bay have a reputation for being difficult—a lot of rocks and a lot of rivers. True, but there are also fewer boats and a wealth of new places to explore.

East of Mount Desert, Maine becomes more austere and challenging. To anchor off beautiful Roque Island beach is the goal of many sailors, and others aim beyond, way down east to the Passamaquoddy Bay region, with sparsely settled shores and awesome tides. Perhaps these are things to do, not on your first cruise to Maine, but after you have savored the more accessible cruising grounds of the western and central coast.

PREPARATIONS FOR CRUISING IN MAINE

Because of the rocky coast, frequent fog, chilly waters, and relative scarcity of marinas, cruising in Maine requires a greater degree of self-sufficiency than in the more forgiving waters to the south. Particularly if you are a newcomer to Maine, consider the following checklist:

Equipment. *Anchors.* All the familiar types of anchors are in use along the coast of Maine, but the most prevalent are the plows and Danforths. We much prefer plows here and have had very good experience with our 45-pound CQR, fitted out with 18 feet of 3/8-inch chain and 250 feet of 5/8-inch nylon. It handles sand and rocky bottoms well and is heavy enough to penetrate the weed or kelp found in certain harbors. Although smaller boats need less heft, your ground tackle should be as heavy as you can reasonably handle.

You can cruise most places in Maine without one, but sometimes a yachtsman or fisherman anchor is the only thing that will work—for example, in a cobblestone bottom. For a stern anchor we use either a light Danforth or another 45-pound CQR, depending on the circumstances.

Fenders and Fenderboards. If you are going way down east, be prepared for the boat to take a beating. Sometimes you will be coming alongside pilings instead of floats and often tying up to draggers and lobsterboats. Commercial gear does a better job than yachting gear. Pick up a couple of those big, red fenders used by fishing boats and make yourself a couple of fenderboards. (A 2 by 6 with lashing lines will do the trick.)

Knife, Face Mask, Snorkel, Wetsuit, Prop Cage. There are more than two million lobster pots in Maine, each with its long tethering rope (potwarp), and each marked by a lobster buoy floating on the surface. Given an opportunity, the potwarp and buoy will wrap themselves around your propeller in no time, particularly under power.

Your first line of defense is to stay alert, steering

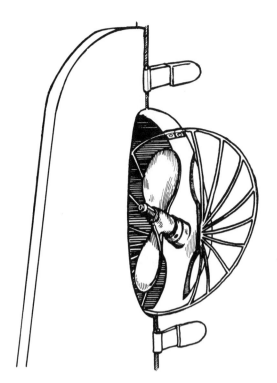

A prop cage is a wise precaution to avoid the expense, embarrassment, and potential danger of tangling your prop in the ubiquitous Maine lobsterbuoys.

over the side and cut the warp off with a big, sharp knife (synthetic rope may fuse into a tough plastic blob). A knife, face mask, snorkel, and wetsuit should be standard equipment aboard your boat. Whenever you have to cut potwarp to clear your prop, try to save valuable gear for a lobsterman by tying the cut ends together.

Since Maine is our home cruising ground, and the loss of half a knot of speed doesn't bother us, we have had a prop cage fitted to our boat, just like the ones on lobsterboats. It has saved us considerable grief. For a single cruise, of course, it's probably not worth the effort and expense.

Warm Clothing and Heater. Nights are cool in Maine, even in midsummer, and the weather is frequently damp and chilly. Bring plenty of warm clothes, especially wool hats, socks, and sweaters. Early and late in the season, a stove or cabin heater is a real blessing.

Screens. Screens are a must to ward off black flies and mosquitoes. At dawn, and especially at dusk, you will be very glad you brought them. In certain marshy spots there are stories of yachtsmen bodily carried away . . . .

Lobster Cooking Pot. The day will surely come when nothing will do but lobsters steamed over an open fire on some remote and rocky beach, and your big, black, 19-quart lobster pot will be your best asset.

Water Container. In many Canadian ports (and some Maine ones) drinking water is not piped to the docks, and it's useful to have a five-gallon container to lug it aboard.

Entering Canada. If you plan to enter Canada, you will want to have a Canadian courtesy flag and long mooring lines (two lines of 100 feet or more). Both Canadian and U.S. Customs will ask for certain documents, including crew identification, boat papers, and rabies certificates for dogs. For further details, see "Entering the United States and Canada" in Region 7.

Float Plan. The Coast Guard urges cruising sailors to file a detailed float plan with a friend or relative. This plan should include the intended route of the vessel, anticipated port calls, and a complete description of the vessel, including all navigation and lifesaving equipment. The persons on board the boat, their ages, and any medical problems should also be listed.

to avoid running directly over the buoys. In many places, it's like weaving your way through a minefield. If you realize that your prop is about to pass over a buoy, put the engine in neutral.

As you sail farther down east, the brightly colored lobster buoy will often be connected to a second float, called a "toggle," which is smaller and less visible—usually a cork or simple white buoy (see drawing on page 7). The two buoys may be 30 feet or more apart; don't pass between them. Normally, lobster buoys float downwind or downcurrent from their toggles.

If you do snag a pot, not an unusual event, you may be lucky enough to remove it with the boathook or back it off with the engine. An experienced sailor, Stuart Gillespie, offers this advice: "Reach for the warp with your boathook, bring it aboard, and wrap it a couple of times around a winch. Nudge the clutch to turn the prop; you'll be able to sense which way it will come off by the pull on the winch. You'll feel the warp come off the prop one blade at a time—thump, thump, thump."

If this procedure fails, someone will have to go

ISLANDS

Some 3,000 islands lie off the coast of Maine, more than any one person can know in a lifetime. There are more islands in the Maine archipelago than in the Caribbean, more than in Polynesia or on the Dalmatian Coast.

About a third of these islands are 10 acres or more in size, of which 14 are inhabited year round, mostly in Casco Bay, Penobscot Bay, and south of Mount Desert. There is scheduled ferry service to about 20 of them—some of it private, some of it

North Haven summer cottage overlooking Penobscot Bay and the Camden Hills. (Christopher Ayres photo)

public and run by the state. It's good to know about these ferries because you will need to keep an eye out for them—and also because they often come in handy for arranging to meet friends and to change crew. For a complete ferry listing, see Appendix B.

Although it might not appear so to look at these remote, secluded little communities today, the outlying islands were in fact the first footholds of European settlement in the New World. Islands such as Damariscove and Monhegan, their history dating back to the earliest years of the seventeenth century, not only were ideal locations for fishing operations, but also were relatively safe from attack by mainland Indians. The mainland itself was not permanently settled until the end of the French and Indian Wars in 1763. Even then, as commerce grew along the coast, the islands remained the most convenient locations, easily serviced by coasting schooners. Fish, lumber, and ships were the early items of trade, followed later by granite, ice, and lime.

With the advent of railroads, coastal transportation was doomed. Steamships replaced sail, and highways changed the pattern of commerce even more. Now the islands were out of the mainstream, and their people started to drift toward the mainland. Island populations peaked around 1900 and have declined ever since. By the end of World War II the islands were almost uninhabited.

Today a new cycle of growth seems to be underway. Islands now are increasingly prized for recreational use and for second homes. Another recent trend has been a resurgence of interest in the traditional uses of islands, such as for lumbering and raising sheep.

Public and Private Property. Although half of Maine's islands are publicly owned, most of these are very small. Not counting Acadia National Park, federal and state agencies and conservation groups

own 1,509 islands totaling 15,457 acres. The other half of the islands—and most of the island acreage—are in private hands.

Mainers have always felt free to land anywhere and use the beach below high water for the traditional purposes of fishing, fowling, and navigation, as provided in the Massachusetts Colonial Ordinance of 1641. But the world has changed. The issue is cloudy when it comes to the use of private beaches for purposes such as sunbathing, picnicking, or simply recreation. Recent court decisions, upholding the rights of coastal property owners, threaten the centuries-old perception that the public has access to the intertidal zone, between low water and the high tide mark. How this will work out remains to be seen.

The state of Maine has recently reviewed the islands it owns and is gradually releasing this information and encouraging public use in cooperation with the Maine Island Trail Association, a branch of the Island Institute. In this guide we have identified state or federally owned land, islands, and parks, as well as nature preserves and areas owned or managed by not-for-profit organizations.

But what about privately owned islands? When is it OK to go ashore? Here are the guidelines we follow ourselves.

● If an island is obviously inhabited, we stay aboard, whether or not the owner is there.

● We feel free to go ashore on an uninhabited island unless it's a wildlife sanctuary or sprinkled with "No Trespassing" signs. Often there are signs indicating how the owner would like you to treat the island.

● If we land on an island we thought was uninhabited, but meet someone ashore, we introduce ourselves and ask permission to explore.

● We try to respect the privacy of people living on islands, and their desire for peace and solitude.

As the islands are repopulated with second homes, and as more yachtsmen, canoeists, and kayakers come to Maine, a new sensitivity is needed. One of the most effective signs we have seen is on a small island near Stonington: "In their absence, the owners know they are dependent on your good judgment and sense of fitness as to what you do. If you value privacy and beauty, surely you will understand that the owners treasure the land on which you stand."

RESPECT FOR THE ENVIRONMENT

Maine is unique; its beautiful coast is relatively unsettled, untraveled, and unspoiled; its waters sparkle, and the air is clean. The environment is fragile, however, and what is carelessly destroyed in a hour may never grow back. Here are some basic guidelines to help preserve this wonderful coast.

● *Leave Only Your Footprints*

Above all, adhere to the fundamental wilderness ethic: Take out what you brought in; leave only your footprints.

● *Wildlife*

Avoid disturbing nesting birds, especially in sanctuaries and important nesting sites. If the parents are driven away, the eggs or young may be abandoned or exposed to predators. Nesting season runs from April to about mid-July.

Seals love to bask on remote halftide ledges. Their uneasy actions will indicate when you are getting too close.

● *Camping*

Most landowners discourage camping on their land. The major fear is fire, which can ruin an island or a headland for a generation.

● *Fires*

Build fires only below the high-water mark: the farther down the beach, the better. If the weather has been dry for a long time, don't build fires at all. (NOAA weather broadcasts will often contain fire-danger information.)

If you find the stones or scars of an old firepit, use that again, and gather driftwood and fallen branches for your firewood, not branches from living trees. Make sure your fire is thoroughly doused and scattered.

● *Trash*

It's OK to throw small organic matter over the side, such as apple cores, but nothing else—especially not cans or Styrofoam or plastic bags, which float and last forever. Don't leave garbage on islands. Save it for some mainland stop where there are facilities to handle it.

● *Human Waste*

If you discharge directly overboard, avoid using the boat's head in a harbor. Use shore facilities if possible.

There are relatively few pumpout stations in the state of Maine. A new law, however, requires facilities that manage 18 moorings or more to have a pumpout station, so the situation is starting to change.

Environmental Advocacy Groups. The pristine beauty of the Maine coast is not just a lucky accident; it is the result of continuing vigilance on the part of many dedicated people who value Maine's unique quality of life. A generation ago, the greatest threat to the environment came from industrial pollution; today it comes from development pressure, particularly along the southern coast. There are many environmental and conservation groups working hard to preserve this beautiful coast. If you would like to support their work, or become more closely involved yourself, here are some of the major not-for-profit organizations influential on a statewide basis:

Hurricane Island Outward Bound School
Box 429
Rockland, Maine 04841
207-594-5548

Island Institute
60 Ocean St.
Rockland, Maine 04841
207-594-9209

Maine Audubon Society
118 U.S. Route 1
Falmouth, Maine 04105
207-781-2330

Maine Coast Heritage Trust
Box 426
Northeast Harbor, Maine 04662
207-276-5156

Natural Resources Council of Maine
271 State St.
Augusta, Maine 04330
207-622-3101

The Nature Conservancy—Maine Chapter
122 Main St., P.O. Box 338
Topsham, Maine 04086
207-729-5181

Yes, the Vikings were here in the New World, though probably not in Maine. Excavation in the 1960s of a Norse settlement at L'Anse aux Meadows, on the northern tip of Newfoundland, confirmed the Norse sagas and the discovery of the New World by Leif Ericson, and probably before him by Biarni Heriulfson. But there was no follow-up to these first voyages, and another half-millenium was to pass before explorers once more braved the western ocean.

The European history of the coast of Maine starts in 1524 with the Florentine explorer Giovanni da Verrazzano. Financed privately by French and Italian bankers, Verrazzano sailed from North Carolina to New York, visiting Block Island and Narragansett Bay, and rounding Cape Cod. His first landfall in Maine was probably at Cape Small. There he encountered Indians, "exhibiting their bare behinds and laughing immoderately," as Samuel Eliot Morison put it, which led him to call the place "Terra Onde di Mala Gente." Estevan Gomez, a Portuguese mariner in the employ of Spain, followed on Verrazzano's heels in 1524–25 and explored the coast of Maine from the other direction.

Meanwhile, the French were busy fighting wars. Though French fishermen had early found their way to the rich banks off Newfoundland, it was not until Cartier's voyages in 1534 to the Gulf of St. Lawrence that France started to develop a real interest in the Americas. Samuel de Champlain, known as "the Father of Canada," established a settlement on an island in the St. Croix River and founded Quebec in 1604. Champlain also explored the coast of Maine as far south as Penobscot Bay and gave us names such as Mount Desert and Isle au Haut.

Many of the early explorers, expecting to be the first to drop anchor in a harbor hitherto unknown, were dismayed to find two or three dirty fishing vessels already there. The fishermen, of course, wrote no accounts of their voyages and kept their favorite fishing banks secret. Thirty-six English, French, Spanish, and Portuguese ships were counted fishing off Newfoundland in 1583.

After a fast early start, with the discovery of Newfoundland by John Cabot in 1497, the English dropped far behind. But by the early seventeenth century, English explorers had arrived in force and were rapidly filling the gap in the chart between Florida and Nova Scotia. John Walker had explored Penobscot Bay in 1580; Bartholomew Gosnold coasted southward from Cape Elizabeth to Martha's Vineyard and Cuttyhunk in 1602. Martin Pring (who named the Fox Islands) explored the coast of Maine and Cape Cod Bay in 1603.

In 1605 George Waymouth made his landfall on Monhegan, visited Allen Island, and explored a great river, probably the St. George. He also captured a few Indians to take home, arousing great interest in London, but also poisoning the relationship between the English and Indians for two centuries. In 1607, George Popham and Raleigh Gilbert founded the Popham Colony near the mouth of the Kennebec River, but this ill-fated attempt at settlement succumbed to one of the severest Maine winters in recorded history—and Jamestown, Virginia (also founded in 1607) went on to claim the title as the first permanent British colony in the New World.

Captain John Smith, Governor of Virginia, sailed up the coast in 1614 to the Isles of Shoals and Monhegan. It was Smith's lyric descriptions of the beauty, lushness, and potential of New England that fired the English imagination and spurred the growth of the new colonies. And it was Smith who realized the real treasure of Maine was not gold or silver, but codfish.

FISHERMEN, LOBSTERBOATS, AND WORKING HARBORS

Generally speaking the native Maine fisherman is a person of honesty, character, and self-reliance; a shrewd observer and a good judge of human worth. Fishermen are also friendly, in our experience, and will go out of their way to help you. More than once in the past few years, a lobsterman has pointed out a ledge we were heading toward, suggested the best place to anchor, or told us whose mooring would be free for the night.

Lobsterboats often run in circles as they haul their traps, and they may appear to be shooting off in unpredictable directions. In fact, the lobsterman is following a pattern, a sequence of carefully defined steps. Knowing what these steps are may help you to keep clear.

Each of those brightly painted lobster buoys dotting the surface of the water is attached by a long length of line (potwarp) to one or more traps (or "pots," as they are known west of Rockland), set on the bottom with a brick or stone to weight it down. Often one buoy marks a string of traps. Lobster buoys are often attached by a length of line to another float, called a "toggle," whose purpose is to keep the line off the bottom at low tide.

In the course of a hauling day, the lobsterman will work his way around to as many of his traps as he can. Using a hydraulic hauler to bring his traps aboard, he throws out seaweed, crabs, female lobsters carrying eggs, and lobsters that are too short. The trap is rebaited and dropped over the side;

then on to the next trap. Each lobsterman has his own buoy colors, registered with the state and displayed on his boat; you can scan the waters for his colors and guess which way he'll head next. Even so, he may surprise you. Stay clear; give him plenty of room; don't insist on your right of way. These people are earning a living.

It's easy to foul your propeller with a lobster buoy, or by running between a buoy and the accompanying toggle. For a discussion of how to avoid the problem and what to do when it happens, see Preparations for Cruising Maine (page 2).

Never haul a lobster trap, even out of curiosity or if you plan to leave money. You're likely to have your mooring line cut (and rightly so, many would say).

Lobstering is not the only fishery in Maine. Fishing boats may be towing nets astern and unable to change course or stop. Don't insist on your right of way. Be alert to nets strung across the

mouths of coves, or in circles marked by little floats or dories. Fouling a net could be a real mess, and expensive—especially if you release a large catch.

Many harbors in Maine shelter yachts and fishing boats side by side in peaceful coexistence, but then there are also strictly working harbors, jammed full of lobsterboats and draggers, with no facilities for yachts and little interest in anything but the fishing business. Cape Porpoise, Friendship, South Bristol, and Carvers Harbor are good examples—as are most of the harbors east of Mount Desert.

For the yachtsman, working harbors can be difficult—no guest moorings, no yacht clubs, no fuel floats, a great bustle of lobsterboats coming and going. Just for this reason, the working harbors are fascinating places to visit. These communities have a culture and language all their own. This is Maine the way it has been for 200 years.

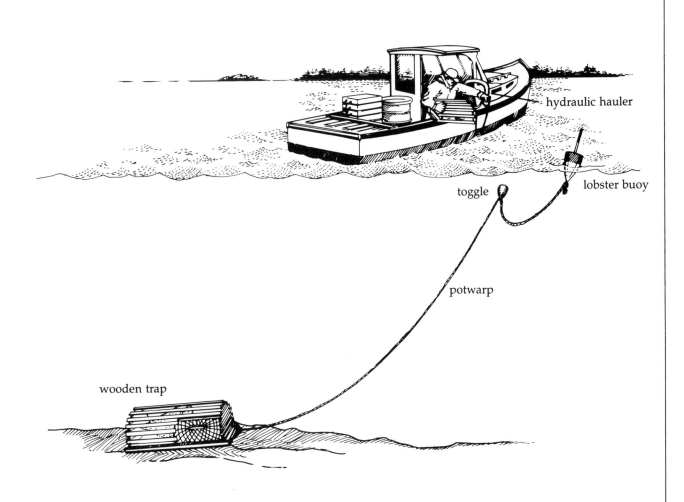

hydraulic hauler

lobster buoy

toggle

potwarp

wooden trap

The lobstering operation. (Pat Rossi illustration)

In these communities, where self-sufficiency and reticence are a way of life, try to adapt to the local mores. Don't feel you have the absolute right to be there; don't demand to be serviced. Give way to the lobsterboats at the fuel dock, and wait for a lull in the activity to seek services or ask questions. Perhaps the less help you expect, the more you will get.

MOORINGS

Rental moorings for transients are common in the western and central part of the Maine coast. East of Mount Desert, they are rare. Be prepared to anchor.

On the subject of mooring etiquette, many cruising yachts seem driven to pick up a mooring, any mooring, as long as it's close to their desired destination, without any apparent regard as to who owns it or whether it's adequate. Violations of reasonable behavior are altogether too frequent.

Here are some suggestions:

• Find out who is in charge of moorings. In harbors with mostly pleasure boats, it may be the yacht club, the harbormaster, or one or more boatyards. Often transient moorings are marked "rental," or identified by a special color or by a club or yard's initials. In working harbors, there usually is a harbormaster; if not, you can inquire at the lobster co-op or ask a fisherman nearby.

• If there is no one around to ask, either anchor or else pick up a mooring temporarily and go ashore to inquire. Leave aboard crew competent to move the boat in case the owner returns.

• Never leave your boat unattended on an unknown mooring. Imagine a fisherman or yachtsman coming home late at night and finding your boat on his mooring, locked up and silent. What does he do? Cut you loose? Where does he moor his own boat?

In certain harbors along the southern coast and Casco Bay, there's no one in charge and it seems to be first come, first served. We still prefer to anchor, unless the holding ground is poor.

• There used to be guest moorings everywhere, maintained by yacht clubs or towns for the convenience of visiting yachts. Unfortunately, with a few notable exceptions, the day of the free guest mooring has passed. Expect to pay a mooring fee of $15 to $20 a night.

SUPPLIES AND SERVICES

The supplies and services that you are used to elsewhere are available on the coast of Maine; they're just stretched a little thinner. Marinas become scarcer as you sail farther east, and almost nonexistent beyond Mount Desert. There you will be dependent on facilities that service fishermen—not as convenient, but a lot more interesting. In fact, this adds a great deal of flavor to cruising down east.

Fuel. Gas and diesel can be found everywhere. East of Mount Desert, you will sometimes have to tie up alongside pilings. In some remote coves, way down east and in Canada, fuel may be delivered by truck.

Water. Good water in reasonable quantities is generally available without charge all along the coast. In certain places dependent on wells, the supply is limited.

Ice. Ice is also easy to find, either in cubes or blocks. Most marinas and many markets have ice machines. Way down east, you may have to go to a fish plant or a lobstermen's co-op and get chipped ice.

Propane and CNG. Propane is available in the larger harbors. In smaller harbors, you may be able to get refills from shops that cater to trailers and mobile homes. CNG can be found in a few places and soon should become more widely available.

Repairs. Hull and engine repairs can be made in boatyards all along the coast, most of them described in this book. Farther east, as marinas and boatyards dwindle, you will become more dependent on your own resources. Remember that lobstermen and fishermen do their own work on their boats, and most of them are good mechanics.

In addition, you should be aware of services that can haul your boat almost anywhere on the coast (wherever there is access to the water), using a large hydraulic trailer. Your boat can then be transported at a very reasonable cost to the nearest yard for repairs. One of the first to offer this service was Midcoast Marine Services, Inc., whom you can call at 207-563-3030. For other such services, see boat transporting in the Yellow Pages.

NAVIGATING DOWN EAST

WEATHER

Weather in Maine is changeable—not only from day to day but from place to place. It is not at all surprising to find quite different conditions in two coastal locations less than 50 miles apart. As Mark Twain put it: "I reverently believe that the Maker who made us all makes everything in New England but the weather. I don't know who makes that, but I think it must be raw apprentices in the weather-clerk's factory . . . . "

A Typical Summer Day. Summer weather in Maine is generally pleasant, especially on the water and in coastal areas. On a typical summer day, the breeze is light in the early morning, gradually building up to 15 knots or so from the southwest, reaching its greatest strength in the afternoon, and diminishing before sunset.

Weather Patterns. The second half of June is often delightful for sailing, cool and sunny. Temperatures are mildest during July and August, but this is also when fog is most frequent. September, too, can bring wonderful sailing weather. In late September and October, you will encounter an increasing number of strong winds, with a northerly component.

And then there are the exceptional years. After five or six summers of normal weather, with a preponderance of bright, sunny days and southwesterlies, a summer will come when nothing is normal, the sun is seldom seen, the fog lingers for a week or two at a stretch, and there are frequent winds from the north or northwest.

Fog. July and August are the most common months for fog, but it can occur any time of year.

There is a general belief that fog comes with calm or light winds. Often this is not the case in Maine; don't be surprised to find fog and a brisk wind at the same time. Be prepared for fog to close in with only a few minutes' notice; take bearings while you still can, and have in mind a destination that is easy to reach in low visibility. For a more detailed discussion of fog, see ahead.

Prevailing Winds. The prevailing wind in the summer is from the southwest, usually no more than 15 or 20 knots, and often less. Morning calms are frequent in sheltered waters along the coast. Winds from anywhere in the east usually bring fog, drizzle, and generally gray, unpleasant weather.

Winds from the northwest are typically clearing winds bringing sparkling visibility but gusty sailing conditions. Strongest right after the front has passed, they tend to taper off after several hours and shift southwesterly.

Gales and Hurricanes. During spring and summer, the strongest winds are generated by fronts and thunderstorms. Although the prevailing summer wind is a moderate southwesterly, don't assume that everything from that direction is benign. When the weather forecasters start talking about southwest winds of 20 or 30 knots, you can expect periods of higher winds as well. In a given summer, there may be two or three gales (34 to 47 knots) from the south.

Hurricane season is June through October, but hurricanes are infrequent in Maine, usually dissipating over land before arriving here, or heading out to sea. Since hurricanes are tracked from their

Wind direction by month, based on observations made over a five-year period in Rockland, Maine. (U.S. Coast Pilot)

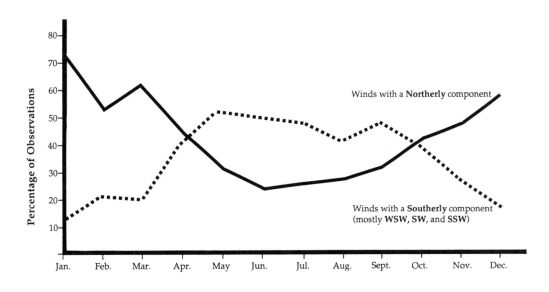

inception in the Caribbean or the Gulf of Mexico, there always is several days' warning. For more on hurricanes and hurricane holes, see ahead.

Downdrafts. There are many places on the coast of Maine where hills and mountains are close to the coast, and where you should be on the look-out for fluky winds and downdrafts unrelated to general weather patterns. Among areas subject to these are the shoreline just north of Camden, Egge-moggin Reach, Somes Sound, and Devils Head in the St. Croix River.

Weather Forecasts. We are fortunate to have reasonably current weather forecasts always available through NOAA Weather Radio on VHF channels 1, 2, and 3, and there are similar broadcasts in Canada. Usually these forecasts are quite good; occasionally they are badly off the mark or too late to be helpful. This happens, in part, because NOAA paints with a broad brush (Eastport to the Merrimac River and up to 25 miles offshore), and, as mentioned earlier, local conditions often vary significantly from the general picture. The forecast for the offshore Gulf of Maine may be seriously misleading for coastal waters.

Caveat Yachtsman. Take all weather forecasts with a grain of salt. Consult the sky and consult your own barometer. A rapidly falling glass may mean much worse weather than the radio is predicting. Have a fallback anchorage to run for if the wind blows up too strong or from the wrong quarter. Use more scope than demanded by weather conditions at the time you anchor.

Weather always seems to clear reluctantly—usually later than suggested by the weather forecast.

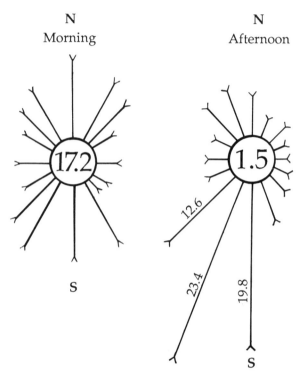

Average direction of morning and afternoon winds, May through September, based on observations made over a 21-year period in Brunswick, Maine. The length of the arrow in the wind rose shows percentage of observations, as measured by the scale below. The number in the circle indicates percentage of calms. (U.S. Coast Pilot)

Percentage of Observations

0   5   10   15   20   25   30

N
Morning

N
Afternoon

17.2

1.5

12.6

23.4

19.8

S

S

Morning observations were made between 0600 and 0800, afternoon observations between 1500 and 1700, local standard time.

HURRICANES AND HURRICANE HOLES

Since the 1938 hurricane, which devastated New England, Maine has been seriously affected by only five other hurricanes, most recently by Gloria in 1985. Here's the 50-year history:

Sept. 21, 1938	Hurricane of '38
Aug. 31, 1954	Carol
Sept. 12, 1954	Edna
Sept. 12, 1960	Donna
Oct. 29, 1963	Ginny
Sept. 27, 1985	Gloria

Although hurricanes can strike anytime from June through October, for the past 50 years all except one have hit Maine in September (give or take a day). Of course, hurricanes and hurricane tracks are highly erratic, and there is no assurance that the next one might not arrive at any time during the hurricane season.

The hurricane of 1938 came more or less as a surprise, in an era when observations of tropical storms and forecasting techniques were rudimentary. Today tropical depressions are usually identified shortly after they form and tracked by plane and satellite until they whirl off to oblivion. Frequent early warnings are broadcast on commercial radio and TV, as well as on NOAA Weather Radio.

Despite their infrequency, hurricanes do hit Maine, so if one is on its way, what should you do?

The first decision is whether to haul the boat or leave her in the water. With a hurricane approaching, many people have their boats hauled. If it's near the end of the season, why not? Even in mid-season, it could certainly be worth the trouble and expense if the hurricane did come through. And it avoids the difficult decision of whether or not to be aboard the boat when the storm hits.

If you decide not to have the boat hauled, or the yard cannot handle you, then you must find the best possible harbor to protect your boat—a hurricane hole.

Scattered along the coast of Maine are a number of coves, harbors, rivers, and hideaways so well protected by surrounding land that they truly constitute hurricane holes. What makes a good one?

- completely landlocked
- good holding ground
- enough swinging room
- deep enough; not so deep as to require excessive scope
- not so large that there is a lot of fetch (waves are more damaging than wind in causing a boat to drag)

Some places that meet these criteria are already crowded with moored boats, and a transient yachtsman wouldn't have a chance (e.g., the western end of Boothbay Harbor). Other places that make excellent hurricane holes are difficult to enter under the best of conditions and impossible in bad visibility or heavy weather, particularly for strangers (e.g., Eastern Branch in Johns Bay). You might be able to use one of these if you arrived well ahead. Some of the best hurricane holes are not normally crowded, but they fill up quickly. Get there early.

It is somehow comforting to be in the same harbor with a lot of other boats. On the other hand, much of the damage in a hurricane is caused by boats dragging, snagging anchor rodes, and crashing into others. There is a lot to be said for being in a safe harbor all by yourself, or with only a few other boats. In Maine, that's still possible.

A sloop on the ledges of Rockport Harbor in the aftermath of Hurricane *Gloria*, September 1985. (Neal A. Parent photo)

For each of the seven regions of this cruising guide there is a chart identifying good hurricane holes. We have anchored in each of these recommended hurricane holes and talked to people who have used them under severe conditions. Nevertheless, each blow is different, and you must make your own choice.

FOG

Fog is a fact of life on the coast of Maine, most likely to occur in the months of July and August, but quite common from May through September. While the monthly pattern is well established, as shown in the accompanying graph, it varies a great deal from year to year. Sometimes you will be shut in for a day or two by fog; sometimes it may last a week or more.

In the western part of the state, the foggiest areas are Halfway Rock, at the entrance to Casco Bay, and Cape Elizabeth. Fog is also frequent around the outlying islands of Matinicus and Monhegan. The farther east you go, the more likely you will encounter it, especially in the area between Petit Manan and West Quoddy Head. Fog is much less frequent as you go up rivers such as the Kennebec and Penobscot.

Fog is formed by warm continental air flowing over colder waters, causing the moisture in the air to condense. Usually this occurs in Maine as the prevailing southwest summer winds blow off the land, producing a "smoky sou'wester." Often you will see a distinct bank of fog lying offshore, or it may just thicken around you without warning. Morning fog may "burn off" by noon or early afternoon.

In his famous book *Summer Island*, photographer Eliot Porter describes typical conditions for a foggy day: "A day that starts with a glassy bay and a clear sky, but with a white band of haze barely obscuring the southern horizon—the kind of day that promises to be warm—is a day to avoid. The faint white blending of sea and sky . . . usually indicates offshore fog that will come rolling in as the prevailing southerly afternoon breezes spring up . . . . "

Coping with Fog. If you are planning a trip to Maine's outlying islands, or to Grand Manan, the best time to avoid fog is during or after a period of northwest winds.

Although fog requires alert seamanship and careful navigation, it is not the end of the world. In

light or patchy fog, it can be an exhilarating experience to find your way from buoy to buoy, occasionally catching a glimpse of an island or headland to confirm your track—all the while sharpening your piloting skills. But when the fog shows signs of shutting down thick and heavy and inpenetrable, then it's good to be safe in port. Break out the books and cards and games and prepare to entertain yourselves. This is a rocky and dangerous coast, and it is no fun to be out there cruising around in zero visibility—Loran or no Loran.

If the fog closes down while you are at sea, get a good visual fix before everything disappears, and head for that safe and easy-to-enter harbor that you had in mind all along. Keep a careful DR, making allowance for current, which can best be judged by observing lobster buoys. Take your time, and use all your senses, particularly sound and smell. Set a bow watch. Use the depthsounder as a check on your DR.

Run for buoys with sound, either under sail or power. Sail has advantages because you can hear better; power has advantages because you can run straight lines and make faster passages, reducing the chances of missing a buoy. Remember that fog often distorts the direction of the sound of a bell or horn, and sometimes it will be almost inaudible upwind.

When sound buoys are scarce, navigate by heading toward bold shores (Great Wass Island and Mount Desert are examples). You will hear the waves breaking and probably see a dim white line of surf through the fog in plenty of time to tack offshore again.

One of the greatest dangers in fog along the Maine coastline is being run down by another boat. Your best insurance is to move slowly, listening for the sound of engines; have a good radar reflector aloft; and sound your own foghorn as required. Fishermen often have radar but seldom use it regularly, nor are they likely to be blowing their foghorns.

In areas of heavy commercial traffic, such as Portland or Penobscot Bay, your knowledge of the "Securité" safety signal on the radiotelephone could be a lifesaver in heavy fog. When you hear large engines in the fog, or have reason to believe a ferry or commercial vessel is approaching, get up

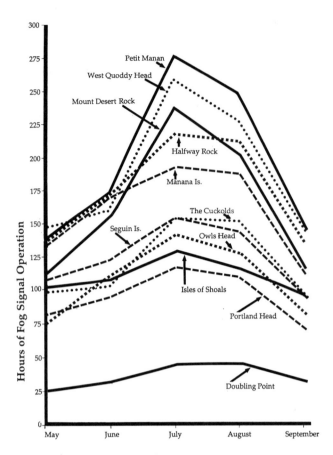

Monthly fog patterns, Isles of Shoals to West Quoddy Head, based on an average of 14 years of observations at U.S. Coast Guard Stations, 1950—63.

on channel 16 of your VHF; call "Securité, Securité, Securité," (pronounced "Say-curitay"). Then, "This is the sailing vessel *Intrepid*, en route North Haven to Camden on course 350 magnetic, speed 5 knots. Vessels in the vicinity please identify."

Loran has made a great deal of difference in low-visibility navigation. It is most useful and reliable in the fog when you have written down the coordinates of important waypoints, or of the sea buoys marking the harbor you want to reach. Great as Loran is, however, it is not infallible, and certainly not a substitute for good visibility or careful piloting.

Radar, of course, is of great value in the fog, both for avoiding collisions and for navigation. It is used by most fishing boats in Maine and increasingly by pleasure craft.

TIDES AND TIDAL CURRENTS

Yes, there is fog here, and the coast is rocky, but the factor most unique to this coast is the great range of tides, and the resulting currents. For the cruising sailor accustomed to a tidal range of 1 or 2 feet in Chesapeake Bay, Florida, or the Caribbean, or even 7 feet in Long Island Sound, a rise and fall of 11 feet in Penobscot Bay and 20 feet in Passa-

maquoddy Bay is a challenge. But remember that sailors and fishermen have been dealing with these tides for hundreds of years. Once you know what to expect, it's just a matter of gaining a little experience.

Spring Tides and Neap Tides. As every school-child learns, tides are caused by the gravitational

Location	Tidal Range (in Feet)	
	Mean	Spring
Kittery Point	8.7	10.0
Portland	9.1	10.4
Boothbay Harbor	8.8	10.1
Tenants Harbor	9.3	10.6
Pulpit Harbor (North Haven)	9.8	11.1
Bar Harbor (Mount Desert)	10.6	12.2
Roque Island Harbor	12.3	14.0
Cutler (Little River)	13.5	15.4
Eastport	18.4	20.9
Calais	20.0	22.8
*North Head (Grand Manan)	17.9	24.0 (Large)
*St. Andrews (Passamaquoddy Bay)	19.6	27.2 (Large)

*Canadian tide tables show "Large Tides" rather than spring tides. The two countries also use different data to calculate tidal ranges; for the same location the tidal range shown in Canadian tables is somewhat larger than the range shown in U.S. tables.

influence of the sun and the moon, primarily the moon. Tides of increased range, called spring tides, occur twice a month, when the sun and moon are in conjunction or opposition (a day or two after new moon or full moon). Tides of decreased range, called neap tides, occur twice a month, when the sun and moon partially counteract each other (first- or third-quarter moon).

Tidal Range. The tidal range gets steadily larger as you sail from west to east along the coast of Maine and into Passamaquoddy Bay. Starting with a range of 9 feet or so at Kittery, it reaches 20 feet or more at Calais.

To understand these great tidal ranges and why they increase as you move east, imagine the Atlantic Ocean as a large basin of water being sloshed back and forth. The motion of the water in the middle of the basin is relatively small, but when it enters the narrow confines of the Bay of Fundy, the water rushes up to a tremendous height. In the upper reaches of the Bay of Fundy, the tidal range reaches an extraordinary 50 feet or more, culminating with a dramatic tidal bore at Moncton, New Brunswick.

Anchoring with Large Tides. There are several practical implications of the large tidal range, especially the need for caution when anchoring. Many a cruising sailor has anchored in a large, open bay, only to find in the night that the water has drained away, leaving him high and dry on an unsuspected ledge. It pays to study the chart carefully before anchoring, trying to visualize the anchorage at low tide, and to consider where a shift in the wind might put you. In a crowded harbor, look with suspicion at any large area free of boats.

As we have noted throughout this book, certain anchorages should be entered for the first time near low tide, so that the dangers can be clearly seen. A study of the charts and some experience will give you a feel for these situations.

Then there is the question of scope. Where the tidal range is small, what you have at low is more or less what you have at high. But consider the situation near Mount Desert, where the tidal range is 12 feet. Suppose you anchor at low tide in 16 feet of water, with 96 feet of scope out and a ratio of 6:1. At high tide, the depth of the water will be 28 feet, and your ratio will have shrunk to a skimpy 3 1/2:1. In Passamaquoddy Bay, with a tidal range of 20 feet, the situation is even more dramatic. The specifics of anchoring and tying up way downeast will be discussed in detail in Region 7. Meanwhile, wherever you cruise in Maine, be sure to allow plenty of scope.

Drain Tides. During the time of spring (large) tides each month, the extreme lows are called drain tides. Where the tidal range is small, these are of little importance. In Maine, however, you must pay attention to drain tides, which are shown in the *Tide Tables* as negative numbers. This means that the tide level falls below the mean water level on which the chart soundings are based. For example, the depth in Kennebunkport at an average low tide is about six feet. Fine, no problem if you draw six feet or less. But on days of drain tides, the water may be as much as a foot or two below that level; your keel will be deep in the mud. If the charted depth in the anchorage is close to your draft, be sure to check the *Tide Tables.* Since Canadian charts use a lower datum to indicate soundings, negative tides are rare and usually small.

In this book, when we mention the depth in an anchorage at low tide, or the depth alongside a float, we are referring to an average low tide. There will be less water during drain tides.

Rivers. Tides in big rivers such as the Kennebec and the Penobscot vary considerably as you go upstream. At the mouth of the Kennebec, for example, the maximum range of tide is 9.7 feet. By the time you reach Bath, upstream, the maximum range is only 7.4 feet, and farther upstream at Richmond, it is only 6 feet.

On the Penobscot River, the reverse is true. The range of tide increases as you go upstream, from about 11.8 feet at the mouth to a maximum of 15.5 feet at Bangor.

Tide Tables. Have a current copy of the U.S. *Tide Tables* aboard (East Coast of North and South America). If there is a chance you will approach Canadian waters, you also will need the Canadian *Tide and Current Tables* (Vol. 1, Atlantic Coast and Bay of Fundy).

Many commercial firms print up little pads each year showing tides in selected locations such as Boston, Portland, Rockland, and Bar Harbor. They are distributed free as a form of advertising. They have convenient tear-off sheets covering a few days at a time, and they save a lot of looking up in the *Tide Tables*. Use with caution; errors are frequent.

Remember the "Rule of One-Twelfth" for estimating how much the sea level rises or falls at different stages of the tide.

Hours after slack	1	2	3	4	5	6
Fraction of tide	1/12	2/12	3/12	3/12	2/12	1/12

For example, if the tidal range is 12 feet, the tide will rise about one foot the first hour after low slack, two feet the second hour, three feet the third hour, three feet the fourth hour, etc.

The state of the tide is so important to your planning when cruising down east that most people find it handy to look up the times of high and low each day and post them somewhere aboard for easy reference.

Tidal Currents. Since the U.S. does not publish tidal current charts for the coast of Maine, we have prepared such charts for Casco Bay, and Penobscot Bay, based on the data in the *Tidal Current Tables*. See Appendix A.

General information can be obtained in the *Coast Pilot*, or by consulting the *Tidal Current Tables* for the United States (a separate publication from the *Tide Tables*), or the Canadian *Tide and Current Tables*.

Canada also publishes an interesting *Atlas of Tidal Currents—Bay of Fundy and Gulf of Maine*. In Region 7, we include a sketch map showing the tidal flow through the various entrances to Passamaquoddy Bay.

Strength and Direction of Tidal Currents. On straight stretches of coast from Kittery and the Isles of Shoals to Casco Bay, the tide floods generally north along the coast, and ebbs south. From Casco Bay to the Canadian border, the tide floods generally east along the coast, and generally north up the bays. It ebbs west along the coast, and southward out the bays toward the sea.

Along the coast of Maine and in the wider bays, the current seldom exceeds a maximum of two knots. In narrow passages, of course, such as Upper and Lower Hell Gate, Oven Mouth, and constricted portions of the rivers, it will run much harder.

Currents are stronger as you approach Canadian waters and the Bay of Fundy. In Grand Manan Channel, the tidal current runs three knots at strength. In Head Harbour Passage, Letite Passage, and Lubec Narrows, the tidal current runs six to eight knots, and sometimes more, with boils, eddies, and whirlpools.

Tidal currents are important to the cruising sailor. In making a passage east or west, plan to use the current as much as possible. This is especially significant down east, where the tides are large and the currents correspondingly stronger. Fighting two or three knots of current from Mount Desert to Roque Island and Grand Manan is frustratingly slow. With the current pushing you along, the headlands slip effortlessly by, and you arrive with hours of daylight to spare.

In fog or limited visibility, an estimate of tidal current is critical for a good DR, especially crossing a big bay such as Penobscot. Remember that the current may be influenced by a strong wind blowing for a period of time.

Wind against Current. In certain places, such as the mouth of the Kennebec River, Bass Harbor Bar, and Petit Manan Bar, the current running against a strong wind will produce a vicious chop that is dangerous to small craft and highly uncomfortable even to 40-footers.

East-West Passages. The direction of ebb and flood in the east-west passages varies. In Fox Islands Thorofare, the flood comes in from both directions, meeting at Iron Point, and it also ebbs in both directions. In Eggemoggin Reach, the current floods northwest and ebbs southeast. In Deer Island Thorofare and Merchant Row, the current floods east and ebbs west, but either can be reversed by strong winds. In Casco Passage and Moosabec Reach, the current floods east and ebbs west. On Bass Harbor Bar, the current floods west.

River Currents. In the rivers of Maine, the ebb usually is much stronger than the flood, since the strength of the river is added to the tidal current. You can expect stronger currents in narrow stretches of the river. Consult the *Coast Pilot* and *Tidal Current Tables* for details.

When you are picking up a mooring in a river, the current usually is a more important consideration than the wind, except at slack water. In the Piscataqua or the Kennebec, for example, you would normally head into the current, regardless of wind direction.

CHARTS, LORAN, SATNAV, GPS, AND RADAR

Despite the new and wonderful instruments that have become widely available, the most important navigational tools for the coast of Maine remain those basic skills of piloting and dead reckoning. You will become alert to the color of rockweed underwater (indicating a submerged rock) and grateful for the fact that swells break on submerged ledges. Most of the piloting along the coast in clear weather is done by eye and instinct and chart. Fog, of course, requires more formal approaches.

Charts. The charts that cover Maine waters are extremely good. In exploring the whole coast, we have found very few errors, and we have had real difficulty only where the scale of the chart is too small. For such cases, we have included a sketch map in this book to help you interpret the terrain.

For each location discussed in this guide, we have shown the appropriate chart numbers. The most useful or most detailed charts for a particular harbor or area are shown in bold type.

Remember that you have a whole auxiliary "navigational" system on the coast of Maine. The ubiquitous lobster buoys are always of value in helping you judge the strength and direction of the current.

Canadian Charts. Canadian charts can often be ordered through your usual U.S. chart agency. Or obtain a catalog of publications and an order form by writing: Hydrographic Chart Distribution Office, Department of Fisheries and Oceans, 1675 Russell Road, P.O. Box 8080, Ottawa, Ontario, Canada K1G 3H6. Or call 613-998-4931, 4932, or 4933.

Unfortunately the Hydrographic Office requires payment in Canadian funds, which may be awkward and expensive to arrange. Some Canadian chart dealers will accept payment in U.S. or Canadian funds, or by credit card (for example, Federal Publications, Inc., 165 University Avenue, Toronto, Ontario, Canada M5H 3B8; tel. 416-581-1552).

Loran, SatNav, GPS. Our experience with Loran along the coast of Maine has been good, using the U.S. Northeast Chain (GRI 9960). As you approach Canada, the Canadian East Coast Chain (GRI 5930) is likely to provide more accurate readings.

Loran signals are badly distorted or completely blanked out intermittently by the enormous naval radio communications towers on Cutler Peninsula, way down east. The towers create interference from the vicinity of Great Wass Island and Jonesport east to Roque Island, Machias Bay, Cutler, and Grand Manan Channel. Be prepared to do without Loran in this area.

Satnav and GPS, of course, are also in use along the coast. With the rapid evolution of electronic navigation in recent years, the best combination of instruments is a matter of individual judgment.

Radar. Radar is now common on the coast of Maine, as elsewhere. Most lobsterboats and commercial fishermen have it, and a growing number of yachts. In heavy fog it is a blessing.

Publications. Below is a checklist of the U.S. and Canadian publications that we have found essential:

United States

1. Charts
2. U.S. *Coast Pilot*, Vol. 1 (Eastport to Cape Cod)
3. *U.S. Tide Tables* (East Coast of North and South America)
4. *Tidal Current Tables*

Canada

1. Charts
2. *Sailing Directions* (Nova Scotia and Bay of Fundy)
3. *Tide and Current Tables*, Vol. 1 (Atlantic Coast and Bay of Fundy)

A number of other publications may be useful, including the *Eldridge Tide and Pilot Book* (published annually by Robert E. White, 64 Commercial Wharf, Boston, MA 02110), and a current Light List (*Light and Buoy List*, CG-158, available from the Superintendent of Documents, U.S. Government Printing Office, Washington, DC 20402; also at many chart outlets).

VHF RADIOTELEPHONE COMMUNICATIONS

There is a chain of VHF marine operators all along the coast. These are independent organizations linking boats at sea with the land-based telephone system. If you have a VHF radio, the marine operators can be useful in ship-to-shore communications, shore-to-ship, and ship-to-ship. The marine operators use the channels listed in the accompanying chart.

Calls can be collect, or charged to a credit card, home phone, or third party. Registration of your boat with a marine operator will save time making calls.

Placing a call from your boat. Call the closest marine operator on one of their working channels, giving the name of your boat and radio call sign. (Channel 16 may also be used to make contact, but this is discouraged by the FCC.)

Marine operators may also keep track (for a short time) of people trying to reach your boat. Ask the marine operator for a "traffic check."

Calling a boat from land. Ask the regular telephone operator for the appropriate marine operator.

Maximum range will vary with the time of day, weather, type of antenna used by the marine operator, and your own equipment. As a rule of thumb, figure a normal range of 50 miles, and a maximum of 80. The signal may be blocked by high terrain. For example, Camden Marine can be heard at sea

Marine Operator	VHF Channels	Land Phone
Portland	24, 28	207-871-0202
Camden	26, 84	207-236-3605
Southwest Harbor*	28	207-236-3605
Yarmouth, Nova Scotia	26	

'Part of Camden Marine Operator

off Mount Desert, but it may be inaudible in Bar Harbor.

Farther down east, check channels 26, 28, and 84 to see which is best. By the time you reach Jonesport, you probably will be out of range of Camden, and there is a dead spot from there until you can reach Yarmouth in Nova Scotia.

GETTING HELP WHEN YOU NEED IT

You are in trouble. The engine has conked out. The dinghy's gone adrift, or you're aground. A lobster buoy has wrapped the propeller. You are lost. Where do you get help? Here's a quick checklist:

- other cruising boats
- lobsterboats
- boatyards
- Hurricane Island Outward Bound School
- U.S. Coast Guard
- Town rescue services
- Marine operators
- Canadian Coast Guard
- Fundy Traffic (Saint John, New Brunswick)

Looking back over our years of cruising on the coast of Maine, we are not ashamed to say we have been in trouble from time to time, and we have been very happy to receive assistance. Below are further details about each of the suggested sources of help.

Other Cruising Boats. The closest and fastest source of help probably is another cruising boat. We've hailed a passing boat and borrowed his dinghy to retrieve our own, which had gone adrift. We've provided information on harbors, assisted boats aground, and lent a wetsuit to someone who had tangled his prop. Most cruising sailors are glad to help.

Lobsterboats. Lobstermen are busy earning a tough living, and yachts must seem to them like frivolous playthings of the rich. Yet they will offer help whenever they can, simply as part of the camaraderie of the sea. Don't ask for trivial assistance, but don't hesitate to yell or wave at a lobsterman for help if you are in real trouble.

In bad weather or poor visibility, you may have to use your VHF. Lobstermen usually don't listen

on channel 16; they have their own favorite local channel their friends are on. It might be channel 6 or 8, or 72 or 79, or something else. Keep switching until you hear local fishing chatter.

Boatyards. Many yards have powerboats that can tow you in, haul you off a ledge, supply a diver, or otherwise render assistance. To most, it's part of the business.

Check this guide for the nearest yard and how to contact it. If they don't monitor a VHF channel (or don't answer), use your VHF to call them on the phone via the marine operator (see "Communications—VHF Radiotelephone").

Hurricane Island Outward Bound School (HIOBS). The Outward Bound school on Hurricane Island (off the southwest coast of Vinalhaven Island) monitors channel 16 round the clock from late April to November, and they are glad to help. They have search-and-rescue capabilities, including several well-equipped powerboats, highly trained seamen, Coast Guard-licensed skippers, divers, and emergency medical technicians. There is usually a doctor in residence on Hurricane Island.

Hurricane has a base in Rockland and outlying bases on Burnt Island (off Port Clyde) and Cross Island (in Machias Bay). Their boats operate up and down the coast, and they are connected by a radio communication network. HIOBS has towed boats off ledges, put out fires, rescued people marooned on rocks, made medical evacuations, and found boats in the fog.

U.S. Coast Guard. The Coast Guard emphasizes to cruising sailors the need to file a detailed float plan with a friend or relative. (See "Preparations," earlier in this section.)

There are six Coast Guard stations in Maine, plus one in Portsmouth, New Hampshire. These

U.S.C.G. Facility	Small Boat Station	Support Base	Tug	Patrol Boat
Portsmouth, NH	★			★
South Portland	★	★	★	★
Boothbay Harbor	★			
Rockland	★		★	
Southwest Harbor	★	★	★	
Jonesport	★			★
Eastport	★			

are listed above, and also charted in each region of this book. Each has search-and-rescue capabilities.

In summer, one patrol cutter 82 feet or greater is either underway off the Maine coast or on standby to proceed within two hours of notification. This cutter may be anywhere between Portsmouth, New Hampshire, and Eastport, Maine. Each small boat station always has at least one boat ready to proceed within 30 minutes.

For help, call the nearest Coast Guard Station on channel 16 of your VHF. After contact on 16, you will be asked to switch to channel 22 or channel 12. See chapter 1 of the *Coast Pilot* for information on radiotelephone procedures, MAYDAY calls, and what the Coast Guard will want to know when you call. Remember that if you call the Coast Guard, they are going to inspect your boat for safety equipment.

The Coast Guard will place first emphasis on saving human life and then on protecting property. The Commander, First Coast Guard District, Boston, comments: "The Coast Guard will always respond to calls for assistance in some way; in particular, we always dispatch units in life threatening situations . . . .

"The Coast Guard may not dispatch boats in nonemergency cases where commercial firms are available, willing and qualified to assist instead. In cases where a private firm does assist, we monitor the situation to completion by means of a radio schedule.

"Coast Guard policy has always been to tow a disabled vessel to the nearest safe port which can accommodate the vessel being assisted.

"In many cases when a vessel goes aground a decision must be made whether to tow it free immediately or wait for the incoming tide to refloat it. When it is a Coast Guard boat that is assisting the grounded vessel, the only one who can make this decision is the Coast Guard Coxswain on the scene. Crucial factors that he considers are the seaworthiness of the vessel aground, its watertight integrity, the possible damage that might result should he tow it off immediately, and the effects that seas and wind are having on the situation.

"It is fruitless to free a grounded vessel only to have it sink in deep water. Therefore, in most cases, sound judgment will dictate waiting for the tide and rigging portable pumps to control any flooding. In all cases the Coast Guard's primary concern will be the safety of the people on board the grounded vessel. Under adverse circumstances, prudence may require removing the people and foregoing any property salvage attempt."

Town Rescue Services. Many coastal towns have rescue boats operated by police or fire departments.

Marine Operators. Like regular telephone operators, marine operators are a good source of emergency help. They can put you in touch with doctors, poison control centers, and so on, or relay a message to the Coast Guard or other sources of assistance.

Canadian Coast Guard. The Canadian Coast Guard and all government coastal radio stations monitor channel 16. The closest Coast Guard ships are based in St. John, New Brunswick, and Dartmouth, Nova Scotia, and two ships patrol from the south coast of Newfoundland to Georges Bank.

Fundy Traffic. The Canadian Coast Guard operates a Vessel Traffic Service (call name "Fundy Traffic"), based in Saint John, New Brunswick, to provide vessel traffic control and assistance to mariners. There is no requirement that yachts participate in the vessel traffic system, but Fundy Traffic is prepared to help you in various ways. They can provide weather forecasts and information on navigation aids, observe you on radar, or locate you with their VHF direction-finding equipment. Fundy Traffic monitors channels 12, 14, and 16; or call 506-648-4865.

APPROACHES TO THE COAST OF MAINE

Sailing Down East is always an adventure, whether it's the first or the twentieth time. At its best, the passage to Maine is a marvelous cruise in itself.

Coming from Long Island Sound and points south, you'll first savor the pleasures of Block Island and Narragansett Bay, the Elizabeth Islands, perhaps a side trip to Martha's Vineyard or Nan-

tucket, then Buzzards Bay and the Cape Cod Canal.

At this point you have a decision to make: whether to do an overnight passage across the Gulf of Maine, or to work your way up the coast by easy stages. If you prefer to avoid an overnight passage—or if you're headed for cruising grounds in southern Maine—there are a number of ap-

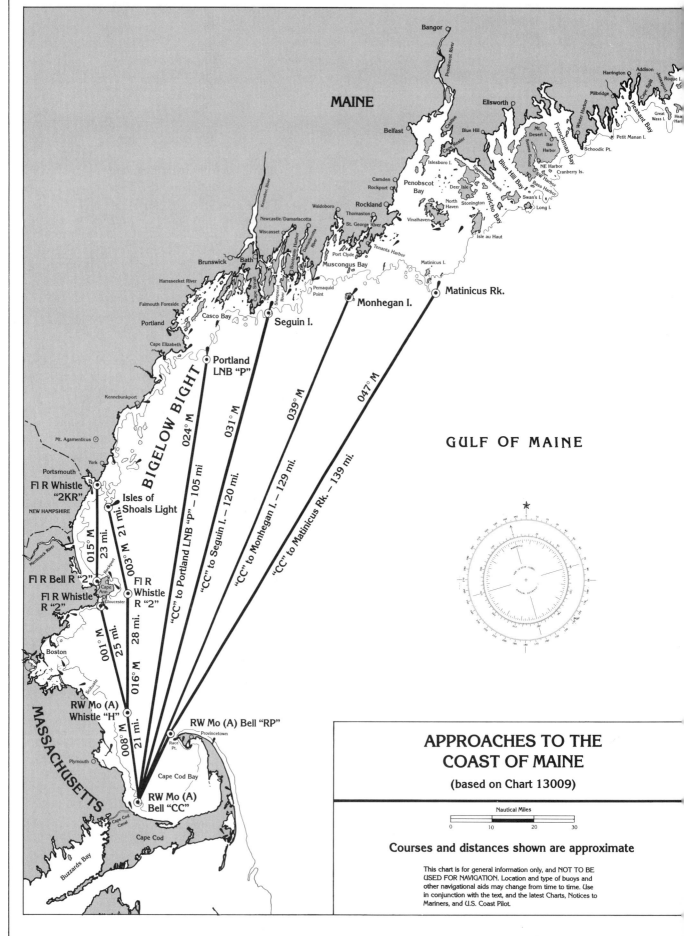

MAINE

Bangor

Harrington
Addison
Roque I.
Cape Split
Jonesport

Milbridge

Pleasant Bay

Ellsworth

Great
Wass I.

Belfast

Blue Hill

Mt.
Desert I.

Frenchman Bay

Great
Head

Bar
Harbor

Schoodic Pt.

Petit Manan I.

Castine

Cape Rosier

Blue Hill Bay

NE Harbor

SW Harbor
Bass Harbor

Islesboro I.

Penobscot
Bay

Deer Isle

Camden
Rockport

Eggemoggin Reach

Cranberry Is.

Swan's I.

Long I.

Waldoboro

Rockland

North
Haven

Stonington

Jericho Bay

Penobscot River

Kennebec River

Newcastle/Damariscotta

Thomaston

St. George River

Vinalhaven

Isle au Haut

Wiscasset

Matinicus I.

Brunswick
Bath

Boothbay Harbor

Port Clyde

Tenants Harbor

Damariscotta River

Muscongus Bay

Harraseeket River

Cape Small

Sheepscot River

Pemaquid
Point

Matinicus Rk.

Falmouth Foreside

Monhegan I.

Casco Bay

Seguin I.

Portland

Cape Elizabeth

Portland
LNB "P"

GULF OF MAINE

BIGELOW BIGHT

Kennebunkport

Mt. Agamenticus

York

Portsmouth

Fl R Whistle
"2KR"

Isles of
Shoals Light

024° M

031° M

039° M

047° M

"CC" to Portland LNB "P" – 105 mi.

"CC" to Seguin I. – 120 mi.

"CC" to Monhegan I. – 129 mi.

"CC" to Matinicus Rk. – 139 mi.

NEW HAMPSHIRE

Merrimack River

015° M
23 mi.

003° M
21 mi.

Fl R Bell R "2"

Fl R Whistle
R "2"

Cape
Ann

Gloucester

Fl R
Whistle
R "2"

Boston

001° M
25 mi.

016° M
28 mi.

Scituate

RW Mo (A)
Whistle "H"

RW Mo (A) Bell "RP"

Provincetown

008° M
21 mi.

Race
Pt.

Plymouth

MASSACHUSETTS

Cape Cod Bay

RW Mo (A)
Bell "CC"

Cape Cod
Canal

Cape Cod

Buzzards Bay

APPROACHES TO THE
COAST OF MAINE

(based on Chart 13009)

Nautical Miles

0   10   20   30

Courses and distances shown are approximate

This chart is for general information only, and NOT TO BE
USED FOR NAVIGATION. Location and type of buoys and
other navigational aids may change from time to time. Use
in conjunction with the text, and the latest Charts, Notices to
Mariners, and U.S. Coast Pilot.

proaches. For example, after leaving the Cape Cod Canal you could spend a night at Provincetown, or at Scituate. The next stop might be Gloucester and the Annisquam Canal, or you might decide to go outside Thacher Island and Cape Ann.

OVERNIGHT PASSAGES

If you want to get down east in a hurry, there are a number of good landfalls on the coast of Maine. Most of those described below are on small, bold islands well off the coast, with lights visible 20 miles or more, foghorns, and some with radiobeacons and racons. See the accompanying sketch map.

Depending on where you plan to cruise, set your course for Portland LNB, Seguin Island, Monhegan Island, or Matinicus Rock. The distance from the Cape Cod Canal to these various landfalls ranges from 108 to 142 miles. For example, a passage to Monhegan Island, which makes a fine landfall for Penobscot Bay or Muscongus Bay, is a comfortable 132 miles.

Portland or Casco Bay. For a destination near Portland, one good landfall is Wood Island Light, near Biddeford Pool (visible 24 miles). Another is Cape Elizabeth Light, near the southern end of Cape Elizabeth (visible 27 miles).

In reduced visibility, however, the safest landfall is Portland Lighted Horn Buoy, "P," also referred to as "Portland LNB," meaning "large navigational buoy." In deep water about 5 miles southeast of Cape Elizabeth, this enormous red buoy is well out to sea and free of all dangers. With a circular base 40 feet in diameter and a 42-foot tower, the buoy is marked "P" and "Coast Guard"; it has a flashing white light visible 14 miles, a fixed white light, radiobeacon, horn, and racon. It also houses meteorological instruments and a flock of deaf seagulls.

Kennebec, Sheepscot, and Damariscotta Rivers, Boothbay Harbor. Head for Seguin Island. Two miles south of the entrance to the Kennebec River, Seguin is small and bold, with a grassy summit 145 feet high. Seguin Light, established in 1795, (fixed white), is shown from a 53-foot white, cylindrical granite tower connected to a dwelling, 180 feet above the sea and visible 18 miles. There is a foghorn at the light.

A second possibility is The Cuckolds Light off Cape Newagen and Booth Bay. Although not offshore like Seguin, The Cuckolds has the advantage of a radiobeacon. The white, group flashing light stands 59 feet above water, visible 12 miles, and there is a foghorn.

Muscongus Bay or Penobscot Bay. The best landfall is Monhegan Island, 9 miles off the mainland, used as a landmark since the earliest days of exploration along the coast. The island is 1.7 miles

long and 165 feet high, with bold cliffs along its southeastern side.

Monhegan Island Light (flashing white), shown from a gray conical tower connected with a white building in the middle of the island, is 178 feet above the water and visible 21 miles. It was first established in 1824. The foghorn and radiobeacon are on Manana Island, a 100-foot-high rocky island close westward of Monhegan Island. Within three miles of the island, the light is obscured between west and southwest.

Another possible landfall is Matinicus Rock, southernmost island in the approach to Penobscot Bay. An enormous, barren granite rock swept by wind and sea, the rock is 56 feet high. First established in 1827, Matinicus Rock Light (flashing white) is shown from a 48-foot gray, cylindrical granite tower 90 feet above the water on the southern part of the rock (visible 24 miles). A foghorn and radiobeacon are at the light, and another (abandoned) light tower also stands on the rock.

Mount Desert Island and Points East. Make your landfall on Matinicus Rock, described above.

An alternative is to head for Mount Desert Rock, 17.5 miles south of Mount Desert Island, marked by a flashing white light 75 feet above sea level (visible 24 miles). However, the rock itself is small and only 20 feet high; this may be a difficult landfall in heavy fog.

Mount Desert Island itself is the highest land feature on the coast of Maine, and visible at sea from as much as 60 miles away in good conditions.

Courses, Distances, and Navigational Aids. Check your chart and *Notices to Mariners* for the most recent information (also the *Coast Pilot* and *Light List*; see "Navigating Down East," earlier in this section, for more details.)

Approaches from Canada. All pleasure boats entering the United States, whether American-owned or foreign, must check in with United States Customs at a port of entry. See "Entering the United States and Canada" in Region 7 for details.

Vessels headed for Maine from the Passamaquoddy or Bay of Fundy area will normally pass through Grand Manan Channel, and continue coasting toward their destination.

Boats approaching the coast of Maine from Newfoundland, the Gulf of St. Lawrence, and Nova Scotia, after rounding Cape Sable can use the same landfalls as discussed above for boats approaching from the south.

To explore the Isles of Shoals, the lighthouse on White Island makes a good landfall. Or if your goal is Portsmouth, head for Whaleback Light at the harbor entrance, or whistle "2KR" off Kitts Rocks.

Region 1 / Isles of Shoals to Cape
The Southern

Aerial view of the Isles of Shoals, showing boats at anchor in Gosport Harbor. (Peter Randall photo)

Elizabeth

Coast

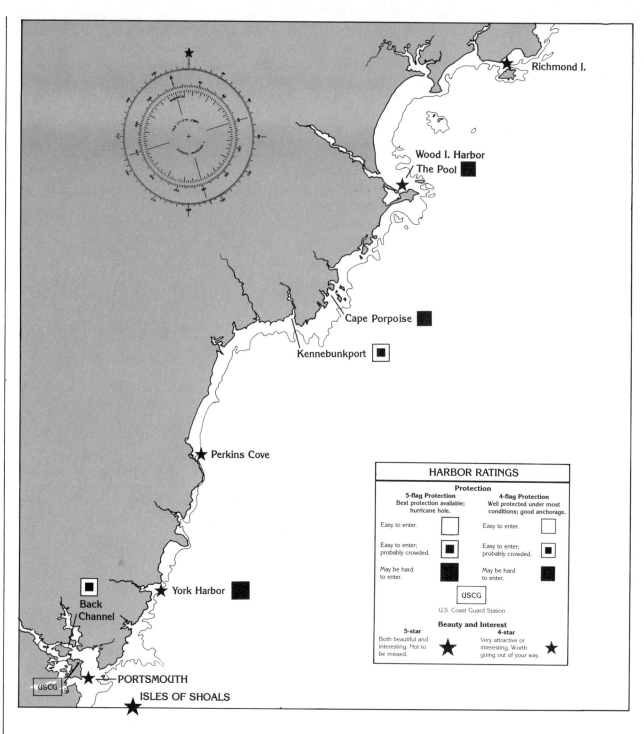

Richmond I.

Wood I. Harbor
The Pool

Cape Porpoise

Kennebunkport

Perkins Cove

HARBOR RATINGS

Protection

5-flag Protection
Best protection available;
hurricane hole.

4-flag Protection
Well protected under most
conditions; good anchorage.

Easy to enter.

Easy to enter.

Easy to enter;
probably crowded.

Easy to enter;
probably crowded.

May be hard
to enter.

May be hard
to enter.

USCG

U.S. Coast Guard Station

Beauty and Interest

5-star
Both beautiful and
interesting. Not to
be missed.

4-star
Very attractive or
interesting. Worth
going out of your way.

Back
Channel

York Harbor

USCG

PORTSMOUTH

ISLES OF SHOALS

On a large chart, the southern coast of Maine, from Kittery to Cape Elizabeth, appears almost featureless, sweeping northward from Cape Cod in a series of shallow bays, punctuated by an occasional rocky headland or tidal river, with relatively few islands. Clearly this is not the fabled rockbound coast of Maine.

Instead, here are Maine's great beaches: Old Orchard Beach, favorite of French-speaking Canadians, Moody, Wells, Kennebunk, Scarborough, and others, some stretching for mile after mile. Another common feature of the southern coast is tidal rivers, from the Piscataqua and the York to the Kennebunk and Saco.

In comparison to the rest of Maine, this portion of the coast is short of harbors, and only a few are first-rate. But there are a number of interesting anchorages that are perfectly adequate in summer conditions and delightful places to visit. We think especially of the fascinating Isles of Shoals and the pleasant towns of Portsmouth and Kittery at the New Hampshire end of Maine.

Then comes York, rich with history, and the contrasting harbors of Kennebunkport and Cape Porpoise—one swarming with "summer complaints" (as tourists are known locally) and the other, only three miles away, a working harbor swarming with lobster pots. Farther north are the marshes and birds and beach of The Pool at Biddeford, and the tranquil anchorages from which you can watch sheep graze on Richmond Island.

Over the lower half of the southern coast broods old Mount Agamenticus, a landmark for Europeans from the early days of exploration. Along the southern coast were several of the earliest settlements in America. In 1616–17, before the Pilgrims landed at Plymouth, Captain Richard Vines wintered over on the Saco River to prove that the Maine climate was not too severe for Europeans. (The failure of the Popham Colony in the terrible winter of 1607 had temporarily discouraged further settlement.) Vines established a permanent settlement on the Saco in 1623, the same year Kittery was founded, and York was settled in 1631. During six Indian Wars, from 1675 to 1763, however, mainland farms and settlements were wiped out time and again by the Indians, and as late as 1713, the only remaining settlements were at Kittery, Wells, and York.

Those who prefer not to make an overnight passage across the Gulf of Maine can coast from Cape Cod to Cape Ann, and then explore these southern shores. But this is not just a stopover en route to better cruising grounds. The southern coast of Maine has much to offer, and many harbors with special charms for the cruising family.

ISLES OF SHOALS ★★★★★

Chart: 13283

The Isles of Shoals lie just six miles southeast of the entrance to Portsmouth Harbor. Of the nine islands, five are in Maine (Duck, Appledore, Smuttynose, Malaga, and Cedar) and four are in New Hampshire (Star, Lunging, White, and Seaveys). The islands are spectacularly scenic, and their long history is crammed with tales of buried treasure, grisly murders, and bloody Indian attacks.

In 1614, Captain John Smith dropped anchor here and was utterly captivated. "Of all foure parts of the world that I have seene not inhabited, could I have but the meanes to transport a Colonie, I would rather live here than any where," he wrote —and named the islands for himself. "Smith's Iles," however, didn't stick. The islands acquired their name not from the surrounding shallow waters, but from the abundant schools, or shoals, of cod. By the eighteenth century, the Isles of Shoals were considered one of England's most valuable colonies because of the great quantities of cod caught, dried, and exported.

The early cod-fishing villages were based primarily on Smuttynose and Appledore islands, but when the Massachusetts Bay Colony started to levy onerous taxes on the islanders in 1680, they crossed over to New Hampshire's Star Island, named their new town Gosport, and continued their thriving fishing industry for another century. During the Revolution, however, everyone was evacuated to the mainland. Those who returned to Star Island after the Revolution acquired a reputation for "laziness, drunkenness, lawlessness, and cohabitation," and the community never returned to its former prominence.

In the nineteenth century, the islands had a modest revival, and a widely read poet, Celia Thaxter, grew up in their midst. Most notable and most charming of the many people associated with the Isles of Shoals, Thaxter was the daughter of Thomas Laighton, the lightkeeper on White Island. Aware and sensitive at an early age, she referred to the area as "these precious isles set in a silver sea."

Around 1850, Laighton built Appledore House, publicized as the first resort hotel between Nantucket and Eastport, Maine. At the peak of their combined popularity in the 1890s, both Appledore House and Celia Thaxter attracted such literary and artistic figures as Nathaniel Hawthorne, Henry Wadsworth Longfellow, Sarah Orne Jewett, Childe Hassam, and John Greenleaf Whittier.

The rival Oceanic House, built on Star Island in 1872, advertised itself as "an ideal summer resort of the highest class and full of historic associations. Pre-eminently the place for the tired worker. No noise. No dust. No trolleys."

With the advent of the automobile, the Isles of Shoals resort business declined, and in 1915, Star Island was sold to an association of Unitarians and Congregationalists as a conference center for religion, natural history, and the arts.

Approaches. From any direction, the approach to the Isles of Shoals is easy. Coming from the south, aim for the 82-foot light on White Island, leaving it to port, then passing between nun "4" on Halfway Rocks and Lunging Island, to red-and-white bell "IS" at the mouth of Gosport Harbor.

Coming from the north, you may be able to see the Appledore tower and the cupola on the abandoned Coast Guard station from as far away as Boon Island. Stay well clear of Duck Island, which is low and featureless and tends to merge with Appledore. After rounding nun "2" at the northwest tip of Appledore, head for red-and-white bell "IS" at the mouth of the harbor.

From Portsmouth, the Isles of Shoals are clearly visible on a good day. Aim for the tower on Appledore in the middle of the group of islands until you pick up red-and-white bell "IS."

Anchorages, Moorings. The only harbor in the Isles of Shoals is Gosport Harbor, between Star, Cedar, and Smuttynose islands, so it is likely to be crowded. On warm weekends, you will be competing with cruising boats as well as day-trippers from Portsmouth and Kittery. Even on weekdays, there may be 10 or 20 boats here, so arrive early in the day to choose a spot.

Holding ground is very poor. In most harbors, you can trust your anchor more than unknown moorings, but in Gosport Harbor, it is better to pick up a mooring. There are a number of large, private mooring buoys scattered around the harbor, and the local custom is first come, first served. The Portsmouth Yacht Club has several moorings marked "PYC."

If you are determined to anchor, try to set your hook in the mud up in the cove between Star and Cedar islands without fouling lobster pots and moorings. Leave swinging room in case the wind switches around to the west. Failing that, find a 21-foot spot farther out, avoiding the eight-fathom areas. Use a good, heavy anchor; the bottom is all ledge, rocks, and kelp.

In a blow from the northwest, get out of the harbor and head for Portsmouth or go to sea. With enough visibility, you can power around Smuttynose and reset the hook on the opposite side of the breakwater between Cedar and Smuttynose. There is a lot of room to anchor here in 8 to 18 feet. The bottom is sand and boulders, and there is good holding ground, protected from the wind, although still exposed to a swell.

Star Island. Although the former Oceanic House is no longer a hotel open to the public, the Star Island Corporation welcomes day visitors to the island from 10 A.M. to dusk. It's fun to go ashore and observe the bustle of the family-oriented conference center. The steamship replica *Thomas Laighton* makes several round trips daily between Star Island and Portsmouth, landing at the end of the stone pier below the hotel.

Land your dinghy at the floats next to the pier. One of the young employees (known as "Pelicans") will welcome you and provide a map of the island with its few simple rules: no pets, no bare feet, no open fires, no picking of wildflowers. No fuel, water, ice, or groceries are available, and there is no trash disposal.

Visitors are welcome on the first floor of the main building, where there are restrooms, a snack bar, and a gift and book shop. Newspapers are available at the front desk. A radiotelephone is for emergency use only, and a doctor is in residence.

A daily guided walking tour of the island leaves from the porch of the main building, but you are free to use your map and wander around by yourself. In June and July, gulls are nesting everywhere, including many sitting right in the middle of the paths, exercising their maternal rights. Look for the Vaughn cottage, which displays Celia Thaxter memorabilia, and the chapel nearby.

Near the eastern shore is Betty Moody's cave, described in Robert Carter's 1858 *Summer Cruise on the Coast of New England*. "Early in the old colony times," Carter relates, "the Indians from the mainland made a descent upon the islands, and killed or carried off all the inhabitants except a Mrs. Moody, who hid herself under the rocks with her two small children." As the Indians combed the island, "the unhappy mother, unable to keep her infants quiet, killed them with a knife to prevent their crying."

From there, walk south along the coast to find Miss Underhill's Chair, a rocky perch from which a romantic young island schoolteacher was swept away by a great wave.

In the evening, as visitors depart from the dock, the Pelicans chant their ritual refrain, "You will come back; you will come back."

Smuttynose and Malaga Islands. Named for the dark rocks at its eastern end, uninhabited Smuttynose boasts enough history for several novels. In a little graveyard behind his 1750 cottage lies Captain Samuel Haley, aged 84, "a man of great ingenuity and industry," according to his headstone. On this little island Captain Haley built a 270-foot ropewalk, a salt-works for curing fish, windmills to grind wheat and corn, blacksmith and

ISLES OF SHOALS

(based on Chart 13283)

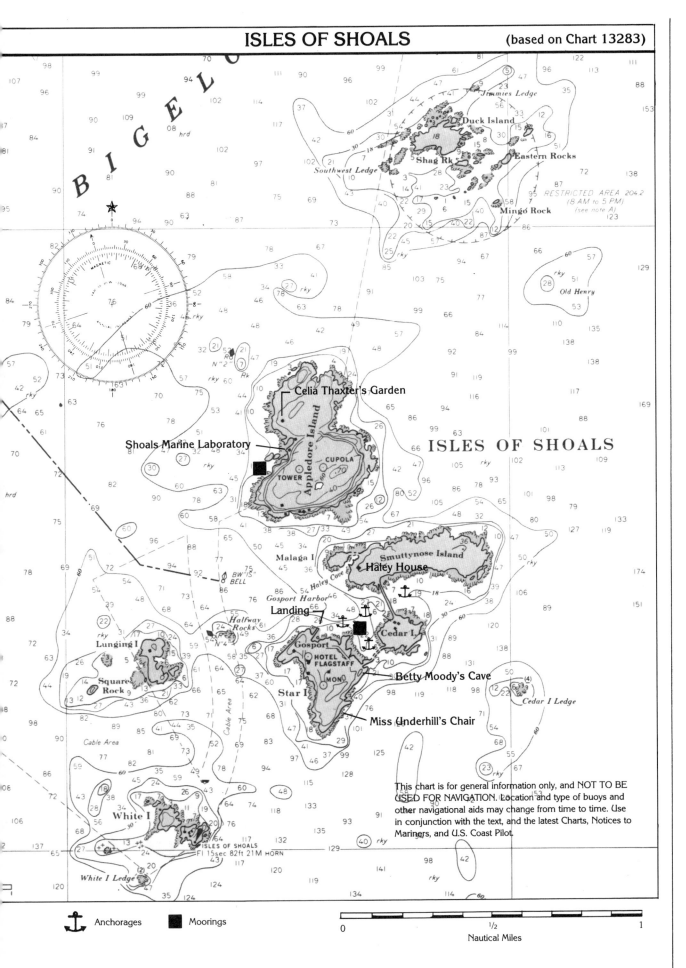

This chart is for general information only, and NOT TO BE USED FOR NAVIGATION. Location and type of buoys and other navigational aids may change from time to time. Use in conjunction with the text, and the latest Charts, Notices to Mariners, and U.S. Coast Pilot.

⚓ Anchorages   ◼ Moorings

0 — ½ — 1

Nautical Miles

cooper shops, a bakery, a brewery, and a distillery.

Pirates reputed to have visited Smuttynose include Blackbeard, Captain Kidd, and Quelch. The ghost of Blackbeard's wife, they say, still roams the shores crying, "He will come back. He will come back," and stories of buried treasure, for once, were true. Captain Haley found four bars of silver under a flat stone and used the proceeds to build a breakwater connecting Smuttynose to little Malaga Island, creating Haley's Cove.

Row ashore at Haley's Cove and land at the little beach behind the stone wharf. This is a lovely spot for a picnic, peaceful and secluded, and you can swim off the beach. Nearby are two houses: Haley's cottage, now dilapidated and dangerous, has a brick chimney. The other house, in reasonable repair, is stocked as a refuge for shipwrecked mariners and fishermen.

If you are considering exploring the island as far as the conical rock cairn at the eastern end, remember that some 3,000 pairs of nesting gulls are likely to defend their nesting grounds with vigorous dive-bombing tactics. Hold a stick over your head to keep them away.

Cedar Island. On tiny Cedar Island, between Star and Smuttynose, are several houses, shacks, and a pier. These are the homes of the Hall and Foye families, fishermen in these waters for six generations. The island is private property.

White and Seaveys Islands. White and Seaveys islands, six acres in total, form a lonely outpost for the two Coast Guardsmen who used to run the light (now automated). To explore these islands, tie up to the white Coast Guard mooring at the north side and take your dinghy ashore near the boathouse (difficult except in relatively calm weather).

The history of White Island is filled with sagas of gales, shipwrecks, and dramatic rescues. In heavy gales, solid water may come halfway up the light tower and spray over the top.

Lunging Island. Lunging Island is a small, privately owned island with a house at one end and a

small cove on the east side. The name is a corruption of the island's original name of Londoners, reflecting its colonial use as a trading center for the London Company. Bought by oil-refinery interests in 1974, the island was slated to be an offshore terminal for unloading oil tankers and pumping to Portsmouth, but the plan was defeated.

Appledore Island. The public is welcome on Appledore until sundown, and there is much to see. It is inhabited mostly by seagulls that tolerate summer students from Cornell University and the University of New Hampshire who work at the Shoals Marine Laboratory field station.

The island is home to thousands of gulls, and it is a migratory way station for more than 125 species of birds. Harbor seals, whales, porpoises, and dolphins are also frequent visitors.

Call Shoals Marine Lab on either channel 16 or 80 as you approach, to check whether a mooring is available. Or, pick up one of the four large moorings in 40 feet of water on the west side, just off the landing. Row ashore, tie your dinghy on the back side of the dock, and inquire whether you can stay on the mooring. Sign in at the dock and pick up a map. There is a delightful, well-protected tidal pool for swimming, just to the left of the dock.

On the island are the foundations of the old Appledore House and the Laighton family graveyard. Celia Thaxter's lovely garden as described in her book *An Island Garden,* illustrated by Childe Hassam, has been re-created here.

Stay on the blazed trails to avoid encountering the impressive poison ivy bushes and disturbing the nesting gulls in June and July.

Duck Island. This 11-acre, low-lying, treeless outpost is, ironically, devoted simultaneously to preservation and destruction. On the one hand, it is a naval aircraft bombing target; on the other hand, it is a wildlife refuge managed by the Shoals Marine Laboratory. The island is home to large colonies of cormorants and gulls, and access is restricted. Leave it for the birds.

LITTLE HARBOR ★★★
Chart: 13283

Located in New Castle, New Hampshire, Little Harbor lies between white sand beaches on the undeveloped shore of Odiorne State Park and the grounds of the old Wentworth-by-the-Sea Hotel, which has been closed for years. Although Little Harbor is an attractive spot, there are some drawbacks. First, the harbor is part of the mighty Piscataqua River, and the current runs strong. Also, its proximity to the city of Portsmouth means that

summer weekends bring out runabouts and day-trippers in force; boats are rafted six or eight on a mooring, and there is joyous partying on the beach at Odiorne.

A major new marina associated with the Wentworth dominates the north side of the harbor.

Approaches. The entrance, protected by two overlapping breakwaters, presents no problems. From Kittery or Portsmouth, head down the coast,

SEAGULLS: THE SCAVENGERS OF THE COAST

At anchor of an evening in a peaceful cove, you sip your drink, nibble on a piece of cheese, and toss a cracker to the gray-backed seagull floating watchfully below. The cracker disappears into a yellow beak and suddenly three more gulls swoop down, then ten. They land gracefully on the water, closing their wings neatly with a final twitch, in attentive formation.

Up high, another gull appears in answer to some magic seagull summons, soaring gracefully on the air, wings never moving. Along the shore, a seagull turns and climbs and drops a clam to break upon the rocks below. Clouds of gulls wheel in the wake of fishing boats as they clean their fish.

Gulls are monogamous and can live for up to 30 years. Parents forage for their young, which peck the orange spot below the beak to get their food. The gull drinks salt water, living on the sea for days (the salt is excreted through its beak), eating fish and crabs, sea urchins, clams, and even kelp. On land, it drinks fresh water and dines on mice and berries and, most especially, garbage. A useful scavenger and con-

noisseur of garbage, the gull is an habitué of open dumps and also follows fishing boats to feed on fish scraps. It has an expandable gullet, a cast-iron stomach, and the manners of a fishwife.

Jonathan Livingston Seagull was a herring gull, with silver-gray wings and black wingtips. Colored the same, but smaller, and with a black ring at the end of its beak, the ring-billed gull is seen in Maine late in the summer.

Not as common as the herring gull, but bigger, tougher, and more aggressive, is the great black-

backed gull, 30 inches long, whose wings and back are black. The black-backed gull is at the top of the pecking order and feeds on the young and eggs of other gulls and terns, shorebirds, and eider chicks.

A much smaller gull easily mistaken for a tern is Bonaparte's gull. Its white body and black head are distinctive, and when you get closer, you can see its red feet. The wings are gray, with a thin white streak near the end.

No match for man, seagulls had been hunted to near extinction in Maine by 1900, their eggs taken by coastal residents for food, their feathers for the millinery trade. With the passage of protective laws, the gulls came back—with a vengeance. Aggressive gulls have sharply cut the populations of other species, particularly terns. The voracious gulls eat tern eggs and gobble up tern chicks. So successful has been the gull resurgence, and so destructive to the other birds, that conservationists reluctantly approved the experimental poisoning of gulls on Green Island in 1984. (The tern population has since recovered.) What next? It is not a simple issue.

being sure to leave the can at Stielman Rocks to starboard. Aim outside Odiornes Point until you see the entrance nun "2" and can "1." The huge, white Wentworth-by-the-Sea buildings are not in sight until you are opposite the first breakwater, with its flashing red light. The inner breakwater to the south has no light, but it is marked by can "3." Stay in midchannel until past the inner breakwater, then stay to the right to avoid the three-foot spot south of nun "6."

When a strong southwest wind is blowing against an ebb tide, a dangerous swell may build up at the entrance. Little Harbor is well protected except for an easterly.

Anchorages, Moorings. The Wentworth Marina has 170 slips, with 10 feet of water alongside, and there is usually room for transients. Vessels as long as 300 feet can be accommodated. Most of the moorings in the harbor are privately owned, and there is no room to anchor. The Portsmouth Yacht Club has a couple of moorings marked "PYC."

Getting Ashore. Call the Wentworth Marina launch on Ch. 71 to get ashore at the marina, which does not allow you to land your dinghy at their

floats. Use your own dinghy to land at Odiorne Park or (if you have enough power) to motor through the back passage to the Piscataqua River and Portsmouth.

For the Boat. *Wentworth-by-the Sea Marina (Ch. 16, 68 and 71; tel. 603-433-5050).* Fuel, ice, electricity, and cable TV are at the marina floats. Potable water is available at the fuel dock by reservation.

For the Crew. On the dock you will find showers, laundromat, and pay phones. The "concierge" in the marina office can make reservations for you at the tennis courts, golf club, or at one of the restaurants in the complex. You may be able to get a lift to the nearest grocery, which is a mile away.

Things to Do. Odiorne State Park boasts lovely beaches, raspberries in profusion, a nature center, and guided nature walks.

APPROACHES TO PORTSMOUTH and KITTERY

Charts: 13283, 13285, 13286

The mighty Piscataqua River is the boundary between Maine and New Hampshire. On the south side of the river lies the charming city of Portsmouth, New Hampshire, while the quiet towns of Kittery and Kittery Point are on the north side, in Maine. Second-fastest-flowing river in the continental United States (after the Columbia, in Washington state), the Piscataqua winds many miles back into the New Hampshire countryside to Great Bay and up various tributaries to the onetime shipbuilding communities of Durham and Exeter.

Kittery, organized in 1647, was Maine's first town. Its early forts, built as protection from the Indians, evolved into coastal defense batteries during the French and Indian Wars, the American Revolution, and the Spanish-American War.

Shipbuilding started early on the banks of the Piscataqua. Dories and gundalows, frigates and clipper ships were launched from shipyards on Seavey and Dennetts islands. It is not surprising, then, that the first U.S. naval shipyard began here too, in 1800. Now known as the Portsmouth Naval Shipyard (located in Kittery), its docks use cannons from old men-of-war as bollards to tie up nuclear subs. Most appropriately, its motto is "Sails to Atoms."

Maine launched the U.S. Navy in 1777, when John Paul Jones's 18-gun sloop *Ranger* slid down the ways at Badgers Island, where remnants of these ways are still visible.

Near the mouth of the harbor, Fort Constitution, originally Fort William and Mary, played a critical role in the Revolutionary War. As discontent with the British grew, Governor John Wentworth and his family moved into the fort in 1774 with a small force of British soldiers and a large supply of gunpowder. The ubiquitous Paul Revere rode to Portsmouth to persuade the citizens to storm Fort William and Mary. Two hundred ardent revolutionaries then marched to Market Square and stormed the fort, with no loss of life. They imprisoned the soldiers and the governor and sent the cannons and gunpowder by gundalows upriver to Durham. Eventually these munitions were used against the British at the battle of Bunker Hill. Portsmouth was where the War of Independence began.

During World War II, an antisubmarine net was stretched between Wood Island and New Castle. Ships proceeding into Portsmouth had to radio ahead to arrange for dropping the net. Sometime in 1943, a German U-boat crept through behind a merchant ship and lay on the bottom just off the Portsmouth Naval Shipyard for three days and three nights, rising after dark to make observa-

tions. The sub escaped undetected, but after the war, detailed drawings of the shipyard were discovered in files captured from the Germans.

Approaches. The dominant factor for navigation in this area is the tidal current, which may run six knots and in certain places more. Be aware of heavy commercial traffic, including very large tankers, tugs, cruise vessels, and Coast Guard ships. Large ships often anchor off the mouth of

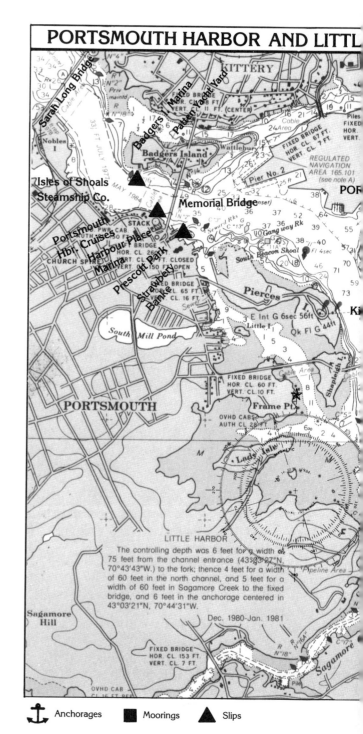

LITTLE HARBOR
The controlling depth was 6 feet for a width of 75 feet from the channel entrance (43°03′27″N, 70°43′43″W.) to the fork; thence 4 feet for a width of 60 feet in the north channel, and 5 feet for a width of 60 feet in Sagamore Creek to the fixed bridge, and 6 feet in the anchorage centered in 43°03′21″N, 70°44′31″W.

Dec. 1980–Jan. 1981

⚓ Anchorages ■ Moorings ▲ Slips

the harbor awaiting a favorable tide or good visibility. This is not a place to be underway in thick fog or limited visibility.

Coming up the coast from Cape Ann, head for Whaleback Light at the harbor entrance, or Fl R whistle "2KR" off Kitts Rocks. On a clear day, you will see the white mass of Little Harbor's Wentworth-by-the-Sea, an obvious landmark whose largest cupola is marked on the chart (see preceding writeup). If the weather is thick, you will hear the horn on White Island, in the Isles of Shoals, to starboard. Pick up bell "I" on Gunboat Shoal to port about 1.5 miles before you reach whistle "2KR."

Coming south from Cape Elizabeth, run down the line of whistle buoys until you reach whistle "24YL," southeast of York Ledge, leaving Boon Island, with its 133-foot lighthouse, to port. Then head in for whistle "2KR" off Kitts Rocks, leaving it well to starboard.

Returning from the Isles of Shoals in good visibility, aim just to the left of the buildings, stacks, and bridge that mark Portsmouth, or run a compass course to whistle "2KR."

After leaving whistle "2KR" well to starboard, head up the harbor, leaving Whaleback Light to starboard. Although this light is visible for 24 miles, the 59-foot tower is dark brown and merges with

RBOR

(based on Chart 13283)

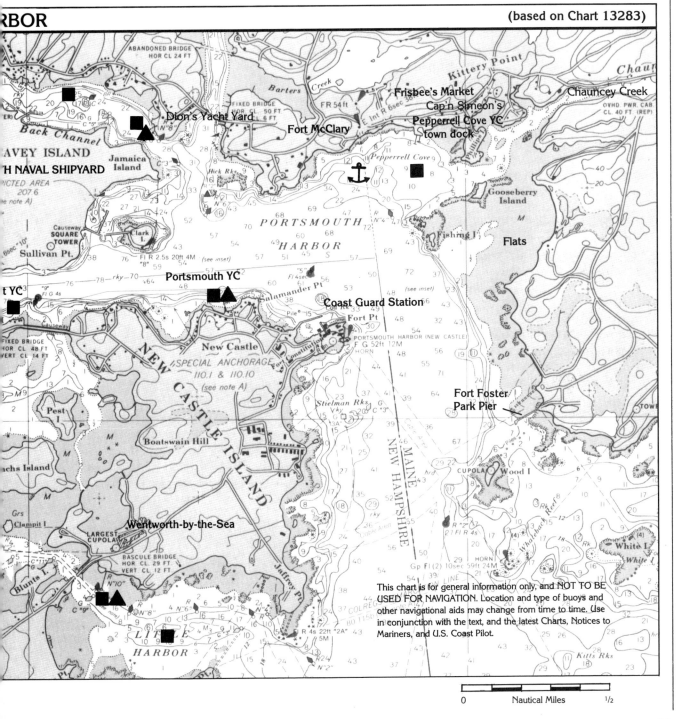

the land behind it. (In 1943, the lighthouse keeper at Whaleback reported that three waves crested over the top of the light while he was in it.)

Leave to starboard buoy "2" off Wood Island, which has an enormous abandoned house, formerly a lifesaving station. Be sure to identify can "3" off Stielman Rocks on the left-hand side of the channel. The white Fort Point lighthouse, with a fixed green light, is conspicuous.

PEPPERRELL COVE
(KITTERY POINT) ★★★ ⬚2⬚ 🛢️ 🚰 ⚓ 🛒 🚿 🍽️

Charts: **13283**, 13285, 13286

Named after Sir William Pepperrell, Kittery's most illustrious citizen and the first colonist to be knighted by King George II, Pepperrell Cove is a very convenient spot. It does have its drawbacks, including exposure to heavy weather from the south. There are crosscurrents as the tide runs in and out of Chauncey Creek, and boats swing around a lot. The moorings are too close together, and it is not unusual to feel a bump in the night from a boat moored nearby or a float bobbing alongside.

Since there are about 50 lobsterboats in the area, there is wake and engine noise in the early hours of the morning, not to mention the wash from large ships passing in the main channel, plus the normal boat traffic in and out of the cove.

On weekends, in particular, there are runabouts with radios blaring, powerboats roaring up the river, and airplanes buzzing overhead. Also, Pepperrell Cove is more than abundantly supplied with mosquitoes and "no-see-ums." Have your screens in place before dusk.

Approaches. Pepperrell Cove is easy to enter. After passing Fort Point, head for nun "4" off Fishing Island, and you will see 100 or more boats that almost fill the cove. A channel leading to the town dock is marked by green spar buoys and red spar buoys.

Anchorages, Moorings. Two separate organizations are responsible for the facilities in Pepperrell Cove: the town of Kittery, and Pepperrell Cove Yacht Club. The dock and adjacent launching ramp belong to the town, which has some guest moorings. The harbormaster (Ch. 16) has a little house on the dock, but he is a busy man (his responsibilities include the Isles of Shoals), so you will probably do better if you check with the PCYC launch. Or you may prefer to anchor west of the moored boats, in 12 to 14 feet, good holding ground.

Getting Ashore. Row your dinghy to the floats where all the other dinghies are tied up. Take your oars and oarlocks with you, or leave them at the Pepperrell Cove Yacht Club.

For the Boat. Gas, diesel, and water are available at the floats of the main dock, with 10 feet alongside at low. Pepperrell Cove Yacht Club (Ch. 68), provides launch service, has two guest moorings, and keeps track of what else is available. The nice little clubhouse, open to visiting yachtsmen, is located under the restaurant, with showers and dressing rooms. If it is closed, ask for the key at Cap'n Simeon's Galley (see below).

For the Crew. There are pay phones nearby. Up the road from the town dock is Frisbee's Market, billed as "North America's oldest family store." It can supply groceries, block ice, and other necessities. The Frisbee family also manages Cap'n Simeon's Galley, a popular seafood restaurant and takeout.

The Kittery Point post office is across the street, next to a long-term parking lot managed by Frisbee's. Kittery has a discount liquor store and a laundromat but no public transportation, so call a taxi or see if you can get a ride at Frisbee's.

Things to Do (Kittery Point and Kittery). There are a number of pleasant things to do within rowing or walking distance. A short walk on Route 103 (down the street to the left as you leave Frisbee's) will take you to the Fort McClary picnic area, a lily pond, and picnic tables in a grove of tall pines. Farther along on the left is Fort McClary State Memorial, whose white, six-sided blockhouse is clearly visible from Pepperrell Cove. (You can also reach it by dinghy.) The fort is worth visiting, especially with kids. There are granite fortifications and good views of the harbor. Farther down the road is the handsome 1760 Lady Pepperrell House—not open to the public, however.

If you are yearning for a lobster dinner, take the dinghy up Chauncey Creek, east of Pepperrell Cove, to Chauncey Creek Lobster Pier, which attracts people from as far as Boston. The lobsters

Anchorages, Moorings. Because of the swift tidal current, it is highly desirable to find a mooring. There are only a few spots where you can lie comfortably at anchor, particularly if you intend to leave the boat for any length of time. Most visiting yachtsmen head for Pepperrell Cove or Back Channel, behind Seavey Island, although there are alternatives. For specifics, see the writeups that follow: Pepperrell Cove; Back Channel; and Portsmouth/Kittery—Alternative Slips and Moorings.

are great and the view superb. BYOB.

To get a feel for the area's natural resources, it's fun to row over to Gerrish Island. This is a good place to watch herons wading through the shallow water and snails progressing across the wet sands at their well-known pace, or to walk over the rippled sand flats.

At the southwest corner of Gerrish Island is a long pier extending from the Fort Foster recreation area. There are good jogging roads running through the park, barbecues, picnic tables, benches, and grassy areas (dogs on leash only). There are World War I concrete bunkers and a watch tower to explore.

BACK CHANNEL (KITTERY) ★★★
Charts: **13283**, 13285, 13286

The major alternative to Pepperrell Cove is Back Channel, behind Seavey Island. It is a little farther to go and less convenient for grocery shopping, but more peaceful and much safer in heavy weather. Back Channel has considerably less current than the main part of the river—an average of 1½ knots and a maximum of 2½ knots. In fact, Back Channel is a hurricane hole, almost entirely landlocked and the place to be when weather is brewing.

Approaches. Leaving the Pepperrell Cove area, head for the huge, white former naval prison on Seavey Island (square tower on chart). The Portsmouth Naval Shipyard occupies all of Seavey Island and adjacent Clark Island. Note the restricted area on the chart. The main channel of the Piscataqua River runs right next to Seavey Island, but stay at least 200 feet away—particularly from the nuclear subs that are moored there—if you don't wish to arouse the interest of the armed security guards at the shipyard.

Locate nun "6" and red daybeacon "2," leaving them to starboard as you turn toward Spruce Creek. After a short distance, turn to port into Back Channel, leaving can "3" to port. You will see nun "8" close inshore to starboard, and just beyond the point on the right is Dion's Yacht Yard (see below).

Anchorages, Moorings. Pick up a convenient mooring and inquire at Dion's, which usually has moorings and space alongside for transients.

(Moorings can be reserved.) There is 22 feet of water along the floats.

Back Channel is full of moorings, so there is no room to anchor. A fixed bridge leads to Seavey Island, and that is as far as you can go. Be careful of the six-foot ledge in midchannel beyond Dion's.

Getting Ashore. Row to the dinghy dock at Dion's.

For the Boat. *Dion's Yacht Yard (Ch. 16; tel. 439-9582).* Founded in 1963 by Elmer Dion, this family business thinks of itself as a boatyard rather than a marina. The yard has facilities to work in wood, fiberglass, aluminum, and steel, and can do extensive restoration work, rebuilding, and hull and engine repairs. The marine railway can handle craft up to 200 tons, and there are two hydraulic trailers for overland transportation of boats up to 55 feet. Ice, water, and electricity are available at the dock, but no fuel. There are showers and a well-supplied marine store.

Kittery Yacht Club (tel. 439-2550). The Kittery Yacht Club has no clubhouse, but it maintains a guest mooring in Back Channel (marked KYC-BC), just west of the midchannel ledge.

For the Crew. It's about a mile east to Frisbee's Market in Kittery Point (see Pepperrell Cove, above), and a mile west to the drugstore and post office in Kittery.

PORTSMOUTH/KITTERY—ALTERNATIVE SLIPS and MOORINGS

There is a growing shortage of moorings for both residents and transients in the Portsmouth/Kittery area, so you may need to seek out alternatives to Pepperrell Cove and Back Channel. Less desirable places to spend the night can be had along the southern shore of the Piscataqua, both east and west of Memorial Bridge (see below).

Although offering proximity to downtown Portsmouth, these anchorages are exposed to the full tidal current. When the tide is running, moor-

ings are tricky to pick up, and may even be pulled under. For those not accustomed to tidal rivers, here is Rule Number One: regardless of wind direction, approach the mooring into the current.

The Bridges. There are three bridges across the Piscataqua River between Kittery and Portsmouth. The first two are lift bridges and the third is fixed. Closed, the lift bridges have vertical clearances of 10 and 19 feet, so you will have to arrange for the spans to be lifted in order to go up the river.

The river runs very swiftly, and the bridges constitute a hazard for incautious skippers or boats with too little power to deal with the current. At full ebb, you will need at least six knots of power and probably more to fight your way upstream. If the current is flooding, you will need the same power to avoid being shoved into the bridge while waiting for it to open.

To minimize the problem, do what the big ships do. The *Coast Pilot* says, "As a result of the combination of rapid tidal currents and hazardous cross-currents, navigation of deep-draft vessels is limited to the three-hour period consisting of 1.5 hours before and 1.5 hours after slack water during daylight." To determine the time of slack water (which does not usually coincide with the time of high or low water), consult the *Tidal Current Tables*. A local rule of thumb is to add three hours to the time of high and low tides (two hours in Great Bay).

During summer daylight hours the bridges now lift only at specified times. They don't lift automatically; you still have to request it. The first lift span is Memorial Bridge, which opens on the *hour* and *1/2 hour*.

Call Memorial Bridge on channel 13 of your VHF as you round Henderson Point on Seavey Island. Here's how a call might sound: "Hello, Memorial, this is the sailboat *Eider* just coming around Henderson Point. May I have a lift?" And the reply might go: "Sure, *Eider*, we can take care of you." Not necessarily the approved language, but it's short and snappy and gets the message across.

If you do not have a VHF, use your horn. The signal is one prolonged blast, followed by one short blast. If the bridge will be opened immediately, the bridgetenders will reply with the same signal within 30 seconds: Check chapter 2 of the *Coast Pilot* for further details or changes. When the bridge cannot be opened immediately, or if it is open and about to be closed, the bridgetenders sound five short blasts in rapid succession.

The second bridge, called Sarah Long (or Long), is about half a mile farther upriver. It lifts at your request *15 minutes before the hour* and *15 minutes after the hour*. Although it monitors the same VHF channel as Memorial, you must call each bridge separately. The current on the Piscataqua is at its strongest between the first two bridges—as much as nine knots—so if you're too early for the second bridge, find an eddy to wait in.

The third bridge, some 900 yards beyond Sarah Long, is a fixed highway bridge with a 135-foot vertical clearance.

Slips and Moorings—East of Memorial Bridge. *Portsmouth Yacht Club (New Castle) (Ch. 78; tel. 603-436-9877).* This attractive club is located just west of Salamander Point, on the south side of the Piscataqua River. It has good facilities for visiting yachtsmen, including moorings, launch service, and space alongside, with deep water at

the outer floats. Gas, diesel, water, electricity, and ice are available. There are reciprocal privileges for members of other yacht clubs, including a key to the handsome 1898 clubhouse, which has showers.

Kittery Point Yacht Club (Ch. 68; tel. 603-436-9303). The Kittery Point Yacht Club is not in Kittery Point, but at the eastern end of Goat Island, on the south side of the Piscataqua—a gray building with the initials "KPYC" along the porch. One or two moorings usually are available, and there is a launch service on weekends. There are floats, ice, water, and trash disposal, but no fuel or other facilities. The clubhouse has showers and a telephone.

Prescott Park Docking Facility (tel. 603-431-8748). The city of Portsmouth provides a docking facility just east of Memorial Bridge, with the entrance marked by nun "2" and can "3." Even inside the buoys, the current can run very strong, so tie up to the outer floats, approaching bow into current. There is reported to be eight feet at low along the outer floats.

This location is convenient to downtown Portsmouth, with its many stores and restaurants. Rules include: "No commercial boats; no boat over 40 feet; 72-hour limit; no rafting." Call ahead to reserve a slip, and register at the little dockhouse if a city attendant is there. Some of the slips have electricity, but there are no other facilities.

West of Memorial Bridge. Several new facilities have grown up in recent years west of Memorial Bridge.

The Marina at Harbour Place (Ch. 16; tel. 603-433-1904). Located in Portsmouth, on the south side of the river just west of Memorial Bridge, this marina has dock space for transients, with 30 feet alongside at low. Facilities include water, electricity, telephones, and cable TV hookups.

Badger's Island Marina (Ch. 16; tel. 439-4456). This marina is in Kittery, on the north bank of the Piscataqua, opposite nun "16." It offers 235 feet of dockage along the outside floats, with 30 feet at low, and 35 slips with electricity and water.

George A. Patten Yacht Yard (tel. 439-3967). Adjacent to Badger's Island Marina, this is a major repair facility capable of tackling any problems. They handle both commercial vessels and yachts, with steel, wood, and fiberglass hulls. The yard has a diesel mechanic and can perform electronic, electrical, and refrigeration repairs. The two marine railways are rated at 20 and 50 tons and there is a hydraulic trailer.

For the Crew (Portsmouth). From locations near Memorial Bridge, you can walk to an A & P that is open 24 hours a day, downtown near Ceres Street, and to all sorts of other stores. The HCA Portsmouth Regional Hospital is at the east end of town (tel. 603-436-5110).

Things to Do (Portsmouth). In addition to the

civilized pleasures of a small city, Portsmouth has some special attractions of its own. The old brick warehouses on Ceres Street now house wonderful little waterfront restaurants and bars. Nearby is Strawbery Banke, a 10-acre historic waterfront neighborhood with fascinating old homes, gardens, and interesting exhibits. Strawbery Banke and Prescott Park sponsor many special summer events, from open-air concerts and arts festivals to craft fairs and gardening workshops.

One of the best ways to see Portsmouth and appreciate its history is to take a harbor cruise, offered by Portsmouth Harbor Cruises (tel. 603-436-8084) leaving from a dock on Ceres Street. You may go the back way from the Piscataqua to Little Harbor, under the bridge between Shapleigh and Goat islands, passing the Wentworth-Coolidge mansion, with the oldest lilacs in the United States. Returning, you will get a good look at forts and lighthouses, the Coast Guard Rescue Station, and the Portsmouth Naval Shipyard. Other cruises take you into Great Bay, with its quiet tributaries and abundant birdlife. Farther west are the docks of the Isles of Shoals Steamship Company, offering excursions to the Isles of Shoals (tel. 603-431-5500).

About a mile west of Prescott Park, just beyond the second bridge, is the Port of Portsmouth Maritime Museum, featuring the U.S.S. *Albacore*, a research submarine. You can walk through the sub, marveling at how people live and work in such tight quarters—well worth the visit.

PISCATAQUA RIVER and TRIBUTARIES; LITTLE BAY and GREAT BAY

Chart: 13285

It is not wise for anyone new to these waters to try to take a boat above Portsmouth on the Piscataqua River. As the *Coast Pilot* says, "General navigation throughout the entire length of the Piscataqua River is severely hampered by rapid tidal currents." There are hazardous crosscurrents, and buoys sometimes are towed under.

If this is your home territory or you are comfortable with fast tidal currents, the Piscataqua River has a number of tributaries above Portsmouth worth exploring, with marshes, birds and good gunkholing. Plan to run upriver with the flood; otherwise, it takes forever.

In addition to the three bridges described in the preceding section, there is a fourth, between Dover Point and Newington. The (fixed) General Sullivan bridge has a clearance of 46 feet at high tide and 52 feet at low tide.

For the Boat. *Great Bay Marine, Inc. (Ch. 9 or 16; tel. 603-436-5299).* In Newington, on the north side of Fox Point in Great Bay, this is a large and well-equipped marina, with many moorings and slips (deep water alongside), water, electricity, gas, diesel, and ice. With a 30-ton boatlift, the yard can handle a wide range of hull and engine repairs. There is also a well-stocked marine store, and showers for the crew.

BOON ISLAND

Chart: 13286

Running north from the Portsmouth-Kittery area, you will pass infamous Boon Island, scene of many a shipwreck in the nation's early days.

Take, for instance, the story of the *Nottingham*, related by Kenneth Roberts. There was a howling gale of snow that night in the winter of 1710 when the *Nottingham*, 135 days out of England, drove on the rocks of Boon Island. Think of those 14 miserable wretches, with no means to build a fire, drenched by spray and frozen by bitter winds, surviving for weeks on shellfish and seagulls, within sight of the mainland, but with no hope of discovery. The little boat they built was destroyed by the sea, and two men were lost on a raft, whose remains, washed up on Cape Neddick finally led to rescue—but not before the body of "the old carpenter" had provided the grisly food for survival.

The granite lighthouse built in 1855 towers 133 feet above the low and menacing rocks of the island and its light and horn warn mariners 18 miles away. It is visible from the Isles of Shoals to the south and Cape Porpoise to the north.

There is no soil on these dismal rocks, and lightkeepers used to carry a few sacks of earth in their boats to plant tiny gardens, only to have it all disappear with the winter storms. Keepers were lost when waves washed over earlier towers, but one William Williams liked the lonely post so much he stayed for 27 years. The light is automated now.

There is a white Coast Guard mooring north of the island, and it is possible to row ashore in calm weather. There is no access to the tower, however, and the keeper's house is gone.

YORK HARBOR ★★★★

Charts: **13283**, 13286

As long ago as 1624, explorer Christopher Levett described the appeal of this historic area when he wrote, "This is a good place for a plantation—a good harbor for ships." Today York Harbor is a delightful little place where lobsterboats, yachts, fishermen and summer visitors coexist in relative peace and harmony. It is also a fashionable summer resort, with many antique stores and galleries, beautiful old homes and historic sites, and many pleasant ways to spend the time.

This is the most secure harbor between Portsmouth and Portland. However, the entrance requires a sharp turn that can be very tricky when the tide is running hard, so it is not a place to enter at night or in the fog. In such circumstances, it would be far better to run for the easy entrance to Portsmouth Harbor, a few miles back down the coast.

York Harbor has long had a reputation as a hurricane hole. It provided protection during the hurricane of 1938 as well as in more recent blows.

Approaches. Entering the harbor is tricky and dangerous on a flood tide because of the sharp right turn at nun "10." Plan to enter against the ebb tide if possible or at slack water. Find the red-and-white bell "YH" off York Harbor and then head halfway between the entrance buoys, leaving nun "4" to starboard and can "3" to port. Aim for Stage Neck Light, a red, triangular shape on a small, white box with a light on top. Stage Neck, a peninsula running along the north side of the harbor entrance, is lined with condominiums.

Observe nun "6" and can "7" with care and stay to port of the line between can "7" and nun "10." If you are coming in with the flood do not cut nun "10" close, because there will not be enough room to turn after the nun and you may be thrown by the current into Harris Island ledge or the boats moored nearby. Instead, leave nun "10" a couple boat lengths to starboard, giving yourself room to make the turn before reaching Harris Island ledge. Head through the narrows between the rocky beach off Stage Neck and the ledge on Harris Island marked with green daybeacon "11," staying just right of midchannel. Leaving York Harbor, stay just left of midchannel in the narrows to avoid the Harris Island ledge. After turning sharp left around nun "10," be careful not to be set to port by a flooding tide. It is very easy to keep aiming at can "7" and end up on the Stage Neck beach.

There is a lot of bottom paint on these ledges, and even the great and famous have come to grief here. One story goes that *Ticonderoga* cut the nun close many years ago when leaving and ended up high and dry on Stage Neck. The embarrassed captain offered the then-astronomical sum of $50 to be towed off in secrecy during the night.

Anchorages, Moorings. Anchoring is no longer allowed in York Harbor, and all moorings are assigned by the harbormaster. Call the harbor master's launch on channel 16. If you can't reach the harbormaster, ask York Harbor Marine for help. There is space alongside at Donnell's Marine and York Harbor Marine.

Getting Ashore. The easiest places to get ashore are at the Agamenticus Yacht Club float or behind the dock at Donnell's. The current runs hard enough so that a little planning pays off. If you are rowing ashore from the cove north of Bragdon Island against a flood current, stick to the shallows and eddies until you are opposite your objective; then strike straight across.

For the Boat. *Agamenticus Yacht Club (tel. 363-9814).* On Stage Neck, the tiny clubhouse of the Agamenticus Yacht Club is identifiable by its flagpole and burgee. Yacht club facilities are limited to water at the floats (six feet alongside at low) and weekend launch service, but the people there are cordial and helpful.

Donnell's Marine (tel. 363-4308). At the north end of the harbor before can "13" is Donnell's dock, with space alongside for the night, water and electricity, but no fuel. Unlikely as it appears, Mr. Donnell says there is 10 feet of water at the outside float at low tide. A pay phone is at the head of the pier.

York Harbor Marine Service (Ch. 16; tel. 363-3602). This operation is located on Harris Island, just past the narrows on the left. To avoid turbulent water when the tide is flooding, go just beyond the yard before turning back through the moorings toward the marina. The yard can provide dock space (six feet of water alongside at low), launch service, water, electricity, gas, diesel, ice, and marine supplies. They have a 60-ton marine railway and can handle normal boat and engine repairs.

For the Crew. York Harbor Marine has showers, washing machines, and a telephone.

The town of York Harbor is at the north side of the harbor, and the post office is about a block from the water and very obvious. York Harbor Market, a deli/convenience store selling newspapers, sundries, ice cream, cheeses, and baked goods, is in the big, gray Lancaster Building, on the same street as the post office. The trolley-bus stops across the street. The next nearest provisions are at the Cumberland Farms convenience store in York Village (a one-mile walk via Route 1A—see sketch map). There is a laundromat next to Cumberland Farms, and a bike rental shop (tel. 363-4070). York Hospital is nearby.

A right turn and another .6-mile walk leads to a

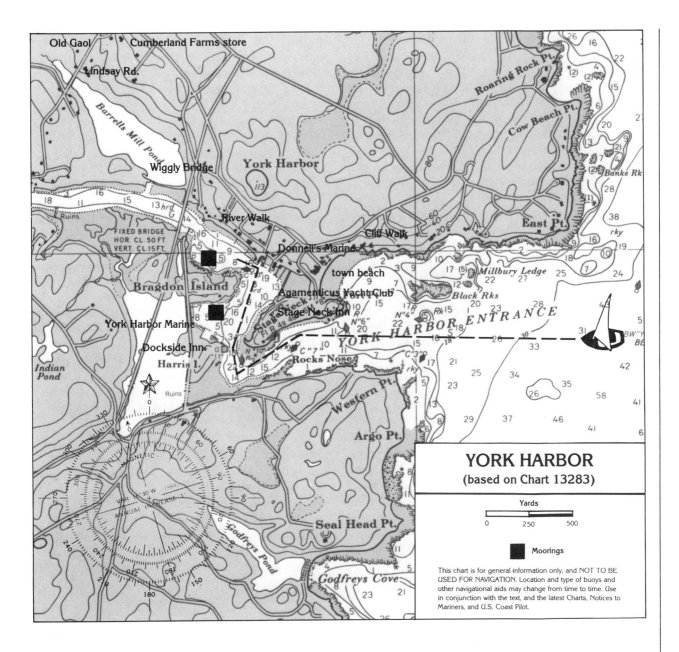

YORK HARBOR
(based on Chart 13283)

Yards

0   250   500

■ Moorings

This chart is for general information only, and NOT TO BE USED FOR NAVIGATION. Location and type of buoys and other navigational aids may change from time to time. Use in conjunction with the text, and the latest Charts, Notices to Mariners, and U.S. Coast Pilot.

shopping center with an IGA grocery store, bakery, hardware store, 5¢ and 10¢ store, and pharmacy. Before you start walking, check to see whether the red trolley-bus is running from York Harbor. The schedule changes from summer to summer; ask a local resident or simply keep your eyes peeled. Restaurants within easy rowing distance are the Stage Neck Inn and The Dockside (see sketch map).

Things to Do. The manicured lawns of the Stage Neck Inn lead to a pleasant lounge overlooking the adjacent town beach. The word *stage* comes not from stagecoaches but from early fishing days when cod was dried and salted on stages or racks. The inn serves lunch and dinner by reservation (tel. 363-3850).

Wonderfully situated at the turn of the channel is the Dockside Inn on Harris Island. Meals are served in a separate building with a screened porch overlooking the ocean and the river. Walk out to

the gazebo on the point and watch new arrivals negotiate (or fail to negotiate) the sharp turn.

The town beach is a crescent of white sand where you can swim in gentle surf. At the far end of the beach is the beginning of the Cliff Walk around the northern side of the harbor. Winding between the sea and beautiful old summer cottages, it is one of the loveliest coastal walks in Maine. Respect the privacy of the landowners.

If you have a dinghy with an outboard, another enjoyable pastime is exploring upriver.

York Village is full of sites with historic interest. York originally was the Indian settlement of Agamenticus, wiped out by plague and resettled by colonists in 1630. Here Sir Ferdinando Gorges, friend of King Charles I, created the first city in British North America in 1640. Anticipating becoming governor of New England, he called it "Gorgeana." With the triumph of Oliver Cromwell, however, Gorges lost his power and the city

of Gorgeana was demoted to the village of York.

For a good walk that offers a taste of York history, start at the Agamenticus Yacht Club dock or Donnell's Marine. Go left on a path along the waterfront called the River Walk. Cross the road and head for the pedestrian Wiggly Bridge, which leads into a wooded nature preserve. Follow the dirt lane until you reach the first paved road (Lindsay). Take a right on Lindsay and walk a half mile until you come to York Village, passing a number of interesting old houses on the way.

At the corner of Lindsay Road and York Street is Jefferds Tavern and nearby is the Old Gaol. Built in 1719 with timbers from its 1653 predecessor, the Gaol is the oldest remaining English public building in the United States. Here you can visit cells and dungeons and the restored quarters where jailer William Emerson and his family lived cheek-by-jowl with the prisoners. His bedroom window opened onto one of the cells. That's togetherness.

Near the Old Gaol are several other buildings open to the public, including the Old Schoolhouse. Nearby is the Old Burying Ground with some fascinating headstones dating back to the early 1700s. A plaque in the cemetery says, "Near this spot are interred the remains of the victims of one of the worst massacres of colonial days. On Candlemas Day, 1691–2, the dawn of a January morning, Abenaki Indians attacked the settlement of York, burning the houses and killing or capturing 300 of its inhabitants. About 40 were killed. The rest marched to Canada, many dying on the way." There the captured inhabitants of York were sold as servants to the French.

Leaving York Harbor, if the weather suits, drop the lunch hook off the town beach outside Stage Neck, in 10 to 12 feet of water at low, and have a swim. Halfway between nuns "4" and "6," head in for the middle of the beach and anchor a little way past Fort Point.

YORK BEACH ★★

Charts: **13283** (Inset), 13286

York Beach is a broad crescent beach tucked behind the north side of Cape Neddick and open from east to north. It is better protected than Cape Neddick Harbor from prevailing southerlies by the bulk of the cape and provides a fine anchorage in settled weather. Entry is easy. The scene ashore includes the beautiful—and very popular—beach, summer cottages and boarding homes, and endless beachfront attractions that appeal to the resort's family-oriented clientele.

Approaches. Coming from the south, pick up the light or horn on Cape Neddick Nubble and skirt the northern shore of Cape Neddick, which is steep-to. Head for the center of the beach. There are no obstructions.

Popularly known as the Nubble, Cape Neddick

light is one of the most photographed lighthouses on the coast of Maine. A narrow channel separates the Nubble from the mainland, and generations of lighthouse keepers' children have walked (or been rowed) across to attend school.

Anchorages. When the fathometer shows about 15 feet at low, it is time to drop the hook. If you go farther in, you will start to feel the roll of the surf. Holding ground is good in sand.

Getting Ashore. The calmest spot to land a dinghy is usually in the southeast corner of the beach, but you'll probably get your feet wet in the small surf.

For the Crew. There are restaurants and markets in town, within a block or two of the water.

CAPE NEDDICK HARBOR ★★

Charts: **13283** (Inset), 13286

Cape Neddick Harbor is comfortable in settled summer weather, but exposed from the east to the south. Although the entrance is easy, there are several unmarked dangers that make it difficult to go far inside.

There are no facilities except the Cape Neddick Lobster Pound and Restaurant across the street from the anchorage, and the view of the trailer park on the western shore is hardly inspiring, but the sand bar at the mouth of the Cape Neddick River is a nice place for wading and swimming.

Approaches. Head in between red bell "2" and

can "1" toward a small, gray house on the beach.

Anchorages, Moorings. Once you are past the northern entrance ledge, the northeast shore to starboard is fairly steep-to, and you can anchor anywhere along it in 10 to 14 feet of water. Resist your instinct to seek better protection by anchoring in the southwest corner. Although you can pick your way among the rocks there and anchor on short scope, it is tricky. A view of the harbor at low tide shows several ledges, some awash and some just below the surface.

PERKINS COVE (OGUNQUIT) ★★★★

Chart: 13286 (Inset)

Perkins Cove is a gem. It is a tiny, working fishing village whose fish shacks have been transformed into shops and galleries, but whose fishermen and charm remain despite a swarm of tourists.

In normal weather, the cove is extremely well protected from every direction. During strong northerlies or easterlies, however, the water piles in and may make it dangerous to enter and completely untenable. Entrance is always rather difficult because of a unique wooden bascule bridge and also because there is so little room inside among the resident lobsterboats.

This tiny harbor is relatively recent. Before the first dredging in 1941, the Josiah's River trickled into Oarweed Cove, and there was no harbor to speak of.

In 1889 the surf-pounded rocks, lobster shacks, and brightly painted dories caught the eye of Charles Woodbury, a Massachusetts artist. He founded the Ogunquit Art Association on Adams Island, where most of the lobster and fish shacks stood. People were attracted to this idyllic spot, and fishermen, artists, and summer people have intermingled here ever since.

Approaches. Pick up the red-and-white "PC" bell offshore, then head for the can and nun marking the entrance. Use power going in; there is no room to maneuver.

The ledges on both sides of the entrance break heavily and are easy to see, even at high water. From nun "2," head for the 13-foot spot, until you can see right up the slot. Then turn to starboard and proceed up the middle toward the bridge.

Land at the floats to starboard just before the bridge and ask for the harbormaster, who is likely to be nearby.

Anchorages, Moorings. The sign on the wooden footbridge says, "Guest Moorings for Emergency Only—$20 per night." And they mean it. Despite the lack of space, however, the harbormaster says, "We'll find room for you." How he does it is a mystery known only to him.

You are the bridgetender in Perkins Cove. Walk up on the bridge and press the button that raises the span. Probably someone will close it for you.

Aim carefully as you go through: The opening is narrow, so boats with upper spreaders may have trouble. Once inside, stay to the right until you can turn toward your assigned mooring. All boats are moored fore and aft to chains laid sideways across the harbor.

How much water is there in the cove? As a local sailor put it, "If you draw more than five feet, you're in trouble." The chart shows four-, five-, and six-foot spots, some of which are soft and silty; others are hard rock. On days with extreme low water, the depth might be a foot or two less.

Getting Ashore. Row to the dinghy dock on the north side of the harbor.

For the Boat. Water is available at the town dock, but there are no fuel or repair facilities.

For the Crew. In the village are public restrooms and pay phones. Perkins Cove has no market; you will need to go into Ogunquit for supplies. This is beyond comfortable walking distance when lugging provisions, but a trolley-bus leaves from Barnacle Billy's Restaurant, right on the harbor. The schedule is changeable; inquire locally. There are several waterside restaurants in this little community. Notable is Barnacle Billy's, Maine's most glorified takeout. Diners stand outside to pick up lobsters, chowders, and blueberry pies when their number is called and then retire to tables with views of the harbor. Founder Billy Tower was a fisherman and harbormaster at the age of 14 before he retired from the sea to become an energetic host.

Things to Do. Visiting Perkins Cove means exploring the many small shops and galleries that are the hallmark of this artists' colony.

One of the most beautiful strolls along the coast of Maine is the 1½-mile-long Marginal Way, which parallels the open ocean from Oarweed Cove to Ogunquit Beach, with spectacular views of the surf dashing on the rocks, wildflowers, and stunted pines. The walk is not strenuous, and there are memorial benches for resting and dreaming. To the north stretch the white sand beaches of Ogunquit, Moody, and Wells.

WELLS HARBOR ★★★

Chart: 13286 (Inset)

This is no place for cruising yachtsmen. The entrance is dangerous and there is hardly any water in the anchorage basin at low tide. As the owner of Wells Harbor Marina says, "Tell 'em to stay away." Still, it is possible to enter Wells Harbor in good

weather at high tide, and the miles of unspoiled marshes behind the coastal beaches, including the Rachel Carson National Wildlife Refuge, have their own special beauty.

Approaches. Wells Harbor is formed by the

Webhannet River. Over the years, several attempts to create a good harbor have cost taxpayers a great deal of money without the slightest hint of success. The two jetties apparently disturb the coastwise flow of sand, and a dangerous delta has built up. As the *Coast Pilot* notes, swells break across the entrance even in a moderate sea, making entry hazardous.

The northern jetty is marked by a flashing red light, the southern jetty by a green daybeacon. Favor the southern one. The controlling depth of the dredged channel in recent years has been 4 feet to daybeacon "5," and 1 foot beyond it. Further shoaling may be expected. The main town dock is on the west side of the basin.

KENNEBUNKPORT ★★★ All facilities

Chart: 13286 (Inset)

Summer Kennebunkport is a madhouse, perhaps the epitome of tourist Maine. The sidewalks are jammed with people, the cars creep along the crowded streets, and the roar of speedboats echoes off the banks of the river. Nevertheless, Kennebunkport has appeal for visiting yachtsmen, with places to explore and tranquil oases here and there. If you can find a mooring or a place to tie up, this is a snug harbor and extremely well protected. Since the Kennebunk River is shallow and tends to silt up, a six-foot draft is probably the most you can carry to enter this harbor comfortably at low water.

The Kennebunk River probably was discovered by Bartholomew Gosnold in 1602 or Martin Pring in 1603. In its natural state, it was a barred harbor, with only two feet of water at the entrance at low water, and navigable for only about half a mile. Settled in 1643, Kennebunk and nearby towns were depopulated several times during the Indian wars. During the nineteenth century, the banks of the Kennebunk River boasted six shipyards that launched 638 vessels.

Approaches. Coming in is easy. You can approach either east or west of Fishing Rock, but the eastern approach is better marked, particularly in poor visibility. From the east, leave green bell "1" and can "3" to port and run in for the two jetties. Drop your sails before entering the river. Jog to the right at can "7" after you pass the jetties. (Boats entering at night sometimes miss the right turn and end up on the shelving beach to port.) As you proceed up the channel, check off the buoys, which often are obscured by boats. Lobsterboats moored on the left side stick out in the channel between cans "7" and "9," creating a tight squeeze to get around them at nun "8."

Anchorages, Moorings. The major area for

Anchorages, Moorings. There are no moorings available in Wells Harbor, and little room to anchor. You can tie up to the floats at the town dock, in seven feet of water alongside.

For the Boat. Gas, diesel, ice, water, and pay phone are available at the town dock.

Wells Harbor Marina (tel. 646-9087). The yard has a marine railway that can handle boats up to 40 feet. Repair and maintenance services are being expanded, and there is a small chandlery.

For the Crew. The popular Lord's Harborside Restaurant is next to the marina, and there is a pleasant little seafood restaurant half a mile inland—clearly visible across the expanse of marshes.

moorings is just past can "11" on the left side of the river channel. About 15 small cruising boats usually are lying in this area. Anchoring is not allowed in the river. Your best bet for getting a mooring is to call Chick's Marina ahead of time (see below). It may be possible to pick up a mooring and check in later at Chick's, but don't count on it. Arundel Boatyard might also have a mooring.

Although dredged to six feet from time to time, the mooring area silts in to four or five feet. But don't worry about damage to your boat: you will merely settle gently into the mud. Just remember, if departing at low tide, you may find you are attached imperceptibly to the bottom.

Although tidal like the York and Piscataqua rivers, the Kennebunk River ebbs and flows with much less fuss and a current of only two or three knots. There may be considerably more current, however, after a few days of heavy rains.

Beyond the mooring area are several marinas where a slip may be available. On the right side of the channel, just past the inlet after can "13," is Chick's, with dozens of boats in front of it. Farther up the right bank, just past can "15," are the docks and clubhouse of the Arundel Yacht Club. Be careful of large shoal areas just before and after the yacht club slips, the corners of which are marked by pilings. Slips are on a first-come, first-served basis, although on weekdays you may be able to reserve one by calling ahead.

Finally, on the left-hand side at the head of the harbor and closest to the town center, you will find Riverview Docks and Arundel Boatyard, both with slips and moorings that can be reserved. There may sometimes be space alongside at the Nonantum Marina. Most of the other slips and moorings in the Kennebunk River are private.

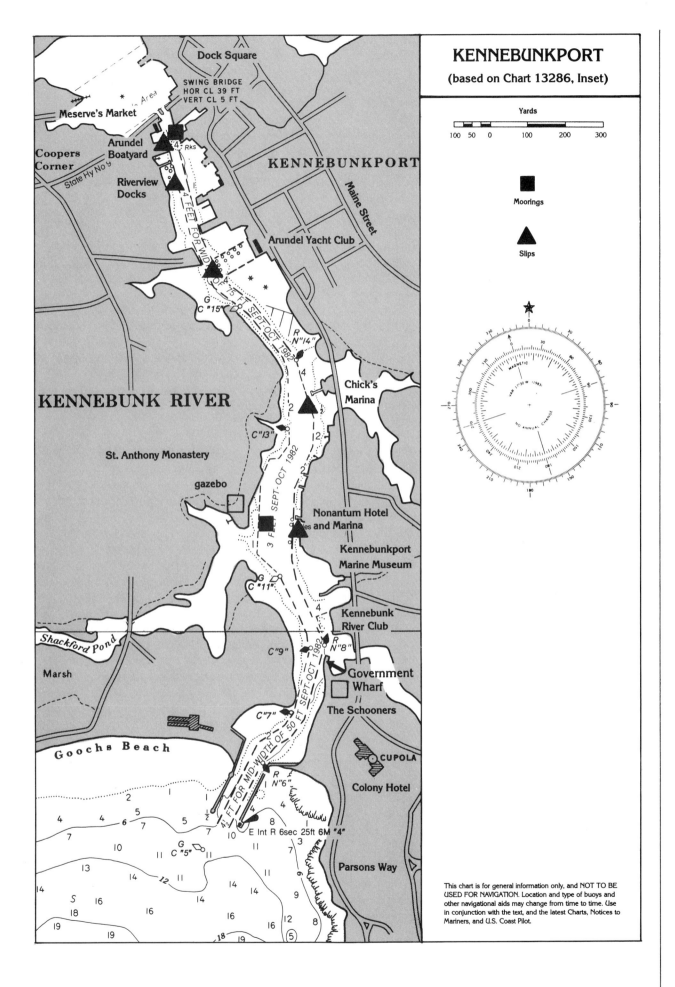

KENNEBUNKPORT
(based on Chart 13286, Inset)

Yards

100 50 0 100 200 300

Moorings

Slips

Dock Square

SWING BRIDGE
HOR CL 39 FT
VERT CL 5 FT

Meserve's Market

Arundel
Boatyard

Coopers
Corner

State Hy No 9

Riverview
Docks

KENNEBUNKPORT

Maine Street

4 "4" Rks

4 FEET FOR WID

75 FT SEPT-OCT 1982

Arundel Yacht Club

G
C "15"

R N"14"

KENNEBUNK RIVER

4

Chick's
Marina

2

3 FEET SEPT-OCT 1982

C "13"

12

St. Anthony Monastery

gazebo

Nonantum Hotel
and Marina

Kennebunkport
Marine Museum

G
C "11"

4

Kennebunk
River Club

Shackford Pond

C "9"

75 FT SEPT-OCT 1982

R N"8"

Marsh

Government
Wharf

C "7"

The Schooners

Goochs Beach

4½ FT FOR MID-WIDTH OF 50

R N"6"

CUPOLA

Colony Hotel

2   1

4   5
6
4   2   5   7   7
7   10   4   8
E Int R 6sec 25ft 6M "4"

Parsons Way

10   11
G
C "5"   11

13   11
14
12   11
14   14   14

14   S   16   14
16   16   12
18   8
19   19   18   19   (5)

This chart is for general information only, and NOT TO BE USED FOR NAVIGATION. Location and type of buoys and other navigational aids may change from time to time. Use in conjunction with the text, and the latest Charts, Notices to Mariners, and U.S. Coast Pilot.

Getting Ashore. Convenient places to take your dinghy ashore include the dinghy float at the Nonantum Hotel, Chick's Marina, the Arundel Yacht Club, and the Arundel Boatyard.

For the Boat. *Arundel Boatyard (Ch. 16; tel. 967-5550).* This is a full-service boatyard and marina. There is six feet of water alongside the main float at low. Facilities include water, electricity, ice, showers, and a marine store. The yard has a 15-ton boatlift and can make hull and engine repairs. They specialize in wooden boat repair and restoration.

Arundel Yacht Club (Ch. 16; tel. 967-3060). The clubhouse is a wonderful old wooden building that once was part of a rope walk (a long building where rope was laid and twisted) and is still called by that name. Services include showers, ice, and a pay phone. Water and electricity are available at the outer floats, with six feet of depth alongside, but no fuel. The water shoals rapidly at the inner floats.

Chick's Marina (Ch. 16; tel. 967-2782). Chick's is the main resource for transients. It handles the moorings north of can "11" and also has space alongside. There is six feet of water at the outer floats, where you can obtain water, diesel, gas, ice, and electricity. On the dock are showers, washing machines, a marine store, and pay phone. Chick's hauls boats up the ramp by hydraulic trailer, and can perform most engine, rigging, and hull repairs.

Nonantum Marina (tel. 967-3338). This informal marina is for guests at the Nonantum Hotel but occasionally has space at the floats for a transient. There is about six feet of water alongside; no facilities.

Riverview Docks (Ch. 16; tel. 967-2612). Just south of Arundel Boatyard, the two-story Riverview shops and condos stretch along the left bank of the river. There are slips with 6 feet alongside at low, water, electricity, telephone and cable TV.

For the Crew. Several of the marinas provide laundromats and a small selection of grocery items. The only market in the town center is a convenience store named Meserve's (also a state liquor store), just west of the bridge. There is a laundromat past Meserve's. The post office is on Temple Street, just east of the bridge and close to Dock Square.

Kennebunkport offers all sorts of gift shops, stores, and restaurants. Upstairs in an old rum warehouse in Dock Square is a great bookstore called the Kennebunk Book Port. Near the handsome, century-old Nonantum Hotel are a fish market, shops, restaurants, a beauty salon, and an ice cream bar.

Things to Do. To appreciate the town's splendid architectural traditions, start at the river and walk two blocks east to Maine Street, then along quiet, shady streets lined with colonial and federal homes. Follow the street north along Grist Mill Pond. For another walk in the most peaceful part of town, land at the Nonantum Hotel dock and walk south along Parsons Way to the oceanfront. En route is "The Floats," used by novelist Booth Tarkington as a boathouse and summer afternoon retreat, now converted to the Kennebunkport Maritime Museum and Shop, with a fine collection of nautical antiques.

If you are moored beyond can "11" near a brown, wooden gazebo in the marshes, go ashore from there and follow the boardwalk. It leads to a shady path through the trees and emerges at the handsome grounds, gardens, and chapel of St. Anthony Monastery and Shrines, the home of Lithuanian Franciscan monks. The grounds and some areas of the monastery are open to the public. Land near high tide, because the banks are steep and muddy. For another nice outing, row your dinghy toward the harbor entrance, inside the moored lobsterboats, until you come to the first little sand beach on the west bank. Walk along the edge of the river to magnificent Gooch's Beach, with its flat, hard sand. For a whale watching expedition, the *Nautilus* leaves from Arundel Boatyard (tel. 967-0707).

CAPE PORPOISE HARBOR ★★★ 

Chart: 13286 (Inset)

The stranger approaching Cape Porpoise Harbor does so with trepidation, having heard of the profusion of lobster buoys and the ledge-strewn entrance. Matters have improved. The Coast Guard has added some navigational aids where they are most needed, and although the lobster buoys are still spread like a colorful carpet in the entrance, the hazards have receded somewhat.

Cape Porpoise, a working harbor, is home to a fleet of 40 or 50 lobsterboats. The anchorage is large and reasonably well protected by the encircling islands and ledges. You will be safe and comfortable here—at least until 4 A.M., when several dozen unmuffled lobsterboats rev up for the day's work. Who wants to sleep after 4 A.M., anyway?

In his 1837 *History of Kennebunk Port*, Charles

Bradbury wrote of Cape Porpoise's renown even then as a safe haven: "Cape Porpoise is a small but very convenient harbor. It lies at the extremity of the cape, and is the only safe harbor for coasting vessels between Portsmouth and Portland, being equidistant from them. Great numbers put in there during the dangerous seasons of the year. Nearly a hundred have harbored there in one day."

Approaches. The entrance to the harbor is marked by red bell "2." From there, run between can "3" and nun "4." As the *Coast Pilot* points out, green daybeacon "5A" on the ledge northeast of Folly Island is not at the edge of the channel, and the same is true of daybeacon "6" southwest of Goat Island. Give both of them a wide berth. A helpful new buoy, can "5," now marks the left-hand edge of the channel coming in, and there is one more pair of channel buoys to observe before the harbor opens up.

The presence of the ubiquitous lobster buoys in midchannel demands caution, but the careful skipper can wind his way through the maze, occasionally gliding in neutral, as in many Maine harbors. Entering at night multiplies the difficulty and is strongly discouraged, except under ideal conditions.

Anchorages, Moorings. The moorings are all private, and are in use mostly by lobsterboats. You might learn of an available mooring for the night by inquiring at the lobstermen's co-op on the town dock.

Anchor anywhere in the area where the channel widens, preferably in the half closest to the entrance, to keep a distance from the many lobsterboats moored farther in. There is a line of floats topped by sheds (lobster cars) moored along the western edge of the anchorage. Holding ground is good, in mud.

If there's a strong wind from the south or southwest, it may get a little lumpy in the harbor, particularly when the ledges are covered at high tide.

Getting Ashore. There are dinghy floats beyond the town dock.

For the Boat. Although gas, diesel, and water are available at the dock, you will have to deal with tall, grimy pilings that are not easy to tie up to without scraping your topsides, fishermen dangling lines off the dock, and a procession of lobsterboats. Furthermore, yachts are not terribly popular here, and lobster bait has been known to fall unexpectedly on pristine decks.

For the Crew. On the wharf you will find a pay phone and ice. Close by are a takeout and restaurant.

The village of Cape Porpoise is small and peaceful, especially compared to Kennebunkport. A ten- or fifteen-minute walk from the wharf leads to the head of the harbor. Continue a little farther along the road to a stop sign at a fork (.7 mile from the harbor), where there are a small hardware store, two restaurants, and a pastry shop. Bradbury Brothers Market, located just beyond them, is one of the best such establishments anywhere on the coast, especially for meat. Bradbury's has even been known to offer a lift to the harbor for grocery-laden customers. The post office is located inside Bradbury's, and ice and newspapers can be obtained there also.

For good seafood and unusual atmosphere, don't miss Nunan's Lobster Hut, one hundred yards down the road to the right, past the hardware store. Don't expect anything fancy. Guests attack their lobsters with gusto and wash up in sinks next to the tables. As the menu says, wine is served "without undue attention to the complication of wine ritual."

In the low-key atmosphere of present-day Cape Porpoise, it is hard to imagine what it was like at the turn of the century, when a lively casino featured a dance floor and restaurant, and patrons availed themselves of romantic strolls by the sea.

STAGE ISLAND HARBOR ★★★

 No Facilities

Chart: 13286 (Inset)

Stage Island Harbor, just east of Cape Porpoise Harbor, is unmarked, and it should be entered by strangers only near low tide, when the ledges on both sides of the entrance are exposed. It is peaceful and private during settled summer weather, but probably should be used only as a temporary anchorage at other times.

Stage Island, as with Stage Neck in York, refers to the stages, or drying racks, used by early cod fishermen. Just south of Stage Island is Fort Island, whose claim to historical significance is as the site of a onetime colonial bastion besieged by Indians in

the early seventeenth century. According to the saga related by Charles Bradbury in his 1837 *History of Kennebunk Port*, a handful of settlers holed up in the fort with dwindling supplies of food and ammunition. One of their number, lame and alone, stole off after dark in a decrepit canoe and headed for Portsmouth. Less than a day later, an armed sloop arrived, sprayed the Indians with gunfire, and loaded the settlers aboard the vessel. Unnerved by their near-tragic experience, the colonists abandoned the area for the next decade.

Approaches. Making for Stage Island Harbor

from Cape Porpoise, go out as far as red bell "2" to get past Old Prince Ledge; then head up the coast. Identify the islands, starting with Goat Island with its lighthouse. Cape Island is wooded at its north end and connected at low tide to the larger Trott Island, which is mostly wooded. Do not enter the cove between Cape and Trott islands. As you round Cape Island, Little Stage Island, with a small, white house, will come into view.

The ledges make out a long way to the north of Cape Island and to the south of Little Stage Island. Run into the harbor halfway between the exposed ledges (at low). The entrance is about 100 yards wide.

Anchorages, Moorings. Anchor in the southwest corner in 10 to 14 feet at low. At low water, the rock awash and the ledge at the western edge of the harbor are easily identifiable.

Stage Island Harbor is exposed to the east and south and may also be exposed to a strong northwesterly.

Getting Ashore. The beach in the western corner of the harbor between the rocks is a good place to land your dinghy.

WOOD ISLAND HARBOR and THE POOL

(AT BIDDEFORD POOL);

WOOD ISLAND ★★★

THE POOL ★★★★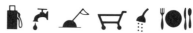

Charts: 13286, **13287**

Wood Island Harbor and The Pool are right next to each other but quite different in character. Wood Island Harbor is fairly open and unprotected. There are moorings and usually a number of large boats along the west side. A narrow channel with swift current called The Gut leads southwest from there into The Pool, a delightful little marshy bay separated from the ocean by Fletcher Neck. It is tight, but once in, you are snug.

Approaches. From the south, the most conservative approach is to head for Wood Island Light, staying well clear of dangers off Fletcher Neck, including Danbury Reef, marked by nun "2." Then skirt the north shore of Wood Island (you can go fairly close) and make a wide left turn into Wood Island Harbor, between the grassy hump of Negro Island and Stage Island (conspicuous for the tall stone monument, an old navigational mark, shaped like the snout of a very large anteater). In good visibility, it is also comfortable to enter or leave between Wood Island and Gooseberry Island. Stay well clear of can "7" at the turn; the shoal that it marks is extending.

From the north, head toward Wood Island Light and find red-and-white bell "SA." Continue into Wood Island Harbor between Negro and Stage islands. Another useful aiming point from a distance is the tall water tank shown behind The Pool on the chart. In thick weather, find offlying red-and-white whistle buoy "WI," then run a compass course to Wood Island Light.

Anchorages, Moorings. *Wood Island Harbor.* The Biddeford Pool Yacht Club launch often meets an arriving yacht and directs it to a mooring. You can anchor or take a mooring west of the channel. (The water is shoal west of a line between Stage Island and The Gut.) Holding ground is good in Wood Island Harbor, but it is exposed to the east, northeast, and northwest. As that old salt and one-time *Yachting* editor Alfred Loomis wrote in 1939 in his *Ranging the Maine Coast*, "I, for one, dislike an anchorage such as Wood Island Harbor that is sheltered only from winds from certain directions." Nevertheless, this is a fine stopover under prevailing summer conditions. At low tide, you can watch the gulls wheeling and protesting as people wade out on the exposed sands to Basket Island and uninhabited Stage Island.

The Pool. To be in The Pool, you must have a mooring, which probably should be reserved in advance through the Biddeford Pool Yacht Club (see below).

The current runs very fast in and out of the narrow Gut; do not even consider anchoring there. Inside The Pool, the deep water is crammed with moorings, and it would be hard to find swinging room. As you go through The Gut, stay in the middle or a bit to the right. A sloping beach making out from the left side claims several victims a year.

In this tiny harbor, have your boathook ready; there is no time for indecision. There probably will be just enough room and deep water to go in among the moored boats, make a tight turn, and head back into the current to pick up the mooring.

Do not go east of the granite mounds that break the winter ice (three little squares on the chart), or

THOSE WHO CAME BEFORE US

A handful of flint spears, crescent-shaped beads, knives, and arrowheads—the only remnants of a culture that flourished on the coast of Maine more than 5,000 years ago. Who produced these artifacts? We know almost nothing about these so-called Red Paint People—except that the red iron oxide found in their burials has been traced to a single source on the slopes of Mount Katahdin, Maine's highest mountain.

More recently, relatively speaking, when Nero was Emperor of Rome, "Oyster Shell Man" roamed up and down the coast of Maine. They were creatures of habit, these people, and lovers of feasting. Year after year, they returned to the same locations for their outdooor feasts, and the evidence is still here: enormous heaps of oyster shells, sometimes rising 25 feet high, line the banks of rivers such as the Damariscotta. Do you suppose our own civilization will leave traces so joyful and innocent?

The next wave introduced the "People of the Dawn," the Abenaki Indians, encountered by the earliest European explorers. The exploits of the Abenakis, as well as those of the French and English who struggled to maintain a toehold here, are chronicled in myriad volumes of Maine's long history. Twentieth-century historical novelist Kenneth Roberts offered a paean to the Abenakis in his *Arundel:*

Little enough is known of them now, God knows, and most of that is erroneous; and I fear that in another hundred years the only memory of them will be the names they gave to ten thousand hills and headlands and bays throughout our eastern country.

By way of background and explanation, Roberts provided the following:

The Abenaki nation is a confederation of tribes living in the river valleys of our beautiful province of Maine, moving up the rivers in the autumn to hunt and gather furs, and down the rivers in the spring to fish and be cool. Between times they plant and harvest their crops on fertile spots along the rivers. . . .

In the Merrimac Valley were the Pennacooks, who went early to Canada to live on the St. Francis River because of the manner in which white men crowded them. In the valley of the Saco live the Sokokis, the Abenakis who came to Arundel for the summer fishing. In the Androscoggin Valley are the Assagunticooks, and in the Kennebec Valley dwell the Kennebecs, sometimes called the Norridgewocks, because the largest of their towns is at Norridgewock on the Kennebec. To my mind the Sokokis, the Assagunticooks, and the Kennebecs are the finest of all Abenakis, just as the Abenakis are the finest of all Indians.

Farther to the eastward, in the Penobscot Valley and on the shores of Mt. Desert, which places have no equal for beauty in any of our provinces, live the Penobscots. Beyond them, along our wildest and foggiest shores, are the wigwams of the Passamaquoddies. All of these together, with the Micmacs of Acadia, which is also called Nova Scotia, form the Abenaki Confederation.

It has been one of the peculiarities of our colonists that they have never kept faith with Indians. They have either stolen their lands outright, or made the Indians drunk and persuaded them to sell vast stretches of territory for a few beads and a little rum and a musket or two, and they have made treaty after treaty with them—treaties which have always favored the white men; and never has there been a treaty that white men haven't broken.

Everywhere throughout New England the colonists lied to them, cheated them, robbed them—an easy matter, since the Abenakis are brought up from childhood to think that all their possessions are safe, that no locks or bars are necessary to guard them. In trade they are fair and honest. Nothing causes them greater astonishment than crimes white men commit in order to accumulate property.

For an Abenaki to tell an untruth to a friend except in jest or in the making of medicine, is accounted a crime. When an injury is done to one of them, all his friends make common cause against the guilty person. In friendship they are faithful and ardent, and grateful for favors, which never vanish from their memories; and if these be not returned in kind, then the Abenakis become contemptuous, revengeful, dangerous.

Because of these traits the English might easily have gained and held their friendship and had their assistance against the French. Instead of that, by insults, cruelties and constant frauds they early aroused the enmity of many of them and drove them over to the French; and the French, by flattery and fair dealing, made them into faithful friends. . . .

It may be I shall be damned for saying so; but unless I have misread my Bible, I have found more Christianity and human kindness in . . . my Indian friends than in the venerated and violent Cotton Mather of Boston, who has declared in his writings that all red men are Scythians, and that the practising of cruelties on them and the breaking of treaties with them are justified in God's sight.

west of nun "10." The Pool silts up continuously and has to be dredged from time to time, so check for local knowledge on depths.

The Pool is not only beautiful but also interesting. Experiencing the rushing of the waters at flood and ebb is rather like living in the neck of a bottle, but you will be well protected. The Pool is enormous at high tide, then shrinks to a sea of marsh grass a few hours later. It is popular among birdwatchers, who are likely to spot egrets, gulls, cormorants, loons, and night herons.

A dozen or so lobsterboats and offshore draggers have moorings in The Pool, right among the pleasure craft. Adjacent to the yacht club is the fish pier, and just down the street you may find fishermen mending their nets on their back lawns. Of course, a working harbor means waking at dawn as the lobstermen rev up, but that only adds to the enjoyment of the place. There are mosquitoes in The Pool, and no-see-ums—minimal drawbacks to a lovely and peaceful setting.

Getting Ashore. The Biddeford Pool Yacht Club launch will pick you up (call on Ch. 16 or 68), or you can take your dinghy to the club floats.

For the Boat. *Biddeford Pool Yacht Club (Ch. 16 or 68; tel. 282-0485).* On the east side of The Gut, the club is small, informal, and friendly. Gas, diesel, and water are available at the float (plenty of depth alongside, even at low tide). Except at slack water, come alongside the float headed into the current, not into the wind.

For the Crew. There is a shower in the BPYC clubhouse. Close by are a good fish-market, a market, ice machines, and pay phones.

A short walk, bearing right, goes past the post office and well-kept summer cottages to Hattie's Deli, with outside tables. Great blueberry pie. The village of Biddeford Pool is peaceful, pretty, and very low-key. It is hard to believe that just three miles away from this tranquil place is the honky-tonk of Old Orchard Beach.

Things to Do. Old sepia prints in the Biddeford Pool Yacht Club show the 1885 herring fleet under sail in The Pool, and the magnificent Fletcher Neck lifesaving station.

From Hattie's Deli, walk toward the ocean and the Biddeford Pool Boathouse and public beach,

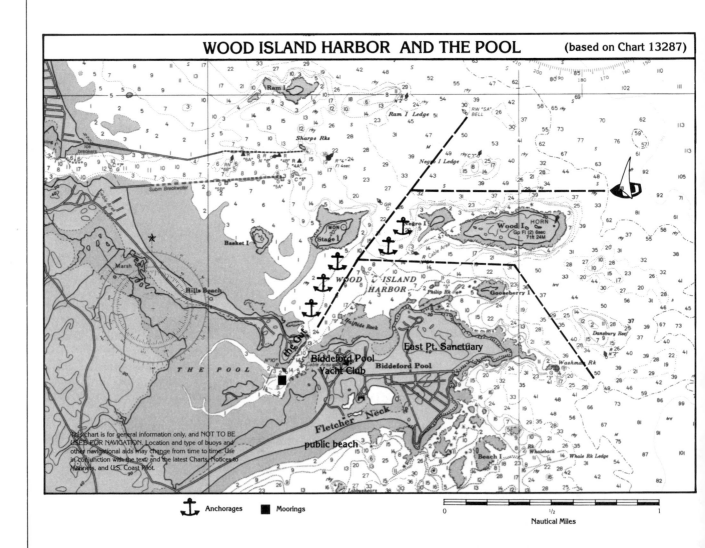

WOOD ISLAND HARBOR AND THE POOL   (based on Chart 13287)

⚓ Anchorages   ■ Moorings

0   1/2   1

Nautical Miles

where there is swimming and even surfing. Bath-houses provide showers, dressing rooms, and phones.

Fishing is great in The Pool. Fishermen perch on every available pier around The Gut and putt around in little boats. Birdwatching is extraordinary here and at East Point Sanctuary (see sketch map). To reach the sanctuary, walk east from the BPYC through an intersection, past The Pool Vol-

unteer Fire Department, and go .7 mile to where the road meets the shore and turns south. The wire fence gate on the left leads past a golf course into East Point Sanctuary, maintained by Maine Audubon Society. Bayberry and wildflowers abound, and there are lovely ocean views out to Wood Island. Wide, grassy paths and trails along the north shore make the walking easy and pleasant.

STRATTON and BLUFF ISLANDS

Charts: **13287**, 13288

These two little islands, just over a mile south of Prouts Neck, are low-lying and grassy, with bushes and a few trees. They constitute the Phineas W. Sprague Memorial Sanctuary of the National Audubon Society. Stratton was colonized as early as 1630 by an Englishman, but it is home now only to gulls, cormorants, and certain exotic species like the glossy ibis.

To explore, anchor in the northeast bight between the two islands and land your dinghy on the west side of Stratton Island. Visiting hours are from sunrise to sunset. Audubon requests: no overnight camping; no fires; do not remove any plants or bushes; animals must be leashed; stay away from bird-nesting areas.

PROUTS NECK ★★★

Chart: 13287

Prouts Neck is a beautiful, exclusive enclave jutting out into Saco Bay and flanked by two of Maine's most popular public beaches, Old Orchard and Scarborough. Here Winslow Homer spent the last 25 years of his life at the turn of the century and produced many of his most famous paintings, including *Eight Bells* and *Fog Warning*.

Approaches. Entering Saco Bay, you will see the headlands of Prouts Neck and then a concrete watchtower planted amid a number of large houses. After you round the headland, go to red-and-white bell "SR," which is the entrance buoy for the Scarborough River and opposite the Prouts Neck Yacht Club breakwater and float. Do not go north of the club or attempt the entrance to the Scarborough River unless you carry shallow draft.

Anchorages, Moorings. Ask the launch operator or inquire at the club about the large guest mooring. Most of the other moorings are small, and there are tales of guests dragging through the fleet. You can anchor west of the yacht club toward the bell, where holding ground is adequate, but there is little protection.

Getting Ashore. Take the yacht club launch or row in to the yacht club float.

For the Boat. *Prouts Neck Yacht Club (Ch. 16;*

tel. 883-9362). There is daily launch service, and water is available on the dock.

For the Crew. There is a pay phone at the PNYC. The posh Black Point Inn (tel. 883-4126) is a short walk off to the left of the club, and its elegant dining room is open to the public (three meals a day; jacket and tie required for dinner).

Things to Do. Walking north from the PNYC, you will catch enticing glimpses of a pristine white sand beach on the left. It is somewhat hard to reach, but just opposite the inn entrance is a path down to it.

Walk south a few hundred yards from the yacht club to Winslow Homer Road and Homer's studio, a National Historic Landmark open to the public. Homer's gravesite is on the lawn, seaward from his studio. The studio is a wing of the second house on the right past the gate.

Near Winslow Homer Road is an access to the magnificent cliff walk, looking out to Saco Bay, the islands, and Wood Island Light. It's a beautiful stroll around the rocky perimeter of Prouts Neck and back to the Black Point Inn. The granite ledges, tidal pools, and coves still appear just as Homer painted them.

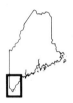

RICHMOND ISLAND HARBOR ★★★★
and SEAL COVE ★★★★

Charts: **13287**, 13288

1 No facilities

3 No facilities

Lying half a mile south of Cape Elizabeth, to which it is connected by a breakwater, Richmond is a beautiful island with two large wooded areas and meadows between. There are white sand beaches on both the island and the mainland, and a wonderful sense of tranquility and remoteness only seven miles from the city of Portland.

The island was settled in 1627 by the English, and French explorer Samuel Champlain had earlier dubbed it "Isle of Bacchus" because of the wild grapes that he found growing there. In the seventeenth century a number of ships were built here, and a fishery employing more than 60 people flourished. More recently, various enterprises have been attempted, including potato farming, herb growing, and sheep raising. A big barn on the island's north shore once was used as a root cellar to store potatoes. There are deer here, many with deep red coloration, supposedly from their diet of salt grass. The island is infested with woodchucks and is home to several pairs of mink.

Approaches. *Seal Cove.* From the south, pick up bell "1" east of Richmond Island before heading in toward the middle of Seal Cove. This will take you clear of dangerous Watts Ledge. After passing East Point, coast along the north shore of Richmond Island, at least 200 yards offshore, toward the breakwater. There is plenty of room to clear the rocks and shoals in the middle of Seal Cove.

Richmond Island Harbor. Give West Ledge a good berth and head for the middle of Richmond Island Harbor, leaving green can "3" to port. What looks like a line of mooring buoys off West ledge marks a mackerel pound; avoid it.

Anchorages, Moorings. *Seal Cove.* In normal summer weather, Seal Cove, east of the breakwater, provides the best protection. Depending on the direction of the wind, anchor near either end of the breakwater in 10 to 15 feet at low. Watch for buoys marking fish nets or pens. The holding ground is good, in sand, but you probably will experience some roll during the night.

Although parts of the breakwater barely clear the surface at high tide, the line is easily visible.

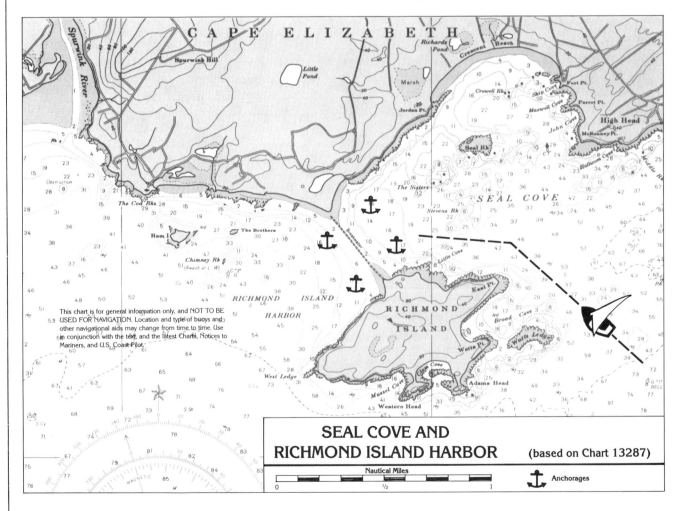

**SEAL COVE AND
RICHMOND ISLAND HARBOR** (based on Chart 13287)

This chart is for general information only, and NOT TO BE USED FOR NAVIGATION. Location and type of buoys and other navigational aids may change from time to time. Use in conjunction with the text, and the latest Charts, Notices to Mariners, and U.S. Coast Pilot.

Nautical Miles

0   1/2   1

⚓ Anchorages

LIBERTY SHIPS

South Portland was the site of an enormous shipbuilding effort that had a major effect on England's survival and the outcome of World War II. Here, "Pete" Newell of Todd-Bath Iron Shipbuilding Corporation supervised the construction of an innovative yard where ships were built on a level keel in concrete basin drydocks instead of the traditional inclined ways, and launched simply by opening the gates.

After a contract was signed in December, 1940, the entire yard rose from the mudflats, and 30 ships were delivered to the British in only 466 days, helping to replace the enormous tonnage of shipping being sunk by German submarines. (Another 30 ships were built for the British by Kaiser on the West Coast.)

The first British ship launched was christened *Ocean Liberty,* and when the yard went on to build ships for the U.S. war effort, they were known as Liberty ships. When the U.S. entered the war, President Franklin Roosevelt called for an Atlantic "Bridge of Ships," and the Liberty ships were the backbone of the enormous building program that followed. Newell was asked to construct a second yard to the west using conventional ship ways. The two yards employed 30,000 workers—mostly inexperienced men and women who were trained on the spot—and built an unprecedented 236 ships in three and a half years. By December of 1944, it took only 52½ days to complete a vessel, from laying the keel to launching.

"Truck horses of the sea," 236 Liberty ships were built in record time in South Portland to replace the tonnage sunk by German submarines and to keep the supply lines open to the Allies. These ships, such as the *Jeremiah O'Brien* pictured above, were 441 feet long, carried 9,146 tons of cargo, and plodded along at 11 knots. The *O'Brien,* all that remains of a once-vast fleet, is now a museum on the West Coast. (Don Patterson illustration)

The remains of the eastern concrete basins were incorporated in Spring Point Marina and Breakwater Marina, and traces of the western yard may be found at South Portland Shipbuilding Co.

Liberty ships were "the truck horses of the sea," 441 feet long, with 57-foot beams. They carried 9,146 tons of cargo in five holds, and were capable of 11 knots with a single 2,500-h.p. reciprocating steam engine. Manned by a crew of 40, plus a naval gun crew of 30, the ships were involved in convoys in the North Atlantic, the Aleutians, the Mediterranean, and the far Pacific. Many were torpedoed and sunk or damaged, but enough survived to carry the precious cargo that was, as

Roosevelt had foreseen, the lifeline of the Allies. Seven of the Liberty ships were deliberately sunk to form a part of the breakwaters used as artificial ports for the Normandy invasion in June of 1944.

The list of Liberty ships is a roster of familiar names—from Winslow Homer to Sarah Orne Jewett, from Noah Webster to Calvin Coolidge and William Lyon Phelps, from George Popham to Ferdinando Gorges, from Joshua Slocum to F. Scott Fitzgerald.

(Much of the information above is from *Portland Ships are Good Ships* by Herbert G. Jones, and from the Spring Point Museum in Portland.)

Supplies for the island's caretaker are driven out to the island on the sands next to the breakwater, which are bare at drain tides. The lively park at Crescent Beach is far enough away so you will not be bothered.

Richmond Island Harbor. Richmond Island Harbor is better protected than Seal Cove if winds are from the east. Again, anchor in either corner of the

breakwater in 10 to 15 feet at low.

Getting Ashore. From any of the anchorages, it is an easy row ashore to gentle sand beaches.

Things to Do. You are allowed to land on privately owned Richmond Island and picnic on the beach, but do not explore inland without checking first with the caretaker, who lives in the gray house at the crest of the meadow.

Region 2 / Cape Elizabeth to Cape

Casco Bay

Small

Past and present seem to merge as this traditional Friendship sloop explores "the placid waters of the bay, spangled by multitudinous gems of emeralds." (Neal A. Parent photo)

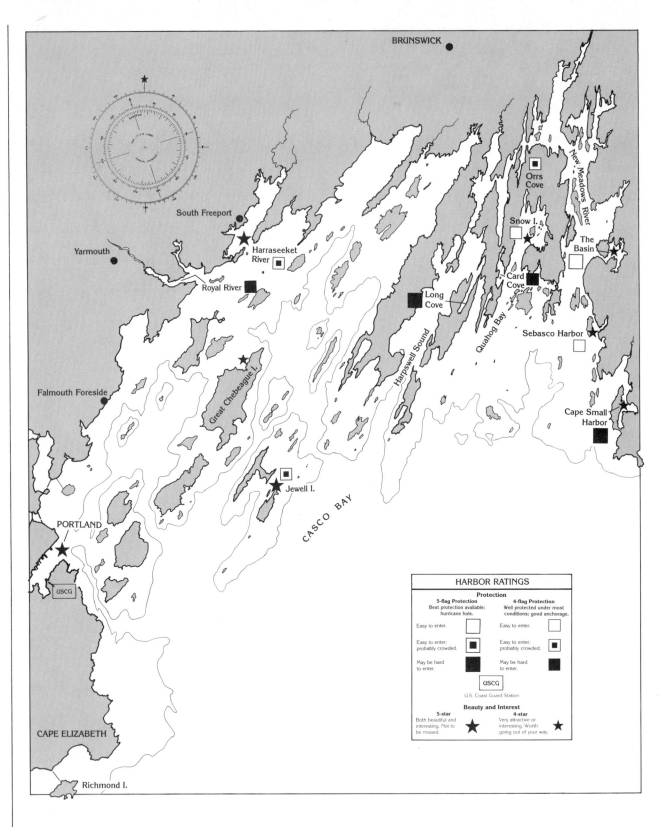

BRUNSWICK

South Freeport

Yarmouth

Harraseeket
River

Royal River

Falmouth Foreside

Great Chebeague I.

Jewell I.

PORTLAND

USCG

CAPE ELIZABETH

Richmond I.

Orrs
Cove

Snow I.

New Meadows River

The
Basin

Card
Cove

Harpswell Sound

Quahog Bay

Sebasco Harbor

Cape Small
Harbor

CASCO BAY

HARBOR RATINGS

Protection

5-flag Protection
Best protection available;
hurricane hole.

4-flag Protection
Well protected under most
conditions; good anchorage.

Easy to enter.

Easy to enter.

Easy to enter;
probably crowded.

Easy to enter;
probably crowded.

May be hard
to enter.

May be hard
to enter.

USCG
U.S. Coast Guard Station

Beauty and Interest

5-star
Both beautiful and
interesting. Not to
be missed.

4-star
Very attractive or
interesting. Worth
going out of your way.

N o element of beauty is wanting. Many of the islands are wildly
picturesque in form,—and from their woodland summits you behold
on the one hand the surges of the Atlantic, breaking almost at your
feet, and on the other the placid waters of the bay, spangled by
multitudinous gems of emerald, while in the dim distance you discern on the
horizon the sublime peaks of the White Mountains."

—Robert Carter, *Summer Cruise on the Coast of New England, 1858*

Here is where the Atlantic coast, trending north all the way from Florida, turns a sudden corner, breaks out in a flourish of islands, and heads for Spain. Here is where the great sand beaches of Maine's southern coast end and the rocky promontories of the mid-coast begin.

As the early explorers reported, there are hundreds of islands, large and small, in Casco Bay. They are the peaks of three parallel ranges whose flanks are drowned in the bay, the valleys between gouged by glaciers that stood a mile thick on this land 13,000 years ago. Thus, Great Chebeague Island and Long and Peaks and Cushing are the extension of Merepoint Neck; Cliff Island and Jewell are remnants of Harpswell Neck, and Halfway Rock is the farthest tip of Orrs-Bailey Island.

The valleys between the ranges are now the great bays and sounds that make Casco Bay so interesting—Hussey, Luckse, and Broad sounds in the middle; Maquoit, Merepoint, and Middle Bay to the north; Merriconeag and Harpswell sounds, Quahog Bay and the New Meadows River to the east.

While far busier with boats and people than Penobscot Bay and points east, Casco Bay is still surprisingly beautiful and unspoiled—a superb cruising ground. The scale of the bay is small—less than 20 miles from Cape Elizabeth to Cape Small. In clear weather, you can see the Portland skyline from Harpswell Neck. The broadest sound is only a mile wide and the nearest island usually is only a short reach away. The pattern shifts constantly on a sail through the bay—one island silhouetted against another, and that one dark against a third; five or six points change shape and arrangement as you sail past. The perspective is always different, always striking. One of the pleasures of sailing here is finding your way among these islands, chart in hand. Even in the fog, land is always in sight. It is easy to become confused about whether red buoys should be left to port or starboard, so check the chart often. Winds fluctuate as you pass into the lee of one island or another, and the current often runs swiftly through the slots.

Unlike any place farther east, the presence of a substantial metropolitan area affects the look and the feel of Casco Bay. Portland is small by most standards, but the islands in the shadow of the city are heavily populated, or soon will be. The attaché case now is more prevalent on these islands than the snowy egret. The influence of the city radiates out to summer and year-round homes on the islands. Little yellow ferries dart back and forth; fishing boats, daysailers, runabouts, cruising yachts, excursion boats are ubiquitous. There are more marinas and more moorings than farther east. But do not bypass Portland just because it is a city—this is one city you can enjoy visiting under sail.

Another striking reminder of man's presence here is the layer of fortifications built over the centuries to guard Portland Harbor, forts in the harbor itself—grim, but picturesque. The modern ruins are less romantic: concrete towers that stood watch for German submarines, 8-inch and 16-inch gun emplacements on many Casco Bay islands, along with concrete bunkers, decaying barracks, old piers, and abandoned military bases.

There are three major yachting centers in Casco Bay: Portland itself, with its harbor recently cleaned up, boasts the Centerboard Yacht Club and several large marinas. Five miles north is Falmouth Foreside, home of the Portland Yacht Club and many splendid cruising and racing yachts. South Freeport is the third sailing center, home of the Harraseeket Yacht Club.

There are plenty of good harbors in Casco Bay and lots of islands to explore. And there is an infinite number of day stops—little gunkholes between islands, picnic spots, beaches the family dog will love, and places of special interest like Eagle Island and the Inn at Great Chebeague. Some narrow spots are worth sailing through just for the fun of it—Whitehead Passage between Cushing and Peaks, for example. Or shoot through the tiny passage between Pumpkin Nob and Peaks Island under sail. Or run between Bustins Island and Little Bustins.

At the eastern end of Casco Bay are two delightful and seldom-visited areas, Quahog Bay and the New Meadows River. Snow Island, in Quahog Bay, may be one of the nicest anchorages anywhere on the coast. The New Meadows offers a variety of places to explore, including working harbors and such

Construction of the Ram Island lighthouse off Portland, 1904. (Frank Claes Collection)

comfortable stops as Sebasco Harbor, with its own resort. Also on the New Meadows is a landlocked harbor called The Basin, a perfect hurricane hole. There is often warm-water swimming at the ends of the shallow fingers of these bays that probe north into the mainland.

Casco Bay is the home of the mooring, and hardly anyone anchors. Everyone seems to pick up a mooring without concern about the condition of the chain, or the size of the block, and it is not unusual to see four, six, or even eight boats rafted on a single buoy.

PORTLAND ★★★★★   All facilities
Charts: 13288, 13290, **13292**

Maine's largest city somehow manages to retain some of the appealing traits of a small town. It is one of the few cities pleasant to visit in a cruising boat. Portland has restaurants, museums, concerts, theatres, and stores of all kinds, not to mention historic buildings and a bustle of activity, much of it near the waterfront in the Old Port Exchange section. It also is a major yachting center.

Approaches. Portland Harbor is easy to make under any conditions. The main approach is from the south. From Portland Lighted Horn Buoy "P" or red whistle buoy "2" off Cape Elizabeth, proceed to gong "7" on Willard Rock, and thence to the bell off Portland Head Light. Follow the channel northward past the lighthouse on Spring Point (South Portland) and bear left into Portland Harbor.

When entering Portland, keep a good lookout for heavy commercial traffic and frequent ferries. Everything you will need in Portland Harbor is east of the first highway bridge. The Fore River west of the bridge is lined with oil tank farms.

Anchorages, Moorings. Once you are in the harbor, you can choose whether to stay on the Portland side or on the South Portland side. In either case, reserve ahead for a slip.

On the north side of the harbor, DiMillo's

Marina has a prime location at the foot of the restored waterfront area, with every convenience nearby. The disadvantages are the absence of moorings and the fact that you are amid the hurly-burly of downtown Portland. Slips also are available at Gowen, Inc., farther west, and there are moorings at Portland Yacht Services at the eastern end of the harbor.

On the other side of the harbor in South Portland, with its many oil tanks and commercial docks, there are four marinas and a yacht club. Here you can enjoy the view of the city in peace and quiet, including the evening spectacle of the cruise ferry *Scotia Prince,* all ablaze with lights, completing her daily run from Nova Scotia. Laundromats and supermarkets are a short cab ride away. With the heavy channel traffic, it is unsafe to take a dinghy across to Portland. As Dodge Morgan puts it, "a dinghy ride across the harbor channel is like making your way across an active airport runway on a tricycle."

For the Boat and Crew: Portland (from East to West). *Portland Yacht Services (Ch. 16; tel. 774-1067).* At the eastern end of the harbor, next to the floating drydock and directly below the Portland Observatory, are the expanding facilities of PYS.

PORTLAND HARBOR (based on Chart 13292)

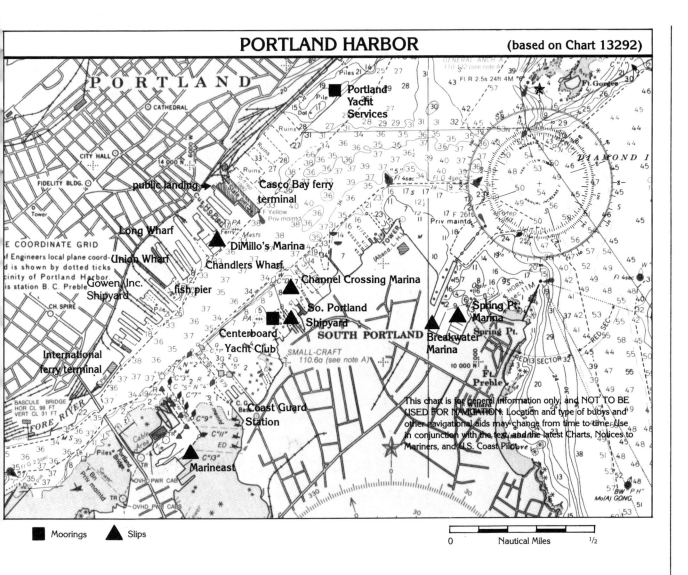

■ Moorings ▲ Slips

0   Nautical Miles   ½

Owned by circumnavigators Phineas Sprague Jr. and his wife Joanna, this new yard is interested in cruising sailors. PYS has 18 moorings, from 700- to 2,000-pound blocks, with considerable exposure. In addition to custom boatbuilding and restoration, PYS handles major repairs for wood, fiberglass, and cold-molded boats, including hull, engine, and electrical work.

Maine Marine Diesel (tel. 773-4618). Located in the PYS complex, Maine Marine Diesel specializes in diesel and electrical repairs. They will service your boat anywhere from Portsmouth to Camden.

DiMillo's Marina (Ch. 9; tel. 773-7632). On the north side of the harbor, west of the blue floating drydock and several piers, is DiMillo's floating restaurant (blue and white, with a big sign) and the adjacent marina on Long Wharf. This is a big, fancy outfit, with 125 slips and 8 to 21 feet of water alongside. DiMillo's has gas, diesel, water, ice, electricity, and engine repairs; marine supplies are available at The Marine Store. For the crew, there is a shower and laundromat. A rich variety of restaurants, shops, and entertainment begins right across Commercial Street in the Old Port Exchange.

The Chart Room at Chase Leavitt (tel. 772-3751). Located in the Old Port Exchange area, Chase Leavitt maintains a large chandlery, with a broad range of marine supplies and equipment, including extensive charts. Life rafts can be reconditioned here.

On the east side of Union Wharf, Chase Leavitt has dock space for repairs of all kinds, including rigging, diesel engines, and electronics.

Union Wharf Market (tel. 774-7397). Three piers west of DiMillo's, Union Wharf Market offers a good supply of meats, fish, produce, groceries, and ice. Open seven days a week, they will deliver to your boat.

Adams Marine Center (tel. 772-2781). On Commercial Street, west of the fish pier, Adams Marine Center is a discount marine outlet, offering a broad range of supplies and accessories.

Gowen Inc. (Ch. 16; tel. 773-1761). West of the fish pier, Gowen, Inc. (Shipyard Division) is now catering to recreational boats. With the huge 150-ton boatlift, large boats can be hauled. Hull and engine repairs are done by the yard, or on a do-it-yourself basis.

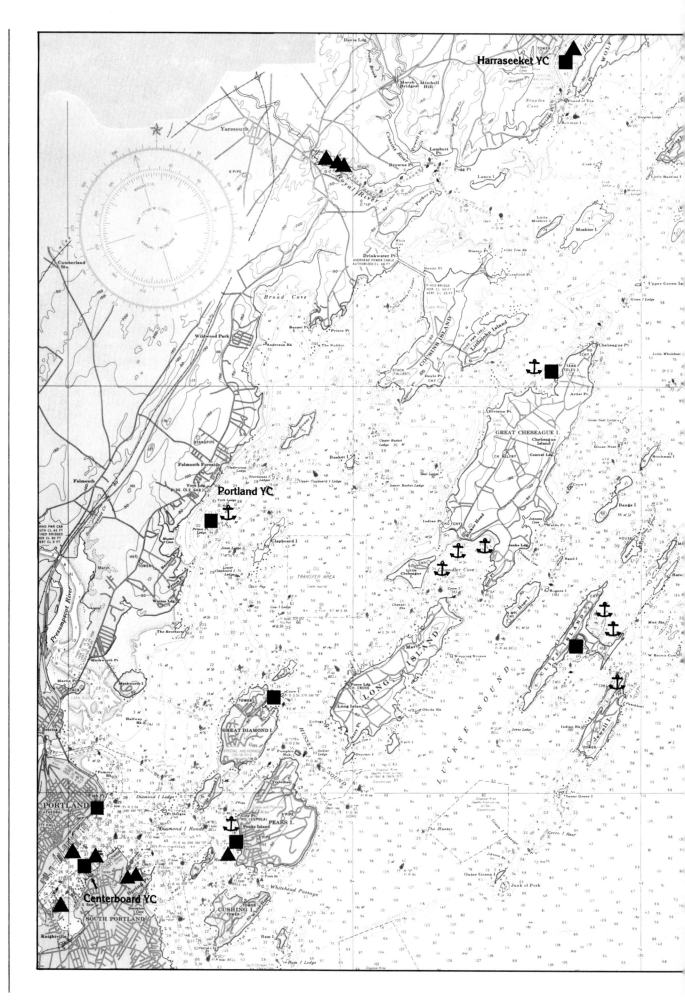

Harraseeket YC

Portland YC

Centerboard YC

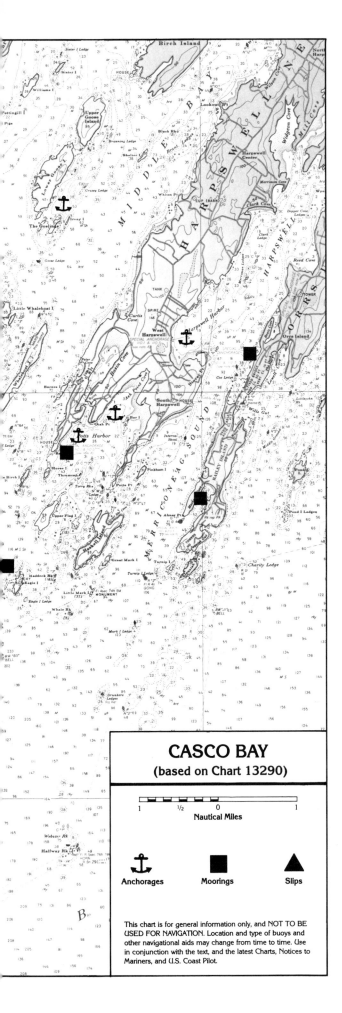

CASCO BAY

(based on Chart 13290)

1 1/2 0 1

Nautical Miles

Anchorages   Moorings   Slips

This chart is for general information only, and NOT TO BE USED FOR NAVIGATION. Location and type of buoys and other navigational aids may change from time to time. Use in conjunction with the text, and the latest Charts, Notices to Mariners, and U.S. Coast Pilot.

For the Boat and Crew: South Portland (from East to West). *Spring Point Marina (Ch. 9 or 16; tel. 767-3254).* First of the South Portland marinas as you enter the harbor is Spring Point, which has slips for 250 boats. There is nine feet of water along the floats, and the marina can accommodate vessels of 100 feet or more. Spring Point Marina is comfortable under normal circumstances but would be bad in a northeaster.

The marina is easy to locate. After passing the lighthouse at the tip of Spring Point, continue past can "1," then head in to port for the masts. Access to the slips is on the left (east) side of the marina (at low tide, there is a five-foot spot at the entrance). The fuel float is on the right (west) side.

Facilities include gas, diesel, water, electricity, and ice. A diesel mechanic is on hand, and repairs of all kinds are possible. There is a canvas shop and marine store. The yard has 15- and 35-ton boatlifts. Every convenience is available for the crew, including snack bar, groceries, showers, and laundry. There is bus and taxi service to downtown Portland; for schedules and fares, inquire at the marina.

The Spring Point Walkway winds along the waterfront just east of the marina, leading to the breakwater and lighthouse, the grounds and buildings of Civil War–vintage Fort Preble, and the pre-revolutionary "Old Settlers Cemetery." On the way you will find the growing Spring Point Museum, which houses the bow of the only remaining American clipper ship, *Snow Squall*, built in South Portland in 1851 and recovered from the Falkland Islands.

Breakwater Marina (Ch. 9 or 16; tel. 799-1899). This new marina is adjacent to Spring Point and fronting a group of gray condominiums. Although it is basically a "dockominium," space alongside is available for transients. The 121 slips offer excellent protection behind a concrete breakwater (recognizable by the series of blue waves painted on it), with seven feet of water at low, electricity, water, and cable TV. In the office building you will find showers, laundromat, and a pay phone. Hull and engine repairs can be arranged.

Channel Crossing Marina (Ch. 9; tel. 767-4729). The next marina as you enter Portland Harbor is Channel Crossing Marina, with 135 slips (no moorings). Transients are welcome.

After passing buoy "5," a group of oil tanks on the left, and the long pipeline terminal pier, you will see the slips of the marina extending well into the harbor. Ashore is the Channel Crossing Restaurant, a gray building with white trim.

The marina has 220 feet of outside dock space (more than six feet of water at low) where they can accommodate boats up to 160 feet. The slips are exposed to the northeast. Gas, diesel, water, electricity, ice and marine stores are available, with six

The *Scotia Prince* enters Portland Harbor after a passage from Yarmouth, Nova Scotia. Portland is a human-sized city, rich in history and culture, and with a pleasant bustle of activity, both on and off the waterfront. (Prince of Fundy Cruises)

feet of water alongside the fuel float at low. Hull and engine repairs can be made using a 25-ton hydraulic trailer.

For the crew, facilities include laundry, showers, and the Channel Crossing Restaurant.

South Portland Shipyard (Ch. 16; tel. 799-5501). Between Channel Crossing Marina and the Centerboard Yacht Club are the old, red buildings of the South Portland Shipyard. With three marine railways that can haul up to 400 tons and a 25-ton crane, the yard can do major hull repairs and arrange repairs for engines, rigging, and electronics. Though much of its work is commercial, pleasure boats are a growing part of the business. New finger floats are planned, as well as a 277-slip marina.

Centerboard Yacht Club (Ch. 68; tel. 799-7084). This friendly and unassuming yacht club has a substantial fleet of cruising boats. To reach Centerboard, run well into the harbor, passing a series of oil tanks, the floats of Channel Crossing Marina, and a group of red buildings with a crane. Then comes the clubhouse, with CYC in big yellow letters on the roof. Pick up a mooring temporarily and check with the launch operator.

The club has several guest moorings, and the launch keeps track of members who are away cruising. There is a long finger float, with four feet of water at low tide, which is easy to come alongside for water. No fuel is available. Facilities include a shower, pay phone, and ice.

It is quite pleasant to lie at a CYC mooring, gazing across at Portland's twinkling lights and listening to the low growl of the city at a distance and occasionally the wash from some large vessel going

by. The harbor is in the path for jet aircraft, but fortunately pilots sleep later in the morning than lobstermen.

Marineast (Ch. 9 or 16; tel. 799-8191). Farthest into the harbor on the South Portland side is Marineast, just before the bascule bridge and surrounded by townhouses. It has the advantage of being closer to downtown Portland than the other South Portland marinas, and is within walking distance of the large Mill Creek Shopping Center. If your boat draws more than 4½ feet, however, enter at half-tide or higher.

To find Marineast, continue down the harbor beyond the Channel Crossing Marina, past the Coast Guard base, and almost all the way to the bascule bridge. Just before the large green oil tank on the left is a narrow channel dredged through mudflats. It is marked by tall pilings and red day markers on the starboard side and small, green spar buoys to port.

There is six feet of water at the outside floats, with water and ice, but no fuel. Boats can be hauled with the boatlift, and repairs made for hull or engine. The Snow Squall Restaurant is at the head of the dock, along with a marine supply store.

Things to Do. Portland is a human-sized city rich in history, arts, shops, and restaurants, and it can be hard to choose from among the myriad activities during a brief stopover. Below are only a few suggestions.

The Portland Museum of Art, located on Congress Square near the heart of the city, has a superb collection of Winslow Homer paintings and works by other Maine artists. There are outdoor concerts by the Portland Symphony Orchestra and a variety

"THE BEAUTIFUL TOWN . . . BY THE SEA"

Henry Wadsworth Longfellow immortalized and idealized Portland, yearning for it as he did in *My Lost Youth:* "Often I think of the beautiful town that is seated by the sea . . . ." Now, more than a century later, he would scarcely recognize the metropolis that has come a long, long way in the last 350 years.

First settled as Casco in 1632, the town became Falmouth in 1658 and finally was incorporated as Portland in 1785. By 1775, most Falmouth families were sympathetic to the revolutionary cause and rebelled against the newly imposed Stamp, Sugar, and Navigation acts. They moved and concealed upriver ship masts that had been marked with the king's broad arrow and destined for the British Navy. Young men of Falmouth participated in the battles of Lexington and Bunker Hill. In October 1775, the British sent a Royal Navy fleet, under Captain Henry Mowatt, into Falmouth Harbor to retaliate. Giving the inhabitants two hours' warning, Mowatt bombarded the city relentlessly for 12 hours, completely destroying it by fire.

It was during the ensuing rebuilding phase that Maine's first lighthouse was erected at Portland Head (Cape Elizabeth) in 1790, its first keeper appointed by President George Washington.

For the next hundred years or so, the city slowly grew and flourished. The economy was based on shipbuilding and the export of lumber from the deep, ice-free harbor with its easy access to the open sea. The Portland Observatory, a tall wooden structure that dominated the skyline, was built in 1807 as a signal tower, and a system of flags alerted townspeople, shipowners, and families to incoming ships hours before they docked.

In 1866, Portland was once again destroyed by fire—this time allegedly by a firecracker from the festivities celebrating the end of the Civil War. "It seemed as if the fires of Hell had erupted on earth," said one observer. More than 1,500 buildings burned, leaving hundreds of homeless who established a tent city. This time, the rebuilding was planned carefully. Brick was used for shops and warehouses, and granite for the public buildings. Streets were widened and lined with Victorian mansions and newly planted trees.

In the last century, Portland's harbor has continued to be the city's focus. Today it ranks third in commercial activity among eastern seaboard ports and second in oil shipments. A large fishing fleet supports a newly constructed fish pier. The Bath Iron Works shipbuilding firm has a huge floating drydock for repairing commercial and naval vessels. Portland has become a major banking and insurance center as well, and has developed an international airport.

Portland's most recent revitalization began in 1966 with the restoration of a host of rundown nineteenth-century brick buildings along the waterfront. Today the Old Port Exchange, its cobblestone streets lined with shops, restaurants, and galleries, is a major reason for Portland's prominence and the core of an unprecedented commercial boom.

of cultural offerings at the Portland Performing Arts Center. You can visit the Wadsworth-Longfellow House on Congress Street, headquarters of the Maine Historical Society, and the public library nearby. The *Maine Sunday Telegram's* "Audience" tabloid is an excellent source for goings-on throughout the city.

Wander around among the unusual shops of the Old Port Exchange area, take guided historical walks through the city, or visit the landmark Portland Observatory. The retired lightship *Nantucket* is worth a visit. If you still yearn to be waterborne, you might enjoy a cruise on the *Longfellow* from Long Wharf to nearby islands, including Peaks, Diamond, and House; or on the ferries of the Casco Bay Line, based near the Casco Bay ferry terminal.

For Maine Medical Center (emergency), phone 871-2381.

SPRING COVE

Charts: 13290, **13292**

Spring Cove, a bight on the north side of Cushing Island, borders Whitehead Passage. With just a glimpse of the Portland skyline, this is a pretty spot for a daytime stop, and it is well protected from southerlies. The eastern exposure, however, allows ocean swells to curl around White Head, so you might spend a rolly night. Though only two miles from Portland, Spring Cove is not jammed with boats like Diamond Cove. Cushing Island is owned by an association that strongly discourages landing on the island.

The cove is clearly identified by two watchtowers (charted) and White Head; there are no problems entering. It is free of obstructions, except along the eastern shore; there is 14 feet or more of water at the end of a big dock, and plenty of room to anchor. Once inside, you will be out of the strong current of Whitehead Passage.

PEAKS ISLAND ★★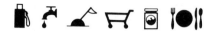

Charts: 13288, 13290, **13292**

In 1689, Indians gathered on Peaks for a successful attack on Portland. Three hundred years later, Peaks is under attack from the mainland, as the growing population of Portland presses out into Casco Bay. Only two miles from the city, Peaks is rather suburban in character, with paved roads, electricity, and city water. The year-round population is about 1,500, swelling to 5,000 or more in the summer. It includes fishermen, artists, summerfolk, retirees, and, more recently, the young professionals who make the 20-minute commute to Portland by ferry. The main street between the ferry landing and the market is full of kids on bikes and happy dogs.

For the cruising sailor, this is not exactly a remote, spruce-clad, rocky island, but it is pleasant nonetheless to stand on Peaks and gaze across the bay at Portland's twinkling lights.

Since moorings and slips are hard to come by in Portland Harbor, an easy way to enjoy the city is to leave your boat at Peaks Island and take the Casco Bay Lines ferry. The ferries run often, and the last ferry leaves Portland for Peaks at 11:30 P.M.

Approaches. The landings on Peaks Island are all on the west side, opposite the north end of House Island. From the south, the easiest approach is between Cushing Island and House Island. From Portland, pass north of House Island, keeping your eyes open for the frequent yellow ferries that follow the same route.

Anchorages, Moorings. All the docks are clustered together on Peaks. Farthest south is a fishing pier. Just north of this are the ferry docks, next to which is the float of the public landing. Continuing north, you will find the slips of Jones Landing Marina sticking well out beyond the ferry docks. Farthest north are the slips and moorings of Peaks Island Marina.

The water is deep outside the moored boats (30 to 35 feet at low). If you want to anchor, it probably is better to choose a spot in the shallower water north of the docks (16 to 22 feet at low). The holding ground is good mud, and the anchorage is reasonably well protected, although there will be wash from ferries and powerboats.

Getting Ashore. Land the dinghy at one of the marinas or at the public landing.

For the Boat. *Jones Landing Marina (tel. 766-5542).* There is deep water at the small finger floats, but no facilities. The marina is used mostly by small powerboats and by restaurant patrons.

Peaks Island Marina (tel. 766-2508). Farthest north of the docks, Peaks Island Marina has more than 50 slips, with a depth of 35 feet at the outside and depths of 10 feet or more near shore. They also have a number of moorings (1,500- to 2,000-pound blocks). Water, electricity, and diesel are available at the slips, with 8 to 10 feet alongside at low. There is a laundromat on shore, near the marina office.

Public Landing. North of the ferry docks, the public landing has a float for loading and unloading, 30-minute tie-up, and no facilities.

For the Crew. Jones Landing Restaurant (tel. 766-5542) is right at the ferry dock on Peaks; tables on the porch provide a great view of the Portland skyline, House Island, Fort Gorges, and all the waterfront activities. There is a pay phone.

Walking left along Island Avenue, you will come to the post office and then Bayview Market, with groceries and ice. Next comes the Dockside, a coffee shop, bakery, and popular gathering spot, where you can eat on the outside deck. Beyond that are a small hardware store and the library. A water-taxi from the public landing offers service to Portland and the neighboring islands.

Things to Do. The east side of Peaks Island has been left largely undeveloped, and it invites exploration. In addition to beaches, nature trails, and lovely coastal walks among beach peas, rosa rugosa, and marshes, there are the eerie remains of huge World War II installations, including tunnels, bunkers, and towers. The island is about five miles around, so it is not too far to walk.

GREAT DIAMOND and LITTLE DIAMOND ISLANDS

Charts: 13288, 13290, **13292**

Hardly a mile from Portland, the islands of Great and Little Diamond are joined by a sandbar that you can walk across at low tide. The Casco Bay Lines ferry from Portland stops at the state pier at the south end of each island.

In a cove on the eastern side of Little Diamond lie the hulks of a barge, a schooner, and a steamship, beached at the ends of their useful lives.

Half of Great Diamond once was Fort McKinley, abandoned after World War II. After nearly four decades as a forlorn ghost town, the three-story brick houses surrounding an oval parade ground are now being developed as McKinley Estates.

The easiest access to the island is through Diamond Cove.

DIAMOND COVE ★★★
Charts: 13290, **13292**

Diamond Cove is a small, pleasant, protected harbor at the northeast tip of Great Diamond Island. However, it is only two miles from Portland, and its accessibility has earned it the nickname of "Cocktail Cove." At the height of the season, the ferry from Portland arrives eight or 10 times a day.

The stately brick houses of old Fort McKinley still surround the parade ground where soldiers marched for a hundred years, but now the barracks and officers' quarters are being transformed to townhouses. Some of the former amenities such as tennis courts and dance hall are being refurbished, and others added, including an art gallery and swimming pool. While most of the facilities are for the benefit of residents, the public is welcome ashore to use the restaurant and general store, and to visit the parade ground from 10 AM to 5 PM.

Approaches. From the west, leave nun "2" to starboard and pass between Cow Island (with overgrown concrete bunkers) and Great Diamond, paying close attention to the rocks at the southeast tip of Cow. Then turn south inside tiny Crow Island to the cove. From the east, pass between can "1" and the Crow Island Light, favoring the can.

An old brown watchtower stands above the trees at the head of the harbor, and there are two piers. Deep water extends to the ends of these piers, with 16 feet at low. There is also an old granite wharf on the west side. Some of these landmarks may well change or disappear as development of the island progresses.

Anchorages, Moorings. The main pier for residents, where the ferry lands, is on the western side of the cove. A 120-slip marina for transients is being developed on the eastern side. For reservations, call McKinley Estates at 797-6241. Some moorings may be available for transients, but there is probably no room to anchor in the cove; note the cable crossing area, and the ferry's path down the western shore.

Diamond Cove is out of the current and well protected under most circumstances, except a strong northeaster. A swell comes in from Hussey Sound, however, and it is likely to be rolly at night.

Getting Ashore. Row in to the dinghy float near land on the western side of the main pier, keeping a good lookout for the ferry. Plans call for a launch to serve the transient marina.

For the Crew. The former storehouse at the head of the main pier is now a restaurant, open for lunch and dinner. Just beyond is the General Store, where you will find ice, beer, wine, deli items, meats, and seafood. Package deals will be available to visiting yachtsmen, including dockage, laundromat, showers, and use of the tennis courts and pool.

Things to Do. By all means go ashore and wander along the roads open to the public, including the oval parade ground and magnificent brick houses of Fort McKinley. You can also visit the administration and recreation building, which houses the art gallery.

If you like World War II fortifications and concrete bunkers, row over to Cow Island to explore.

FALMOUTH FORESIDE ★★★ All facilities
Charts: 13288, 13290, **13292**

Home of the Portland Yacht Club, second-oldest yacht club in the United States, Falmouth Foreside is one of Maine's great boating centers. Overlooking a large fleet of handsome yachts, the PYC offers a hospitable welcome to visiting yachtsmen in its lovely old clubhouse. Handy Boat Service next door can serve every need.

Approaches. The various dangers near Falmouth Foreside are well marked, and the approach is easy from north or south. Your goal is visible from miles away: a forest of masts and a sea of hulls. Watch for York Ledge, hidden among the boats. It is small, and clearly marked by green beacon "YL" and can "17."

Anchorages, Moorings. The big complex of buildings and docks to the south belongs to Handy Boat Service. The dock farther north belongs to the Portland Yacht Club. Check with the PYC launch to see if a mooring is available. If not, hail the Handy Boat launch. Handy's maintains a sizable number of very heavy moorings. Reserve ahead (tel. 781-5110). Falmouth Foreside is on an exposed stretch of coast without much protection, and a strong chop can build up over the long fetch from the south.

There is plenty of room to anchor out beyond the moorings; the bottom is mud and apparently excellent holding ground. It may be possible to lie along the floats at Handy's if there is not too much wind. Check with the dockmaster.

Getting Ashore. The Handy Boat launch monitors channel 9 and the PYC launch monitors channel 68. Row in to either dock. The next float north of the PYC is the town landing; land your dinghy there for convenient access to the Town Landing Market, .2 miles up the hill.

For the Boat. *Handy Boat Service (Ch. 9; tel. 781-5110).* Founded more than 50 years ago as a boatyard, Handy Boat now offers almost every conceivable service, including an elegant chandlery and the Hallett Sailmakers loft. Major repairs of all sorts can be done, and facilities include fuel, ice, water, CNG, and electricity. There are two docks at Handy's, the southern one for fuel and the northern one for service, with 8½ feet of water at the ends and six feet alongside.

Portland Yacht Club (Ch. 68; tel. 781-9820). The Portland Yacht Club welcomes members of recognized yacht clubs (be prepared to show your club membership card) and asks that you sign the guest register. The "facility use fee" includes the mooring and use of club facilities.

The club was founded just after the Civil War, when Portland Harbor was still crowded with great sailing ships and coasting schooners. Having survived fire and the Depression, the PYC almost foundered during World War II. It was born again with the acquisition of a Falmouth Foreside summer cottage on a bluff with grand views of Casco Bay. Today the club is a bustling, family-oriented sailing center, with a vigorous program for juniors and popular races on weekends and Thursday evenings.

Launch service is provided from 8 A.M. to 9 P.M., or you can tie up alongside for a brief period (six feet of water at the floats). You will find water and ice, but no fuel.

For the Crew. Mail will be held for your arrival at the PYC. There are showers, a washing machine, and a dryer. The dining room is open to visiting yachtsmen for lunch and dinner; dress is informal, but not too informal; BYOB. No credit cards.

Handy Boat has a waterfront restaurant called The Galley, the Scaramouche Lounge, and a pay phone. The closest source of groceries and provisions is the Town Landing Market, ½ mile north on Route 88. Check with Handy's for transportation. The Falmouth Shopping Center is 2½ miles away.

BASKET ISLAND

Charts: 13288, 13290, **13292**

Basket, a nine-acre island off Falmouth Foreside, northeast of Clapboard Island, belongs to The Nature Conservancy, which maintains it jointly with the Portland Yacht Club. This is a popular spot for a picnic and exploration, but only in the daytime.

No fires or camping are allowed (much of the island was burned over by a fire in 1979).

You can anchor west of Basket (note the rocks shown on the chart) and land your dinghy on the gravel beaches at the island's northern tip.

CHANDLER COVE ★★ No facilities

Charts: 13288, 13290, **13292**

Chandler Cove is formed by three islands: Great Chebeague, Little Chebeague, and Long. It may be a good anchorage for substantial vessels, as the *Coast Pilot* suggests, but not for cruising yachts. The cove is wide open to the southeast and the southwest, deeper than comfortable for anchoring, and too large to provide a feeling of protection. As one Portland yachtsman observed, "It's a thoroughfare."

With the wind in a northern quadrant, however, Chandler Cove would provide excellent shelter. This is the base for a small fishing fleet, and the Portland ferry docks at the wharf on the east side.

Approaches. Chandler Cove is well marked for entry from either southwest or southeast.

Anchorages, Moorings. Note the cable areas. In settled summer weather, you might find good anchorage in the northeast corner of Chandler

Cove, or off the eastern shore of Little Chebeague Island.

Another possibility is to anchor off the long sand bar that connects Great and Little Chebeague, either inside Chandler Cove or outside. The beach uncovers at low water, and in good weather it would be pleasant, although entirely exposed.

Things to Do. Explore Little Chebeague Island, a state park. Once a flourishing farm with open meadows, and later several homes, the island still draws the eye and welcomes the stranger.

GREAT CHEBEAGUE ISLAND ★★★

Charts: 13288, **13290**, 13292

Chebeague is an Indian word meaning "Island of Many Springs," and locally pronounced "sha-bíg." At 3½ miles long and a mile or so wide, Great Chebeague is the largest and highest of the Casco Bay islands. Great Chebeague once was a summer resort for the Indians, who retreated to the mainland in winter, and much the same pattern is evident today. The 2,000 summer folk retreat to the mainland on Labor Day, leaving this beautiful island to 400 year-round residents.

The first white owner of Great Chebeague was Sir Ferdinando Gorges, "Father of Maine." In the eighteenth century, the island was settled by Scots, among them Ambrose Hamilton. This energetic and prolific Scot fathered 14 children and built the "stone sloops," a large fleet of schooners that carried granite from quarries farther east to build libraries, post offices, and other public buildings in New York, Boston, and Philadelphia.

The isolation of Great Chebeague has been threatened from time to time by plans for a bridge from Littlejohn Island, but so far the idea has been rejected.

Approaches. Approaching from the south, note the rocks that make out a long way from Great Chebeague Island, forcing you well over toward the shore of Littlejohn in order to leave nun "18" to starboard. From there, you will see the large, white Chebeague Island Inn.

Anchorages, Moorings. The best anchorage is in the northwest bight, off the stone pier and the Chebeague Island Inn, which maintains several moorings in deep water north of the stone pier, or you can anchor comfortably nearby in 12 feet at low. Shallow water extends a long way from the stone pier, so anchor well out beyond the moorings. The bottom is grass and mud and the holding ground is good. Although open to the north, this anchorage is well protected from prevailing winds and a long way from ocean swells—an ideal choice for a peaceful night.

Getting Ashore. Bring your dinghy in to the east side of the float, leaving the west side free for the ferry from Cousins Island.

For the Crew. Near the landing is the Stone Pier Variety, a convenience store/takeout that has ice and limited groceries, but no fuel or water. There are public phones here and cabs are available. The larger Island Market and the post office are a short walk up the road to the right. As you come ashore, you'll pass a tiny golf tee on the right for the challenging par 3 waterhole—fun to watch.

Walk up the road through a fairway of the nine-hole public course to the Chebeague Island Inn (tel. 846-5155). Many people come here to enjoy dinner (by reservation) and contemplate the peaceful scene from a rocking chair on the porch. Dress is informal. Other attractive features of the inn include a massive stone fireplace and the Bounty Pub.

Things to Do. Aside from golf and rocking on the porch, Great Chebeague lends itself well to exploration on bicycles, which can be rented at the Chebeague Island Inn.

Great Chebeague has several nice beaches, most convenient of which is Hamilton Beach, on the northeast tip of the island, close to the inn. Hamilton Beach can also be approached from the sea by anchoring just south of can "1." Another pleasant beach that can be reached from the water is the sand spit connecting Great Chebeague to Little Chebeague.

CROW ISLAND

Charts: 13288, **13290**

Tiny Crow Island, off the east side of Great Chebeague, is owned by the state of Maine. With granite ledges, a few spruce trees, and an abandoned cabin, this is an idyllic island to explore.

COUSINS ISLAND
Charts: 13288, **13290**, 13292

Cousins Island is hard to miss. A huge power plant occupies the southwest end—with a green rectangular blockhouse, one enormous stack, and another merely large stack. Lights on these stacks blink at you day and night from almost any part of Casco Bay, but time heals all, and eventually you can ignore them altogether. During the summer, a ferry runs from Cousins to Great Chebeague.

Cousins Island is connected to the mainland by a bridge at Drinkwater Point in Yarmouth. The point's name comes from an early nineteenth century family that produced 14 sons. Each Drinkwater son in turn became a master mariner and captain of his own square-rigger. Being Mainers of independent spirit, they found government regulations irksome and decided to strike back. The story goes that one summer day, 14 square-riggers, each commanded by a Captain Drinkwater, each registered from Cousins Island, Maine, entered New York Harbor and applied to Customs for clearance. It was a rough day for the fledgling federal bureaucracy.

MOSHIER and LITTLE MOSHIER ISLANDS
Charts: 13288, **13290**

Between the southern tips of Moshier and Little Moshier Islands, anchor in 6 to 12 feet of water.

Linger awhile, have a picnic, and savor a lovely location.

ROYAL RIVER (YARMOUTH) ★★★
Charts: 13288, **13290**

The Royal River is a narrow, winding stream leading from Casco Bay to a fixed bridge at the falls below the town of Yarmouth. Its marshy green banks are reminiscent of *Wind in the Willows*—the kind of river that conjures up images of Indians in their birchbark canoes.

Thanks to the forested banks, the Royal River offers excellent protection from just about any blow. At worst, you will ground out on a soft mudbank. "Best-protected harbor on the coast," says a local yard employee.

Although surrounded by busy boatyards and civilization, the basin at the head of the river attracts its share of wildlife—you might see herons at dusk or perhaps flocks of ducks flying upstream in the early morning.

Approaches. Enter on a coming tide, preferably at half-tide or better. Make your approach between Little Moshier and Cousins islands, heading for flashing green buoy "1," which marks the beginning of the channel. From there to the first turn, there are no great problems. Follow the marked channel, remembering that it may be no wider than 50 to 100 feet, and that it probably has silted up in places. Much of the channel is deep, but it is narrow and has some bad spots—especially where the Cousins River joins from the north. It can be very disconcerting to find yourself aground in the middle of a marked channel, but that is not uncommon here. The shoalest area is between nuns "8" and "10."

The channel buoys are reset each spring. Some helpful stakes have been placed between buoys, at the edge of the mudflats, with little green and red markers on top.

Anchorages, Moorings. Approaching the basin at the head of navigation, you will come to three yards. First, on the right, is the Royal River Boat Yard, which maintains floats parallel to the channel, with seven feet of water alongside, and 80 slips.

On the left, where the channel broadens out to a turning basin, is Yankee Marina, Inc., which has 110 slips with deep water alongside.

Yarmouth Boat Yard, Inc., is the last yard on the left, at the head of navigation. It has 150 slips, with six to eight feet of water alongside.

Proceed slowly; the turning basin is tight and jammed with boats.

Getting Ashore. Take your dinghy to the floats at any of the yards. The town landing and float, and a landing for fishermen, are at the north side of the turning basin.

For the Boat. *Royal River Boat Yard (tel. 846-*

9577). This yard is owned by members of the Dugas family, whose grandfather started a small operation here many years ago. With a 50-ton boatlift and a 100-ton marine railway, the yard can make extensive repairs on both commercial and pleasure vessels in steel or fiberglass. Alan Dugas himself repairs and restores wooden boats.

Gas, diesel, water, ice, and electricity are available at the floats along the river.

Yankee Marina Inc., (tel. 846-4326). Yankee Marina specializes in fiberglass repairs, with a 15-ton boatlift and plans for a 35-tonner. Water and electricity are available at the slips, but no fuel. The yard dredges to 12 feet or so alongside its floats. If you get stuck in the river, Yankee Marina can tow you off.

Yarmouth Boat Yard, Inc. (Ch. 16; tel. 846-9050).

Gas, water, and electricity are available here, and there is a marine store. The yard has a 4-ton forklift; facilities exist for fiberglass and wood hull repairs as well as engine repairs.

For the Crew. The former fish factory near Yankee Marina has found new life as Lower Falls Landing, a handsome complex of marine-related facilities, including the Landing Boat Supply chandlery, Harbour Books, with a great selection of marine titles, and The Cannery Restaurant, which serves lunch, dinner, and Sunday brunch on the waterfront. The town of Yarmouth, where you can obtain groceries and other supplies, is about a mile away from the harbor. From the boatyards, turn right on Route 88, then left under the bridge on Route 115.

BANGS, SAND, ROGUES, and HOPE ISLANDS
Charts: **13290**, 13292

East of Great Chebeague Island stretches 55-acre Bangs Island, owned by the state. High and wooded, Hope Island lies just east of the south end of Great Chebeague Island. Nearby are tiny Rogues Island and larger Sand Island, both uninhabited. Anchor at the northern end of Hope Island in 21 feet of water or west of Sand Island in 12 feet for a convenient and enjoyable day stop.

CLIFF ISLAND ★★★   No facilities
Charts: 13288, **13290**

The striking H-shape of Cliff Island intrigues many a sailor. Perhaps this explains why it originally was named Crotch Island. This is the home of the famous Crotch Island pinky, one of Maine's most distinctive small craft.

North of the crossbar are protected anchorages far from civilization, with beaches to explore. Tucked in the corner south of the crossbar is the little harbor of Fisherman's Cove, where you may be able to obtain fuel.

The state pier (ferry landing) and public float landing are on the west shore of the island, about .7 mile from the south end.

Approaches. Since the dangers in the anchoring area north of the crossbar are unmarked, it is best to arrive near low water if you don't know the territory. You can approach easily from the west between Cliff and Stave Islands, or from the east, leaving nun "6" close aboard to starboard. The current is strong through these narrow passages.

Anchorages. North of the crossbar, you can anchor either side of the ledge that divides the cove in half (see sketch map). Note that the eastern section has an unmarked 3-foot spot.

In the western half of the cove, identify the rock on the chart shown as uncovering six feet at low, pass to the east of it, and anchor south of it in 15 to 17 feet of water. The bottom is rocky, so be sure your anchor is well set.

Getting Ashore. It is an easy row in to the white sand beach.

Things to Do. Once anchored in the northern sector, you will see only one house and a great long beach that you can walk all the way over to the cliffs on the east side of the island, which are now protected by Oceanside Conservation Trust, and open to the public.

Cliff has one of the few remaining one-room schoolhouses in Maine.

BATES and MINISTERIAL ISLANDS

Charts: 13290

Northeast of Cliff Island, Bates and Ministerial are low and partly wooded islands with only a few houses. As you can see on the chart, there is a little slot between the two islands at the north end where you can sneak in and drop the hook in 13 feet of water for a day stop.

JEWELL ISLAND ★★★★★ No facilities

Charts: 13288, **13290**

Jewell is an ideal stopping point when traveling east or west. On the outer fringes of the Casco Bay islands, it's right on your way and provides a secure anchorage for the night, although it is likely to be crowded on weekends. If you have time, take advantage of the opportunity for easy walks and spectacular views.

This state-owned island is a mile long and no more than a quarter of a mile wide. The anchorage is at the northwest corner between Jewell and Little Jewell (connected at low tide). The attractive harbor is lined with low cliffs on the east side, fringed by birches mixed with evergreens.

There are sundry tales of pirate treasure buried on Jewell, so you may be disappointed to know that the island was named not for loot but for George Jewell of Saco, who bought it from the Indians in 1637.

Approaches. Coming from seaward, make your landfall on Halfway Rock, which has a 76-foot lighthouse visible for 19 miles, a foghorn, and a radiobeacon. Be careful that a flooding tide does not push you toward dangerous Drunkers Ledges to the north. In thick weather, favor Halfway Rock, listening for the horn or trying for a glimpse of the lighthouse.

Then run halfway between the tip of Jewell Island and West Brown Cow, staying well clear of the ledges making out to the east from Jewell. West Brown Cow is a little rock plateau 36 feet high, grassy on top, and normally quite visible even in haze. In clear weather, you can also use the high face of Cliff Island as a reference.

Note that nun "4" and can "5" are *not* entrance buoys for the harbor at Jewell, but channel markers for the passage between Jewell and Cliff.

After you round the north tip of Jewell Island, head into the harbor on a course roughly southwest, staying well away from the ledge making out from the north tip of Little Jewell.

As you approach Jewell from the south, the tall watchtower on the southern tip of the island is obvious from a long way out. Run up between Cliff Island and Jewell, passing between nun "4" and can "5" before turning right, leaving the nun well to starboard as you enter the harbor.

Anchorages, Moorings. The state has ordered all moorings removed from the cove, which leaves more room for anchoring in this tight little harbor. Holding ground is good anywhere in the cove, with bottom of sand and mud. Anchor on the midline and not too close to the cliffs on the eastern shore, where the beach shelves very gradually. There is good water past the house on Little Jewell Island, but be careful of two pilings just beyond, one of which is submerged at high tide. Beyond the pilings, the cove shoals rapidly.

This harbor is well protected from every direction except the north. The wind can funnel down the slot from the south, however, so anchor with enough scope to keep your boat from dragging through the fleet.

Getting Ashore. Getting ashore is easy with your dinghy. Except at high tide, there is a gradual slate pebble beach, and several places to climb the low cliffs.

Things to Do. For a quick and delightful way to stretch your legs, walk straight across the island on a well-trodden trail to the Punchbowl on the eastern side, a wide, crescent-shaped beach and (at low tide) a completely encircled body of shallow seawater warmed by the sun. This is a great place for a picnic—with lots of driftwood, birds, beach roses, beach peas, and sand. The young, the old but foolish, and dogs will enjoy bathing in the quiet pool, which can be quite bracing even in July. On the way to the Punchbowl, raspberries and blackberries are abundant in season. Be prepared with bug spray.

For a longer walk, head south along the eastern shore of the anchorage, on a path carpeted with pine needles. The path narrows, but persist until you arrive at the ruins of buildings, and eventually an eight-story tower. It is worth the climb up the concrete steps for marvelous views of Casco Bay to the north, east, and south (be careful of rusted ladders). During World War II, this structure was a lookout tower, one of several scattered along the coast. Round concrete pads with bolts supported telescopes that were aimed through the slits. Observers in two or more of these towers reported cross-bearings on a sub or periscope, from which its position could be fixed.

Walk a little farther, past collapsed tarpaper barracks, and you will find another but lower concrete tower. Warning: The path leads next to a deep pit, on the right, which apparently held oil tanks for the whole facility.

Just beyond you will come to an enormous concrete circle with a hole in the middle for an eight-inch-gun emplacement. For those who love concrete tunnels with water dripping from the ceiling, massive steel doors on rusty hinges, open floor pits, and dark passages leading off to unknown destinations, there is a fascinating underground system of tunnels and bunkers to explore, with another gun emplacement beyond. Just be sure to carry a flashlight.

HARRASEEKET RIVER

(SOUTH FREEPORT) ★★★★★

 4   All facilities

Charts: 13288, **13290**

The Harraseeket, a tidal river, creates a splendid, well-protected harbor at the north corner of Casco Bay, in the town of South Freeport. This major yachting center has almost every facility, yet it remains simple and attractive. Close by in Freeport is the fabled L.L. Bean store.

Although a bit out of the way for a yacht traveling east or west along the coast, the Harraseeket is a good place to change crew, find a diesel mechanic, or make some shore excursions.

This area has a long shipbuilding history, one that parallels the history of the whole coast of Maine. Boats have been built on the Harraseeket River for 2½ centuries, ever since the first settlers cut pine in the virgin forests to build England's Royal Navy. Ships of 300 to 400 tons were built at what is now South Freeport Marine before 1816, and 40 percent of the men in Freeport were employed by the yard. Since then, this location has seen boatyards come and go, and some of the pilings and stone abutments at South Freeport Marine still date from the mid-nineteenth century.

Approaches. The entrance to the Harraseeket River is narrow and bends sharply right, and the current runs swiftly here most of the time. It can be tricky for a stranger in thick weather.

The approach starts between Little Bustins Island and nun "2A" at Moshier Ledge. Note the line of mudflats on the left, from Moshier Island to the entrance. Crab Island is almost on the edge of these flats, so leave it well to port. There are two good landmarks for the entrance itself: tiny Pound of Tea Island, with its single house and a few trees (yes, that was the original purchase price from the Indians), and The Castle, which stands near the shore in South Freeport (shown as "Tower" on the chart).

After leaving flashing red buoy "2" to starboard, hug the left side of the channel, particularly near can "3," since rocks make out in that direction from Pound of Tea. After leaving can "3" close aboard to

port, curve gradually to starboard around Pound of Tea, leaving can "5" to port as well.

Local boats take great joy in passing inside Pound of Tea, especially at high tide. Resist the impulse.

Beyond can "5" is a deep and fairly narrow channel to the marinas, marked by small buoys. Don't stray far from this channel, and do *not* go where there are no moored boats. At high tide, the Harraseeket River looks like an enormous quiet lake; at low, the deepwater area is much narrower than it appeared.

Anchorages, Moorings. The first dock on the left belongs to the Harraseeket Yacht Club, which sometimes has guest moorings available. There is a gap after the yacht club, and then the remaining facilities and docks are all cheek-by-jowl. First come the floats of Strouts Point Wharf Co., which has moorings, then the town docks and public landing (above which are the red buildings of Harraseeket Lunch); farthest to the north are the floats of South Freeport Marine, which also has moorings. Ring's Marine no longer has a base in South Freeport, although it does have moorings (see below).

Most of the available space in the Harraseeket River, from Pound of Tea to Weston Point, is occupied by moorings, spaced just far enough apart. Do not anchor.

Many people like to be north of the docks, where the protection is best and there is little wake from commercial boats. You may prefer a mooring near the entrance, where you can have a good view of The Castle, hear the cows mooing on Wolf Neck, watch the many harbor seals, observe the constant procession of interesting boats, and listen for the splashing of the pogies. This is a calm harbor and a very pleasant place to be under most circumstances.

Getting Ashore. Take your dinghy ashore to

MASTS AND THE BROAD ARROW

Not more than one man in a thousand who looked at a ship of the line reflected that her great mainmast had been cut in the forests of Maine. . . .

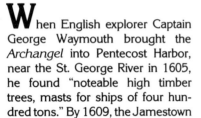

Robert Albion,
Forests and Sea Power, 1926

When English explorer Captain George Waymouth brought the *Archangel* into Pentecost Harbor, near the St. George River in 1605, he found "noteable high timber trees, masts for ships of four hundred tons." By 1609, the Jamestown Colony was sending home the first shipment of masts from the New World.

Softwoods such as firs and pines are superior to hardwoods for use as masts, being far more flexible and carrying less weight aloft. England's forests were cut for firewood in the Middle Ages, and by the seventeenth century, the closest supply for mast timbers was in the Baltic. There she competed with the French, Spanish, and Dutch for the great Baltic firs, prized by the British Admiralty for their resilience and durability.

But the Baltic was 1,000 miles away and not under England's control, and the route could be blocked easily at the straits of Denmark. New sources were needed.

By about 1650, the colonists in America had established a flourishing trade in masts, lumber, and other naval stores to Europe and the Caribbean. They were not pleased when the British Admiralty awoke to the fact that its supply of mast trees in North America was in danger. In 1685 a Surveyor of Pines and Timber was appointed to survey the Maine woods "within 10 miles of any navigable waterway" and mark all

suitable trees with "the king's broad arrow," the symbol used since early times to designate Royal Navy property. Now the broad arrow was to be blazed with an axe on "all trees of the diameter of twenty-four inches and upwards at twelve inches from the ground." And woe to anyone who damaged or stole the king's property—the fine was £100. The Broad Arrow Policy was observed with all the enthusiasm that greeted Prohibition more than two centuries later, and the same native ingenuity was applied to circumventing it.

Mast trees were partially burned in mysterious fires or splintered in unusual gales. Loopholes apparently excluded certain properties, whose great pines were promptly felled and sawn into profitable lumber. And never, under any circumstances, would the floorboards of any colonial home exceed 23 inches in width. The law was tightened again and again, but still the king's pines continued to disappear.

Mast trees usually were cut in the fall, when they were full of resin. The trees were carefully felled on prepared beds, limbed, and squared. During the winter, the baulks of timber were then dragged by brute strength onto sleds and hauled out of the woods by teams of oxen. Since one great tree could weigh as much as 18 tons, this was a difficult and dangerous process, requiring great skill and the efforts of as many as 100 oxen.

Where mast roads met, communities sprang up, and often the shape of the town square was determined by the clearance needed to turn the long timbers. An example of this remains in Freeport, opposite the L. L. Bean store, where the former Bliss-Holbrook Tavern (now stores) was sited at a strange angle for that very reason.

Every mast road led to the nearest navigable waters, often a tidal marsh. Here the baulks were delivered to a mast agent, slipped into the water, and towed to a mast depot. ("Mast Landing" is a title that still appears on charts for many locations along the Maine coast.)

At the mast depot, the baulks were graded and hewn to the specified 16 sides. Then they were loaded aboard special mast ships, through large stern ports, for transportation to England, where the final trimming and fitting of the mast was done. Some of these mast ships were of 400 to 600 tons burden and could carry 30 to 50 of the enormous baulks below decks.

Although the Broad Arrow Policy never could be effectively enforced, and the colonists continued to cut the mast trees for sale on the black market, the supply of great pines was sufficient to provide a crucial resource for the Royal Navy for 125 years, until the monopoly finally was ended by the American Revolution.

the floats at the Harraseeket Yacht Club, Strouts Point Wharf, or South Freeport Marine. The strong current may help or hinder you. Use channel 9 or your horn (one long, one short blast) to call the launch from South Freeport Marine. The Ring's launch, based at the town landing, responds to channel 9 or three toots on the horn.

For the Boat. *Harraseeket Yacht Club (tel. 865-4949).* This is an informal and friendly place whose burgee carries a drawing of The Castle. To assist visiting yachtsmen, members who are off cruising post notices on the bulletin board giving the locations of their moorings. There is no launch, and no one visibly in charge, so ask the sailing instructor or a member for help or advice. Water is available at the floats, with 10 feet alongside, but not fuel. There is a pay phone.

Strouts Point Wharf Company (Ch. 16; tel. 865-3899). This marina has 100 slips, with 16 feet at low along the outer faces. Gas, diesel, water, and electricity are available, plus showers. There is a marine store, and a 25-ton boatlift; repairs of all kinds can be accomplished. The marina has about 15 moorings, but no launch service.

Ring's Marine Service, Inc. (2 Main Street, Freeport; Ch. 9 or 16; tel. 865-6143). Based in Freeport, Ring's also has a presence on the waterfront, including 100 moorings. The Ring's launch will direct you to a mooring. The yard has a boatlift and chandlery; mechanical, electrical, and electronic repairs can be arranged through the Freeport base, which also can supply divers.

South Freeport Marine (Ch. 9 or 16; tel. 865-3181). South Freeport Marine manages 160 moorings for local yachts and visitors and provides all the normal services, including gas, diesel, electricity, water, ice, and showers. The marina has 215 feet of dock space at the outside floats, with 12 feet of water at low.

The yard has a 25-ton boatlift, and can handle hull and engine repairs of all kinds. Associated with the yard are the Casco Bay Rigging Company (865-3183) and Maine Compass Services (865-6645), which provides compass adjusting, sales, and service.

With 24 hours' notice, South Freeport Marine provides transportation to and from the Portland airport.

For the Crew. Harraseeket Lunch and Lobster provides takeout and restaurant service in the red building next to South Freeport Marine.

The post office and Mom 'n' Pop's, a market and variety store, are a 15-minute walk up the hill and to the left. For a more extensive grocery selection, plus liquor and good meat, try to get a ride to Bow Street Market in Freeport, about three miles away (865-6631). Or take the free shuttle bus provided by L.L. Bean (inquire at South Freeport Marine); once in Freeport, you can walk to the Bow Street Market, and they will take you back to the boat. The market is open seven days a week. For Freeport Taxi, call 865-9494.

Things to Do. If you have a strong consumer urge, don't miss L.L. Bean, open 24 hours a day in Freeport. Attracted by the store's popularity, more than 80 other stores, factory outlets, and boutiques now cluster in the town.

Land your dinghy at the yacht club float and take a 10-minute walk to the picturesque Castle. Casco Castle was a large Victorian hotel built around the turn of the century by Amos Gerald "the Electric Railway King." A trolley completed in 1902 brought guests to the hotel, which burned in 1914, leaving only the stone tower.

For a much longer trip, run up the estuary at the northeast end of the harbor in your dinghy to Mast Landing, named for the enormous pine trees felled and shipped to England for masts (see sidebar). Just beyond is Mast Landing Sanctuary, operated by Maine Audubon, with trails and nature exhibits.

Or explore the trails of Wolf Neck Woods State Park, on the eastern side of the river. To get there, take your dinghy ashore at one of the two little indentations to the right of the word "Harraseeket" on chart 13290. The end of Wolf Neck is private property.

MEREPOINT BAY ★★★

No facilities

Charts: 13288, **13290**

Merepoint and Maquoit are shallow bays on either side of Merepoint Neck, only about three miles from the town of Brunswick. Many of the residents of this area are based at the Brunswick Naval Air Station and are avid yachtsmen.

This northern corner of Casco Bay feels remote and peaceful. As with many of Maine's long, shallow fingers that stretch inland, the tidal water here is often comfortably warm for swimming.

Approaches. Beyond Bustins Island a row of lovely little wooded islands—Sow and Pigs, Pettingill, Williams, and Sister—lines the route to tranquil Merepoint Bay. Except for Bustins Ledge, which is visible, and a rock just south of Sister

Island, there are no unmarked dangers along the way.

Anchorages, Moorings. As you enter Merepoint Bay, the flagpole and clubhouse of the Merepoint Yacht Club will be to port near the tip of the peninsula. The club is a small one, however, and offers no facilities for the visiting yacht.

Farther up the bay, opposite the northern end of Birch Island, is a substantial fleet of boats and Paul's Marina, where you might be able to get a mooring for the night. The bay shoals rapidly at this point, so stay a good distance off Merepoint Neck. The outer moorings are in deep water. You can also anchor here, in good sand bottom.

BIRCH ISLAND

Charts: 13288, **13290**

Birch is a large island between Merepoint and Middle bays. In the southwest end is a long slot with eight feet of water at the entrance—a pleasant spot to drop the lunch hook for a peaceful picnic.

UPPER GOOSE ISLAND

Charts: 13288, **13290**

Upper Goose is a 94-acre wooded island on the western side of Middle Bay. The Nature Conservancy owns most of the island, which has the largest great blue heron rookery in New England. According to that organization, more than 250 nests have been counted in the island's hemlock, beech, and yellow birch trees. Some trees have held as many as 10 nests.

Since herons are susceptible to human disturbance, particularly during the nesting season, when disruptions can cause them to abandon their nests, *The Conservancy urges that you refrain from visiting the interior of the island between early April and mid-August.*

To explore the shoreline's rocky ledges, gravel beaches, and salt marshes, land at the large gravel beach on the western shore or in the north cove. Common sights are osprey, eiders, and other sea ducks, as well as harbor seals on the southeast ledges.

THE GOSLINGS ★★★ No facilities

Charts: 13288, **13290**

North of the Goslings (two small, privately owned islands off the southern end of Lower Goose) is one of the nicest anchorages in Casco Bay. With the wind anywhere in the south, you can lie here with a surprising degree of protection and choose from several islands to explore. A minor detraction from the beauty of the scene is a platoon of oil tanks marching in ranks down to the water on Harpswell Neck, across the bay.

On a weekday, there may be nobody here. On summer weekends, however, the Goslings take on the air of a small and festive town, with the constant arrival and departure of picnicking groups.

Approaches. Run halfway between Irony Island and Grassy Ledge.

Anchorages, Moorings. Find a spot in 12 to 16 feet of water, north of the eastern Gosling or a bit farther west. Holding ground is good in mud.

Getting Ashore. It is easy to go ashore on the Goslings and other nearby islands with your dinghy.

Things to Do. There is a picnic table on the eastern Gosling and a lovely little shell beach. The water is clear, and swimming is excellent. At low tide, the reason for the anchorage's protection becomes evident as you watch people wading across the sandbar between the two Goslings. The owners request that there be no fires except on the beach, and that no wood be cut for the fires.

When the tide is right, you can watch seals sunbathe and belch on the north tip of tiny Irony Island. By July, seal pups have joined the entourage and often are basking on the rocks with their mothers. Also on Irony is a bronze plaque in memory of a captain of the Portland Pilot Boat, lost off his cutter near this island in 1962.

POTTS HARBOR ★★★

Charts: 13288, **13290**

Potts Harbor is a great, wide-open bay at the southern end of Harpswell Neck. At first glance, it appears exposed to prevailing winds. Inside, however, the surrounding islands and ledges provide reasonable protection all the way around.

Easy to enter, with adequate facilities, Potts is a good stop for yachts traveling east and west.

Approaches. Coming from outside Casco Bay, the key to the approach is Halfway Rock, with its 76-foot lighthouse. Run from there to red-and-white bell "BS" at the entrance to Broad Sound, and then between gong "3" and nun "4." Turn to starboard between red bell "6," off Little Birch, and the red-and-green nun. From there, it is a wide and easy entrance between Horse Island and Thrumcap into Potts Harbor.

There is an eastern entrance to Potts Harbor from Merriconeag Sound. It is a bit confusing, and a fair current may be running, so strangers should use this passage only in good visibility. Start at nun "2," north of Haskell Island, leaving red buoys to starboard and green ones to port. Follow the channel around the hairpin turn to the south and then return northward into Potts Harbor.

Anchorages, Moorings. On the charts, the anchorage is shown inside the southwest tip of Harpswell Neck. Look for the moored boats. You can probably obtain a mooring from Dolphin Marine or lie alongside (ask the dockman). There is plenty of room to anchor.

Potts Harbor is almost a mile across, so it may not be a quiet anchorage in heavy weather. Quite a chop can build up. In a blow from the north or east, consider anchoring east of Ash Point.

Getting Ashore. Row your dinghy in to the floats.

For the Boat. *Dolphin Marine Service, Inc. (tel. 833-6000).* This laid-back, fisherman-oriented marina has gas, diesel, ice, and a pay phone. Water is limited, however, because the marina gets its supply from a well. A mechanic is available and there is a small chandlery.

For the Crew. There is a nice restaurant with both table and counter service at Dolphin Marine. To top it off, the nearby field is loaded with succulent blueberries in August.

Things to Do. At the end of the narrow slot leading northeast from Potts Harbor is a large lobster dock, dredged to 10 feet some years ago. Row west through the narrow spot, across the remnants of a rock dam, into Basin Cove, a primordial and magical place. The cove's western shore, for a long way, is privately owned and a sanctuary for birds. You may see great blue herons roosting high in the trees, or perhaps night herons, little green herons, and snowy egrets.

Make this trip near slack water. The tide pours hard in and out of Basin Cove. And be sure to row; an outboard will frighten the birds.

EAGLE ISLAND

Charts: 13288, **13290**

One of the outermost islands in Casco Bay, 17-acre Eagle is a state park best known as the site of Admiral Robert E. Peary's house. Announcing discovery of the North Pole in 1909, Peary was beset by controversy that did not subside until Congress officially proclaimed him the discoverer in 1911 and awarded him a pension. He spent the last nine years of his life with his family here on Eagle Island. The question of whether Peary actually reached the North Pole continues to fascinate people, perhaps because the issues are those of character and obsession as much as fact and scientific proof.

Standing high on the northern tip of the island, the Peary home is built like a ship, with a deck all around, and it is full of the admiral's collected arti-

facts and furnishings. This is well worth a visit, but plan it for a weekday to avoid the crowds.

The dock at Eagle Island is near the northwest tip. In the approach, nun "4" marks the end of a long ledge from the west side of the island. Some moorings are available, but you probably will have to anchor off in 16 to 30 feet of water. The anchorage is exposed and the current in Broad Sound can run swiftly, so you may want to leave someone aboard when you explore the island.

Eagle Island is high, with spectacular views of Casco Bay in every direction. Near the landing is a nice little wading beach, and a trail leads all the way around the island.

MACKEREL COVE
(BAILEY ISLAND) ★★★

 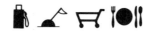

Charts: 13288, **13290**

Mackerel Cove is a very deep harbor in the south end of Bailey Island, home to many lobstermen and tuna fishermen. The shores of this picturesque

cove are lined with pine-topped cliffs and docks piled high with lobster traps.

Approaches. The entrance to Merriconeag and

Harpswell sounds is clearly marked by the metronome-shaped monument on Mark Island and the two square concrete towers at the tip of Bailey Island. Once you have found green flashing buoy "1" at Abner Point, left to port, entering is no problem. As you approach the marina at the northwest end of the harbor, maneuvering is tight among the moored boats, floats, and moorings.

Opinions vary as to whether the rock shown on the chart at the head of the harbor really exists. Local fishermen say they've never had trouble with it.

Anchorages, Moorings. Mackerel Cove Marina has moorings for rent and 200 feet of space alongside, with 10 feet of water at low. If these are occupied, anchor out beyond all the moorings. Holding ground is good mud anywhere in the cove, but the 50-foot depth makes it uncomfortable for anchoring.

Although Mackerel Cove is well protected from every direction except due southwest, there are entering swells even in calm weather. Once in a long while the harbor suffers heavy damage from a southwest storm.

Getting Ashore. Land your dinghy at Mackerel Cove Marina.

For the Boat. *Mackerel Cove Marina (Ch. 16; tel. 833-6656).* Mackerel Cove Marina also answers to its former name of Dockside Marina. Depth alongside is ample. Gas, diesel, electricity, and ice are available. Water is limited because it comes from a well and the supply usually is low in summer. There is no mechanic here, but the marina can find one for you.

For the Crew. Right next to the marina is a little coffee shop with lots of local flavor. Next door is a fancier restaurant and lounge. A 15-minute walk up the road will take you to the Bailey Island post office and the General Store, which has a good selection of groceries, ice cream, and sundries.

Things to Do. A big event for deepsea fishermen, the annual Bailey Island Tuna Tournament is held here the last full week in July. The largest tuna ever caught by the Casco Bay Tuna Club weighed 1,009 pounds. Some tuna is eaten here, but most of it is flown to Japan, where bluefin is highly prized.

ORRS-BAILEY YACHT CLUB ★★

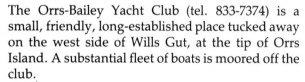

Charts: 13288, **13290**

The Orrs-Bailey Yacht Club (tel. 833-7374) is a small, friendly, long-established place tucked away on the west side of Wills Gut, at the tip of Orrs Island. A substantial fleet of boats is moored off the club.

Approaches. Examine the chart closely. You must go north of the red daybeacon on Cox Ledge and nun "6" before turning south into the harbor.

Anchorages, Moorings. Guest moorings are available at the club; inquire at the dock. Be aware that the yellow ferry from Portland comes right past the moorings on its way to Cook's Wharf. There is no room to anchor.

According to the harbormaster, the harbor is well protected from the south, but "can be clobbered in September or October with a brisk wind across Harpswell Sound from the northwest."

Getting Ashore. Take your dinghy in to the float.

For the Boat. There is 15 feet of water along the yacht club fuel dock, where gas and water are available, but no diesel.

For the Crew. The clubhouse has a pay phone.

Things to Do. From the yacht club, walk across the famous Orrs Island/Bailey Island bridge, a national historic civil-engineering landmark and the only cribwork bridge in the world. Granite slabs are laid in a filigree pattern, without cement, to create a strong and beautiful structure. Beyond the bridge is a selection of several restaurants. The nearest market is at least another mile.

If you yearn for a lobster dinner in a picturesque setting, take your dinghy down past the cribwork bridge to the floats next to Cook's Lobster Pound (see following writeup). The entrance by road is circuitous, so it is faster by water than by land.

COOK'S LOBSTER POUND ★★

Charts: 13288, **13290**

Cook's Lobster House and Pound (tel. 833-6641) are just south and west of the Orrs-Bailey cribwork bridge. The little cove full of working lobsterboats and the restaurant on the peninsula make a pic-

turesque spot for dinner if you are moored at the Orrs-Bailey Yacht Club or elsewhere in the vicinity.

Approaches. Head south from the Orrs-Bailey Yacht Club (see preceding writeup), staying far enough west to clear the ledge west of Wills Gut. The small can and nun are located to help boats heading under the bridge clear this ledge.

Anchorages, Moorings. Cook's Lobster Pound has a long line of floats running north and south, with 10 to 12 feet along the outer edges at low. The floats are in active use by lobstermen, who congregate toward the south end. Space along the middle

is intended for visitors and restaurant patrons. You can also tie up here for the night. Do not tie up, however, at the northern end of the floats. This area is reserved for the Casco Bay Lines ferry from Portland.

For the Boat. Gas, diesel, and water are available at the floats.

HARPSWELL HARBOR ★★ No facilities

Charts: 13288, **13290**

At the entrance to Harpswell Sound, this is a big wide-open bay, easy to enter and well protected from prevailing winds. As such, it may come in handy, even though it is not the area's most scenic anchorage.

The Merriconeag Yachting Association is based here, but it has no facilities for visiting yachtsmen.

Approaches. Entering the harbor, leave can "5" to port and take a wide swing around toward the center of the harbor. On the chart, note the rock and a 1-foot spot, which have hung up more than one yacht in recent memory. One way to avoid the hazard is to leave most of the lobster pots to port.

Anchorages, Moorings. The bottom shoals gradually, and you will want to anchor in about 12 feet of water at low, just outside the lobsterboat moorings. Holding ground is good. You will be well protected here from the southwest wind, without a hint of roll.

Getting Ashore. Land at the road where the chart says West Harpswell. Don't make the mistake of going ashore at low tide; there is no dock and you'll be squelching through clamflats.

Things to Do. The road leads up the hill to nowhere. The walk is pretty and bucolic, but there are no stores nearby.

BEALS COVE

Charts: 13288, **13290**

On the east side of Harpswell Sound, just above the Orrs-Bailey Yacht Club, Beals Cove opens up to the south. The shores are rocky, with houses set way back, and a tiny island in the middle adds a nice touch.

This is a good sheltered anchorage for shoal-draft boats but of little use for deep-draft ones.

REED COVE

Charts: 13288, **13290**

About a mile north of Beals Cove, on the east side of Harpswell Sound, Reed Cove is an open bight fringed with shingle beach and marsh.

Although it is exposed to the north and west,

you can find protection here in normal summer weather. Feel your way in as far as you can toward the beach, which shoals rapidly.

MILL COVE

Charts: 13288, **13290**

Near the head of Harpswell Sound, this shallow cove stretches north on the west side of High Head peninsula. It contains several houses and many shoals, but you might want to explore it as a gunkholing adventure.

Head for the tip of land between Mill Cove and Widgeon Cove, then enter Mill Cove just east of this tip. Even at dead low, there is as much as 14 feet of water here.

HIGH HEAD YACHT CLUB ★★

Charts: 13288, **13290**

High Head Yacht Club (tel. 725-8440) is a pleasant little club six miles up Harpswell Sound, on the west side, just north of High Head.

Approaches. Coming up Harpswell Sound toward High Head, aim for a modern white house on the southwest tip of the peninsula. This will keep you away from Dipper Cove Ledges, which make out a long way from the eastern shore. Opposite Wyer Island, coast around the high, wooded section of High Head. You will first see the moored boats, then the yacht club. The fixed bridge at Ewin Narrows is visible to the north.

Anchorages, Moorings. The yacht club maintains a guest mooring, and the steward keeps track of members who are away so that visiting yachtsmen can use their moorings.

There is plenty of room to anchor among the moorings in 8 to 10 feet of water at low. While the anchorage is good, there is exposure both to the northeast and the southwest.

Getting Ashore. Row in to the yacht club float.

For the Boat. Water and gas are available on an emergency basis only (club policy) at the yacht club floats, with 10 feet alongside at low. There is no diesel. An ice machine is in the clubhouse.

For the Crew. There are showers in the clubhouse. The nearest supplies are at Harpswell Mall, four miles away. You may be able to get a ride from someone at the club.

LONG COVE ★★★

 No facilities

Charts: 13288, **13290**

Long Cove, an intriguing narrow slot that bisects the northern part of Orrs Island, is out of the way and seldom used by cruising yachts. Here is a delightful and remote spot, with high, tree-lined shores of spruce, cedar, and oak, and hardly a sign of habitation. The only drawback is the noise of occasional cars on the Orrs Island road.

Long Cove is a bit tricky to enter. The entrance is surrounded by unmarked ledges, so do not try it in poor visibility. Study the chart carefully and eyeball your way in, preferably near low tide, when the ledges are visible. Once in, you will be extremely snug.

Approaches. Make your way up Harpswell Sound, favoring the west side to avoid Dipper Cove Ledges and aiming for High Head. At High Head, turn east, leaving tiny Dogs Head Island to starboard (it has a house with a cupola and a sign saying "Dogs Head").

Go well past Dogs Head to avoid the rocks (visible at low) to the east. Then start your turn southward, heading for a point south of the narrow peninsula bordering Lumbos Hole; note the ledge that makes out from the tip.

Once inside Long Cove, favor the east side to avoid a line of rocks that make out halfway across the cove about 400 yards inside the entrance. They are visible only at low tide. The channel is eight feet deep at low, and a hundred yards or so wide.

Anchorages, Moorings. Anchor in 8 to 10 feet at low in the eastern half of the cove, either before the rocks or beyond them. Holding ground is good, in mud bottom.

There is excellent protection here, and it would be suitable as a hurricane hole. In a strong northwester, however, the wind can funnel down the cove and create a stiff chop.

GUN POINT COVE

Charts: 13288, **13290**

This is a long, wide-open slot that separates Orrs Island from the Gun Point peninsula. The upper end of the cove has numerous unmarked rocks.

The cove is easy to enter but entirely exposed to the southwest and of no particular interest to a cruising sailor.

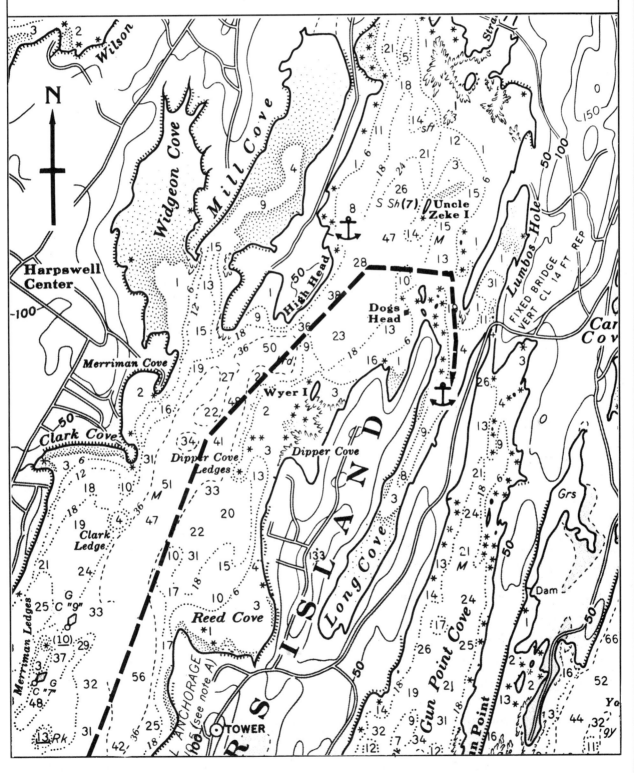

QUAHOG BAY

Charts: 13288, **13290**

Quahog Bay, at the eastern end of Casco Bay, is one of the loveliest spots along the western Maine coast. Only five miles from the city of Brunswick, it somehow has managed to remain unspoiled, with a character quite different from adjoining Harpswell Sound. Cedars line the edges of the bay; there are flights of snowy egrets; and osprey nests appear on almost every point. Lobsterboats here favor a dark green color not seen elsewhere in Maine.

Like most good things, Quahog Bay is hard to reach, and the direct route is not the best. The approaches include an abundance of ledges and rocky islands, matched by a scarcity of buoys. A stranger should enter only with good visibility.

Study the chart carefully beforehand and run a course that puts the least emphasis on identifying ledges (which may or may not break) and makes the best use of easily recognizable islands and what few buoys there are.

One useful preliminary is to trace the buoyed channel from the New Meadows River to Orrs-Bailey Islands (mentioned by the *Coast Pilot*). Once you have hooked up with this channel, which crosses the entrance to Quahog Bay, you are home free (see sketch map).

Approaching From the West. Coming from the west, round Drunkers Ledges and associated nun "2." Then run a course to red-and-white bell "JI" off Jaquish Island and beyond to the red-and-green nun at Charity Ledge. Continue up the eastern shore of Bailey Island, leaving nuns "2" and "4" to starboard. You are now in the buoyed channel between New Meadows and Orrs-Bailey Islands. Head for Gun Point Cove, then turn east toward nun "6," off Gun Point, leaving it close aboard to starboard. Leave Long Point Island (it has a house and telephone poles) to port and continue north into Quahog Bay.

Approaching From the East. To reach Quahog Bay from the east with a minimum of anxiety, first approach the entrance to the New Meadows River. After rounding Fuller Rock off Small Point and the red bell off Bald Head, run to flashing red bell "4"

off Wood Island, then north to flashing red buoy "6," off Harbor Island (noting the can to starboard and the green can off Jamison Ledge to port). Now cut across to can "1" off Rogue Island, leaving to port the red-and-white daybeacon on Goudy Ledge. You are now in the buoyed channel from New Meadows to Orrs-Bailey Islands. Turn southwest, leaving to starboard can "1" off Rogue Island, nun "2," and Jenny Island. Continue west, leaving nuns "2" and "4" also to starboard. After passing between nun "4" and the Elm Islands, turn northward into Quahog Bay.

Other Approaches. It is also possible to enter Quahog Bay from Ridley Cove to the eastward. Because of unmarked dangers, attempt this only at midtide or better, and then with caution.

There are other, more direct approaches to Quahog Bay. For example, after leaving red-and-green buoy "RR" off Round Rock to port, it is a straight shot directly into Quahog Bay. However, this requires positive identification of islands and ledges and should not be attempted by strangers or in poor visibility.

Entering Quahog Bay. From a distance, you will see two dark, high, rounded islands in the mouth of Quahog Bay. The eastern and smaller of the two, identified only as "15" on the chart, is Raspberry Island, just west of Yarmouth Island. The western and higher one is Pole Island, farther up the bay, identifiable by a conspicuous white boathouse at the southwest tip. There is an impressive number of lobster pots in these waters.

Leave Raspberry Island to starboard, then follow the name "Quahog Bay," printed on chart 13290, leaving nun "2" at South Ledges well to port and Pole Island to port. A long ledge continues to the north from Pole Island. An alternative route, deep but narrower, runs along the western side of the bay, leaving nun "2" and Pole Island to starboard. As you approach Center Island, note the ledges that stick out to the south; bear to starboard and turn east to the 16-foot area southeast of Snow Island. You've arrived.

CARD COVE ★★   No facilities

Charts: 13288, **13290**

Card Cove, a well-protected little harbor on the west side of the entrance to Quahog Bay, has a mixture of summer residences and fishermen's homes. Most of the lobstering activity is outside

the harbor on Pinkham Point, site of the large building of the Quahog Bay Co-op.

Approaches. Run up Quahog Bay west of nun "2" on South Ledges. The entrance to Card Cove is

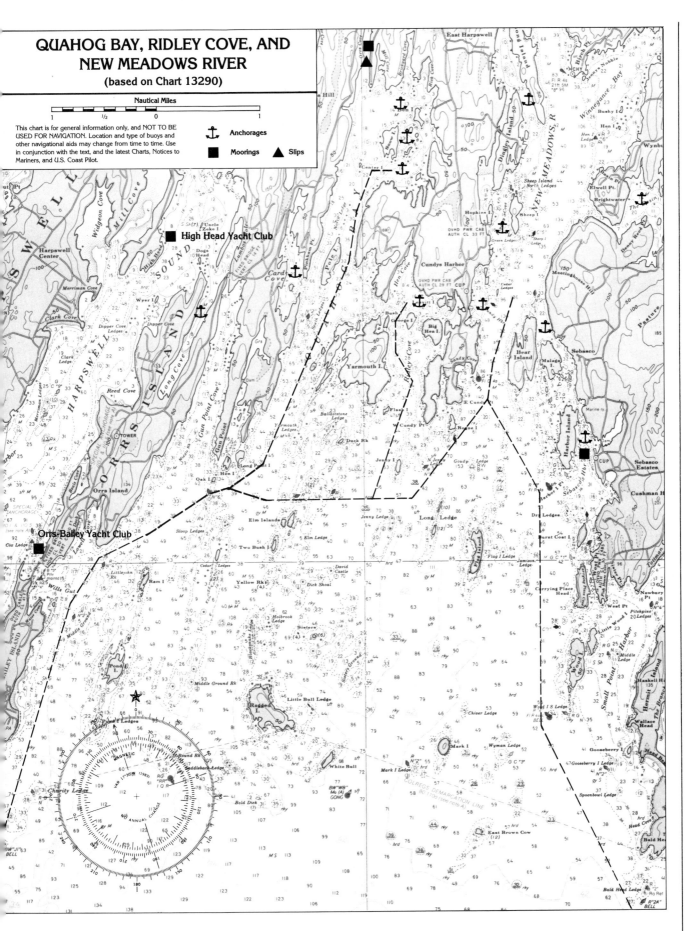

QUAHOG BAY, RIDLEY COVE, AND NEW MEADOWS RIVER
(based on Chart 13290)

Nautical Miles

This chart is for general information only, and NOT TO BE USED FOR NAVIGATION. Location and type of buoys and other navigational aids may change from time to time. Use in conjunction with the text, and the latest Charts, Notices to Mariners, and U.S. Coast Pilot.

⚓ Anchorages

■ Moorings   ▲ Slips

High Head Yacht Club

Orrs-Bailey Yacht Club

tricky, and best done at midtide or higher. Overlapping ledges make out from each side of the entrance, the larger southern ledge being outside and the northern one inside. Line up the white boathouse on the southwest tip of Pole Island, with the middle of the small, unnamed island (Ham Loaf) in Card Cove and run in gently on that line. Once safely past the northern ledge, turn northward past Ham Loaf.

Anchorages, Moorings. Anchor north of Ham Loaf Island in 29 feet at low. This is a quiet and comfortable spot for the night. If you go farther north in the cove, the road runs alongside the water, bringing reminders of civilization in the form of traffic and headlights.

SNOW ISLAND ★★★★ No facilities
Charts: 13288, **13290**

Snow Island, at the head of Quahog Bay, is one of those idyllic anchorages you dream about in the dead of winter. It is a very special place—uncrowded, beautiful, tranquil. The only counterpoint to nature's music here is an occasional military plane lumbering overhead from Brunswick Naval Air Station.

Approaches. As you pass Pole Island, note the ledges extending northward. Tiny Center Island, with a spray of trees, is very obvious ahead. Bear to starboard to avoid the ledge south of Center, then turn east and run south of Snow Island (which has a red house on its southeast tip).

Anchorages, Moorings. Anchor south and east of Snow Island in 16 feet of water at low. The bottom is mud and good holding ground.

You can also anchor between Snow Island and the several islets to the east, or work your way up along the mainland east of Snow Island and anchor near Ben Island, in 9 to 11 feet. Each of the islets has an active osprey nest in a tall, dead tree.

The anchorage north of Snow Island is also good, but perhaps not quite as pretty because you are closer to civilization. Protection is excellent either north or south of Snow Island.

Things to Do. Take your dinghy beyond Ben Island at high tide and turn right to explore a beautiful inlet. Southernmost of the islets is Little Snow Island, owned by the state.

In these upper reaches of Quahog Bay, the water temperature is delightful, and swimming is a pleasure rather than an ordeal—even for those from the three-quick-strokes-and-you're-out school.

ORRS COVE ★★★
Charts: 13288, **13290**

Orrs Cove is the most western of the fingers extending north from Quahog Bay, and the deepest. It is well protected under most circumstances, although local sailors report that a strong southerly can funnel up Quahog Bay and make it very rough indeed. In that situation, escape to the north of Snow Island.

Approaches. The cove is easy to enter and identifiable by the masts and hulls of boats moored off Great Island Boat Yard (see below). Deep water in midchannel (eight feet at low) extends as far as the first boatyard dock to port.

Anchorages, Moorings. Moorings usually are available from Great Island Boat Yard, or there is ample room to anchor south of the moored boats. Holding ground is good, in mud.

Getting Ashore. Take your dinghy in to the Great Island float.

For the Boat. *Great Island Boat Yard (Ch. 9; tel. 729-1639).* The yard has 65 slips and 30 moorings. Facilities include water, electricity, ice, and a marine store. Gas and diesel are available at the fuel dock (which parallels the land), but there is only four feet alongside at low.

The yard hauls boats to 50 feet and 45,000 pounds up the ramp by hydraulic trailer. It can perform most repairs on boats and engines and has a large shed for indoor work.

For the Crew. The yard has showers and a pay phone.

There is no grocery store in Orrs Cove, but you probably can arrange for a ride to Brunswick, five miles away.

MILL COVE, BRICKYARD COVE, and RICH COVE

Charts: 13288, **13290**

Four little coves extend north like fingers from the hand of Quahog Bay; from west to east, they are Orrs, Mill, Brickyard and Rich. Orrs Cove is discussed in the previous writeup. Of the other three, Mill Cove is the easiest to enter and makes a fine day stop. Anchor in nine feet at low with mud bottom.

Brickyard and Rich coves are guarded by unmarked ledges, and they are difficult to enter except at low tide. The adventure is worthwhile primarily for the pure pleasure of gunkholing.

RIDLEY COVE

Charts: 13288, **13290**

Ridley Cove is attractive, but open and unprotected. With reasonable care, you can work your way in past several unmarked dangers. Handsome, wooded Yarmouth Island borders the cove on the west.

To enter Ridley Cove, leave Jenny Island to starboard and Flash Island to port, then come up the middle of the cove. Ledges make out a short distance from both sides. Just south of Big Hen Island is a nice day anchorage.

Ridley Cove can be used with care as an entry to

Quahog Bay, although other approaches are safer. As you near the north end of Yarmouth Island, stay well to the west to avoid the shoals that extend southwest from George Island. Run between Bush and George islands and turn west into Quahog Bay before you come to the charted ledge at the mouth of Hen Cove (which uncovers at halftide). There are three-foot spots in the channel to Quahog Bay, so make the attempt only at midtide or better. Several yachts find bottom here every year.

RIDLEY COVE (NORTH) ★★★   No facilities

Charts: 13288, **13290**

Located north of George and Big Hen islands, Ridley Cove (North) offers reasonable protection and opportunities for a bit of exploration by dinghy.

Approaches. As you near the north end of Yarmouth Island, stay well to the west to avoid the shoals marked by a generous sprinkling of lobster buoys extending southwest from George Island. Continue between Bush and George.

Caution! Abreast of George Island, look dead ahead for the large charted ledge, which uncovers at halftide. Bear to starboard around George Island to avoid the ledge.

Anchorages, Moorings. The approach described will bring you to a lovely spot to anchor in 14 to 16 feet of water at low, with one or two houses and a private dock. The mast and super-

structure of a sunken ship are visible north of the hole between George and Big Hen islands. The best anchorage is west of this hulk.

Things to Do. Take your dinghy and poke around the eastern end of the harbor, where there are little inlets to explore. Several old ships have been run up on the shore here. In the tickle between Big Hen Island and the mainland, the bows of the freighter *Surf* nestle incongruously in a grove of white birch. At low tide, water pours from the hull as though her ghostly crew had just started the engines.

It would be easy to tie up to one of the docks and walk across the narrow peninsula to Cundys Harbor.

One of the great experiences of sailing the Maine coast is to watch an osprey hover 50 feet in the air, plunge into the sea, seize a fish in its talons, and carry it away to its nest in triumph. The osprey, or fish hawk, is a magnificent creature, with a wing-spread of 5 or 6 feet, and a curved beak that lends it an air of ferocity. It is white underneath, dark brown on top, and has a beautiful brown-and-white pattern under wings and tail.

Like storks, ospreys build large, messy nests of sticks, and the same nest is occupied year after year, presumably with a few renovations. Daybeacons are a favorite spot; many an osprey chick spends its youth watching boats enter or leave a harbor. One of the biggest osprey nests along the coast is on a can buoy at the turn of the Sheepscot River near Wiscasset. Another nest familiar to yachtsmen has been at the mouth of Pulpit Harbor as long as anyone can remember. When not using aids to navigation, ospreys tend to nest in dead spruce trees.

Ospreys fish tirelessly all day and carry their catch back to the nestful of noisy and insatiable young. The osprey defends its nest vociferously, screaming "Kee, kee, kee" and making passes at intruders. It is crucial to avoid disturbing an osprey during nesting season (late April until early July), because the chicks may be abandoned as a result.

Not so long ago, fish hawks had disappeared almost entirely from the coast of Maine. The pesticide DDT accumulated in the food chain, reaching heavy concentrations in fish, the birds' total diet. Subsequently, osprey chicks were deformed or failed to hatch. Thanks to the alarm raised by the 1962 publication of Rachel Carson's *Silent Spring*, the life-threatening pesticides and other chemicals no longer are legal, and the osprey has been saved.

Large as it is, the osprey has enemies other than man. Crows are fond of osprey eggs, and bald eagles have the strength and flying ability to rob ospreys of their catch in midair—a spectacular duel of giants that is infrequent but fascinating to witness.

NEW MEADOWS RIVER

Charts: 13288, **13290**, 13293

The New Meadows River rises in lakes and salt marshes west of Bath, flowing gently southward to form the eastern border of Casco Bay. It has neither the strength nor the majesty of the neighboring Kennebec River, and seems more like another of the long bays and sounds of Casco Bay.

The cruising sailor bound east or west should be aware of the New Meadows River, where attractive and well-protected Sebasco Harbor is only four miles north of Cape Small. Three miles farther north is The Basin, easy to enter, completely land-locked, and a marvelous harbor of refuge.

For the sailor with time to explore, the New Meadows river and its approaches offer a dozen attractive and remote anchorages that are little known to cruising boats—a mixture of working harbors and summer havens well worth the visit.

Proceeding in or out of the New Meadows River, it is fun to run inside Malaga Island and also inside Burnt Coat Island, farther south. Both channels are well marked and easily navigated, despite the moored draggers and lobsterboats.

Where the river turns west above Sebascodegan Island, it has the feel of a long and peaceful lake; only a tiny bit of open horizon is visible, way to the south. On the east bank, near Houghton Pond, there are iron rings in the rock where old ice schooners used to tie up to take on the pond's winter harvest. Beyond the turn, the river winds north past Bombazine Island, approaches a highway and small marina near coastal Route 1, and loses much of its charm.

SMALL POINT HARBOR

Charts: 13288, **13290**, 13293

Small Point Harbor lies west and north of Cape Small, between Hermit and Wood islands. Exposed to the southwest and wide open to the ocean, this usually would be a very uncomfortable place to spend the night. "Harbor" it may be—but certainly not a recommended one.

CAPE SMALL HARBOR ★★★★

Charts: 13288, **13290**, 13293

Cape Small Harbor, an interesting little hideaway between Hermit Island and the mainland, is difficult to enter but peaceful and extremely well protected. Locally known as "Small Point," this is no place to visit casually or try to enter for refuge on a dark and stormy night. In difficult conditions, it would be far better to make for easily entered Sebasco Harbor or The Basin, a short way north.

The harbor itself is relatively undeveloped, with a mixture of commercial craft, a few daysailers, and cruising boats. Blue herons pose silently along the tree-lined shores at low tide; there are snowy egrets here, as well as terns and other interesting birds.

Approaches. The approach to Cape Small Harbor depends on the state of the tide, and the chart information leaves much to be desired (see sketch map).

First enter Small Point Harbor, leaving the red-and-green nun on Middle Ledge to starboard. Then head for nun "4" on Pitchpine Ledges, also left to starboard, and go north of Goose Rock to start your entry into Cape Small Harbor. At a distance, Goose Rock seems to merge with the mainland, but there really is a channel east of it.

Turn southward past Goose Rock and favor the eastern side of the channel. A long, sandy beach curves south from Flat Point, ending at an outcropping of white rocks. This is followed by a shorter sand beach and a second set of white rocks, which mark the beginning of the channel obstructions.

Two overlapping bars together block the channel southeast of Goose Rock. The first bar is sand and extends from the rocks on the mainland. A short distance farther south is a large rock ledge making out from the southern end of Goose Rock. At midtide or lower, you probably cannot run a straight course over these bars.

The channel past the bars is marked by two red spar buoys (not the nun and can shown on chart 13290, 29th Ed.). Run a straight course from the first red spar buoy to the second, leaving both to starboard. The channel at low is about 60 feet wide, with a depth of five or six feet.

Once past the bars, stay on the eastern side past

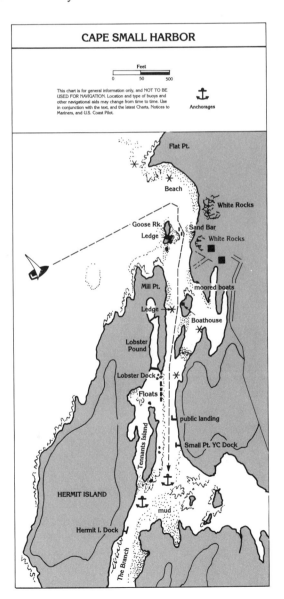

CAPE SMALL HARBOR

Feet
0   50   500

This chart is for general information only, and NOT TO BE USED FOR NAVIGATION. Location and type of buoys and other navigational aids may change from time to time. Use in conjunction with the text, and the latest Charts, Notices to Mariners, and U.S. Coast Pilot.

Anchorages

Flat Pt.

Beach

White Rocks

Goose Rk.
Ledge

Sand Bar

White Rocks

moored boats

Mill Pt.

Ledge

Boathouse

Lobster Pound

Lobster Dock

Floats

public landing

Tenmants Island

Small Pt. YC Dock

HERMIT ISLAND

mud

Hermit I. Dock

The Branch

Mill Point and the two islets (left to port). The second danger is opposite the first islet, where a ledge extends halfway across the channel from the west side. Avoid it by staying close to the eastern side.

After this ledge, you have almost a clear shot to the anchorage. There is deep water near the lobster dock on the west side of the channel. Go right up the middle among the moored boats.

Anchorages, Moorings. Anchor among the moored boats if there is room, or just beyond them, opposite the tip of Tennants Island, in six to eight feet of water at low. The bottom is mud and good holding ground. Note that the channel curves west after Tennants Island into The Branch, and shoals.

The anchorage appears to be a wide-open pond at high tide, but it becomes a narrow slot at low, lined with clam flats and mussel beds. The prevailing southwest wind funnels down The Branch and normally will keep you lined up with the channel. However, any shift of wind direction could easily put you over the mud, and the surge of the incoming tide could do the same. A stern anchor is good insurance here.

By all means, try to find a local yachtsman for advice. One local summer resident says that there may be as many as eight or nine transients here on a given night, but that's about the limit.

Hermit Island Campgrounds, privately owned, sometimes has a mooring available, or space alongside at the floats extending south from the lobster pound. It is best to call ahead (tel. 443-2101).

Getting Ashore. Depending on your goal, take the dinghy to the Small Point Yacht Club float or to the Hermit Island dock.

For the Boat. The Small Point Yacht Club has a dock on the east side of the channel, north of Tennants Island. You will search in vain for a clubhouse. No boat larger than 12 feet is allowed to stay at the float.

For the Crew. Land at the yacht club float, scramble up the hill to the paved road and walk right a half mile to the main road. Turn right, and it's a quarter mile to the Lobster House, featuring fish and lobsters; no frills, but good meals. You can also approach the restaurant by dinghy, heading east from the anchorage, but a falling tide may leave you stranded; the water is adequate about an hour either side of high tide.

Food is also available on Hermit Island, described below.

Things to Do. From the Lobster House it is half a mile east to spectacular Small Point Beach, from which you can see Seguin Island in the distance and the mouth of the Kennebec River. Small Point Beach is an Audubon sanctuary for the least tern.

Looking southward up The Branch from the anchorage, you can see a dock that is part of Hermit Island Campgrounds. Row your dinghy to their float and walk to the entrance of the campground, right at Head Beach. The campground store has a snack counter and is well stocked with fresh food.

CARRYING PLACE COVE

Charts: 13288, **13290**, 13293

This small and busy fishing community lies snugly between Carrying Place Head and the mainland. A tiny island with a fish wharf sits in the center of the cove.

You can't take your boat through Carrying Place Cove because of shoal waters and overhead power cables with 30-foot clearance. You can, however, anchor at the northeast tip of the island—just outside the moored lobsterboats and a wharf on the mainland—in 21 feet at low, and explore with your dinghy. The bottom here is mud and old potwarp.

The southern part of Carrying Place Cove is known locally as West Point Harbor, and the village of West Point has a general store. Snug Harbor General carries beer, wine, groceries, and lobsters.

We mourn the disappearance of the West Point General Store, where seaboots hung from the ceiling, and the motto was, "If we don't have it, you don't need it."

SEBASCO HARBOR ★★★★

Charts: 13288, **13290**, 13293

Sebasco Harbor is a welcoming spot, well protected under most conditions and easy to enter. It is probably the most convenient harbor at this end of Casco Bay, not far out of the way for boats traveling east or west.

What makes this harbor unusual is the presence

of Sebasco Lodge, a well-appointed resort whose resources are available to visiting yachtsmen.

Approaches. Coming from the south, leave green can "5" off Jamison Ledge to port and head for flashing red buoy "6" at Harbor Island Point, keeping well clear of Dry Ledges. At red buoy "6" turn east toward the harbor, continuing well beyond can "1" before making a turn to the north. The ledges that make out a long way southeast from the tip of Harbor Island are exposed except at high tide. On the right side, less prominent ledges are marked by a privately maintained beacon. It is safe to turn north when you can see up the channel between the boats moored on the west side of the harbor and those on the east side.

Anchorages, Moorings. Sebasco Lodge maintains a dozen or so large moorings for visitors, with granite blocks of 2,000 to 5,000 pounds, to let you sleep well. These are grouped on the western side of the harbor. Hail the resort's launch for directions.

If no mooring is available, there is room to anchor in midharbor, in 15 to 26 feet of water.

With normal summer winds, the ledges at the harbor entrance provide good protection, and this is a comfortable anchorage. A strong southwester, however, will bring in swells.

Getting Ashore. The Sebasco Lodge launch will pick you up in response to the usual three toots, or you can take your dinghy in to the float.

For the Boat. *Sebasco Lodge (tel. 389-1161).* The cupola marked on the chart is a many-layered octagonal green-and-white wedding cake of a house, referred to by Sebasco Lodge as its "Lighthouse," and used for guests. Just north of the lighthouse is the dock and float, with five feet of water at low tide. Gas, water, and ice are available, but no diesel. There are laundry facilities and showers.

For the Crew. There are limited provisions more than a mile away at the small market in West Point.

Things to Do. The Sebasco Lodge is a convenient and pleasant place to meet guests coming aboard or to put them ashore after a cruise. There is plenty of parking space. This great old resort provides a variety of services and entertainment, including golf, tennis, swimming in a harborside saltwater pool, a snack bar, movies, dancing, concerts, bowling, and a gift shop—all of which are available to visiting yachtsmen. Sunday brunch is served by the pool.

The *Anne C. Maguire* on the rocks near historic Portland Head light, Christmas Eve, 1886. (Frank Claes Collection)

SEBASCO ★★★　　

Charts: 13288, **13290**, 13293

North of Malaga Island and east of Bear Island, near the fishing village of Sebasco, is a sizable harbor used by large draggers and fishermen. It is an attractive spot, an unspoiled working harbor well protected from prevailing winds and open only to the north.

Approaches. The harbor can be entered from either north or south. From the north, pass between nun "2" and the mainland.

Entering from the south, leave cans "1" and "3" to port. Can "3" seems a surprisingly long way out from Malaga Island, but be sure to observe it. After rounding can "3," aim for midchannel to avoid the ledge making out from the southeast end of Malaga Island. The rock shown on the chart on the east side of the channel is marked with a pipe.

Anchorages, Moorings. North of Malaga Island and east of Bear Island, there is plenty of room to anchor among the moorings in 10 to 22 feet at low. Very little swell enters the harbor. While there might be even better protection in the channel east of Malaga Island, that area usually is occupied by draggers and lobstermen, and there is no room.

Getting Ashore. Take your dinghy ashore at Sebasco Wharf.

For the Boat. *Sebasco Wharf (tel. 389-2756).* Gas and diesel are available at Sebasco Wharf, on the mainland, with six feet of water off the end of the wharf at low. Approach cautiously; there is a ledge just north of the wharf.

Brewer's Boatyard (tel. 389-1388). In the little indentation northeast of Harbor Island, Brewer's provides "moorings, salvage, railway service, repairs, and dock building." The yard is equipped with a 12-ton boatlift and a 75-ton marine railway. Approach either from Sebasco Harbor or around Harbor Island from the north. Both approaches are bare rock at low tide.

H & H Boatworks (tel. 389-1000). Just north of Brewer's, this yard is recognizable at a distance by its big, red shed. Round Harbor Island into the buoyed channel, giving the tip of the island a wide berth, then head back into the center of the cove from the north. There is good water along the end of the yard's float. H & H specializes in spray painting, woodworking, and repairing and restoring wooden boats, although other repairs can be handled as well. Boats up to 40 tons and 65 feet are hauled by hydraulic trailer, and there is a 15-ton crane. No slips, moorings, or other facilities.

For the Crew. At Sebasco Wharf, you will find the pretty Waters Edge takeout.

CUNDYS HARBOR ★★　　

Charts: 13288, **13290**, 13293

At the western entrance to the New Meadows River this little working harbor is simple and authentic. Fuel and lobster docks stand on ancient pilings and the harbor is full of large draggers, lobsterboats, and only a few pleasure craft.

Approaches. The harbor is easy to enter. First find flashing green buoy "7" at Fort Point. Then follow the coast north until you have identified can "3" at the entrance, marking the end of the ledges that form the eastern side of the harbor. Leave the can to starboard and go straight in toward the docks.

Anchorages, Moorings. Get a slip at The Pier at Cundys Harbor or find an open spot anywhere in the harbor and anchor in 22 to 29 feet at low. Cundys Harbor is not very well protected, so there is an uncomfortable roll even on a calm night. In the words of one local observer, "No, it ain't much of a harbor. Sea piles in here when the wind blows southwest. But it's deep water, and the fishermen keep their boats here."

Getting Ashore. Tie up your dinghy to the floats at Holbrook's Lobster Wharf to the south, or at The Pier, or at Watson's dock, farther north.

For the Boat. *The Pier at Cundys Harbor.* Gas, diesel, water, ice, and supplies are available at The Pier.

Watson's General Store (tel. 725-7794). You can obtain gas, diesel, and water at Watson's float, with eight feet alongside at low. Approach from the east to avoid a large rock awash at midtide, just south of the float.

For the Crew. Holbrook's Store (tel. 725-5697) offers beer, soda, ice, lobsters, a few basic groceries and supplies, and yesterday's newspaper. There is a pay phone, and the post office is in the store. Holbrook's Lobster Wharf has a snack bar and takeout. There is no place in town to dispose of trash, unless you are prepared to separate out glass and cans, in which case Holbrook's will take it.

Watson's General Store has a similar selection of items, (including lobsters), but more hardware. Started by the Watson family in 1819, this is Maine's oldest family-operated general store. It is currently run by the fourth and fifth generations of Watsons.

Things to Do. A pleasant half-mile walk north on the main road will take you to the Block and Tackle, an eat-in or takeout restaurant open for three meals. This basic, no-frills Maine eatery serves huge early breakfasts for fishermen and var-ious seafood items for lunch or supper.

En route, you may catch a glimpse of the wrecked ships in Ridley Cove on the other side of the peninsula.

DINGLEY COVE ★★ No facilities
Charts: 13288, **13290**, 13293

Dingley Cove, on the west side of the New Meadows River, just north of Cundys Harbor, is a small working harbor with no facilities for yachtsmen. Strangers should enter this harbor carefully, and not at night.

Approaches. Enter near the southern tip of Sheep Island and head toward Hopkins Island, to avoid Green Ledges.

Anchorages, Moorings. Anchor outside the moored lobsterboats in 16 to 20 feet at low, mud bottom. The harbor is exposed to the south, but some protection is provided by Cedar Ledges.

THE BASIN ★★★★ No facilities
Charts: 13288, **13290**, 13293

Here is what many yachtsmen dream about when they ponder the ultimate safe harbor: a small lake surrounded by rocky points and dark green trees, with hardly a sign of human habitation, completely protected from every direction, and the water still as a millpond.

The Basin is an extraordinary harbor on the New Meadows River, about two miles north of Sebasco Harbor. It is worth going out of your way to make the passage through the deep, narrow entrance and into the broad sanctuary beyond. For this part of the world, this is the best site for a hurricane hole.

Approaches. Coming north up the New Meadows River, leave can "5" on Sheep Island Ledge to port, then look for the indentation in the eastern shore that marks the entrance. A house on the north shore of the entrance has a pointed stone chimney, a good mark to head for.

Turn right into the channel, perhaps 150 feet wide at low tide, and run straight down the middle. It narrows to 75 feet or so at the left turn. Turn wide around the bend to the left, then up into The Basin.

Anchorages, Moorings. Anchor in the middle of the western part of The Basin, in 14 to 20 feet of water at low, with mud bottom. Even at the height of the summer season The Basin usually has only a handful of boats—and there is room for a fleet.

Some boats work their way in close to the small island in the eastern part of the bay (Basin Island), or close to the rocky point of land that juts down from the north. The ledge shown on the chart as a star, between the two 11-foot spots, has claimed its share of unsuspecting yachts. There is room to pass either north or south of it, with care.

Lying in The Basin on a calm night, you will feel as though you are in a mountain lake far removed from the sea.

Things to Do. Explore beautiful one-acre Basin Island, which is owned by the state. You'll find some of the warmest water on the Maine coast here for swimming (67 degrees Fahrenheit on the Fourth of July).

LONG ISLAND ★★★ No facilities
Charts: 13288, **13290**

Between Long Island and Dingley Island is a slot that provides shelter except from the south and is easy to enter.

Approaches. Give the ledge at the southwest tip of Long Island a good berth and head north into the slot.

Anchorages, Moorings. Anchor in 17 to 20 feet between the northern part of Dingley Island and the southern part of Long Island. This section is lovely, with woods on both sides. If you go up farther, past the northern tip of Dingley, you may be able to find better protection, but the view is less appealing.

The narrow, shallow fingers of Quahog Bay and the New Meadows River are fun for gunkholing in the dinghy. (Dick Durrance II photo)

BRIGHAMS COVE ★★ No facilities
Charts: 13288, **13290**

At the north end of Winnegance Bay, this little cove is perhaps 100 yards wide, surrounded by rocky shores, summer houses, and docks. It feels like a small lake. The cove is well protected from every direction but the southwest.

Approaches. Approach through pretty little Winnegance Bay, graced with small islands, rocky points, and summer homes. Enter Winnegance leaving red daybeacon "6" on Hen Island Ledge to starboard and keeping more to the western side until you are even with the word "Meadowbrook" on chart 13290. Brighams Cove is easy to enter, the only danger being the rocks off the western tip of the entrance.

Anchorages, Moorings. There are several private moorings, and plenty of room to anchor outside the moorings in 10 to 15 feet at low, mud bottom.

THREE ISLANDS
Charts: 13288, **13290**

Three Islands, just south of Bragdon Island at the turn of the New Meadows River, are small, rocky, and wooded. They are connected with each other and with Bragdon by sandbars at low tide.

Run in halfway between the most southerly of the Three Islands and the tip of Long Island, in 60 feet of water. Then turn north around this first island until you are opposite the northern tip, where you can anchor in 18 to 25 feet.

There is exposure in several directions, so consider this only as a lunch stop.

MILL COVE ★★★ No facilities

Charts: 13288, **13290**

Where the New Meadows River turns west, two long, narrow fingers of water continue north on either side of Rich Hill. Mill Cove to the east is very pretty, but more inhabited than Back Cove to the west.

Approaches. Red daybeacon "10" on Bragdon Rock is visible against the trees from a long way off. Go to either side. There is a huge osprey nest on the beacon, with birds in residence.

The farther into Mill Cove you go, the prettier it becomes, with rocky shores and handsome houses. The passage is easy and open; favor the western shore to avoid the ledges to starboard, especially before the little islands near the upper end.

Anchorages, Moorings. There is a beautiful spot to drop the hook opposite Dam Cove in 17 feet at low, or you can go farther in to anchor. The bottom is mud. Mill Cove has good protection from any winds except a strong southerly.

BACK COVE ★★★ No facilities

Charts: 13288, **13290**

The finger of water west of Rich Hill in the New Meadows River is Back Cove, a tranquil and lovely spot.

Approaches. Leave red daybeacon "10" on Bragdon Rock to starboard and head straight up the middle of the slot between Merritt Island and Williams Island. Keep your eyes open for fishnets, hung from floats, which may partially block the channel in this area. It is an easy glide between high, rocky, tree-lined shores, with only a single house in sight. You may well find you have the place to yourself.

Anchorages, Moorings. You can anchor in 17 feet near the northern tip of Williams Island, but the current against the breeze may cause you to swing, so you might want to consider a stern anchor if you spend the night. Holding ground is good, in mud bottom.

BOMBAZINE ISLAND

Just above the turn in the New Meadows River lies small, wooded Bombazine Island, home of Indian Sagamore Bombazeen, who was killed by the English in 1724.

As related in *Beautiful Harpswell,* by Margaret and Charles Todd, half a century later "Granny" Young visited the island to pick berries:

"After filling her pail, she set out for home in her canoe. Hearing a noise behind her, she turned to see a huge black bear gaining on her fast.

"Granny had only a stave for a paddle. The bear quickly overtook the canoe and tried to overturn it; but Granny, with pioneer resourcefulness, struck the bear a stunning blow on the head with her stave, and then held his head under water until he was dead. Then, after tying the carcass to the canoe, she continued to paddle homeward, towing the bear until she reached shore."

Region 3 / Cape Small to Marshall

Midcoast and

Lonely, austere Pemaquid Point Light guards the southern entrance to Muscongus Bay. (Dick Durrance II photo)

Point
the Rivers

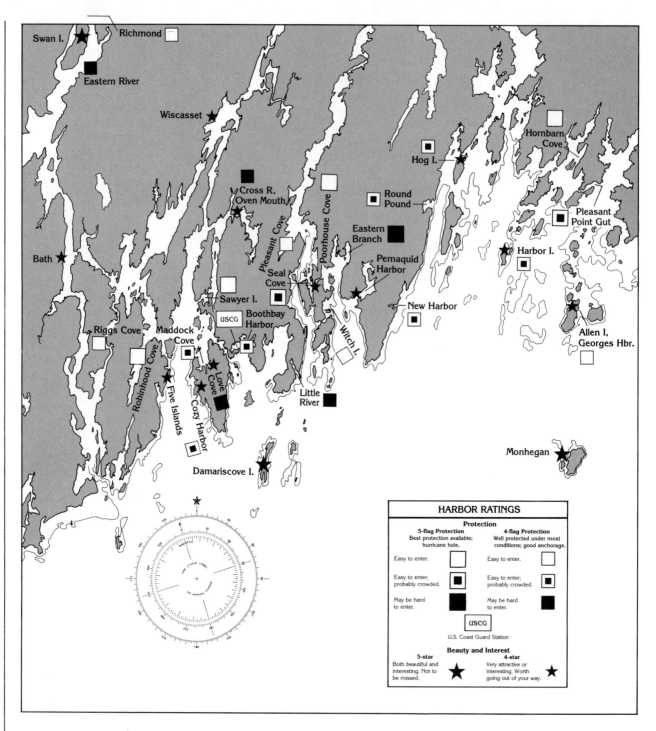

The region from Cape Small to Marshall Point, from the Kennebec River to the western side of Penobscot Bay, is less familiar to cruising yachts than any other portion of the coast of Maine—except, perhaps, for way down east. It has many charms.

Here the land and the sea hold equal sway. The chains of hills and mountains running north and south are separated by long, narrow bays. Rivers great and small run down to the ocean in a complex pattern of coves and estuaries, marshes, and back channels. Large islands just off the mainland are themselves indented by intruding arms of the sea.

Here the mighty Kennebec, rising far to the north, surges past the cities of Augusta and Bath, past the site of the ill-fated seventeenth-century Popham Colony, and past Seguin Island, before spilling into the Gulf of Maine. The Inside Passage, cutting across faults of granite from Bath to Boothbay Harbor, winds through narrow guts where the current rushes with impetuous force. The Sheepscot, Damariscotta, and St. George rivers, each with its own history and special character, glide past small towns and quiet anchorages.

These midcoast rivers offer a new kind of exploration for the cruising yacht: islands that are as remote as any off the coast, with natural beauty, wildlife refuges, picturesque villages, historic sites, and plenty of adventure.

Beyond Pemaquid Point, the character of the coast again starts to change; now there is less land and more salt water. Sparsely populated and beautiful Muscongus Bay harbors dozens of islands, rocks, and ledges, and a maze of passages among them.

Offshore are some very special, very unique islands: lonely Seguin, with its towering light; Damariscove, a busy fishing station long before Plymouth was settled and now left to nesting birds; spectacular Monhegan, known by Verrazzano and Champlain, one of the most fascinating places on the eastern seaboard.

For the sailor seeking cruising grounds that offer unexpected adventures and unheralded charms, this region rates high.

KENNEBEC RIVER and Inside Passage

Charts: 13288, 13293, 13295, 13296, 13298

The mighty Kennebec River, linked inextricably with Maine's history, is the longest river in the state, rising in Moosehead Lake and flowing 150 miles to the sea. From the head of navigation at Augusta, the Kennebec runs 45 miles to its guardian offshore island of Seguin. The tide pushing up from the ocean makes the river salt as far as Bath, but only a few miles farther north the Kennebec is fresh. Majestic in its lower reaches, with wooded islands and bold promontories, the river northward mingles with lesser streams at Merrymeeting Bay, and wanders sometimes into marshlands. But everywhere it is big and strong and worthy of attention and respect.

For two centuries, until not so long ago, the Kennebec was white with sails of ships newly launched from a dozen yards along its banks, heading downstream to every port in the world. Today, a sailboat on the river south of Bath is rare enough, and farther north is seldom seen.

For much of its past, the waters of the Kennebec were choked with logs floating down to build the ships and cities of America. There still are logs in the depths of the river, and every spring, the deadheads emerge like ghosts to threaten the unwary sailor.

More recently, the waters of the Kennebec have recovered from the scourge of toxic waste. The bluefish are back, as are the salmon.

Cruising the Kennebec is an extraordinary experience, and often a difficult one. Most of the time you will be under power, and always you must wait for the tide. Much of the uniqueness comes not from the places you visit (though some are indeed special), but from the river itself.

Plan to visit the historic city of Bath, where the shipbuilding tradition has endured for hundreds of years. Or continue on to Swan Island, above the bridge, near Richmond, a fascinating state-owned wildlife preserve, where you can camp or simply visit.

To make a trip upriver to Bath, enjoy the town, and return, allow two days. To go all the way to the fixed bridge at Gardiner, visiting both Bath and Swan Island, allow three or four days. Running down under power from Gardiner with the ebb, you should be able to reach Bath in 4¾ hours. Allow at least another 2½ hours from Bath to Pond Island, at the mouth of the river. Yet another cruising itinerary—challenging but fascinating—is to follow the meandering Inside Passage from Bath to Boothbay, via the Sasanoa and Sheepscot rivers.

A trip up the Kennebec has its drawbacks: There are few safe anchorages, the current is strong, and the river can be very rough when the wind is against the ebb. Going aground is easy, and getting off in the current is hard. The trip requires alertness and a basic familiarity with river seamanship (see sidebar).

The dominant fact of life in the Kennebec is the current. You go upstream with the flood and downstream with the ebb. Unless you have a powerboat, any other schedule means slow going indeed.

With a summer southerly you can sail upriver, of course, as all the schooners used to do, but be prepared to lose your wind in certain stretches like Fiddler Reach. Sometimes you may be lucky enough to get a wind that will help you downstream. Because of the funneling effect of the high banks and escarpments, the wind usually blows either straight upriver or straight downriver.

As in most rivers, the natural flow of the river is added to the tidal effect, so the ebb is much stronger than the flood. The flood normally runs one to two knots, and the ebb 3½ to four knots. Ebb velocities up to six knots have been observed, and even higher during spring freshets. Heading upriver, the mean range of tide is 8.4 feet at Fort Popham, 6.4 feet at Bath, 5 feet at Gardiner, and 4.1 feet at Augusta.

According to the *Coast Pilot*, the channel above Bath is subject to considerable annual changes caused by the spring freshets. Have an anchor on deck ready to let go; you may need it on short notice. Be prepared to kedge yourself off.

Brush up on your bridge techniques (see chapter 2 of the *Coast Pilot*). The huge lift bridge that carries Route 1 across the Kennebec at Bath has a vertical clearance of only 10 feet. There is no need to go under the bridge in order to visit Bath, but if you want to go farther upstream, read about the Carlton Bridge in the Bath section of this book. A swing bridge at Richmond is much less of a problem. Then, just above the towns of Gardiner and Randolph, a fixed bridge with a vertical clearance of 35 feet prevents most cruising boats from going farther upriver to the state capital, Augusta.

The river can be extremely rough with a southerly wind against the ebb current. The mouth of the Kennebec is notorious for an ugly chop, as is the stretch between there and Bath. Disquieting tide rips occur in certain places, with strips of foam or brown discoloration, but no change in depth. The chart will reassure you.

It is usually easier in a river to pick up a mooring or come alongside into the current, rather than into the wind. But the swiftly running river is deceiving to the eye. It can be very hard to judge whether your anchor is dragging or whether it's an optical illusion. Watch the land rather than the surface of the water.

Safe anchorages on the Kennebec are few and far between, so allow plenty of time to reach your destination, and have a fallback plan. Do not travel on the river at night; there are few lights and many dangers. If necessary, you can always anchor in the river, but it is hard to get out of the current, and you are likely to spend a sleepless night.

SEGUIN ISLAND

Charts: 13288, 13293, **13295**

Most imposing of all Maine lighthouses, the light on lonely Seguin Island stands 180 feet above the sea, two miles off the entrance to the Kennebec River. This is the second-oldest lighthouse in Maine (only Portland Head was built earlier), and the deed for the island was signed by President George Washington. In clear weather, Seguin— grassy and almost treeless—can be seen from a great distance. The powerful foghorn, however, is in frequent use. A brief visit to Seguin is an unforgettable experience.

Seguin stands like a rock in the slipstream of the great Kennebec River current. From the island's summit you can clearly see the line of demarcation of ebb tide. If the wind is running against the ebb, the waters north of Seguin form a nasty chop.

Seguin was automated in 1985, after almost 200 years. Unfortunately, the new automatic devices lack the human qualities of watchfulness, devotion, and judgment. A few years ago, a sailboarder blown helplessly offshore was sighted and saved by the Coast Guardsmen then stationed at Seguin —only one of thousands of rescues. One of the great comforts and safeguards of the coast is gone.

The Friends of Seguin have now leased the island from the Coast Guard, so there is usually someone living here during the summer months who has the key to the lighthouse. Climb the beautiful spiral iron staircases of the light tower and watch the rainbows refracted on the walls by the huge first-order Fresnel lens. This is one of only two such lenses in New England (the other is in Boston). To replace such a lens today would cost at least $8 million.

Approaches. To approach Seguin from the east, head for Ellingwood Rock (bare rocks, white along the top), then head into the center of the cove on a southerly course. Note the ledge making out northward from the northeast tip of Seguin.

Coming from the west, leave Ellingwood Rock close aboard to starboard, passing south of Seguin Ledges. Then head for the cove.

Be aware that within a mile of Ellingwood Rock is a local magnetic disturbance, and your compass could be off by as much as eight degrees.

Anchorages, Moorings. Pick up the Coast Guard mooring deep in the north cove of Seguin Island (no anchoring allowed because of an underwater cable) and row ashore to the tiny sand beach.

Walk past the beach peas, the seagulls roosting in the trees, and the boathouse, then climb the long ramp and railway to the lighthouse on the crest. From there you have magnificent vistas westward to Cape Small and the dim islands of Casco Bay, and eastward to The Cuckolds and Monhegan on the horizon.

FORT POPHAM

Charts: 13288, 13293, **13295**

The shoreline at the mouth of the Kennebec River came very close to being the site of the first permanent English settlement in the New World. The Plymouth Company, assigned the rights to colonize "Northern Virginia," from 38 to 45 degrees north latitude, sent out colonists in early 1607. Led by George Popham and Raleigh Gilbert, the group crossed the Atlantic in two small ships, the *Gifte of God* and the *Mary and John,* during the summer of 1607 and established the Popham Colony. According to the August 17 journal entry of Captain Robert Davies, "Captain Popham in his Pynnace with 30. persons, & Captain Gilbert in his long boat, with 18. persons more, went early in the morning fromm their shippe into the River of Sachadehoc, to view the River, and to search where they might fynd a fitt place for their plantationn." Fort St. George and a number of houses were finished that fall on Sabino Head, along with the 30-ton pinnace *Virginia,* first English vessel constructed in the New World.

But winter struck with extraordinary severity that year, and many of the colonists died, including Popham. Although resupplied the next sum-

mer, the survivors refused to face another winter, and they were evacuated in the fall of 1608. And so it chanced that Jamestown, founded by the London Company in May 1607, instead became the first permanent English colony in the New World.

Near the site of the original colony, Fort Popham was built during the Civil War to defend the important Kennebec shipbuilding industry against the Confederates. It was manned again during the Spanish-American War. The massive fort is now part of a state park, and fun to explore.

To stop here for a visit, round Fort Popham and you will see a number of small moored boats. Anchor outside the boats in 20 feet or so of water, getting in as close as you can. If possible, leave someone aboard, since the anchorage is not too secure. Row in to the dinghy float at the dock on the northwest tip of Hunnewell Point. The narrow slot of deep water in Atkins Bay is full of private moorings, with no room to anchor.

Just south of the fort, you can walk along the beautiful sands of Popham Beach or go for a swim. Spinney's Restaurant is near the fort, and groceries can be found at Percy's nearby.

BATH ★★★★

Charts: 13288, 13293, **13296**, **13298**

Bath is an interesting small city of 10,000 inhabitants on the west bank of the Kennebec, about 12 miles above the river's entrance. It has a long history of shipbuilding, elegant old houses, many marine-related activities, and a flourishing arts program. This is the home of the Maine Maritime Museum and Bath Iron Works, one of the country's leading naval shipyards. It is easy to spend an enjoyable day or two here.

Opposite Bath, on the east shore of the Kennebec, is the entrance to the Sasanoa River, the beginning of the Inside Passage that leads east and south to Boothbay Harbor.

Ever since the 1607 launching of the pinnace *Virginia* at the nearby Popham Colony, the history of the Kennebec River and of Bath has been linked

to ships and shipbuilding. Century-old Bath Iron Works—adhering to its motto, "Ahead of schedule and under budget"—maintains that tradition.

Founded in 1884 by young Brigadier General Thomas W. Hyde, Bath Iron Works has had a roller-coaster history, soaring to periods of greatness and surviving a devastating fire and two bankruptcies. When it went up for public auction in 1925, the yard was sold to a scrap metal dealer and stripped, and BIW's proud heritage for a while launched nothing but pie plates.

But new entrepreneurs stepped forward, the yard was rebuilt, and the next decades saw the launching of a series of famous yachts. In 1930, J.P. Morgan's 343-foot black-and-gold *Corsair* slid down the ways. "What does it cost to maintain

Guided missile frigates (FFGs) nested at Bath Iron Works, under the tallest crane in the Western Hemisphere. (Bath Iron Works photo)

her?" This was the yacht about which Morgan replied, "If you have to ask, you can't afford it." Then followed trawlers for F.J. O'Hara's fishing fleet, destroyers for the U.S. Navy, and Harold Vanderbilt's famous J-boat *Ranger* which defeated *Endeavour* in 1937 for the America's Cup and won every race she ever entered.

During World War II, BIW built 82 destroyers, more than the number produced by the entire Japanese Empire. More recently, it has been building guided missile frigates, cruisers, and the new Arleigh Burke class of destroyers.

"Number eleven," the tallest crane in the Western Hemisphere, broods over Bath like some prehistoric monster. With its 220-ton capacity, the crane can handle enormous modular sections of ships, a building method that has contributed to BIW's success. The yard also takes pride in its tradition of hard work, high quality, and low turnover in the experienced workforce.

Approaches. Be aware that the current runs hard, normally three or four knots and occasionally more. With a southwest wind and an ebb current it can be very rough here.

All of the facilities near Bath are on the west bank. They are listed below in sequence as you would find them coming upstream. You will usually want to come alongside or pick up a mooring into the current, rather than into the wind.

Anchorages, Moorings—Below the Bridge. *(For additional anchorages and moorings above the bridge, see ahead.)* Below the bridge the only choice for a berth or a mooring is at the Percy and Small Shipyard, part of the Maine Maritime Museum, about a mile south of the bridge, just south of can "33." There are two piers; the *Sherman Zwicker* normally lies along the pier to the south, while the fitting-out pier to the north is available for large vessels.

At the northern end of the yard are several floats; it may be possible to lie alongside one of these for the night, with 15 feet of water.

There are two lines of moorings in the river available to visitors. The larger moorings in the outside line (each with at least a 1000-pound granite block) are marked by numbered white balls and a lobster buoy pickup. Moorings for smaller boats, with mushroom anchors, are on the inside line. For dockage (when available) check with the dockmaster. Reserve ahead.

Don't make the mistake of trying to pick up the white cylinder with red markings near the *Sherman Zwicker* dock; it marks a sandbar with 4½ feet at low.

If no mooring is available, anchor in some convenient spot on the river, in 15 to 25 feet at low.

Getting Ashore. Row in to the floats at the northern end of Percy and Small. Remember that the current runs very strong, so take all precautions and avoid overloading your dinghy.

For the Boat. *Percy and Small Shipyard (Ch. 9 or 16; tel. 443-1316).* The yard offers water and electricity at the floats, but no fuel.

For the Crew. Just about anything you need can be found in Bath close to the waterfront, including a drugstore, hardware, bank, beauty shop, gift shops, and restaurants.

For groceries, walk west on Center Street (a block north of the bridge). There is a small convenience market catering to BIW employees (Roy's), but you will do better to continue west another block to Burgess Market, which has an excellent meat department.

The post office is a large brick building west of BIW, on Washington Street. There is a laundromat about half a mile west of the waterfront, along the road that parallels Route 1 just north of the bridge. Continuing west along this road, .8 mile from the waterfront, you will come to the Bath Shopping Center, with a Shaw's supermarket, pharmacy, beauty shop, hardware, laundromat, McDonald's, a good bookstore with many marine titles, and a liquor store. Call a cab to get your groceries back to the boat.

Kristina's Bakery and Restaurant, serving breakfast, lunch, and dinner, is worth the 10-minute walk up Center Street; good food and wonderful pies (tel. 442-8577).

The Bath Memorial Hospital provides 24-hour emergency service (tel. 443-5524).

Things to Do. There is plenty to do here for grownups and children as well, much of it related to small boats and shipbuilding, the river, and the great maritime tradition of the "City of Ships."

The Maine Maritime Museum (tel. 443-1316) offers a wide variety of sights and activities, and families are encouraged to visit.

The core of the museum is the Percy and Small Shipyard, the only surviving shipyard in the country where large wooden sailing ships were built. The yard is home to the Grand Banks fishing schooner *Sherman Zwicker*, and during the summer is visited by sailing vessels such as the *Westward* and the restored arctic schooner *Bowdoin*.

There is a collection of classic wooden small craft at the yard, and impressive exhibits on boatbuilding and lobstering. You can also watch apprentices working on small craft with traditional tools. There are splendid displays of marine art, ship models, and life at sea in the new Maritime History Building, and a museum store. Live exhibits on sailing, shipbuilding, navigation, and other nautical subjects are presented during the summer.

The museum offers frequent 45-minute narrated boat rides, downstream from the shipyard to the Squirrel Point lighthouse and upstream past Bath Iron Works.

The Bath area Chamber of Commerce, at 45 Front St. (near the waterfront; tel. 443-9751), can provide information about other activities, including a suggested walking tour. Below are some highlights.

Check out The Laughing Whale, a shop on Front Street with models of classic craft including Friendship sloops, dories, whaleboats, the *Seguin*, the *Joseph Conrad*, and the *America*.

It's exciting to walk across the Carlton Bridge, staring down at the river swirling way below, examining at leisure the ships at BIW and the beckoning entrance to the Sasanoa River across the way. There's a sidewalk on the downstream side.

For security reasons, the public is not allowed to visit Bath Iron Works except on rare occasions, such as launchings. The Chamber of Commerce or BIW (tel. 443-3311) will give you the launching schedule. The ships under repair and construction are plainly visible from the bridge or the water.

The Center for the Arts is the formal name of the local arts organization, "the Chocolate Church," which uses a wonderful old dark-brown church on Washington Street, near Center Street, for a wide variety of exhibits, concerts, and plays. There is an art-gallery annex and a small theatre downstairs. Call 442-8455 for schedule information.

The Carlton Bridge. The big, green Carlton Bridge over the Kennebec River was built in 1927 to replace a ferry service. The Maine Central Railroad crosses the river under the highway bridge, so there is vertical clearance of only 10 feet under the lift span when the bridge is down (135 feet when it's up). The clearance rises toward the east bank, and there is about 22 feet under the easternmost fixed span. There is not much traffic under this bridge—mostly small powerboats, and an occasional sailboat or ship. In daytime during the summer months the bridge will lift for recreational vessels *only at specific times*, 10 AM and 2 PM, or at any time between 6 PM and 6 AM.

The bridge moves fast, and the whole process of passing under it should take only five minutes or so. Call the bridgetenders on Channel 13 of your VHF, or use your horn: one prolonged blast, followed by one short blast. (That's what the regulations stipulate, but the bridgetender says, "Just give us two toots on your horn.") Check chapter 2 of the *Coast Pilot* for further details or any changes.

If you have difficulty attracting the bridgetender's attention, an alternative is to telephone the bridge through the marine operator on your VHF. The number is 443-2482.

As with all bridges, you must be careful not to be swept down on it by wind and current, which may be as much as 6½ knots here at maximum ebb.

The mammoth crane that dominates the sprawling shipyard of Bath Iron Works, on the banks of the Kennebec, represents the contemporary incarnation of an industry that has thrived on the Maine coast since 1607. Sleek gray destroyers and missile frigates are today's versions of the 30-ton pinnace *Virginia*, built at the turn of the 17th century by the ill-fated settlers of the Popham Colony. Much has changed in the ensuing 400 years, but the tradition remains strong in communities all along the Maine coast.

For more than three centuries after the construction of the *Virginia*, ships were built up and down the coast, along riverbanks, and on islands, wherever there were settlers. They were built from the materials on hand, supplemented by special items cannibalized from older boats or brought from Europe. They were built mostly by farmers and by fishermen-turned-boatbuilders, often for their own use.

Shipbuilding as a business flourished from the middle of the 18th century, with a series of booms and busts, as entrepreneurs from Kittery and Kennebunkport, Wiscasset and Bath, Waldoboro and Camden, Belfast and Roque Island built ships for the Caribbean trade and the trade with Europe. All this halted abruptly with the Napoleonic Wars and President Jefferson's Embargo Act in 1807.

The great era of building wooden sailing ships in the United States lasted about a century, from 1800 to 1900. The boom years were even shorter, from 1843 to an all-time national peak in 1855, and then to successively lower peaks until 1890.

During most of the era of sailing ships, Maine built the largest number of them in the United States. The center of shipbuilding was Bath, where shipyards lined the banks of the Kennebec. In the boom year of 1854, only Boston and New York City built more. The Waldoboro region was second to Bath in that peak year, and their cumulative total placed Maine well out ahead as the nation's leading shipbuilding state. Ships and barks, barkentines and brigantines, brigs and schooners

slid down the ways to meet an endless demand for Maine-built vessels to carry the world's cargo.

The efficient carrying of freight was the watchword for the two centuries before the 1840s, when speed became an important factor for the China trade. When gold was discovered in California in 1848, speed became everything.

The beautiful, fast clipper ships were developed to meet this demand, and shipbuilding surged during the 1850s. It is 15,000 miles from New York to San Francisco around Cape Horn. The clippers were able to make the passage in an average of 130 days, and some did better; Bath-built *Flying Dragon* once made it in 97 days. But the Gold Rush was short-lived, and so was the clipper-ship era.

Then it was California again, and wheat was the new gold, wheat for the markets of Europe. Both speed and cargo capacity were important, and the "Downeasters" built for this trade were the pride of Maine. Shipbuilding surged again.

But the profitability of voyages halfway round the world declined with foreign competition, and new markets developed for coastwise trade—mundane traffic in coal, lumber, lime, ice, and granite. To transport these bulk cargoes, Maine developed the economical "coasting" schooner, with its fore-and-aft rig, and much-reduced crew ("two men and a boy," they used to say).

The two-masted schooner soon evolved into the three-master, correspondingly larger and more profitable. Four- and five-masters were built after the 1880s. The first six-master was built in Camden in 1900, and the second at Percy and Small Shipyard in Bath that same year.

In this enormous growth and in new technologies were the seeds of destruction. One Bath builder saw the possibility that oceangoing tugs, towing strings of barges, could carry cargo at a fraction of the cost of the great schooners. In 1890, 36 wooden sailing vessels were built in Bath; in 1910, none were built.

It's interesting to speculate on what has happened to all these hun-

dreds and hundreds of great sailing ships. Many were lost, of course, on rocks and ledges from Bishop Rock, off Land's End, to the Straits of Magellan, on lonely Pacific reefs, and in the roaring 40's and the Tasman Sea. Many more were wrecked within sight of home, on Portland Head, and Matinicus and the Libby Isles. Fire claimed the lime ships, and storms the granite schooners.

Those that survived 25 or more years of profitable voyages often were converted in their later years to ignominious uses as storage hulks or barges. The famous clipper *Red Jacket* ended her days in obscurity as a coal hulk in the Cape Verde Islands; four-masters *Luther Little* and *Hesper* lie rotting in Wiscasset Harbor for tourists to photograph.

Many ships were simply junked when their useful days were over—run up in some convenient cove and left to fall apart. Their ribs emerge from the bottom at times when the tide is low or the sands are disturbed by winter storms.

A few have fared better, like the schooner *Lewis R. French,* built in 1871 and now the oldest documented pure sailing vessel in the U.S. merchant fleet. She and the *Stephen Taber,* also built in 1871, in New York, still sail as windjammers out of Rockland. Admiral Donald MacMillan's famous arctic research schooner *Bowdoin* was refurbished at Percy and Small in Bath, and launched anew in 1985.

In modern times there has been something of a renaissance for traditional wooden sailing ships, still being built in small numbers on the coast of Maine, most destined for the windjammer trade.

Large non-traditional wooden sailing ships have also been built in Maine in recent decades, designed by Bruce King of East Boothbay and built by Phil Long. The magnificent cold-molded ketch *Whitehawk,* reminiscent of *Ticonderoga,* was launched in Rockland in 1979, followed by the 90-foot sloop *Whitefin,* constructed on a Rockport tennis court in 1983. In 1990 the luxurious 100-foot ketch *Signe* went down the ways at the Renaissance boatyard in Thomaston.

The magnificent five-masted schooner *Cora F. Cressy* on her launching day in 1902. She was built by Percy and Small in Bath; length, 273 feet; beam, 45.4 feet; draft, 27.9 feet. The hulk of the *Cressy* now shelters a lobster pound in the Medomak River, north of Hog Island. (Frank Claes Collection)

Anchorages, Moorings—Above the Bridge. There are three possible places to stop just north of the bridge, all on the west bank. Though convenient to town, they cater mostly to small powerboats and are exposed to strong current.

BFC Marine (tel. 443-3022). Just above the bridge, BFC Marine has floats with 18 feet alongside, where boats up to 22 feet can be accommodated. Gas and water are available, and diesel by truck. There is a small chandlery.

Town Float Landing (tel. 443-5564). Transients may stay at the main float (between the large dolphins), with 15 feet alongside, for one hour, and three hours at the side floats. Three guest moorings are available free of charge on a first come, first served basis.

Bathport Marine (tel. 363-3540). North of the Town Landing, Bathport has floats with deep water alongside, and can provide gas and water. Bathport maintains several moorings in the river, with 150-pound and 250-pound mushrooms.

WOODS, CRAWFORD, and RAM ISLANDS ★★★ ⬛3 No facilities

Charts: 13288, 13293, **13298**

Three miles above Bath is a sharp turn in the river, which broadens and forms three channels leading to The Chops and on into Merrymeeting Bay. Among these channels are nestled several small and beautiful islands, all trees and granite.

Approaches. Of the three channels leading to The Chops, by far the most difficult is the one to the right, east of Thorne and Lines islands. The section above Lines Island is full of rocks—don't try it.

The channel to the left, south of Woods, Crawford, and Ram islands, is far easier but contains some unmarked rocks.

The easiest channel is straight through, north of Woods, Crawford, and Ram. On an ebb tide, leave nun "10" well to starboard to avoid being set down on Thorne Island Ledge.

Anchorages, Moorings. The key to finding a comfortable anchorage is to get out of the main current. Anchor between Woods and Crawford or between Crawford and Ram, putting your hook down in 7 to 20 feet at low. Do not anchor in the area west of Ram Island, where you will be exposed to the full strength of the current.

THE CHOPS and MERRYMEETING BAY

Above Lines Island the Kennebec passes into Merrymeeting Bay through The Chops, a deep passage between high Chops Point and West Chops Point. The overhead power cables across The Chops have a vertical clearance of 145 feet. Sturgeon Island and its small companion just to the west are state owned and have lovely beaches. Anchor in the 14-foot slot southeast of Sturgeon Island to explore.

Merrymeeting Bay is formed by the confluence of five rivers (the Androscoggin, Muddy, Cathance, Abagadasset, and Kennebec). The extensive shoals and marshes of the bay make it a haven for waterfowl, but no place for deep-draft boats.

The Kennebec continues in a northeasterly direction past Abagadasset Point to Swan Island.

EASTERN RIVER ★★★   No facilities
Charts: 13288, **13298**

This is a short river for true gunkholers. Starting at the southern tip of Swan Island, Eastern River meanders for about two miles through expanses of marsh until it reaches a fixed bridge with vertical clearance of 16 feet. Feel your way up the river very carefully at dead low so that the banks and all hazards are clearly visible.

The south end of the "training wall" shown on the chart is marked by a granite block, and there are some small and undecipherable private marks

in the area. Using chart and fathometer, work carefully past the rocks at Carney Point. At the left turn, the channel shoals. Stay way over to the right. From there on, it is relatively easy: You just run up about halfway between the marshy shores.

This would be an excellent place to hide during a storm, or to find refuge from the Kennebec current if no mooring is available farther up in Richmond.

RICHMOND ★★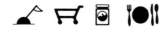
Chart: 13298

Eleven miles north of Bath and 23 miles above the entrance to the Kennebec, Richmond is a small and remote town tucked away on the west bank of the river near the northwestern end of Swan Island. In town are several handsome old red brick buildings, one of which has been recycled to manufacture electronic parts. Richmond is the point of departure for nearby Swan Island, a visit well worth making.

Approaches. The usual approach to Richmond is up the main (eastern) channel of the river. Just before you reach the swing bridge, curve left around the end of Swan Island, leaving to port can "33," which marks the end of a submerged jetty.

You will see a pier and float on the north tip of Swan Island to port before you get to the red brick buildings of Richmond.

Anchorages, Moorings. There are three Swan Island YC guest moorings near the northwest bank, just before you reach the first floats. Or go in to the town dock and inquire if a private mooring off the waterfront is available.

As you come around the northern end of Swan Island, the first landing on the Richmond side belongs to the state. It is used by the Department of Inland Fisheries and Wildlife to ferry visitors to Swan Island.

Next comes the town float landing at a waterfront park, with 16 feet of water alongside at low. You can tie up here for two hours, but overnight stays are not allowed, except with permission of the harbormaster. There are no facilities.

Getting Ashore. Row in to the town float landing.

For the Crew. Just across the street from the town landing is a convenience store with beer, ice, and groceries. A bank is nearby.

Walk a few minutes west, up Route 197, and you will find a market, liquor store, hardware store, laundromat, barbershop, dairy bar, and drugstore. There is a beauty shop nearby. The post office is farther up the same street, .4 mile from the waterfront.

ICE

Teams of horses scraping snow off a field of ice on the Kennebec River, preparatory to cutting blocks for storage in the enormous sheds of the American Ice Company. Ice was harvested after the river froze in mid-December and shipped south starting in early April. (From *Tidewater Ice of the Kennebec River*, by Jennie G. Everson, courtesy Eleanor L. Everson)

Soft music floated on the warm evening breeze, and on the veranda ladies in long white gowns whispered to their escorts. Ice tinkled in the tall mint juleps . . . .

Ice—from the Kennebec River. All up and down the coast of Maine, ice was harvested in every available pond and river to satisfy the growing markets down south. The center of the industry was the Kennebec River, with 60 icehouses between Bath and Augusta harvesting 1,185,000 tons of tidewater ice in 1886–87. Other important areas were the Penobscot River, Boothbay, Wiscasset, and Bristol.

An acre of ice 12 inches thick produces 1,200 tons of ice, or 1,000 tons after shrinkage. In 1870 Kennebec ice was sold for $10 a ton delivered on board.

During its heyday in the latter half of the 19th century, the ice business was very substantial, employing considerable numbers of men and considerable capital. Enormous icehouses were built to hold the harvest. In 1868 the "Ice King of the Kennebec," James Cheeseman, built a dozen icehouses, each 700 feet long by 40 feet wide by 30 feet high. Together they could hold 70,000 tons of ice.

Ice harvesting usually began as soon as possible after the river froze in mid-December. Once the ice was thick enough to bear the weight of men and horses, the area to be harvested was scraped after every snowfall. When the ice thickened to a foot or more, the field was laid out and marked by hand, then grooved by plow-like implements drawn by spans of horses. A hole was chiseled, and the cutting began. As the saw cuts gradually opened up a canal through the frozen river, blocks of ice were prodded along with picks to the icehouses, where they were drawn up a ramp by chainbelt, then stored inside in tiers, insulated with dunnage. Hay was the most satisfactory, followed by sawdust.

In the spring, when the river was again open for navigation, the process was reversed. The ice was run down from the houses, loaded aboard the hundreds of waiting schooners, and shipped south. In the later years, when the schooners were replaced by tugs and barges, strings of barges were often a mile long.

New York was the biggest market, taking 500,000 tons a year by 1874. The main source of supply for New York was the Hudson, so a poor ice year on the Hudson meant "ice fever" on the Kennebec. Philadelphia took 400,000 tons, Baltimore 100,000 tons, and so on down the Atlantic coast to Washington, Norfolk, and Savannah. Shipments were made to Cuba, Panama, the coastal cities of South America, and even halfway around the world to India and China.

During the season's storage, about five to ten percent of the ice was lost by melting. Further shrinkage took place during shipment, despite huge quantities of dunnage. As an example, the schooner *John F. Randall* in 1898 carried a cargo of 2,169 tons of ice to Cuba, and 200 cords of shavings were required as dunnage. Ice was an unpopular cargo with ship captains, awkward to load, and turning to fresh water in the bilges.

And indeed, the handwriting soon was on the wall for Maine's flourishing ice industry. Refrigeration was in growing use by the turn of the century, and no ice was cut at all on the Kennebec in 1907–08. By 1921 only one icehouse was left.

SWAN ISLAND ★★★★★

  No facilities

Chart: 13298

Four miles long and half a mile wide, Swan is the largest island in the Kennebec River and the most unique. Named *Swango,* or "Island of Eagles" by the Abenaki Indians, Swan has the westernmost bald eagle's nest in the state of Maine. If you are lucky, you may experience the thrill of seeing one of these magnificent birds flying up the river.

The island is now the Steve Powell Wildlife Management Area, owned and managed by the Department of Inland Fisheries and Wildlife as a sanctuary for migratory waterfowl, particularly Canada geese. Some 300 acres are kept as open field, and in the spring, as many as 5,000 geese at a time may be grazing in the meadows. The bright-green fringe around the island is wild rice.

The island also is home to a large herd of white-tailed deer, which are able to come and go as they please by swimming the river or crossing the ice. The woods on Swan Island are bare of underbrush and low branches—as high as a deer can reach on its hind legs. This vegetation contrasts vividly with the areas inside various fenced "exclosures," which are used for protecting gardens and for experimental purposes.

Swan Island has a long and colorful history, including European visitors in the early seventeenth century. In 1750, it was inhabited by the Whidden family when Indians attacked, captured 11 family members, marched them to Canada, and sold them as slaves to the French. The price for four adults was reported as $29 each.

During the fall and winter of 1775, when Benedict Arnold's bold and futile expedition to Quebec struggled up the Kennebec, Aaron Burr and Benedict Arnold spent the night on Swan Island in the Dumaresq house, which still stands today.

For centuries a farming and fishing community, and at one time an exporter of lumber and ice, Swan declined during the Depression, and eventually the island was abandoned. The state bought it for back taxes during the 1950s.

Swan Island is lovely and interesting. It is worth going this far up the Kennebec if you have the time.

Approaches. Follow the route to Richmond (see preceding writeup).

Anchorages, Moorings. Visit Swan Island from Richmond.

Getting Ashore. Fisheries and Wildlife people request that visitors come through Richmond, so that they can maintain control over this important and delicate waterfowl staging area.

Things to Do. Swan Island is open to the public on a limited basis—only 60 people a day. No pets. Make reservations ahead of time, whether for a brief visit or for an overnight stay at the island campground. Call 289-1150, or write: Reservations Clerk, 8 Federal St., Augusta, ME 04333. People who arrive without a reservation sometimes can get on the island, but it depends on how many already have reservations for that day.

Visitors are ferried across from the state landing at Richmond, loaded on a stake truck, and driven the length of the island with an Inland Fisheries and Wildlife guide.

A mile from the Swan Island landing is a beautiful meadow looking south to the river and across to Little Swan. Three-sided lean-tos with fireplaces in front are available by reservation for overnight campers, who are free to wander around the northern part of the island. South of the campground, visitors are permitted only with the resident wardens.

THE SWING-BRIDGE ABOVE RICHMOND

Chart: 13298

The road running east from Richmond carries relatively little traffic, and the swing-bridge above Richmond will open promptly for your horn signal.

GARDINER ★★

Chart: 13298

About 33 miles above the entrance to the Kennebec, Gardiner is a town on the west bank that marks the limit of navigation for most cruising sailboats. Just above the town, an old swing bridge has been replaced by a fixed bridge with 35 feet clearance.

Approaches. From Richmond, continue north about 10 miles through the buoyed channel at Tarbox Flats to the twin towns of Gardiner and Randolph, marked by oil tanks on the west bank.

Anchorages, Moorings. North of the oil tanks, next to a small park, is the town wharf and float landing, along a steel bulkhead, with 12 feet of water alongside. You can tie up to the floats for a reasonable daily rate, although you will have to cope with the glare of arc lights and the rumble of an occasional truck. Be sure to stay clear of can "47A," upstream from the landing, which marks the end of submerged pilings left over from the old swing bridge. For moorings, see the following writeup on Randolph.

Getting Ashore. Row in to the float at the town landing.

For the Boat. Water and electricity hookups are available upon request at the town landing float.

For the Crew. On the waterfront, the town has posted a useful map showing all the nearby stores and facilities. Among these are a market, laundromat, bakery, hardware and liquor stores, and restaurants.

Things to Do. Gardiner is the finish-point for the annual Great Kennebec River Whatever Week Race over the Fourth of July weekend—an eight-mile regatta run downriver from Augusta that features homemade craft of great imagination but doubtful ancestry.

RANDOLPH ★

Chart: 13298

Opposite Gardiner, on the east bank of the river, is the village of Randolph, with a wharf, float, and marina.

Anchorages, Moorings. Bowen Marine maintains about 40 moorings in the river, with 950-pound blocks. One or more usually are available for transients, except over the Fourth of July weekend. Reserve ahead. The marina float—to be used only for pickup and dropoff—reportedly has 10 feet alongside.

Getting Ashore. Row in to the float at Bowen

Marine or across the river to the town landing at Gardiner.

For the Boat. *Bowen Marine (tel. 582-2520).* Moorings, water, and electricity are available, but no diesel. There are marine supplies, and the marina can handle minor repairs.

For the Crew. There is a pay phone next door to Bowen Marine. Walk a couple of hundred yards north up the road to find a market, laundromat, ice, and a restaurant.

INSIDE PASSAGE (BATH TO BOOTHBAY)

Charts: 13288, 13293, **13296**, 13298

The Inside Passage from Bath to Boothbay Harbor is one of the adventures of the Maine coast. Like marriage, however, it is not to be entered into lightly, but advisedly...and soberly. The current in two of the stretches, Upper and Lower Hell Gates, can be awesome for those of us not accustomed to running whitewater rivers in deep-keeled boats.

The 11-mile passage cuts southeast and northwest across the grain of glacial valleys, broadening into placid bays and narrowing into sluices through which the current rushes with great force. The current floods northwest from Boothbay Harbor to Bath and ebbs southeast. You must pass under a fixed bridge with 51-feet vertical clearance at the western entrance near Bath, and through a swing bridge near Boothbay.

If you contemplate this passage, be sure you know the height of your masthead above water (including antennas), study the chart carefully ahead of time, and study the *Tidal Current Tables.*

The western part of the Inside Passage, including Upper and Lower Hell Gates, is by far the most difficult. Currents here are driven by a differing water level between the Kennebec and Sheepscot rivers. A number of bays and rivers empty into the passage, however, making the timing of the currents complex and variable.

Powerboats that know the territory come through at any tide, but cruising sailboats should come through near slack water or with a minimum of current. Much of the time the current in the narrows will be running three or four knots, and eight knots or more at maximum in Upper and Lower Hell Gates. What makes these spots dangerous is not so much the force of the current as the turbulence, which may cause you to lose control.

Most cruising sailboats power all the way through the passage. It is possible to sail in certain areas, but you will often be blanketed and simply drifting with the current. There is no room to tack in the narrows. During the summer there is often a lot of traffic, especially powerboats, in the Inside Passage. There may also be floating debris like logs and branches.

There are four narrow places in the Inside Passage where the current runs strongest: Upper Hell Gate, Lower Hell Gate, Goose Rock Passage, and Townsend Gut. The amount of current and difficulty of the passage is highest at the western end and least as you approach Boothbay Harbor.

The description below assumes that you are entering the Inside Passage at Bath, and heading southeast. At the end of the section are pointers on making the passage the other way, from Boothbay Harbor to Bath.

Sasanoa River Entrance (Bath). Making the passage from west to east, the best time to enter the Sasanoa River is just before high slack water at Upper Hell Gate (assuming you can get under the Arrowsic bridge—see below). You will have a minimum of current at Upper Hell Gate and the ebb to help you through the rest of the passage.

Use the *Tidal Current Tables* to determine the time of high slack water, which is not the same as high tide. If you are too early, you can anchor on the eastern side of Hanson Bay in the area between can "37" and nun "34," in mud bottom. A former captain of the cruise boat *Argo* reported that sometimes high slack at Upper Hell Gate lasts only a few minutes. "Then it starts to ebb like hell."

It is possible but inadvisable to make the passage starting at low slack water instead. The current will become strong against you, and the margin of error in the narrow and shoal places will be reduced by the fall of the tide.

Arrowsic Bridge. The fixed bridge across the Sasanoa River to Arrowsic Island, near Bath, has a vertical clearance of 51 feet at mean high water. Remember that every tide is different, and remember your flagstaff and antenna.

The mean tidal range at Bath is 6.4 feet. On a normal low tide, therefore, you can carry about 57 feet under the bridge.

Sasanoa River and Upper Hell Gate. This is the narrowest and most difficult part of the Inside Passage. Follow the channel buoys carefully around the slow S-turn through Hanson Bay and into the narrows, leaving green to starboard and red to port.

Watch carefully now for turbulence and cross-channel currents. As you approach Money Point, leave cans "31" and "29" fairly close to starboard to keep you away from Carleton Ledges (visible at any tide).

The chart shows several tiny islands. At high tide they are very hard to find, being flat rocks and grass only barely above water.

Shortly after can "27," you will come to the

narrowest part of the passage at Upper Hell Gate, about 60 yards wide. Stay close to the left-hand bank as you approach green daybeacon "23" at Lime Rock, which you leave to starboard. You can almost reach out and touch the rocks on the bank with your left hand. Then pass between red daybeacon "22," which you leave close aboard to port, and the little island (barely visible above water at high), which you leave to starboard.

It is also possible to go to the other side of this little island, leaving it to port; at low tide that would be preferable. There is deeper water here, but it requires a sharp turn to the right after green daybeacon "23."

Once past red daybeacon "22," the worst is over, but note the small island off Tibbett Point and the ledge beyond marked by nun "20."

At maximum there may be 8 knots of current or more in Upper Hell Gate, with boils, turbulence and standing waves in the narrowest spots. Bill and Barbara Hadlock once tried to fight their way against the full current in their Friendship sloop, which can do six knots under power, and didn't make it. It was too narrow to turn around, so they were actually flushed back.

Hockomock Bay and Lower Hell Gate. At Mill Point you enter Hockomock Bay, a broad, calm area, filled with flats and shallows, fringed by marsh grass and featureless shores, named for the Hockomock Indians. Montsweag Bay and the Back River trend off to the northeast, and you may catch a glimpse of the dome of the Maine Yankee nuclear plant in the distance.

Follow the buoys through Hockomock Bay, north of Castle Island, checking them off carefully. Can "5," north of Bareneck Island, is often dragged under water. The maximum current in Lower Hell Gate occurs near The Boilers, where a velocity of nine knots has been observed, and there may be dangerous boils and eddies which can spin you around.

The main danger is the ebb current that sets you cross-channel to the southeast, toward The Boilers. After rounding Bareneck Island, steer well to the right of nun "4," making a sharp turn to port when you are sure you can clear The Boilers.

Fortunately, the passage is clear and reasonably wide. But stay alert because you never know what kind of traffic you may meet. Beal Island belongs to the Appalachian Mountain Club, which has built portaging trails so canoeists can avoid Lower Hell Gate.

Knubble Bay and Goose Rock Passage. Now you pass through Knubble Bay, a broad and beautiful expanse of water bordered by handsome saltwater farms. Near Thomas Great Toe you may see the skiffs of a small-scale industry harvesting seaweed for fertilizer.

Give Little Knubble a comfortable berth and

enter Riggs Cove, where you can pick up a Robinhood Marine mooring, or continue on through Goose Rock Passage. (Robinhood and Riggs are discussed in more detail later; see the Sheepscot River.)

The current flows hard through Goose Rock Passage, but the channel is quite wide and you should have no problem. Entering from the west, run past Lowe Point and southward along the shore in deep water toward flashing green light "5," on a skeleton tower ashore. Find nun "2" at Boiler Rock as early as possible and keep track of its location. The buoy is often dragged under until only the tip is showing, or nothing at all. The flotation collar recently added to the buoy should help. If you can see nun "2," leave it well to port. If not, run along a line from light "5" on the shore to a point north of can "3," which you leave to starboard.

The remainder of Goose Rock Passage is wide and clear. Leave green daybeacon "1" north of MacMahan Island to starboard as you enter the Sheepscot River. Two or three anchorages in Goose Rock Passage are discussed later (see the Sheepscot River).

Townsend Gut. Work your way across the Sheepscot River and approach Townsend Gut north of Dogfish Head and Ebenecook Harbor. Dogfish Head can be recognized by the skeleton tower 1/4 mile south (shown on the chart), and by the round house with white roof on the bare rocks of the point.

A second approach to Townsend Gut is north of Isle of Springs, first locating green daybeacon "1" at the end of the ledge, and turning wide to starboard to avoid the ledge just beyond.

The passage through Townsend Gut, anchorages, and the swing bridge are discussed later (see the Sheepscot River).

The Inside Passage—east to west. In order to encounter a minimum of current, Glen Baldwin (of Robinhood Marine) recommends that you leave Robinhood about one hour after low slack water at Upper Hell Gate. The alternative, leaving Robinhood about one hour *before* high slack water at Upper Hell Gate, seems to work equally well.

MONTSWEAG BAY and BACK RIVER

Charts: 13288, 13293, **13296**

As you shoot through the Inside Passage and enter Hockomock Bay, you will glimpse to the north in Montsweag Bay the huge dome of the Maine Yankee nuclear power plant, operating since 1972. It is located on the west side of the Back River, on Bailey Point. Although you cannot enter the plant itself, visitors are welcome at the interesting Information Center next door (tel. 882-6321).

The Back River, running south from Wiscasset to Montsweag Bay and Hockomock Bay, passes under a fixed bridge (vertical clearance 48 feet) at Cowseagan Narrows, and the area south of the bridge is filled with ledges and very turbulent.

Therefore, the easiest way to reach Maine Yankee is to come up Montsweag Bay from the south.

The size and lack of shore features in Montsweag Bay make navigation difficult, but Maine Yankee maintains a Coast Guard–approved system of red buoys and green buoys from May 15 to October 15 and produces a sketch chart with navigational notes.

Anchor off Bailey Point, or pick up any vacant mooring for a short visit. Take your dinghy in to a float just north of Little Oak Island. There is no sign, but it is only a short walk from there to the Information Center.

SHEEPSCOT RIVER and Boothbay Harbor Region

Charts: 13288, 13293, **13295**, **13296**

Of all the rivers on the coast of Maine, the Sheepscot offers the best cruising, perhaps because it is more like a bay than a river. The entrance opens invitingly between Southport and Georgetown islands, two miles wide and almost free of dangers. For an hour's sail, the river remains a broad sound,

with islands and passages of great beauty and interest beckoning on either side. Flags flutter on the headlands, ospreys nest on every beacon, and shores are white granite.

The Sheepscot has many good harbors and anchorages—enough so that you could discover a

101

different place every night for two weeks. Deepest of all the Maine rivers, the Sheepscot is also cold, and lobsters hauled from here are reputed to be the tastiest.

Unlike many of the other midcoast rivers, there are few narrow spots or shoals here, and usually only a moderate current. You can find good places to shelter in heavy weather, and one or two spots that even qualify as hurricane holes. Two major harbors provide supplies or repairs (Ebenecook and Robinhood).

Harbors such as Cape Harbor, Cozy, Five Islands, and Love Cove are a delight. One short but lovely Sheepscot sail runs north of Ebenecook Harbor, tucking in behind the Green Islands, going past Cameron Point, and emerging back into the river north of Isle of Springs. Or circumnavigate MacMahan Island, through Goose Rock Passage and the Little Sheepscot River.

The Sheepscot River bisects the Inside Passage, an interesting, meandering route between Bath and Boothbay Harbor. The portions of this passage adjoining the Sheepscot are relatively benign and enjoyable to explore.

Wiscasset, at the head of navigation 14 miles from the sea, is an historic town of considerable charm. From here, a fleet of sailing ships once traded to every part of the world.

Until her death in 1964, writer Rachel Carson spent summers along the shores of the Sheepscot, north of Hendricks Head on Southport Island. The river was both her home and her laboratory. Her first great and influential book, *The Sea Around Us*, followed by *The Edge of the Sea*, introduced us to the beauties and complexities of the oceans. And then her *Silent Spring* opened the eyes of the world and launched the environmental movement.

CAPE HARBOR ★★★

Charts: 13288, 13293, 13295

At Cape Newagen, the southern tip of Southport Island, is this beautiful little harbor that provides reasonable protection except in a strong southwesterly. The entrance is narrow, deep, and exhilarating. It will test your convictions about "red right returning." If the harbor is new to you, do not enter it at night or in poor visibility.

Both Hunting Island and Cape Island (locally known as Witch's Island), to the south of the harbor, are privately owned. Cape Harbor is the site of the handsome old Newagen Seaside Inn, whose meals and facilities are available to visiting yachtsmen.

The area's long history is commemorated here in a large bronze plaque: "Newagen—the earliest locality visited and named by English explorers in the Boothbay region. Here Capt. Christopher Levett and the Indian Sagamores Menawarmet, Samoset and Cogawesco met for four days in December 1623. Indians destroyed the fort and settlement in 1675."

Approaches. Enter Cape Harbor from the west. Leave nun "2" to starboard, but do not run a straight line to the entrance. To avoid the three-foot spot, run north from the nun before turning

toward the beacon at the entrance.

The entrance is only 50 to 75 feet wide, but it is deep, and Southport Island is steep-to. Pass between Southport Island to port and red daybeacon "4" to starboard. (The beacon is not on the edge of the channel; you must be at least 10 or 15 feet north of it.)

Anchorages, Moorings. The Newagen Seaside Inn maintains several moorings for visitors. To reserve ahead, call 633-5242. There is little room to anchor among the lobster buoys and boats, and the northern cove is foul.

Getting Ashore. Take your dinghy to the inn float at the western end of the harbor or to the town landing floats at the eastern end.

For the Crew. The inn has a cocktail lounge and serves breakfast and dinner (reservations recommended). Ice and showers are available. There are no nearby stores or markets.

Things to Do. There is a heated freshwater pool, a large saltwater pool, croquet, horseshoes, badminton, and volleyball. The inn is set in a forest preserve, with nature trails and deserted rocky beaches to explore.

HARMON HARBOR ★★★

Charts: 13288, 13293, **13295**

As you enter from the sea, this long narrow cove is the first on the west side of the Sheepscot River. The harbor is well protected except from southerly gales, but it is likely to be rolly when the entrance

ledges are covered at high tide. The shores are rocky and wooded, with an occasional house and a dozen or so moored lobsterboats.

Few cruising boats use this harbor, so it is far

more peaceful than neighboring Five Islands. However, many mosquitoes and two impressive screech owls make Harmon Harbor their home, so have your netting ready at dusk.

Approaches. The harbor is easy to enter only in good visibility. After you round Griffith Head, coming in from the sea, the sun will gleam on the white granite of Five Islands. To the left of them is the green indentation of Harmon Harbor. Head for a massive, gray, turreted building high on a hill.

At the entrance leave nun "2" close aboard to starboard; there is 16 feet of water a boat length away from the nun at low tide. The ledges to port and starboard are both clearly visible at low.

Anchorages, Moorings. Come in past the first two or three docks until it shoals to 16 or 20 feet at low, and anchor in the middle of the harbor. There is plenty of swinging room, and holding ground is good, in mud buttom.

The Grey Havens Inn (shown on the western shore of the harbor on chart 13295) has a mooring available, or it may be possible to lie along their float, with 17 feet of water at low. Reserve ahead (tel. 371-2616).

Getting Ashore. There are convenient spots to land the dinghy along the rocks of the eastern shore, or land at the Grey Havens Inn float.

For the Crew. Dinner at the Grey Havens Inn is open to the public, except Sundays. BYOB.

Things to Do. Walk south along the rocks of the peninsula and around Dry Point, where it connects to Wood Island at low tide, to find sandy beaches.

From the tip of the peninsula, a narrow macadam road runs through piney woods, past a few summer cabins, and eventually reaches Five Islands. Just opposite the first island is a lovely path through the woods to the high cliffs on the eastern side.

COZY HARBOR ★★★

Charts: 13288, 13293, **13295**

This is truly a cozy harbor, and a most charming spot. Home of the family-oriented Southport Yacht Club, Cozy Harbor is full of kids splashing in and out of the water, a fleet of sailboats, and an altogether wonderful atmosphere. It is crammed with small boats, both lobsterboats and sloops. Even moderate-sized yachts seldom come in here, although a windjammer has been known to spend a night in the mouth of the harbor.

Approaches. Coming up Sheepscot Bay, you will have no trouble spotting the square white lighthouse on Hendricks Head. Look for the nun and the red daybeacon a quarter mile south of the lighthouse marking the entrance to Cozy Harbor. Note that nun "6" is a river mark, so you leave it to *port*.

From nun "6," run between can "3" to port and red daybeacon "2" on Nick Ledge to starboard. Then enter the harbor, leaving green daybeacon "5" close aboard to port, but no closer than 10 feet.

Although the entrance is very narrow, it is easy with good visibility. Do not try this harbor for the first time if you can't see where you're going.

Anchorages, Moorings. There are two possibilities. Pick up the single Southport Yacht Club guest mooring identified by a club burgee. There is about six feet here at a low tide, and you may then rest gently in the mud.

The second possibility—and this is what the windjammer did—is to anchor just inside the mouth of the harbor after you pass the green beacon. Wherever you are, swinging room is limited, so you may need to put out fenders.

Getting Ashore. Take your dinghy in to the yacht club float, used by everybody in the harbor including the lobstermen (who are members of the club).

For the Boat. *E.W. Pratt (Gus's)* Gas and water are available at Gus's dock next to the yacht club. But plan ahead. It dries out at low.

Southport Yacht Club (tel. 633-5767). There is water at the club float, with four feet alongside at low.

For the Crew. Next to the club is a white building with a sign saying, "E.W. Pratt, General Merchandise." This is Gus's place, a turn-of-the-century ice cream parlor and sandwich counter, plus two candlepin bowling lanes. Gus can supply delicious sandwiches, limited groceries, lobsters, and ice cubes. There is also a pay phone.

Walk half a mile up the road to the left to Southport Island Market, well stocked with plain and fancy items and big-city newspapers. They'll give you a ride back (tel. 633-2849). The post office is a block down the road.

Sometimes you can buy lobsters from one of the lobsterboats moored near you—a splendid example of convenience shopping.

Things to Do. Row under the bridge leading to Pratts Island, or north through the rocky guzzle inside David Island, which will take you to the beach in a corner of Hendricks Harbor. Or take the first road to the right from the yacht club and walk over to Pratts Island.

Bowl a few games of candlepins at Gus's.

FIVE ISLANDS ★★★★

Charts: 13288, 13293, **13295**, 13296

On the west side of the Sheepscot River, Five Islands is a beautiful and well-protected harbor, easy to enter. The bold, granite-fringed islands contrasting with the dark green trees make this a lovely anchorage.

The harbor is surrounded by modest homes on the mainland and the handsome summer cottages on Malden Island that have been in the same families for six generations. This is both a working harbor and a haven for pleasure craft.

Approaches. The usual entrance is just north of Malden Island, largest of the group, high and wooded with several substantial summer cottages on the north side. Find green can "1" inside the entrance and head for it on a westerly course about halfway between Malden Island and the ledge to the north. The can may be left on either side.

There is also a northern entrance. Having identified wooded Crow Island, look for red daybeacon "2" in the north channel. Approaching the beacon, favor the Crow Island side to avoid the unmarked ledge making out from Georgetown Island. Pass westward of the beacon, leaving it close to port.

There are other unmarked entrances from the south, but they are difficult without local knowledge.

Anchorages, Moorings. The Five Islands Yacht Club maintains four guest moorings with a club burgee on the pickup buoy. Sheepscot Bay Boat Company has about 20 moorings, granite blocks up to 2,000 pounds.

Getting Ashore. To get to the village, use the dinghy floats at the town dock, next to the red buildings of Five Islands Seafood, or land at the Sheepscot Bay Boat Company.

For the Boat. *Five Islands Town Dock.* Next to Five Islands Seafood, the town dock provides a place to tie up briefly, and a dinghy float.

Five Islands Yacht Club. There is no clubhouse, but the club maintains guest moorings for yachtsmen.

Sheepscot Bay Boat Company (Ch. 16; tel. 371-2442). The yard is easily identified in the northwest corner of the harbor by its docks and blue crane. Facilities include moorings and slips, two docks with 8 to 10 feet alongside the floats at low, gas and diesel. The yard does engine and hull repairs for boats to 30 feet, and there is a small chandlery.

For the Crew. Five Islands Seafood has a take-out, offering lobsters and clams that can be enjoyed at trestle tables on the dock. In the Love Nest Snack Bar next door are limited groceries, newspapers, and some fresh produce. Outside is a pay phone, plus ice and a mailbox.

Things to Do. Row under the footbridge between Malden Island and its neighbor to the west, or between the northern islands.

For a pleasant walk, take the road inland from the harbor and the first left down the shore toward Dry Point. This beautiful little road runs a mile through piney woods to Harmon Harbor.

WESTERN REACHES of the Sheepscot

LITTLE SHEEPSCOT RIVER and MACMAHAN ISLAND

Charts: 13288, 13293, 13295, **13296**

The Little Sheepscot River is a pleasant passage of a mile or so, west of MacMahan Island. Current floods north and ebbs south, and is strong in the narrow places. If it is flooding, the Little Sheepscot is the best route to the Inside Passage. If it is ebbing strongly, you will do better to take the longer route around MacMahan Island, through Goose Rock Passage.

Entering the Little Sheepscot from the south, leave Turnip Island to starboard (Turnip is rocky, with granite and cedar-lined shores). Run through the narrows, leaving nun "2" to starboard.

You can certainly sail through the Little Sheepscot with the current, but you are likely to lose your wind part way along. If the current is running strong, you may find boils and eddies here, but nothing alarming.

Just past the narrow section is the landing for MacMahan Island, with its pleasant little summer community. Anchor off the dock and row in to the float to explore the island. Walk inland from the landing, then take a left up the hill to the Episcopal church, an unusual landmark on such a small island.

GOOSE ROCK PASSAGE

Charts: 13293, **13296**

From the Sheepscot River, enter Goose Rock Passage north of MacMahan Island, leaving green daybeacon "1" to port. The passage may also be entered through the Little Sheepscot River.

The current flows hard through Goose Rock Passage. Leave can "3" to port and locate nun "2" at Boiler Rock as soon as possible; nun "2" is often dragged under until only the tip is showing, or nothing at all. If nun "2" is invisible, run a straight line from north of can "3" toward flashing green light "5" on a skeleton tower ashore, then follow the shoreline up around Lowe Point.

There are two little coves in Goose Rock Passage that will provide anchorage and shelter from the current if you need it. On the north side of MacMahan Island the chart shows a break in the ledges. Head straight in for the docks, and you can anchor outside the moored boats in 13 to 15 feet of water at low. This is easiest to do at half tide or lower, when the ledges are visible.

On the north side of Goose Rock Passage is Brooks Cove, on Westport Island. Head straight in the middle of the cove and anchor near the moorings in 15 to 20 feet at low.

RIGGS COVE (ROBINHOOD) ★★   `4`   All facilities

Charts: 13288, 13293, **13296**

Riggs Cove, just south of Knubble Bay, is full of moorings put out by Robinhood Marine Center. This is an excellent place to get anything you need for the boat, and to wait until the tide is right for the passage through Lower and Upper Hell Gates. There usually are lots of big cruising boats in the harbor.

Approaches. Approaching from the east through Goose Rock Passage you will see the boats moored at Robinhood as soon as you come around Lowe Point. The only danger is Blacksmithshop Ledge, just south of Robinhood Marine, marked with green daybeacon "3."

Anchorages, Moorings. Robinhood Marine has 40 slips or more and at least 70 moorings, of which a dozen usually are available for transients. No one objects if you pick up a mooring temporarily while waiting for the tide to turn. There is no

room to anchor among the moorings, but you can anchor past the moorings toward Robinhood Cove; the water, however, is deep.

Getting Ashore. Take your dinghy in to the Robinhood Marine floats.

For the Boat. *Robinhood Marine Center (Ch. 16 or 68; tel. 371-2525).* Robinhood Marine is a large, full-service yard, with every facility for the boat— gas, diesel, water, ice, electricity, and a chandlery. The fuel dock is midway along the line of floats, with 10 feet of water alongside. The yard has a crane and a 35-ton boatlift and can perform most engine, electronics, and hull repairs.

For the Crew. There are showers, laundromat, and a pay phone at Robinhood Marine. Best of all, the Osprey Restaurant above the chandlery serves an extraordinary lunch and dinner. Reserve ahead on the radio.

ROBINHOOD COVE ★★   `5`   No facilities

Charts: 13288, 13293, **13296**

South of Knubble Bay, this long, narrow slot stretches more than two miles into Georgetown Island. The little-used cove has low, wooded shores and few houses. An unbuoyed tongue of deep water extends about a mile from the entrance.

Robinhood Cove is landlocked and offers good protection in every direction except southwest, where the length of fetch detracts somewhat from its value as a hurricane hole.

Approaches. Head straight down the middle of Robinhood Cove. Just past the narrows at the entrance, a large hulk lies near the east bank. Feel your way down the deepwater tongue as far as you wish.

Anchorages, Moorings. Anchor anywhere at the edge of the channel in 8 to 20 feet, mud bottom. You are not likely to have much company.

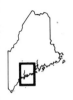

EASTERN REACHES of the Sheepscot

As you enter the Sheepscot, the first major harbor on the east side is Ebenecook, on the northwest corner of Southport Island. The harbor is easy to enter and consists of three separate arms of water, each quite different in character. From west to east, these are Maddock Cove, Pierce Cove, and Love Cove.

MADDOCK COVE
(EBENECOOK HARBOR) ★★

Charts: 13288, 13293, 13295, **13296**

Maddock Cove, the westernmost cove in Ebenecook Harbor, is the well-protected home of Boothbay Region Boatyard, whose docks and moorings fill most of the available space. On a typical summer day, there might be 70 or 80 boats.

Approaches. Dogfish Head is easily identified by a skeleton tower one-fourth mile from the end, and by a round house with a white roof on the granite ledge at the northwest tip, both shown on the chart.

Passing between Dogfish Head and Green Islands, turn to starboard before nun "2" to enter Maddock Cove. Run down the channel between two lines of moored boats. Be cautious of the ledges that separate Maddock from Pierce Cove. There is a pole on the highest part of the long ledge.

Anchorages, Moorings. Check with Boothbay Region Boatyard for moorings or slips. It is also possible to anchor in midchannel northwest of the marina in 8 to 16 feet of water at low.

Getting Ashore. Row your dinghy to the floats on the east side of the Boothbay Region Boatyard.

For the Boat. *Boothbay Region Boatyard (Ch. 16; tel. 633-2970).* This is a full-service boatyard with 50 berths and 40 moorings. Facilities include electricity, water, and ice. You can get gas and diesel at the fuel floats, with six feet of water alongside at low.

The yard has a 30-ton boatlift and crane and can perform all types of hull, electronics, rigging, and engine repairs. The chandlery carries charts and other marine supplies.

For the Crew. The yard has a separate little house with showers and laundry, and there are pay phones.

Southport Island Market (tel. 633-2849) in West Southport, with a variety of grocery items, and the post office are a half-mile walk up the road. They'll give you a ride back with the groceries.

PIERCE COVE (EBENECOOK HARBOR) ★★

 No facilities

Charts: 13288, 13293, 13295, **13296**

The middle arm of Ebenecook Harbor, Pierce Cove, is less well protected than Maddock Cove or Love Cove when winds are from the northwest. The cove harbors a dozen moored boats, with no facilities.

Approaches. After passing Dogfish Head, leave nun "2" to starboard before heading down into the slot of Pierce Cove. Favor the east side to avoid the ledges on the west.

Anchorages, Moorings. Anchor in 10 to 15 feet of water at low either before you reach the moored boats or among them. Do not go past the tip of land on the west side of the cove.

LOVE COVE (EBENECOOK HARBOR) ★★★★

Charts: 13288, 13293, 13295, **13296**

Farthest east of Ebenecook's arms, and best protected of all, is serene Love Cove. A bit tricky to enter, it is a delightful place for watching seals, herons, and osprey, exploring in a dinghy, and savoring the tranquility.

Approaches. After you pass Dogfish Head, leave nun "2" to starboard and continue east until you can see down into Love Cove. The chart shows an unmarked ledge at either side of the entrance, so coming in at high tide requires some guesswork.

Better still, enter at midtide or lower, when the ledges are visible.

Anchorages, Moorings. Note the cable area shown on the chart. There are signs on both shores showing the location of a pipeline. Anchor south of this area in 8 to 10 feet of water at low. An unex-pected find in Love Cove is a mooring maintained by the resident harbor pilot, marked "guest"—first come, first served. Appreciative cruising folk have left messages to the pilot in a pickle jar attached to the float.

TOWNSEND GUT
Charts: 13288, 13293, **13296**

In his 1858 book *A Summer Cruise on the Coast of New England*, Robert Carter described Townsend Gut: "We . . . had a delightful sail through a most singular strait narrow, like a river of moderate size, and bordered on both sides by meadows green to the water's edge, with occasional groves ringing the banks. We should have had no suspicion that this passage was not a river had it not been for the seaweed growing on its rocky edges."

Townsend Gut is the eastern end of the Inside Passage leading from Bath to Boothbay Harbor. Narrow in several places, and about a mile long, the banks of this stretch are still lined with meadows, trees, and handsome summer homes. There are secure anchorages here, protected in every direction. The passage is clear and well defined.

From the Sheepscot River, the entrance to Townsend Gut is easy to find; look for flashing light "7" off Cameron Point, leaving it to starboard. The current runs from zero to moderately strong at the entrance near Cameron Point and in the other constricted areas, but it is no problem for sailboats with power. Pass through the narrow space between this and nun "6," marking the long ledge to port, partially visible at almost any tide; then turn left into the channel.

Townsend Gut Swing Bridge. For half a century or more, this swing bridge has been tended by members of the Lewis family, who take pride in how often the span opens for water traffic (perhaps 60 times on a busy summer day).

The bridge is manned 24 hours a day, and it will open promptly on demand. They may see you coming, but be ready with your horn (one prolonged blast, one short), or call on channel 16 and switch to 13.

The bridgetender has to walk to the middle of the span and climb the stairs to a little house from which he operates the bridge. Surprisingly, it all takes a very short time—perhaps a minute or so from your signal.

The current here at maximum is five knots, more or less, and there is about 20 feet in the channel at low. Pass through the swing bridge, staying to the right and noting nun "4," which marks a midchannel rock just beyond. As you go through, the bridgetender will ask for the boatowner's name.

In the narrow section south of the bridge, hug the Southport Island shore, favoring the deeper western side of the channel.

OAK POINT (Cove west of) ★★★
Charts: 13288, 13293, **13296**

Just west of Oak Point, on the north side of Townsend Gut, is a lovely cove, unnamed on the chart, with some handsome homes, oaks on the lawns, and often several classic yachts at private moorings. Well protected from every direction except northwest, the cove offers good anchorage and splendid sunsets.

Approaches. Head for the center of the cove; there are no dangers.

Anchorages, Moorings. Anchor just outside the moored boats in 17 feet at low, mud bottom.

For the Crew. If you feel like eating out, there is a dock at the Ocean Gate Motor Inn in Southport, across the bay, or you can go through the swing bridge to Robinson's Wharf, an excellent and informal seafood place (see Hodgdon Cove writeup).

HODGDON COVE ★★
Charts: 13288, 13293, **13296**

Halfway through Townsend Gut, east of Oak Point, Hodgdon Cove is out of the current and offers excellent protection. There are just a few boats in the cove and usually there is plenty of room to anchor.

Approaches. The approach is straightforward.

Favor the eastern side of the cove to avoid the ledges in the north corner, but do not go east of the moorings.

Anchorages, Moorings. Anchor near the moorings on the east side of the cove in 13 to 20 feet at low, mud bottom.

For the Crew. While waiting for the tide or anchored for the night, run over in the dinghy to Robinson's Wharf, in Deckers Cove, just beyond and east of the swing bridge—one of those atmospheric clam-and-lobster, outdoor-trestle-table restaurants.

Northern Reaches of the Sheepscot

INDIANTOWN ISLAND

Charts: 13288, 13293, **13296**

Indiantown Island lies just north of Cameron Point, at the western entrance to Townsend Gut. The island is high and wooded, with a rock bluff on the southeast tip. Huge shell mounds on the southern side remain as mute testimony to the large Indian summer village for which the island was named. The island is currently uninhabited, but proposals have been made for a bridge from the mainland and intensive development.

On the west side of Indiantown Island, opposite the northern of the two Spectacle Islands, is a pretty little cove, unnamed on the chart, a good place for a day stop. Anchor just outside the cove itself (note the ledge on the chart), in 10 to 15 feet at low, mud bottom.

Take your dinghy and circumnavigate Indiantown Island, going through the shallow passage between the island and the mainland. Half a dozen blue herons live on the eastern shore of the island.

ISLE OF SPRINGS ★★★

Charts: 13288, 13293, **13296**

Two miles north of Ebenecook Harbor is the large, wooded Isle of Springs, which sustains a rustic summer community (more than a century old) of several dozen cottages. Residents arrive at the landing on the northeast side via a ferry from Sawyer Island.

Approaches. From the east, the approach is easy around the northern tip of the two Spectacle Islands. Then coast along the Isle of Springs. Note the four- and five-foot shoal in the middle of the bay.

Approaching from the west, leave green daybeacon "1" at the northern end of Isle of Springs to starboard. Make a wide right turn to avoid the ledge extending from the northern tip of the island,

passing halfway between Isle of Springs and Sawyer Island.

Anchorages, Moorings. The dock has an "Isle of Springs" sign. Next to it is a guest mooring stake with a pendant. Pick it up or anchor outside the small moored powerboats in 10 to 15 feet of water at low, mud bottom. Protection here, in the lee of the island, is good.

Getting Ashore. Row in to the back of the dinghy float, leaving the sides open for the ferry. Watch out for water skiers.

Things to Do. The island is circled and crossed by a network of lovely grassy paths and boardwalks.

SAWYER ISLAND ★★   No facilities

Charts: 13288, 13293, **13296**

Amid Sawyer, Hodgdon, and Barters islands is a small, landlocked bay that is easy to enter and offers good protection from every direction. Of no great beauty, this unnamed bay is little used and would make an excellent hurricane hole.

The bay forms part of the approach into Back

River via the Trevett swing bridge, which has overhead power cables with authorized clearance of 50 feet. The current runs strong through the narrows at the bridge. Even if you could pass safely under the cables, there is little in the unbuoyed Back River to attract you.

Approaches. Approach the entrance from the west between Sawyer and Barters islands, starting near nun "18" through a reasonably wide channel. At the end of this channel, leave to port can "1," marking a ledge, and enter the unnamed bay north of Sawyer Island.

Anchorages, Moorings. Work your way south in the middle of the bay, anchoring in 8 to 20 feet of water at low, in mud and sand bottom. You will have plenty of swinging room.

CROSS RIVER and OVEN MOUTH ★★★★ No facilities
Charts: 13288, 13293, **13296**

At the north end of Barters Island, the Sheepscot River divides into two branches, the main western branch continuing up to Wiscasset and the smaller, eastern branch forming the pleasant diversion of the Cross River. (Since chart 13296 stops just past the entrance to the Cross River, you must rely on chart 13293 for Oven Mouth, which makes it look narrower and more difficult than it is.)

Cross River is lovely and open, with just a few houses in sight. The river narrows down to 50 yards or so as you shoot between the bold cliffs of Oven Mouth in deep water, a delightful little passage.

You can run through Oven Mouth and out across the basin to the east, but do not head southward on the Cross River without local knowledge.

Approaches. The fork on the Sheepscot is marked by a red-and-green lighted buoy, left to port. Give the northern tip of Barters Island a wide berth. Immediately afterward, make a slow, wide turn to port past the shoals on the north side before High Head. The privately maintained buoy shown on the chart is not always in place.

As you continue upriver past High Head, you will see a high, wooded bluff marking the north-

west corner of the entrance to Oven Mouth. A red house marks the southwest corner.

In passing through Oven Mouth, stay in mid-channel until you emerge into the basin beyond, which is 500 yards across. The current is particularly strong near the eastern end, where it may run five or six knots.

Anchorages, Moorings. There are several places to anchor in the area. The basin to the east of Oven Mouth is deep, but it shoals on the east side. Perhaps you can locate the 13-foot area in the middle. There is a comfortable and quiet anchorage in 30 feet of water between the tips of land directly east of Oven Mouth, out of the current.

The basin probably is a little too large, with too much fetch from the south, to be considered the perfect hurricane hole, but it comes close.

Another anchoring possibility is west of Oven Mouth, in about 25 feet at low, just north of the 45-foot spot, near some private moorings. This will put you north of the current that pours through Oven Mouth and hits High Head about in the middle. Watch your depths and do not go too far north here; it shoals rapidly.

WISCASSET ★★★★ All facilities
Charts: 13288, **13293**

Proclaiming itself "the prettiest village in Maine," Wiscasset is well worth the 14-mile trip up the Sheepscot River. There are wonderful old homes open to the public, antique shops, museums, stores, and good restaurants. Best of all, this is a delightful and peaceful spot for strolling.

Once alive with shipyards and great schooners, the waterfront today is strangely silent. Only the rotting piles and sad wrecks of two four-masters hint of what once was.

Approaches. The approaches to Wiscasset could not be simpler. Deep all the way to the town, the Sheepscot River makes a dramatic left turn around the northern tip of Westport Island. Leave

to port one of the world's largest osprey nests, on can "25" at the turn.

The wooden blockhouse of Fort Edgecomb will be to your right, and ahead will loom the huge red-brick Central Maine Power plant and communications tower on Birch Point. On your starboard bow is the village of Wiscasset, through which Route 1 passes before it crosses the Sheepscot on a graceful new fixed bridge (vertical clearance 25 feet). Near the bridge lie the decaying hulls of the schooners *Hesper* and *Luther Little*.

Anchorages, Moorings. You can anchor anywhere south and southwest of the docks off Wiscasset in 25 to 30 feet, with good holding ground in mud bottom. Protection is good unless a heavy southerly is blowing. The boats ride to the strong current.

Check with the Wiscasset Yacht Club to see whether a member's mooring might be available. There are a number of empty moorings festooned with kelp and with unknown ground tackle. Beware.

Another less convenient possibility is a mooring or float at Sheepscot Marine or The Eddy (see below).

Getting Ashore. If you are on a mooring, take the dinghy in to the floats at the town pier, the town landing, or the yacht club. As in all swift-moving tidal rivers, be careful and do not overload the dinghy.

For the Boat. *Town Pier.* South of the schooners, the big town pier is marked by a tall flagpole. There is 15 feet alongside at low. You may stay for two days with the permission of the harbormaster, and use the dinghy floats. Gas and diesel may be obtained by tank truck.

Town Landing. Next southward is a smaller town landing and float.

Wiscasset Yacht Club (tel. 882-9275). Next come the docks and floats of the Wiscasset Yacht Club, whose low, white clubhouse has a green roof and a sign on top. This is a nice, friendly little club which offers showers and a pay phone. There is 15 feet of water at low along the float landings, and water is available. Moorings are put out by the town's harbormaster, but the club steward may be able to tell you if one is available.

Sheepscot Marine, Inc. (Ch. 16; tel. 882-7152). Sheepscot Marine is on the west side of Clough Point (the tip of Westport Island), about three-quarters of a mile across the harbor from Wiscasset. Owner Vic Churchill has been vigorously expanding facilities, both for sail and power. Moorings are available, some with 1,500-pound blocks, or you can stay alongside the floats, with 12 feet of water at low. Water and electricity are available, but no fuel. The yard makes all kinds of repairs, and there is a 15-ton boatlift that can handle boats up to 45 feet. There are showers and marine supplies.

The current off the yard is strong, five knots or more. It is also peculiar, almost always running in the same direction (north), tailing off in strength near high tide. If your dinghy is inadequate for the passage, you could ask the yard to run you over to town.

The Eddy Marina (Ch. 16; tel. 882-7776). Located on the east side of the Sheepscot, southeast of Davis Island, in North Edgecomb, The Eddy has 34 moorings and space alongside the floats with 17 feet at low. Gas, diesel, water, electricity, and ice are available, and a shower. There is a small chandlery that carries charts. The yard will run you over to Wiscasset in their skiff.

Fort Edgecomb and the Muddy Rudder Restaurant are within walking distance, and it is about a mile across the bridge to Wiscasset. The house prepared for Marie Antoinette (see sidebar) overlooks the marina.

For the Crew. Within a few minutes' walk of the Wiscasset waterfront you will find just about anything you need. There are drugstores, a market, hardware stores, laundromat, beauty shops, bank, pay phones, and the bus station. The post office is not far up Main Street (Route 1). The nearest liquor store is the Quik-Stop, out Route 27 and one-fourth mile from the center of town.

You might have lunch or dinner at Le Garage, a big yellow building on the waterfront looking out over the abandoned schooners and the bay.

Things to Do. Much of Wiscasset looks as it did a century ago, and is included in a National Historic District. Stores in town offer a Wiscasset area guide, which identifies the historic buildings and museums and suggests a walking tour. There are many examples (some open to the public) of the splendid architecture made possible by the prosperity of this shipping town and its cosmopolitan citizens.

Near the town landing is the handsome, red-brick Old Custom House, now a gift shop. On the hill overlooking the harbor, the elegant 1807 Castle Tucker will catch your eye, and in town is the Nickels-Sortwell house (also 1807). The Carlton house (1804), on High Street, was bought by shipowner Moses Carlton for 100 puncheons of rum. Before the days of banks, he had his cash wheelbarrowed up the hill in kegs and dumped into chests in the cellar.

The Musical Wonder House (1852), close by on High Street, has a fascinating collection of antique music boxes and Steinway player pianos that are shown and played in rooms furnished with antiques of the period.

Wander along the waterfront and ponder the fate of the *Hesper* and the *Luther Little*. As the sign says, "You are looking at the last 4-masted schooners in the world . . . . History tells us that 562 four-masters were built in the USA. The only evidence that they ever existed lies before you."

In the other direction, along the railroad tracks past the yacht club, is a tiny island reached by a footbridge. Once the site of a shipyard, deserted Whites Island is a good spot for a picnic or just a rest in the shade.

A couple of blocks up Main Street, and then north out Federal Street (Route 218), you will find the Ancient Cemetery, and beyond that the Old Gaol and Lincoln County Museum (.7 mile from the waterfront). The jail is built of solid granite blocks—walls, floor and ceiling—and windows are barred with strap iron. Several deaths and a birth were recorded here, but no escapes. The orig-

WISCASSET—DAYS OF GLORY, DAYS OF GLOOM

At one time the busiest port north of Boston, with its large, protected, and ice-free harbor, Wiscasset has known both great prosperity and economic oblivion.

For the first settlers, fish came in great quantities from the Sheepscot River, and the surrounding forest provided almost limitless lumber. The early fortunes of Wiscasset men were made in the Caribbean trade: fish and lumber to build the plantations and feed the slaves, barrel staves to ship their rum.

Shipbuilding began in earnest in the late 1760s, and more fortunes were made in trade with Europe. Francs and pieces-of-eight were accepted as good currency in Wiscasset, and the local schools taught French, Italian, and Spanish. Citizens of Wiscasset were citizens of the world.

Perhaps this explains why such a pragmatic sea captain as Samuel Clough risked himself and his ship in an attempt to save Queen Marie Antoinette from the guillotine. His ship, the *Sally*, was loaded with furnishings, objets d'art, and the queen's personal belongings in preparation for her escape, while back home in North Edgecomb, Captain Clough's simple farmhouse was being prepared to receive a queen.

As Maine author Louise Dickinson Rich suggests, Mrs. Clough may have resented her husband's news that "he was refurnishing the house for this woman." Mrs. Clough undoubtedly was nervous about entertaining a royal guest and wondering if "she'd be satisfied with a good clam chowder and a slab of johnnycake."

As it turned out, before she could be brought aboard the *Sally*, Marie Antoinette was seized by the mob. All of Captain Clough's generous and romantic plans went for naught, and he was lucky to escape with his own head.

This golden age came to an abrupt end with the Napoleonic Wars. Both France and Britain seized neutral ships trading with the enemy. President Jefferson's resulting Embargo Act of 1807 and the War of 1812 left New England's shipping tied up at the docks. Rigging was stowed, topmasts sent down, and the mainmast trucks covered with tar barrels, known as "Jefferson's nightcaps."

Fortunes dwindled, and a period of economic decline set in from which Wiscasset never recovered. In 1866 and 1870, great fires consumed the waterfront—all the piers, docks, and marine enterprises that had been the heart of the town—and many of the old houses. Such setbacks destroyed the will to dream and risk that marked Wiscasset men. In 1913, the Custom House was closed, and for the first time in more than a century, Wiscasset no longer invited ships from abroad.

---

inal graffiti are still on the walls.

For another good outing, walk the bridge across the Sheepscot, take the first right at the Muddy Rudder, and go right again at the sign for Fort Edgecomb (about 1¼ miles each way). Here, surrounding the wooden blockhouse built to defend Wiscasset during the War of 1812, you will find a lovely state park with picnic tables.

BOOTHBAY HARBOR REGION

DAMARISCOVE ISLAND ★★★★★ No facilities
Charts: 13288, **13293**

Long before Plymouth and Jamestown, Damariscove was a bustling harbor filled with as many as 30 ships, and a major trade center. "Here was the chief maritime port of New England," according to historian Charles Bolton.

The earliest years are unrecorded, but it's clear that fishermen have known Damariscove for at least 400 years. Humphrey Damarill was the resident entrepreneur in 1608 at Damarill's Cove, with ships arriving from European ports to trade for fish and furs, and fishermen bringing their catch ashore to split and salt and dry on stages.

There was a year-round fishing community here in 1622, under the ownership of Sir Ferdinando Gorges. That year, Edward Winslow of Plymoth Plantation came to Damariscove to plead for rations of food, which were offered generously. When the first Indian War broke out in 1676, settlers in Maine fled to the safety of the outlying islands. Some 300 went first to Damariscove and then to Monhegan. Damariscove was attacked by Indians in 1676 and again in 1689.

As every local child has heard by the fire on a winter's night, that was the year that Captain Richard Pattishall, owner of Damariscove, was killed by Indians aboard his sloop at Pemaquid and thrown into the sea. His body came ashore on Damariscove, and to this day the lonely traveler walking on the foggy headlands may encounter the headless Captain Pattishall, or hear the howling of his faithful dog.

For another 2½ centuries, the people of Damariscove fished and farmed, until modern times. Alberta Poole, who grew up on Damariscove between 1910 and 1922, related her experiences in *Coming of Age on Damariscove Island*. At the time, there were 25 or 30 residents: her father Isaac and her uncle Chester, who raised garden produce, poultry, eggs, and milk for sale to the resort on Squirrel Island; the fishing community; and the seven members of the lifesaving station. With the Depression, Isaac and Chester Poole and their combined 13 children moved to the mainland. The Coast Guard station was abandoned in 1959, when the only residents remaining were the summer fishermen.

In 1966, Damariscove was given to The Nature Conservancy, and it has reverted to the remote and uninhabited spot it was before the Europeans came. For the cruising yachtsman with a sense of history, it is an extraordinary experience to visit what may well have been the first permanent settlement in the New World and find only a few fish shacks and a crumbling granite pier.

If you are making a passage along the coast and have no need for services, Damariscove is a convenient and reasonably protected harbor under normal conditions. It is also a place of wild and desolate beauty worth going a long way to visit. The proximity to the Boothbay region means that day-trippers are attracted to Damariscove, so avoid arriving on weekends or holidays.

Damariscove Island is 1.7 miles long and divided almost in two by a narrow neck. The northern portion, called Wood End, was once forested before a series of disastrous fires. It is now a nest-

Boats anchored in the inner pool of Damariscove Island, past the dilapidated stone pier, on a busy weekend. (Peter Ralston photo)

112

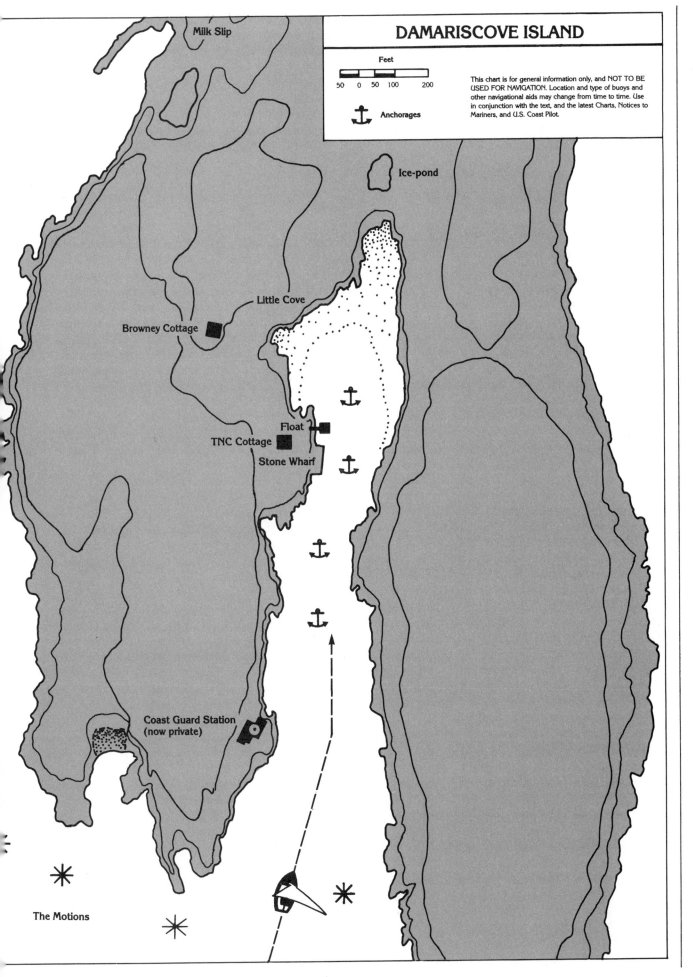

DAMARISCOVE ISLAND

Feet
50 0 50 100 200

⚓ Anchorages

This chart is for general information only, and NOT TO BE USED FOR NAVIGATION. Location and type of buoys and other navigational aids may change from time to time. Use in conjunction with the text, and the latest Charts, Notices to Mariners, and U.S. Coast Pilot.

Milk Slip

Ice-pond

Little Cove

Browney Cottage

Float

TNC Cottage

Stone Wharf

Coast Guard Station
(now private)

The Motions

ing island for several species of birds, including the major site for eiders in this country.

The southern section is almost treeless as well. There are a few lobstermen's shacks, a small house for Nature Conservancy interns, one cottage dating from the years when there was a farming and dairy community on the island, and the abandoned Coast Guard station at the mouth of the harbor, now a private home.

Approaches. The harbor itself is a deep, narrow slot in the southern end, no more than 100 feet wide at low tide but easy to enter (see sketch map). From red-and-white gong "TM," steer a compass course toward the center of the harbor, leaving The Motions to port. Swells breaking on these ledges show clearly where they are.

As you come abreast of the western tip of the island, favor the left-hand side of the channel to avoid a ledge making out from the eastern shore. From there on, the harbor is clear of dangers, so simply run down the middle.

Anchorages, Moorings. There are two choices for anchoring: the outer pool just north of the Coast Guard station and the inner pool past the narrow neck and the stone pier.

The outer pool has a sand bottom and 11 feet of water, with room for three or four boats to anchor comfortably, far enough north of the Coast Guard station to be reasonably protected from ocean swells and southwesterlies. A stern anchor will help keep you lined up with the narrow channel. In these tight quarters, consider using chain and short scope. A fisherman anchor would be useful in dealing with the kelp. There are two private moorings with 800-pound blocks in deep water just off the Coast Guard station.

There is better protection in the inner pool and six feet of depth, but also a lot of kelp on the bottom, which makes anchoring very difficult. It shoals rapidly beyond the halfway point of the inner pool. A resident fisherman, Dick Hammond, lives here year round with his family aboard the green sloop *Otok;* he acts as informal harbormaster, and is knowledgeable both about anchoring and about the island itself. If the harbor is crowded or a strong southwesterly is bringing in a surge, go somewhere else for the night; it's easy to get in trouble here.

Getting Ashore. Land your dinghy at The Nature Conservancy float just north of the stone wharf. The Nature Conservancy asks that you sign in at the registration box nearby, and read the posted regulations.

Things to Do. Damariscove is open to the public "for careful day use." That means no camping, no open fires, no trash; dogs on leashes. Subject to those guidelines, you are free to hike around the island. Nature Conservancy interns may be available to show you the way to some petroglyphs, or to lead you on a delightful hike around the cliffs of the southeastern tip. In season there are abundant blueberries, blackberries, strawberries, raspberries, and wildflowers.

Walk along the main trails through the meadows to the spring at the head of the harbor, which used to supply the fishing ships. The smaller trails are made by muskrats, which can be ferocious when cornered. From there, you can work your way north to the large freshwater pond shown on the chart, but stay high along the eastern ridge to avoid deep puckerbrush and poison ivy. Bird- and muskrat-watchers will love this pond, but don't get your hopes up for a swim—it's not too pleasant.

There's another nice walk to the Milk Slip, from where Isaac Poole rowed his dory to Squirrel Island to sell milk to summer residents, never missing a day from the first of June until October, no matter what the weather.

The southwestern tip of the island is dominated by the handsome Coast Guard station, built in 1897, originally a U.S. Lifesaving Station.

The northern end of the island is a bird-nesting area, off-limits until mid-August.

SQUIRREL ISLAND

Charts: 13288, **13293**

Right in the middle of Booth Bay stands high, wooded Squirrel Island, an exclusive summer retreat for generations. Lawn tennis championships were held here in the 1920s and 1930s, and there are wonderful old turn-of-the-century cottages with an air of calm assurance. Members have a 99-year lease on their homes, renewable for $1.

Despite this apparent exclusivity, visiting yachtsmen are welcome, and you can land to explore. The island's exposed location makes it a poor choice for an overnight anchorage, but it's a delightful day stop, with inviting paths most of the way around the coast.

On the western side are two coves. The smaller and more northerly one is used by the boat from Boothbay Harbor to unload supplies. Squirrel Cove, to the south, is the home of SIBA (Squirrel Island Boating Association), which usually maintains a guest mooring on the outer fringe of the cove.

Pick up a mooring and row ashore to the SIBA floats. There is deep water alongside the floats, and water is available. Behind the boathouse are two pay phones, but there are no other facilities.

When you land, you will immediately see a concrete path with railings. This takes you around the island, perhaps an hour's walk. By all means, take it. The paths lead to every house on the island and afford wonderful views of the surrounding islands and peninsulas. Only service vehicles are allowed on Squirrel, and no bikes, roller skates, or skateboards are permitted on the path, but you are likely to meet a summer resident carting his groceries in a little red wagon. The northern section of the path turns into a beautiful woodland trail, and there is a private sand beach on the north side.

If you walk left from SIBA's floats, past another beach and the chapel, you will reach "downtown" Squirrel Island, which boasts a post office, pay phones, Town Hall, and a tearoom (open to members only).

BOOTHBAY HARBOR ★★★

Charts: 13288, 13293, **13296**

⬚ 4 All facilities

Boothbay Harbor is one of the best harbors on the Maine coast. Not only is it large and well protected, but it is easy to enter under all conditions. There are all the services a yachtsman might need. If you are coasting east or west, it is very convenient, less than five miles off the direct route.

The harbor—alive with a bustle of boats of every description—has the general air of a city of the sea. The town, like Kennebunkport, is crowded and touristy, but offers a great variety of shops and restaurants and plenty of special summer activities.

The town's annual Windjammer Days festival and the Friendship Sloop Races are wonderful spectacles, but reserve ahead if you want a berth or a mooring during those times.

Approaches. Coming from the west, round green bell "1C" off Southport Island, leaving The Cuckolds (two little bare islets) to port. The Cuckolds Light is a distinctive white octagonal tower 48 feet high on a dwelling, with a foghorn and radio beacon. Pass either side of high Squirrel Island, observing red lighted buoy "4." Head for red lighted buoy "8" off Tumbler Island, leaving Burnt Island (with a lighthouse) and Mouse Island to port. Do not go inside Tumbler. Leave lighted green buoy "1A" to port at McFarland Island and enter the inner harbor.

Coming from the east, find red-and-white bell "HL" at the beginning of Fisherman Island Passage, sailing north of the Hypocrites, Fisherman Island, and small, grassy Ram Island (with a lighthouse and foghorn). Once past nun "2A," leave high Squirrel Island to port, and enter as above.

Anchorages, Moorings. There are a dozen or more places to find a mooring or berth (see sketch map). The most convenient locations are in the inner harbor, at the northeast corner of Boothbay Harbor. Tugboat Inn Marina and Boothbay Harbor Marina are right in town. There is no room to anchor in the inner harbor.

Carousel Marina and Brown's Wharf Marina, along the eastern side of the harbor, are well down Spruce Point and half a mile or more from town. The distance has some advantages since this part of the harbor is less noisy.

Best bet is the Boothbay Harbor Yacht Club, which has a good number of moorings in the western part of Boothbay Harbor, inside McKown Point. Facilities are good, although it is not close to town. Other possibilities are listed below.

For The Boat: Inner Harbor, Western Side. *Boothbay Harbor Marina (Ch. 16; tel. 633-6003).* Right in town, next to the footbridge, this is a full-service marina. There are several finger floats and ample room for transient berthing, with 16 feet of water along the outer floats, and a few moorings. Electricity, water, and ice are available. There are showers, pay phones, and a laundromat in the building on the dock.

Public Landing. Just south of Fisherman's Wharf Inn and Pier 6 are the floats of the public landing, with six feet alongside and a three-hour maximum tie-up. There are no facilities. The harbormaster keeps his launch here.

Tugboat Inn Marina (Ch. 16; tel. 633-4434). The Tugboat Inn has a large marina and many moorings just south of Pier 8. This is the first facility on your left as you enter the inner harbor. The marina provides a large amount of dockage, with 12 feet of water at the outer floats. Electricity, water, ice, and phones are available, but no fuel; there are showers and a laundromat.

Down East Yacht Club. The club has no clubhouse, but it maintains several moorings off the Tugboat Inn Marina. These are white balls marked with a burgee and DEYC, available to members of other yacht clubs for boats of 40 feet or less, for a fee. At the northern section of the Tugboat Inn Marina, the club also has one side of a dock where you can tie up briefly for water and electricity.

Sample's Shipyard (Ch. 16 or 68; tel. 633-3171). Around to the west from the inner harbor, Sample's is recognizable by its yellow buildings and two marine railways. One of these is a 700-ton giant on which the huge windjammers regularly are

Boothbay Harbor is large, well protected, and easy to enter. The town itself can be crowded and touristy, but offers all the services a yachtsman might need. (Hylander photo)

hauled. Wooden minesweepers were built here during World War II. While the yard no longer builds ships, it has complete vessel repair facilities. A mechanic is available at all times, including weekends. There is a chandlery, and the yard maintains 24 moorings nearby, which are quite exposed.

Signal Point Marina (Ch. 16; tel. 633-6920). This marina is near McFarland Point, with 57 slips at the southern end of Wotton's Lobster Dock (see sketch map). Gas, diesel, water, electricity, showers, laundry facilities, and cable television are available, plus minor repairs.

For the Crew: Inner Harbor, Western Side. In this part of town, you are within a few hundred yards of every kind of shop imaginable, including Carbone's Market. The state liquor store is in the shopping center north of town, .8 mile from the waterfront. Note the free trolley-buses from Rocktide (see below). For a water taxi, contact Brown's Wharf (see below).

One of the unique facilities serving Boothbay Harbor is St. Andrews Hospital (tel. 633-2121), where you can take your dinghy right up to the back door and walk to the emergency room. The

hospital's dock and float are on the west side of Mill Cove, opposite the lobster dock.

For the Boat: Inner Harbor, Eastern Side. *Rocktide Motor Inn (tel. 633-4455).* The floats at Rocktide are available for people coming to eat at the restaurant or stay at the inn. You can bring your boat along the floats on the outside, with 12 feet of water at low, or take your dinghy to the inner floats. Rocktide is popular among residents and tourists alike, so reservations are a good idea. Rocktide and the town of Boothbay Harbor run convenient free trolley-buses all around town and also to the shopping center.

Cap'n Fish's Motel and Marina (Ch. 16; tel 633-6605). There are seven moorings here, and 125 feet of dockage, as well as ice and electricity. Reserve ahead. Breakfast is served in the restaurant.

Brown's Wharf Marina (Ch. 9 or 16; tel 633-5440). Brown's has 40 slips, with 8 to 20 feet alongside, and a number of transient moorings. Water, electricity, ice, and showers are available, but no fuel. The restaurant is right at the water's edge. A water taxi into town leaves Brown's Wharf on an hourly schedule, visiting Fisherman's Wharf. It is also available on call to any dock or moored boat.

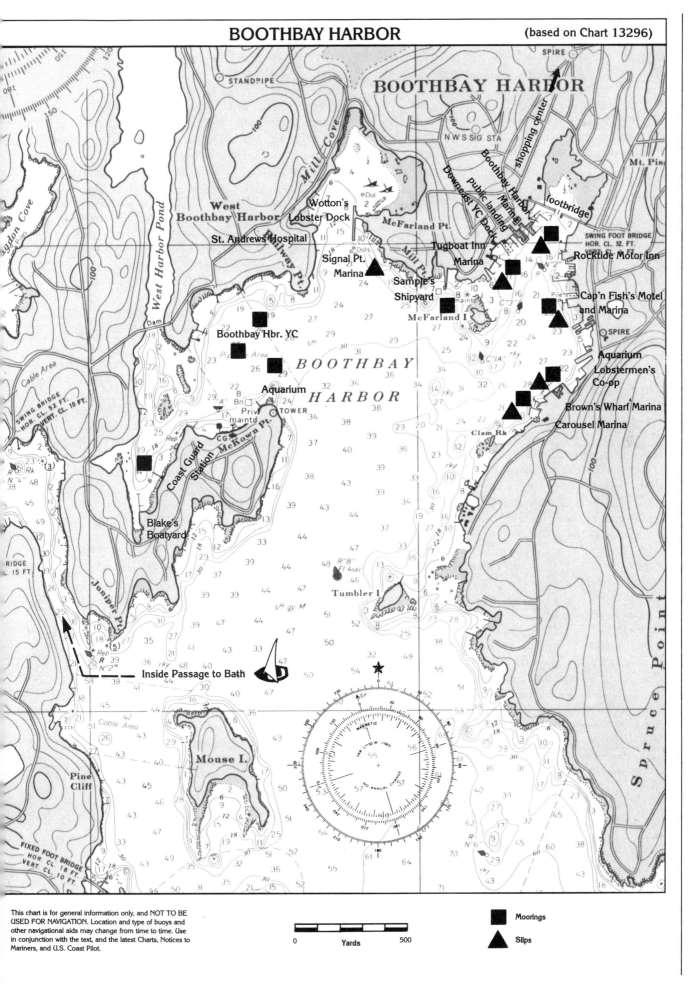

BOOTHBAY HARBOR

(based on Chart 13296)

BOOTHBAY HARBOR

SPIRE

STANDPIPE

N W S SIG STA

Mt. Pis

Mill Cove

West Boothbay Harbor

Wotton's Lobster Dock

McFarland Pt.

Boothbay Harbor Marina

shopping center

footbridge

St. Andrews Hospital

Downeast YC Dock

public landing

SWING FOOT BRIDGE HOR. CL. 32. FT.

Signal Pt. Marina

Mill Pt.

Tugboat Inn Marina

Rocktide Motor Inn

Sample's Shipyard

McFarland I

Cap'n Fish's Motel and Marina

West Harbor Pond

Millway Pt.

Dam

Boothbay Hbr. YC

BOOTHBAY HARBOR

Aquarium Lobstermen's Co-op

Aquarium

Priv maintd

TOWER

Brown's Wharf Marina

Carousel Marina

Clam Rk

Cable Area

SWING BRIDGE HOR. CL. 52. FT. VERT. CL. 10 FT.

Coast Guard Station McKown Pt.

CG

Blake's Boatyard

Juniper Pt.

Tumbler I

BRIDGE 15 FT.

Inside Passage to Bath

MAGNETIC

VAR 17°30'W (1983) NO ANNUAL CHANGE

Pine Cliff

Cable Area

Mouse I.

Spruce Point

FIXED FOOT BRIDGE HOR. CL. 18 FT. VERT. CL. 10 FT.

This chart is for general information only, and NOT TO BE USED FOR NAVIGATION. Location and type of buoys and other navigational aids may change from time to time. Use in conjunction with the text, and the latest Charts, Notices to Mariners, and U.S. Coast Pilot.

0   Yards   500

■ Moorings

▲ Slips

117

Carousel Marina (Ch. 16; tel. 633-2922). At the southern end of the harbor, below a block of gray condos, Carousel has a large, full-service marina, with 340 feet of dockage and 22 moorings. You can reserve ahead. Facilities include gas, diesel, water, and electricity; groceries, produce, beer, wine, ice and marine supplies at the store; laundry facilities, breakfast and lunch counter, a sitting room with television, and showers. A yacht mechanic and a diver are available, there is a canvas shop, and electronic repairs can be made.

For the Crew: Inner Harbor, Eastern Side. Groceries are available at the small market at the eastern end of the footbridge, in addition to Carousel Marina. There is a fish market next to Cap'n Fish's. For supplies and shops of all kinds, walk across the footbridge into town.

For the Boat: West of McKown Point. *Boothbay Harbor Yacht Club (Ch. 9 or 16; tel. 633-5750).* At the northwest side of the bay, opposite McKown Point, the active Boothbay Harbor Yacht Club has a low, white building over the water on pilings, with a "BHYC" sign, a dock, and floats. The club maintains a large number of moorings, but it is a good idea to reserve ahead for weekends during big events. Launch service is provided (three blasts). There is 20 feet of water alongside the floats, with water and electricity but no fuel. Overnight dockage is not permitted. Bring your dinghy in to the inner float.

The club has showers, telephones, ice, and laundry machines. Visiting yachtsmen are welcome to use the bar and restaurant; jackets and ties are required for evening meals. There are also two tennis courts that visitors may use. The West Boothbay Harbor post office is next to the tennis courts.

Blake's Boatyard (Ch. 16; tel. 633-5040). Tucked down in the western corner of the bay, Blake's is a good, small yard with probably the best protection in Boothbay Harbor; this is where to be if bad weather is threatening. Unfortunately, most of the moorings here are rented on a seasonal basis, with only occasional room for a transient. Water and electricity can be obtained at the floats, but no fuel. The yard has three marine railways and can perform most repairs. There is a well-stocked chandlery that carries charts.

For the Crew: West of McKown Point. To get into town, call a cab or hitch a ride. Another possibility is to phone the quick and reliable Brown's Water Taxi (Ch. 16 or 633-5440).

Things to Do. Wandering around town, window-shopping, eating ice cream cones, and looking at the tourists—those are the favorite occupations in Boothbay Harbor.

Check what's playing at the Carousel Music Theatre at the shopping center (tel. 633-5297).

A delightful evening outing is to row across the harbor to the Lobstermen's Co-op, tie up at the float, and have a lobster or clam dinner outdoors, overlooking the lobsterboats next door. Good food at reasonable prices. Next door is the entertaining Oceans East aquarium. You can also get there by walking across the footbridge at the head of the harbor, passing en route the beautiful Catholic church, Our Lady Queen of Peace, whose reassuring chimes float across the busy harbor. Nearby is the striking memorial "in honor of the proud, independent fishermen of Maine who lost their lives at sea."

From the waterfront in town, all sorts of excursions are available. For example, you can take a trip up the Inside Passage through the Hell Gates and the Sasanoa River to Bath. Or circumnavigate beautiful Southport Island, or run out to historic Damariscove Island.

Go deepsea fishing, cruise to a lobster feast, or explore the neighboring islands on a bright pink vessel, the *Pink Lady*. There is a wonderful all-day cruise to Monhegan Island, and short cruises through the harbor and out to Squirrel Island. Information booths for all these trips are easily located dockside. Noted sailor and author Roger Duncan offers daylong and half-day trips on his Friendship sloop, *Eastward*, by reservation only (tel. 633-4780).

In the western part of the harbor, you might enjoy a visit to the little aquarium at the end of McKown Point, operated by Maine's Department of Marine Resources. There you will find displays showing various fisheries, old sailing directions, and a "touch tank" full of live marine animals that you touch at your own risk.

LINEKIN BAY ★★★

Charts: 13288, **13293**

Almost deserted compared to Boothbay Harbor next door, Linekin Bay is a lovely, wide-open place to sail, with the encircling arms of a wooded shore all around. There are some ledges and rocks in the bay, but they are obvious or well marked.

The approach to Linekin Bay is easy. Leaving large Squirrel Island to port, pass between small, wooded Negro Island and can "1." There you are.

Good anchorage may be found in Lewis Cove at the northwest end of the bay (see below).

Paul E. Luke, Inc. (tel. 633-4971). As you enter Linekin Bay, you'll see a large installation on the eastern shore near nun "4," with several sheds, a crane and a dock and float—but no signs of any kind. This is the well-known yard of boatbuilder Paul E. Luke. Luke has several moorings and space alongside, with 15 feet at low. Visit the interesting little museum with memorabilia of 50 years of boat-building.

LEWIS COVE ★★★ No facilities

Charts: 13288, **13293**

In the northwest corner of Linekin Bay, Lewis Cove provides tranquility and good protection, from south and southwest around to the northeast. If you're not in the mood for the bustle of Boothbay Harbor, this is a delightful alternative.

Approaches. After entering Linekin Bay, run up along the coast of Spruce Point, leaving can "3" and Cabbage Island to starboard.

Anchorages, Moorings. Anchor in 24 feet of water at low near the Spruce Point shore, as far up into Lewis Cove as you can get. Note the arc of rocks extending from the spit of land to the north and curving about 250 yards down to the Spruce Point shore. You may find it helpful here to put out a stern anchor.

Getting Ashore. Land at Barrett Park, on the spit of land to the north.

For the Crew. Although there are no facilities of any kind in Lewis Cove, you can easily walk across the neck of Spruce Point from Barrett Park to the eastern shore of Boothbay Harbor. It is a five-minute row plus a 10-minute walk, emerging on Bay Street.

Things to Do. Row to Barrett Park, where you'll find pleasant greenery, picnic tables, stone piers, and beaches. Another possibility is to explore Cabbage Island, used by the local people for clambakes and picnics.

DAMARISCOTTA RIVER and Johns Bay

Charts: 13288, **13293**

The Damariscotta is a modest river, with neither the grand scale of the Kennebec nor the cruising charms of the Sheepscot. It is also a relatively easy river to navigate, where the current asserts itself only in one or two narrows and the upper reaches are well marked. From the mouth to the head of navigation is only 14 miles, so it can be explored in a day or two.

On the river are two or three harbors of special interest to the cruising sailor. Christmas Cove is small and crowded, but cozy, hospitable to sailboats, family-style, and low-key. Nearby, the Thread of Life is charming not only for its name but for the beauty of this little passage.

The river is famous for its boatbuilders—Gamage in South Bristol; W.I. Adams, Rice Brothers, and Hodgdon Brothers in East Boothbay. Goudy & Stevens bought the Adams yard in 1924, merged with Hodgdon Bros., and continues to this day. They can fix whatever is wrong with your boat, or build you a trawler or an exquisite 100-foot schooner yacht.

Above Christmas Cove are handsome stretches of river, with high wooded banks and few houses, not much changed since the Indians called it the "river of many fishes" and used it in their annual spring migrations to the sea.

The current runs strong through the Narrows off Fort Island, but the passage is wide enough and well marked.

Three miles upriver from Christmas Cove is one of the great secluded spots of the midcoast. Seal Cove is a special place—hard to enter, hard to leave.

Beyond Seal Cove are two agreeable harbors, Pleasant Cove and Wadsworth. Across the way from them is the Ira C. Darling Center of the University of Maine, which offers the opportunity to spend a fascinating hour or two learning about lobsters, clams, and aquaculture.

Thereafter, the river winds peacefully northward to Damariscotta and Newcastle, lovely, quiet little towns at the river's head of navigation.

Beyond the Damariscotta River to the east lies Johns Bay—only five miles long, but lovely and unspoiled, and offering three extremely well-protected anchorages. Although Johns Bay is physically connected to the Damariscotta River by The Gut, the two bodies of water are entirely different in character. Even the two halves of the harbor at South Bristol—bisected by a small swing bridge—are quite different in feeling and will be treated as two separate entries.

LITTLE RIVER ★★★
Charts: 13288, **13293**

Little River is a long, narrow inlet extending northward into Linekin Neck at the west side of the entrance to the Damariscotta River. While impossible to enter in bad weather, and a bit daunting to enter under any conditions, it will reward you with a peaceful anchorage in a working harbor seldom visited by yachtsmen.

Approaches. Do not try to enter the harbor in heavy weather; the sea breaks all across the entrance. Go in on a rising tide; there is a five-foot spot in the channel. Much of the problem with entering under normal conditions is that the chart has too small a scale, so you can't tell where to go. The following notes should be of help.

Starting at the green-and-red gong at the entrance, leave to port the red-and-green nun (not shown on the 29th Ed. of chart 13293) and run just east of the abandoned daybeacon, which stands near the north end of a rock right in the middle of the entrance. This rock is not large and runs roughly north-south. Leave it quite close aboard to port (perhaps 40 feet).

After passing the rock with the beacon, continue on almost the same course toward the point at the western side of the entrance. On the point is a gray house with three dormer windows. As you get within about 100 yards of the point, bend right into midchannel (note the five-foot spot here), leaving to starboard the long ledge shown on the chart, which is visible at most tides.

The worst is over. Run down the middle of the channel, leaving to starboard little Treasure Island and its handsome brown house, with bell and binnacle on the lawn, and enter the inner harbor. You will find good water as far north as the dock on the left with the gray-shingled boathouse.

Anchorages, Moorings. After the inner harbor opens up north of Treasure Island, there is room to anchor midchannel in 13 to 18 feet of water. Moorings are available from Spar Shed Marina.

Getting Ashore. Row in to the dinghy float at Little River Lobster or Spar Shed Marina.

For the Boat. *Little River Lobster (tel. 633-2648).* Look for a two-story shingled building on the eastern shore, with a series of floats. Little River Lobster can provide gas and diesel at the float, which has 14 feet alongside at low.

Spar Shed Marina (tel. 633-4389). Just beyond Little River Lobster, on the opposite side, is the dock and gray boathouse of Spar Shed Marina. In addition to moorings, Spar Shed has six slips, with seven feet of water at low, water, ice, and electricity.

For the Crew. Groceries may be found at the East Boothbay General Store, two miles north.

Things to Do. Row your dinghy north to the far end of the cove. You can land at either end of the dam to the east, and then take a pleasant walk north or south on a dirt road. Rent bicycles from Spar Shed Marina and pedal a mile south to the Ocean Point Inn for a good dinner, or bike around scenic Ocean Point.

CHRISTMAS COVE ★★★
Charts: 13288, **13293** (Inset)

Ever since Christmas 1614, when Captain John Smith dropped anchor in this picturesque spot, Christmas Cove has been a favorite of sailors. Protection is excellent from all directions except the southwest, so there seldom are problems during the summer. Christmas Cove is a busy little place, always full of movement, but it retains its low-key atmosphere. Seals, mallards, and ospreys are fellow residents.

Approaches. The usual approach is west of Inner Heron Island, starting at the red-and-green gong off Little River. Pick up nun "4" north of Inner Heron Island and then aim for the square, shingled tower near the head of Christmas Cove.

The entrance to the cove is tight, about 35 yards wide, and you are likely to find kids racing small sailboats right in the narrowest part of the channel.

As you can see on the chart 13293 inset, there are two tiny dots of land on each side of the entrance. Red daybeacon "2" is on your right coming in, but do not cut it close, since it is 50 feet or so from the end of the ledge. Green daybeacon "3" stands at the edge of the shoal water on the left side of the entrance. Pass about halfway between the two beacons, and expect to find boats moored just inside.

Anchorages, Moorings. Most of the moorings belong to Coveside Marina, with several available for transients. Get here early if you want one; they often are taken by early afternoon.

Christmas Cove is packed with moorings, so it is doubtful you could find enough swinging room to anchor.

Getting Ashore. Row your dinghy in to the Coveside dinghy float.

For the Boat. *Coveside Marina (Ch. 16 or 68; tel. 644-8282).* Coveside Marina is the complex of red buildings on the north side of the harbor. To reserve a mooring, call "The Admiral" on VHF. There is limited dockage, with 12 feet alongside the floats at low, electricity, gas, diesel, and ice. Water is for your tanks only, since it is drawn from a well. There is a small chandlery.

The dock and float at the southeast corner of the harbor belong to the private Christmas Cove Improvement Association.

For the Crew. Because of the well water, there is no laundromat, but there are showers and a pay phone at Coveside Marina. The popular marina restaurant serves three meals a day, and dinner reservations may be made for five or more. In good weather, you can eat on the deck.

Across the road is Coveside Inn, with separate accommodations at The Shorefront. The owner and host of the whole complex is cordial Mike Mitchell, who likes to see cruising friends returning year after year.

For provisions, walk 1.2 miles along the Damariscotta River to the Island Grocery and Lunch in South Bristol (tel. 644-8552). It is open daily, well stocked, and has a good supply of fresh seafood. To get there, turn left past the inn and take the next left at a house called "Wigwam" on Westside Road. Coveside Marina can probably arrange a ride back with the groceries, or ask someone in the store.

Things to Do. The walk along the Damariscotta River to South Bristol is pretty and shaded. When you arrive, it is fun to observe one of Maine's most active swing bridges at The Gut and the busy scene in South Bristol Harbor to the east as lobsterboats unload their catch.

For a shorter walk, turn right from Coveside Marina and then walk south on Route 129. You will find a spectacular view of the Thread of Life, and maybe see a sailboat or two tacking through.

THE GUT—WEST OF THE BRIDGE
(SOUTH BRISTOL) ★★ 3
Charts: 13288, **13293** (Inset)

The Gut is a narrow passage between the Damariscotta River and Johns Bay, separating Rutherford Island from the mainland at South Bristol. The west side of The Gut is home to the boatyard made famous by shipbuilder Harvey Gamage. The east side of The Gut is an active lobsterman's harbor with several commercial docks. The boundary between west and east is a small swing bridge that can open up for you on short notice—but check your mast height and the clearance before trying it. Do not assume that you can get through this swing bridge until you have read the fine print on the chart. Overhead power and telephone cables allow a vertical clearance of 55 feet at mean high water.

Depth at the bridge is just under six feet at low, according to the bridgetender, and the current runs two to three knots at most.

Approaches. Coming from the west (Damariscotta River), leave red daybeacon "2" well to starboard and run for the middle of the opening. The bridgetender says that he will open up for one toot, or two toots, or if he sees you coming. This may be the busiest swing bridge in New England, but it is very small-scale and friendly.

Anchorages, Moorings. There is very little room to anchor in The Gut. Your best bet is to get a mooring from Gamage, or lie alongside. There is dockage at the floats east of the long dock, with 12 feet of water at low.

Getting Ashore. Row in to the float at the Gamage yard.

For the Boat. *Gamage Shipbuilder, Inc. (Ch. 16; tel. 644-8181).* Gamage is west of the bridge on the north side of The Gut. Electricity and water are available at the floats, but no fuel. There is a chandlery. The yard has two marine railways and a 25-ton boatlift and can perform most hull and engine repairs.

Many famous boats were designed and built at the Gamage yard, including the 95-foot gaff-rigged sloop *Clearwater*, used to spur the cleanup of the Hudson River.

If you are desperate for fuel, there are a number of commercial operations in the eastern part of The Gut that could provide gas, diesel, and boating supplies. See ahead, under The Gut—east of the bridge.

For the Crew. From the Gamage yard, walk across the swing bridge to the Island Grocery and Lunch, close by in South Bristol, to find a good selection of fresh fish and produce, groceries, beer, and wine. Farrin's Lobster Pound, right next to the bridge, serves lobsters on its outdoor deck.

Things to Do. It is a delightful, shady walk of just over a mile along the Damariscotta River to Christmas Cove. From Gamage, cross the swing bridge and turn right after the Island Grocery.

FARNHAM COVE ★★★   3   No facilities

Charts: 13288, **13293**

On the west side of the Damariscotta River, within sight of East Boothbay, is Farnham Point. Inside of the point is a tiny harbor to which you might repair if there is no room at Christmas Cove.

This little cove is out of the current, pleasant, and well protected from all directions except north. At the head of the cove is a lobster pound.

Approaches. Avoid the six-foot spot north of Farnham Point and come straight down the middle of the slot.

Anchorages, Moorings. Anchor outside the moored boats, in about 16 feet at low, good mud bottom.

EAST BOOTHBAY ★★   3

Charts: 13288, **13293**

East Boothbay is a small community on the west bank of the Damariscotta River, about four miles from its mouth. More of an open roadstead than a harbor, it is exposed to wind and current up and down the river. There are good moorings, however, and almost any repairs can be accomplished.

East Boothbay is an interesting place to visit. Boats under construction at any one time may range from large wooden schooners to state-of-the-art longliners to ferryboats and other commercial craft. This has been the home of Goudy & Stevens for more than half a century, as well as other shipbuilding firms now departed, including Hodgdon Brothers and Rice Brothers. One of the buildings now occupied by G & S belonged to Hodgdon Brothers, founded in 1826, builders of the *Bowdoin*, the schooner that logged 300,000 miles in her 26 trips to the Arctic under Admiral Donald MacMillan. Many famous vessels have gone down the ways at Goudy & Stevens, including a replica of the 104-foot *America*, for which the coveted trophy was named.

Approaches. As you come up the Damariscotta River and pass Farnham Point, the moored boats and large boatsheds at East Boothbay become visible just past can "5."

Anchorages, Moorings. It is too deep to anchor in East Boothbay, so pick up a Goudy & Stevens mooring (in 50 or 60 feet of water). If none is available, there may be space alongside. Or you can run back to Farnham Cove (see preceding writeup) for the night.

Getting Ashore. Take your dinghy to a convenient spot at any of the Goudy & Stevens floats.

For the Boat. The huge, blue shed toward the south end of the anchorage is the shipbuilding firm of Washburn & Doughty (no facilities for yachts). Then come some abandoned structures, followed by Goudy & Stevens, whose several large sheds and buildings stretch around to the north end of the village.

Goudy & Stevens (Ch. 16; tel. 633-3971). Gas and diesel may be obtained along the north side of the floats, with 12 feet alongside. Also available at G & S are water and electricity (at the floats), and ice. There is a chandlery, and the yard has a 100-ton marine railway, a 25-ton boatlift, and two cranes. Repairs of all kinds can be made.

Coastal Marine Electronics (tel. 633-7090). This electronics sales and repair shop is right next to Goudy & Stevens.

Nathaniel S. Wilson (tel. 633-5071). Well-known sailmaker Nat Wilson is based on Lincoln Street in East Boothbay (turn right when you leave Goudy & Stevens, right again on Lincoln, and go up the hill). He can handle sail or rigging repairs as well as new sails. Wilson made the sails for the sloop *Clearwater*, built at the Gamage yard in South Bristol.

For the Crew. The East Boothbay post office is directly across the street from Goudy & Stevens. A short walk up the hill to the left will lead you to the East Boothbay General Store, a small market with limited groceries, beer, wine, newspapers, and ice-cream cones.

Lunch and dinner are served at Lobsterman's Wharf, whose dock and sun umbrellas make it easy to spot, just south of the G & S floats. Customers can tie up at the restaurant's float, and there is a pay phone.

JONES COVE ★★★   1   No facilities

Charts: 13288, **13293**

On the east side of the Damariscotta River, opposite East Boothbay, Jones Cove is a pretty and seldom-used anchorage. There are horses grazing in the meadows and a small sand beach at the head of the cove. It offers no protection from prevailing summer winds but would be useful if the wind came around to the north.

Approaches. The cove is easy to enter. Stay on the west side to avoid the rocks shown on the chart (always visible).

MEADOW COVE

Charts: 13288, **13293**

Meadow Cove is just above East Boothbay, on the west side of the Damariscotta River. While it offers protection from the southwest, it is too deep for comfortable anchoring until you get close to land.

Anchorages, Moorings. Anchor past the southernmost rock, in 12 to 14 feet at low, good mud holding ground.

For a temporary stop, anchor in the little bight just west of Montgomery Point, in 13 feet of water at low.

SEAL COVE ★★★★   No facilities

Charts: 13288, **13293**

Seal Cove, on the eastern bank of the Damariscotta River, must be one of the most beautiful and peaceful harbors in Maine. A family of harbor seals is usually in residence. You may catch them lounging lazily on their favorite haul-out rocks—or suddenly, there they'll be, heads popping up out of the water to eye the visitor with curiosity.

It takes some careful eyeball navigation to enter Seal Cove, but once in, you are perfectly protected and set for a tranquil night.

Approaches. The current runs four to five knots at maximum ebb through The Narrows off Fort Island, with some eddies and boils, but the passage is 100 yards wide and well marked, so you should have no real trouble. Nun "10," marking Eastern Ledge, sometimes tows under.

It is difficult to enter the inner harbor of Seal Cove at high tide, when you can't see the ledges. If you are going all the way in, make your entry on a rising tide, from an hour after low to midtide.

After coming through The Narrows at Fort Point, identify the ledge to your right and long, wooded Hodgsons Island to the east. Continue upriver until you can turn north of Hodgsons Island, leaving its tip to starboard. Then turn south down the slot between Hodgsons and the unnamed island farther east. Go more or less down the middle.

The overhead cable shown on the chart across the entrance to Seal Cove (authorized clearance 40 feet) seems to have disappeared, and ospreys have taken over the poles on each side of the cove. Thus far, however, the Coast Guard has not confirmed that the cable is gone for good, so take a careful look.

Focus now on the long ledge extending south from the head of land on the east bank and the five-foot spot just west of the ledge. Separated from the head of land on the east bank is a small, round island covered with trees. There is then a gap of 100 feet or so, followed by the long ledge, which is now your main concern. Only the northern bit of the ledge shows above water at high tide—as a piece of whitish rock covered with grass. At low tide, the whole ledge is visible.

Having passed the five-foot spot, continue south, paralleling the ledge, but not too closely. About 50 feet west of the long ledge is another little ledge, identifiable by rockweed until mid-tide, but invisible at high tide. When you reach the end of the long ledge, turn to port past its southern tip and enter the anchorage.

It would be wise to sight a compass course that will take you clear of the southern tip of the ledge, in case you decide to leave when the ledge is covered.

Anchorages, Moorings. If you prefer not to enter the inner harbor, or the timing is wrong, anchor almost anywhere along the slot between Hodgsons Island and the unnamed island to the east, in 20 to 22 feet of water at low. This is a well-protected and attractive anchorage, with more breeze and fewer mosquitoes than in the inner one.

If you have entered the inner harbor, anchor east and south of the ledge in 12 to 14 feet of water. Holding ground is good, in mud bottom. You can work your way south quite a way along the east bank, but there will be less swinging room. Watch out for a line of blue buoys strung out for oyster cultivation.

Getting Ashore. You can go ashore on the tiny island at the north end of the ledge, but stay away from the seals on the rocks to the south.

PLEASANT COVE ★★★

No facilities

Charts: 13288, **13293**

This tranquil harbor well deserves its name. Here, surrounded by saltwater farms, you can spend a night out of the river current and away from the world.

Approaches. The entrance to Pleasant Cove is wide and easy. As it narrows, stay in the deeper water near the south bank.

Anchorages, Moorings. You can anchor in 10 to 20 feet of water at low in the mouth of the cove, west of Carlisle Point, north of Pleasant Cove Island.

For better protection and surroundings, go half a mile farther in, anchoring just east of the point that sticks down from the north, in 13 to 14 feet at low, mud bottom. Opposite this point are several moored boats and a dock.

Things to Do. Take your dinghy and explore the rocky points and piney nooks at the end of the cove, or state-owned Pleasant Cove Island.

WADSWORTH COVE ★★★

No facilities

Charts: 13288, **13293**

This anchorage on the Damariscotta's west bank, just above Pleasant Cove, is protected by an encircling arm of ledges to the south and east, and big enough to harbor a number of boats. A handsome hayfield sweeps down to the water from the north and a private dock and float are at the rocky point in the southwest corner.

Approaches. The ledges that make up the eastern and southern parts of this cove are visibile from

low to halftide. Approaching from the south, leave can "11" to port and make a wide left turn into the harbor. The northernmost ledge is considerably west of the can, so do not cut it close.

Anchorages, Moorings. Anchor east of the rocky point (between Wadsworth and Burnham Coves) in 14 to 20 feet of water at low, mud bottom. You will be well protected here by the surrounding ledges and Carlisle Point.

IRA C. DARLING CENTER
(WENTWORTH POINT)

Charts: 13288, **13293**

At Wentworth Point, on the east bank of the Damariscotta, is the Ira C. Darling Center, which conducts research to benefit all state fisheries, traditional and potential. Visitors are welcome at the center, which is part of the University of Maine. Projects range from the restoration of alewives in the Medomak River, smelt in Portland, and Atlantic salmon in the Kennebec, to developing a strain of blue lobsters (to help in tracking lobster movements along the coast).

The laboratory is partly funded by the federal Sea Grant Program and actively supports Maine's growing aquaculture industry. For example, stud-

ies are made of water temperature, flow, and salinity to optimize the growth of shellfish, and genetic experiments to improve the breed of oysters, clams, mussels, and scallops. You may never have tasted a triploid oyster, but they grow 40 percent faster than their backward diploid cousins.

Stop here for a visit, particularly if you appreciate lobsters or other shellfish. You will receive an interesting briefing on research in progress.

There is a guest mooring off the concrete dock and float at Wentworth Point, about three miles north of the Narrows. Call the center on channel 16 or 69 to reserve the mooring, or phone 563-3146.

SALT MARSH COVE

Charts: 13288, **13293**

On the west bank of the Damariscotta, two miles above Pleasant Cove, Salt Marsh Cove mostly dries out, and you are likely to see clammers here on the mudflats. It is possible to sneak in just far enough

past the headlands to get protection, and anchor in 13 to 20 feet at low, mud bottom. Nearby Wadsworth and Pleasant coves are better choices.

HARBOR SEALS

Helena nuzzling her two-day-old male pup. Helena is an important participant in an ongoing research project conducted by *Maine Seal*, a nonprofit organization focusing on research, education, conservation, and management of harbor seals. (Leslie Cowperthwaite photo)

Seals—those appealing creatures with sleek round heads, soft black eyes, and whiskers, friendly and curious, a cross between a golden retriever and a mermaid.

Of the four species of seals most likely to be seen in the Gulf of Maine, the harbor seal is by far the most common. (The others are gray seals, harp seals, and hooded seals.) They vary in color from brown to gray to reddish, and may appear light or dark from a distance, depending on how heavily spotted they are. Their summertime population, sunning themselves on halftide ledges all along the coast of Maine, amounts to 15,000 or more. This is a major increase from a decade or two ago, when a seal sighting was a rare and wonderful event.

Seals eat fish, and fishermen have long resented the competition. Seals are also accused of destroying nets and other valuable gear, and suspected of spreading the cod worm. To reduce their numbers and presumably increase the fish catch by humans, Maine and Massachusetts in the late nineteenth century instituted a bounty on each seal destroyed. The seal population, historically high along the coast, plummeted—without a noticeable effect on the fish catch.

When Maine repealed its bounty in 1905 and Massachusetts in 1962, seals began to increase in number. Further aid was given to all marine mammals in 1972 with the passage of the federal Marine Mammal Protection Act, and the seal population has rebounded dramatically. Only since 1972 have fishermen grudgingly abandoned the habit of taking a shot at any seal within range. The increase in seal population undoubtedly is a direct result of federal protection.

Female seals have their single pups in the spring, and rear them for three to four weeks without help from the males. The pups sometimes are in the water swimming within a minute or two of birth, and most are weaned by the end of June. After the May–June pupping season, the cycle starts all over again with the breeding season, June through August. This is followed by a period of molting, July through September, when the seals retreat to the outer islands and ledges to replace their coats. In captivity, seals can live 30 to 35 years; in the wild, males live 15 to 20 years and females 25 to 30 years. A female may bear as many as 25 pups in her lifetime.

"Seal Bay," "Seal Cove," and "Seal Harbor" are common names along the coast of Maine, but there are concentrations of seals in southern Penobscot Bay, Jericho Bay, Machias Bay, and near Mount Desert Island and Swan's Island.

Seals are disturbed by nearby people and fast motorboats. Instead of heading straight toward a group of seals, sail a course that will take you past. If they appear nervous, you're close enough. If they are alarmed, you're too close. It is particularly important during the May and June pupping season to approach slowly and keep your distance, so as not to risk separating a pup from its mother.

Unless the seals are accustomed to your boat, they will wiggle and slither down to the water and disappear, often popping up suddenly to inspect you with great curiosity from different directions. Seals can stay down for 20 minutes or more, though the normal dive is much shorter. Their streamlined shape and powerful flippers make them formidable in pursuit of fish.

Seals have been observed fishing cooperatively. One sailor reports watching four of them attack a school of fish in unison, from north, east, south, and west. The dark, sleek heads disappeared under water, and a few seconds later a great white patch appeared, accompanied by violent splashings, tiny fish catapulting through the air, and an occasional quick glimpse of a swiftly plunging seal. Then the waters quieted and the seals reappeared, swimming away in different directions. It was an extraordinary spectacle.

DAMARISCOTTA and NEWCASTLE ★★★

Charts: 13288, **13293**

Some 13 miles from the open ocean, Damariscotta and Newcastle are twin towns separated by a short bridge at the head of navigation of the Damariscotta River. There are beautiful old homes here, and the pace is slow.

Approaches. The channel in the upper two miles of the Damariscotta River is narrow and winding, but reasonably well buoyed. After can "15," follow the chart carefully and do not run straight lines between buoys. Above nun "18," favor the left-hand side; once past the southern tip of Hall Point, favor the right-hand side to avoid the shoal marked by can "19." After nun "22," the deeper water is on the left side of the channel.

Anchorages, Moorings. There are several choices. Get a slip from Schooner Landing at the head of the harbor, anchor off the public landing, or pick up a Riverside Boat Co. mooring in the channel between can "21" and nun "22."

Getting Ashore. If you are up near the bridge, come ashore in your dinghy at the town landing floats or at Schooner Landing, and you will be right in town.

If you are on a mooring near Riverside Boat, you have a choice of the town floats or of landing at the yard and walking the three-quarters of a mile into town.

For the Boat. *Public Landing.* The public landing in Damariscotta is identifiable by the flagpole and launching ramp just east of the bridge. A line of floats juts out into the river next to the ramp. You are allowed to use the end float for short periods of time, and the west side for tie-ups, with a two-hour limit.

Although a sign will tell you to ask the harbormaster about overnight guest moorings, there haven't been any for some time. The harbormaster says, "Anchor anywhere and nobody'll bother

you. We're pretty easygoing here."

Riverside Boat Company (tel. 563-3398). Riverside Boat is about three-quarters of a mile downriver from the bridge, on the west side of the river. You will see a small dock and float (which dries out at low), a marine railway, and a flagpole. The railway can handle boats up to about 40 feet for repairs.

Schooner Landing (Ch. 16; tel. 563-3380). At the head of the harbor, this marina caters especially to sailboats. It has 38 slips with seven to nine feet alongside at low. Water and electricity are available, and fuel delivery can be arranged. Emergency repairs can be made and there is a chandlery.

For the Crew. Everything you need is close at hand in Damariscotta, including groceries, drugstores, bookstore, hardware store, takeouts, some nice restaurants and gift shops, and a movie theatre. Just off Main Street is a little shopping center with a laundromat, liquor store, and barbershop. Miles Health Care Center is nearby (tel. 563-1234).

The restaurant at Schooner Landing serves lunch and dinner daily, and brunch on weekends. If you feel the need for a night ashore, reserve one of the suites upstairs.

Things to Do. If you have an archeological bent, take your dinghy upriver a mile to visit the Indian oyster-shell heaps, on the west bank of the river, just below the next fixed bridge (Route 1). Though the heaps are of modest proportions compared to, say, the pyramids, it's fun to imagine the hundreds of years of picnics and oyster feasts required to create the 12-foot-high mounds of shells, now covered with trees. Some striking columbines now thrive on the alkaline soil. En route, you may be lucky enough to see one of the seals that live in these protected waters. There is a lot of current, so plan your trip to go up with the last of the flood and return with the ebb.

THREAD OF LIFE

Charts: 13288, **13293**

If you have an opportunity, sail through Thread of Life, between the Damariscotta River and Johns Bay. This little passage with the evocative name is one of the prettiest on the coast. It is wide enough to tack through against a southwesterly, and there are no dangers in the channel.

Coming from Christmas Cove or the Damariscotta River, run east of Inner Heron Island. Aim

for the wooded portion of Thrumcap Island and identify can "1" off Turnip Island. Make a gradual left turn around the can and Turnip, which has a little brown house and a number of trees. Then run up the middle of Thread of Life, with bold ledges on either side. From Turnip Island you will be able to see the nun and the can that mark the exit to Johns Bay north of Crow Island.

JOHNS BAY

Charts: 13288, **13293**

Johns Bay, just west of the Pemaquid peninsula, is short but pithy. Named for Captain John Smith, who explored the area in 1614, it's a very pretty bay and includes a lot in a five-mile stretch.

The fort and the state park at Pemaquid Harbor are definitely worth a visit, whether you are interested in the tumultuous early history of our country or simply like spectacular views and climbing around forts. Also well worth a visit is the eastern part of The Gut, a crowded and picturesque working harbor.

There are three extremely well-protected anchorages in the bay, only one of which is easy to enter (west of Witch Island). Poorhouse Cove provides excellent shelter but should be entered at halftide or below. Eastern Branch is the third hurricane hole, but very difficult to enter.

This is not a major cruising area, so you won't find many boats here, but you will enjoy the experience.

McFARLANDS COVE

Charts: 13288, **13293**

North of Witch Island, on the west side of Johns Bay, McFarlands Cove is a small indentation full of moored small craft, with a rocky beach at the north end. There is heavy kelp on the bottom, so use it only as a day stop. Anchor in the western portion near the mouth, outside the moored boats, making sure the hook is well set.

WITCH ISLAND ★★ No facilities

Charts: 13288, **13293**

On the west side of Johns Bay, just north of the entrance to The Gut, lies densely wooded Witch Island, a sanctuary of Maine Audubon. To the west of the island there is an excellent anchorage with protection from every quarter except northeast. You'll be sleepily aware of lobstermen leaving South Bristol in the early morning.

Approaches. The approach from Johns Bay is easy. Pass between green can "1" on Corvette Ledge and nun "2" on McFarlands Ledges, taking a wide curve around the north end of Witch Island.

Anchorages, Moorings. There are moorings on both sides of the channel west of Witch Island, but plenty of room to anchor anywhere in midchannel, in 21 feet of water at low, with excellent holding ground in mud.

THE GUT—EAST OF THE BRIDGE
(SOUTH BRISTOL)

Charts: 13288, **13293** Inset

The eastern part of The Gut is a picturesque working harbor, full of lobsterboats going about their business, dories loaded with nets, seagulls quarreling over fish, and a busy little swing bridge connecting the town of South Bristol to the mainland.

Approaches. Coming from the east (Johns Bay), pass between can "1" and nun "2," then curve wide around densely wooded Witch Island,

leaving it to port. As you get to the narrow entrance to The Gut, favor the right side of the channel to avoid the isolated ledge on the left. Inside, pick your way carefully among the moored and moving boats.

Anchorages, Moorings. Don't even think of anchoring here. It is too busy and you'll just be in the way. There are moorings available at the

Lobster pots piled on a pier at The Gut, South Bristol. Not much room for a yacht here. (Boutilier photo)

Gamage shipyard, west of the bridge.

To eat at Farrin's Lobster Pound tie up to their floats.

For the Boat. The eastern part of The Gut is a working harbor, not particularly geared toward visiting yachtsmen. In a pinch, there are three commercial operations that could provide gas, diesel, and boating supplies, as well as lobsters. Starting at the bridge and going eastward, these are: Farrin's (tel. 644-8500), Eugley's (tel. 644-8609), and the South Bristol Fishermen's Co-op (tel. 644-8224).

Farrin's and Eugley's have 10 feet along their floats at low.

Bittersweet Landing Boatyard (tel. 644-8731). This small yard, in the sheltered waters on the south side of the Gut, can haul and store boats up to 40 feet, using a hydraulic trailer on its private launching ramp. They can handle some hull and engine repairs and provide marine supplies.

For the Crew. Farrin's Lobster Pound serves lobsters upstairs on an outdoor deck with a great view of the harbor.

PEMAQUID HARBOR ★★★★

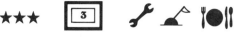

Charts: 13288, **13293**

Four flags fly from the round stone tower overlooking Pemaquid Harbor—American, British, French, and the State of Maine. All have been deeply involved in this historic place on the west side of Pemaquid Neck, three miles north of the entrance to Johns Bay.

The fort at Pemaquid was the eastern bastion of English territory and a counterbalance to the French fort at Castine, farther up the coast. All the territory in between was in dispute, and there was open warfare between the British and French between 1613 and 1759.

Much of the early history of our country can be read in the succession of forts at Pemaquid. The first Fort Pemaquid was erected in 1631, and a year later it was attacked and plundered by pirate Dixie Bull. Its successor, Fort Charles, was built in 1677 but destroyed by the Penobscot Indians in 1689. Fort William Henry was erected in 1692. Although it mounted 28 guns, an attack from land and sea by a force of French and Indians led by Baron de Castin destroyed the fort once more in 1696. Governor David Dunbar restored it and renamed it Fort Frederick in 1729. This last fort was razed by the town of Bristol in 1775 to keep it from falling into the hands of the English.

Approaches. The round stone tower shown as "FORT" on the chart is visible a long way; so is Pemaquid Beach, just to the south. There are two approaches to Pemaquid Harbor, both unmarked but easy. Coming from the south, pass halfway between high, wooded Johns Island and Knowles Rocks. These rocks are low and blend with the background, but are always visible.

From the west, pass halfway between the grassy mound of Beaver Island and the ledge to the north off Thurston Point. Several bits of this ledge usually are visible even at high water, but give it plenty of berth because the part that extends farthest is visible only near halftide or below.

Anchorages, Moorings. There are two anchorages with reasonable protection, either north or south of the fort. If you choose to anchor in Pemaquid Harbor, north of the fort, pass midway between the point on which the fort is located and the tiny island (usually a peninsula) on the left-hand side of the channel.

Having entered the harbor north of the fort, you may be able to get a rental mooring from Konitzky (see below). Or you can anchor on either side of the channel. On the north side, however, outside the moored boats, there is more swinging room.

This little harbor is the entrance to the Pemaquid River, and there is a fair amount of current.

Your boat may swing to the current or the wind, depending on which is stronger. The anchorage is exposed to the southwest.

It is possible to go farther up the Pemaquid River, near the Pemaquid Fishermen's Co-op on the northern shore (where all the workboats are), but it is unmarked and tricky. Be careful of the ledge extending from the northern shore near the eight-foot spot (chart 13293). Check with the harbormaster, at the Co-op, for a possible mooring.

The second anchorage is off Pemaquid Beach, between the fort and Fish Point, where you will see a number of boats moored. Anchor near the private moorings in 17 feet of water at low, sand bottom. This anchorage is out of the river current and protected from the south, but exposed to the southwest.

Getting Ashore. If you are in Pemaquid Harbor north of the fort, do not land at the dock next to the fort; it's private. Instead, take your dinghy to the long Pemaquid pier farther east and tie up behind the float.

For the Boat. There are no boatyard facilities visible from the anchorages. Konitzky Boatworks, however, is not far away.

Konitzky Boatworks (Ch. 6; tel. 677-3726). This shop is a short distance inland and can be reached by walking along the road from the fort. Although it has a ramp on a creek off the Pemaquid River and can haul boats up to nine-foot draft, most boats arrive by trailer overland. Konitzky is equipped to do engine and hull repairs as well as substantial restoration of wooden boats and new construction.

For the Crew. Located in an old clam factory on Pemaquid pier, the Pemaquid Chart House (tel. 677-3315) restaurant is open for lunch and dinner, and there is a takeout. There are picnic tables outside where you can enjoy your lobster and clams. Ice and a pay phone are on the pier.

A one-mile walk south on the road marked "Pemaquid Beach Rd. and New Harbor" will take you to the center of New Harbor, where you will find C.E. Reilly & Son—a marvelous market (tel. 677-2321). Also there are a post office, bank, gift shop, art gallery, and dairy bar.

On the way back, take a rest at Captain's Catch and enjoy their crabmeat rolls. You can also buy fresh fish, crabmeat, and ice there.

Things to Do. A short walk and a small admission charge will get you in to beautiful white-sand Pemaquid Beach.

At the head of Pemaquid pier is a wonderful little museum run by the Bureau of Parks and Recreation, and well worth the admission fee. Walk around the grassy park, where excavations

Less than 24 hours after they leave the shell, tiny eider ducklings pop boldly into the water and swim earnestly around under the tolerant and protective eye of an adult female. Flotillas of little puffballs. In *The Salt Book,* Willie and Elizabeth Ames, who grew up on Ragged and Matinicus islands, reminisce: "The mother ducks would baby-sit for each other. A lot of the times, we'd see one mother with two flocks, while the other mother was probably off feeding or something. . . . Black-back gulls were the worst enemy they had . . . . They're miserable birds. They'd goffle up a whole flock of them little ducks all a-kickin'. Made me some angry to see them do that."

Eiders spend much of their lives at sea, pairing off in the spring and returning year after year to the same nesting site. Maine is the only state (other than Alaska) where eiders nest; this is the southern edge of their breeding grounds. The female eider is a mottled dark brown, good camouflage as she incubates her

eggs. The male eider, who takes little or no part in rearing the ducklings, is striking: white back and breast, black sides, and wearing a black cap. In summer, eiders molt, during which time they are flightless. Cruising yachtsmen will see the birds paddling rapidly away from their approach.

Both males and females have characteristic sloping foreheads and wedge-shaped bills. Eiders are the largest ducks in North America, running 3½ to 5½ pounds and as

much as 18 inches long. Graceful on the sea and under water, eiders are ponderous fliers.

To incubate properly, an egg must lie next to a patch of skin. The mother plucks the down from her breast to expose this patch, and lines the nest with the eider down. Indians and white settlers collected eggs and gathered down from the nests, having learned that it made superior insulation. In moderation, this practice caused no great problem, but in the last half of the nineteenth century, eider down became commercially valuable for parkas and pillows, and hunters descended on nesting sites, killing birds indiscriminately and robbing the nests. By 1907, only one nesting pair of eiders remained in Maine, on Old Man Island. Protective federal and state laws came none too soon.

The National Audubon Society was influential in protecting outlying nesting islands, and there has been a rapid resurgence. By the 1980s, the eider population was estimated at more than 20,000 nesting pairs.

---

have revealed the sites of early buildings (including the Customs House, where clearance was required of all ships between the Kennebec and St. Croix rivers). Wander through the Old Burial Ground, dating from 1695.

Nearby is the round stone William Henry Memorial Fort, a 1908 replica of the last fort to have stood on this strategic spot. There are interesting exhibits inside, and the view from the battlements is unsurpassed.

POORHOUSE COVE ★★ No facilities

Charts: 13288, **13293**

Poorhouse is a very well-protected cove on the west side of Johns River at the head of Johns Bay. Although much easier to enter than neighboring Eastern Branch, it is best to come in at halftide or below so you can see the ledges.

Wooded High Island forms the eastern side of the cove. There are a number of houses and docks lining the west side, but usually only a few boats.

Approaches. Entering within an hour or two of low tide, note the ledge outside the entrance at the northern end of High Island. Inside Sproul Point is a larger ledge coming down from the north, which you leave to starboard, aiming for the north corner of the entrance to Bradstreet Cove. As you ap-

proach the boats moored near Bradstreet, turn to port and run down the west side of Poorhouse Cove.

Anchorages, Moorings. There are a number of private moorings. Anchor nearby in 8 to 11 feet at low, in good mud holding ground. You can go as far south as the fourth dock and still find good water.

The protection is good all around in Poorhouse Cove. You should be safe and comfortable here under almost any conditions.

There is an agreeable day stop with 16 feet of water just outside the entrance, in the little bight south of Sproul Point.

EASTERN BRANCH ★★★ |5| No facilities

Charts: 13288, **13293**

Eastern Branch is an arm of Johns River at the head of Johns Bay. Beautiful and extremely well protected, the branch has just a few homes set in woods and tranquil meadows.

It is common to find 30 or more seals slouching and snorting on the ledges west of Foster Island as you enter. You are also likely to see terns, osprey, gulls, herons, egrets, cormorants, and others.

The entrance is dangerous, and many yachts with experienced skippers have left bottom paint on the rocks. As you can see on the chart, the mouth is cluttered with unmarked rocks. For the uninitiated, safe passage through the 35-foot opening requires a combination of low tide, a keen eye, and good luck.

Approaches. Come in within an hour or so of dead low, and proceed as slowly as you can. As you approach Foster Island, running roughly northeast, pick up the halftide ledges on the northern side of the entrance, but do not get too close—they make out quite far under water. On the right-hand side of the entrance, you will see the tips of several pinnacle rocks. Others are submerged, even at low.

Make a sharp turn to starboard, passing about halfway between the pinnacle rocks on your right and the ledges on your left. Local resident Stuart Gillespie says, "Stay among the lobster buoys; they are most likely in deep water." Once past the ledges on your left, make a slow turn (about 90 degrees) to port and head up the branch, favoring the western shore.

Anchorages, Moorings. There are a number of private moorings in the harbor and plenty of room to anchor nearby in 13 to 15 feet of water at low. Holding ground is good, in mud, and there is little current. This would be an excellent place to ride out a hurricane.

Things to Do. The water is unusually warm here, a good place for your annual dip in Maine waters.

Land your dinghy way up the eastern shore, just where the green appears on the chart, and walk through the old cemetery. Across the road is the Harrington Meeting House (1773) and Museum.

Muscongus BAY, Monhegan, and St. George River

Charts: 13288, 13301

Muscongus Bay has a bad reputation for rocks. As one sailor put it, "You have to navigate all the time, and I'd rather be enjoying myself." There *are* a lot of rocks and unmarked ledges, but also lovely islands and passages. In 1524 Verrazzano glowingly described ". . . islands lying all near the land, being small and pleasant to view, high, and having many turnings and windings between them, making many fair harbors and channels, as they do in the gulf of Venice in Illyria and Dalmatia. . . ." Verrazzano had it right. Muscongus Bay is a beautiful place to sail, and comparatively uncrowded. It has a number of interesting harbors, plenty of gunkholes, and, yes, lots of navigation.

The scale of Muscongus Bay is fairly small, and in a week or so, you can comfortably see most of it. Two narrow, winding rivers at the head of the bay, the Medomak and the St. George, lead respectively to Waldoboro and Thomaston. Both have strong tidal currents, so cruising is better in the bay, but Maple Juice and Otis coves, up the St. George, make it worth the effort.

There are the large working harbors of Port Clyde and Friendship, and the tiny ones of New Harbor and Pleasant Point Gut. The unspoiled cove at Harbor Island is lovely, as are Greenland and Davis coves. The National Audubon Society maintains a fascinating preserve on Hog Island, in the northwest corner of the bay.

Among the many interesting passages in the bay are Georges Harbor, Port Clyde Harbor, the slot between Allen Island and Burnt, Davis Strait, the passages between Louds and Marsh islands, and north of McGee.

Best of all is magnificent Monhegan, 10 miles offshore, guarding Muscongus Bay—probably the most spectacular island on the coast of Maine.

PASSAGES THROUGH MUSCONGUS BAY

Charts: 13288, 13301

Passages North and South. The islands and ledges of Muscongus Bay are oriented in long, north-south lines. Therefore, passages north and south are fairly simple and well marked—for example, from Burnt and Allen islands northward to the St. George River, and from Pemaquid Point up Muscongus Sound (see sketch map).

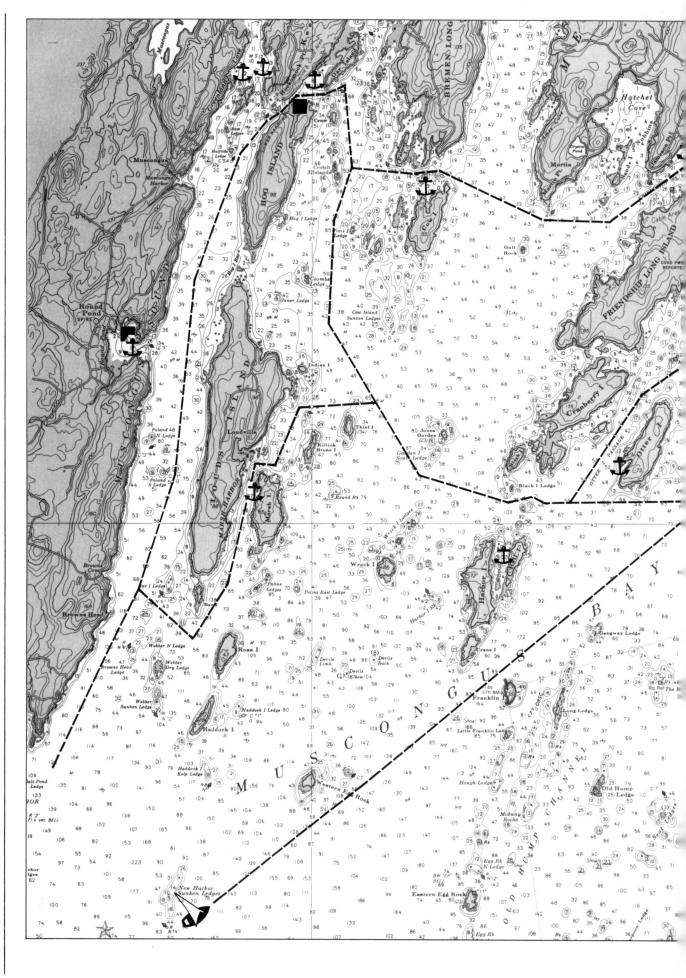

PASSAGES THROUGH
MUSCONGUS BAY

(based on Chart 13301)

This chart is for general information only, and NOT TO BE USED FOR NAVIGATION. Location and type of buoys and other navigational aids may change from time to time. Use in conjunction with the text, and the latest Charts, Notices to Mariners, and U.S. Coast Pilot.

Nautical Miles

⚓ Anchorages

■ Moorings

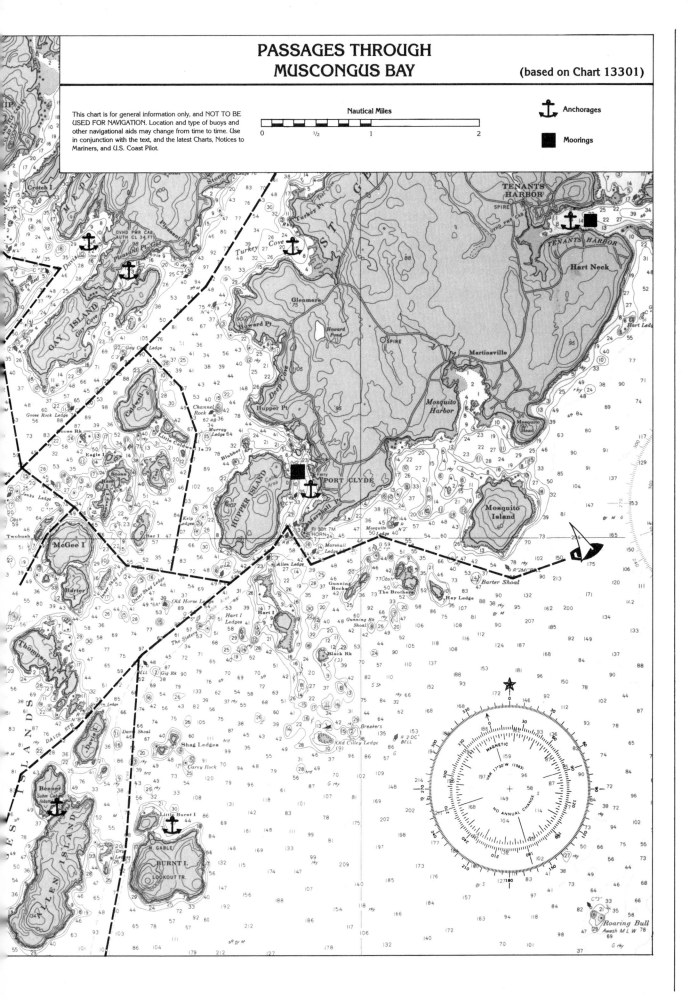

Passages East and West—The Outside Route. Passages east and west through Muscongus Bay run against the grain of the islands and are much trickier. For boats headed east or west, with no particular interest in Muscongus Bay itself, the normal route would be outside everything—outside Allen and Burnt islands, outside Old Woman Ledge and Old Man Ledge, seaward of red whistle "2 OM."

In poor visibility, unless you are intimately acquainted with the area, avoid the dangers of a passage through Muscongus Bay and take this outside route.

Northern and Middle Routes. Coming from Tenants Harbor or points east, round Mosquito Island, leaving red bell "2MI" to starboard, then following the red nuns to Marshall Point, leaving them to starboard as well. Pass between can "3" and Hupper Island, leaving nun "6" to starboard.

From this point, there are several possible paths through the chain of islands that runs from Caldwell south to Allen. If your destination is in the area of Friendship Harbor, run north of Caldwell, or north of McGee. If your destination is Round Pond or New Harbor, pass north of McGee and then through the hole between Otter and Cranberry on the north, and Hall and Harbor on the south.

From there, run north of Hog Island into Muscongus Sound, or between Marsh and Louds, then south of Bar, into Muscongus Sound.

These routes are shown on the sketch map and discussed in the pages that follow. They are not necessarily the most direct routes, but they take advantage of easily recognizable islands, deep channels, and navigational marks. You will discover many possible variations—which is, after all, part of the pleasure of Muscongus Bay.

NEW HARBOR ★★★

Charts: 13288, **13301** (Inset)

You do not have to go far out of your way to find New Harbor, on the eastern side of Pemaquid Point. It's a small, busy, working harbor filled with lobsterboats and draggers—a classic Maine fishing community.

New Harbor has the distinction of being the site where the Indian Chief Samoset gave a deed to John Brown of New Harbor on July 15, 1625, and acknowledged it before Abraham Shurte—this being the first deed properly executed in New England.

Approaches. Approaching from the east, run in from nun "14" to red bell "2" marking the entrance. The harbor is too small for much maneuvering, so drop your sails near the bell.

Do not run a straight line between bell "2" and nun "4," but stay north of this line to avoid the ledge at the southern point of the entrance. Leave nun "4" to starboard and green daybeacon "5" to port.

There is a narrow path clear of lobster buoys in the winding channel, which runs along the northern side of the harbor.

Anchorages, Moorings. This is a tight harbor, and there is no room to anchor, or harbormaster to help you.

You may be able to find space alongside at either Shaw's Wharf or the New Harbor Co-op (second large dock on the right). Shaw's also has a couple of moorings. Or ask at the Co-op if a fisherman's mooring will be empty for the night.

The Gosnold Arms (tel. 677-3727) has several moorings, with 500-pound concrete blocks, next to their dock at the entrance to the harbor. Or lie alongside their float, with 10 feet of water at low.

If there is no room in New Harbor, your best bet is to go north to Round Pond or Greenland Cove.

Getting Ashore. Use the dinghy float at Shaw's.

For the Boat. *Shaw's Wharf (tel. 677-2200).* Gas, diesel, and water can be obtained at Shaw's Wharf, where there is 10 feet alongside at low.

New Harbor Co-op (tel. 677-2791). Gas and diesel are also sold at the Co-op, with eight feet alongside at low. There is an ice machine.

For the Crew. There is a pay phone at Shaw's Wharf. Better yet, they offer a great lobster supper that you can enjoy outside overlooking the harbor.

The Co-op serves lobsters and clams on their outside deck or will steam them for you to enjoy on your own boat.

Across the street, on the north side of the harbor, the Gosnold Arms serves breakfast, Sunday brunch, and suppers. The inn is named after Bartholomew Gosnold, who stopped here in 1602.

For supplies, downtown New Harbor is a pleasant 15-minute walk. Make a left as you leave Shaw's parking lot and continue on the paved road to Route 130. Turn left up the hill and continue to the center, which includes a bank, service station, art gallery, dairy bar, gift shop, and C.E. Reilly & Son (tel. 677-2321), which has everything from the *New York Times* to fresh crabmeat, and is open Sundays.

To find the post office, take a right on Route 130.

Things to Do. Row the dinghy to Back Cove, which branches off the southern side of the harbor.

It is full of fishing boats and lobstermen's shacks, with a small reversing falls at the head—reputedly the most-photographed cove in Maine.

The *Hardy* (tel. 882-7909) runs excursions to Eastern Egg Rock and Monhegan from Shaw's Wharf.

LOUDS and MARSH ISLANDS
Charts: 13288, **13301**

There is a delightful passage between Marsh and Louds islands, near the western side of Muscongus Bay. Loudville, on the eastern shore of Louds, is a small fishing community.

Approaching from the east, the best-marked path is north of state-owned Thief Island (high and wooded), leaving to port nun "2" north of Killick Stone Island (low and rocky, with grass). It is also possible to pass between Killick Stone and Marsh. (Note the four-foot spot east of Marsh.)

Find the ledge that makes out to the east of Loudville and is partially visible at most tides. Leaving the ledge to starboard, run down the middle of the passage between Marsh and Louds islands.

The cove at Loudville dries out at low tide and is studded with rocks; stay clear. Pass south of Bar Island to enter Muscongus Sound.

Ross Island, at the end of the passage, is grassy and treeless, a nesting site for cormorants. Haddock Island, beyond, is wooded.

Shortly after passing the northern tip of Marsh Island, you will see to port a tiny sand beach tucked inside the rocks, facing south. This is Marsh Island Harbor, with room perhaps for one boat to anchor off the beach in about nine feet of water. The anchorage is small and exposed to southerlies; it is fine as a day stop.

ROUND POND ★★
Charts: 13288, **13301**

In *Sailing Alone Around the World* Joshua Slocum recorded his visit to this snug harbor on May 8, 1895: "The wind being free, I ran on into Round Pond harbour, which is a little port east from Pemaquid. Here I rested a day while the wind rattled among the pine-trees on shore."

Today, Slocum might have trouble finding a place to anchor in Round Pond. The harbor is crammed with more than 100 boats and there's not much room for transients. Round Pond is partly a working harbor for lobstermen, partly a port for pleasure craft.

Approaches. A bar makes out from the southern point of the entrance, so be sure to leave can "5" to port. Thereafter, you will be meandering among moored boats and lobster cars. Stay away from the shoals at the southwest and northeast ends of the harbor.

Anchorages, Moorings. Padebco maintains a number of moorings, ranging from 500- to 1,800-pound granite blocks, with floats marked "Padebco" and the weight. On the average night, two or three moorings are available for transients. Arrive early.

There usually is some room to anchor in 15 to 20 feet of water at the southeastern corner outside the moorings. Protection is excellent. Round Pond is landlocked except for due east, and even there, Louds Island provides cover.

Getting Ashore. The most convenient spot to take your dinghy is the town landing. The floats at Padebco ground out at low.

For the Boat. *Muscongus Bay Lobster Company (tel. 529-5528).* Just below the Anchor Inn on the north shore are the dock and floats of Muscongus Bay Lobster Company, much in use by lobsterboats. There is 10 feet of water at the end floats at low; gas and diesel are available.

Padebco (tel. 529-5106). The family enterprise of Bruce and Paul Cunningham, Padebco occupies the large gray building and small shingled house farthest east along the waterfront. The yard provides hauling, storage, and repairs, with a marine railway that can handle boats up to 45 feet.

Mid-Coast Lobster (tel. 529-5622). This lobster dock is separated from the others and farther west. Gas and diesel are available, with four feet of water reported alongside the floats at low.

Water is not available at the lobster docks, and the water at Padebco is bad (highly mineralized).

Town Landing. Just west of Muscongus Bay Lobster Company is the town float landing, with a launching ramp.

For the Crew. Have a meal at the Anchor Inn, (tel. 529-5584) right by the waterfront. You can eat inside or on the deck. There is an ice machine. Just below, Muscongus Bay Lobster offers steamers and lobsters on their deck. Lobsters can be bought at either of the lobster docks, or at Round Pond Lobster near the town landing.

Just up the road is the Granite Hall Store, which offers toiletries, gifts, magazines, ice cream, and ice. Curving left up the hill, past the Little Brown Church and the white church with the shingled steeple, the road will take you to King Ro Market, with a limited selection of groceries, plus beer,

wine, newspapers, and a pay phone.

Things to Do. There is a very pleasant walk starting at the waterfront, turning right at the Granite Hall Store, and back down to the old boathouse on the northern point of the harbor entrance. This is a peaceful road, with little summer homes tucked among the trees.

GREENLAND COVE ★★★ No facilities

Charts: 13288, **13301**

Near the northwest corner of Muscongus Bay, north of Hog Island, lies Greenland Cove. A favorite of cruising yachtsmen, this large and attractive cove offers good protection except from the southwest, with lots of swinging room. There are only a few docks and summer cottages around the shores, and the swimming is good.

Several dories are moored near the west side of the cove, and you may be able to watch fishermen purse-seining here.

Approaches. As you run up Muscongus Sound west of Louds and Hog islands, there are two possible entrances to Greenland Cove, on either side of Ram Island. Ram is wooded, with a house and a flagpole on the east; ledges make out a long way south of the island. The easier entrance is to the east, leaving can "5A" at Halftide Ledge to port and running up the middle of the channel between Ram Island and Hockomock Point.

Stay clear of the three-foot spot marked by can "7," and the ledge just north of it, bits of which are visible at high tide. There is plenty of room in the entrance.

Coming from the east and passing north of Hog Island, leave cans "7A" and "7" (in the Lower Narrows) to starboard before turning north into Greenland Cove.

Anchorages, Moorings. There is good water for anchoring over a large part of Greenland Cove. Holding ground varies: good mud in some areas, but grass in others. Be sure your anchor is well set. With normal southwest winds, the best place to be is in the lee of Ram Island. But be careful. There is a ledge making out some distance to the north of Ram, as shown on the chart. Greenland Cove can get choppy in a strong southwesterly.

HOG ISLAND ★★★★

Charts: 13288, **13301**

Established in 1936 in the upper reaches of Muscongus Bay, Hog Island was the first of four National Audubon Society ecology camps. It is a 330-acre wilderness area with a variety of habitats, including rocky intertidal zones, mudflats, salt marshes, spruce-fir forests, and freshwater ponds. Visitors are welcome to hike the trails and visit the collections of birds, plants, and rocks.

People come here from all over the country to attend workshops emphasizing firsthand observation and study of the interrelationships among plants, animals, and their physical environments. Over the years, many famous naturalists have taught here, including Roger Tory Peterson and, more recently, Stephen Kress, founder of the Eastern Egg Rock Puffin Project.

Approaches. From the east, run up outside the

Crotch Islands and higher Crow Island (both state-owned). Then leave nun "6" to port, turning westward between Hog and Oar islands and aiming just right of the dock at the northern tip of Hog Island. Sail past the dock to the mooring area.

From the west, coming up Muscongus Sound west of Louds and Hog islands, leave cans "5A," "7," and "7A" to port. Just past can "7A," in the Lower Narrows, run close to the mainland at Hockomock Point, leaving to starboard the rocks making out from Hog Island. Once past these rocks, you are in the mooring area.

Anchorages, Moorings. Do not anchor here. There is a cable crossing that you are likely to foul. Audubon maintains three or four moorings identified by white lobster buoys and a small white float. There is probably seven feet of water at low here,

Purse-seining for herring in Greenland Cove. After the fishermen in the dory close the purse and haul the net, the herring will be pumped out into a sardine carrier. This traditional Maine fishery has shown remarkable resistance to the pressures of modernization. (Boutilier photo)

and the location is extremely well protected by the surrounding land. Use the moorings for a brief visit or to stay overnight.

Getting Ashore. Take your dinghy to Audubon's dinghy float. Leave the main float open for the launches, which make frequent trips to the mainland and outlying islands.

Things to Do. Introduce yourself at the Audubon office, ask permission from the warden to use the mooring, pick up a map, and enjoy exploring the island.

OAR ISLAND COVE ★★★

Charts: 13288, **13301**

Between the south end of Oar Island and Keene Neck is a little cove of some interest, the final resting place of the five-masted schooner *Cora F. Cressy*. This is a working harbor that yachts seldom visit. If the moorings at Hog Island are occupied, you might choose to spend the night here instead.

Approaches. The approaches are the same as for Hog Island.

Anchorages, Moorings. Anchor outside the lobsterboats, in about 14 feet of water at low. The lobster buoys in the cove are probably moorings for lobsterboats, so do not anchor next to one.

The anchorage is well protected except from the south, and the bottom is mud; it would be a good place in a northerly.

Getting Ashore. Row your dinghy in to the floats, hidden behind the schooner's great hull.

For the Boat. *Keene Narrows Lobster.* Gas and diesel are available at the floats, with about four feet alongside at low water.

Things to Do. It is worth rowing in to the float just to feel the awesome bulk of the *Cora F. Cressy* looming over you. The *Cressy* (2,499 tons) was built in Bath by Percy and Small and launched in 1902. Her length is 273 feet; beam, 45.4 feet; and draft, 27.9 feet. (See photo on page 95.) When her sailing days were over, she lay alongside a dock in Boston, as wharfage charges accumulated. She then was transformed into a casino, and her last crew were ladies of the night.

Walk ashore from the floats and investigate the huge double lobster pound.

It is a short hop over to the Audubon camp on Hog Island.

MEDOMAK RIVER

Charts: 13288, **13301**

The Medomak River empties into the northwest corner of Muscongus Bay. Despite its rich ship-building history—Waldoboro, at the head of navigation, was once one of Maine's major 19th century shipbuilding centers—this is not a place for deep-draft cruising boats. The channels are winding, studded with rocks and ledges (generally unmarked), and the tidal currents are strong.

If you want to explore the river, do so at low slack, when most of the dangers are visible and the tide will be rising in case your keel finds bottom. There are several approaches on either side of Bremen Long Island, but the widest and easiest to navigate is Hockomock Channel, to the west.

Entering Hockomock Channel at low slack tide, leave can "9," north of Oar Island, to port. Tucked in around the ledge north of Oar Island is a small working harbor filled with lobsterboats.

Proceeding up Hockomock Channel, look for the ledge north of Clam Island, which is low and hard to see. After passing this ledge, favor the right-hand side of the channel to avoid the line of rocks and ledges on the west side. The farthest-outlying rock on the west side, opposite the C in "Channel" on the chart, is visible for an hour or so after low tide.

Having negotiated Hockomock Channel, leave wooded, state-owned Hardy Island to port and head for the small island on Havener Ledge, which has some trees. Turn sharply to starboard and pass through the narrows between Locust Island and Havener Ledge, between can "1" and nun "2." The current starts to run strong in the narrows within half an hour of low.

Here is what the *Coast Pilot* says about the channel leading farther north: "For the next 2.5 miles to within 1.6 miles of Waldoboro, the channel leads between flats nearly bare at low water, and shoals gradually to 5 feet. The controlling depth to Waldoboro is about 3½ feet . . . . The channel can best be followed at low water when the flats are visible, or on a rising tide."

COW ISLAND★★★   No facilities

Charts: 13288, **13301**

Large, wooded Cow Island south of Bremen Long Island, offers an attractive little anchorage at the northern tip.

Approaches. Approaching from the west, pass south of nun "4" next to Palmer Island, then enter the anchorage south of can "3," giving it some space to avoid the three-foot spot.

Anchorages, Moorings. Work your way far enough east to get protection from southwesterlies, then anchor in 13 feet at low.

WHARTON ISLAND★★   No facilities

Charts: 13288, **13301**

East of Hungry Island, at the entrance to the Medomak River, Wharton Island provides a seldom-used anchorage that is easy to enter but exposed to prevailing winds.

Approaches. Run into the Medomak River east of Cow and Bremen Long Island. As you approach the southern tip of Hungry Island stay well to the east to avoid the ledges south of Wharton (there is a small house on one of the ledges). Note the four-foot spot at the southeast end of Wharton.

Anchorages, Moorings. Anchor halfway along Wharton Island, midway between Wharton and the mainland, in seven to 12 feet at low.

HATCHET COVE ★★   No facilities

Charts: 13288, **13301**

Just west of Friendship Harbor, Hatchet Cove is a precarious place to enter and has little to offer once you get in.

Pretty little Ram Island, in the mouth of Hatchet Cove, has been used for decades by Friendship people for Saturday-night parties.

Approaches. The cove is divided down the middle by a line of attractive islands and not-so-at-

Two traditional Friendship sloops racing. *Gladiator* (71) coming up to the leeward of *Chrissy* (18). (Boutilier photo)

tractive ledges, starting at the mouth with Ram and Sand islands. Do not attempt the eastern entrance, in which even local sailors have trouble.

Use the entrance west of the islands and come in at dead low or within an hour of that time. This will allow you to see most of the rocks, which reach from the middle almost to the western shore. These rocks, which start opposite the remains of a granite pier on the western shore, are locally called the "Chocolate Chips." Hug the shore, perhaps 100 feet off. The channel here is about 100 yards wide.

As the cove opens out, you will see a small, isolated ledge to starboard opposite the 15-foot depth on the chart. Leave this ledge to starboard.

Anchorages, Moorings. Anchor in 11 to 17 feet at low, just past the isolated ledge.

FRIENDSHIP ★★★ 　 3 　

Charts: 13288, **13301**

If you want to see a real Maine coastal harbor with few yachts and tourist facilities, go to Friendship. Located on the mainland, halfway across Muscongus Bay, Friendship shelters one of the largest fleets of lobsterboats in Maine. The harbor is full of their colorful comings and goings as they load traps and gear and unload their catch at the various commercial docks.

Friendship remains resolutely a working harbor, and can be a difficult—some would even say unfriendly—place for yachts. The harbor is busy with its own affairs, with little time to cater to yachtsmen's needs and problems. Be prepared to accept the place on its own terms.

This is the birthplace of the famous Friendship sloop. The beautiful design with long bowsprit, topmasts, and graceful sheer evolved a century ago as a workboat, before the advent of engines. These lovely craft have now become pleasure boats that still return to Friendship on special occasions—as they did in the summer of 1987 to celebrate their 25th anniversary gathering.

Approaches. The easiest approach is from the west. Note that nun "8" at Martin Point marks the Medomak River and not the entrance to Friendship Harbor. After leaving Ram Island to port, sail between red daybeacon "10" to port and green daybeacon "9" to starboard. There is plenty of room between them. From a distance, the green beacon may be difficult to see against a background of trees.

Coming from the east requires a winding approach among the nearby islands, which will vary depending on where you start. From Port Clyde, for example, you might head north of Caldwell Island, then southward around Gay Island, up between Gay and Morse Islands, leaving can "3" off N E Point Reef to port, then nuns "4" and "6" to starboard. Be sure to observe can "7" at the eastern end of Friendship Harbor, leaving it to port. It is tempting, but potentially disastrous, to cut this can and follow a shoal-draft lobsterboat directly into the harbor.

Anchorages, Moorings. Almost all of the moorings in Friendship Harbor belong to lobstermen. You might be lucky to find someone who can point out a lobsterman's mooring available for the night, but don't count on it. If you pick up a mooring temporarily, be prepared to move your boat on short notice.

You can anchor outside the moored boats, but the water is rather deep—21 to 28 feet at low.

Getting Ashore. Row your dinghy in to the float of the town landing.

For the Boat. The commercial docks in Friendship cluster in two groups, one at each end of the harbor, with a beach between. The town landing

and Hall's Wharf are in the eastern group.

Friendship Town Landing. The town landing and floats can be identified by the road leading directly down to them on the east side of the harbor. There are no facilities, and only about 1½ feet alongside at low. You can tie up briefly, but do not leave the boat for any length of time, or you will interfere with lobstermen who may need to use it.

Hall's Wharf. Directly west of the town landing, Hall's Wharf has gas and diesel. It exists, however, to serve fishermen, and "yachts get in the way." If you do come in to the floats (three feet alongside at low), choose a time when they are not busy.

For the Crew. To find pay phones, the post office, ice, and provisions, walk about three-quarters of a mile north to Friendship Village, where you will find the Archie Wallace grocery store, the Friendship Market, and a takeout. You probably can hitch a ride, and the market may be able to arrange a lift back with your groceries. Friendship is a dry town.

Things to Do. Visit the Friendship Museum, in the former schoolhouse. It has local memorabilia and an interesting exhibit on Friendship sloops.

HORNBARN COVE ★★★ No facilities

Charts: 13288, **13301**

Just east of Friendship Harbor, three-mile long Meduncook River might easily be overlooked. Hornbarn Cove, a short distance up the river on the east side, is easy to enter and offers excellent protection.

Approaches. There are two entrances to the Meduncook River, one on each side of Crotch Island. The western approach is foul and not recommended.

Although entry to Hornbarn Cove is almost a straight shot, you will be happier if you plan it between low and halftide, when the rocks on the right-hand side of the entrance and in the cove are visible.

Coming from Friendship, round nun "4," leaving it to port. Aim for the slot east of Crotch Island,

favoring the western bank. The river here is about 100 yards wide, deep and clear of obstructions, except for the ledge making out from the eastern shore just as you enter. There are several docks along the eastern shore of the river, and usually some moored sailboats.

Pass the end of Crotch Island and the ledge and rocks just beyond. The midharbor ledge and four-foot spot south of Bradford Point are marked by an informal beacon.

Anchorages, Moorings. Anchor in 14 feet at low, beyond the midharbor ledge and to the east of it, opposite a meadow on the right bank. There are a couple of private moorings. The holding ground is good, in mud and grass.

DAVIS COVE ★★★ No facilities

Charts: 13288, **13301**

A mile or so east of Friendship Harbor, this beautiful little cove has spectacular panoramic views, including a glimpse of Franklin Island Light to seaward. There are a few summer cottages well hidden among the trees, and two islets set in the northern end of the cove. Protected in all directions

except southwest, Davis Cove is likely to be quiet at night but pretty lively during the day.

Approaches. Coming from the south, pass between Gay and Morse islands, leaving nun "2" to starboard and favoring the Morse Island shore. The rocks northeast of nun "2" uncover about four

CORMORANTS

Cormorants on a granite pier. (Christopher Ayres photo)

On every ledge in Maine, it seems, cormorants stand in solemn rows drying their wings. With long, black, snaky necks, green eyes, and hooked beaks, they look malevolent, throwbacks to an age of dinosaurs and sharks and pterodactyls —and so they are.

While later-model ducks have oil glands with which to preen their feathers, cormorants do not. The water soaks their feathers, and they stand sopping wet—like someone who has fallen in with all his clothes, elbows up, hung out to dry. No oil glands, and no sweat glands either; cormorants dissipate the heat via the bright-orange throat pouch. The most common species in Maine during the summer is the double-crested cormorant, although its crests are hard to see.

On land the cormorant is awkward and ungainly, with short legs and a fan-shaped tail, but in the water it is a champion. Like the loon, it uses its legs to propel itself underwater, with powerful thrusts of its webbed feet, and can stay submerged a minute or more.

The cormorant is neither loved nor much admired. Shags, they're called in Maine, when fishermen are feeling kindly toward them, which is not often. (At other times they are called lawyer birds, or crow ducks.) No sooner has a fisherman made a catch of herring in a weir or net than shags arrive. Not only do they gorge themselves on young fish, but they panic the fish in the nets, causing many of them to be wounded or destroyed. They descend ravenously on young salmon that the state releases in the Machias, Penobscot, and other rivers, thus earning the enmity of sportfishermen.

Cormorants often roost in large dead trees, which have been killed by the shag droppings. Entire small islands have been denuded in this way. Shag droppings whiten the tops of ledges, where they do no harm, and the tops of open boats, where they are less popular.

With such annoying habits, it is not surprising that cormorants were shot by fishermen and their eggs sprayed with kerosene to reduce the population. By the turn of the century, they came close to extermination. In 1972, however, Maine passed a law that protected many birds, the cormorants among them. Some, no doubt, still are shot by irate fishermen, but a recent count indicated there were more than 26,000 pairs nesting in Maine.

The cormorants build their nests of twigs and dry seaweed, three to five eggs to a nest, and the parents take turns incubating the eggs. The urgent cries of the cormorant chicks induce the adults returning with their catch to open their beaks and regurgitate the food into their throats, from which the babies feed.

Duck Island in the Isles of Shoals is one of the important nesting sites for shags. Another is Ross Island in Muscongus Bay, where the National Audubon Society has banded young cormorants for years to track their movements and breeding success. One early result of the banding program was the discovery that cormorants are particularly fond of Tampa Bay, Florida, for the winter months.

feet at low. As you reach the end of Morse Island, aim for the center of Davis Cove, leaving well to port can "3" and N E Point Reef, which it marks.

Anchorages, Moorings. Most of the cottages around the cove have docks and private moorings. There is ample room, however, to anchor in 8 to 15 feet of water, with good mud bottom.

CRANBERRY ISLAND

Charts: 13288, **13301**

There is a pretty little working harbor between Friendship Long Island and the northeastern end of Cranberry Island. Although it is well protected from the southwest, the holding ground is poor, so it is recommended only as a day stop. The bottom is soft mud and eel grass.

In approaching from the east, note that Morse Ledge consists of two separate ledges. Green daybeacon "1" stands on the south end of the more easterly ledge. The second ledge lies west of the beacon and is submerged at halftide.

OTTER ISLAND

Charts: 13288, **13301**

There is an intriguing little slot in the southwest corner of Otter Island, no more than 50 yards wide and 200 yards long. Reportedly one or two schooners would snuggle up in here in the old days, but with another boat already there, you may find that swinging room is scarce. This would be an uncertain place to spend the night anyway, since it is open to the southwest.

The entrance is straightforward but full of lobster buoys. There is a depth of seven to eight feet of water at low along the centerline of the cove, back as far as the large rock that sticks out from the eastern shore.

This is a delightful place for a lunch stop. The island is private, but you can row ashore at the head of the cove and walk through the woods either east or west to a nice little beach. No fires, please.

HARBOR ISLAND ★★★★ No facilities

Charts: 13288, **13301**

What a special spot. Harbor Island is privately owned, but the owners have put up a welcoming sign:

Welcome to Harbor Island, which for Us is Home. Please Respect our Privacy as We Would Yours.
—the Lev Davises.

From this beautiful and well-protected anchorage between Harbor and Hall islands, you can gaze south to the lighthouse on Franklin Island, to the lobsterman's house on Hall Island, and to the owners' old stone Cape on Harbor. There may be guillemots in the cove, or eiders, or great blue herons.

Approaches. Hall Island to the east is wooded; the northern tip of Harbor Island is mostly grassy.

The approach is less difficult than it appears on the chart. You must pass between two isolated rocks, one just north of Harbor Island and the other just north of Hall, but there is at least 250 yards between them. The rock north of Harbor Island sticks farther out from the shore, and the rockweed floating above it is visible at halftide. The rock north of Hall Island is visible only at dead low, but it is in line with the western edge of the island and therefore easy to avoid. Favor the eastern side of the entrance.

It is helpful to start at small, bare Black Island Ledge to the north, and then run a compass course for the entrance to the harbor.

Anchorages, Moorings. Most cruising boats anchor near the Hall Island side of the harbor, in 27 feet at low.

The Harbor Island side of the anchorage is shoal for quite a distance from shore, and "for the most part foul for anchoring—kelp ledges, and lots of lobster trap buoys," according to Mr. Davis. But it is possible to find an anchorage there in 12 feet or so. A stern anchor would be a good idea, however, to keep you from swinging into the ledge.

Further advice from Mr. Davis: "The middle ground ledge makes up from the south of the harbor as far as a line at right angles to the lobsterman's dock on Hall. Stay north of this line when crossing the harbor. The five-foot spot charted has only about two feet of water on a drain tide."

At high tide, it appears that the harbor is exposed to the south, but the whole passage between Hall and Harbor islands is blocked by ledges, which provide good protection.

Getting Ashore. Land on any of the beaches, or use the stone dock opposite the house on Harbor Island.

Things to Do. The Davises have expressed their desire to be generous with the island, so please use it with respect, care, and discretion. Stick to the shorelines, no fires above the high-water mark, and no camping. The northern end of the island is the Duryea Morton Audubon Sanctuary; avoid it entirely during the eider nesting season up to mid-July.

Walk around the southern end of the island. Take the path north of the white house over to the western shore, then walk south along the beach. It takes an hour or more, past a cave, nesting osprey, and interesting rock formations. The beaches are lined with beach peas, beach roses, and wild iris.

It is also fun to explore the tiny southern tip of Hall, which becomes a separate island when the tide comes in.

EASTERN EGG ROCK

Charts: 13288, **13301**

In the middle of the entrance to Muscongus Bay is seven-acre Eastern Egg Rock, no more than a patch of boulders and grass. It lies in an area full of unmarked ledges; plan to be nowhere near it when the fog closes in. In sunlight, however, this is a fascinating island to sail around. Here Cornell University ornithologist Stephen Kress and the National Audubon Society have reestablished a colony of puffins—the most southerly nesting ground for these strange and wonderful birds, with their colorful beaks and comical posture.

Puffins and terns were both here before the turn of the century. Terns were hunted for the millinery trade and puffins were eaten. Their eggs were collected from the outlying islands to supplement the farmers' meager subsistence. By 1900, both species were gone, replaced by aggressive herring gulls.

To nest, puffins need tumbled rocks to provide burrows and drainage, they need good fishing grounds nearby, and they must be free of mammalian predators. Eastern Egg Rock, far out in the bay, has no mammals, not even a mouse, so it is ideal. In the 1970s, researchers laboriously hand-dug burrows for puffin chicks transported from Newfoundland. Their efforts have been highly successful: The puffin colony has been growing, and more than 1,000 pairs of arctic terns nest on Eastern Egg Rock today as well.

You may be lucky enough to see puffins near Eastern Egg Rock during June and July, but the population is much larger on Matinicus Rock to the eastward. (For the best view of puffins, plan a journey to lonely Machias Seal Island, way down east, where, hidden in a blind, you can observe puffins, terns, and razor-billed auks at close range.)

MONHEGAN ISLAND ★★★★★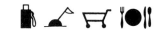

Charts: 13288, **13301**

Places that are hard to get to are often the best. By all means, visit Monhegan if you possibly can. Unspoiled and beautiful, 1.4 miles long and .7 mile wide, it stands majestically alone, 10 miles out to sea, with a personality all its own and a wonderful sense of remoteness. Monhegan was important in the early history of Maine, and to this day remains as independent in spirit and fact as it is possible to be in these United States. As one islander put it, "What makes Monhegan different is that it's hard to get to and hard to live on, and anything that makes it easier is a step in the wrong direction."

The first European to pass this way was Giovanni da Verrazzano in 1524, searching for a passage to China. Other early explorers associated with Monhegan include Estevan Gomez in 1525, also searching for Cathay on behalf of Spain. Then came Martin Pring for the English in 1603, and Samuel de Champlain for the French, all of whom must surely have seen the island during their voyages along the coast.

First to describe the island was probably George Waymouth in 1605. James Rosier's contemporaneous narrative of this voyage says, "It appeared a meane high land, as we after found it, being but an Iland of some six miles in compass, but I hope the most fortunate yet discovered."

When Captain John Smith sailed north from the Virginia Colony with two ships in 1614, he was looking for gold and copper. Arriving at Monhegan, however, he soon discovered the island's true wealth: "the strangest fish-pond I ever saw." Smith was a wonderful publicist, and his enthusiastic accounts led to early attempts at colonization of these northern regions. "During the 16th and 17th centuries," as a placard at the museum explains, "Monhegan steadily gained a reputation among European traders and explorers as the richest fishing area in the New World. It became the landfall for European mariners westward-bound."

Today there are 12 working lobstermen on Monhegan, and a unique six-month season designed to preserve the fishery. Lobstering starts on "Trap Day," January 1, and ends in June—just when the season begins for many Maine lobstermen.

Two-thirds of Monhegan is protected woodlands, and the hiking is unsurpassed. And so is the birding. Monhegan is on the flyway for spring and fall migrations of hundreds of species of land and sea birds. The woods are alive with their sounds.

The cliffs of Monhegan tower 160 feet above the sea like an enormous beacon, highest on America's east coast. Today the island marks the first landfall for sailors coming from the south, just as it did for explorers crossing the Atlantic more than 400 years ago. Little Manana Island forms the western part of

Monhegan Harbor, and tiny Smuttynose protects the north end.

It is never easy to spend the night with your boat at Monhegan. It is a difficult anchorage exposed to a big ocean. If the weather is bad or threatening, you should not be here at all.

Getting There. The most direct way to get to Monhegan, of course, is to sail there in your own boat, either on your way down east or from a base on the mainland, such as Tenants Harbor or Port Clyde. But since the anchorage is difficult, you may well want to spend time here without worrying about your boat. There is no airport on Monhegan; the only alternatives are by water.

The easiest way is to take the mailboat *Laura B.*, leaving Port Clyde two or three times daily. In good weather, it is about an hour's trip. But fair or foul, Captain Jimmy Barstow gets her there every time. Advance reservations are required; call the Monhegan Boat Line (tel. 372-8848).

The *Balmy Days* operates out of Boothbay Harbor to Monhegan during the summer (tel. 633-2284) and the *Hardy* out of New Harbor (tel. 882-7909).

Approaches. From any direction, the high island of Monhegan is easy to find, and the lighthouse on Monhegan is visible 21 miles. The foghorn and radiobeacon are at the Coast Guard station on Manana Island. Two miles west is Manana Island lighted whistle buoy, where pilots board ships headed up Penobscot Bay.

Do not arrive at Monhegan late in the day. There may be no moorings available and no time to retreat to the mainland before dark.

From the North or East. Find gong "3" north of Eastern Duck Rock and then coast down the western side of Monhegan. Or find green bell "5" and pass west and south of Duck Rocks.

Smuttynose sits in midchannel between Monhegan and Manana. The main channel, Herring Gut, is on the Monhegan side and has 12 feet of water. The town wharf is just south of Smuttynose. There is plenty of room to pass through Herring Gut, even with a boat alongside the wharf.

The passage between Smuttynose and Manana is called Drunken Gut. It is very narrow and has about three feet at low water. Use it only if in need of adventure.

From the South or West. After finding red whistle buoy "14M" west of Monhegan, you can sail directly into Monhegan Harbor from the south.

Anchorages, Moorings. The simplest solution is to find a mooring in Monhegan Harbor. Find the harbormaster and see if a lobsterman's mooring is available. If he is not at the wharf, ask at the Island Inn or the Island Spa. Island Inn may have a rental mooring (tel. 596-0371).

The harbor is exposed to the southwest and northeast. Even in calm weather, ocean swells fun-

nel into the harbor and make it unpleasant. During a blow from the south, the swells are awesome, and it would be an extremely difficult and dangerous place to be.

The lobsterboats have great granite blocks for moorings, half the size of a house, and the harbormaster claims the boats have ridden out winds of 120 m.p.h. You might be safe enough on one of these moorings, but very uncomfortable. As is true anywhere on the coast, but even more so here, do not under any circumstances pick up a lobsterman's mooring and leave your boat unattended.

Do not anchor in crowded Monhegan Harbor. Depths are 15 to 25 feet, with poor holding ground, and the bottom is foul from 300 years of heavy use.

For comfort and safety, the best solution is to be on the *Balmy Days* mooring or the *Hardy* mooring, just inside Inner Duck Rock (locally called Nigh Duck). These excursion boats arrive with their day-trippers around 10 A.M. and leave about 3 P.M.

Inquire at the wharf to see whether any rental moorings have been put out inside Nigh Duck or in Deadman Cove. The moorings here provide fairly good protection if the wind is southerly, but they are not as convenient to the village center.

Another possibility is to anchor in the area from inside Nigh Duck up toward Deadman Cove, although it is deep and there is a lot of tidal current.

It seems impossible to combine safety, comfort, and convenience at Monhegan. If you can't find a good mooring, do not stay. The nearest anchorages are at Burnt and Allen islands, Port Clyde, and Tenants Harbor.

Getting Ashore. You can bring your boat up to the town wharf temporarily, but do not stay for more than an hour, especially if the *Laura B.* is due to arrive. Dinghy passengers can land at the town wharf anytime; there are ladders on each side. Do not leave the dinghy there.

If you intend to spend some time ashore, land at one of the two tiny beaches south of the town wharf. The one closest to the wharf is Swim Beach; the one farther south is Fish Beach. Fish Beach is the official public access for boats, but there is also lots of broken glass and rusty iron, so Swim Beach is preferable.

For the Boat. Diesel fuel is available at the town wharf by truck, from the Monhegan Store, but not drinking water. There are no repair facilities. If you have engine troubles, ask for the island mechanic.

For the Crew. Groceries, wine, beer, and ice cream are available at the Monhegan Store (see sketch map). North End Pizza is nearby. There are pay phones in several places and restrooms behind Monhegan House.

Meals are served at the Trailing Yew and the Island Inn.

Straight up the path, 100 yards from the wharf,

144

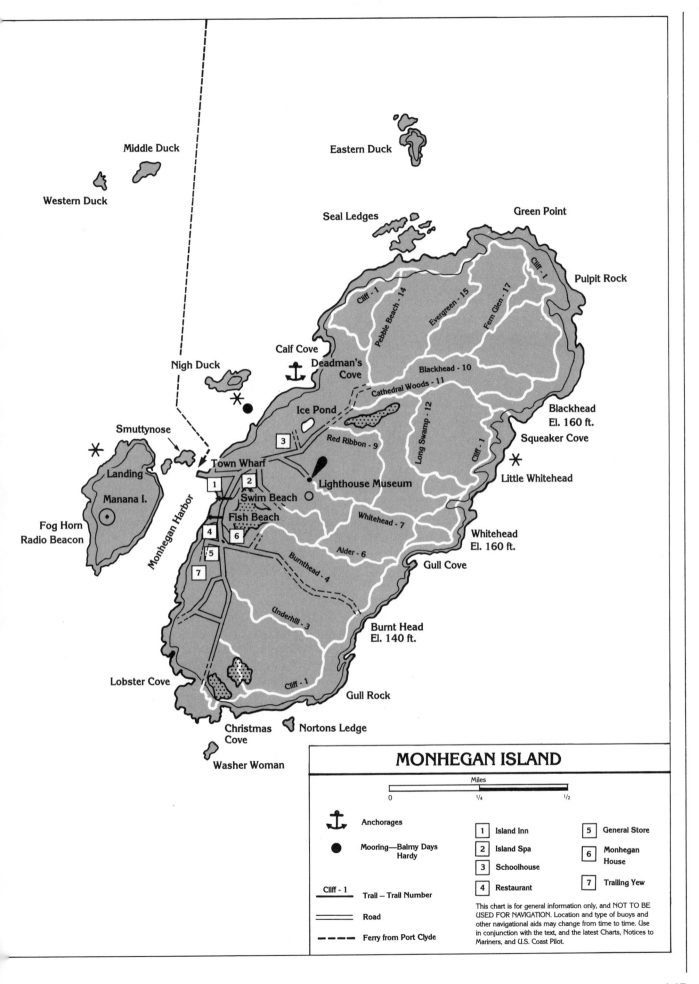

Middle Duck

Western Duck

Eastern Duck

Seal Ledges

Green Point

Cliff - 1

Pulpit Rock

Pebble Beach - 14

Evergreen - 15

Fern Glen - 17

Calf Cove

Nigh Duck

Deadman's Cove

Blackhead - 10

Cathedral Woods - 11

Blackhead
El. 160 ft.

Ice Pond

Long Swamp - 12

Squeaker Cove

Smuttynose

Red Ribbon - 9

Cliff - 1

Little Whitehead

Town Wharf

Lighthouse Museum

Landing

Swim Beach

Manana I.

Fish Beach

Whitehead - 7

Whitehead
El. 160 ft.

Fog Horn
Radio Beacon

Alder - 6

Gull Cove

Burnthead - 4

Burnt Head
El. 140 ft.

Underhill - 3

Lobster Cove

Cliff - 1

Gull Rock

Christmas
Cove

Nortons Ledge

Washer Woman

MONHEGAN ISLAND

Miles

0   ¼   ½

⚓ Anchorages

● Mooring—Balmy Days
Hardy

Cliff - 1 Trail — Trail Number

Road

Ferry from Port Clyde

1	Island Inn		5	General Store
2	Island Spa		6	Monhegan House
3	Schoolhouse		7	Trailing Yew
4	Restaurant			

This chart is for general information only, and NOT TO BE USED FOR NAVIGATION. Location and type of buoys and other navigational aids may change from time to time. Use in conjunction with the text, and the latest Charts, Notices to Mariners, and U.S. Coast Pilot.

The harbor at Monhegan in the late 1800s, showing a steamship at the town wharf and gaff-rigged fishing boats; photo taken from Manana Island. (Frank Claes Collection)

is the Island Spa, which sells gifts, postcards, books, and coffee. Posted here is a sign that advises: "If you can't enjoy the natural beauty of this island without the *New York Times*, the boat leaves at 11:30 and 4:00. Have a happy crossing . . . seasick pills 27 cents."

Years ago, things were pretty Spartan on Monhegan, but nowadays, most of the comforts of home are available, thanks not only to generators, but more recently to solar energy. Monhegan has an impressive amount of photovoltaic power, including the world's first solar-powered post office. Even a shack on Manana boasts a single solar panel, which powers the lights, a five-inch TV, and an electric guitar.

Things to Do. Watching the daily boats come in at the wharf is probably the big entertainment on Monhegan. Don't underestimate the show. Everyone crowds down to the dock to meet guests or send them on their way, or just to see the arriving passengers. Pickup trucks are waiting to carry bags to the inns; a torrent of propane bottles, lumber, and all the other fascinating miscellany needed for island life pours from the hold of the *Laura B.* After a day or two on the island, you wouldn't miss the boat parade for the world.

Be sure to allow time to hike the beautiful trails that run across and around the island. The protected woodlands are controlled by Monhegan Associates, and this group of citizens has preserved an extraordinary private park for the public to enjoy.

The family that established the present colony in 1784 (Henry Trefethern and his two brothers-in-law) believed that "the rocks belong to everyone." By the mid-twentieth century, however, summer people had arrived in force, and cottages were encroaching on the wild back side of the island. With the formation of Monhegan Associates in 1954, this trend was halted, and even some existing buildings were removed.

The result today is a great expanse of beautiful land more or less in its virgin state, 17 miles of maintained rustic trails, and breathtaking walks along the cliffs. There are forests and swamps, rocky headlands, and spectacular views to the distant mainland and the islands.

Trail maps are available at the Island Spa and other shops, as well as at the inns. If you have only a short time, try Trail #7 to Whitehead. It is 20 minutes or so one way. From the cliffs of Whitehead, there is a high, wonderful view of Ragged Island and Matinicus on the eastern horizon; lobsterboats working their pots; and herring gulls, eiders, guillemots, and cormorants. Anywhere on the island you can hear the clanging of a distant bell or gong.

For a more strenuous hike, follow the cliffs south from Whitehead on Trail #1 to Burnt Head, then back across the island on Trail #4 to the church. Or continue south around the end of the island to Lobster Cove. Another lovely trail across the island is #11, Cathedral Woods. See if you can find the fairy houses.

As the trail map warns, "The trails are rough and wild, especially cliff trails. Walk with care." No

146

smoking is allowed in the wild area, nor any outdoor fires. One further warning: On the headland side of the island (the eastern shore), stay well above the tide line. There are currents and undertows that make a rescue unlikely if you fell in. The town library was founded in memory of two children washed out to sea by a huge wave.

Even though Monhegan is relatively small in area, do not try to walk all the way around it the first day, unless you are in great shape and want to be thoroughly tired. A trek around half of the island is more than enough for most people.

Besides the great natural beauties of this island, there are many other things to enjoy. Artists have been attracted to Monhegan for more than a century, and today there are 20 or more studios scattered around the town, some open to the public at specified hours. A listing of these can be found on the maps posted on various bulletin boards all over the island. Among the familiar names that have been linked to Monhegan are George Bellows, Rockwell Kent, and Jamie Wyeth.

It is worthwhile visiting the lighthouse, now automated and run from the Coast Guard station on Manana Island. The lightkeeper's house has become a museum, with an interesting collection of old photos, books, artifacts of the lobstering trade, and mementos of this extraordinary island.

On the way to the lighthouse, near the old schoolhouse, is a bronze plaque dedicated to Captain John Smith, "Adventurer in many old world countries; a pioneer in the new world, Governor of Virginia. Came here with 2 vessels in 1614, anchored in this island harbor and explored the coast from Penobscot Bay to Cape Cod, discovering a large opportunity for adding to England's glory by colonization."

A boat operating out of Monhegan makes trips to Eastern Egg Rock, only 40 minutes away, to see the puffins.

Manana Island. Row your dinghy over to the Coast Guard ramp at Manana Island, at the northwest corner of the inner harbor. There is no float, so tie up to the railings and walk to the top of the hill for a magnificent view. The Coast Guard fog signal station is on the west side of the island.

As you approach the Coast Guard station, look for a yellow X on the rocks across the gully to your right. This marks the "Norse runes," reportedly inscribed by Norse explorers.

The ramshackle estate that cascades down to the harbor was owned by Ray Phillips, known as "The Hermit." A food inspector in New York City during the 1920s, he came to Monhegan in 1931, bought one-sixth of Manana Island, and built a 12-by-15 driftwood building, living there unmarried, with his goats and sheep and geese, until he died in 1975 at age 83. His ashes are buried on the island.

ALLEN ISLAND and GEORGES HARBOR ★★★★

 No facilities

Charts: 13288, **13301**

On Sunday, May 19, 1605, English explorer George Waymouth anchored his vessel *Archangell* in "Pentecost Harbor," probably the bight formed by the Georges Islands—Allen, Benner, and Davis. There they fished, filled their water tanks, and gave thanks for their safe arrival and the fortunate discovery. Waymouth made a preliminary reconnaissance up the St. George River and also mounted a cross on one of these islands to guide future explorers. Although the original has long since disappeared, a granite cross has been erected in modern times on the northwest tip of Allen Island to commemorate this brief but fertile exploration.

After meeting a group of Pemaquid Indians and trading with them in cautious but friendly fashion, Waymouth and his men captured five Indians and took them back to England. Although this seemed of minor significance at the time, it was one of the most important events in the early history of America.

The appearance and dignified demeanor of the Indians greatly impressed the people of London and the Court, creating a surge of interest in New World colonization.

The capture of the Indians by Waymouth was reported by Chief Arrossac shortly afterward to Samuel de Champlain, sailing in the same area. "He told us," wrote Champlain, "that there was a vessel ten leagues from the post that was fishing, and that those on the vessel had killed five savages from this river, under the guise of friendship; and according to the way they described the people of this vessel, we believe them to be English . . . ."

The enmity and distrust of the British that this engendered among the Indians was encouraged and exploited by the French, who allied themselves with the Indians in a series of bloody wars that destroyed English settlements along the coast for a hundred years.

Covering 400 acres, Allen Island, high and mostly wooded, is due west of Burnt Island and four miles south of Port Clyde. The private owner of Allen has cooperated with Maine's Island Institute to develop Allen as a model of island self-sufficiency. Once home for a number of lobstering families, Allen is now home for a flock of sheep. The northeast point has been cleared and the spruce used to build houses and a wharf.

The purpose of the experiment is to see whether there are practical and economic ways to use Maine islands today—rather than abandon them entirely to nature or to the onslaught of vacation homes. Salmon aquaculture is the most promising recent development.

Signs on the beach at the northern tip of the island say, "No fires, no dogs, beware dangerous ram." All of these are serious warnings. To protect the sheep, the shepherd will shoot dogs found on the island, and the ram has his own set of standards.

Georges Harbor (between Allen and Benner islands) is a cozy anchorage about 100 yards wide. The ledge on Benner breaks the seas, and the harbor often is calm when it's roaring outside.

Approaches. Enter Georges Harbor from northeast or southwest. Coming in from the northeast, pass down the middle of the slot, leaving to port the dock on Allen and probably some fish pens. Favor the east side as you emerge, to avoid a ledge making out from the south end of Benner.

Anchorages, Moorings. Note the submerged mooring cables shown on the chart crossing Georges Harbor. You can anchor comfortably in midchannel north of the large dock on Benner Island in 19 feet of water at low. Or run past the cable area and anchor where the channel widens on both sides. Holding ground is good.

Getting Ashore. Allen is a private island. While visiting is allowed, it is not encouraged. Scramble ashore near the Waymouth cross, or take the dinghy around to the little sand beach at the northern end of the island. Do not use the island's only wharf. Keep an eye out for the ram, who cares more about sheep than you do and can run much faster.

BURNT ISLAND ★★★ No facilities

Charts: 13288, **13301**

High, wooded Burnt Island marks the southeast corner of Muscongus Bay and is recognizable by the watchtower on the highest point, associated with the former Life Saving station. The island is privately owned, and a caretaker usually is in residence.

Little Burnt Island is connected to the northwest corner of Burnt by a sandbar that bares at low tide. In the bight on the west side between Burnt and Little Burnt are the dock and buildings left by the Life Saving (later Coast Guard) station.

Burnt Island has been used for many years as an outpost of the Hurricane Island Outward Bound School (HIOBS), so do not be surprised to see students heaving at the oars of a pulling boat, or jumping off the dock.

Approaches. Coming from Monhegan, run between Dry Ledges and Burnt Island. From Port Clyde, observe cans "3" and "5" and bell "7," all of which should be left to port.

Anchorages, Moorings. There may be some HIOBS moorings off the former Coast Guard dock (they are removed periodically, so don't count on their being there). These probably are all right for a short stop, but they are intended to hold 30-foot whaleboats and not heavy cruising yachts. This area also has considerable exposure.

The best anchorage in settled summer weather is north of Burnt Island, east of Little Burnt. Feel your way in until you find a comfortable depth for anchoring. The holding ground is good, in sand bottom.

Getting Ashore. If the state of the tide allows, take your dinghy over the sandbar at Little Burnt and tie up at the dock; there are no floats. If the tide is too low, land on the sandbar and walk around.

Things to Do. Check with the caretaker, who lives in the largest house next to the dock, for permission to land and explore.

All the way around the island (rough in places) is a trail built by the Life Saving Service, whose crews patrolled the perimeter of the island and occasionally launched lifeboats from the exposed outer shores to make a rescue. The Tower Trail leads south from the Life Saving station to the lookout tower (which is in dangerous condition). The Pooh Trail leads east from the Tower Trail and down across a swamp to the high cliffs at the southeast corner of Burnt. You may well see Outward Bound students scaling these cliffs. Camping facilities for the Outward Bound students are primitive on this island; they build their fires on the rocky beach of the north shore. If you are up at 5:30 A.M., you may also see them running around the island and jumping into the chilly water from the dock.

McGEE ISLAND

Charts: 13288, **13301**

McGee Island is part of the chain of islands running north and south from Caldwell Island to Allen Island. The passage north of McGee is a good one to know about—easy to find and well marked. The island itself is privately owned, and visiting is not encouraged.

Coming from Port Clyde or farther east, identify the red beacon on Old Horse Ledge. Run north of Outer and Inner Shag ledges, and close along the north shore of McGee Island, which is steep-to. Pass between can "1" and nun "2," north of McGee, or down the narrow slot between McGee and Twobush Island, into open water.

CALDWELL and TEEL ISLANDS

Charts: 13288, **13301**

Among the most attractive of the many islands in Muscongus Bay are the Caldwell Islands and neighboring Teel Island, at the mouth of the St. George River, west of Port Clyde. It is fun to make the passage from east to west between Caldwell and Teel, but you need to exercise some care. If you are unfamiliar with this passage, do it within an hour or so of low tide so that you can find the ledge shown on the chart halfway between Stone Island and Caldwell Island.

Approaching from the east, enter the passage south of the southernmost and smallest of the three Little Caldwell Islands. This high rock is grassy on top and crowned with a rock cairn. Continue through the passage north of Teel Island, identifying the midchannel ledge as soon as you can.

There is a small, privately maintained radar reflector buoy just east of the ledge, which also serves to mark the north-south passage between Stone and Teel islands. Leave the ledge fairly close to port to avoid the rock shown on the chart south of Caldwell Island. Once past the ledge, head for can "1" on Goose Rock Ledge, which will take you safely out.

There is a large home and dock on Teel Island, and often a yacht moored off. The holding ground is poor here, however, in mud and grass.

ST. GEORGE RIVER

Charts: 13288, **13301**

In 1605, English explorer George Waymouth and his crew encountered an impressive river along the Maine coast. The expedition's chronicler, James Rosier, wrote: "The River it selfe as it runneth up into the main very nigh forty miles toward the great mountaines beareth in bredth a mile, sometimes three quarters, and halfe a mile is the narrowest."

Rosier's description, intended to impress and perhaps to mislead certain folks at home, is a trifle exaggerated. After comparing the river favorably to the Orinoco, Rio Grande, Loire, and Seine, he modestly adds: "I will not prefer it before our river of Thames, because it is England's richest treasure."

The first reaction of most people reading Rosier's laudatory account is that he must have been talking about the Kennebec or Penobscot, or some other great river, and a hot historical debate has raged on the subject for centuries. But despite some discrepancies, it seems evident that it was the St. George River that Waymouth explored.

Burnt and Allen islands look as though they were especially lined up to lead Waymouth and every subsequent mariner directly into the St. George River. Even today, the *Laura B.*, in her passage to Port Clyde from Monhegan, runs between those two islands.

At the eastern entrance to the river is the busy working harbor of Port Clyde, not well protected, but fun to visit. At the western entrance is the much smaller and better-protected harbor of Pleasant Point Gut, which you can hardly squeeze into.

The river is easy to enter, and, for the first five miles or so, broad and deep. The banks are wooded, with saltwater farms and meadows lining the route. On either side are the wide coves described by Rosier: Turkey Cove, Maple Juice, Otis,

149

and Watts. Most of these are pleasant and secure anchorages for the cruising boat, although relatively shoal.

The whole river from Marshall Point to the head of navigation at Thomaston is less than 10 miles long. The upper section is narrow, with strong tidal currents, and bordered by mudflats. As discussed under the approaches to Thomaston, the channel near that town does not stay put, and the buoys are shifted frequently. This can be a tricky place for a deep-draft boat. Go up on a rising tide.

PORT CLYDE ★★★

Charts: 13288, **13301**

Port Clyde is easy to enter and a reasonably good harbor. It can be miserable, however, in strong winds from the southwest or northwest. It is primarily a working harbor for draggers and fishermen, whose picturesque houses and docks line the northern shore. Efforts are being made to improve facilities and attract yachtsmen.

This is also the starting point for the *Laura B.,* which takes passengers to Monhegan Island (see earlier writeup) at the rate of 1,000 a week in midsummer. Although this generates good business for local residents, the parking lots for Monhegan passengers threaten to overrun the town. Center of activity is the old-fashioned and delightful Port Clyde General Store.

Before the Revolution, the channel inside Hupper Island bore the euphonious name of Lobsterfare. This was changed by the pragmatic British to Herring Gut at about the time the town was first settled. In 1891, the town's name became Port Clyde.

Shipbuilding was the major industry here during the 1800s. When that declined, the town turned to canning lobsters, clams, and fish, and finally back to lobstering and fishing today.

Approaches. Coming from Tenants Harbor or farther east, turn at red bell "2MI," south of Mosquito Island. Passing north of The Brothers, bend left around green can "1" and sharp right at nun "4." The passage is easy and well marked, and you will have Marshall Point Light in sight. This lighthouse has a white tower, and the distinctive bridge leading out to it looks like a small Roman aqueduct.

Approaching from the west or south, there are two routes often used. The first is west of the Georges Islands through Davis Strait (narrow but straightforward), leaving nun "8" close aboard to port. Leave bell "7," can "5," and can "3" to starboard and enter the harbor.

The second approach is to run between Allen and Burnt islands, leaving Dry Ledges to port and then bell "7" to starboard, as above. This is more or less the track of the cable area shown on the chart.

There is a northern entrance to Port Clyde between Hupper Island and Hupper Point, which can be used by most boats except at dead low. Note the five- and six-foot spots between Hupper Island and Raspberry Island (the small, wooded island, unnamed on the chart, northeast of Hupper).

There is also a back entrance with deep water between Raspberry Island and the mainland, but it is difficult, and to be avoided without local knowledge. The ledge at the northeast corner of Raspberry Island extends at least 150 feet northeastward from the portion visible at low tide; stick close to the mainland, at dead slow speed, and with a lookout on the bow.

Anchorages, Moorings. The Port Clyde General Store puts out 25 heavy moorings (inquire at the store). There is plenty of room to anchor if you prefer, but the depths in midharbor are substantial (26 to 35 feet at low).

Getting Ashore. Land at the town landing dinghy float, or at the Port Clyde General Store floats.

For the Boat. *Port Clyde General Store (Ch. 10 or 16; tel. 372-6543).* The docks of the Port Clyde General Store lie between the Monhegan Boat Landing to the south and the town landing to the north. At their floats, with 10 feet of depth at low, they provide gas, diesel, electricity, water and ice; maximum stay is 30 minutes. The store carries marine hardware and charts.

Town Landing. The town landing has short-term dockage, with floats in front and a dinghy float around in back next to the launching ramp, but no other facilities.

For the Crew. Almost anything you need, from groceries and ice to lobsters, newspapers, and wine—and lots of things you don't need but might like to have—is available at the Port Clyde General Store. This is a colorful, old-fashioned general store and an experience to visit. The store also has showers, a takeout, and picnic tables where you can enjoy pizza, crabrolls, or lobsters on the deck.

There is a pay phone at the Monhegan Boat Landing, and another on the front porch of the Ocean House (a bed-and-breakfast up the hill to the right). The post office is just beyond. In town are a used-book store, a gallery or two, and the Black Harpoon Restaurant.

Just past the post office, turn left on a dirt road and follow the signs to the Fishermen's Co-op seafood market.

Things to Do. In any town with a ferry, one of the principal occupations and greatest pleasures is to go down to the dock and watch the boat loading or unloading. This is particularly true in Port Clyde, where the *Laura B.* loads up for the Monhegan Island trip. Don't miss it.

If you have time, make a day-trip to Monhegan on the *Laura B.* (tel. 372-8848); it's always an adventure. Normally, it would be logical to take your own boat, but you should think twice about taking it to Monhegan.

For a pleasant walk (a mile each way), take the first right along the shore to the Marshall Point Light, from which the view is spectacular. The lighthouse dates from 1833 and the lightkeeper's house has been restored as an historical museum.

PLEASANT POINT GUT ★★★

 No facilities

Charts: 13288, **13301**

Pleasant Point Gut is a working harbor on the west side of the entrance to the St. George River, north of Gay Island. It offers extremely good protection under almost any conditions, and the current through the Gut is not strong. People who were born here know how to get through the western end of the Gut safely at high water, but this is not recommended for strangers. The western entrance dries out a couple of hours before low tide.

Approaches. The best time to enter is at dead low tide, from the east, so the ledge making out from tiny Flea Island (unnamed on the chart), midway through the Gut, is fully visible.

Note that can "5" is a river marker, not a harbor buoy, and you leave it to starboard on entering the Gut. After rounding the northern tip of Gay Island,

favor the northern shore of the Gut. The major danger is the ledge making out north and northeast of Flea Island, which is about the same length as the island itself.

Anchorages, Moorings. You may be lucky enough to find an available mooring by asking around, but be prepared to anchor.

Drop the hook in 10 to 13 feet of water, at low, before the slot of deep water along the northern shore runs out, if you can find space among the moored boats. Holding ground is good, in mud, and the harbor offers extremely good protection under most conditions. There is not, however, a great deal of extra room.

TURKEY COVE ★★   No facilities

Charts: 13288, **13301**

First of the large, open coves on the east side of the St. George River, Turkey Cove offers a well-protected anchorage for a small fleet. Forty cruising boats have been known to rendezvous here at one time. The south shore is wooded, but there are a number of houses on the north shore and a road at the head of the harbor.

Approaches. The entrance is wide and easy.

Anchorages, Moorings. Anchor in the center or southern part of the cove in 8 to 15 feet of water at low. For the best protection, get east of the rounded point of the south shore. The water starts to shoal rapidly just before the dock on the south side. Holding ground is good, in mud.

MAPLE JUICE COVE ★★★

Charts: 13288, **13301**

Maple Juice Cove is a large, round bay half a mile across, on the west side of the St. George River, two miles or so above the entrance. Access is easy and the cove provides a calm and secure anchorage. This must have been one of the "very gallant Coves" described by James Rosier, chronicler of

George Waymouth's expedition. Philip Conkling, director of the Island Institute, suggests that this cove probably was named for the encircling stands of large sugar maples.

The surrounding shores have no intrusive features, and some handsome old houses are set on the meadows of Stones Point. The arm of the cove extending to the north is the home of a small fishing community.

It is not unusual to see 10 or more cruising boats in Maple Juice Cove on a summer day, with plenty of swinging room for all. Seals like it here, too. The water is warm enough for swimming.

Approaches. Coming up the St. George River, leave can "7" to port.

Anchorages, Moorings. Anchor anywhere in the cove in 9 to 15 feet of water at low, mud bottom.

Getting Ashore. Row your dinghy in to the far end of the Maine Mussel floats and climb the ladder. Or land at the tiny island west of Burton Point—if it is not occupied by the cows that amble over at low tide.

For the Boat. *Maine Mussel Company (tel. 354-6961).* Gas, diesel, and ice may be obtained at Maine Mussel, whose red buildings are visible at the northern entrance to the cove. There is about five feet of water at low along the outer float (you will need fenders). There is also a small selection of marine supplies.

For the Crew. Maine Mussel Company sells lobsters, clams, and, of course, mussels. There are no grocery stores or other facilities within walking distance.

Things to Do. Row over and examine the hulk near Maine Mussel Company. Referred to as "the old tug," her superstructure now forms the restaurant for the Tugboat Inn in Boothbay Harbor, and there are plans to make her hull into a pier.

Maine Mussel seeds and harvests mussels locally, and also buys mussels from farther down east for processing here. You might enjoy observing the operation.

A quarter-mile up the road, on the right, is the distinctive weathered farmhouse made famous by Andrew Wyeth's painting *Christina's World*.

Do not be tempted to land on Stones Point; you are likely to encounter an irate property owner.

LOONS

The mournful tremolo of the loon sends shivers down your back— eerie and old and very wild. Loons are impressive and fascinating birds, equally at home on the lakes of Minnesota and the salt water of Maine.

Almost as big as Canada geese, loons are easy to recognize, with their glossy black heads, ruby eyes, white necklace, long pointed beaks, beautiful black-and-white-checkered backs, and white breasts.

Loons mate for life, and they are territorial, so you are likely to find only one or two birds in a cove, no more. If you run across them underway, they are capable of submerging like a submarine, by exhaling and sinking slowly out of sight without a ripple. Or they may swim off with just their heads showing above water, still watching you.

Taking off is hard work for the loon. As with the cormorant, there is a long struggle just above the water, wings beating hard, feet paddling the water. And ashore, loons are equally awkward. But underwater they are in their element, diving as deep as 200 feet, driving their streamlined bodies with powerful thrusts of their webbed feet.

The weird ululating cry of the loon covers a lot of situations: courting, greetings, and alarm. There are other calls as well: the yodel, de- scribed as "thrilling and blood- curdling," often heard among competing males in the springtime; and the wail, like the cry of the wolf, which causes campers and sailors to stir uneasily in their sleep. Sometimes the cry is a wild, maniacal laugh.

The population is declining in Maine now—perhaps because of growing intrusions into their habitat, perhaps because of fluctuating water levels—and the Maine Audubon Society, among others, is taking steps to save this handsome symbol of the wilderness.

OTIS COVE ★★★ No facilities

Charts: 13288, **13301**

Otis Cove, on the east side of the river, is probably one of the loveliest spots on the St. George. It has pretty, wooded, rocky shores with only a few houses in sight, broad views all around, including fields and farmhouses across the river and the Camden Hills to the north. In the middle of the cove is small, uninhabited Ten Pound Island. Protection is good.

Approaches. To stay clear of the rock and six-foot spot at the southern end of the cove, head in for the island on a southeasterly course.

Anchorages, Moorings. There is a good anchorage either southwest or northeast of the island. The northeast one provides a little better protection from prevailing winds, and somehow seems cozier. Anchorage is good, in mud and grass.

WATTS COVE ★★ No facilities

Charts: 13288, **13301**

Watts Cove, on the east bank of the St. George, opposite Broad Cove, is shallower than some of the other anchorages on the river and therefore less useful to cruising boats. If you draw less than five feet, however, this would be a secure anchorage. It is mostly wooded, with a few houses and a lovely encircling cove.

Approaches. The entrance is wide open. Go in as far as your draft allows, to get protection from the southwest. Note the ledge extending from the south shore.

Anchorages, Moorings. With shoal draft, you will be comfortable here. Boats drawing five or six feet probably will simply ground gently in the mud, which provides good anchorage.

THOMASTON ★★★ 4 All facilities

Charts: 13288, **13301** (Inset)

Nine miles up the St. George River from Muscongus Bay, Thomaston was one of the great Maine coast shipbuilding towns of the nineteenth century. But its history goes back much farther—to 1605, when Captain George Waymouth landed here. Just above the waterfront today is a wooden cross that commemorates the event: "That We, The Menne of Englande, have marked this spot for home."

Settled in the 1630s as a trading post between Plimoth Plantation and the Indians, Thomaston had its heyday in the 19th century. Burning of lime to make plaster was the first industry, followed by the shipbuilding necessary to transport the lime. For half a century, the major interest of Thomaston was building great schooners and other vessels, which made the name of this small town well known in foreign ports. Eight major yards were engaged in building these ships, and whoever was not a sailor or captain was a rigger, cooper, sailmaker, or merchant. It was indeed, as its motto proclaims, "the town that went to sea."

Today Thomaston remains a working town linked with past and present. Although the great shipyards are long gone, there has been a boatbuilding renaissance, and five builders are active along the waterfront. A contemporary town landmark is the immense brick structure of the Maine State Prison, the state's only maximum-security facility.

Approaches. The channel at Fort Point is still wide and deep enough so you should have no trouble working your way from buoy to buoy. Above nun "16," opposite Hospital Point, the situation changes. There are frequent shifts in the channel near the sharp turn in the river toward Thomaston, and many boats have grounded in the mud here.

As noted on the inset to chart 13301, "Buoys "17," "18," "19," and "23" are not charted because they are frequently shifted in position." The Coast Guard tries to keep up with the shifting channel, but there is no guarantee that these buoys are in the right places. Flashing green light "21" is fixed in position on a pile of granite blocks, but do not cut it close; the channel probably is some distance to the east.

Come in on a rising tide, either at dead low—when the mudflats appear and the channel becomes obvious—or after midtide, when there is plenty of water.

The current in the river may run two or three

knots above Fort Point and four or five knots off the Thomaston waterfront.

Anchorages, Moorings. The head of navigation is a fixed bridge just beyond the docks of Thomaston. With the strong current in the river and that fixed bridge nearby, you may be uncomfortable anchoring here. Moorings can be obtained from Thomaston Marine or Lyman-Morse, or you can lie alongside at either. If you simply want to explore the town, tie up at the Thomaston town dock (see below).

Getting Ashore. Row your dinghy in to the floats at Thomaston Marine, Lyman-Morse, or the town dock.

For the Boat. As you approach the Thomaston waterfront, the gray buildings toward the east belong to Wallace Marine boatyard. Next comes the float and dock of Lyman-Morse Boatbuilding, whose shop is just up the hill. Then, past a sloping wall of granite blocks, comes the town dock, followed by the floats of Thomaston Marine.

Jeff's Marine Service (Ch. 16; tel. 354-8777). Hidden on the left side of the harbor, just before the fixed bridge, is Jeff's, which has floats with water and electricity, and eight feet of water alongside at low. The yard specializes in the sale and repair of outboards and stern-drives, and has a related chandlery.

Lyman-Morse Boatbuilding Company (Ch. 9; tel. 354-6904). This is the yard that became famous building John Alden's Malabar schooners and the Friendship sloops. Today, Lyman-Morse produces handsome custom-designed sail and power craft, including Seguin 44s. The yard uses a 50-ton mobile crane and can make repairs of all kinds. Showers are available. Their floats near the eastern end of the waterfront have 10 feet alongside at low, and they have rental moorings.

Thomaston Marine (tel. 354-2200). This marina offers gas, diesel, water, and ice at the pier, with 8 feet of water alongside at low. Thomaston Marine has rental moorings, or you can lie along the floats, with depths of eight feet. There is a small selection of marine supplies, including charts, and snack foods.

Thomaston Town Dock (Public Landing). The town dock has a launching ramp and floats, with a 30-minute tie-up limit on weekends and a three-hour limit during the week.

Wallace Marine Services (tel. 354-8898). Wallace concentrates on restoration of wooden boats and new construction, and is also equipped for repairs and emergency towing. The yard maintains one mooring and has three marine railways, the largest of which can handle 100 tons.

For the Crew. Just above Thomaston Marine is the Harbor View Tavern, offering food and spirits and a pay phone. It is a half-mile walk up the road to Main Street, where you will find a post office, drugstore, laundromat, bank, a small grocery, and a variety of other stores. Jameson's Grocery will drive you back to your boat.

Things to Do. Just up Knox Street from the waterfront, on the right, is the museum of the Thomaston Historical Society. It is housed in the last of nine brick buildings that formed a semicircle at the rear of Montpelier, Major General Henry Knox's mansion built on this spot in 1795. Knox, military historian and tactician and Commander of Artillery under George Washington in the American Revolution, was the most renowned citizen of Thomaston. He served as the fledgling nation's first Secretary of War. Through his marriage to Lucy Flucker, Knox was able to acquire large landholdings in Maine and build his splendid mansion.

Montpelier fell on hard times and was torn down, but a replica, open to the public, was built east of town in the 1930s. It is a magnificent building, containing much of the original furniture and other Knox memorabilia, and worth the 1.2-mile walk.

The route to Montpelier takes you up Knox Street, lined with beautiful old houses, then to Route 1, where you will pass the refurbished Thomaston Academy, home of Mid-Coast Community College and the town library. Farther along Route 1 is an imposing cemetery, a good place to make some unusual grave rubbings. One of the stones is for the "Captain of the unfortunate *Pacific*," and one for the first officer of a ship lost at sea between Le Havre and New York. Mehitabel McCallum is there, and so is Mrs. Margaret George, "Relict of Capt. George." Edward O'Brien stands there full size in stone, wearing his frock coat and bow tie, leaning on an anchor, looking out over a garden of lesser relatives.

The walk eastward along Main Street will also take you past a wonderful row of handsome homes built by merchants and sea captains. Now designated a National Historic District, this area's homes reflect the sophistication of world travelers: European styles ranging from Federal to Greek Revival and Gothic, to Italianate and French Second Empire—splendid reminders of those days of glory.

If the weather is poor, you might want to visit the Maine State Prison showroom on Route 1, where inmate-produced artifacts are sold at reasonable prices.

Cruising sailors may be especially interested in visiting Thomaston's many boatbuilders. In addition to Lyman-Morse and Wallace Marine, already mentioned, there are three more yards near the western end of the harbor: Renaissance Yacht Company, Edward T. Gamage, Inc., and Phoenix Boat Building Company.

LIGHTHOUSES

The storm howls, the waves pound endlessly on shore, breaking into driven white spray. A small boat wallows in the surf and is flung, helpless, toward the rocks. In the beam of the lighthouse, frightened faces are lit for a flash, yellow-slickered arms flung outward; then lost in the black, chaotic night. The vessel strikes the rocks. Unperturbed, the great beam of the lighthouse sweeps its appointed circle, briefly lighting the splintered planks, the gear sucked out in the backwash of the waves, the yellow bodies tossed ashore. No one sees.

In 280 BC the Pharos of Alexandria was one of the Seven Wonders of the World, its fires blazing 440 feet above the sea. More than 2,000 years later, the 84 lighthouses of Maine are direct descendants, gems of functional architecture that gladden the heart of the mariner. First was the Portland Head light on Cape Elizabeth, built during George Washington's first term, in 1791. Next came the tower on Seguin Island, off the mouth of the Kennebec, which much later became the only one in Maine with a first-order Fresnel lens.

Whale oil was the fuel at first, followed by lard oil and eventually kerosene. One of the duties of the keeper was to trim the wicks, and every few hours he wound the weights that turned the panels to make the light flash. Electricity made things easier, and the invention of large refracting prism lenses in 1922 by Augustin Fresnel greatly improved the range and brightness of the lighthouse beam. Powerful airway beacons cast the lights today.

Fog bells were struck by hand in the early days, then by a clock-wound mechanism. Finally lighthouses were equipped with steam whistles to produce the familiar and sonorous notes that reverberate through the fog. *Whooo-aaah. Whooo-aaah.*

First managed by a Lighthouse Board, then the U.S. Lighthouse Service, the lights came under the U.S. Coast Guard in 1939. During the austerity programs of the late 1980s, the Coast Guard decided to de-activate many lighthouses, and to automate the remaining ones over a period of several years. This process is now complete.

Some lighthouses, like Hendricks Head at the mouth of the Sheepscot River and Indian Island off Rockport, are now private residences. The lighthouse on Marshall Point at the mouth of the St. George River is now an historical museum. The facilities on Matinicus Rock are leased to the Audubon Society, and the keeper's house on Seguin Island is occupied during summer months by the Friends of Seguin.

These lighthouses remind us of Captain Joshua Strout, who served more than half a century at Portland Head light, and of William Williams, who spent 27 years on lonely Boon Island, off York. And of 17-year old Abbie Burgess, who was tending the light on Matinicus Rock when a great wave swept over the rock in 1856. For two hundred years there was a great tradition of lighthouse keepers—families willing to live alone on a rock in the sea, their only communications and resupply by small boat, often isolated for weeks on end during winter storms. They minded the lights, they rescued sailors in distress, they raised their families. That way of life has passed, and it will take a while to understand what we have lost.

Region 4 / Marshall Point to Isle Au
Penobscot Bay

A windjammer ghosting into Pulpit Harbor on North Haven as the sun sets over the Camden Hills. (Neal A. Parent photo)

Haut

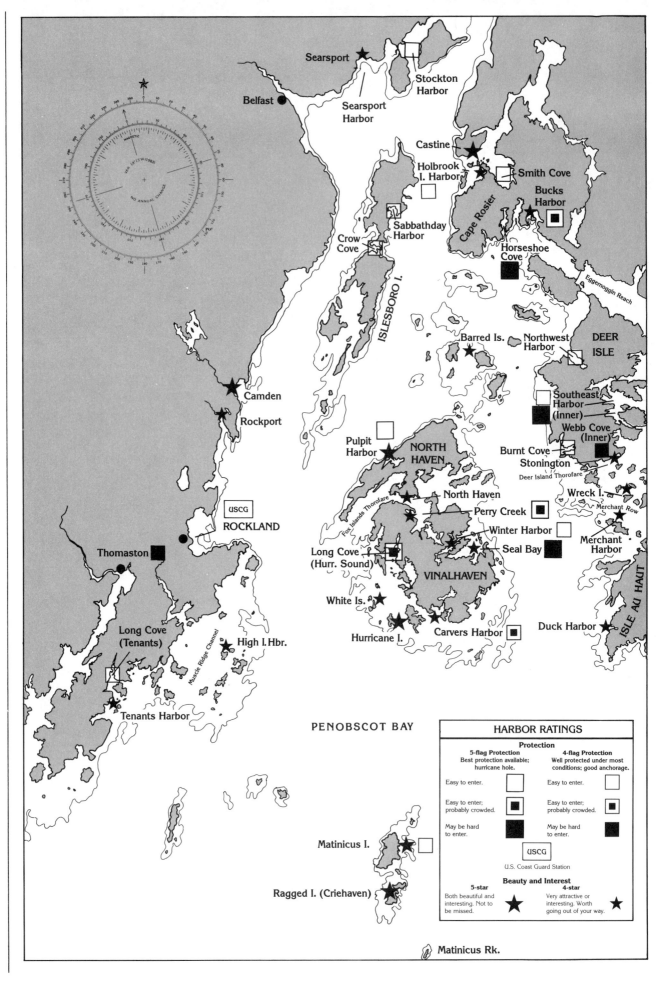

Searsport

Stockton
Harbor

Belfast

Searsport
Harbor

Castine

Holbrook
I. Harbor

Smith Cove

Cape Rosier

Bucks
Harbor

Sabbathday
Harbor

Crow
Cove

Horseshoe
Cove

Eggemoggin Reach

ISLESBORO I.

Barred Is.

Northwest
Harbor

DEER
ISLE

Camden

Rockport

Southeast
Harbor
(Inner)

Webb Cove
(Inner)

Pulpit
Harbor

NORTH
HAVEN

Burnt Cove
Stonington

Deer Island Thorofare

USCG

ROCKLAND

North Haven

Wreck I.

Merchant Row

Fox Islands Thorofare

Perry Creek

Winter Harbor

Merchant
Harbor

Thomaston

Long Cove
(Hurr. Sound)

Seal Bay

VINALHAVEN

White Is.

Long Cove
(Tenants)

High I. Hbr.

Muscle Ridge Channel

Hurricane I.

Carvers Harbor

Duck Harbor

ISLE AU HAUT

Tenants Harbor

PENOBSCOT BAY

HARBOR RATINGS	
Protection	
5-flag Protection	**4-flag Protection**
Best protection available; hurricane hole.	Well protected under most conditions; good anchorage.
Easy to enter.	Easy to enter.
Easy to enter; probably crowded.	Easy to enter; probably crowded.
May be hard to enter.	May be hard to enter.

USCG
U.S. Coast Guard Station

Beauty and Interest

5-star
Both beautiful and interesting. Not to be missed.

4-star
Very attractive or interesting. Worth going out of your way.

Matinicus I.

Ragged I. (Criehaven)

Matinicus Rk.

I t's a beautiful, beautiful bay! Spruce-covered headlands jut boldly from its shores, jewel-like islands float on its surface, and the gentle, glacier-rounded contours of the Camden Hills look down on its broad reaches."

The Coast of Maine, Louise Dickinson Rich

One of the best cruising grounds in Maine, and perhaps the world, Penobscot Bay is 40 miles long and 15 miles wide, graced with more than 200 islands. Here there is everything from busy fishing communities to small, sophisticated resort towns, from large commercial harbors to uninhabited islands.

Well marked, with great stretches of open water and generally predictable and moderate winds, Penobscot Bay is a sailor's delight. There are gentle sails with sunset on the Camden Hills; there are exhilarating passages, rail down, surrounded by an ever-shifting scene of dark islands and distant headlands. There are winding thoroughfares to thread, endless gunkholes to explore, and a hundred harbors tucked away.

At the entrance to the bay are the outlying islands, remote and hard to visit: lonely, sea-swept Matinicus Rock, where puffins fly between your masts at sunrise; Ragged Island and Matinicus, most seaward communities on the coast of Maine; Metinic, Green, Seal, and Wooden Ball islands. They have their own rules, these distant islands, their own priorities, hardly part of Maine at all.

Along the shores of Penobscot Bay are a variety of interesting harbors, from safe and welcoming Tenants Harbor to the very different towns along the western shore: the large, industrial fishing harbor of Rockland; small and charming Rockport; beautiful Camden nestled at the base of the Camden Hills.

In Camden is based the largest fleet of windjammers on the Maine coast, whose tall masts and gaff-rigged sails on the horizon add so much pleasure to cruising in the bay.

Up north lie Searsport and Sears Island, destination of the tankers, tugs and tows, cargo ships, and container vessels that steam up Penobscot Bay. A century ago, Belfast and Searsport were homeports for ships that sailed for every corner of the world, home to a hundred sea captains. The Penobscot Marine Museum in Searsport preserves this heritage.

Northward runs the Penobscot River, past Fort Knox and 24 miles up to Bangor, once a brawling frontier town and lumber capital of the world. Near the eastern head of the bay, the Bagaduce River empties past Castine, stronghold of the French, and later the British, site of America's first great naval defeat during the Penobscot Expedition, and now home of the Maine Maritime Academy.

South of Cape Rosier lie Bucks Harbor, Little Deer Isle, Deer Isle, and the broad passageway of Eggemoggin Reach. On the eastern side of the bay, the fishing town of Stonington looks out on Deer Island Thorofare and the magnificent islands of Merchants Row. And at the eastern entrance of Penobscot Bay stands rugged Isle au Haut, much of which is now part of Acadia National Park.

The islands of Penobscot Bay are as interesting as its shores. At the western entrance lies the archipelago of Muscle Ridge, once important for its granite quarries, now sparsely settled by fishermen. Among these islands and ledges are two or three delightful anchorages hardly changed from Indian times.

In the center of the bay are the Fox Islands—the twin islands of North Haven and Vinalhaven. Separated by the narrow, winding, and altogether delightful Fox Islands Thorofare, they are separated also by a wider gulf. North Haven is a fashionable community settled long ago by Boston yachtsmen and summer people. Vinalhaven is a working island, where Carvers Harbor is the base for lobstermen and seiners and draggers. Around the convoluted shores of the Fox Islands are some of the best harbors in the bay: Pulpit Harbor, Perry Creek, Winter Harbor, and many more.

South of Vinalhaven, volcanic Brimstone Island stands all alone, twin crescent beaches piled with black and polished stones. And at the southwest edge of Vinalhaven is Hurricane Sound, with five separate entrances. This is the home of the Hurricane Island Outward Bound School, whose students roam the coast of Maine in open, ketch-rigged whaleboats.

Beyond North Haven is a scattering of islands—Pond and Pickering, Butter, Eagle, Great Spruce Head, and the Barred Islands, to name a few. Dividing the northern part of Penobscot Bay is Islesboro, a long and lovely island also discovered by Boston Brahmins, who established the fashionable summer and sailing community of Dark Harbor a century ago.

Lime was quarried on the western shores of Penobscot Bay and shipped to Boston and New York for plaster and for mortar. Granite was cut in dozens of quarries, from Dix Island to Stonington, to build the banks and post offices, museums and monuments, breakwaters, bridges, and cobblestone streets of Boston, Washington, Philadelphia, and New York.

But always the main preoccupation has been with the sea—with building ships, with fishing, with lobstering.

MATINICUS and the Outlying Islands

Charts: 13302, **13303**

Scattered for 20 miles across the mouth of Penobscot Bay lie the outlying islands: Metinic and the Green Islands, Matinicus and Ragged, Wooden Ball and Seal. Beyond them all, standing as the first rampart to the sea, is lonely Matinicus Rock, whose lighthouse has guided mariners into Penobscot Bay since 1827. These rocks and islands are the ends of mountain ranges depressed by the glaciers long ago, then drowned by the returning sea.

Ocean islands are different from bay islands. Each stands isolated, exposed to unending waves that sweep across 3,000 miles of ocean to crash upon the shore. Even on the calmest of days, swells break in spray and spume on every ledge, and in the worst of gales, a great wave will break entirely over Matinicus Rock.

The people, too, are different here. Like the ocean islands themselves, they stand alone—tougher perhaps, independent to a fault. Most were born here; they stay because they love the islands, or perhaps because they have no choice.

Of all these outlying islands, only one—Matinicus—has a permanent year-round settlement. The ferry runs once a month to Matinicus and not at all to Metinic. Ragged Island was inhabited for generations, but now it supports only a small seasonal community of fishermen and summer people.

Peregrine falcons, soaring over these barren islands, glide down to land on Wooden Ball and Matinicus Rock during spring and fall migrations. The National Audubon Society is trying to reestablish a puffin colony on Seal Island; the other islands are visited occasionally by fishermen, naturalists, Outward Bound students, and sometimes an intrepid yachtsman.

METINIC ISLAND ★★★

Charts: 13302, **13303**

Metinic, an Indian word meaning "far-out island," is largely owned by the Post family of fishermen. Long and low, it is wooded in the middle and has meadows at both ends. The island has a group of homes toward the southern end, and two unoccupied houses standing gray and lonely near the northern end.

In 1750, enterprising Ebenezer Thorndike took a 99-year lease on Metinic Island from the Abenaki Indians. For 250 years, the island has been owned, farmed, and fished by his descendants.

Though less than five miles from the mainland, Metinic might just as well be on another planet. This remote outpost is the home of eiders, gulls, guillemots, arctic terns, white-faced Metinic sheep, and fishermen as self-reliant as any in the world.

Walter Wotton, who grew up on Metinic, remembers his father rowing him to church in Tenants Harbor every Sunday.

The flock of wild, white-faced sheep has been here since the Civil War, roaming the island at will and living off the land. The rams are kept on a neighboring island until February so that lambs are born in the late spring. Then the sheep are driven the length of the island into a corral for shearing.

This is a hard place for a cruising yachtsman to visit. Attempt it only during settled weather, and not when the wind is from the east or the north.

Approaches. If you are coming from Muscle Ridge Channel, be sure to switch from chart 13305 to chart 13303; the latter shows red bell "2SB" off South Breaker, which must be left to port before heading toward Metinic. From the north, the island appears as a smooth, rounded meadow with a fringe of dark trees.

Head for green bell "1W" off the north end of Metinic Island, then run down the east side until you are opposite the houses at the narrow waist of the island. Stay far enough out to be well clear of Cat Ledge. Having identified The Nubble (small and rocky) and larger, grassy Hog Island, head north of The Nubble toward the little cove.

Anchorages, Moorings. Do not enter the cove without local advice. There are ledges at each corner of the entrance, and not much water inside.

Hail a fisherman and ask if a mooring is available. Most likely, he will direct you to the stake moorings north of Hog Island, in 13 feet of water at low. The one "to nor' ard" has a four-ton block, and the other two have two-ton blocks; you probably will need to rig a pendant. Hog Island, The

Nubble, and Metinic together provide pretty good protection in normal summer weather. If the wind comes in from the north or east, *leave*.

Anchoring temporarily is fine, but you probably will not be happy spending the night here except on a big mooring.

Getting Ashore. Take your dinghy in to the float, which dries out at low.

Things to Do. This is a private island, but you are welcome to go ashore (ask permission from one of the fishermen). There are no public facilities of any kind. If you take a dog ashore, keep it leashed so it won't worry the sheep.

Walk through the red spruce woods to the north end and contemplate the lonely lives of the families who lived in these old houses, exposed to the fury of the northern gales. Metinic is a major nesting area for many seabirds, especially eiders, until July 15. Stay on the trails.

MATINICUS ISLAND ★★★★★
Charts: 13302, **13303**

 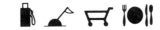

Matinicus is the outermost Maine island inhabited year round. With its true remoteness, air of independence, and long occupation by the same families, Matinicus is reminiscent of other extraordinary islands like Tangier in the Chesapeake and lonely Pitcairn.

As islander Donna Rogers writes, "I guess what Matinicus offers most is her stubborn refusal to keep up completely with the rest of the world. There are no factories, no traffic, no noise, except for the sound of waves breaking on shore or the bell buoy on a blowy day."

This is a beautiful and fascinating place to visit, but also difficult. Choose your time carefully; it can be uncomfortable and dangerous in heavy weather, and frequent fogs arrive with little warning.

The local fishing fleet numbers 25 or 30 boats. On a given summer day, there may be half a dozen visiting yachtsmen, or you may be the only one. Don't expect to be greeted warmly, but Matinicus men, in the best tradition of the sea, keep a watchful eye on all passing or visiting vessels; if you are in trouble, you can count on them for help.

The central occupations of the island are lobstering and fishing, and the islanders like it that way. "We don't want to become like Monhegan," they say.

Matinicus is almost two miles long, with one good harbor on the east side, meadows, woods, and white sand beaches of great beauty. The fields are alive with wildflowers that last into October, and there are hundreds of species of plants on its 720 acres.

The state runs a ferry from Rockland to Matini-

cus once a month, so most communication with the mainland is by private boat or plane. Air-taxi service, provided by Penobscot Air Flying Service from Owls Head, is an important lifeline. There is a private boat service four days a week between the Rockland ferry terminal and Matinicus (tel. 366-3700 or 366-3926 at night).

Winter population varies from 35 to 50, and grows to 150 or more during the summer. Most important to the survival of Matinicus as a year-round community is the small school, which sometimes has seven children, sometimes nine, occasionally only three.

Approaches. *From the South.* If you are coming from Matinicus Rock, give the east coast of Ragged Island a good berth as you head north for Matinicus.

You will see the gap of Matinicus Roads and long, rocky Tenpound Island (grassy on top). Work your way north toward the red-and-green bell off Matinicus Harbor, passing between Wheaton Island and West Black Ledge.

Both East and West Black ledges are high and easy to identify by the breaking surf. Note the shoal spots at the southeast end of Wheaton Island.

From the North. Set your course for red-and-white bell "WP" north of Matinicus and then to green lighted buoy "5," off Zephyr Rock. Coast past barren, rocky No Mans Land—a forbidding place even in sunny weather and loud with herring gulls—to can "5" north of Mackerel Ledge. From can "5," a straight course to the red-and-green bell at the mouth of Matinicus Harbor will clear The Barrel, a small rock, 10 feet awash at low, on which the swells break with enthusiasm. Note Harbor Ledge northeast of the bell.

From the red-and-green bell just off the harbor, run directly through the middle of the entrance, between the rocky tip of Wheaton Island to the south and the small, lighted beacon on the end of the breakwater to the north, aiming for a two-story white house with a red roof on the far shore.

It is not unheard-of for the mouth of the harbor to be closed off by fishing nets. On one occasion, the crew of a visiting windjammer lowered the net to enter, and the trapped herring escaped. There was hell to pay.

Anchorages, Moorings. Inside the harbor on your line of approach, fisherman Victor Ames has put down heavy nylon cables, in the shape of a "Y," to which are attached a number of rental moorings; most have white pick-up lobster buoys; marked "rental." In maneuvering to pick up a mooring, do not enter the area between Wheaton Island and Matinicus, where mooring cables stretched across could snag the keel of a deep-draft

MATINICUS: 'A DIFFERENT BREED'

In *Matinicus Isle: Its Story and Its People (1926)*, Charles Long tells the story of Ebenezer Hall, first permanent settler on Matinicus in 1751. Hall was not well received by the Penobscot tribe of the Tarratine Indians, who resented his presence in their traditional fishing and birding lands. They complained to the govenor when Hall burned over Green Island to improve the hay, thus disturbing the habitat for eiders, on which the Indians relied for food and feathers. Hall continued the practice.

In June of 1757, a band of Indians laid siege for several days to Hall's house on Matinicus. It ended with the scalping of Hall and the capture of his wife and daughters. Mrs. Hall was finally ransomed in Quebec, but her four daughters were never heard from again. A son, Ebenezer, who escaped only because he had been out fishing, returned to live on the island in 1763 and married Susannah Young. Many of the islanders today can trace their ancestry from this couple.

In an interview in the annual *Island Journal*, Dorothy Simpson of Criehaven reminisced: "Matinicus ancestors go way back to the Revolution and before that, even to the Indian Wars. There's something grown into them I think. They are a different breed . . . . The people fish there and work there and their kids keep coming along in the steps of their fathers . . . . They say, 'My grandfather fished over there and my father and my uncle and I got a right.' "

A group of Matinicus ladies preparing a lobster cookout, 1901. (Frank Claes collection)

Much of the land on Matinicus has been owned by the same families for 200 years; Ames, Young, Philbrook, Bunker, and Ripley are some of the familiar names. More recent settlers are now prominent, but fishermen still outnumber rusticators.

"Matinicus, eh? They have their own sense of justice out there. They're either the best people you ever met or the worst, depending on how they accept you," says one observer. "Don't cross 'em. Somebody was cutting lobster traps and one of the boys flew over his lobsterboat in his airplane and dropped this great big field stone right through the boat. Sank him.

"And don't fool around with the things they love, like churches and graveyards. A man threw a rock through the window of *Sunbeam* once, and before you knew it, he was off the island."

Sunbeam is the 65-foot vessel of the Maine Seacoast Missionary Society in Bar Harbor. It is important to this community, and its monthly winter visits are much anticipated. In addition to sponsoring religious and medical services, and a scallop dinner each spring, *Sunbeam* is relied on for marriages and burials. Many are born, live all their lives, and die on the island; then *Sunbeam* takes them to a funeral home in Rockland and returns them to Matinicus for burial. One elderly lady requested in her will that she be spared the rigorous trip to the mainland. Her wish was granted.

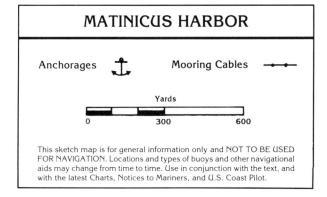

MATINICUS HARBOR

Anchorages ⚓   Mooring Cables •—•—

Yards

0   300   600

This sketch map is for general information only and NOT TO BE USED FOR NAVIGATION. Locations and types of buoys and other navigational aids may change from time to time. Use in conjunction with the text, and with the latest Charts, Notices to Mariners, and U.S. Coast Pilot.

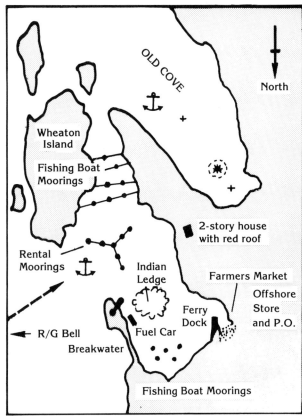

sailboat. There may be room to anchor just west of the moorings and also in the entrance of the harbor (see sketch map), but the bottom is hard sand and not good holding ground. If an easterly is predicted, be prepared to leave.

There is good protection here in settled summer weather; the only real exposure is to the east. Because of the ocean swells, however, you are likely to spend a rolly night.

Most of the fishing fleet is moored at the north end of the harbor behind Indian Ledge, near the state ferry dock. It is possible to pass to either side of Indian Ledge, but the water inside is shoal, so this is no place for yachts.

During the night, you will see the sweep of Matinicus Rock Light through the slot inside Wheaton Island. Lying at anchor here is not the same as in the protected islands of the bay; the sounds of the sea are loud and relentless.

Old Cove. If the harbor at Matinicus is full, it's possible to anchor in Old Cove, just around the corner to the south. This seldom-used anchorage offers reasonable protection from southwesterlies but is open to the southeast. Ledges line the western shore; stay well over to the east and do not go much beyond the first house on the eastern shore.

Getting Ashore. Landing your dinghy is difficult here. There are no floats in the harbor. The best solution is to run the dinghy up the beach just left of the ferry dock to land passengers and cargo. Then tie up to a ladder near the end of the ferry dock.

Do not bring trash ashore; there is no place to leave it. There are no public toilets on the island.

For the Boat. Fuel may be obtained at the lobster car near the breakwater on the eastern side of the harbor. If you need engine repairs, ask around. Matinicus lobstermen are experts.

For the Crew. Matinicus fishermen use channel 19, (and sometimes channel 10) on which you can also reach some of the local businesses. Store hours vary from time to time; check posted notices. Near the ferry landing is the Off Shore Store (with groceries, ice cream, beer, and wine), open weekday afternoons until 4 p.m. and Saturday morning.

Also nearby are the post office, a pay phone, and a takeout. To the left of the beach is a refurbished lobster shack with a wide deck. Called the Farmers Market, it is operated two days a week by the Matinicus Ladies Aid Society. They sell sandwiches, bread, fresh vegetables, and crabmeat. The Farmers Market also will open on request to sell local crafts, including a most unusual cookbook, *Recipes from Matinicus Island, Maine* (with recipes for baked dog bones, a homemade Boursin cheese, and homemade goat-milk fudge). Matinicus Island women may serve lobster suppers in their homes Friday or Saturday nights. Look for notices. Lobsters can be purchased from one of the two buying stations in the harbor.

If you need transportation, Monique's Island Tours and Taxi is based at the Off Shore Store. The Tuckanuck Bicycle Shop (tel. 366-3830) is located at Tuckanuck Lodge.

Things to Do. Walking is a delightful activity on Matinicus. There are paths along the ledges and through the woods, and everyone is free to walk them. The main road runs down the center of the island. You are welcome to pick strawberries, blueberries, and raspberries along the roadside, but stay off private property. The islanders will wave and may give you a ride in their pickups.

Markey's Beach is at the northeastern end of the island, and the magnificent crescent of South Sandy Beach, at the south end, looks out to Criehaven. Birding is good on Matinicus, especially during spring and fall migrations.

Friendship sloops and the S.S. *William J. Butman* at anchor in Matinicus Harbor, 1905. This midharbor anchorage, still the obvious choice for today's yachtsmen, offers good protection in settled summer weather, but the ocean swells are likely to make for a rolly night. (Frank Claes Collection)

RAGGED ISLAND (CRIEHAVEN) ★★★★★ No facilities
Charts: 13302, **13303**

Even more remote than Matinicus, beautiful Ragged Island is the farthest outpost on the coast of Maine. There's no store, no school, no post office, hardly any way to get there, and no place to stay. There are lovely walking trails through woods and meadows, a profusion of wildflowers late into the fall, and excellent birding. This was "Bennett's Island" of Elisabeth Ogilvie's famous trilogy, *Storm Tide*, *The Ebbing Tide*, and *High Tide at Noon*.

"Racketash" it was to the Indians, which became "Ragged Arse" to the British. Prudish American cartographers later shortened the name. After the Revolution, a British soldier named John Crie retired to live on Matinicus. His grandson Robert set up housekeeping on neighboring Ragged Island in 1848, and for half a century was the leading citizen and entrepreneur. Like many Maine islands, Ragged produced hay and lumber, sheep and wool, and fish for the city folk in Boston—all under Robert Crie's jurisdiction. Eventually, he bought up the whole island and was known locally as "King Crie." At the head of Criehaven Harbor, the right-hand path leads to the dark and overgrown cemetery where Crie is buried.

The fishermen of Ragged Island tried for decades to get federal funding for a breakwater for their harbor. Matinicus got its breakwater in 1912, but Criehaven had to wait until 1938. It was breached during the 1978 Groundhog Day storm, and considerable damage was done to the boats and docks.

Ragged Island appears to be in a state of transition between the year-round community it was until 1941 and the abandonment that has overtaken many coastal islands. Perhaps the present summer community will suspend or halt this seemingly inexorable process.

As George Putz wrote in the annual *Island Journal*, "Though island communities are elegant in their social orders, they are for the same reason more prone to reverses brought about by only one or two events. The death of an influential man, the loss of a mailboat, a teacher, a store, or a breakwater, may have influence all out of proportion to comparable events in mainland communities where more options are available."

There are no year-round residents on Ragged Island today, but 10 lobstermen fish here, prizing their independence and the good lobstering grounds. By unwritten law, one of the lobstermen has to relinquish his rights before another lobsterman can start fishing here. They work out of Criehaven 10 or 11 months a year, usually returning to their mainland homes and families on weekends. Another 10 families summer at Criehaven in relative harmony with the fishermen.

To row ashore in Criehaven on a fall day is to enter a ghost town. There are dinghies at every mooring and fishing gear piled on the surrounding docks. Little clapboard houses surround the harbor, but there is no visible movement—no dogs, no women and children, no sound except the gulls. In summertime, there is activity, of course, but, as a Mainer would say, "It's real peaceful."

Approaches. Coming from Matinicus Harbor, run south past West Black Ledge and turn westward between Tenpound Island (long, rocky, grass on top) and The Hogshead (small and dark, with swells breaking heavily). Leave Pudding Island to port (35 feet high, rounded and cliffy, with a few windblown trees). Criehaven Harbor and the granite breakwater are hidden at first (except for the beacon), but will open up as you coast westward through Matinicus Roads.

Pass the seven-foot spot west of Pudding Island before turning into Criehaven Harbor on a southerly course, leaving the breakwater to starboard. Harbor Ledges, just west of the harbor (marked by nun "6"), are covered two hours after low tide, but swells continue to break on them.

Anchorages, Moorings. *Criehaven.* The harbor is very small and full of lobstermen's moorings. These are secured to cables laid on the bottom—four cables and three moorings each. There is little or no room to anchor outside the moorings, and the bottom is reported to be solid granite ledge. Somewhere near the mouth of the harbor is a pile of rusting metal junk, dumped there by the lobstermen to snag the gear of draggers. This is not a healthy place to anchor.

If you want to spend the night, pick up a mooring near the entrance and wait until a fisherman appears; ask him if there's an empty mooring with enough water and swinging room. If you go ashore, leave someone aboard who can move the boat. The harbor is well protected except from the north and northwest.

Getting Ashore. There are no floats in Criehaven Harbor, and the wharves are both high and private. To get ashore, row your dinghy in to the little beach at the head of the harbor; tie up to the mooring cable on the right end of the beach.

Wilson Cove. On the north side of Ragged Island, south of Pudding Island, Wilson Cove (unnamed on the chart) provides a possible anchorage in summer weather, protected from ocean swells and the prevailing southerlies.

Pass inside either Pudding Island or Shag Ledge to reach the cove. A ledge makes out 50 yards from the eastern shore, so favor the deeper water in the western part of the cove. Stay a good distance off the beach, which slopes gradually. The bottom is cobblestone; use a kedge anchor and not a Danforth.

There is a big, grassy field above the cobble beach, and trails leading to Criehaven.

Seal Cove. Seal Cove, on the east side of the island offers another possible anchorage. The cove itself is filled with ledges; stay near the entrance.

Land at the semicircular beach; a footpath leads over to Criehaven.

Things to Do. As you walk the narrow paths from Criehaven toward Seal Cove, you can see Matinicus Rock in the distance. A path runs down the eastern shore, then cuts across to the western shore and down to the southern tip of the island, passing through a grove of yellow birch. Wildflowers and birds are everywhere.

MATINICUS ROCK

Charts: 13302, **13303**

Matinicus Rock is an impressive place—"the outermost, loneliest rampart," as photographer Eliot Porter puts it in *Summer Island*. Here great swells surge and break on the cliffs as they did before the memory of man. The rock is the first outpost of land at the entrance to Penobscot Bay and one of a series of outlying islands seen by the early explorers as well as modern-day coasting mariners: Seguin, Monhegan, Matinicus Rock, and Mount Desert Rock.

A lighthouse was first built here in 1827. It was replaced again and again. Today's stone tower shows a powerful light 90 feet above the sea, visible 23 miles, with a foghorn and radiobeacon. Scientists and birdwatchers come here to see puffins, terns, petrels, auks, and other rare species. "Be there at dawn," says Peter Willauer, founder of Hurricane Island Outward Bound School. "Sail along the cliffs on the eastern side, and puffins intent on feeding will fly between your masts."

Manned from the earliest days until automation in 1983, the Coast Guard facilities on Matinicus Rock were licensed to the National Audubon Society to ensure a human presence on the island. You may encounter a group of Island Institute volunteers camped on the rock, counting migrating peregrine falcons.

In bad weather, access to the island by sea is cut off altogether. Even in normal weather, landing is extremely difficult, so don't try it except in a dead-flat calm. Then it is possible to go ashore on the western side, near the Coast Guard station. The instructions given in the 1891 report of the Lighthouse Board still apply: "The lightkeeper effects a landing by steering his boat through the breakers on top of a wave so that it will land on the boat ways, where his assistants receive him and draw his boat up so far on the ways that a receding wave cannot carry it back to the sea."

To avoid disturbing the nesting birds, do not go ashore at all before July 15. You can sense the power and presence of this lonely outpost from your boat, without having to land.

Best known of the lightkeepers who lived on Matinicus Rock was the Burgess family. Keeper Samuel Burgess spent much of his time away fishing, and he depended on his daughter, Abbie, to maintain the light while he was gone.

Writing to a friend, Abbie described the great gale of January 19, 1856, when she was 17 years old: "Early in the day, as the tide rose, the sea made a complete breach over the rock, washing every movable thing away, and of the old dwelling not one stone was left upon another. The new dwelling was flooded, and the windows had to be secured to prevent the violence of the spray from breaking them in. As the tide came, the sea rose higher and higher, till the only endurable places were the light towers. If they stood we were saved, otherwise our fate was only too certain. But for some reason, I know not why, I had no misgivings, and went on with my work as usual . . . .

"You know the hens were our only companions. Becoming convinced as the gale increased, that unless they were brought into the house they would be lost, I said to mother: 'I must try to save them.' She advised me not to attempt it. The thought, however, of parting with them without an effort was not to be endured, so seizing a basket, I ran out a few yards after the rollers had passed and the sea fell off a little, with the water knee deep, to the coop, and rescued all but one.

"It was the work of a moment, and I was back in the house with the door fastened, but I was none too quick, for at that instant my little sister, standing at the window, exclaimed, 'Oh look! Look there! The worst sea is coming.' That wave destroyed the old dwelling and swept the rock. I cannot think you would enjoy remaining here any great length of time, for the sea is never still and when agitated, its roar shuts out every other sound, even drowning our voices."

During a storm in 1975, the keepers watched from their tower as a great wave once again swept across the entire rock.

A 1904 photo of the twin lighthouse towers on lonely Matinicus Rock, 25 miles offshore. Only one tower is in use today, automated in 1983. Landing here by sea is always difficult; it is impossible during heavy weather. (Frank Claes Collection)

WOODEN BALL ISLAND

Charts: 13302, **13303**

Three miles east of Matinicus, high, rocky Wooden Ball Island is narrow and a mile long. There is enough pasturage on the island to graze sheep and do some farming, but it is hard to believe that two families lived here year round during the 1840s and 1850s. A couple of small fish shacks remain near Back Cove.

Today the only inhabitants are birds, and occasional birdwatchers; this is a favorite nesting island for the usual gulls, cormorants, and eiders. Two rarer species—laughing gulls and arctic terns—also can be seen here as well as peregrine falcons during their migrations. Birds are nesting until mid-July.

The two most likely anchorages are Northeast Cove and Frenchman Cove, but neither offers much protection or an easy landing. Even in calm weather, the ocean swells break hard on the eastern ledges. Holding ground is rocky and poor.

SEAL ISLAND

Charts: 13302, **13303**

All alone, six miles east of Matinicus and three miles northeast of Wooden Ball, Seal Island looks on the chart like a sea serpent. The rocky island, owned by the United States Fish and Wildlife Service, is a mile long, 77 feet high, and covered with grass and arctic plants. The southern shore is formed of sheer white cliffs.

Although used by fishermen from early times, remote Seal Island has never had permanent inhabitants. It has probably seen more action in the past 50 years than in its entire previous existence.

During World War II, the island was used as a bombing range. This broke up the surface rocks, leaving ideal nesting terrain for seabirds, especially petrels. Their existence changed suddenly, however, when a fire broke out during the dry summer of 1978. A team from the Hurricane Island Outward Bound School landed on Seal to help put out the fire, but long-buried shells suddenly started to explode from the heat and the effort was abandoned. The fire smoldered for weeks. Since that unnerving experience, the island has been cleaned up again, but the chart still shows it as a danger area. A haunting portrait of the burning of Seal Island can be found in the book *Amaretto,* by Joe Upton (International Marine Publishing Company; 1986).

The National Audubon Society is trying to reestablish puffins here, as they did on Eastern Egg Rock. Puffin chicks transplanted from Newfoundland have been installed in burrows painstakingly dug by hand. The task now is to feed all those hungry young birds by hand, make them feel that Seal Island is home, and convince them to return to breed.

Because of the surge, it usually is difficult to land on Seal Island. Your best bet is to anchor in Western Bight, which provides the most protection, and row ashore on the boulder beaches. Because this is a nesting site for several species of seabirds, do not land before mid-July.

TENANTS HARBOR to Muscle Ridge Channel, Rockland, and Camden

TENANTS HARBOR ★★★

Charts: **13301**, 13302

This is an attractive working harbor, and a convenient stop on your way east or west. Sarah Orne Jewett, who called it "this quietest of seaside villages," in *The Country of the Pointed Firs,* wrote much of that famous book here. Deep and reasonably protected except from the east or southeast, Tenants Harbor is very easy to enter under most conditions—with good anchorage, moorings, and plenty of room. The town is on the north side, and private homes are scattered around the harbor. The handsome bell tower at the seaward end of privately owned Southern Island has been immortalized by Andrew Wyeth.

On the south shore of the harbor is the boathouse that houses *Dyon,* a 52-foot gaff-rigged sloop designed and built by Luders in 1924 for Philip L. Smith of New York and Tenants Harbor. The old man had a reputation for pushing her hard and being reluctant to shorten sail (1,350 square feet in the huge main). The harbor looks right when this graceful, classic yacht is at her mooring, waiting for the third and fourth generations of Smiths to sail her east.

Approaches. Southern Island, with its abandoned lighthouse, clearly marks the entrance to Tenants Harbor. From the south, the lighthouse is seen as a series of white buildings. From the east, all the buildings merge into one. Pick up green lighted bell "1" just to the east of Southern Island and leave it to port. The entrance is wide and open except for a profusion of lobster buoys. Head up the middle of the channel, staying clear of the bar at the western end of Southern Island.

Anchorages, Moorings. Anchor anywhere with swinging room in 14 to 22 feet, mud bottom. There is some kelp on the bottom, particularly near the head of the harbor, but the holding ground is very good elsewhere.

Moorings are available from several sources: Cod End moorings have a yellow lobster buoy marked "Cod End Rental." Lehtinen's Boat Shop moorings are marked "LBS." Art's Lobsters moorings have green lobster buoys marked "Rental." Witham's Lobster moorings are white balls marked with lobsters.

Getting Ashore. Take your dinghy to the Cod End float or the town landing, and you will be right in the heart of Tenants Harbor.

For the Boat (from East to West, along the North shore). *Witham's Lobsters.* Witham's owns the first dock on the north side; gas and diesel are sold here, with deep water off the end of the dock (not the floats). You can also buy lobsters.

Art's Lobsters. The second set of docks on the north shore belongs to Art's Lobsters. Except for mooring rentals, this is strictly a commercial lobstering operation. They also sell lobsters retail.

Lehtinen's Boat Shop (tel. 372-6327). Next door to Art's Lobsters are the red buildings of Lehtinen's Boat Shop, which builds and repairs mostly wooden boats. The yard has a marine railway and a machine shop.

Cod End (Ch. 16; tel. 372-6782). The "cod end" is the bag at the end of a funnel-shaped trawl where the fish accumulate. When the cod end is lifted from the sea, you find out whether you have a good catch. A shingled shack with red trim, Cod End has a dock and float with four feet alongside at low. Gas, diesel, ice, and water are available at the float. Some marine supplies can be obtained, and there is a selection of charts.

Cod End is owned by the Miller family, who offer fresh fish, lobsters, and other seafood at the takeout restaurant and picnic area on the deck. Another service associated with Cod End is a delivery boat, which makes the rounds of the harbor, providing hot muffins, groceries, ice, cooked lobsters, clams, and trash pickup. Very convenient!

Town Landing. Just beyond Cod End are the launching ramp and town dock and float, with about four feet alongside at low.

For the Crew. To get to Hall's Market, with a good selection of fresh meat and produce, beer and wine, and the town's only pay phone, go up the hill to the right from Cod End. Continue a short distance to the post office and laundromat.

The East Wind Inn (tel. 372-6366), a large white building on the north shore, serves breakfast and dinner in pleasant surroundings. Visitors to the inn may use a small float just east of the Cod End dock. There are a couple of other restaurants in town.

The nearest taxi service is in Rockland, 10 miles away. Call R & H Taxi at 594-5525.

LONG COVE ★★★★   No facilities
Charts: **13301**, 13302

If you prefer an anchorage that is quieter and more isolated than Tenants Harbor, tranquil Long Cove is right next door. The anchorage is well protected under almost all circumstances, and far preferable to Tenants Harbor when the wind is blowing strong from the east or southeast.

So many English stonecutters came to work in the granite industry here at the end of the 1800s, the local historical society relates, that a section of Long Cove was called Englishtown. They were followed by Finns and Swedes and other nationalities, so that Clark Island and Long Cove developed a cosmopolitan air. In those days, the village boasted stores, a post office, boardinghouses, and

even a bandstand. Only the silent quarries remain to remind us of that fascinating era.

Approaches. The approach to Long Cove is easy. Run between nun "2" at Northern Island and the ledge making out from the mainland, staying close to the nun.

Anchorages, Moorings. Anchor almost anywhere in Long Cove up to green can "1," in 9 to 14 feet of water at low. There are no moorings. With normal summer winds, you will have good protection and a peaceful night. Even when the wind is from the southeast, the ledge between High and Northern islands blocks most of the swells, except at high tide.

MUSSELS—OR THE BEST THINGS IN LIFE ARE FREE

Lobsters you can buy from a lobsterman. Clams you can dig on a clam flat, if you have the equipment and the license. Oysters you can find in the fish market. But mussels, delicious mussels, are free for the taking, and easy to collect from the cold, clear waters of Maine.

As tiny seed, mussels attach themselves to rocks and pilings in the intertidal zone, or clump together with other mussels. They lead sedentary lives, straining the seawater for microscopic organisms brought to them by the rising and falling of the tides.

To collect them, just wait for low tide, survey the scene, and pry the clumps of mussels from the most convenient rocks. They come off easily, and you need no special tools. You can also collect them from mussel beds on the bottom, but that may be a bit messy.

As the Maine Department of Marine Resources points out, be sure that the location you select is not closed to the taking of mussels because of red tide or similar biological phenomena. Restriced areas are announced daily on NOAA Weather Radio. *Never eat shellfish from a closed area.* And, of course, do not take mussels in populated harbors or in areas that obviously are polluted. Also, some people have allergic reactions to shellfish that are unrelated to red tide.

The best mussels are those just exposed or below water at low tide. They will last several days if refrigerated, or indefinitely if hung over the side in moving water. It is best to eat them fresh right away.

Cleaning mussels is simple. With your fingers or a knife, pull out the byssus threads by which they attach themselves to rocks. Rinse them in cold water (salt water is fine) to get rid of sand. Throw away any mussels that remain open or are heavy with sand.

You can substitute mussels in almost any recipe calling for clams or oysters, but there is no need to be fancy. Steam them in white wine—with onion, garlic, and other herbs—until the shells open (5 or 10 minutes). They're ready to eat. Serve with French bread and a nice Chablis or Montrachet.

Outward Bound students learn to build a little fire below the high-water mark and steam mussels in salt water in a #10 can. The results are better than you can find in any French restaurant—and the price is right.

If you go beyond can "1," stick to the western half of the cove to avoid the shoals extending southwest of the Spectacles. Two yachtsmen who rode out a 50-knot northerly just north of can "1" reported that the water barely rippled.

While it is possible to go as far as nun "4" and beyond, do it only with local knowledge. There is excellent protection deep in the cove if you know how to get there. It becomes very ledgy and narrow, full of lobster buoys and strong currents.

Getting Ashore. The easiest place to go ashore is at the floats of Atwood Brothers, recognizable as a two-tone red and green building on the west side, opposite can "1"—or you can scramble up on the rocks nearby. Spectacles, Northern, and High islands are private and inhabited.

For the Crew. In the shallow cove due west of can "1" there is a takeout on the lobster pound wharf. It can be reached directly by dinghy, or by walking from Atwood Brothers to the main road and then one-quarter mile south. Lobsters are available at Atwood Brothers and mussels at Great Eastern Mussel Farms (see below).

Things to Do. If you have a sailing dinghy, explore the ledges north of the anchorage.

An interesting outing is a visit to the plant of Great Eastern Mussel Farms, tucked in the cove on the west shore opposite the north end of Clark Island. Take your dinghy around the corner past nun "4," about a mile from can "1." Great Eastern has a gray building on a granite wharf, and you can land at their floats. Be aware, however, that this upper part of Long Cove bristles with ledges, and the tidal currents are strong.

If you prefer to walk, it is about 1½ miles. Land at Atwood Brothers and walk past the quarry, turning right on Route 131. Continue half a mile or more to the next right-hand turn, Long Cove Road. There is a sign for the mussel farm. Walk another quarter of a mile and take the first right turn.

Wild mussels from lowtide ledges have always been a local Maine delicacy. Early attempts to culture oysters and mussels relied on rafts moored in bays and rivers, with the seeds arranged in trays or clinging to long vertical strings. Better methods have been developed since the passage of a 1973 law making it possible to lease parcels of sea bottom for aquaculture. In recent years, Great Eastern has learned how to improve the quality of wild mussels and reduce the time they take to grow.

Great Eastern sows mussel seed on acreage leased from the state. After two years, when they have grown to sufficient size, the mussels are harvested by local fishermen and brought to the Great

169

Eastern plant. There they spend a day in tanks of clear seawater to siphon themselves clean, before declumping, washing, and inspection to remove broken shells and grit. Finally, the shiny black mussels are shipped all over the country in special refrigerated trucks. You can buy mussels right here, and Great Eastern provides recipes in English and French. They also sell a T-shirt printed with the comparative nutritional values of mussels and a T-bone steak (95 calories versus 395 calories, just for a start).

Despite the popularity of these succulent mollusks, the mussel industry remains highly controversial. Fishermen have objected strenuously to the harvesting of seed mussels and to the leasing of mussel beds. "One man's seed mussel is another man's catch," they say, and lobstermen complain of damage done to good lobstering ground.

MUSCLE RIDGE CHANNEL

Charts: 13302, 13303, 13305

Muscle Ridge Channel runs northeast-southwest inside the islands of the Muscle Ridge archipelago, at the western entrance to Penobscot Bay. The name is an English variation of "mussel." Muscle Ridge Channel is the usual approach for small vessels and cruising yachts. Deep-draft ships must use Two Bush Channel, which is farther out, much wider, and well marked with light and sound buoys.

Muscle Ridge is a good passage in daylight and clear weather. It has the advantages of being somewhat shorter than Two Bush, offering protection from the ocean swells, and providing a degree of shelter from the wind. It is also an interesting passage, with a variety of unspoiled islands and headlands stretching from the lighthouse on Whitehead Island to the dramatic Owls Head Light—about nine miles.

The current through Muscle Ridge Channel is strong, so time your passage accordingly (the tide floods northeast and ebbs southwest). The channel is relatively narrow and bordered with a number of ledges and rocks; good piloting is essential. If you are heading south past Whitehead Island, use

chart 13303, which shows red bell "2SB" marking South Breaker. The dangers are well marked, but only one buoy has sound. Going through in a moderate fog, you can catch enough glimpses of the land, and the marks are just close enough together, to make the passage without much difficulty. In a thick fog, it is very sticky.

There are no really good harbors on Muscle Ridge Channel, the closest refuges being Tenants Harbor to the south and Rockland to the north. If you were fogged in or wanted to stop for some other reason, you might find a mooring in Seal Harbor or Owls Head Harbor. Both are easy to enter but crowded with lobsterboats.

Consider these "Directions from Tennant Harbour to the Muscle Ridges," from *The American Coast Pilot* of 1806: "In sailing from this harbour you may steer E. by N. 1 league to Whitehead, but be careful not to haul in for it till it bears N.E.; . . . a pistol shot from the shore, is safe navigation. There is a good harbour called Seal Harbour, on your larboard hand as you pass this head (bound to the eastward), where you may lie safe from all winds."

WHITEHEAD ISLAND

Charts: 13302, 13303, **13305**

On the northeast side of Whitehead Island is a little bight that shows 17 feet on the chart. It is fun to poke into, but it would be uncomfortably exposed for the night, being open from southeast to northeast and to the ocean swells.

From Muscle Ridge Channel, work your way in south of the large ledge with two little rocky islands (Seal), favoring the bold shore of Whitehead Island. There is a granite pier on Whitehead, after which the water shoals. The ways formerly used by the Coast Guard lightkeepers are just beyond.

SEAL HARBOR ★★

Charts: 13302, 13303, **13305**

On the west side of Muscle Ridge Channel, between Whitehead Island and Sprucehead Island, Seal Harbor was much used by coasting schooners waiting out the tide during the days of sail. Today it is a working harbor with a fleet of some 50 lobsterboats. These are concentrated along the south shore of Sprucehead Island; the big, open bay shown as Seal Harbor on the chart is hardly used.

Approaches. Enter between green can "1" and the red-and-green can south of Burnt Island. (There is a large gray house on the southeast end of Burnt.) Head toward nun "4," near Sprucehead Island, north and east of which the fishing fleet is moored. Note the rocks and ledges just west of nun "4."

Anchorages, Moorings. This is a friendly place. Ask a lobsterman where there is an available mooring. You can spend a night here, but it may be somewhat rolly because of exposure to the ocean swells.

If no mooring is available, there are two alternatives, neither of which is particularly satisfactory. The first is to anchor southwest of nun "4" in the main part of Seal Harbor. This is a mile across and does not offer very good protection. Furthermore, the bottom is reported to be poor holding, in kelp. Parts of Long Ledge are visible until two hours before high.

The second alternative is to run up north of Slins Island and anchor in the strip of deep water running westward above Rackliff Island. This is narrow, crowded, and unmarked, except by a line of moored boats, and it would be easy to find yourself aground on the mudflats. Go on a rising tide.

Getting Ashore. Take your dinghy in behind the float at the Fishermen's Co-op.

For the Boat. The main part of the harbor is in the small cove northeast of nun "4," with the dock and little gray-and-white building of the Spruce Head Fishermen's Co-op. You can get gas and diesel at the Co-op float (seven feet reported alongside at low). The docks on the right side of the cove and near the bridge to Burnt Island serve two lobster-buying stations.

For the Crew. You can buy lobsters, clams, and fresh fish at the Co-op, and there's a takeout at W.M. Atwood next door. It's about 1.2 miles to the Off Island Store, which offers groceries, newspapers, and wine.

Things to Do. Turn right as you leave the dock and walk toward the private bridge to Burnt Island. There is granite everywhere, rough and partly finished blocks. It protects the shoreline, lines the road, and forms unusual fences between neighbors.

FALSE WHITEHEAD HARBOR ★★
Charts: 13302, **13303**, **13305**

False Whitehead is the indentation on the north side of Sprucehead Island, west of Muscle Ridge Channel. Although it provides a lee in southwest winds and gets you out of the ebb current in Muscle Ridge, the harbor shoals rapidly just inside the entrance and the holding ground is poor, with kelp and eelgrass. Take a mooring.

Approaches. The approach from the channel is clear between Sprucehead Island and can "7" on Sunken Ledge. Note the ledge at the northeast tip of Sprucehead.

Anchorages, Moorings. Moorings are available for boats up to 50 feet from Merchant's Landing Moorings, located on the left side of the harbor as you enter.

Getting Ashore. Go into the float at Merchant's Landing.

For the Boat. *Merchant's Landing Moorings (tel. 594-7459).* There is about seven feet alongside the floats at low; water, ice, electricity, and a telephone are available.

For the Crew. A walk of about 1.7 miles north takes you to the Off Island Store, which has a lunch counter, groceries, newspapers, and wine; the Spruce Head post office is nearby.

SPRUCE HEAD MARINE (SPRUCE HEAD)
Charts: 13302, 13303, **13305**

Just east of the village of Spruce Head, a point of land jutting north forms a shoal cove. Tucked away in this cove is Spruce Head Marine (Ch. 16; tel. 594-7545). The yard has no landings or floats, but hauls boats for storage with a 30-ton boatlift. Hull and engine repairs can be made by the yard, or you can do them yourself. No fuel is available, but you can get water and some marine supplies.

The Spruce Head Marine dock on the western side of this cove should be approached only during the two hours before or after high tide. From the eastern tip of Sprucehead Island, run toward Waterman Beach. Leave close aboard to port the ledge with a tiny island (visible at high water) east of Spruce Head, heading for a house with a blue roof. When you have rounded the point of land, head for the marina dock. If the tide is wrong, pick up a mooring at Merchant's Landing (see above).

Close by on the main road to the left, the Off Island Store has a lunch counter and offers groceries, wine, and newspapers. The Spruce Head post office is around the corner.

DIX ISLAND HARBOR
Charts: 13302, **13303**, **13305**

Dix Island Harbor is south of Dix Island and west of The Neck. More of a rocky gunkhole than a harbor, it is exposed to prevailing southwesterlies.

The *Coast Pilot* notes that it can be entered "from the southwestward through a narrow and crooked channel leading between the ledges north of Hewett Island," but it advises that the channel and harbor are unsafe for strangers.

HIGH ISLAND HARBOR
and DIX ISLAND ★★★★ ☐ 3   No facilities
Charts: 13302, **13303**, **13305**

High Island Harbor is our name for the anchorage surrounded by Dix, Birch, and High islands at the north end of the Muscle Ridge archipelago. In summer weather, it is a delightful place for a short visit. The two larger islands—High and Dix—were important quarries during the nineteenth century.

Approaches. The approach to the anchorage is direct, with few dangers. From Muscle Ridge Channel, run halfway between nun "10" and red daybeacon "12" on Otter Island. Otter is partly wooded with clearings at the west end and along the south shore. Leave Little Green Island (a few low trees and small house) to port and Oak Island (small, rocky, and treeless) to starboard.

High Island is high and densely wooded, with two large granite wharves at the west end. Note the three-foot spot reported west of it. Dix Island is lower and partially wooded, with a clearing and house at the northwest end. Granite rubble lines the northeast shore. Birch Island is low-lying, treeless, and grassy, with a number of small beaches.

Anchorages, Moorings. You can choose a number of different spots to anchor, depending on the wind. For access to the islands, drop the hook in the middle of a triangle formed by Dix, Birch, and High, not far off the stone wharf on High, in about 15 feet of water at low. The bottom varies in spots from rocky to sand and mud. Exposed only to the northwest and north, the anchorage provides good protection for prevailing summer winds.

Things to Do. *High Island.* Row over to the granite wharf and scramble up. Then work your way inland, through the alders and apple trees, along the path of granite tailings. Be careful; you may come suddenly upon the water-filled quarry at the west end of the island, with its high ledges and clean granite. Usually the water is clear, but sometimes it is green with algae.

Quarrying by the High Island Granite Company started here in 1894—about 16 years after the last stone was cut on neighboring Dix—and lasted until World War I. Life was not easy in the boardinghouses where 200 quarrymen lived. As Charles McLane reports in *Islands of the Mid-Maine Coast,* "Local liquor laws led to periodic raids by the county sheriff and confiscation of the red wine necessary to the morale of the luckless Italians."

Dix Island. You are welcome to come ashore on privately owned Dix Island, but access is limited to a short stretch on the eastern shore. No camping, fires, or swimming in the quarries. Land at the beach well north of the dock on the east side, and walk south on the path as far as the row of carved granite pediments. There they lie in the grass, as they have for a hundred years, waiting for some edifice that will never be built.

There are at least three layers of history on Dix Island starting with this mysterious account by a local historian (reported in the August 1982 issue of *Down East* magazine): " . . . many skeletons, much decayed, seem to have been buried in a circle, with their feet pointing towards the centre." One leg bone was said to have been several inches longer than those of today's tallest people.

Today there is no trace of these giant early inhabitants, but the later residents have left their mark everywhere. It is hard to imagine that there were more than 2,000 quarrymen on Dix in its heyday. There were more than 150 buildings, including the Shamrock Boardinghouse for the Irish, the Aberdeen for the Scottish, and even an opera house.

All this was started by Horace Beals of New York and carried on by his wife, Jennie, with cost-plus-15-percent contracts for granite to build post offices in New York City, Charleston, and Philadelphia. Legends accumulated around Jennie Beals—beautiful, sophisticated, blessed with business acumen, but not satisfied to spend her life here. After her husband's death in 1863, she moved to New York City, later becoming the Duchess of Castellucia by a second marriage.

Today the island is owned by the Dix Island Association, whose members aspire to self-sufficiency. They live here simply, without electricity, and pump water by hand. The land is owned in common. The few houses, individually owned, are like summer camps, built to blend into the landscape—except for one at the northwest end that was the maid's quarters and laundry for Horace Beals's mansion.

The association is fighting to keep the fast-growing spruce trees from reclaiming the open meadow. One owner wears a glove at all times to pull up the seedlings as she goes. Sheep are another weapon in this struggle.

HOME HARBOR ★★★ No facilities

Charts: 13302, **13303**, 13305

If you need a place to stop for the night on your way north or south through Two Bush Channel, Home Harbor (on the eastern side of the Muscle Ridge islands) is a lovely harbor under normal conditions. Seldom used, the harbor is nestled in the encircling arms of several islands and ledges, with a distant view of Heron Neck and Hurricane Island to the east.

Approaches. Start your approach south of nun "2B," off Halibut Rock. The easiest path is north of Yellow Ledge, then southwest between Hewett Island Rocks and Hewett Island, favoring the shore.

Yellow Ledge, its top whitened with bird droppings, is a smooth rock eight feet above water at high. At first it merges with the shoreline, but persist until you can see that there is plenty of room between Yellow Ledge and Hewett Island. Stay well north of the ledge; there is a shoal spot near it.

Hewett Island Rocks are visible at halftide but covered at high. The entrance between the rocks and Hewett Island is about 150 yards wide. Once past the southeast tip of Hewett Island, you are in Home Harbor. Aim for the little cobble beach at the head of the cove on Pleasant Island.

Lobsterboats often cut through to Home Harbor via the narrow, rock-infested channels from the west. A deep-keeled boat can do so too, but it requires great caution.

Anchorages, Moorings. Work your way in to 16 or 20 feet at low, noting the ledges that make out from the west side of the harbor. Holding ground is good in mud, and you will be well protected from prevailing southerlies, although exposed to the east and somewhat to the north-northwest.

If you leave near high tide, remember to stay west of Hewett Island Rocks.

CRESCENT BEACH ★★ No facilities

Charts: 13302, 13305, **13307**

South of Owls Head Harbor and west of Sheep Island is Crescent Beach. Although protected from the southwest, it is open to the south and southeast and is likely to be rolly.

Approaches. Coming from the north, pass through Owls Head Bay and then between can "3" and nun "4," west of Sheep Island. It is easy to confuse Crescent Beach with a similar cove just to the south. One distinguishing feature is green daybeacon "1," east of Emery Island.

Anchorages, Moorings. Anchor north and east of Emery Island in 15 to 20 feet, mud bottom.

Getting Ashore. Land on the crescent-shaped beach.

OWLS HEAD HARBOR ★★★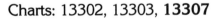

Charts: 13302, 13303, **13307**

Owls Head, a working harbor, is home to a fleet of 35 or more lobsterboats and draggers. Served by a large dock and lobster pound, the harbor is located just south of Owls Head Light and protected by Monroe and Sheep islands to seaward.

In his 1858 book, *A Summer Cruise on the Coast of New England*, Robert Carter noted: "At 6 P.M., we reached Owl's Head, an exceedingly picturesque promontory where a large white lighthouse crowned a high rock rising abruptly from the water. Here we anchored in a broad channel between the mainland and two islands, amid a fleet of vessels. This channel is much frequented by coasters and fishermen, and five hundred sail have been seen passing Owl's Head in one day."

Approaches. Coming from the north, round Owls Head with its lighthouse, then leave to starboard can "7" and green daybeacon "5" on Dodge Point Ledge.

Coming from the east, round the red skeleton tower at the north end of Monroe Island. (Note that there is a similar tower on the north end of Sheep Island—both are Navy maintained—marking a measured mile.)

Anchorages, Moorings. The harbor is full of moorings, so the only room to anchor is at the

outside edge, almost into the channel. The holding ground is poor.

Your best alternative is to pick up the guest mooring with the cordial inscription, "Strangers Welcome," located outside the fleet. Otherwise, inquire at P.K. Reed and Sons, who will know of any empty moorings.

Getting Ashore. Row in to the dinghy float.

For the Boat. *P.K. Reed & Sons (tel. 594-4606).* Gas, diesel, and ice are available at the dock, with depth alongside reported as seven feet at low. The setup is geared for fishing boats, however, with pilings and a wonderfully strong fishy smell to everything.

For the Crew. Clams and lobsters are available from P.K. Reed. The post office is a short way up the hill.

Things to Do. The "picturesque promontory" on which the lighthouse stands is now Owls Head State Park, about a one-mile walk from the harbor and a delightful picnic spot.

DEEP COVE ★★★ No facilities
Charts: 13302, 13305, **13307**

Deep Cove lies just west of Owls Head. Although the shoreline is private property, there are no houses, and the little beach at the head of the cove probably has not changed since the Indians camped here.

Approaches. Deep Cove is easily identified by green daybeacon "9" on Shag Rock, just east of the entrance. Favoring the eastern side because of the ledge making out from the west, work your way in slowly to a comfortable depth. It shoals very rapidly. Do not go beyond the first point to port after the entrance.

Anchorages, Moorings. Anchor here in 15 feet at low. Your anchor is likely to come up clean, suggesting a rocky bottom.

BROAD COVE ★★★ No facilities
Charts: 13302, 13305, **13307**

Opposite the Rockland breakwater and slightly east of it, Broad Cove provides an attractive setting and good protection from prevailing summer winds. There are spectacular views of the Camden Hills and the city lights of Rockland. The New Jersey–based Bancroft School has a summer camp here, and there are several private homes.

Fishermen sometimes set a circular net that occupies much of the southern cove. It will be marked by dories and floats.

Approaches. Coming from Rockland, between the breakwater and can "1," you will see Broad Cove open up to starboard. The complex of buildings at the eastern end of the cove is the Bancroft camp.

Anchorages, Moorings. Anchor in 10 to 15 feet at low near the private moorings in the southern part of the cove (note the ledge making out from the west side). Or anchor in 20 feet at low in the eastern bight of the cove, outside a line between the end of the Bancroft dock and a point to the southwest. The bottom is both mud and kelp, so be sure your anchor is well set.

ROCKLAND ★★★ All facilities
Charts: 13302, 13305, **13307**

A busy commercial harbor on the west side of Penobscot Bay, Rockland is the largest city in the area and has facilities for any yachting need. Rockland also has a major Coast Guard base with search-and-rescue capabilities.

Fishing has been a central part of Rockland from the earliest days, although in recent years the fish plants have closed and major commercial operations have moved elsewhere.

For visitors, there are several hidden gems here, especially the Farnsworth Art Museum, the Shore Village Museum, and the nearby Owls Head Transportation Museum. The Samoset Resort is located at the north end of the breakwater. Hurricane Island Outward Bound School and the Island Institute have their land bases here.

Rockland has a regional airport nearby, and ferries to North Haven, Vinalhaven, and Matinicus leave from Rockland's waterfront (tel. 596-2202).

In 1765, Isaiah Tolman of Massachusetts moved with his 21 children to form an instant settlement at "the shore," part of Thomaston, which became

Shore Village and eventually Rockland. Not long afterwards, John Lermond moved from nearby Warren to establish a logging camp at Lermond Cove (earlier called Catawamteak, "great landing place," by the Indians), the present-day Rockland waterfront.

The story of Rockland is one of lime, granite, ships, and fish. Lime was shipped to market in 50- to 150-ton schooners, and it was natural that a shipbuilding industry should flourish in Rockland. Half a dozen well-known yards grew up, and a large number of ships were launched over a century or more—until lack of business closed them down in the 1930s.

Approaches. Rockland is easy to find. Even from a distance, it looks like a city, with conspicuous high structures isolated in a comparatively low-lying area well south of the Camden Hills. Owls Head Light, on its dramatic wooded bluff, is visible a long way. Beware of ferries coming and going, not to mention barges, fishing boats, and lots of commercial traffic.

Approaching the harbor, you will pick up the lighthouse at the end of the mile-long breakwater forming the eastern part of the harbor. Leave the end of the breakwater to starboard and head in toward the radio towers on the hill. The Coast Guard station is on the large granite pier that sticks out farthest to the east. Here the channel divides. Bear southwest for the public landing, Hurricane Island, and National Sea Products Shipyard. The northeast channel will take you to the marinas, ferry terminal, and North End Shipyard.

If you are headed for the Samoset Resort, run north along the west side of the breakwater.

Anchorages, Moorings. If you need facilities or intend to explore Rockland, your best bets are Knight Marine, which provides slips and moorings, Journey's End Marine, or the public landing.

Anchor or get a mooring near the Samoset Resort, west of the breakwater, to enjoy its amenities (see below). If you are visiting the mainland

THE CLIPPER SHIP *RED JACKET*

During all her long life, *Red Jacket* was considered the most handsome of the great clipper ships, and the swiftest. Designed by young genius Samuel Harte Pook of Boston, she was launched November 2, 1853, at the Thomas yard in Rockland. *Red Jacket* was 251 feet long; beam, 44 feet; depth, 31 feet; 2,305 tons.

Red Jacket was built for speed, and she proved her worth on her first Atlantic crossing. She was towed to New York for rigging, and then dispatched to Liverpool in January 1854, before her bottom was copper-sheathed. Manned by an indifferent crew but a determined captain, *Red Jacket* logged more than 343 miles a day for six days running, and on January 19 made a run of 413 miles, a record surpassed only two or three times in the history of sailing ships. In spite of constant snow, rain, and hail during the midwinter crossing, Captain Asa Eldridge stayed on deck day and night and drove her hard, arriving in Liverpool in 13 days, one hour, and 25 minutes, dock to dock—still a record for single-hulled sailing ships.

Shrugging off lines from waiting tugs, *Red Jacket* drove up the River Mersey, all sails flying in a brisk

northwester, toward a great crowd awaiting her arrival. Then, with enormous daring, Captain Eldridge performed a feat of seamanship that still sends shivers down a sailor's back a century later. The maneuver was described by one of Eldridge's descendants. Still under full sail and abreast of the pier, "He took in his kites, his skysails, royals and top gallants, hung his course—or lower sails—in their gear, ignored the tugs which by that time had caught up, and throwing *Red Jacket* into the wind, helm down hard, he backed her alongside the berth without aid."

Sailing next from London to Melbourne, she made the passage in 67 days and 13 hours. There she was bought by a British firm carrying freight and passengers to Australia and India, never again to sail under the American flag. In her later years, she carried lumber from Canada. Sadly, she ended her career of 30-plus years as a coal barge, fueling steamers in the Cape Verde Islands.

A bronze plaque at Jordan's Market in Rockland marks the location of the Thomas yard where the *Red Jacket* was built.

headquarters of Hurricane Island Outward Bound School, pick up one of the moorings (one-ton granite blocks) off their dock at the southern end of the harbor. You will see several reddish buildings and a dock, and probably some of the double-ended whaleboats moored nearby.

For the Boat. E.S. Bohndell & Co. (tel. 236-3549). Based in nearby Rockport, Bohndell is a sailmaker and also provides full rigging service.

Hurricane Island Outward Bound School (Ch. 16; tel. 594-5548). The school maintains several power vessels with search and rescue capability and monitors channel 16 around the clock.

Journey's End Marine (Ch. 16, 18 or 68; tel. 594-4444). Turn north at the Coast Guard pier and skirt the station, leaving it to port. The marina is tucked in just west of the station, on the north side. It has been dredged to 12 feet alongside the floats, where diesel, water, and electricity are available. The store has ice and marine supplies, and there are showers and a sauna.

Knight Marine Service (Ch. 9 or 16; tel. 594-4068). Knight's is a full-service boatyard. To get there, branch right at the Coast Guard pier and follow the channel around to the right of the ferry terminal. Gas, diesel, and water may be obtained here, with eight feet of water alongside at low. Also here are an ice machine, and a small chandlery. The yard has a tugboat, 20- and 35-ton boatlifts, hydraulic trailer, and a crane, and can handle most repairs. Row your dinghy in to the right behind the floats.

There are showers, laundry facilities, and a pay phone. The Captain Hornblower takeout is on the premises, and there is an IGA supermarket across the street. The state liquor store is about a mile away, next to a good Shop 'n Save supermarket.

North End Shipyard, Inc. (tel. 594-8007). This unusual yard was started on a shoestring by Doug and Linda Lee and John Foss, to rebuild and maintain some of the area's windjammers. It is located north of the ferry terminal, between nuns "10" and "12." There they launched the new 93-foot schooner *Heritage* in 1983 and the restored 90-foot fishing schooner *American Eagle* in 1986, both additions to the windjammer fleet. Three other windjammers are also based at the yard. North End can handle major repairs. It is also one of the few yards where you can do your own repairs, leasing their space and heavy woodworking equipment. The yard has a 14-foot dredged channel leading to a substantial marine railway. On occasion, a berth might be available for a large vessel.

Rockland Boat Inc. (tel. 594-8181). This is the kind of old-fashioned, no-nonsense chandlery and boating supply shop you wish you had at home. Once a boatbuilding shop, and catering now mostly to fishermen, Rockland Boat has great seaboots (at half the price of those fancy catalog items), paint, potwarp, sailmaker's palms, marine

hardware, and a thousand other items. It is tucked in among the fish plants, on Wharf Street, a couple of blocks inland from the Coast Guard station.

Rockland Municipal Dock (Ch. 16; tel. 596-0376—Chamber of Commerce). To reach the public landing, branch left at the Coast Guard pier. The floats and dock are opposite a yellow nun at the end of the channel. The dock itself has a green trestle bridge and lands you near a little park with a white building that houses the Chamber of Commerce.

You can tie up at the floats for a maximum of two hours (longer with permission), with eight feet alongside at low, water, and electricity. Obtain a rental mooring by checking with the harbormaster based here, or anchor outside the moorings.

There are showers in the Chamber of Commerce building, ice, and pay phones behind. A block away you will find Sears, a drugstore, taxi stand, and Rockland's business district.

Samoset Resort Inn (tel. 594-2511). Anchor off the Samoset, near the northwestern corner of the breakwater and the little float, in 10 to 20 feet of water at low. The Samoset has only a few moorings for visitors, so reserve ahead. The anchorage is exposed because of the size of Rockland Harbor, although fine for settled summer weather or a short stop. There is kelp on the bottom, so make sure your anchor is set.

For the Crew. The Knox County Airport in Owls Head serves Portland and Boston. Rental cars are available. For a cab, call R & H Taxi (tel. 594-5525). Penobscot Bay Medical Center, a few miles north of the city, has an impressive staff with emergency-room service (tel. 596-8000).

For a splendid dinner try Jessica's European Bistro (tel. 596-0770), a one mile walk south on Main Street from the public landing.

Things to Do. Stop in at the Chamber of Commerce at the public landing for information on area activities and attractions. Two highlights of the summer include windjammer races and other events ashore during Schooner Days in early July, and the Maine Lobster Festival early in August at Harbor Park. Several vessels offer short sightseeing trips out of Rockland.

Walk out to the end of the mile-long Rockland breakwater. Begun in 1881, it required 700,000 tons of granite (most of it brought by stone sloop from Vinalhaven) and took 18 years to build. It starts near the Samoset Resort and takes you out to the automated lighthouse on a 17-foot granite causeway.

On your way to the breakwater, take advantage of the spectacular Samoset Resort Inn, looking out to sea over an 18-hole golf course. Facilities include tennis, swimming, a health club, and a good restaurant.

The Farnsworth Library and Art Museum in Rockland is only a few blocks from the waterfront.

This handsome building has a notable collection of works by American artists, especially coastal landscapes and ships. Most remarkable is the large collection of works by three generations of Wyeths. Next door is the family homestead of the Farnsworth lime barons, with its original elegant furnishings. It is considered one of the finest Victorian homes in the country and is open to the public.

Two miles south of Rockland, near Knox County Airport, is the famous Owls Head Transportation Museum, with a unique collection of antique airplanes, cars, and engines. On weekdays, these are on static display; on weekends, they are hissing, puffing, creaking, and flying. There are horse-drawn carriages, Stanley Steamers, Model-T

Fords, and Rolls-Royces, as well as World War I fighter planes and a Ford Trimotor. The museum has special events all summer long. For the schedule, call 594-4418. The best way to get there from Rockland is by taxi. (The taxi stand is on Rockland's Main Street, two blocks from the public landing.)

Another interesting place to visit is the Shore Village Museum, with the largest collection of lighthouse artifacts on display in the United States. These include Fresnel lenses removed from Petit Manan, Whitehead Island, and Matinicus Rock when they were automated. The museum is at 104 Limerock Street, an easy half-mile walk from the waterfront (tel. 594-4950).

CLAM COVE★★ No facilities
Charts: 13302, 13305, **13307**

This little-used harbor between Rockland and Rockport offers good protection from prevailing winds and is easy to enter. Although the shores are attractive, Route 1 passes along the head of the cove.

Approaches. Enter north of can "3" off Ram Island and proceed up the middle of the harbor. There are no obstructions.

Anchorages, Moorings. Anchor a short distance past the point on the north shore in 10 to 20 feet of water at low, mud bottom. The cove shoals

rapidly to clam flats after this point.

Getting Ashore. When the mud flats are covered, it's possible to land at the little park at the head of the harbor.

For the Crew. Local produce is often sold on Route 1 nearby, and it's a mile and a half south to the outskirts of Rockland. Turn right at McDonald's for a nearby Shop 'N Save market. Penobscot Bay Medical Center is a short distance north of Clam Cove on Route 1 (tel. 596-8000).

ROCKPORT ★★★★
Charts: 13302, 13305, **13307**

On the west side of Penobscot Bay, between Rockland and Camden, Rockport is small and beautiful.

Fifty years ago, Rockport was home for fishermen who built their weirs in the harbor, and for lobstermen, but today the harbor is mainly for pleasure boats. With all of the boats moored here, it is a wonder that the 70-foot windjammer *Timberwind* can make her way among them without an engine. It's a lovely sight to see her glide past Indian Island under sail, drop all canvas, and come boldly in, pushed by her little yawlboat, turning in the last possible open space at the head of the harbor to nestle alongside her float.

Although Rockport is popular as a harbor, it often is not a comfortable one. Exposed to the south, the harbor gathers up the ocean swells; the "Rockport roll" is well known to those who live

aboard.

In the nineteenth century, Rockport was at the heart of the mid-coast lime industry, and you can still see remnants of several old kilns on the waterfront. The kilns inspire images of the night sky aglow with fires, the harbor crowded with kiln-wooders unloading cords of four-foot spruce and limers loading casks for Boston and New York. Great piles of white lime tailings are still visible in Walker Park and on the banks of the Goose River. One story has it that a locomotive is buried in one of these piles, and small boys dig and dream.

Approaches. Rockport is an easy harbor to enter, the only danger being Porterfield Ledge, topped with a granite marker. In poor visibility, find red-and-white bell "RO" off Indian Island, and then the light on Lowell Rock.

From Thomaston to Warren, from Rockland to Rockport to Lincolnville, there are deposits of limestone all along the shore, perhaps laid down originally as seashells in a shallow sea. When limestone is burned to eliminate carbon dioxide, what's left is lime. For building materials and fertilizer, lime has been useful to man from prehistoric times. Lime from Rockland was used mostly for plastering walls and ceilings and to make mortar for laying brick.

The first lime kiln in the area was built about 1733, in Thomaston, near the site of the present-day Maine State Prison, and there limestone was burned for shipment to Boston. By 1828, there were 160 lime kilns in the midcoast area of Maine; by the Civil War, they were burning more than a million casks of lime a year. Rockland split off from its parent town of Thomaston and became the lime-producing center of the world.

It took 30 cords of wood to fire one lime kiln, and still more wood to build the casks for shipment. Cordwood came from islands in the bay, from down east, and from Canada. Farmers cut birch and alder to split and bend for hoops, and built cooper shops to make the casks for winter cash.

To fetch the cordwood and carry the lime casks to market, mostly for construction in New York City, ships were needed. More than 500 ships were engaged in this trade by midcentury. The countless "kilnwooders" were rough-built vessels, their decks piled high with cords of wood. Ships used to carry lime to market, on the other hand, were carefully constructed, because this cargo had one enormous drawback: if the slightest amount of water reached the lime in the casks, it caught on fire, and the fire often was un-

"Kiln-wooders" unloading cords of wood in Rockport Harbor, 1894. It took 30 cords to fire one lime kiln. Most of the houses shown on Amsbury Hill still exist. (Frank Claes Collection)

quenchable. As W.H. Rowe explains in his *Maritime History of Maine*, "The master needed a keen sense of smell. The odor of lime being slaked by water was an ominous danger signal . . . . Every crack and crevice through which air might get into the hold and the doors, ports, and smokestack were quickly sealed with plaster made from the lime.

"Then the craft was headed for the nearest harbor and anchored some distance from the shore and away from other vessels. For at any time she might burst into flames. The schooner was stripped of all movables and the captain and crew sat down to await developments. Sometimes three months would go by before their patience was rewarded and the vessel saved. If, however, the fire could not be smothered, the vessel was towed to some secluded place and scuttled." Not until steel barges replaced the sloops and schooners in the twenti-

eth century was the fire problem solved.

Technology came to the industry in the last half of the 19th century, with oil- or coal-fired, continuous-process "patent kilns." In 1900, the three largest lime manufacturing firms merged to form the Rockland-Rockport Lime Company. By this time, railroads transported the limerock from the quarries, 100,000 tons a year, to burn in Rockland's kilns.

But within 30 years, the quality of Rockland lime declined and there was price-cutting and new competition. New materials and building methods cut the market for lime: wallboard instead of plaster, concrete instead of brick. The kilns went cold, the railroads were abandoned. Today there is hardly a trace of the whole flourishing industry—a few kilns preserved on the waterfronts of Thomaston and Rockport, white limestone tailings on the shores.

Do not cut the abandoned lighthouse on Indian Island close; a ledge makes out well south of the lighthouse to the present light structure on Lowell Rock, which you leave to starboard.

Continue in among the moored boats to the head of the harbor, noting red beacon "4" on Seal Ledge to starboard, and green beacon "5" on the rocks to port, well inside the harbor and often hidden by the moored boats.

Anchorages, Moorings. Rockport Marine, at the northeast end of the harbor, maintains moorings for rent and also offers space alongside, with 10 feet of depth at low.

At the northwest end of the harbor, Rockport Marine Park has several floats with six feet at low. An overnight tie-up can be arranged, but space is limited and this location is uncomfortable with any sea.

Across the Goose River from the park is the small red building of the Rockport Boat Club, with floats for temporary tie-up, recently dredged to six feet of water at low. The club also maintains a guest mooring.

Rockport Harbor is now full of moorings, with little or no space to anchor except well outside, where the depths run 50 feet or more.

Getting Ashore. Take your dinghy in to the public landing floats at the head of the harbor, Rockport Marine on the east side, or the floats at the Marine Park on the west side.

For the Boat. *E.S. Bohndell & Co. (tel. 236-3549).* Half a mile from Rockport Harbor, on Route 1, the Bohndell sailmaking and rigging firm has been in business more than a century.

Rockport Boat Club. Water and electricity are available at the floats, but no other facilities. Visiting yachtsmen are welcome to use the clubhouse.

Rockport Marine, Inc. (tel. 236-9651). Taylor Allen's recently expanded Rockport Marine specializes in building, restoration, and repair of wooden boats. They can, however, provide hull and engine repairs for boats of all kinds, and they have a 35-ton boatlift. In addition to dockage and moorings, the yard offers gas, diesel, water, and electricity at the floats, with nine feet or more alongside. Ice and marine hardware are available.

For the Crew. There are pay phones at the public landing. Rockport Marine has a shower for yachtsmen, and upstairs is the popular Sail Loft Restaurant, offering lunch, dinner, and Sunday brunch overlooking the harbor. Call 236-2330 for reservations. The marine influence shows in the plaque inside that says, "Lat. 43° 11' 13.2" N, Long. 69° 4' 21.9" W." Check your loran.

Just up the hill is The Corner Shop, a wonderfully un-fancy eatery with pine bench booths, where carpenters and fishermen rub elbows with students from the Maine Photographic Workshop. Breakfast and lunch are available at reasonable prices. At Graffam Brothers, right next to the Sail Loft, you can buy lobsters for the boat or have them shipped anywhere. It's worth the three-quarter mile walk to The Market Basket (tel. 236-4371), a gourmet deli with a good variety of wines, cheeses, French bread, and fresh produce. Cross the bridge to Pascal Avenue and walk south along the western side of the harbor, then right on West Street to the intersection with Route 1.

Camden, with a wide selection of restaurants and shops, is only a few miles away. For a cab, call Don's Taxi (tel. 236-4762). For local use, you can rent a car at Smith's Garage (tel. 236-2320).

Things to Do. Walk east out of town, then turn northward on Russell Avenue, past the golf course and the Lily Pond. By the pond grazes a herd of Belted Galloways, a decorative breed of cattle, black with broad white belts. Continue past a cemetery with an ocean view and eventually to Camden.

For good views of the harbor walk up Russell Avenue to Mechanic Street, and then along the eastern side of the harbor toward Beauchamp Point.

Visit the Marine Park, with the last of the lime kilns once so important here. There is a tiny Vulcan steam locomotive that used to haul limestone from the quarries on a three-mile narrow-gauge railway. Also here is a statue of Andre the seal, with a plaque that says,

Abandoned at birth, he was found, befriended, raised and trained by Harry Goodridge of Rockport, Maine. Andre is honorary Harbormaster of Rockport Harbor and is a celebrity of more than local renown. His antics have delighted people far and wide. Andre is a harbor seal (Phoca vitulina), the only species that occurs regularly in New England waters.

During the summer of 1986, Andre, aged 25, disappeared. His body washed up in Rockland Harbor in July, and he was buried at the end of the lawn on the Goodridge place. He is gone, mourned by young people and adults alike, but his life-size statue remains in Rockport Marine Park, for children to sit on and hug. He would have liked that.

Just north of the bridge is another pleasant park along the west side of the Goose River. Continue south along the harbor on Pascal Avenue, turning left at Elm Street toward the Rockport Apprenticeshop, where you can see beautiful traditional wooden boats under construction by the apprentices, under the supervision of a master builder. The visitors' loft has some interesting exhibits and a variety of small craft on display.

Plan a picnic right on the harbor—at the Marine Park near the head of the harbor, or at Walker Park next to the Rockport Apprenticeshop, where you can also swim.

Right up the hill, opposite the Corner Shop, is the Maine Photographic Workshop, a mecca for people from all over the country who come for its acclaimed courses in photography. During the summer, special lectures and shows are open to the public. The workshop also operates a well-stocked camera store.

Up Main Street, to the right, is the Rockport

Opera House, where Bay Chamber Concerts are held Thursday nights (and some Friday nights) with well-known piano soloists, string quartets, and other performers. Just beyond the Opera House, the Maine Coast Artists Gallery, housed in a one-time livery stable and firehouse, displays the works of Maine artists. The public library is across the street.

CAMDEN ★★★★★ All facilities
Charts: 13302, 13305, **13307**

Camden is one of the jewels of Penobscot Bay. This beautiful harbor is home to a large fleet of picturesque windjammers and cruising boats of every kind. Curtis Island, with its lighthouse, guards the entrance; the steeples of the small town are white against the hills; a stream cascades down into the head of the harbor. There are excellent marine facilities, good restaurants and stores, entertainment, mountains and lakes.

All of these attractions have not escaped notice, and the town is aswarm during July and August. Despite all the activity, however, Camden remains a pleasure for the cruising family.

The inner harbor is extremely well protected but crowded, and you are likely to end up on a mooring in the outer harbor. Exposure there is to the south and southeast, and some nights are rolly.

Shipbuilding was a major industry in Camden from well before the Civil War. Best known of the Camden builders was Holly M. Bean, whose yard stood where Wayfarer Marine is today. The Bean yard built the world's largest five-masted schooner, and the first six-master in 1900.

Approaches. Nestled at the base of the Camden Hills, Camden is easy to recognize from a distance. As you approach from south or east, a clear marker is The Graves, a jagged spine of rocks about a mile southeast of the entrance to Camden, marked by a green gong to the east and a flashing green light on the rocks themselves.

There are two well-marked entrances to Camden Harbor—from the southeast and from the northeast—skirting a group of ledges in the mouth. Most boats use the larger entrance from the southeast.

Coming from the south, leaving The Graves on either hand, you will see the small lighthouse on Curtis Island. The sea buoy is red bell "2," .3 mile off Curtis, and from there it is a straight shot into the outer harbor. You can come quite close to the

Aerial view of Camden, showing Curtis Island and the outer and inner harbors. (Barbara Hatch photo)

Windjammers at the head of the inner harbor in Camden. (Neal A. Parent photo)

northeastern shore of Curtis. Do not use the unmarked entrance west of Curtis unless you carry shoal draft.

The entrance from the northeast is much narrower, but well marked and perfectly safe. The sea buoy is red-and-white bell "CH," .3 mile to the northeast. If it is blowing hard, be alert for strong puffs coming down off the mountains in the area north of Camden.

There will be 200 or more boats moored in the outer harbor, and there is a marked channel through the moorings leading to the inner harbor. Do not cut the corner at Eaton Point; there are rocks making out from the end of the seawall just before the turn into the inner harbor.

There is a channel down both sides of the inner harbor, and a place to cross over at the head. When the windjammers are in port, however (on weekends), things get pretty tight.

Anchorages, Moorings. Much of the outer harbor is filled with moorings. Often the only place to anchor is near the entrance, north of can "1," or in the outer part of Sherman Cove. Do not anchor inside the line of moorings along Eaton Point, or you will find yourself aground. Anchoring is not allowed in the inner harbor.

Most of the moorings for transients are managed by Wayfarer Marine and are located in the outer harbor. To request a mooring call Wayfarer on channel 9; during working hours its launch will come out to show you the way. The white mooring buoys for transients are marked with a Wayfarer burgee and the maximum length boat allowed. Willey Wharf also maintains a number of transient moorings.

Boats up to 42 feet may lie along the outer floats at the public landing, with permission of the harbormaster (channel 16; tel. 236-3269). His office is in the Chamber of Commerce building at the public landing, near the head of the inner harbor, and his launch is the *Welcome*.

Getting Ashore. If you are on a Wayfarer mooring, the usual three toots on the horn will summon the launch from the Camden Yacht Club (or call on channel 68); it will take you either to Wayfarer or to the yacht club. There is a small charge for this service. On summer weekends, be patient; there is a lot of traffic in the harbor. The yacht club has a dinghy float, but more convenient is the public landing, near the head of the harbor on the left. If you can find a place to insert the bow of your dinghy, you will be right next to the Chamber of Commerce, pay phones, and the heart of Camden.

For the Boat. *E.S. Bohndell & Co. (tel. 236-3549).* In business for more than a century, sailmaker and rigger Bohndell is on Route 1 in adjacent Rockport.

Camden Yacht Club (Ch. 68; tel. 236-3014). The low red building of the Camden Yacht Club is at the left-hand entrance to the inner harbor. The club has no guest moorings, and 15-minute tie-up at its floats. The inner harbor is extremely busy and crowded, and the easiest spot to fill your water tanks is at the yacht club floats. The steward of this friendly club will help you any way he can. No fuel is available.

Cannell, Payne, and Page (tel. 236-2383). One of the best-known brokers of wooden boats, Cannell, Payne, and Page have their office at Wayfarer Marine.

Downeast Trading Co. (tel. 236-8763). This marine supply store is located at the public landing.

Shore Sails. Shore Sails is located at Wayfarer Marine.

Wayfarer Marine (Ch. 9 or 16; tel. 236-4378). Wayfarer's docks and floats line the east side of the inner harbor. There is more than 12 feet of depth at low. In midseason, boats are rafted three or four deep in every available space. All services are available. This is a major yard with a large staff of experienced craftsmen capable of repairs on wood, fiberglass, or metal hulls, engines or electronics. On a site where ships have been built for a century or more, the yard has two marine railways (one of 115-ton capacity), a 15-ton boatlift, a rigging crane, a 60-ton hydraulic trailer, and a yard tug, the *Barbie D.*

The fuel dock (first float on your right as you enter the inner harbor) offers gas, diesel, ice, and water. Also available are showers and laundry facilities. There is a good marine store, with charts.

Willey Wharf (tel. 236-3256). Just across the harbor from Wayfarer, Willey caters to very large power- and sailboats (often with reservations made far ahead), although anyone is welcome. Willey does not have the boatyard facilities of Wayfarer, but it has the advantage of being right in town. Gas or diesel in large quantities may be obtained at the floats, with 10 feet alongside at low. Willey can refill CNG and propane tanks, and provide water, electricity, ice, and showers.

For the Crew. Visiting yachtsmen are welcome to use the handsome old clubhouse of the Camden Yacht Club, which serves an excellent lunch. Next door is The Convenience Store (run by Wayfarer), which carries groceries, beer, wine, ice, and some marine supplies.

Groceries also may be found at well-stocked French and Brawn, at the main intersection in Camden. Also nearby, at the northern end of Main Street, is Ayer's Seafood Market (fresh produce—and they'll cook lobsters for you). At the other end of town, on Elm Street, is Stop N Go, open late and on Sundays. Worth a short taxi ride, perhaps, is the IGA Supermarket, south on Route 1, or the Megunticook Corner Market a few miles up Washington Street (Route 105). Call Don's Taxi at 236-4762.

The state liquor store is at the Camden Market Place, just south of town. A short way from the main intersection in Camden is The Wine Emporium (at Highland Mill Mall), with a good selection

of wines, cheeses, and other delicacies.

There is a laundromat (Clothes Care Unlimited) on Mechanic Street, just beyond the main intersection, open seven days a week (tel. 236-3332). You can drop off laundry there and have it done by the pound.

In summertime, there is a wide choice of places to eat within a few minutes of the public landing, ranging from pizzas to nouvelle cuisine, delis, and takeouts. Overlooking the harbor is The Waterfront Restaurant, a popular spot with a delightful outdoor deck.

Other favorites in town are Cappy's and Peter Ott's, or try Cassoulet for gourmet dining.

For local use, you can rent a car at Smith's Garage in Rockport (tel. 236-2320).

Penobscot Bay Medical Center (tel. 596-8000), on Route 1 about six miles south of Camden, is a large, modern acute-care hospital with 24-hour emergency-room service and a helicopter pad.

There are pay phones at the public landing and at the main intersection in town. The post office is a block away on Chestnut Street, and there are several banks.

One of the most unusual bookstores anywhere is the Owl and Turtle, on Bayview Street. Downstairs is a whole section where you can browse among marine books.

Things to Do. Walking the streets of Camden, window-shopping, and observing the activity in the busy harbor can keep you well occupied for quite a while. If you have a little extra time, however, there are many interesting things to see and do. Start at the Chamber of Commerce, in the little house on the public landing, in the heart of town.

If you haven't had enough of the water, there are several ways to explore the harbor and nearby islands on someone else's boat. Several boats offer short trips at frequent intervals, leaving from the public landing.

With your own dinghy you can reach Camden's waterside parks, including Curtis Island, a town park in the harbor entrance. Land at the end toward town. There is a grassy area for a picnic, plus a working lighthouse and the whole little island to explore.

Check to see what plays or concerts are scheduled in the beautiful outdoor amphitheatre at the head of the harbor. For movies, there is the old-fashioned Bay View Street Cinema.

In its brick building on Chestnut Street, the Camden YMCA has unusually good facilities for a small town, including a swimming pool, squash and racquetball courts, bowling alleys, exercise rooms, showers, and a gym. All are open to the public for a small fee.

Camden Hills State Park is a mile or so north of town on Route 1. Including Mount Megunticook and Mount Battie, the park covers some 8,000 acres

The schooner *Helen J. Seitz* was launched in late October 1905, fully rigged and ready for sea, the 71st vessel built by the Bean yard in Camden (now Wayfarer Marine). Next to the ways is the turreted steamboat wharf, with Curtis Island in the background.

Her keel was 272 feet, length overall 308 feet, and length from end of jibboom to end of spanker boom 399 feet. Her beam was 48.4 feet and depth 23 feet; she spread 9,000 yards of canvas, and carried two stockless anchors weighing 8,000 pounds each. The *Seitz* was destined to carry a cargo of 4,500 tons of coal from Newport News to Boston.

As described in *The Camden Herald*, "A very large crowd saw the launch, many coming from out of town. Steamer *Rockland* brought a large party down from up river and Steamer *Castine* made a special excursion from Belfast with a crowd. The electrics were crowded all day and many came in from the country in teams." (Frank Claes Collection)

and for a small entrance fee offers hiking trails, modest climbs, and spectacular panoramic views. With the exception of Cadillac Mountain on Mount Desert Island, 1,385-foot Mount Megunticook is the highest point on the Atlantic seaboard. The road to the top of Mount Battie was built originally for cannon, and then for horse and carriage. From the summit, the view is breathtaking, with the peaks of Mount Desert in the distance, Isle au Haut, Deer Isle, Blue Hill, and dozens of spruce and granite islands dotting the bay.

You can easily climb Mount Battie on foot. Walk north up Main Street and turn left on Mountain Street (Route 52). Take the first right on Megunticook Street and follow it up to the beginning of the trail, perhaps 15 minutes from the center of town. It is about a 25-minute hike to the top, with just a couple of spots where you have to scramble.

Bikes can be rented at Maine Sport, on Route 1 in Rockport. Camden Hills State Park is one good destination, or go out Mountain Street (Route 52) to Lake Megunticook, where there is a swimming and picnic area at Barrett Cove. Nearby is the start of the Maiden's Cliff trail, which connects with the state park trail system.

The Camden-Rockport Historical Society has a pamphlet outlining a 2½-mile tour on foot, and a more extensive bicycle or car tour. (Get a copy at the Chamber of Commerce.) Noteworthy on the tour is the Whitehall Inn, north of town on Route 1, where in 1912 Edna St. Vincent Millay, then a schoolgirl, first read her poem "Renascence," beginning the literary career that won her a Pulitzer prize. Her statue looks out over the harbor.

Half a mile south of Camden, on Route 1 and Conway Road, is the Old Conway House (c. 1780), Blacksmith Shop, and Museum. At the end of Conway Road is Merryspring Nature Park, with 66 acres of fields and woods, an arboretum, and marked trails.

A lovely walk that takes in one of the town's quieter residential districts goes out Bay View or Chestnut street, past Aldermere Farm, home of the intriguing Belted Galloway cattle. If you go beyond the farm, all the way to Rockport, it is about three miles each way.

Windjammers have operated out of Camden for more than half a century. Not only do they offer a wonderful experience for their guests, but their tall sails provide a glorious sight on the horizon. Some are a century old and converted from the coastal trade, some brand new and built for the purpose. Monday mornings, you will see a procession of these magnificent vessels departing Camden Harbor, their decks colorful with passengers. Some proceed under their own power, but many are pushed by yawlboats until they reach open waters and can hoist sail. After leaving Camden, the schooners spread to all points of the compass to spend the week exploring the remote harbors, small villages, and deserted islands of Penobscot Bay and beyond.

LASELL ISLAND
Charts: 13302, **13305**

There is an attractive beach at the north end of Lasell Island, east of Camden. Approaching Lasell from the northwest, find the long ledge (visible except near high tide) extending north from Lasell.

After rounding this ledge, anchor in a comfortable depth off the sand beach. This anchorage is exposed, but provides a pleasant day stop with views of the Camden Hills and the surrounding islands.

PASSAGES EAST FROM CAMDEN
Charts: 13302, **13305**

Going east from Camden, you will have to pass through the chain of islands that splits Penobscot Bay—Mark, Saddle, Lasell, Lime, and Islesboro. If you are heading for the Fox Islands Thorofare, the easiest route is south of the whole chain, picking up red whistle "8" at the end of Robinson Rock and leaving it to port.

However, if you are bound for Pulpit Harbor on North Haven, or points north, there are several slots through the islands. The cleanest and safest route is between Mark Island and Robinson Rock, leaving the daybeacon south of Mark Island 100 yards or so to port.

The next choice, a bit more direct but not quite as easy, is to pass between Mark and Saddle islands. Be sure to identify East Goose Rock (always visible) and leave it to port. To avoid the ledge east of East Goose Rock, stay south of a line between East Goose and the southern tip of Saddle Island. Give Mark Island a fair berth to starboard, noting the outlying rocks on the chart.

Next north is the passage between Saddle and Lasell islands—less comfortable because of the ledge (usually invisible) northeast of East Goose Rock. (At least one schooner has fetched up on this ledge.) The safest route is to stay within 100 or 200 yards of Lasell Island. The rocks running out like a breakwater at the southwestern tip of Lasell are visible, and there is a privately maintained marker off the end of the cove formed by these rocks. Leave it to port. Once past the tip of Lasell, continue southeast, leaving Goose Island to port. Or turn northeast between Lasell and Mouse islands, emerging north of can "3" and Mouse, on which there often are seals basking.

Do not try going between Lasell and Lime islands. North of Lime is a treeless islet known locally as "Little Bermuda." The chart shows five feet just north of Little Bermuda, and you can cross this bar with caution on a rising tide.

All of these routes are shown on the accompanying sketch map, with approximate magnetic courses from red bell "2" at the entrance to Camden Harbor.

NORTH HAVEN, VINALHAVEN and Fox Islands Thorofare
Charts: 13302, **13305**, **13308**

Known collectively as The Fox Islands, North Haven and Vinalhaven are a paradise for cruising sailors. Fox Islands Thorofare provides a convenient and fascinating passage from west to east, and there are enough harbors and coves, passages and bays in the deeply indented shores of these large islands to keep you well occupied for a week. Pulpit Harbor on North Haven is one of the finest harbors in Maine, and one of the most beautiful.

The Fox Islands were named by Martin Pring, in command of *Discoverer* and *Speedwell*, who saw foxes on the islands during his voyage of exploration in 1603. Separated by only a few hundred feet of water, North Haven and Vinalhaven are worlds apart.

North Haven and the Thorofare are home to summer people from Boston, Philadelphia, and New York: Saltonstalls and Lamonts, Cabots and

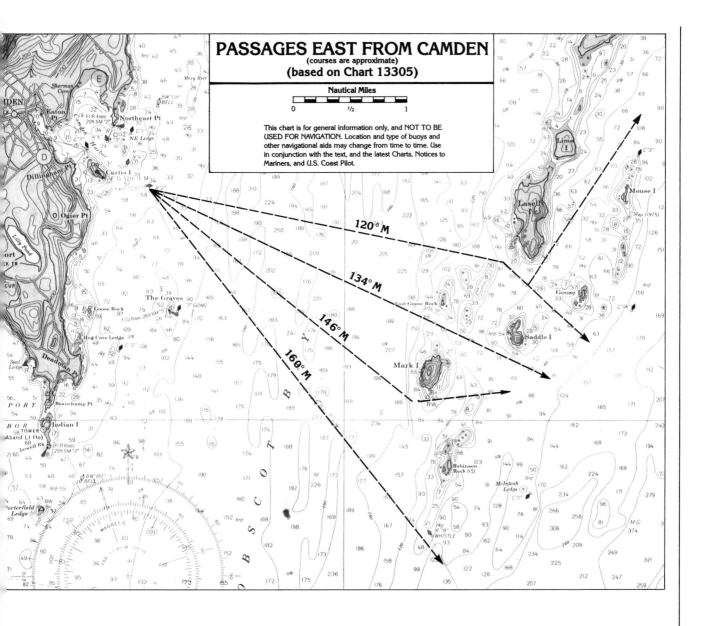

Watsons. Splendid summer cottages and docks line both sides of Fox Islands Thorofare, and a working lobsterboat here seems like a quaint anachronism.

Vinalhaven is entirely different. Although the population swells in summer, this island never has become fashionable, and the year-round residents are still in charge. The people of Vinalhaven are fishermen and lobstermen from generations back.

Here the names are Dyer and Carver, Arey and Vinal, Calderwood and Coombs. The Reach, the entry to Carvers Harbor, is a working man's thoroughfare, bordered with modest homes. A Hinckley yawl here seems out of place.

As if to emphasize the difference, each island has its own separate ferry departing from the same terminal in Rockland.

PULPIT HARBOR ★★★★★

Charts: 13302, 13305 **13308**

On the northwest coast of North Haven Island, Pulpit is only a two-hour sail from Camden, or less than an hour from the Fox Islands Thorofare. It is a marvelous harbor, the favorite of many skippers, with a hidden entrance that reveals itself at the last moment, an osprey nest guarding the mouth, and

excellent protection under any conditions for a fleet of a hundred boats. Once inside, there are plenty of choices for an anchorage, and through the entrance the sun sets over Penobscot Bay and the Camden Hills.

It is customary for several windjammers to an-

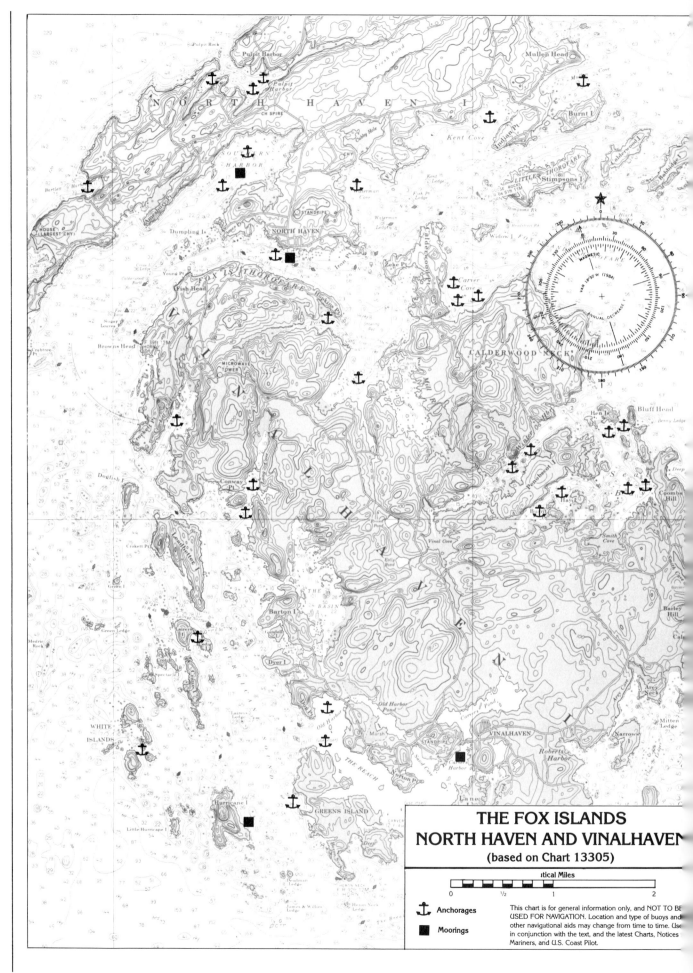

THE FOX ISLANDS
NORTH HAVEN AND VINALHAVEN
(based on Chart 13305)

Nautical Miles

0   1/2   1   2

⚓ Anchorages

⬛ Moorings

This chart is for general information only, and NOT TO BE
USED FOR NAVIGATION. Location and type of buoys and
other navigational aids may change from time to time. Use
in conjunction with the text, and the latest Charts, Notices
Mariners, and U.S. Coast Pilot.

Aerial view of Pulpit Harbor, showing Pulpit Rock (note the shoals and ledges to starboard). Once past the rock, Cabot Cove is to the immediate right; the town landing (out of sight in this photo) is to the left, at the head of the harbor. (Hylander photo)

chor here Friday nights, to give them a short sail back to Camden Saturday morning. What a glorious sight to watch these stately schooners glide into Pulpit and drop the hook nearby! Occasionally they even tack in when the wind is from the east.

Pulpit Harbor once was the center of population for the island, with three general stores, a post office, and a customs house. All this has disappeared.

Approaches. Pulpit Harbor is hard to find, especially from the south or west. At a distance, look for a clearing in the woods and a meadow sloping down to a barn-red house, which marks the left-hand side of the entrance.

Coming from the north, find the large, yellow house on the crest of the hill north of the entrance and look for a cluster of small gray cottages visible inside the harbor.

Pulpit Rock, a bold pinnacle that gives the harbor its name, is notoriously hard to see against the shore. Sometimes you can distinguish it at a distance by its white speckle of seagulls. The entrance is northwest of Pulpit Rock. Leave it to starboard, giving it a berth of 50 to 100 feet, passing halfway between Pulpit Rock to starboard and the small cliffs on shore to port. Then stay in the middle, away from the ledges making out from the north side.

As you shoot past Pulpit Rock, check the status of the enormous osprey nest that has crowned the rock for more than 150 years. In the early summer, you can watch the parents returning to the nest to feed their chicks, grasping a fat fish in their talons and landing with loud chirps of triumph.

Anchorages, Moorings. Just after you enter, a cove extends to your right. The land surrounding this cove has been owned for generations by the Cabot family, and it is known locally as Cabot Cove. The several moorings here are private. You can anchor in 15 to 20 feet at low, a long way in. Holding ground is good, and Cabot Cove is the best-protected portion of Pulpit Harbor.

For an unobstructed view of the sunset on the Camden Hills, head for the southeast end of Pulpit Harbor, anchoring in 16 to 20 feet anywhere along the perimeter. Latecomers and the big schooners anchor more in the middle of the harbor, where depths are 20 to 30 feet.

Another cove stretching out to the east has a number of private moorings maintained by Thayer's Y-Knot Boatyard. During July and August, they are likely to be occupied, but you might be able to find an empty one in the spring and fall.

Holding ground is generally good in Pulpit Harbor, with mud bottom. There are also patches of kelp, however, so be sure your hook is set. The encircling hills provide good protection from winds of any direction, and it is a superb harbor under all conditions.

Getting Ashore. Take your dinghy to the floats at the public landing, at the head of the cove stretching east.

For the Boat. Water may be obtained at the public landing, with seven feet at the end of the floats at low tide. There is a trash bin at the head of the dock.

Thayer's Y-Knot Boatyard (Ch. 16; tel. 867-4701). Based a short distance away in Southern Harbor (see writeup), the yard keeps a boat in Pulpit and can be reached for help easily by phone.

For the Crew. There is a phone at the public landing. Tiny Taxi (tel. 867-2076) can take you to the town of North Haven.

Although Pulpit Harbor is wonderfully rural, the Pulpit Harbor Inn and Restaurant (tel. 867-2219) is a short walk from the public landing. It is open every day except Monday for dinner (reservations required). Walk south over the little bridge, following the harbor around past the graveyard, and continue until you find the inn on your right. Take a flashlight if you go for dinner. If you phone the inn from the public landing, they will pick you up. The inn has showers and laundry facilities, available only in the afternoon.

Just beyond Pulpit Harbor Inn is the Islander Grocery Store (tel. 867-4771), which will deliver substantial orders to the public landing; they have a good line of groceries, beer, wine, and ice.

Things to Do. Allow an hour to walk to the town of North Haven, plus time for collecting raspberries. Aside from taking walks, it's fun to poke around with the dinghy. Row up under the little bridge to the east. This provides a lovely, peaceful passage, and you can go for a mile, if you wish, at high tide.

BARTLETT HARBOR ★★★ No facilities

Charts: 13302, 13305, **13308**

This is a quiet little harbor on the west side of North Haven Island, a couple of miles west of Pulpit Harbor. Although exposed to the west and southwest, it would be a pleasant place to anchor in settled summer weather, with a beautiful view of the Camden Hills.

Approaches. The only danger in the approach is the long ledge making out from the north side of the entrance, which is visible almost until high tide.

Anchorages, Moorings. At the northeast end of the harbor is a cluster of boathouses and sheds. There are several private moorings, and room to anchor outside the moorings in 12 to 20 feet. The holding is good.

FOX ISLANDS THOROFARE

Charts: 13302, 13305, **13308**

Fox Islands Thorofare is one of the great east-west passages of Maine. Winding seven or eight miles between the islands of North Haven and Vinalhaven, it is sometimes 500 yards wide and sometimes as narrow as 100 yards. Because of the many turns and shifting winds, and places where you will be blanketed by the land, it is a challenge to sail all the way through. Like all passages in Maine, the Thorofare is buoyed from east to west.

In the town of North Haven, on the north side of the Thorofare, you can satisfy most of the needs of boat or crew. The ferry from Rockland docks here several times a day, making it a convenient place to meet people without retracing your steps to the mainland.

The Thorofare is lined with great summer cottages, each with its own dock and float. It provides its own form of entertainment, with a constant stream of every kind of boat—classic and modern, wood and glass, large and small. It is hard to come here without meeting someone you know.

Currents in the Thorofare are not usually very strong, unless it has been blowing hard from west or east. The critical area is in the narrows at Iron Point, where you may find strong currents and eddies. The ebb flows in both directions from Iron Point, and the flood meets here.

Approaches from the West. Approaching from the west, the entrance to Fox Islands Thorofare is hard to see because of the way North Haven curves down around Vinalhaven. From Camden, aim just north of the outermost islands on the horizon (Hurricane and the White Islands), passing north of The Graves and south of Robinson Rock.

The first mark you will pick up probably will be the large granite monument on Fiddler Ledge. Before reaching Fiddler, keep a careful watch for dangerous Drunkard Ledge, half a mile to the west. The currents are especially strong in this area, and the flood will set you toward this ledge, which is submerged at high tide, uncovering seven feet at low. The red daybeacon marking Drunkard Ledge is near its eastern edge; do not cut it close. Leave the granite monument on Fiddler Ledge to port. The ledge extends a short distance south of the monument, so give it a little room.

In thick weather, find red gong "26" or red-and-white bell "FT" in the entrance.

Near Fiddler Ledge, you will sight inconspicuous Browns Head Light, in a clearing on the northwest shore of Vinalhaven. The white sector marks the safest approach to the Thorofare. This lighthouse is more than 150 years old, built during Andrew Jackson's presidency.

The Sugar Loaves are high, barren rocks, grassy on top and usually dotted with cormorants drying their wings. Leave them on either side. Beyond are the Dumpling Islands, low, wooded, and rocky.

From there on, the Thorofare is obvious and well marked. Can "17" sticks out in the channel farther than you expect, and it always seems to be at one of these narrow points that you look astern and find the ferry coming with a bone in its teeth.

There is a substantial fleet of boats moored off the town of North Haven, often obscuring the nun at Lobster Ledge, covered two feet at low.

The most difficult point to sail through is the narrows off Iron Point, where you may find strong current and eddies. The wind often heads you just enough so you must tack between Dobbin Rock, marked by nun "10," and Iron Point Ledge, marked with green daybeacon "11" near the northwest end of the ledge.

In the eastern end of the Thorofare, marked by huge meadows and saltwater farms, the wind often is fluky, but there are few dangers. The lighthouse on Goose Rocks (known as "The Sparkplug") has been fitted with a solar panel that is probably highly efficient but looks incongruous.

There is plenty of room on either side of Widow Island, which has a beach on the western side and a house near its peak on the southeast. Once used as an insane asylum, the island later housed a large government sanatorium for tuberculosis victims.

Approaches from the East. Approaching from the east in thick weather, run for red bell "4" off Channel Rock, and the foghorn on Goose Rocks behind it. If you are fogbound or caught by darkness, Carver Cove in Calderwood Neck is extremely easy to enter, and it provides good anchorage and protection except from the northeast. Kent Cove is another alternative, also easy to enter.

In clear weather, you can identify the white tower of Goose Rocks Light at a distance.

SOUTHERN HARBOR ★★★

Charts: 13302, 13305, **13308**

A large body of water on the southwest side of North Haven Island, Southern Harbor extends northward from Fox Islands Thorofare and is easy to enter. Because of the exposure to prevailing southwesterlies, there may be an uncomfortable chop here at times. With the wind from the north and east, however, it offers very good protection.

Southern Harbor is the home of well-known artist Eric Hopkins, many of whose paintings show views of the harbor.

Approaches. Coming from the west, leave the Sugar Loaves (high, barren, grassy on top) to starboard and continue up into the harbor.

Coming from North Haven, leave the Dumpling Islands and nun "20" at Calderwood Rock to starboard, then double back toward Southern Harbor.

Avoid the two-foot spot west of Turnip Island by favoring the left side of the channel at this point. Near low tide, Seal Ledge probably will be occupied by a large and lethargic group of these creatures. Seal Ledge, Lobster Island, and the subsequent little bits of land lie more or less in a straight line, so you should have no trouble steering a safe course past them, even if the tide is high.

Anchorages, Moorings. Anchor in 10 to 16 feet at low on the centerline of the harbor in good mud bottom, or pick up one of the moorings established by Y-Knot Boatyard. The outer moorings are suitable for boats drawing seven feet.

Getting Ashore. Row into the floats at Y-Knot Boatyard.

For the Boat. *Thayer's Y-Knot Boatyard (Ch. 16; tel. 867-4701).* This yard is on the eastern side of the harbor, past the cove east of Pigeon Hill. There has been a substantial expansion here in recent years. A channel marked with red stakes and green stakes has been dredged to the stone dock and floats ($3\frac{1}{2}$ feet in the channel at low); you can get water and electricity, but no fuel; there is a chandlery.

The yard has a 25-ton marine railway and boatlift and can handle most repairs, including diesel engines and electronics; a diver is available.

For the Crew. There are showers at Y-Knot. The boatyard can provide transportation to the Pulpit Harbor Inn and Restaurant, or you may prefer to walk there, a mile or so north. (See Pulpit Harbor writeup.) Reservations are required for dinner (tel. 867-2219). The inn also has a van that will take you back and forth. For Tiny Taxi, call 867-2076. The village of North Haven is about .7 mile south of the harbor; there you will find services of all kinds, including a market and laundromat.

NORTH HAVEN ★★★★

All facilities

Charts: 13302, 13305, **13308**

North Haven is a pleasant village on the north side of the Fox Islands Thorofare. One of the first summer communities in America, it was founded by Boston yachtsmen who saw it as a wonderfully protected but challenging area to race small boats. The 14½-foot, gaff-rigged North Haven dinghies started racing in 1887 and are still racing today—probably the oldest formal class boat in the country. Another popular class in North Haven is the beautiful little Herreshoff 12½'s.

Although the Thorofare is lined with private docks and floats, most of those of interest to visiting yachtsmen are clustered around the ferry landing. The car ferry from Rockland makes frequent trips, so keep your eyes open.

Approaches. North Haven is midway through the Thorofare, centered on the ferry landing. While maneuvering among the moored boats, do not ignore nun "14," marking two-foot Lobster Ledge to the east.

Anchorages, Moorings. The North Haven Casino (as the Yacht Club is officially known) has several guest moorings (marked "NHC") and extensive floats west of the ferry landing. Tie up to the yacht club floats, with five feet alongside at low, for short periods only. The J.O. Brown & Son boatyard also has moorings (marked "JOB"), opposite the yard.

If no mooring is available, anchor outside the moored boats in 16 to 25 feet of water at low. The holding ground is good, in mud, with exposure to the west and southeast.

Getting Ashore. Row your dinghy in to the town landing or the yacht club floats. The small building at the seaward end of the dock is the clubhouse; the buildings at the land end are private homes.

For the Boat. *J.O. Brown & Son, Inc. (Ch. 16; tel. 867-4621).* Located east of the ferry landing, this yard was started in 1899 at the old clam and lobster processing factory. Fourth-generation Foy Brown is still building wooden boats here, ranging from a traditional lobsterboat to a radical Phil Bolger design. In addition to their moorings, there is space alongside, in five feet of water at low.

Gas, diesel, water, ice, and electricity may be obtained at the floats, and there is a chandlery. The yard has a 15-ton boatlift and can handle hull and engine repairs. Or you can do it yourself.

North Haven Casino (tel. 867-4696). Water is available at the floats.

Town Landing. There are no facilities at the town landing, which is tucked inside the ferry slip on the west side.

For the Crew. Showers are available for yachtsmen at J.O. Brown's yard, and Brown's Coal Wharf Restaurant serves dinner (tel. 867-4739). There is a laundromat on the main street nearby. Across from the ferry landing is the Waterman Co. variety store and market, and the post office. Phones and restrooms are at the ferry landing.

Opposite Waterman's is Roman's Fish Market, and a snack bar. There are several galleries and gift and craft shops in the little town.

When the ferry is due, a cab will be down at the landing. Otherwise, call Tiny Taxi at 867-2076.

The Pulpit Harbor Inn and Restaurant serves dinner (except Mondays). Call 867-2219 for reservations (required). The inn is about 1.5 miles north out of town; you can go by cab, or the inn will send a van to pick you up. The inn has showers and laundry facilities, available for afternoon use.

Things to Do. If you have your own bikes, there are 27 miles of paved roads and much to enjoy, from sparkling coves to archaeological sites.

This is a great area to explore by small boat. Take your dinghy and poke around in the Thorofare, or up Perry Creek. An interesting run, well seeded with rocks and ledges, goes through the Mill River (dry at low tide), under the bridge, and into Winter Harbor. Both sail and powerboats can be rented at Brown's yard.

Across from J.O. Brown's is Calderwood Hall, with a display of island arts and crafts.

Aerial view of North Haven, looking west through Fox Islands Thorofare. (Christopher Ayres photo)

PERRY CREEK ★★★★ 5 No facilities

Charts: 13302, 13305, **13308**

Perry Creek is a beautiful well-protected anchorage, tucked away around the corner from North Haven Village. Arrive early to find room in this popular spot. It is small and very peaceful, with only one farmhouse visible, fields leading down to the water, and a picturesque little island guarding the entrance.

Approaches. Coming from Fox Islands Thorofare in either direction, bear south toward Hopkins Point and the entrance to Seal Cove. Skirt the little island off Hopkins Point (which has a clump of trees), noting that the ledge makes out southward a distance equal to the island itself.

Enter Perry Creek between the island and the unmarked ledge making out from the south shore. (The stake reported on the chart no longer exists.) At low tide, the ledges on both sides of the entrance are visible. At high tide, come in halfway between the southern tip of the island and the shore to your left.

Local sailors report they have been unable to find the four-foot spot shown on the chart just past the entrance (see sketch map). Curve northward past the rocky point to port until you are beyond the cable area shown on the chart.

Anchorages, Moorings. There are a few private moorings in Perry Creek. Anchor in 8 to 11 feet of water at low, just west of the cable area, near the green boathouse on the north shore. Holding ground is good, in mud.

You can also work your way farther up the creek, although the deep water narrows rapidly. The farther in you go, the prettier it becomes.

Things to Do. On a high tide, you can row about a mile all the way up to the head of the creek—a most delightful experience. The shores are lined with sloping rocks and bits of marsh, where sanderlings and kingfishers play. There are pines and spruce and stands of birch. Musseling is good here.

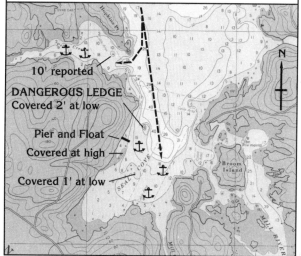

SEAL COVE and PERRY CREEK
(based on Chart 13308)
(notes courtesy of L. Emmett Holt III)

Yards
0   500   1000

Anchorages

This sketch map is for general information only and NOT TO BE USED FOR NAVIGATION. Locations and types of buoys and other navigational aids may change from time to time. Use in conjunction with the text, and with the latest Charts, Notices to Mariners, and U.S. Coast Pilot.

10' reported
DANGEROUS LEDGE
Covered 2' at low

Pier and Float
Covered at high —

Covered 1' at low

SEAL COVE ★★ 3 No facilities

Charts: 13302, 13305, **13308**

Seal Cove cuts into the northern end of Vinalhaven Island halfway through the Fox Islands Thorofare. It is well protected and easy to enter. Caution! The charts are dangerously misleading, as pointed out by Mr. Emmett Holt, who has anchored here for 50 years. The six-foot spot shown on the west side of the entrance is actually a large ledge covered by two feet of water or less at low. An informal marker may be placed on the ledge during summer months.

Approaches. Coming through Fox Islands Thorofare from either direction, head southward into the middle of Seal Cove, staying well east of the ledge mentioned above.

Anchorages, Moorings. Anchor in the southeastern part of the cove in 10 to 25 feet of water where the cable area is shown (reported nonexistent), or in the other areas shown on the sketch map. Mr. Holt reports that it is also possible to tuck inside, between the "six-foot" ledge and the western shore, with plenty of swinging room. The holding ground is good mud.

WATERMAN COVE ★★   No facilities

Charts: 13302, 13305, **13308**

Due north of the narrows at Iron Point, halfway through Fox Islands Thorofare, Waterman Cove is of little interest under normal cruising conditions. If the wind was in the north, however, it would provide a good refuge, easy to enter.

Approaches. Leave nun "8" to port and head up the middle of the cove toward the huge meadow.

Anchorages, Moorings. Anchor in the middle of the cove, west of Fish Point, in 7 to 10 feet of water at low. The holding ground is good, in mud.

KENT COVE ★★   No facilities

Charts: 13302, 13305, **13308**

This large cove, with two bights, is at the eastern end of Fox Islands Thorofare, north of Goose Rocks Light. Like adjoining Waterman Cove to the west, it is of little interest during the summer months. However, the eastern bight here would provide good protection for winds from the north or northeast.

Approaches. Coming through Fox Islands Thorofare from the east, leave Goose Rocks Light to starboard and head up the middle of Kent Cove. Identify the high, little, wooded island and proceed into the northeast bight, leaving the island to port.

Anchorages, Moorings. Anchor in 8 to 10 feet of water at low, just past the island. Holding ground is good, in mud. (In the western bight of Kent Cove, the holding ground is poor, in grass.)

CARVER COVE ★★★   No facilities

Charts: 13302, 13305, **13308**

Carver Cove is at the eastern end of Fox Islands Thorofare, making into Calderwood Neck on Vinalhaven Island. It is extremely easy to enter and provides good protection under normal summer conditions. It is the prettiest of the several large coves in the Thorofare, and a convenient stop if you are coming in late at night from the east. Even if the wind is blowing a gale from the southwest, you can spend a comfortable night here.

There are only a couple of houses on the cove, with several little gravel beaches. Herons and ospreys live nearby, and you probably will have a visit of inspection from a seal.

Approaches. Pass to either side of Widow Island and head southward for the center of the cove.

Anchorages, Moorings. Go well up to the head of the cove and anchor in 9 to 17 feet of water at low. Holding ground is good, in mud.

LITTLE THOROFARE, STIMPSONS, CALDERWOOD, and BABBIDGE ISLAND PASSAGES

Charts: 13302, 13305, **13308**

At the eastern end of Fox Islands Thorofare, Stimpsons, Calderwood, and Babbidge islands, together with Burnt Island, provide an interesting series of passages that require considerable attention. Both Stimpsons and Babbidge are heavily wooded, while Calderwood between them has several meadows and clearings.

Between Stimpsons and Calderwood. The easiest passage is between Stimpsons and Calderwood, providing a good day stop and beaches to explore.

Run along the south coast of Stimpsons until you see the southern tip of Calderwood, rocky with just a few trees. The only danger is the rock near the southeast corner of Stimpsons. It uncovers nine feet at low and normally is easy to find. Run up halfway between this rock to port and Calderwood Island to starboard. The best place to anchor is on the bar, which shows 7, 8, and 10 feet on the chart.

Between Calderwood and Babbidge. The passage between Calderwood and Babbidge has more obstructions. One person reported hitting an uncharted ledge, covered only two or three feet at low, while sailing through this passage at six knots.

It is best to go through here at halftide or better. Coming from the west, stay close to either side of the seven-foot rock in midchannel to avoid the ledge making out from Babbidge. Then stay to the right of midchannel, to avoid the ledge off Calderwood.

Little Thorofare. The Little Thorofare, between Stimpsons and Burnt islands, is clear at the eastern end (except for the three little islands off Burnt), but the western end is a rock garden.

Coming from the west, run close to the northern shore of the Thorofare toward the dock east of Indian Point. From the dock, turn sharply to starboard and strike across the Thorofare toward a spot west of the little island off the coast of Stimpsons. As you approach the little island, turn to port and continue down the midline of the Little Thorofare.

MULLEN COVE ★★ No facilities
Charts: 13305, **13308**

Mullen Cove, on the east side of North Haven Island, north of the Little Thorofare, looks good on the chart, but it is not a secure anchorage.

There is a town-run park with nice trails on Mullen Head.

Approaches. As you leave Fox Islands Thorofare and run north past Babbidge and Calderwood islands, high, wooded Mullen Head is easy to find. Note the unmarked rocks off Burnt Island and off Mullen Head, and stay well out until the cove opens up. Then run down the centerline. There is a red house at the head of Mullen Cove.

Anchorages, Moorings. The cove is easy to enter, but don't go in too far because of numerous unmarked rocks. Anchor in 12 to 17 feet at low. The holding ground is likely to be poor, with an ample supply of kelp. A southwest wind may funnel into the cove through the slot west of Burnt Island.

MARSH COVE ★★★ No facilities
Charts: 13302, **13305**

At the northeastern end of North Haven Island, just south of Oak Hill, Marsh Cove offers good protection from prevailing summer winds, a pleasant beach, and one of the few totem poles to be found in the Penobscot Bay region. A substantial stone dock marks the north side of the cove, and there are views of Isle au Haut and Deer Isle on the eastern horizon.

Occupying 330 acres of Oak Hill is the family compound of Thomas J. Watson, Jr., retired chairman of IBM (and former ambassador to the USSR). Complete with half a dozen houses, a private airfield, a flock of deer, and a fleet of Model-Ts, the estate is designed, as Watson says, as "a grandchildren trap."

Approaches. The cove is easy to enter, south of Hog Island (two little islands connected at low). Head for the middle of the beach.

Anchorages, Moorings. There are several private moorings, but plenty of room to anchor in 15 feet or so at low, west of Hog Island, off the center of the beach. Holding ground is fair, in mud and grass.

Things to Do. If you arrive here after the nesting season ends in mid-July, row over to state-owned Dagger Island to the east.

WINTER HARBOR ★★★★ No facilities
Charts: 13302, 13305, **13308**

Here is another special spot—with a remoteness and beauty nearly unsurpassed. On the east side of Vinalhaven Island, south of Calderwood Neck, Winter Harbor is a long, narrow slot providing excellent protection except from the northeast. The harbor is home to several fishing and lobsterboats, and the back reaches of the harbor are used for seeding and harvesting mussels.

Approaches. The approaches to Winter Harbor are easy. As you come from Fox Islands Thorofare and coast around Calderwood Neck, the highest, rounded, wooded bump to the south is Bluff Head. Just west of Bluff Head is Big Hen Island, with conspicuous white granite shores. Aim for Big Hen until you are well past the southeast corner of Calderwood Neck, from which the rocks make out a long way. Then make your turn into Winter Harbor, going right up the middle. Note the two-foot spot just past the island on the right side of the entrance.

Anchorages, Moorings. Anchor anywhere you wish in 17 to 30 feet. The depth varies considerably, so find a reasonably shallow spot, such as near the first little island to port. Another good spot is in midchannel between the second little island to port and the imposing 100-foot cliff of Starboard Rock.

It is also possible to go farther in past Starboard Rock, squeezing right to avoid the two-foot spot and anchoring in 17 to 26 feet before the next set of little islands. Or work your way even farther in to the pool off the entrance to Mill River.

There is current in Winter Harbor (which connects with Mill River), and you may find yourself lying to either the current or the wind, whichever is stronger. Under normal conditions, Winter Harbor is exposed only to the northeast. If the wind is blowing very hard from the southwest, however, the fetch from the inner harbor will make it uncomfortable.

Things to Do. If the tide is up, the estuaries of Winter Harbor are fun to explore by dinghy.

You are likely to see Hurricane Island Outward Bound students camped out alone in various spots around Winter Harbor, one of the locations used during the course's "solo" experience. Wave, but respect their solitude.

SEAL BAY ★★★★ No facilities

Charts: 13302, 13305, **13308**

Adjacent to Winter Harbor, at the northeastern end of Vinalhaven, Seal Bay provides a variety of delightful and well-protected anchorages, but it is unmarked and requires considerable care in navigation.

The wooded, rocky islands near the entrance to the bay are particularly beautiful, and yes, there still are seals here.

Approaches. The approach to Seal Bay is the same as for Winter Harbor. Rounding Calderwood Neck from the north, pick up the high, rounded, wooded bump of Bluff Head. Turn in toward Winter Harbor when you can safely pass the rocks making out a long way from the eastern end of Calderwood Neck. The Hen Islands are easy to identify, with their long, sloping, white granite ledges leading up into the trees.

The usual entrance to Seal Bay is just west of Little Hen Island. Leave it close aboard to port to avoid the rocks off Penobscot Island (visible at low). There are a number of islands, rocks, and peninsulas in the bay, and it is helpful to check them off carefully as you enter.

It is also possible to enter Seal Bay through the narrow passage between Bluff Head and Big Hen Island, favoring the eastern side.

Anchorages, Moorings. There are several good anchorages in the bay (see sketch map). One of the most beautiful is south of Big Hen, in 10 to 14 feet of water at low, east of the four-foot spot. The bottom is rocky, and there is some exposure to the northeast, but otherwise good protection all around. You can also anchor nearby between the large, unnamed island south of Big Hen and the peninsula of Bluff Head, although the deep water is quite narrow.

Another possibility is to enter the deeper recesses of Seal Bay. Coast south and then southwest along Penobscot Island on the right, looking for Turning Rock, a long and jointed bare rock just west of the 33-foot spot on Chart 13308. The entrance to the inner bay is between Turning Rock and a rock awash two feet at low about 200 yards to the southeast. Follow the deep water around to your right, leaving Turning Rock about 50 yards to starboard. Note the submerged rock 150 yards southwest of Turning Rock. Pass north of Hay Island, curving left and avoiding the rocks on the northwest side of the channel. Anchor north or west of Hay Island, in 7 to 16 feet, with good holding ground in mud. The bay here is fairly wide, but you are surrounded by land.

To reach a similar and more protected anchorage in a smaller bay, continue west of Burnt Island and anchor in 7 to 10 feet. Most of the western end of Seal Bay is still natural, and only one or two houses are visible.

It is also possible to anchor in the southeastern corner of Seal Bay, off Coombs Neck, but the approach is a bit daunting the first time. After entering Seal Bay west of Little Hen, run down the narrow tongue of deep water toward Coombs Neck. Leave to port the smaller of the two unnamed islands (rocky, with a bunch of trees). Also leave to port the ledge beyond, which is awash 10 feet at low and identifiable at high by a patch of rockweed. Beyond the ledge is a rock marked by a green stake; leave the green stake to port also. Note the shallow spots along the western edge of the deep water.

Anchor near the first moored boats beyond the stake in 10 to 18 feet at low. Other boats are moored in shoal water farther in.

Getting Ashore. Many of the islands and

points in Seal Bay are deserted, and you can row ashore to explore. However, be extremely careful of fires, which you should only build well below the high-water mark. There have been a number of fires here in recent memory, and the owner of this land is weary of desperate forays to extinguish them.

Like Winter Harbor, Seal Bay is often used by Outward Bound students for their solo camping experience.

Things to Do. Explore the nooks and crannies of this lovely bay in your dinghy, including state-owned Little Hen.

EAST COAST OF VINALHAVEN ISLAND

Charts: 13302, 13303, **13305**

The east coast of Vinalhaven is the lee shore of the Atlantic Ocean and exposed to its full strength. Even in the calmest of weather, the swells burst on the rocky headlands and shores. Between Seal Bay and Carvers Harbor, there is no safe refuge for a cruising sailor.

The islands along this coast are mostly barren, battered rocks with grass and a few stunted trees; the only one where you can land easily is Brimstone.

The offlying dangers along the coast are marked by a long line of buoys, from can "5" on Triangle Ledge, past nuns "2," "4," "6," and "8," to red beacon "10" on Point Ledge, and finally the light on Green Ledge at the entrance to The Reach. (Leave them all to starboard.) It is an impressive coast to run, easy enough in clear weather but no place to be in the fog.

BRIMSTONE ISLAND

Charts: 13302, **13303**, 13305

Standing well out to sea, southwest of Vinalhaven Island, is high, beautiful Brimstone Island, covered with grasses and wildflowers. On the double-crescent beaches at the northwest corner are piles of wonderfully smooth, black stones, rolled and polished for eons in the endless surf of the Atlantic.

From the 112-foot summit of the island, there are unsurpassed views in every direction—to Blue Hill and Isle au Haut, to Matinicus and the other seaward islands, and to the Camden Hills—not to mention a spectacular view of your own boat anchored far below. Brimstone and Little Brimstone belong to The Nature Conservancy.

Be aware of strong tidal currents running between Brimstone Island and the islands to the west.

For a day stop in prevailing summer winds, anchor on the northeast side of the double-crescent beach. Come in to the center of the beach until you reach a comfortable depth, which will be quite close to shore. The cobble beach of greenstone pebbles continues down to larger rocks, so consider buoying the anchor. At least one competent sailor has lost an anchor here.

The beach is steep. Depending on the size of the waves, it might be easier to get your dinghy ashore at the rocks on the west end of the beach rather than to land on the beach itself. From there,

it's a good scramble up grassy trails to the summit; be careful of your footing.

Foragers will appreciate the island, not only for the usual selection of edible land plants (including a profusion of wild strawberries in season) and tasty intertidal varieties, but especially for the clumps of spearmint near the northwest end.

Brimstone Island is one of the few nesting areas for the increasingly rare Leach's petrel, a small nocturnal bird that comes ashore only to breed. As Peter Blanchard, a volunteer for The Nature Conservancy, says, "They make a riotous laughter when they return from the sea, combined with a purring noise. It's like being in a room with thousands of children, all giggling at once. It's a magical experience." The female digs her burrow in the tussocky ground on the east side of the island, lays one egg, and incubates it on the nest for 90 days. Avoid this area entirely: the petrels nest all summer long.

Although it is possible to anchor for the night between Brimstone and the little islands to the south, do it only when assured of fine weather. Brimstone is a lonely outpost in the ocean and much exposed to waves and wind. The best protection is north and slightly east of Little Brimstone (westernmost and largest of the islands).

CARVERS HARBOR ★★★★

Charts: 13302, 13303, **13305** (Inset)

Carvers is a busy fishermen's harbor, full of activity and interest. It is a difficult place for a yachtsman to visit since there are few moorings and facilities; the attention of the town is on business. But this is the main port of Vinalhaven Island, one of the most fascinating places on the coast of Maine, so it is worth making an effort to stop here.

The Carver family settled Carvers Harbor in 1766. Fishing, farming, and shipbuilding were the early occupations, and at one time the Carvers were the world's largest manufacturers of horse-nets—used to protect horses from flies. Granite quarrying became the dominant industry of Vinalhaven from its beginning in 1826 until the last of the paving quarries closed in 1939.

Signs of the granite industry are everywhere here—the magnificent wharves that surround the harbor, the quarry tailings on the hillsides, the elaborate memorial horse troughs decorating many Vinalhaven intersections, the unusual granite curbing around family plots in the Carver cemetery, and the quarries themselves.

Sands Quarry opened in 1860. The Bodwell Granite Company employed more than 600, including workers from England, Scotland, and Ireland, and stone carvers from Italy, Finland, and Norway. Stone was cut here for the Brooklyn Bridge, but the most famous contract was for four enormous columns to surround the high altar of the Cathedral of St. John the Divine in New York. The rough granite monoliths were 64 feet high and eight feet in diameter, and weighed 360 tons—the largest single pieces of stone ever cut and moved.

Approaches. Carvers Harbor is at the southern end of Vinalhaven Island. The usual approach is from the west, through The Reach. Red lighted buoy "4" marks the right-hand side of the entrance to Carvers Harbor; can "5" marks the left.

Anchorages, Moorings. While it may be possible to anchor in Carvers Harbor outside the fishing

A rough granite column lying on rollers in a quarry on Vinalhaven, 1892. Some of the largest pieces of stone ever quarried were cut here as columns for the Cathedral of St. John the Divine in New York City. (Frank Claes Collection)

fleet, there is very little room, the bottom is soft mud, and the holding ground is not good. You are far better off to try to obtain a mooring. Calderwood's Wharf has several moorings of its own and keeps track of other private moorings not currently in use. The Hopkins Boatyard also has several moorings, and the town maintains two moorings along the south shore, marked with red balls. Do not pick up an unknown mooring without leaving someone on board who can move your boat when the owner returns. Calderwood's is planning to build slips at the wharf, with water and electricity.

Getting Ashore. Take your dinghy in to the floats at Calderwood's Wharf, but tie up out of the way; the face of the floats is much in use by refueling lobsterboats. To get closer to town, row to the public landing floats, at the head of the harbor on the west side, near the millrace.

For the Boat. *Hopkins Boatyard (tel. 863-2551).* On the west side of the harbor, near the north end of the commercial docks, Hopkins has no signs, but it is recognizable by the 15- and 30-ton boatlifts and the cradled boats. The yard has some marine supplies, and can do repairs. There is a small dock and a float with eight feet alongside.

Calderwood's Wharf (Ch. 16; tel. 863-4831). Right next to the fish plant, Calderwood's can be recognized by the gray building with the sign, "Calderwood's Wharf." There are floats (15 feet alongside) where you can obtain gas, diesel, ice, and marine supplies.

For the Crew. Calderwood's Wharf has groceries, wine, beer, and liquor. You can rent bikes and cars here; showers and laundry services are planned. Pay phones are located at the public landing and the ferry terminal. Across from the eagle at the public landing, the Carvers Harbor Market has groceries, wine, beer, ice, and a bakery.

The tiny Haven Restaurant is recommended for dinner; reservations required (tel. 863-4969). The Millrace Restaurant, a local institution, is open for breakfast, lunch, and dinner. For soups, sandwiches, and salads try the Night Hawk Country Store. There are other restaurants and several takeouts. Lobsters can be bought at the Vinalhaven Fishermen's Co-op, close to the ferry slip.

The post office is on Main Street, as is The Paper Store, for books and newspapers. Pick up a copy of "The Wind," the island newsweekly, to find out what's going on.

Things to Do. If you happen to be here on the Fourth of July, don't miss the parade up Main Street and right back down Main Street. There are many interesting walks and outings in the vicinity of Carvers Harbor, either on foot or by bike. Bikes can be rented at Calderwood's Wharf, or at the Tidewater Inn on Main Street; reserve ahead (tel. 863-4618). Start by buying a local street and bicycle route map at The Paper Store.

Carved granite eagles ready for shipment from Vinalhaven, 1907. (Frank Claes Collection)

The few blocks of Main Street are well worth a short stroll, past the millrace and the historic Star of Hope Lodge built in 1885. This extraordinary mansard-roofed building has been restored by pop artist Robert Indiana. Built during the heyday of Vinalhaven's granite industry, it is one of the few remaining buildings from those prosperous times.

For information on history (or anything else), you may be referred to one of the colorful institutions of Vinalhaven—the "Historians"—three old men who hold court in Fifield's Hardware Store on Main Street.

From Main Street, go left up over the hill on High Street past the Historical Society (worth a visit) to the John Carver cemetery, with a most interesting array of granite memorials. Past the cemetery, turn left at the round granite memorial horse trough. Walk a short distance along Old Harbor Road until you reach a dirt road, on your left, leading into Sands Quarry, with spectacular cliffs.

Returning to Carvers Harbor along the Sands Road, you'll pass a great 60-foot granite monolith abandoned in the grass by the roadside. It had been cut for the General Troy monument in Troy, NY, but discarded when a flaw was discovered. The Sands Road will take you back to the ferry terminal, next to which is pretty little Grimes Park on the waterfront.

There are two attractive public swimming quarries, shown on the town map. Booth Quarry is about 2½ miles east of town on the Pequot Road, and Lawson's Quarry is about the same distance out of town on the North Haven Road.

For another interesting walk, go out of town eastward on Main Street until you reach a bandstand and a little park displaying a blue galamander. These awesome machines, with rear wheels nine feet in diameter, drawn by teams of oxen, carried granite blocks from the quarries to the cutting sheds at Sands Cove.

Take your next right onto Atlantic Avenue and walk south until you reach the driveway of the Island Community Medical Center, on your left. Walk up the driveway to the parking lot in back, to the start of delightful, grassy trails leading through the Armbrust Hill Wildlife Reservation and passing several of the oldest quarries on Vinalhaven.

A short walk will bring you back to Atlantic Avenue. Then continue south across the bridge to Lane's Island. Forty-five acres of Lane's Island were bought by residents of Vinalhaven and given to The Nature Conservancy as a preserve. Follow the signs into the preserve and walk around the perimeter of Lane's, enjoying the views of Indian Creek (site of Susquehanna Indian and Red Paint villages from 4,000 B.C. to colonial times), Brimstone Island in the distance, and Carvers Harbor. The terrain is heath, marsh, and bayberry, with many different kinds of grasses, wildflowers, and berries. At the tip is a simple memorial plaque to Vinalhaven men lost at sea. On your return, you will pass the old Lane family cemetery, dating from the early nineteenth century.

THE REACH

Charts: 13302, 13303, **13305** (Inset)

Part of the ferry route from Rockland, the Reach connects Hurricane Sound with Carvers Harbor. It's an interesting passage, though hard to enjoy because you are so busy piloting.

As the *Coast Pilot* says, The Reach is a "narrow, much obstructed channel." It is well marked but winding, with considerable current (which ebbs southeast and floods northwest). Red marks are left to port going eastward, green marks to starboard.

The narrowest part of The Reach is at a sharp S-turn near the little island at green daybeacon "5." Here it is only 100 feet wide, so be especially careful, because you are likely to meet a lobsterboat or the ferry right at the tightest spot.

REINDEER COVE ★★★ No facilities

Charts: 13302, 13303, **13305** (Inset)

The little cove at the northern tip of Greens Island, just opposite Old Harbor, is unnamed on the chart, but locally it is called Reindeer Cove. On the west side is a granite wharf piled with old lobster traps. As the wharf suggests, there once was a quarry on Greens Island, and an old lumber mill.

Approaches. Coming from Hurricane Sound and the west, enter The Reach between can "13" and nun "12" and continue until you see the cove and the granite wharf. Head straight into the middle of the cove.

Anchorages, Moorings. Anchor in a comfortable depth just inside the north end of the wharf. Holding ground is good in mud, but there is some kelp. There is good protection here from prevailing summer winds.

Getting Ashore. Row your dinghy to the granite wharf and clamber up (quite a process at low tide). The clearing next to the wharf is a delightful spot for a picnic.

OLD HARBOR ★★★ No facilities

Charts; 13302, 13303, **13305** (Inset)

This is an attractive old working harbor at the western end of The Reach, surrounded by small houses and lobster shacks. A number of lobsterboats are moored here, and lobster cars for storing the catch, but no yachts whatsoever. There is ample room to anchor.

Approaches. Enter The Reach from the west between can "13" and nun "12," then curve northward into the western portion of Old Harbor, leaving to starboard the wooded island that splits the harbor.

Anchorages, Moorings. Anchor in 10 to 15 feet of water at low in the western portion of the harbor, but do not venture much north of the small whaleback rock to starboard. In an old working harbor like this, all sorts of gear and traps are likely to lie on the bottom, and the *Coast Pilot* warns of "many old fish stakes." You should have no difficulty anchoring here, however. You will be exposed to prevailing southwesterlies but protected if the wind is from the north or east.

HURRICANE SOUND

Charts: 13302, 13303, **13305**, **13308**

On the southwest side of Vinalhaven Island, a series of beautiful islands form Hurricane Sound: Leadbetter, Laireys, Cedar, Crane, Hurricane, and the Whites. There are five separate entrances to Hurricane Sound, several of which are exhilarating (see sketch map).

Hurricane Island Outward Bound School is based here, with a welcome for yachtsmen. There is one harbor in the sound offering extremely good protection (Long Cove), and an unusual tidal pool (The Basin).

Leadbetter Narrows. Coming from the west, or from Fox Islands Thorofare, the usual entrance is at the northern end of the sound, inside Leadbetter Island. Use chart 13308. From the monument on Fiddler Ledge or green daybeacon "25" on Dogfish Ledges, the large granite dock on the eastern end of Dogfish Island is conspicuous. The slot of Leadbetter Narrows will be visible, with land behind it.

Green beacon "25" is not at the easternmost point of Dogfish Ledges, so give it a wide berth. Note the ledge at the mouth of Crockett Cove, some part of which is visible at every tide. The narrow spot in Leadbetter Narrows in marked by can "1," which you leave to starboard.

Laireys Narrows. South of Leadbetter Island is the interesting passage called Laireys Narrows. Some of the passage is shown on chart 13308, but you will need 13305 as well.

Laireys Narrows is hard to find from a distance, and difficult in poor visibility. Coming from the west, work your way in from buoy to buoy, starting at red-and-white bell "FT," leaving to starboard the cans at Inner Bay Ledges and Seal Ledge, until you reach red-and-white bell "GI" off Green Island. From there, aim for red lighted buoy "2A," which you leave close aboard to port, at the entrance to the narrows.

As you slide through the passage north of Laireys Island, you will probably lose your wind for a minute or two and may even need a boost from the engine.

The end of Laireys Narrows is marked by green lighted buoy "1," which you leave to starboard. Turn south into Hurricane Sound immediately past this buoy, running west of the little unnamed island (known locally as Tobacco Juice, since it looks as though it has been chewed and spat out).

As you pass Laireys Island on your way through the narrows, look for the bell mounted on the shore, with a long lanyard reaching up to the porch of a beautiful log house. The owners like to sit on the porch and salute passing vessels. On the tip of Cedar Island is the bow of a wrecked steamship turned upside down and made into a little house.

The ferry from Rockland to Vinalhaven passes back and forth six times a day through this narrow passage, so keep your eyes open. Once you find the outlying buoys, Laireys Narrows is an easy passage in good visibility, but always an exciting one.

North of Hurricane Island. The passage between Hurricane Island and the White Islands is wide and easy, marked by two small cans.

Coming from the west, a good landmark visible a long way is the standpipe at Carvers Harbor. The southwestern of the White Islands (Big White) is wooded and identifiable by high granite ledges at the southwestern end. State-owned Little Hurricane Island is low and has grassy granite ledges, with a few trees. Hurricane Island is high and wooded. As you approach Big White Island, look for cans "17" and "15" inside the passage, to be sure you are in the right place, and leave both to starboard.

Heron Neck. The southern entrance to Hurricane Sound is also wide and easy. As your mark, use the conspicuous lighthouse on Heron Neck, high on a granite bluff with a spine of trees. Deadman Ledge to port is a 20-foot granite island with a little grass.

The Reach. The fifth entrance to Hurricane Sound is The Reach (see earlier writeup).

HURRICANE ISLAND ★★★★★

Charts: 13302, **13303**, **13305**

Hurricane is one of the outlying islands at the southwest corner of Vinalhaven, and the home of the Hurricane Island Outward Bound School (HIOBS). Founded by Peter Willauer in 1964 to challenge and inspire young people, the school each year attracts men and women of all ages to a

great variety of courses year round, on land and sea, at several bases from Maine to Florida.

The Hurricane Island pulling boats, with their distinctive spritsail ketch rigs, sail the coast of Maine from Muscongus Bay almost to the Cana-

*Hurricane Island Expedition
August 1974
Outward Bound*

A 30-foot Hurricane Island pulling boat meets the 90-foot yawl *Gitana IV.*

dian border. If you see a lone figure sitting in contemplation on a rocky point of some deserted island, it probably is a Hurricane student on "solo" —an essential part of the Outward Bound experience.

HIOBS is part of a worldwide network of 30 Outward Bound schools whose purpose is to motivate. In the wilderness and on the sea, students cope with the challenges of the natural world and in the process develop self-confidence and self-esteem. They learn to work with others as a team, giving help and accepting it. They learn wilderness skills, and respect for and care of the environment.

Visitors are welcome on Hurricane Island, and there is much to see—not only student activities like rock climbing in the quarry and a hair-raising ropes course, but also the remains of an earlier period when Hurricane was an important source of granite.

Of interest to cruising sailors is the school's significant search-and-rescue capability. HIOBS has several well-equipped power vessels, and channel 16 is monitored 24 hours a day. HIOBS staff members are highly experienced seamen, many with Coast Guard licenses and EMT training. They probably know the coast better than anyone else.

Fire-fighting equipment, diving gear, and first aid supplies are kept on hand, and a doctor usually is in residence. Helping others is part of the Outward Bound philosophy, and Hurricane has participated in many rescues.

Hurricane's history is an intriguing one. In 1870, a Civil War general named Davis Tilson bought the island for the preposterous sum of $50, and within four years, the island had a population of 1,200 Italian and Irish immigrants. By 1880, the island had been set off from Vinalhaven and become its own town. It had a post office, six boardinghouses, 40 cottages, a pool hall, bowling green, bandstand, company store, and two major quarries and several smaller ones scattered throughout the island.

The island's polishing mill was particularly well known, and many other quarries shipped their stone here to be finished. Hurricane Island became one of the nation's largest, most productive, and famous granite sources. The island's granite helped build such imposing structures as the New York City Public Library and the Metropolitan Museum of Art.

But, like much of the history of quarrying, the Hurricane era was short. The end of the Hurricane

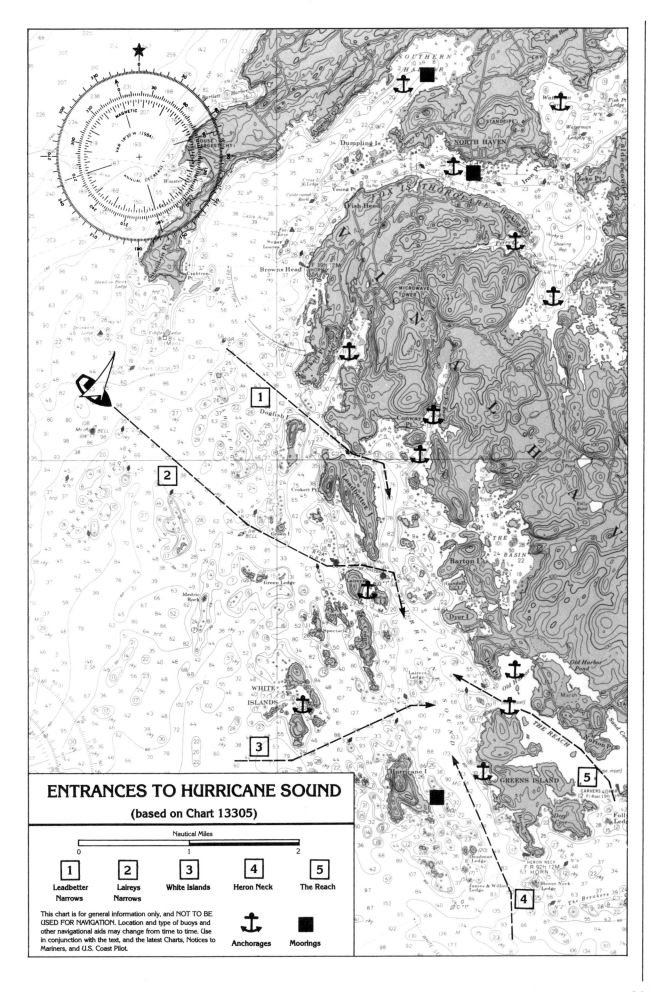

ENTRANCES TO HURRICANE SOUND
(based on Chart 13305)

Nautical Miles

0   1   2

1 Leadbetter Narrows   **2** Laireys Narrows   **3** White Islands   **4** Heron Neck   **5** The Reach

This chart is for general information only, and NOT TO BE USED FOR NAVIGATION. Location and type of buoys and other navigational aids may change from time to time. Use in conjunction with the text, and the latest Charts, Notices to Mariners, and U.S. Coast Pilot.

⚓ Anchorages   ■ Moorings

Island Granite Company came in 1915, with the death of the superintendent of works on the island for 20 years. A mild panic ensued when it was announced that the goods in the company store were being moved to the mainland, and workers and their families rushed to catch the last scheduled boat, in many cases leaving behind most of their worldly possessions. Hurricane was transformed, literally overnight, into a ghost town. It remained so until Outward Bound established its base here.

Approaches. The landings on Hurricane Island are all on the east side, in Hurricane Sound. If you have come through any of the northern entrances, head down the east coast of Hurricane Island toward the moored boats.

Be careful of the ledge shown on the chart east of the 41-foot spot, marked with a pipe with a triangular beacon. Run through the moored fleet, between the ledge and Hurricane Island.

Anchorages, Moorings. Although the anchorage here is only moderately well protected, and may be rolly, there are heavy guest moorings. If you are planning a visit, call the Rockland office at 594-5548, or call Hurricane Island directly on channel 16 and reserve a mooring. The moorings are red balls, marked "HIOBS," opposite the big gray mess hall. Pick one up and make your presence known at the rescue station, the small shingled building on the dock, or at the mess hall. It is wise not to anchor here, since the water is deep and the bottom rocky.

Getting Ashore. Row your dinghy in to the back of the float just below the rescue station. Sign the guest register and pick up information for island visitors, including a trail map.

For the Crew. Check to see if the mess hall can accommodate visitors for a meal; you will meet a lot of interesting people in the midst of a very intense experience. You may also be able to get a shower.

Things to Do. When you check in at the rescue station or the mess hall, find out what student activities are going on that day. It's fascinating to observe students rock climbing and rappelling on the granite cliffs of the quarry, or negotiating the ropes and beams and zip wire of the ropes course. There may be a capsize drill in a pulling boat or sea kayaking instruction. You might want to observe the daily "run and dip" at 5:30 A.M.—a run around the island followed by a dip in the icy waters of Hurricane Sound.

Be sure to walk the 2½-mile trail around the island. It takes you out on great granite slabs into the ocean: offers vistas all around Penobscot Bay; leads past quarries, old machinery, and piles of granite blocks still waiting to be shipped; provides raspberries in profusion, and thoroughly exercises you. HIOBS asks that you stay on the paths and not be tempted to try the ropes course, climb the cliffs, or swim in the quarry. No fires or smoking are allowed; keep dogs on a leash.

SANDS COVE★★★ No facilities
Charts: 13302, 13303, **13305 (Inset)**

The northernmost cove on the west side of Greens Island, opposite Hurricane Island, can be identified on the chart by the 11-foot sounding.

Approaches. Be sure you have the right cove; find the narrow, rocky point forming the southern entrance, and the house at the head of the cove. Leaving the ledge at the southern entrance well to starboard, enter on the midline.

Anchorages, Moorings. Go in far enough past the southern point to obtain protection from southwesterlies. Don't go too far; there are ledges halfway up the cove. Anchor in 12 to 16 feet at low. There is plenty of room to swing, but be sure your anchor is well set because the bottom appears to be rocky.

WHITE ISLANDS ★★★★ No facilities
Charts: 13302, **13303**, **13305**

Off the southwest shore of Vinalhaven lies a tiny archipelago that is among the most beautiful in Maine. Shown as the White Islands on the chart, the group includes Big and Little White and Big and Little Garden. Charles Lindbergh and his wife, Anne Morrow Lindbergh (author of *Gift from the Sea*), donated Big Garden to The Nature Conser-vancy, which also owns part of Big White. Little Garden and Little White are privately owned.

The islands are wooded, with tiny beaches and steep, sloping shores of white granite. Anchored in the lagoon, with vistas of the Camden Hills and not a house in sight, any yachtsman can feel fortunate indeed.

Approaches. The southernmost islands of the group are Big White to the west and Little White to the east. Enter from the south between these two islands, favoring the eastern side.

Although the entrance is clear and straight, it also is narrow, so it is more comfortable to come in near low tide, when you can see the ledges bordering the channel.

Anchorages, Moorings. Anchor between Big and Little White in approximately 24 feet at low. There is not much swinging room, so a stern anchor might be appropriate. One of the windjammers that sometimes lies here puts a line ashore.

You can also continue past the end of Big White and anchor near the 20-foot mark on the chart. Here it opens up a bit, with more swinging room, better views, but also greater exposure to the west. Again, you might want to use a stern anchor in case of a middle-of-the-night wind shift. There is good holding ground here, in mud.

Getting Ashore. Land on Big White with your dinghy on the little beach at the northeastern tip. The landing on Big Garden (northernmost of the group) is in the little cove formed by South Big Garden, a separate little island at the southwest end.

Things to Do. Visitors are welcome on Big Garden and Big White, for day use only. There are no trails on the islands, but there is a salt marsh and a wide variety of plants, including abundant blueberries and beach peas. An old field on Big Garden has wild iris and primroses in early June and July. The birding is good, especially during spring and fall migrations. As Anne Morrow Lindbergh wrote, "I must remember to see with island eyes. The shells will remind me."

LAIREYS and CEDAR ISLANDS ★★★ No facilities

Charts: 13302, **13305**

Tucked between Laireys and Cedar islands is a snug little anchorage that is not as secluded as it seems at first. There are houses and docks overlooking the anchorage, so you may feel as though you are intruding on someone's privacy.

Approaches. Approach from Hurricane Sound, either along the east coast of Crane Island or south of Cedar Island. Note the several tiny islets (one with trees) off the southern tip of Cedar. Enter halfway between Laireys and Cedar.

Anchorages, Moorings. There are several private moorings at the head of the cove; anchor just south of these in 14 to 20 feet. You may hold well here, but the bottom appears to be rocky. There is protection except from the southeast, and some exposure to the northeast. Do not be startled when you see the Rockland–Vinalhaven ferry pass through Laireys Narrows, a stone's throw away.

THE BASIN

Charts: 13302, 13305, **13308**

The Basin is a magnificent tidal lake on the west side of Vinalhaven Island. Here you will find a scattering of little islands, depths as great as 111 feet, and good swimming. The only problem is a narrow, crooked, and obstructed entrance through which the current usually rushes like a millrace.

Entering The Basin is definitely not recommended except for the most daring of gunkholers. The passage may be more of a challenge than you care for, but others have done it. According to local lore, schooners used to winter over inside. The best time to enter or leave is within an hour of high slack tide.

There is a rock directly in the middle of the entrance, as shown on the chart. The channel runs south of this rock and immediately branches at a small island; you can enter The Basin either left or right of the island, but the right branch is wider.

LONG COVE ★★★ No facilities

Charts: 13302, 13303, **13308**

At the northeastern end of Hurricane Sound, opposite Leadbetter Island, is the beautiful little harbor of Long Cove, easy to enter and offering excellent protection. This lovely spot is ringed by rock and spruce, with only a couple of cottages visible. The owners request that you not go ashore.

Approaches. Be careful of the ledge midway along the eastern shore of Leadbetter Island. It extends farther than it seems, and more than one cruising boat has spent a tide here.

The entrance to Long Cove is north of Fiddlehead Island, which is quite large, high, and wooded, with a small dock and house at the north end. Pass halfway between Fiddlehead and the unnamed island to the north, which looks like a smaller replica. Near the top of the hill on your right, you will see a great pile of granite tailings and a granite loading dock.

Follow the curve of the channel around to the left and into the inner harbor, staying in midchannel.

Anchorages, Moorings. There are a number of private moorings. These should not be used except with prior permission. Anchor outside the moorings in midharbor in 8 to 13 feet at low. Beware the south shore, which shoals. The holding ground is good in mud, but there is some kelp, so make sure your anchor is set.

On summer weekends, there may be a lot of boats here. If there is no room, head back to the outer harbor, anchoring north of Fiddlehead in 13 to 20 feet. This is not quite as landlocked, but still a lovely anchorage and well protected.

As you can see on the chart, there is an inner sanctum, providing almost perfect protection. At midtide or higher, it is possible to work your way up beyond the rocks into the head of Long Cove, with 14 feet or more of water. Be aware of a ledge on your right before heading in, after which favor the right side.

CROCKETT COVE ★★   No facilities

Charts: 13302, 13305, **13308**

Crockett Cove is a deep indentation at the northwestern corner of Vinalhaven Island, opposite Dogfish Island. It is exposed to the prevailing southwesterlies, but otherwise well protected. Although the cove is easy to enter, the entire anchorage is a cable area, so you take your chances.

Approaches. Note the ledge between Dogfish Island and the entrance to the cove. The more visible portions of the ledge are at the south end, showing two feet at high. Pass south of the ledge and then head up the middle of Crockett Cove.

Anchorages, Moorings. Anchor in 10 to 20 feet at low about where "Crocket Cove" is printed on chart 13308. There is good holding ground here in mud.

ISLESBORO, WEST PENOBSCOT BAY, and Penobscot River

ISLESBORO

Charts: 13302, 13305, **13309**

Stretched out for 10 miles of bays and headlands, harbors and coves, Islesboro divides the upper reaches of Penobscot Bay into east and west. Long ago, its beauty caught the eye of a young Bostonian, Jeffrey Brackett, and the exclusive community of Dark Harbor was established in 1889 on the southern third of the island, much like those in Bar Harbor, Winter Harbor, North Haven, and Prouts Neck. The great "cottages," the yacht club, tennis club, and golf club remain today for the fifth and sixth generations of families who have loved it ever since.

The major harbor is in the southern portion of the island. In Gilkey Harbor are several places of interest, including Ames Cove (Tarratine Yacht Club), Cradle Cove, the state park on Warren Island, and Grindel Point, where the ferry lands.

There are two or three interesting anchorages northward on the west coast of Islesboro, particularly Crow Cove and Turtle Head. On the east coast of the island, several coves offer protection from prevailing winds, the nicest of which is Sabbathday Harbor. Dark Harbor, for which the summer community is named, was long ago dammed to form a pool.

The island is served by a state ferry that runs from Lincolnville Beach on the mainland, and there is a small airport. The frequency of the short ferry ride has made Islesboro less insular than one might expect, and some islanders commute to the mainland for work and school.

Islesboro is a lovely island to explore by boat, and a biker's paradise because it is very flat. Facilities are few, but the islanders are friendly. You

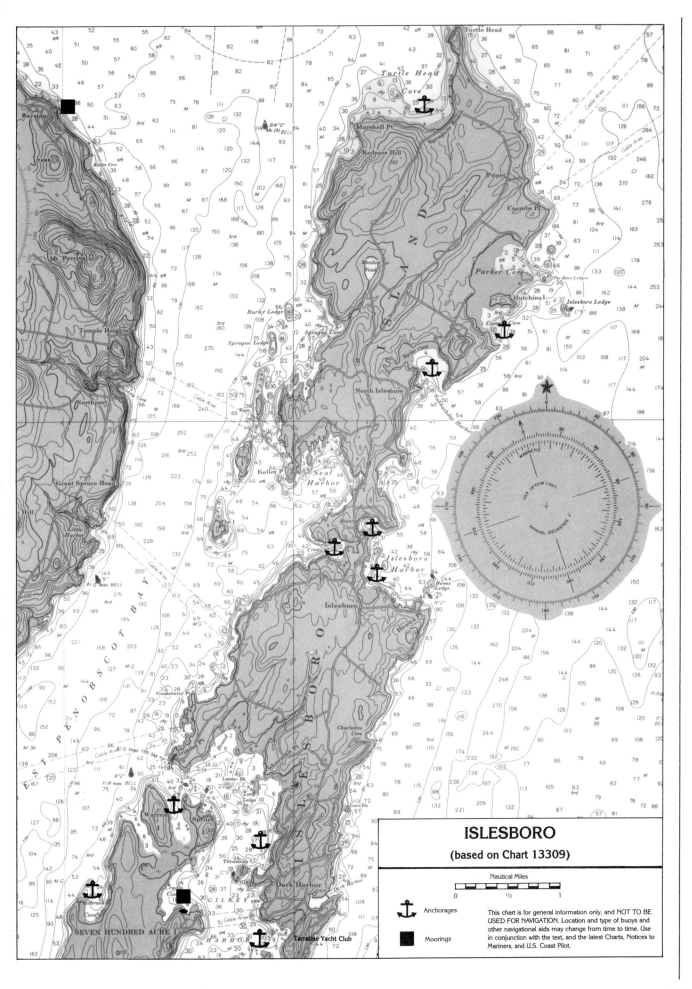

ISLESBORO

(based on Chart 13309)

Nautical Miles

| 0 | 1/2 | 1 |

⚓ Anchorages

■ Moorings

This chart is for general information only, and NOT TO BE USED FOR NAVIGATION. Location and type of buoys and other navigational aids may change from time to time. Use in conjunction with the text, and the latest Charts, Notices to Mariners, and U.S. Coast Pilot.

can't go anywhere on the north-south road without returning waves from every passing car. And always there are views of the Camden Hills across the sparkling waters.

Indians used to summer on Islesboro, fishing and trapping. Early white settlers earned a living with subsistence farming and fishing. In the nineteenth century, the island-based F.S. Pendleton fleet sailed to all corners of the globe. The influx of wealthy summer people in the 1890s changed the character of the Dark Harbor area, and the islanders became increasingly dependent on the summer residents for their livelihoods. The summer people, in turn, depended on the fishermen-turned-carpenters-and-gardeners for many of life's necessities. However, relationships were not always entirely cordial, as Michael Kinnicutt describes:

"A salmon fisherman was setting out his nets," he relates, "when a private steam yacht dropped anchor a ways out. Someone waved the fisherman over. He rowed across. A fancy fellow climbed into the boat and told the fisherman to take him ashore.

As they approached the shore, the passenger said, 'My name is George Washington Childe Drexel and I just bought that land and intend to build a large house with stables.' The fisherman squarely regarded the passenger and replied, 'My name is George Robeson, and this is my punt.'"

The summer community continued almost unchanged for half a century, with horse-drawn carriages and a slow-paced, elegant way of life, keeping at bay the annoyances of the modern world. Finally, in 1932, the islanders waited until the summer people went home, then voted to allow cars on the island for the first time.

In 1984, the threat of further radical change hit Islesboro: two subdivisions were proposed. With the enthusiastic help of the summer community, a land trust was formed in conjunction with Maine Coast Heritage Trust. Hutchins Island and much of Spruce Island came under the trust's guardianship. Further acquisitions and easements are contemplated as Islesboro girds to preserve its peaceful beauty.

GILKEY HARBOR

Charts: 13302, 13305, **13309**

The handsome body of water between Islesboro and neighboring Seven Hundred Acre Island is Gilkey Harbor. More of a thoroughfare than a harbor, Gilkey is wide, deep, and exposed to the southwest. Most boats spend the night in Cradle Cove, at the Tarratine Yacht Club in Ames Cove, or at various private docks and moorings along the shore.

Gilkey Harbor and its approaches are wide enough so you can sail in under most conditions, enjoying the summer cottages, each larger than the last, and changing vistas of the Camden Hills.

Dangers are well marked, except for Long Ledge, in the northeast corner of Gilkey Harbor. The red buoy and flag in its vicinity does not mark the ledge—it's a racing mark. Stay well over to the Spruce Island shore in this area.

Approaches From the South. Sail through the wide and well-marked entrance between large Job Island and the smaller Ensign Islands. Another entrance east of Job Island, called Bracketts Channel, is narrow in spots and tricky; in recent years, this has been privately marked.

Seven Hundred Acre Island can be identified by the complex of white buildings on its eastern tip, and the miniature Norman castle (see Cradle Cove writeup).

Approaches From the North or West. The approach between Warren Island and Grindel Point is also easy and well marked. Look for the former lighthouse and the ferry slip on Grindel Point, and stay alert for the ferry, which makes frequent runs between here and Lincolnville Beach.

AMES COVE ★★★

Charts: 13302, **13305**, 13309

Home of the Tarratine Yacht Club, Ames Cove is just opposite the eastern tip of Seven Hundred Acre Island. On any summer day, handsome yachts are moored here and at the surrounding private piers.

Approaches. To get your bearings, identify the rock shown on the chart at the north end of Ames Cove, and approach south of this rock. The yacht club is a single-story building on the east side of the cove with a flagpole, a green roof, a dock, and several floats.

Anchorages, Moorings. The yacht club has no guest moorings. Anchor outside the fleet in 10 to 15 feet at low. You probably will be exposed to the prevailing southwesterlies, but in little danger of dragging. The holding ground is excellent, in mud. If you need better protection, hop over to Cradle Cove on Seven Hundred Acre Island.

Getting Ashore. Tie up behind the dinghy float at the yacht club.

For the Boat. *Pendleton Yacht Yard (Ch. 16; tel. 734-6728).* At the northern end of Ames Cove, Pendleton has a dock and float that dries out at low and has five or six feet alongside at high. Keep your eyes peeled for rocks when entering this part of Ames Cove. Gas and diesel are available. The yard has a boatlift and marine railway, and offers "major and minor repairs," as well as a chandlery.

Tarratine Yacht Club (tel. 734-6994). Yachtsmen may visit the pleasant old clubhouse, where you can eat lunch on the porch overlooking the cove or use the showers. Established in 1896, the yacht club runs a racing series for the beautiful, old Dark Harbor 20s; you might be lucky enough to see half a dozen of these sleek little sloops some Saturday at the starting line. There is also an active program for youngsters in smaller boats.

For the Crew. Within walking distance north of the yacht yard club is the Dark Harbor Shop, with ice cream, sandwiches, and gifts. You will also find the Blue Heron Restaurant, serving lunch and dinner (tel. 734-6611) and Dark Harbor House (tel. 734-6669).

The post office, a laundromat and the well-stocked Village Market (tel. 734-6672) are a couple of miles north. Try to arrange a ride or hitchhike.

CRADLE COVE ★★★
(Seven Hundred Acre Island)
Charts: 13302, **13305**, **13309**

Seven Hundred Acre Island, forming the west side of Gilkey Harbor, is best known as the summer residence of Charles Dana Gibson, creator of the turn-of-the-century "Gibson Girl" (modeled after his Virginia belle wife, Irene). Cradle Cove, on the east side of the island, is the home of a full-service yacht yard.

On the eastern tip of Seven Hundred Acre is a miniature Norman castle, complete with dungeon, a great hall, and a maiden's chamber. This pleasant folly was built by Gibson in 1926 for his grandchildren (not open to the public).

Approaches. Entering Gilkey Harbor from the south, you will see a large white house on several levels at the eastern tip of Seven Hundred Acre Island. Just around the corner, in Cradle Cove, are the moored boats, fuel tanks, and stone dock of the Dark Harbor Boat Yard. Do not cut the point too close; a small, yellow floating barrel marks the end of the ledge.

Coming from the north, you will see the sheds and moored boats ahead as soon as you round Spruce Island.

Anchorages, Moorings. The Dark Harbor Boat Yard has about 20 moorings. There may also be room to anchor north of the moorings, in 14 feet at low, mud bottom.

Getting Ashore. Row your dinghy in to the boatyard floats.

For the Boat. *Dark Harbor Boat Yard (Ch. 16; tel. 734-2246).* The yard has gas, diesel, electricity, water, and ice at the floats, with about six feet alongside at low. There is a bit less depth in the approach to the floats, however, so choose a time other than dead low. The end of the ledge to the west is marked with a pipe. The yard has a chandlery, a 20-ton marine railway, and a hydraulic trailer; most repairs can be made.

For the Crew. The Dark Harbor Boat Yard has showers and laundry facilities.

Things to Do. Although Seven Hundred Acre Island is private, there is a town-maintained dirt road leading off to the right from the boatyard. It traverses the island and provides a pleasant walk.

GRINDEL POINT
Charts: 13302, **13309**

To visit the Islesboro Sailor's Memorial Museum on Grindel Point, anchor among the private moorings east of the ferry landing and row in to the floats (about six feet alongside at low). Stay out of the way of the ferry, which makes frequent runs from Lincolnville Beach.

Located in the old lighthouse built in 1850, the museum has a charming display of local history and memorabilia (open daily except Monday). There is a pay phone at the ferry landing, and picnic tables nearby.

WARREN ISLAND ★★★

No facilities

Charts: 13302, **13309**

Opposite the Islesboro ferry landing, at the northern entrance to Gilkey Harbor, is 76-acre Warren Island State Park, "Given for the benefit and enjoyment of visitors to coastal Maine" by the Town of Islesboro in 1959, and enjoyable it is. There are spruce-needle trails through the woods past various rustic campsites, west to a view of the Camden Hills, and south to a shale beach overlooking Cradle Cove. For information about the park, call 236-4617.

Approaches. Approaching from east or west, head southward down the middle of the slot between Warren and Spruce islands.

Anchorages, Moorings. The state usually puts out several moorings, marked "W.I." Anchor anywhere in the middle of the slot, in 9 to 12 feet of water at low, but do not go much past the pier on Warren Island, where it starts to shoal rapidly. The bottom is mud and good holding.

Getting Ashore. Row your dinghy to the floats at the state pier.

For the Crew. There are a number of campsites, fireplaces, picnic tables, privies, and shelters. Water is available near the dock, and the central water pump has a wonderfully antique design. Trash cans are at the head of the dock.

Things to Do. Walk the shady paths across the island. If it is sunny, try a dip from the beach at the south end. This is particularly enjoyable at high tide.

As you explore, you can still see the 100-foot-by-100-foot foundation of one of the most expensive log cabins ever built in New England. The dream cabin of William Folwell from Philadelphia, it contained 22 bedrooms and a living room 60 feet by 30 feet. Seldom occupied, but often used for parties, this grand structure burned in 1919.

PHILBROOK COVE ★★★

No facilities

Charts: 13302, **13305**, **13309**

On the west side of Seven Hundred Acre Island is a very pleasant little cove that offers good summertime shelter. Philbrook Cove is easy to enter and affords a view of the Camden Hills at sunset and the twinkling lights of Lincolnville Beach.

Approaches. The approach is straightforward,

toward the center of the cove from the north. Note the large ledge along the western shore, visible at half tide.

Anchorages, Moorings. Anchor in 10 to 15 feet of water at low. The bottom seems to be rocky.

CROW COVE ★★★

No facilities

Charts: 13302, **13309**

On the west coast of Islesboro, just south of Seal Harbor, is a little gunkhole called Crow Cove. The crows are there to greet you in the morning, and so are the seagulls and ospreys. In the evening you can watch the sun setting over the Camden Hills, lulled by the distant cries of a thousand herring gulls on Flat Island, to the west.

The cove offers extremely good protection except from the west, and you should have a restful night under almost any conditions. The Islesboro airport, serving small private planes, is a bit close, as is the main island road, but neither presents major problems.

Approaches. As you come up the west side of Islesboro, head for Flat Island, which is low and

grassy, with only a few trees. Crow Cove is almost due east of Flat Island, below the large bight of Seal Harbor.

Come straight down the middle of the opening into the cove, past the moored boats, toward the eastern marshes. Both shores are reasonably bold, except for some rocks making out from the southern shore.

Anchorages, Moorings. Note the indentation to the north, which dries out at low tide. You can find good water for a short distance past the headland on the western side of this indentation. Anchor on the midline of the cove in 13 to 15 feet of water at low, in mud bottom.

SEAL HARBOR

Charts: 13302, **13309**

Seal Harbor is a big, wide-open bight on the west coast of Islesboro, north of Crow Cove. The harbor has little to recommend it to cruising boats, being exposed to prevailing winds from the southwest and generally too deep for comfortable anchorage.

TURTLE HEAD COVE ★★★   No facilities

Charts: 13302, **13309**

Turtle Head forms the northern tip of Islesboro, pointing toward Sears Island, across the way. The head is high, wooded, bold, appropriately named, and delightful to explore. Turtle Head Cove, a broad bight to the west of the head, offers good protection from prevailing southwesterlies in settled weather.

Approaches. A course from green-and-white bell "II," off Marshall Point to a point just north of Turtle Head will keep you clear of the shoals and rocks at the western edge of the cove. When you are well past Marshall Point and close to the peninsula of Turtle Head, turn south into the cove.

Anchorages, Moorings. To explore Turtle Head, anchor opposite the narrowest part of the neck, where the water shoals to 10 to 15 feet at low.

If you plan to spend the night, the best protection would be in the southeast corner of the cove, off Spragues Beach, in 12 to 20 feet at low.

Getting Ashore. Row in to the beach.

Things to Do. This is private property, and the owner requests no fires and no camping. To explore Turtle Head, land at a gravel beach near the narrowest part of the neck. Climb up and strike inland to a ferny, wooded path leading to the northern tip. You'll know you have arrived when the path skirts the very edge. (There are one or two cliff-hangers.) There is a beautiful little grassy plateau with interesting uptilted rocks, and a natural ramp down to the water. The whole walk should take less than an hour.

COOMBS COVE ★★★   No facilities

Charts: 13302, **13309**

Coombs Cove, at the northeastern end of Islesboro, is easy to enter and provides sweeping views from Castine down to the islands of upper Penobscot Bay. Hutchins Island is owned and protected by a local land trust.

Approaches. From can "9" at Islesboro Ledge, enter the middle of the cove, halfway between Hutchins Island and the point to the south. You can go in about three-fourths of the way toward the west end of Hutchins.

Anchorages, Moorings. Anchor in 12 to 15 feet at low, mud bottom and good holding ground. You will be protected from the prevailing southwesterlies, but there is exposure from the south around to the east.

SABBATHDAY HARBOR ★★★   No facilities

Charts: 13302, **13309**

This is a very pretty cove with a beach at the head and a dramatic wooded, rocky point guarding the right-hand entrance. The harbor offers good protection except from due south and lovely views of the Penobscot Bay islands.

The cottages in Ryder Cove, in the northern part of the harbor, are the remnants of Islesboro's first development, in the late nineteenth century, which included a large pavilion, a dance hall, and a dock. This was a summer colony for Bangor residents, who arrived by steamboat.

Approaches. Look for the prominent point at the east side of Sabbathday Harbor. It is crowned with spruce and has a house nestled in the woods. The low, rocky points at the west side of the entrance are lined with summer cottages.

Anchorages, Moorings. There are several private moorings in the harbor, and plenty of room to anchor outside the moorings in 11 to 15 feet at low. The holding ground is good, in mud.

BILLY'S SHORE

Charts: 13302, **13309**

The shoreline south of Sabbathday Harbor is known as Billy's Shore. It leads to Russell Point, a knob of land standing out to sea, high and wooded, crowned by one of Maine's classic nineteenth-century summer cottages. Anchor to the north and west of the cottage, in 12 to 15 feet at low. A lunch stop here affords dramatic views of Castine, Blue Hill, and the islands of Penobscot Bay.

BOUNTY COVE ★★   No facilities

Charts: 13302, **13309**

In the northwestern corner of Islesboro Harbor are two rocky headlands leading to small Bounty Cove, which offers protection except from south to east. There are houses on each headland, and a road at the head of the cove with many signs of civilization.

The cove is of interest for its brief moment in history. In 1780, when Harvard College was mounting the first formal expedition to observe a total eclipse of the sun, the astronomers calculated that tiny Bounty Cove on Islesboro was the best viewing location. Islesboro was British territory at the time, but solar phenomena are no respecters of the affairs of men. Always devoted to the interests of science, especially among gentlemen, the British gave permission for the scientists to go behind enemy lines and witness the event. A simple marker, along the roadside a short distance north of the cove, commemorates the occasion.

Approaches. Pass north of can "1" at Hewes Ledge and head for the northwestern corner of Islesboro Harbor. Enter the middle of the cove, favoring the right side a little to avoid the rocks and ledges on the left (not visible at halftide).

Anchorages, Moorings. Anchor in the middle, in 11 to 15 feet at low, mud bottom. The holding ground is good.

Getting Ashore. Land your dinghy at the small beach.

ISLESBORO HARBOR ★★   No facilities

Charts: 13302, **13309**

Islesboro Harbor is a large, wide-open bay that provides a lee for prevailing winds.

Approaches. Enter Islesboro Harbor north of can "1" on Hewes Ledge. There is a big house surrounded by birches on Hewes Point.

Anchorages, Moorings. There are several private moorings along the south shore. Anchor toward the southwestern corner of the harbor, near the moorings, in 10 to 20 feet of water at low. Go in cautiously, because it shoals rapidly here.

WEST PENOBSCOT BAY

DUCKTRAP HARBOR

Charts: 13302, **13309**

Ducktrap Harbor is a broad, open bay on the mainland, opposite the northern entrance to Gilkey Harbor on Islesboro. The ferry runs frequently back and forth between Lincolnville Beach and Grindel Point.

The Ducktrap River empties into the northwest corner of Ducktrap Harbor. The mouth of the river and the cove once were the location of 11 salmon berths or weirs, whose catch was shipped daily by steamer to ports as far away as Boston. Upriver today is a thriving fish farm, raising trout much prized in markets and restaurants along the east coast.

LINCOLNVILLE BEACH

Charts: 13302, **13309**

Lincolnville Beach (Lincolnville on the chart) can be identified by the cluster of houses and the terminal for the Islesboro ferry, near the northern end of the Camden Hills. This is not a protected spot for the night, but you might enjoy making a lunch stop at one of the restaurants or shops.

Staying south of nun "2" on Haddock Ledge, run in toward the boats moored north of the ferry terminal. Do not go much past the outside moorings because the beach is steep and shoals very

rapidly. For the same reason, it is difficult to anchor here. The Lobster Pound Restaurant maintains a couple of convenient guest moorings.

There is a float at the public landing (north of the ferry wharf), with three feet alongside at low, where you can leave your dinghy and go ashore. You will pass the Lobster Pound takeout and picnic area. Lincolnville Beach has a small market, post office, a takeout, and several restaurants and shops. Public phones are at the ferry wharf.

SATURDAY COVE

Charts: 13302, **13309**

This is the fictional home of all those wonderfully wacky characters who appear in the Cap'n Perc Sane columns in *National Fisherman*. Cap'n Sane—in reality, journalist and author Allen D. ("Mike") Brown—peoples his columns with such figures as Shorty Gage, the lobsterman; Bubba Beal, the clam cop; and the Dodge girls, who sell "homemade dandelion wine n'chokeberry brandy, which is somewheres around 190 proof. They giggle a lot."

The Cove is visited occasionally by yachtsmen, and in one of his columns Cap'n Sane describes the big Cove event of the year. "The Marblehead Yacht Club pulled inta the Cove for n'overnighter. We were ready for 'em . . . . There was 35 yachts, a self-propelled fuel barge n'a seaplane tender. They wanted just one mooring. Said they'd raft up. Short rented 'em just the ticket, his guest mooring, which is a 1932 Buick Roadster with a chain run right through her, stem to stern."

A few lobsterboats are here, but the real Saturday Cove belongs primarily to the summer people as a fashionable residential area in the village of Northport.

The little harbor is full of boats. There is not much room to anchor, and no place to go ashore. The dock near the head of the cove is for the use of resident boatowners only.

Saturday Cove was the scene of a skirmish in the War of 1812 in which fisherman Zachariah Lawrence singlehandedly repelled a landing force of two barges of British Marines. Returning in greater strength, the Marines fired one-pound shot into several homes, pillaged and plundered, and took away Captain Amos Pendleton's gold watch. Wars were different in those days. Captain Pendleton went to Fort George in Castine to demand his valuables, and the watch was returned.

BAYSIDE ★★★

Charts: 13302, **13309**

Three miles south of Belfast, this is a charming summer community of small Victorian gingerbread cottages surrounding a common. Although located on an open stretch of coast, Bayside has a bit of protection from prevailing winds.

Bayside was founded in 1859 as a Methodist campground—tents at first, followed by the small Victorian cottages that remain today. By the 1930s, it was no longer a religious community and became part of the village of Northport.

Approaches. Bayside can be identified by the fleet of pleasure boats moored off a long dock, and by the water tank above the trees (shown south of the town on the chart).

Anchorages, Moorings. The Northport Yacht Club has its little clubhouse here, with a vigorous sailing program but no facilities for visiting yachts. Check with the harbormaster, who usually can find you a mooring.

Getting Ashore. Row in to the south float at the public landing.

For the Boat. Water may be obtained at the public float, with 15 feet of depth at low.

For the Crew. The nearest provisions are a mile away at a place known locally as Bell's Corner.

Walk north until the road intersects with Route 1, where you will find the Dos Amigos Mexican restaurant and a small market. The Bayside Corner Store has groceries, ice, a deli, takeout, and phone.

BELFAST ★★★ All facilities
Charts: 13302, **13309** (Inset)

At the northwestern corner of Penobscot Bay, Belfast is a town where history is just being rediscovered, where grand old buildings are in the process of renovation and conversion to new uses, where a young professional class is moving in and a new cycle beginning. An interesting place to visit.

Belfast once was an important shipbuilding town; hundreds of schooners slid down the ways here into the Passagassawaukeag River. Forest products were shipped all along the coast, and one historian reports that 10,000 cords of wood were stacked on Belfast's wharves in 1844. After the discovery of gold in 1848, the first direct voyage from Maine to California was made by the bark *Suliote* of Belfast.

Largely destroyed by two great fires in 1865 and 1873, Belfast rebuilt in brick, and splendid blocks of Victorian Gothic and Greek Revival buildings mark the downtown section today. These and much of the residential area of Belfast are on the National Register of Historic Places.

More recently a center for raising chickens and the home of the annual "Bay Festival," Belfast is now mostly out of the chicken business, and into processed potato skins. One result is a vast improvement in the quality of air and water.

Belfast is the home of the Penobscot Bay Area Pilots, who guide large tankers and freighters up the bay to Searsport and up the Penobscot River to Bangor.

Approaches. Belfast is easy and safe to approach. Leave to starboard the granite monument and red bell at Steels Ledge, then run up the middle of the channel toward the bridge and nun "6," among the moored boats, which extend a long way past of the town.

Anchorages, Moorings. The city provides some guest moorings, or you can tie up at the city landing. Belfast Boatyard has rental moorings, and dockage. It is also possible to anchor near the moorings in 7 to 15 feet at low.

Getting Ashore. Land at the dinghy floats at the city landing.

For the Boat. *Belfast Boatyard (tel. 338-5098).*

Past the city landing and the tugboats on the south shore, Belfast Boatyard has eight feet alongside the floats at low, with water and electricity but no fuel. Diesel can be obtained by truck. The yard offers storage, repairs, and marine supplies.

City Landing (Ch. 9 or 16; tel. 338-1340, harbormaster). The Belfast city landing is on the south shore, opposite nun "6." There are a number of finger floats for small craft, and large boats can come alongside the outer floats and dolphins, with 13 feet of water at low. Overnight dockage requires permission of the harbormaster. There are attendants at the city landing who can arrange a tie-up or direct you to a mooring. Gas, diesel, water, and electricity are available.

For the Crew. The town provides showers and restrooms at the city landing and next door the Chamber of Commerce has a helpful information booth. The Weathervane, a combination fish market and restaurant, is also there. Within walking distance, you will find a supermarket and a laundromat. There are stores of all kinds in town.

A few blocks up Main Street is the delightful Belfast Cafe, where the food is good and the decor eclectic. Young's Lobster Pound and Restaurant (tel. 338-1160) is the red building on the north side of the harbor. The easiest way to get there is by dinghy. For a good dinner in pleasant surroundings try Penobscot Meadows Country Inn and Restaurant (tel. 338-5320), 1.7 miles from the waterfront, south of Belfast. Walk out High Street, or take a cab. Waldo County General Hospital (tel. 338-2500) is about a mile out Northport Avenue.

Things to Do. Aside from enjoying the architecture and the shops and the flourishing art galleries in town, you might like to walk across the former Route 1 bridge at the head of the harbor (now converted to a footbridge). Belfast's excellent public library has an active concert and lecture series.

The Belfast and Moosehead Lake Railroad runs roundtrip scenic excursions from the waterfront to Waldo and Brooks, several miles inland.

SEARSPORT HARBOR ★★★★

Charts: 13302, **13309**

Because the harbor is wide open, exposed from southwest to southeast, and the view is dominated by elevators and oil tanks, Searsport would seem to have little appeal to visiting yachtsmen. But the town has a fascinating history as the onetime scene of bustling shipyards and the home of more than 200 ship captains who roamed the globe, and this heritage has inspired the splendid Penobscot Marine Museum, well worth going out of your way to visit.

A century ago, one of every 10 American ship-masters hailed from this small town. Several shipyards flourished in Searsport, supplying the demand and providing steady employment.

As Gretchen Ebbesson reported in *Maine Times*, "Square-rigged Down-easters brought raw sugar from Hawaii and the West Indies; hemp from Manila; rice from India; Japan's silks and sulphur; China tea and coolies for railway labor; flax and tallow from Australia; copper ore, wool and hides from Chile; and guano from the Peruvian islands. To the homes of the seafarers came ostrich eggs, coral beads, clothes, pottery and carvings from China, teakwood chests, tropical shells, curry powders and Canton ginger.

"Some wives waited at home; others went to sea with their families. Many sea births were listed by latitude and longitude on the birth certificate . . . .The Nichols family of Searsport had 35 members born at sea."

Searsport is known for its antique shops, vying with inland Hallowell as the antiques capital of Maine.

Approaches. The approach is straightforward and without dangers. Sears Island to the east is high and wooded, with a tall radio tower near the southern tip. Mack Point, to the northeast, is readily identified by the elevators and oil tanks. Head for the group of boats and the pier at the northwestern corner of Searsport Harbor.

Anchorages, Moorings. The town maintains a guest mooring. Or, if you plan to visit the Penobscot Marine Museum, call ahead (tel. 548-2529) to reserve their guest mooring, a big granite block often used by the windjammers. Otherwise, you can anchor anywhere near the moorings, in 15 to 23 feet at low, in good mud holding ground.

Getting Ashore. Land your dinghy at the town landing floats.

For the Boat. *Town Public Landing (Harbormaster, at Hamilton Marine: Ch. 9, 10, or 16; tel. 548-2985).* One float on the north side of the pier is just for loading and unloading; you can stay alongside the others for longer periods, as indicated. Water and electricity are provided.

Hamilton Marine (tel. 548-2985). Located north of town, Hamilton Marine is probably the largest chandlery in Maine. You'll find just about any marine item there, plain or fancy, including books and charts. It's 1.3 miles from the town landing, but worth the walk or the taxi ride if you need something for the boat.

For the Crew. Walk up Steamboat Avenue to Route 1, turn right, and you will shortly be in town—half a mile from the landing. There you will find a market, laundromat, drugstore, bank, post office, doctor, and restaurant.

Things to Do. In town is the group of seven 19th-century buildings of the Penobscot Marine Museum. For anyone interested in the history of Maine and of the great sailing ships, this is a wonderful place to visit. The museum is a gem.

One of the houses is furnished with the belongings of a sea captain and his family: beds, bureaus, commodes, paintings, and personal articles. The old captain might stomp in at any moment.

In the Old Town Hall is a splendid exhibit that traces the development of sailing vessels from early days to the square-rigged Downeasters built in the 1870s and 1880s.

The museum has a wonderful collection of fine ship paintings, including 24 by noted artists Thomas and James Buttersworth, and many examples of ship portraits commissioned in Chinese and European ports.

Another building houses a beautifully displayed collection of small wooden craft, including a salmon wherry, a dory, a peapod, a yawlboat, a smelt scow, a river punt, and a lumberman's bateau.

LONG COVE ★

No facilities

Charts: 13302, **13309**

Long Cove is one of the most industrialized areas in Maine, with cargo piers, conveyors, warehouses, and oil tanks, and it has nothing recreational to offer a yachtsman. This may become even more true if nearby Sears Island is developed as a cargo port, as planned. Long Cove then will become entirely commercial.

Major General Henry Knox, George Washington's first Secretary of War, acquired ownership of Sears Island as part of his wife's dowry. If Knox had not choked to death on a chicken bone in 1806, the history of the island might have been different. After his death, it passed through other hands to the Bangor and Aroostook Railroad, which envisioned a profitable resort with vacationers arriving, of course, by train. "Penobscot Park" opened in 1906, complete with dance pavilion and amusement park. Doomed by the automobile and new patterns of travel, however, it lasted only until 1927. For several decades, the island was used only for picnicking and hunting. Then came a rash of development proposals for Sears Island, spurred by the advantages of a deepwater port. A 1978 report commissioned by then-governor James Longley recommended construction of a cargo port. Now that a causeway to the mainland has been built, it appears a matter of time before the cargo port becomes a reality. While the full impact will take decades to evolve, clearly it will have a major effect on the marine environment of Searsport, Long Cove, and Stockton Harbor, and substantially increase ship traffic up and down Penobscot Bay.

Approaches. The approach to Long Cove, west of Sears Island, is deep and well buoyed for the use of oceangoing vessels. High, wooded Sears Island can be recognized by the radio tower near its southern end.

Anchorages, Moorings. There is good anchorage in the middle of Long Cove, in depths of 10 to 20 feet at low.

STOCKTON HARBOR ★ No facilities
Charts: 13302, **13309**

East of Sears Island, Stockton Harbor is larger and better protected than Long Cove. Presently the home of the Delta Chemical Company, it probably will share with Long Cove the further commercialization and traffic resulting from development of a major cargo port on Sears Island.

There are plans afoot to build a town landing at the head of the harbor and a large marina. Meanwhile, it is a convenient place to spend the night before running up the Penobscot River.

Approaches. The approach is easy and well buoyed for large ship traffic. Sears Island is high and wooded, with a tall radio tower near the southern end. As you enter Sears Island and Cape Jellison, you will see the tanks, sheds, and stacks of the chemical plant on the west side of the harbor.

The only danger is a Delta Chemical offshore loading platform standing in the water in the left-hand side of the entrance as shown on the chart. (Often there is a barge alongside.) Leave nun "6"

to starboard and then the loading facility to port. There is ample room to pass safely.

There are pilings and ruined wharves along the eastern side of the harbor, but they present no dangers.

Anchorages, Moorings. The harbor shoals gradually toward the head, and there is room for a fleet to anchor, in 9 to 16 feet of water at low. Holding ground is good in mud, and protection is good in every direction except due south. Just past the ruined wharves on Cape Jellison are moored a dozen or so lobsterboats, draggers, and small pleasure craft.

It is a bit eerie here at night—not a single light on the Cape Jellison shore, just the blinking red signal on the Sears Island radio tower and the low hum of the chemical plant to lull you to sleep.

Getting Ashore. Land at the launching ramp or the beach on Cape Jellison, opposite the moorings.

PENOBSCOT RIVER

Chart: 13309

The Penobscot is a grand, wide river, 24 miles long from the entrance at Fort Point to the head of navigation at Bangor. It is the second-longest river in Maine, rising near Mount Katahdin, coursing 240 miles to the sea, and draining one-third of the state.

Somewhere on the Penobscot was the fabled Indian city of Norumbega, reported by Verrazzano in 1524 (see sidebar). Legends of its opulence slowly faded, but by the second half of the nineteenth century, the Penobscot was a prosperous thoroughfare for ships of all kinds, that brought goods from every nation and returned downriver loaded with lumber, granite, and ice. Steamships were seen daily on the Boston-to-Bangor run. The Penobscot was big time, and Bangor was lumber capital of the world.

Today there are splendid miles of river with scarcely a house, almost unchanged since Verrazzano's time. The only river traffic is occasional

Eight schooners being towed up through the Penobscot River narrows toward Bangor, 1912. Fort Knox is in the background. (Frank Claes Collection)

NORUMBEGA

Norumbega was a magnificent city on the banks of the Penobscot, it was reported, three-quarters of a mile long, with streets as broad as London's and splendid houses. The Indians there wore furs and pearl-studded ornaments of gold and silver.

"Aranbega" first appears on Verrazzano's map drawn from a 1524 voyage, and many later explorers sought the fabled city. One adventure that gave it credence was the extraordinary journey of an Englishman named David Ingram in 1568. A sailor who was abandoned with a hundred companions on the shores of the Gulf of Mexico for lack of provisions, Ingram walked along Indian trails with two companions all the way up the east coast through Maine, and to the Saint John River, where he embarked on a French ship that took him back to Europe.

Remarkable though such a journey may have been, Ingram made an even better story of it, providing just what his audience wanted to hear and probably ensuring free drinks for the rest of his life. His report, printed in 1589 by Hakluyt, chronicler of many early voyages of exploration, did much to embellish the reputation of Norumbega. According to historian Benjamin De Costa ("The Lost City of New England," 1884), Ingram claimed to have seen "the spectacle of native monarchs borne to public audiences on sumptuous chairs of silver and crystal, adorned with precious stones. In all the houses pearls were common, and in some cottages were seen a peck or more."

Later explorers searched for Norumbega on the Penobscot River, and several reported finding it. The legend grew. More honest or more politic explorers maintained a discreet silence. In 1583, Sir Humphrey Gilbert sailed to establish a colony at Norumbega, but his ship was lost en route, and Gilbert drowned. It was not until after his 1604 voyage that Samuel de Champlain reported he could find no trace of the fabulous city on the Penobscot. Even then, the myth faded slowly and reluctantly. People wanted to believe in Norumbega.

Later maps applied the name to a wider region, and all of New England was known as Norumbega until the 17th century. The name still appears from time to time, most recently as a splendid turreted estate built in Camden at the turn of the century, now turned bed and breakfast.

small powerboats. Near Bangor are rotting piles and cribs where ships and barges used to crowd, and Bangor itself scarcely knows the river is there.

Cruise up the Penobscot to experience the river itself, not to reach any particular destination. One sight worth the trip is Fort Knox, imposing and wonderful on its escarpment, still guarding the river from British invaders. The prettiest stretch is Crosby Narrows, lined with cliffs and cedars. Ships returning from the West Indies loaded with rum dropped off a barrel here to keep the tax collector happy.

Once you have left Belfast or Castine, places to stop and facilities to the north are few and far between so plan your trip accordingly. Along the river, the best source for fuel or repairs is the yard at Winterport, the head of navigation during winter months. Sea captains built elegant homes here.

Going upriver in daylight, with the flood, is easy for cruising boats. Navigation at night is dangerous, since there are few lighted buoys. There are a number of shoal areas, particularly off Lawrence and Luce Coves and Frankfort Flats, but you will have no trouble if you follow the buoys and the chart carefully. The wind usually blows straight up- or downriver, and you probably will be under power. The *Coast Pilot* notes that currents of five knots are not unusual between Odom Ledge and Orrington. The ebb is stronger than the flood, and

with the wind against the ebb, the river can be rough. As a legacy of the lumbering business, spring freshets and very high tides may float off many logs, dangerous to small craft in the river.

At the lower end of the river, in the Narrows, there is a wonderful Grandma Moses view of Bucksport, framed under a soaring bridge, the buildings scattered in primitive forms on the banks and carefully colored. It would make a lovely quilt design.

There are two fixed bridges on the main channel of the Penobscot River, both with ample clearance. The first carries Route 1 across the river to Verona Island, just south of Bucksport; the second is a new bridge routing I-95 just south of Bangor.

Turtle Cove is a burying ground for sailing ships. Sloops and brigs and schooners were run up here and scuttled when their useful days were done. Some of the hulks that line the Penobscot River were sunk in 1785 during the disastrous Penobscot Expedition (see sidebar), led by Commodore Dudley Saltonstall, who destroyed his flagship, *Warren*, near Oak Point.

More than 400 sawmills lined the river in the days of glory; sawdust still coats the banks (and perhaps the bottom). Smelt were plentiful here a hundred years ago, and salmon too, until pollution drove them out. The river is clean again today, and the salmon are coming back. The first salmon of the season is presented to the White House.

FORT POINT COVE ★★★ No facilities
Chart: 13309

North of Fort Point, at the entrance to the Penobscot River, Fort Point Cove is a large, open bay with good anchorage. In the days when Bangor was lumber capital of the world, the cove was full of ships and barges waiting out the ebb tide before heading upriver to pick up their cargoes, or pausing before setting out to sea. It still serves that purpose today, although you are likely to be the only boat in sight. Fort Point State Park and the lighthouse at the southern end of the cove are worth the stop here.

Approaches. Fort Point is wooded, with a bold cliff topped by the square white lighthouse tower and a substantial residence attached. Nearby is the white bell tower. Fort Point Ledge is marked by a granite structure with a red beacon on top. Leaving this to starboard and can "1" to port, curve left around the point and into the cove, well outside the long pier.

Anchorages, Moorings. Anchor anywhere north and west of the pier in 8 to 29 feet of water at low. Holding ground is good, in mud. The cove is

big enough so that there is considerable fetch if the wind is blowing.

Getting Ashore. Row in to the float at the pier, or land on the sand beach to the east.

Things to Do. Walk up the wooded paths of the state park, working your way east toward the lighthouse. You will find the earthworks and foundations of old Fort Pownall, built in 1759.

The Coast Guard station adjacent to the park has a long history. Marking the entrance to the Penobscot River, it was established in 1836 during the administration of Andrew Jackson. The beautiful fourth-order brass-and-crystal Fresnel lens was made in France and mounted in 1857.

The bell tower northeast of the light originally housed a clockwork mechanism that struck the 1,200-pound bronze fog bell every 20 seconds. Survivor of a decade when similar towers were burned as useless structures, this is the only bell tower still owned by the government, and it is listed on the National Register of Historic Places.

MORSE COVE ★★

Chart: 13309

Morse Cove is on the eastern shore of the Penobscot River, near the entrance, opposite Fort Point.

Approaches. The approach is straightforward. Devereux Marine can be easily identified by the rusting hulk that acts as a breakwater (and which is shown on the chart). It's shoal inside the moorings except near high tide.

Anchorages, Moorings. Moorings (mostly 200-pound mushrooms) are available from Devereux Marine.

Getting Ashore. Take the dinghy in to the float behind the sunken ship.

For the Boat. *Devereux Marine (tel. 326-4800).* This high-tide storage yard has a 20-ton boatlift and can perform hull, rigging, and engine repairs, or do-it-yourself.

FORT KNOX

Chart: 13309

Standing high on the battlements at imposing Fort Knox, you can gaze up and down the majestic Penobscot River, daring the British to send ships past your great cannon. (So far they never have.)

This is a fort for every taste. If you like exploring dark and possibly spidered chambers, or plunging down tunneled staircases, they are here. Or if you prefer open air and grand vistas, you can climb the spiral granite staircases and walk along the upper battlements. Some of the great 10-inch and 15-inch smoothbore cannons still command the river, and the hotshot furnaces remain.

During the American Revolution and the War of 1812, the British controlled the river, so when a border dispute erupted far north in Fort Kent in 1839, there was a natural fear that the British might once more sail up the Penobscot and seize Bangor, a critical source of lumber.

Fort Knox was started in 1844 to forestall this possibility. Granite for the construction was quarried five miles upstream at Mount Waldo and barged downriver. The fort was manned during the Civil War and the Spanish-American War, but by then it was obsolete. This was the prototype of many granite forts built in Maine, including Popham, Gorges, Preble, and Scammell. It was named for Major General Henry Knox, who trained gun crews for George Washington during the Revolution and became the nation's first Secretary of War.

Most visitors arrive at Fort Knox State Park by car. If you are feeling bold, however, it is possible to visit from the water. There is a boat basin just north of the tunnel that emerges from the green embankment, north of the fort itself. The main part of the basin is about 120 feet long and has a flight of stone steps at the end.

There is a lot of current in the river, so plan to arrive near slack tide. At low slack, when the basin is almost dry, anchor in the river just off the basin in about 30 feet, and row your dinghy in to the stone steps. The bottom is rocky and the anchorage is a bit precarious; leave someone aboard.

If you arrive near high slack, it is possible to bring your boat itself into the basin. Have your fenders ready for the granite walls and tie up to the iron rings. A visual inspection of the basin at low tide indicates no obstacles, but enter cautiously.

BUCKSPORT ★★

Chart: 13309

Located at the fork in the Penobscot River above Verona Island, Bucksport is a small town with a splendid view of Fort Knox across the river and a less exciting view of the huge paper mill next door. Although supplies and provisions are available, facilities for yachts are minimal, and the anchorage is exposed.

Approaches. There are no dangers in approaching the town dock, except the five-foot spot shown on the chart if you stray to the east.

Anchorages, Moorings. It may be possible to lie alongside the floats overnight (see below). Otherwise, anchor outside the private moorings off the town dock, in 15 feet of water, mud bottom.

Getting Ashore. Tie your dinghy up in back of the town landing.

For the Boat. *Bucksport Town Landing.* The town landing can be identified by the flagpole. There is eight feet alongside the floats at low: the maximum tie-up is limited to one hour, but call the harbormaster (whose phone number is posted on the dock) for permission to stay overnight.

For the Crew. Almost everything you may need is within a short walk. Turn right to find the Jed Prouty Tavern and Inn, which dates back to 1798. It is said to be the fifth-oldest continuously run hostelry in America. Built entirely of hand-hewn timbers, it was host to Presidents Jackson, Van Buren, Harrison, and Tyler, not to mention Daniel Webster and Jefferson Davis. On display is a guest register from 1875, with the copperplate signatures of visitors from all over.

Beyond the tavern are a laundromat, 5¢ & 10¢ store, bank, and other restaurants. Just where the bridge touches the mainland, there is a convenience store with ice, and a takeout. If you have major shopping needs, continue on the same road to the Bucksport Plaza, half a mile from the landing, which has a Shop 'n Save supermarket and liquor store.

Left from the landing, you will encounter a barbershop and a variety and convenience store.

Things to Do. The Champion International Corporation mill, which dominates the horizon to the west, is the second-largest paper mill in Maine,

and perhaps the only one you can visit by water. There are hourly guided tours weekdays (call 469-3131 for information). No children under 12 are allowed.

If you feel like a stroll, turn right and walk to Mercer's, about .8 mile from the landing. This must be the original convenience store. There is no sign displaying the name, but there are gas pumps and placards of varying ages offering "ammo," fresh homemade butter, whole slack-salted fish, ice, several varieties of worms, and "clams, dressed and undressed."

En route to Mercer's you will pass Buck Cemetery, on the north side of the street. The tall monument nearest to the street belongs to Colonel Jonathan Buck. Observe on the stone the dark outline of a woman's leg, which has resisted all efforts at removal. One story goes that before coming to Maine, magistrate Buck sentenced a woman to be burned for witchcraft. The mark is her curse, which followed him to the grave. Locally, other stories allude to a mistress and a jealous wife.

WINTERPORT ★★★

Chart: 13309

Winterport is an old river town, settled in 1766. Eleven miles south of Bangor, it was the head of navigation during winter months when the brackish water upstream froze. Many steamboat captains chose to settle here, and their stately homes are a reminder of the days when the Penobscot River was a major channel of commerce.

The only yard with repair facilities on the Penobscot River is Winterport Marine, two miles above Marsh River, on the west bank.

Approaches. Below the Winterport Marine yard are long, flat-sided tin sheds and a big barge moored in the river—used for storage of potatoes and frozen chicken. Continuing upriver, you will

notice a cluster of Quonset huts on the west bank, marking Winterport Marine.

Anchorages, Moorings. Winterport Marine has 30 moorings (most are 4,000 pounds), or you can come alongside. It is possible to anchor in the river, but the current here often runs six knots or more, so you are likely to be more comfortable on a mooring.

Getting Ashore. Because of the heavy current in the river it would be wise to use the launch provided by the marina. If you use your own dinghy, take every precaution.

For the Boat. *Winterport Marine (Ch. 16; tel. 223-8885).* This full-service marina was once a ship

Schooners loading at Bangor, lumber capital of the world, in 1880. (Frank Claes Collection)

dock, and the floats have 13 feet of water alongside at low.

Gas, diesel, water, ice, electricity, and marine supplies are available here. Winterport Marine has a full-time mechanic and can perform hull and engine repairs, with a boatlift rated at 12 tons. The yard also offers towing and diving services.

For the Crew. Winterport Marine has a pay phone, head, and showers. By prior arrangement,

it offers pickup and delivery at Bangor International Airport.

To reach civilization, walk straight up the road to the small town of Winterport, no more than .2 mile away. Turn left on Route 1A, and you will find everything from a convenience store and market to a restaurant, pizza place, and inn. Also in that direction are a variety store, laundromat, and public phone.

HAMPDEN ★★
Chart: 13309

A new boating facility is being developed by the town of Hampden on the west bank of the Penobscot, not far below East Hampden. This is the last stopping place before Bangor, two miles upstream. It is pleasantly rural.

Anchorages, Moorings. Turtle Head Marina maintains a number of moorings in the river, with 1,000 pound granite blocks.

Getting Ashore. Take your dinghy in to the marina float or the launching ramp.

For the Boat. *Turtle Head Marina (Ch. 16; tel. 941-8619).* Gas, diesel, and water are available at the marina float, with ice and marine supplies ashore. The buoyed approach channel is dredged to 10 feet, but the channel is narrow, and there is not enough room for large boats to maneuver.

For the Crew. Dana's Grill is next to the marina.

Half a mile from the parking lot, left on Route 1A, is a convenience store.

BANGOR ★
Chart: 13309

Once Bangor was the lumber capital of the world, a great roaring, brawling frontier town full of lumberjacks, sailors, shipwrights, merchants, prostitutes, warehouses, sawmills, bars, and boardinghouses—its face turned toward the river and the seven seas. But since the decline of lumbering and a disastrous fire in 1911, Bangor has turned its back on the Penobscot River, and that grand highway to the sea now slips by the town in obscurity.

During the lumbering heyday, an army of lumberjacks felled trees all winter long—first nearby and then deep in the northern woods as the forest became depleted. When the ice went out in April, the great river drives began, and the Penobscot was choked with logs on their way to the mills at Bangor. A hundred million board feet were shipped in 1842, and it was 200 million by midcentury. The records show that 3,376 ships cleared Bangor in 1860, and the river between Bangor and Brewer was crammed gunwale to gunwale.

Today Bangor is experiencing a revitalization. Although the view from the waterfront still encompasses oil tanks, railroad cars, and expanses of pavement, efforts are being made to improve the waterfront with new floats, landscaping, and riverside walks.

Approaches. The approach to Bangor is easy

and clear, passing under the new fixed bridge for I-95 (vertical clearance 78 feet) and to the head of navigation just beyond, at the fixed highway bridge between Bangor and Brewer (vertical clearance 22 feet).

Examining the chart carefully, you will discover a number of little squares scattered along each side of the river for a couple of miles south of Bangor. These are cribs—little green islands defined by cribwork—used for mooring deep-draft vessels. You could still tie up to one of them today, but they are quite dilapidated.

The Bangor Public Landing is on the west side of the river, just below the second fixed bridge, north of the private floats of Bangor Dock Facility.

Anchorages, Moorings. The city has placed a number of guest moorings in the river next to the town landing. Anchoring is discouraged.

There is about 15 feet of water alongside the floats, but tie-up time is limited. Arrangements for an overnight stay can be made with the harbormaster (tel. 947-5251).

Getting Ashore. Take your dinghy in to the public landing floats farthest north, just beyond the bridge.

For the Boat. *Bangor Public Landing.* There is water at the floats, and electricity at the top of the ramp (you need a long cord). Restrooms, showers, and a phone are in the harbormaster's building in the parking lot.

For the Crew. To get to the main part of the city, walk northward on the gravel path along the waterfront, crossing the tracks and continuing up Broad and Water streets, to Main Street. It is about .3 mile from the waterfront.

Turning right on Main Street, you will find a drugstore, bank, bookstore, deli, restaurants, and bakery. A Shop 'n Save supermarket and a drugstore are farther west on Union Street. There's a laundromat .4 mile from the waterfront, on Route 1A on the way to Miller's (see below).

There are a number of restaurants nearby, including one right next to the public landing. About .6 mile from the landing, Miller's Restaurant has what must be the world's largest salad bar, complete with soup, roasts, and desserts—at reasonable prices. To get there from the landing, cross the tracks and continue west until you reach Route 1A. Turn left on 1A (south) to the restaurant.

Bangor International Airport is nearby.

Things to Do. Bangor has six historic districts with 20 landmark buildings, and there are stately Victorian mansions along West Broadway. One way to see the city is to take a bus or walking tour; inquire at the Tourist Information Bureau on Main Street. The Bangor Historical Society Museum is at 159 Union Street (tel. 942-5766).

On lower Main Street stands a 31-foot statue of Paul Bunyan. A birth certificate on file at the Chamber of Commerce attests that the mythical lumberjack was born in Bangor, Maine, on February 12, 1834.

EAST PENOBSCOT BAY, Western Coast of Deer Isle, and Isle au Haut

CASTINE ★★★★★   All facilities
Charts: 13302, **13309**

Castine is a beautiful town north of Cape Rosier at the mouth of the Bagaduce River, on a high and almost isolated peninsula. It has a long and colorful history and is full of lovely old homes in various architectural styles.

Samuel de Champlain stopped here in 1604, on his way up the Penobscot River, and John Smith followed in 1614. A Plymouth Company trading post had been established by 1629. From then on, Castine changed hands regularly between the French and English, and once, for a few days, the Dutch. Something like 16 different fortifications were built on the peninsula, of which Fort George and Fort Madison are still recognizable today.

One of the earliest, Fort Pentagoet, built by the French in 1635, has recently been excavated, revealing that Brittany slate, used as ships' ballast, was one of the building materials. Ceramic stew pots, soup ladles, and stemware for Rhennish wine uncovered here suggest that the French brought civilization with them to the wilderness. Baron Jean-Vincent d'Abbadie de Saint-Castin was a 22-year-old ensign at Fort Pentagoet when it was destroyed in 1674. Returning from France after his discharge, the baron married Mathilde, daughter of Madockawando, a Tarratine Indian sagamore, and rebuilt Pentagoet.

A century later, it was the British turn, and during the Revolution they started construction of Fort George—thus instigating the disastrous Penobscot Expedition (see sidebar). When the 1783 Treaty of Paris unexpectedly ceded Castine to the United States, a number of Tories who had settled there dismantled their houses and shipped them north to found the town of St. Andrews on Passamaquoddy Bay.

Castine was the last British post to be surrendered at the end of the American Revolution—only to be recaptured during the War of 1812. The British left at last in 1815.

Approaches. Approaching from the south, you can coast safely along quite close to Cape Rosier, which is high, wooded, and steep-to. From well south of Cape Rosier, you will be able to see the round, white tower of the abandoned lighthouse on Dice Head.

A surprising number of boats have discovered the rock shown on the chart on the northwestern corner of Nautilus Island. Do not cut the island close. Find red-and-white bell "CH," marking the entrance to Castine Harbor and proceed up the middle of the river, leaving can "1" to port and red daybeacon "2," on its granite pile at Hosmer Ledge, well to starboard.

The Castine waterfront is opposite nun "2," marking the western edge of Middle Ground. Be sure to locate the nun, which is well over on the left-hand side of the river and just outside the moored boats. Obvious landmarks are the large brick buildings of Maine Maritime Academy, and probably the training ship *State of Maine* alongside.

Anchorages, Moorings. The Bagaduce River empties out past Castine, and the current is swift. This, and the extreme depth, make it impractical to anchor off Castine. The Castine Yacht Club has several guest moorings; Eaton's Boatyard has

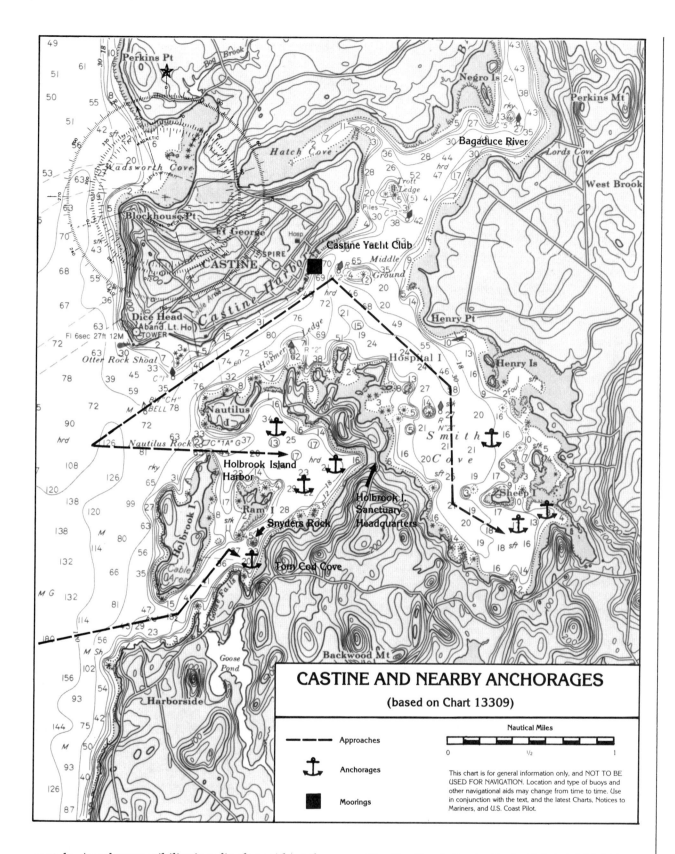

CASTINE AND NEARBY ANCHORAGES

(based on Chart 13309)

- – – – Approaches

⚓ Anchorages

■ Moorings

Nautical Miles

0   ½   1

This chart is for general information only, and NOT TO BE USED FOR NAVIGATION. Location and type of buoys and other navigational aids may change from time to time. Use in conjunction with the text, and the latest Charts, Notices to Mariners, and U.S. Coast Pilot.

rentals. Another possibility is to lie alongside at the yacht club, Dennett's Wharf, or Eaton's overnight. You could pick up a mooring for a few hours while exploring the town, and anchor elsewhere for the night, such as in Smith Cove or Holbrook Island Harbor.

Getting Ashore. Row in to the dinghy float at the yacht club, Eaton's Boatyard, or the floats of the town dock, farther west.

For the Boat. *Castine Yacht Club (tel. 326-9231—pay phone).* CYC is located in a modern gray building with a peaked roof directly opposite nun "2." In addition to their guest moorings (limited to yachts up to 40 feet, for 24 hours), dockage is allowed on the west float, weather and space permitting. There is water at the float, with 20 feet of depth alongside at low.

Dennett's Wharf (tel. 326-9045). The floats along the face and side of Dennett's Wharf have 10 feet of water at low. Call ahead to reserve.

Eaton's Boatyard (Ch. 9 or 16; tel. 326-8579). Eaton's dock and floats and big red-shingled shed are west of the yacht club and just east of Dennett's Wharf. The yard provides dockage with 16 feet alongside at low. Eaton's offers gas, diesel, ice, and water; they have a marine railway and can handle hull and engine repairs. Call the yard for a tow if you end up on a nearby ledge. (The night number for Kenny Eaton, harbormaster, is 326-4916.)

Four Flags (tel. 326-8526). On Main Street, Four Flags is a gift shop with nautical items, including boating supplies and a good selection of charts.

For the Crew. The Castine Yacht Club has showers and a pay phone; Eaton's nearby sells lobsters. For dinner in a charming room with a 360-degree mural of Castine, walk a short way up Main Street to the Castine Inn (tel. 326-4365). Or try the graceful old Pentagoet Inn across the street (tel. 326-8616). Make reservations in either case.

There is a laundromat on Water Street. The Tarratine Market, at Main and Water streets, has good fresh meat, fish, and produce and is also the state liquor store.

Dennett's Wharf, built in the 1830s as a sail loft, boasts "Maine's longest oyster bar" and is the

THE PENOBSCOT EXPEDITION

On August 14, 1779, the fledgling American Republic suffered its worst naval defeat until Pearl Harbor, 162 years later. The history books generally omit mention of this embarrassing episode—one in which we lost 17 armed vessels, 24 transports, and 474 men to a much smaller British force.

Castine was a village of 20 houses or so in June of 1779, when the British landed 750 men and began construction of Fort George. They figured that this would secure the Penobscot River, gateway for masts and lumber for the Royal Navy, and establish a refuge for loyalists as the Revolutionary War drew toward a close.

In less than a month, the Commonwealth of Massachusetts assembled a fleet of militia and marines, under the command of Commodore Dudley Saltonstall, with Generals Solomon Lovell and Peleg Wadsworth in charge of the troops and Colonel Paul Revere commanding the artillery.

On July 19, the fleet headed northeastward, bearing a sorry lot. Many were old men or young boys, entirely lacking in military training. Sighting the fleet sailing up Penobscot Bay, the British started to arm the partly finished fort in Castine, and three British warships were anchored in a line across the harbor. On July 25, the American fleet was repulsed as it tried to enter Castine Harbor, opting instead for Nautilus Island, where the revolutionaries captured the British battery. A few days later, under British fire, the marines scaled Dice Head, capturing the battery there and opening the way to Fort George. General Lovell's journal noted: "It struck me with admiration to see what a Precipice we had ascended . . . . it is at least where we landed three hundred feet high, and almost perpendicular & the men were obliged to pull themselves up by the twigs and trees."

At this point, the British (by their own account) were on the verge of surrender, yet for more than two weeks, discussion continued among the American officers about the wisdom of launching an attack by sea. Things came to a head when a local American commander, Colonel Brewer, having visited Fort George on routine business and having incidentally observed the British defenses and small naval force, reported to Saltonstall, "I thought that as the wind breezed up he might go in with his shipping, silence the two vessels and the six-gun battery, and in half an hour make everything his own. In reply to which," Brewer wrote, "he hove up his long chin, and said, 'You seem to be d-n knowing about the matter! I am not going to risk my shipping in that d-n hole!'"

On August 13, Lovell took command of a 400-man army reinforcement and prepared to storm the fort, a condition imposed by Saltonstall before he would agree to involve his ships. By noon of that day, five American ships got underway and anchored in line, waiting for the tide. Too late. At 5 P.M., a British relief squadron of five warships, under Sir George Collier, was seen entering Penobscot Bay. The American ships and Lovell's men retreated. Ignoring Lovell's pleas, Saltonstall led his fleet up the Penobscot River, pursued by the British. Most of the American ships were scuttled by their own crews, run aground, or set on fire. The British captured two warships and nine transports, losing only 70 men and no ships. The American officers and their men melted into the forest and walked home. The Penobscot Expedition was over.

General Lovell's journal entry for August 14 reports the sorry occasion: ". . . to attempt to give a description of this terrible Day is out of my Power . . . . To see four Ships pursuing seventeen Sail of Armed Vessells nine of which were stout Ships, Transports on fire, Men of War blowing up, Provisions of all kinds, & every kind of Stores on Shore . . . and as much confusion as can possibly be conceived."

A subsequent inquiry by the Commonwealth of Massachusetts concluded that the principal reason for the failure was "want of proper spirit & Energy on the part of the Commodore." Saltonstall was cashiered from the Navy. A complaint was filed against Revere, citing disobedience of orders, neglect of duty, failure to take care of his men, and "unsoldierlike behavior during the whole expedition to Penobscot, which tends to cowardice." The Court did not rule on this complaint, and it took Revere more than two years to obtain a court-martial, which acquitted him "with equal Honor as the other Officers in the same Expedition."

home of the annual Maine state oyster-eating championship. Dennett's also offers showers and desserts and meals to go.

For the Castine Community Hospital, call 326-4348.

Things to Do. The first thing to do is pick up at any store the free pamphlet entitled *The Story of Castine*, which includes a map and suggested walking tours. Particularly enjoyable is the walk up Main Street to the earthworks at Fort George, passing various old buildings and historical plaques scattered throughout the town. One such plaque, at small-boy eye-level, has a graphic description of torture by the Indians.

The *State of Maine* is usually open to the public for guided tours when she is in port. Look for the schooner *Bowdoin,* once commanded by Admiral Donald B. MacMillan on 26 voyages of exploration to the arctic, and now a training ship for Maine Maritime Academy.

Perkins Street, westward along the shorefront, takes you past a number of old homes, including the J.A. Webster House (known as "The House of Sin" because the owner worked in a shipyard on Sundays) and the John Perkins House, built in 1665, with demonstrations of colonial crafts and activities. Next door are a blacksmith shop and the Wilson Museum, containing prehistoric and local treasures. Continue along Perkins Street, passing the earthworks of Fort Madison on the shore, to Battle Avenue and then Dice Head, with dramatic views of Penobscot Bay. The old lighthouse is a private residence, but a short public path leads down to the rocks. It is 1.5 miles from the town dock to Dice Head.

The Castine Golf Club, up Main Street, welcomes visitors to use its course and its tennis courts. Cold Comfort Productions puts on summer theater in various halls, and outdoor performances at Fort George. Look for the posters.

SMITH COVE ★★★ No facilities
Charts: 13302, **13309**

Due south of Castine, Smith Cove provides a convenient and secure anchorage under most conditions. Consider spending the day exploring Castine and then anchor in Smith Cove for the night. Most of Smith Cove south of nun "2" provides good depth for anchoring and is landlocked on all sides. However, it is also a mile across, so there is considerable fetch.

Approaches. Leaving Castine Harbor and observing nun "2" at the west end of Middle Ground, head for the opening between Hospital Island and Henry Point. The fleet of boats moored off Hospital Island belongs to Maine Maritime Academy. The Henry Islands are small, high, and wooded. At low tide, the islands are joined, and the wreck shown on the chart is visible. Leave nun "2" in Smith Cove to starboard.

Sheep Island is low and grassy, with a few trees and one small house on the south side. The deep-water entrance into the lower part of the cove is about 200 yards wide. Estimate a point halfway

between Sheep Island and the mainland to the west and stay west of this halfway point.

The rock off the western shore is visible for about an hour after low.

Anchorages, Moorings. To obtain the best protection from the winds, anchor anywhere convenient in the southeast corner of the cove beyond Sheep Island. You can also work your way in to the eight-foot spot at the east end of the cove and obtain the protection of the ledges there. Holding ground is good, in mud.

Things to Do. There is a pleasant day stop in the upper portion of Smith Cove. Head for the little beach at the narrow neck of land on the west side, anchor in 15 to 20 feet, and row in to the beach. A short distance to the left is the headquarters of the Holbrook Island Sanctuary, with a network of interesting walking trails (see Holbrook Island Harbor writeup).

At the southeast end of Smith Cove is a favorite picnic and swimming spot at the tidal pool.

BAGADUCE RIVER
Charts: 13302, **13309**

The Bagaduce River drains a large area of land at the northeastern end of Penobscot Bay and forms Castine Harbor. Currents are swift, particularly at the Narrows (about three miles in), and the river above Castine is best explored in a small power-boat. Beyond the Narrows, at Jones Point, the pas-

sage is full of rocks and shoals, most of which are unmarked.

On the passage en route to the Narrows, be sure to find nun "2" just off the docks of Castine, marking the western end of Middle Ground. After leaving nun "2" to starboard, cross to the other side of the river, leaving can "3" to port. Head upriver toward Negro Island, which is high and wooded, then around the bend, leaving can "5" to port, and proceed up the middle of the river. This section is quite wide, with summer cottages, banks covered with deciduous trees, and occasional farmhouses with fields down to the river's edge. The river appears to end about a mile ahead, where the Narrows turns eastward. From this point, you can see can "7" at the far end of the Narrows.

In a small powerboat, this would be the intriguing beginning of a river exploration, aiming for the Bagaduce Lunch takeout near the fixed bridge at Brooksville, but this is not a very comfortable place for a cruising boat. The river beyond is treacherous.

HOLBROOK ISLAND HARBOR ★★★★ No facilities
Charts: 13302, **13309**

Just south of Castine is a beautiful harbor formed by Holbrook and Nautilus islands and the northern tip of Cape Rosier. Not only is there good protection, but you will be treated to glimpses of the Camden Hills, Islesboro, Castine, and Dice Head Light. It is unnamed on the chart, but Holbrook Island Harbor seems apt.

Approaches. From the west, Holbrook Island appears with a high, wooded point at each end and a lower saddle between. Nautilus Island is high and wooded, with a large house and a flagpole on the north end. Ram Island, inside the harbor, is low and wooded, with shelving rocky shores, and divides into two islands at high tide.

Enter the harbor between Nautilus and Holbrook islands, leaving can "1A" to port on an easterly course, taking a short jog to the left to avoid the north tip of Holbrook Island. The entrance is fairly narrow but easy.

It is also possible, but hazardous, to approach this harbor through the entrance south of Holbrook Island. The isolated ledge in midchannel, south of Ram Island, shows only two to three feet above water at low, which makes it highly dangerous at midtide or above. "Snyder's Rock" has been located the hard way by many yachts—a dozen or more in recent memory.

Anchorages, Moorings. The best anchorage is at the eastern edge of the harbor, near the narrow neck of land. Work your way in toward the beach and anchor just past the headlands in 16 feet or so at low. You can also anchor northeast or east of Ram Island, in somewhat deeper water.

Getting Ashore. Row in to the beach at the narrow neck of land.

Things to Do. Turn right after landing at the beach and walk toward the headquarters of the Holbrook Island Sanctuary, a state-owned nature preserve on Cape Rosier. (Note that it is not on Holbrook Island, where "No Trespassing" signs are posted.) The sanctuary has an extensive system of trails leading inland and along the shore; a trail map is available at headquarters. One interesting walk is west to Goose Falls and Goose Pond. Another nice trail goes inland to Fresh Pond.

The wildlife sanctuary, covering 1,230 acres, was donated in 1971 by Anita Harris "to preserve for the future a piece of the unspoiled Maine that I used to know." She lived in the big house on Holbrook Island until she died in 1985, leaving Holbrook Island and a trust fund to maintain it as a wildlife refuge and research station.

Holbrook Island Sanctuary can also be approached from Smith Cove, on the other side of the narrow neck.

Ram Island, long a local favorite for picnics and beachcombing, has been acquired by the Castine Conservation Trust to be preserved in its natural state for enjoyment by the public.

TOM COD COVE ★★★ No facilities
Charts: 13302, **13309**

On the north shore of Cape Rosier, due south of Ram Island, is a spot known locally as Tom Cod Cove. Much of the cove usually is occupied by moored lobsterboats, but if you can find room, it is a lovely and well-protected anchorage.

Approaches. Do not approach from Holbrook Island Harbor to the north. The rock in midchannel south of Ram Island is a catcher of boats. Instead, use the wide and clear entrance south of Holbrook Island. If you are coasting north along Cape Rosier, it will be the first opening. On the south side of the entrance are a gazebo, a breakwater, and a boathouse. Leaving these well to starboard, proceed up the middle of the channel. Leave to starboard Goose Falls, with its little bridges, and continue past the next rocky point to starboard, turning right into Tom Cod Cove.

Anchorages, Moorings. If there is room among the lobsterboats, anchor in 15 to 20 feet at low, with good holding ground in gray mud. The anchorage, pretty and unspoiled, is protected from prevailing southerlies but somewhat exposed to strong northwesterlies.

The rock shown on the chart on the west side of the cove is just a bit farther out than the private float, and south of it.

WEIR COVE ★★★ No facilities
Charts: 13302, **13309**

Although it offers less protection than neighboring harbors to the east, Weir Cove, on the southeast side of Cape Rosier, is a lovely anchorage in settled summer weather and a good harbor if the wind is from the north.

At the head of the harbor stands abrupt and rocky Weir Cove Mountain, now protected by the Maine Coast Heritage Trust.

Approaches. Run between Blake Point and the Spectacle islands. When far enough past the Spec-

Things to Do. Go ashore at Goose Falls with your dinghy and enjoy the trails of Holbrook Island Sanctuary.

tacles to clear the seven-foot spot, head for low-lying, rocky Buck Island (which has a little grass on top). Before reaching Buck Island, head north into Weir Cove. The ledges on the west side of the entrance, opposite Buck Island, are visible at half-tide.

Anchorages, Moorings. Anchor just outside the moored lobsterboats in 15 to 20 feet at low. There is exposure from the southeast to southwest, but holding ground is good.

HORSESHOE COVE ★★★
Charts: 13302, **13309**

On the eastern side of Cape Rosier, not far from the entrance to Eggemoggin Reach, Horseshoe Cove on the chart looks impossible to enter. Once you know the secret, it is still a bit tricky but well worth the effort. This beautiful, unspoiled harbor has almost perfect protection.

The cove was named for the abundance of horseshoe crabs that annually migrate and lay their eggs here.

Approaches. The easiest approach is from the east, from the direction of Bucks Harbor and Eggemoggin Reach, passing north of low, grassy Thrumcap Island. Leave to starboard the small, hard-to-see, red daybeacon (privately maintained) at the end of the ledge marking the right side of the entrance to Horseshoe Cove.

Continue westward until the cove opens up; then turn northward up the middle of the channel, passing a dock extending from the west shore and a series of mooring stakes in midchannel. Leave these stakes to starboard and aim for the small red daybeacon some distance ahead. You will also see one or two green spar buoys (left to port) near the red daybeacon (left to starboard).

The first spar buoy serves to nudge you over toward the east shore; the second spar buoy marks the left side of the tiny entrance to the mooring area. The red beacon is set on top of a large, rounded rock (covered about an hour before high tide) at the right-hand side of the entrance. It is not, however, at the edge. Stay at least 30 feet west of the red beacon, favoring the second green spar buoy.

Do not be surprised if you can't find one or both of the spar buoys; they are anchored, and they

tend to drag under at high tide. You can get into the harbor safely with only the red beacon to guide you.

Pass into the mooring area, leaving the second green spar buoy close to port and the red beacon at least 30 feet to starboard.

Anchorages, Moorings. Mooring floats and stakes, with 500- to 2,000-pound granite blocks, are set out by Seal Cove Boatyard, whose sheds are just out of sight farther up the cove on the west side. Pick one up and check with the yard. Protection is extremely good, with the only exposure south-southwest. The tiny, wooded island in the mouth of the harbor helps to break up entering waves.

There is no room to anchor in the mooring area. You could, however, anchor farther south in the approach channel.

Getting Ashore. Take your dinghy in to the floats at Seal Cove Boatyard.

For the Boat. *Seal Cove Boatyard, Inc. (tel. 326-4422).* Owner Bob Vaughan specializes in the rebuilding and restoration of wooden boats. You are likely to see some great old classics at the moorings and up in the yard.

The route from the mooring area to the yard is narrow and crooked; don't try it without someone from the yard to guide you. There is no fuel or ice, but water is available at the floats. The yard has a mechanic for engine repairs and a marine railway. Repairs can be made on wood and glass hulls, but there usually is a waiting list.

Things to Do. Past the boatyard, the river turns west and then north, running a long way back into Cape Rosier, and at midtide the water comes rushing in or out of the narrow passage between granite banks. There is a strong current of at least five or six knots, white water, a salt pond, and two sets of reversing falls, which attract intrepid kayakers and even occasional yachtsmen in their dinghies. To explore this fascinating channel, Bob Vaughan suggests going upstream about an hour before high slack tide and returning with the first of the ebb.

ORCUTT HARBOR ★★★ No facilities

Charts: 13302, **13309**

Orcutt Harbor, on the east side of Cape Rosier, is just west of Bucks Harbor. The harbor is attractive, easy to enter, and well protected except from the southwest; it would be a wonderful refuge in a northerly. Orcutt is little used by yachtsmen, who perhaps prefer the amenities and security of Bucks Harbor next door.

Approaches. Go right up to the head of the harbor, favoring the eastern side to avoid two five-foot spots on the western side. There is good water almost to the rock at the head.

Anchorages, Moorings. Anchor in midchannel in 7 to 14 feet at low, mud bottom, good holding ground.

BUCKS HARBOR and ★★★★ LEM'S COVE

Charts: 13302, **13309**

Bucks Harbor (shown as Buck Harbor on the chart) is one of the best protected and most attractive harbors on Penobscot Bay. The *American Coast Pilot* of 1806 called it a hurricane hole, and nothing has changed since then.

Just east of Cape Rosier and west of the entrance to Eggemoggin Reach, the anchorage is formed by Harbor Island at the entrance. Bucks Harbor Yacht Club, third oldest in Maine, is home to a substantial fleet of yachts. The best-protected portions of Bucks Harbor are behind Harbor Island and in the bight at the southeastern end called Lem's Cove. This is the setting for Robert Mc-Closkey's famous children's books, *One Morning in Maine, Time of Wonder,* and *Blueberries for Sal.*

Approaches. Northwest of Little Deer Isle, there are several rocks and ledges, most of which are marked. Of the various paths among them, the best approach is to find red-and-white bell "ER," then pass between nun "32" to port and cans "33" and "31" to starboard. (These cans are small and hard to see.) Cans "29" and "27" are also left to starboard, on your way to red-and-white bell "EG," south of the harbor. From there, enter Bucks Harbor either east or west of Harbor Island.

Identify green can "1," marking a ledge in the harbor that bares at extreme lows. It may be hard to see among the moored boats.

Anchorages, Moorings. Check first with the Bucks Harbor Yacht Club, which maintains a couple of guest moorings and keeps track of members who are away. Then ask at Bucks Harbor Marine, which rents moorings.

Protection in Bucks Harbor generally is superb, depending somewhat on where you are located.

The best shelter is north of Harbor Island, where you are completely landlocked, but there is not likely to be space for visitors. The protection way east in Lem's Cove is also extremely good.

There is room to anchor outside the moored boats on either the east or the west side of the harbor, in good sand bottom, although the depth may run from 24 to 30 feet at low.

Getting Ashore. Row your dinghy in to the yacht club floats.

For the Boat. *Bucks Harbor Marine (Ch. 9 or 16; tel. 326-8839).* Recognizable by its white fuel tanks east of the yacht club, Bucks Harbor Marine provides many facilities for its size. Its "daily membership" fee includes a mooring, dinghy space, garbage disposal, and outdoor shower. Overnight dockage is available at the floats, with 15 feet alongside, and there is gas, diesel, water, electricity, ice, and some marine supplies. Mechanics and divers are on call for emergency repairs.

Bucks Harbor Yacht Club (tel. 326-9265—pay phone). Water is available for filling tanks only, with a depth of 17 feet at the floats.

Condon's Garage (tel. 326-4964). Welding and some engine repairs can be done at Condon's Garage in South Brooksville, just up the road from the yacht club.

The Golden Stairs (tel. 326-4369). In the shallow cove at the northwestern tip of the harbor is The Golden Stairs, accessible by dinghy or by a short walk from the yacht club. Here you will find marine supplies, charts, a gift shop, and facilities for outboard repairs.

For the Crew. Bucks Harbor Marine has limited provisions, including beer, soda, ice cream, and canned goods. Long- and short-term parking is available there. Visiting yachtsmen are welcome to use the yacht club's clay tennis court and clubhouse.

Just up from the yacht club are the Landing Restaurant (tel. 326-9445) and Harbor View Takeout. Up the street from the yacht club, at the first (and only) intersection in South Brooksville is the post office. The market just beyond may or may not be open; it varies from year to year.

Things to Do. The pace is slow in South Brooksville, and people like it that way. Try sitting in a rocking chair on the porch of the yacht club and observing the yachting scene below. Wander through the clubhouse, which was built around 1912, and note the "first private burgee taken through the Panama Canal; also the Cape Cod Canal."

POND ISLAND

Charts: 13302, **13309**

On a nice summer day you might find a small armada anchored off the beach at Pond Island, just south of Cape Rosier. This 55-acre island has been used for generations by local residents for picnicking and beachcombing. The island was bought by the Philadelphia Conservationists to keep it undeveloped and open for public use, and is now managed by the Island Institute. This is a lovely day stop.

The western end of Pond Island is high and wooded, but the southeastern end is long, low, and sandy, with a single clump of trees. Come in from the north and head for that single clump. Work your way in to a comfortable depth of 15 to 20 feet and anchor off the beach in sand bottom. Check the depth carefully and the state of the tide, since the beach shoals rapidly. Lots of boats have grounded out here while their owners were relaxing ashore.

Several stone campfire sites are here already—no need to establish any more. The Indians liked Pond Island too, as shown by clamshell middens near the pond, the site of recent archaeological digs. A delightful walk around the beaches of the southeastern end takes in driftwood, wildflowers, and the marshy pond that gives the island its name.

Composed entirely of sand and gravel, and once part of a glacial river delta, Pond is atypical—more characteristic of islands around Cape Cod than islands in Maine.

HOG and FIDDLE HEAD ISLANDS ★★★ No facilities

Charts: 13302, **13309**

Just east of Pond Island lies Hog Island. No doubt it came by the name honestly, but "Hog" scarcely describes one of the prettiest islands in Penobscot Bay. Partially wooded, with open meadow, privately owned Hog Island is connected by a sand bar to rocky little Fiddle Head.

Approaches. Come in from the north.

Anchorages, Moorings. Near the northeastern end of Hog Island are some private moorings off the dock. Anchor outside these moorings, roughly on a line between the dock and Fiddle Head Island, in 15 to 25 feet at low, with good holding in sandy bottom. You are well protected here during normal summer conditions. When the sandy bar is exposed, there is the feeling of a peaceful lagoon.

PICKERING ISLAND ★★★ No facilities

Charts: 13302, **13305**, 13309

High, wooded Pickering Island lies at the northeastern end of Penobscot Bay, just south of Little Deer Isle. Two pleasant coves on the north side of the island provide good protection from prevailing winds.

The island is privately owned and frequently occupied during the summer months. It is also a preserve of The Nature Conservancy. You are welcome to go ashore at the western cove, but not at the eastern cove, where the owner has experienced "a constant intrusion of visitors."

Approaches—Western Cove. The easiest approach to either cove is from the west. Sailing up East Penobscot Bay, stay west of a line drawn between the western tips of Bradbury and Pickering islands to avoid the foul ground between them. Make your turn around the western tip of Pickering and coast along the north shore until the western cove opens up. Run up the middle of the cove toward the sand beach at the head.

Anchorages, Moorings—Western Cove. Anchor in 10 to 12 feet at low, with good holding ground in sandy bottom and good protection except from the northeast. There are lovely birch trees along the shore and no houses in sight.

Approaches—Eastern Cove. To reach the Eastern Cove, continue coasting fairly close along the north shore of Pickering. Little Eaton Island has a high, rocky bluff at the western end and a clump of spruce trees in the middle. Eaton Island is mostly wooded, with several beaches. A third, unnamed island is connected to the eastern tip of Pickering by a bar. Enter the middle of the cove formed by Pickering and the offlying islands.

Anchorages, Moorings—Eastern Cove. Anchor in 12 to 15 feet at low anywhere along the southern or eastern perimeter of this cove. The bottom is rocky. The north shore of Pickering is quite shoal, so favor the east end, close to the little unnamed island.

This is the cove where the owner of the island lives. Respect his privacy and do not land here.

CROW ISLAND

Charts: 13302, **13305**

Small Crow Island, just east of Bradbury Island, off Deer Isle, is partly wooded and partly meadow, with abundant wildflowers. It is owned by the state and enjoyed as a day stop by local residents and visiting yachtsmen. Under normal summer conditions, the anchorage is on the north side of the island. Crow Island's somewhat exposed location, combined with a dangerous ledge at each end of the island, makes this a dubious overnight stop.

The approach is easier from the east. A solitary boulder is resting on the eastern ledge, but the ledge continues well beyond the boulder, so give it a good berth.

From the west, coast along the north shore of Bradbury Island, to avoid the rocks between Bradbury and Pickering islands. Near the east end of Bradbury, turn northward to avoid the nasty ledge at the west end of Crow Island. This ledge extends some distance north of the two rocks shown on the chart, which are visible at high tide.

Anchor off the second little shingle beach from the east. The fringing ledge stops at the east side of this beach. The cove shoals rapidly, and you will have to get in quite close to find a comfortable depth. The bottom apparently is rocky.

GREAT SPRUCE HEAD ISLAND

Charts: 13302, **13305**

Many lovers of Maine received their introduction to the state from that wonderful book of photographs by Eliot Porter, *Summer Island: Penobscot Country,* published by the Sierra Club in 1966. "Summer Island" is Great Spruce Head, still owned by the Porters.

The houses, barn, boathouse, and enormous bell are all on the east side of the island, opposite the Barred Islands. There is a float and dock, and a number of private moorings. Feel free to anchor, but do not go ashore on this private island.

BARRED ISLANDS ★★★★   No facilities

Charts: 13302, **13305**

Just southeast of Great Spruce Head Island and west of Butter Island is a tiny archipelago forming a little lagoon and one of the prettiest anchorages in Penobscot Bay. There is a private dock here, but no houses are visible.

The northernmost island is Escargot, with Bartender eastward toward Butter. Big Barred, the largest island, forms the eastern side of the harbor, and Little Barred forms the western side.

Approaches. The entrance to the Barred Islands is from the northwest. Run south past can "3" off Great Spruce Head Island and enter between Escargot (the northernmost island) and Little Barred (at the southwest corner). Because of the submerged ledges at the entrance, avoid entering at dead low; a lookout on the bow is a good idea.

A ledge, shown on the chart and visible at mid-tide, makes out a long way northeast of Little Barred; it is marked with a privately maintained beacon. Don't cut the beacon close; the ledge extends underwater a considerable distance beyond it. You will find good water about halfway between the beacon and Escargot. A second ledge, also shown on the chart, lies beyond, east of the tip of

Little Barred. When past this second ledge, turn right and run southward down the middle of the harbor, between low, wooded Little Barred to starboard and high, wooded Big Barred to port.

The approach from the south, between Great Spruce Head Island and the Barred Islands, is very narrow and lined with rocks. Use it with caution, on a rising tide.

Anchorages, Moorings. Once you have turned south between Little and Big Barred and passed the ledge east of the tip of Little Barred, anchor anywhere in 20 to 34 feet at low, on the midline of the harbor or toward Little Barred. There is good water almost to the gravel bar that connects Little and Big Barred, at the south end of the harbor.

From just opposite the dock you can see across the way to the houses, flagpole, and enormous bronze bell on Great Spruce Head Island. Most summer nights you will find several other boats in this anchorage. Arrive early. Off season, you may be lucky enough to have it all to yourself.

Holding ground is good. Although you will be comfortable here in settled summer weather, the anchorage can be rough and untenable with strong winds from the southwest, north, or northwest, especially at high tide when the bars are covered. If these conditions are expected, *leave*.

Getting Ashore. The owners of Big and Little Barred have established a No Trespassing policy.

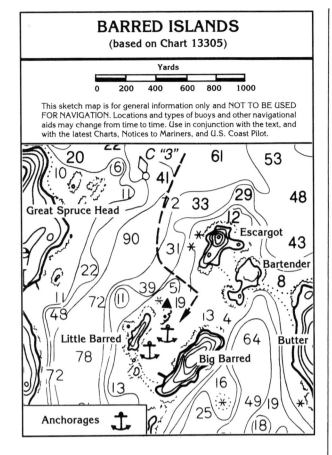

BUTTER ISLAND

Charts: 13302, **13305**

Butter Island, west of Deer Isle and north of Eagle Island, has long been a popular day stop for cruising yachtsmen and local residents. There are lovely beaches to explore, spruce forests, open meadow, abundant berries, and a 186-foot peak to climb.

Butter is owned by Tom Cabot of Boston, who for more than 50 years has played a leading role in the preservation of Maine islands. The Cabot family welcomes visitors ashore and asks that you protect and enjoy this beautiful island and "Avelinda Forest." No fires are allowed.

From the time of its settlement in 1785, Butter was no different from a hundred other islands in Penobscot Bay, home to fishermen and farmers. In 1895, however, the island caught the attention of George and Emory Harriman of Boston, who envisioned an "Arabic-like town of tents and cottages" for genteel Bostonians of good social standing. Butter was renamed Dirigo, after Maine's state motto, and a hotel was built to accommodate as many as 100 guests. The New England Tent Club provided comfortable quarters and vigorous outdoor activities for their enthusiastic guests, who arrived by steamer from Boston. The round trip cost $5.50,

leaving Boston at 5 P.M. and arriving at Dirigo at 7 A.M., after a change at Rockland.

Like other Maine island resorts, the New England Tent Club succumbed to the advent of the automobile and the decline of steamships. The end came in 1916, with cancellation of ferry service, and today there is hardly a trace of the resort.

Depending on the direction of the wind, there are several possible anchorages for a day stop at Butter. With a southwesterly wind, anchor in the little bight just north of the rocky nub at the east end. If the wind is from other quarters, anchor east or west of the peninsula extending from the southwest corner of Butter. Another possibility is at the northwest corner of Butter, south of the sandbar connecting Butter and Bartender and east of the 64-foot spot.

The approach to any of these anchorages is straightforward. Work your way in to a comfortable depth and drop the hook. Note that there are ledges making out a short way from shore near the southwest peninsula.

The bottom in most locations is mud, providing good holding ground, but there is also some kelp.

The anchorage north of the rocky nub at the east end offers the best views and the easiest access to the meadows and the hill at the northern end of the island.

WESTERN COAST OF DEER ISLE

NORTHWEST HARBOR ★★★
Charts: 13302, **13305**

On the chart, Deer Isle is like a butterfly, and Northwest Harbor the deep indentation between its wings. This little-used harbor is wide, free of dangers, and easy to enter in normal visibility. Its shores are tree-lined, with a few summer homes. The cluster of houses at the far end is the village of Deer Isle.

Approaches. The only dangers in the approach are the ledges to the south, marked by can "1" and nun "2," and unmarked Gull Ledge between. At high tide, Gull Ledge is a small, flat rocky island; at low, it is revealed as a sizable ledge to be respected.

Coming from the south, your mark is high, barren Hardhead Island, with impressive cliffs. Then, leaving green can "1" well to starboard, head for Heart Island, north of the entrance. Heart is a small, steep island, with a cleared section facing southwest.

After leaving Gull Ledge and nun "2" to star-board, turn right, down the middle of the harbor.

Anchorages, Moorings. Anchor wherever you wish in 10 to 15 feet at low. You can go in comfortably as far as the large dock on the northeast shore; the water then begins to shoal rapidly.

Holding ground is good, in mud, and protection is excellent except from the northwest. Since so few boats use Northwest Harbor, there is as much swinging room as you could want.

Getting Ashore. It is a long way from the anchorage to the village, which is inaccessible by water at low tide. When there is water at the head of the harbor, land at one of the tiny beaches on either side of the causeway.

For the Crew. In Deer Isle Village, you will find ice, a market, hardware store, bookstore, library, bank and post office. There is also a takeout, and the Pilgrim's Inn, which serves dinner. For reservations, call 348-6615.

SYLVESTER COVE ★★★
Charts: 13302, **13305**

Pleasant, friendly little Sylvester Cove, on the west side of Deer Isle, is shared by working fishermen, a summer colony, the Deer Isle Yacht Club, and the mailboats that transport the residents to Eagle and Great Spruce Head islands. It is a pretty place but not a well-protected harbor.

Approaches. Several clues will help you pick out Sylvester Cove from a distance. It is directly east of the lighthouse on the tip of Eagle Island, which is visible for a long way. Hardhead Island, to the north, is easy to recognize, being high, treeless, and grassy, with impressive cliffs. And you will usually see a little cluster of masts in Sylvester Cove.

As you approach Sylvester Cove on an easterly course, leave nun "2" to starboard. This marks the end of a long ledge to the southeast that is not visible at halftide. You will see the yacht club dock on the north side of the cove and a miniature flag-pole on the dock itself.

From the nun, you can run in among the moored boats if you wish, but do not go beyond the floats at the dock. Local yachtsmen say that staying south of a line between the lighthouse on Eagle Island and the yacht club float will keep you in good water.

Anchorages, Moorings. The Deer Isle Yacht Club maintains a couple of guest moorings outside the fleet near nun "2." You can also anchor in the same vicinity.

Getting Ashore. Row in to the back of the yacht club floats.

For the Boat. The Deer Isle Yacht Club has no clubhouse. Aside from parking and use of the floats (with five to six feet alongside at low), the only facilities are the guest moorings.

For the Crew. The nearest market is in Deer Isle Village, about two miles away. The Pilgrim's Inn (tel. 348-6615) may come pick you up for dinner (by reservation), or call a taxi.

CROCKETT COVE ★★★ No facilities

Charts: **13305**, 13313

On the southwest corner of Deer Isle, near Burnt Cove, Crockett is a pretty anchorage with bold shores and is relatively unused. It is open to the southwest, but offers good protection from the north. There are a number of cottages and docks along the south shore, but no commercial activity.

Approaches. Coming from the west, use the steeple in West Stonington at the head of Burnt Cove as a mark. Once you have identified Burnt Cove, Crockett is the next one north. Run up the middle of the entrance.

Anchorages, Moorings. There is plenty of room to anchor. Go in as far as the little peninsula to port, and anchor in 15 feet or so at low, in mud bottom.

BURNT COVE ★★

Charts: 13305, 13313, **13315**

Burnt Cove is on the southwestern corner of Deer Isle, about a mile north of the entrance to the Deer Island Thorofare. A working harbor with a few small pleasure craft, it is easy to enter and offers good protection.

Approaches. Coming from the direction of Fox Islands Thorofare, steer for the white church spire in West Stonington. As you get closer, check off the islands: Mark Island (lighthouse), Andrews and Second (both wooded), and, farthest north, The Fort, which is a huge granite ledge with a bit of grass and just a few trees. A cleft in the rock on the end of Fifield Point suggests a missing front tooth. Stay in the middle as you enter Burnt Cove to avoid rocks along the south shore.

Anchorages, Moorings. The inner part of the cove is full of moored boats. Anchor west of the moorings in nine feet at low, good mud bottom. Billings Marine, in Stonington, maintains a number of moorings here; the pickup buoys have whip antennas. Reserve ahead (tel. 367-2328).

Getting Ashore. Row in to the Fifield Lobster Co. float.

For the Boat. *Fifield Lobster Co.* The first dock on the south shore is Fifield Lobster. Catering mostly to lobsterboats, Fifield sells gas and diesel at the floats, with about six feet alongside at low.

For the Crew. Try Fifield for lobsters. Walk to the head of the cove to find Burnt Cove Market, which has groceries, ice, and a pay phone. The Island Medical Center (tel. 367-2311) is two miles away.

Things to Do. The 100-acre Crockett Cove Woods Preserve was given to The Nature Conservancy by the well-known artist and architect Emily Muir. It can be reached best by water from Burnt Cove. Walk up to the head of the harbor and turn left on Whitman Road, which leads to the entrance of the preserve. There is a self-guiding nature trail through the woods, with deep mosses and old man's beard lichens hanging from the trees in this quiet sanctuary.

ISLE AU HAUT

Charts: 13302, 13303, 13305, 13312, **13313**

Lying five miles off Deer Isle, beautiful Isle au Haut is remote and hard to reach—probably the reason why the year-round population has always been low, and why this rugged island looks little different now from when it was named by Samuel de Champlain in 1604.

"High Island," he called it, and so it impresses the visitor today—rising to 556 feet, six miles long, two miles wide, and heavily forested. There are lots of deer on the island, and a large variety of birds. The deer are protected, and the islanders have built high wire fences around their gardens to keep them out.

More than half the island is part of Acadia National Park. Millions of people a year visit Mount Desert Island, but park visitors to Isle au Haut are limited to 50 a day. As a result, Isle au Haut remains a wonderful place to explore, with 30 miles of hiking trails, rustic campsites, fishing for salmon and trout in Long Pond, mountains to climb with splendid vistas, and rugged shorelines to walk.

The harbors on the west and northwest coasts are small, and marginal in terms of protection. But they are fine for settled summer weather. The two most useful ones are Isle au Haut Thorofare, adjoining the little village of Isle au Haut, and Duck

Harbor, providing access to the park and trails.

The east coast of Isle au Haut is a forbidding place, with great Atlantic rollers crashing on high cliffs. York Island, at the northeast corner, is private, inhabited, and difficult to approach. Head Harbor, at the south end of the island, is attractive but very much exposed to both prevailing winds and ocean swells.

Electricity came to the island around 1970, but there were no telephones until 1988. Cars are expensive to transport by barge to Isle au Haut, so their owners keep them going as long as possible. As a result, the few "island cars" are in an extraordinary state of life-after-death. About 55 people stay on the island all winter, lobstering being their main occupation.

A ferry runs from Stonington to the village of Isle au Haut, and in summer it continues on to Duck Harbor. The *Miss Lizzie* was named for a much-loved lady who was postmistress for more than 50 years.

The major trails on the island are shown on the accompanying sketch map. The most popular hikes are around Western Head, up Duck Harbor Mountain, and along the high ridge of Jerusalem Mountain. For information on the park, write: Superintendent, Acadia National Park, Box 177, Bar Harbor, ME 04609. Or call 288-3338.

Fishermen settled the island first in 1772, and the population grew gradually to a peak of 274 in 1880. By the mid-1800s, lobstering had become the main occupation, and a lobster cannery was established here in 1860, shipping delicacies as far as London. The cannery closed in 1873, but live lobsters then were shipped from Isle au Haut to customers in Boston and New York.

In 1879, a young Bostonian named Ernest Bowditch (grandson of *American Practical Navigator* author Nathaniel Bowditch) saw the island across the sea one summer day and was enchanted by its wild beauty. With a few friends, he formed the Point Look-out Club, and eventually they bought up most of the available acreage on the island. It was a bachelor club at first—no children, no dogs, and no women. But the bachelors went the way of all flesh, and it developed into a family resort.

There was a large clubhouse for meals, and each member had a little cabin nearby, connected by a boardwalk. Entertainment was simple: sailing, deepsea fishing, hiking, and tennis. There were church fairs, and it was the custom on Sunday nights to go to someone's cabin and sing hymns.

For half a century, this was an exclusive paradise for a few families. Then, in 1945–46, the same summer families donated the land to Acadia National Park. Most of the 300 or so summer residents on the island today are descendants of the original club members.

How is the island's name pronounced? This may help: "Says the summer man, when the fog hangs low, 'There's a bridal wreath on Isle au Haut.' But the fisherman says as he loads his boat, 'It's thick-a-fog on Isle au Haut.'"

ISLE AU HAUT THOROFARE ★★★

Charts: 13302, **13305**, 13313

The narrow channel between Kimball Island and Isle au Haut is known as Isle au Haut Thorofare. It offers reasonable protection and access to the village of Isle au Haut, but the anchorage is not an easy one. A dredged channel makes it possible to continue northward to Merchant Row or Jericho Bay.

Isle au Haut village is a pretty little community, settled partly by fishermen and partly by summer people, and served by a ferry from Stonington, privately owned by island residents. The pace is slow.

Approaches. Approaching from the west, pick up Kimball Rock, awash 10 feet at low, and can "1" off Marsh Cove Ledges, passing outside of both. The lighthouse on Robinson Point is clearly visible, with its round granite base and white brick upper half.

Inside the Thorofare, a large weir has been built on the Isle au Haut side, between green daybeacon "3" and the narrows. Leave the weir to starboard, and stay in midstream through the narrow part of the channel that follows.

Unless you have shoal draft, avoid passing through the dredged channel at dead low. Continuing through the Thorofare past Isle au Haut village, be careful of the ledge, marked by red daybeacon "4," which extends at least 30 feet north of the beacon. Immediately after the beacon, you enter a narrow, buoyed channel dredged to 6 feet and 75 feet wide, marked by a can and a nun at each end plus a green can part way through. Some stakes along the Kimball Island side of the channel help keep you lined up. Proceed slowly, steer straight, and you will have no trouble. Approaching from Merchant Row and the north, pass between Hardwood and Merchant islands, following the cable track shown on the chart. Leave to port the two cans marking the ledges off Flake Island, and enter the dredged channel.

Anchorages, Moorings. There is not much room in the Thorofare. Anchor opposite the vil-

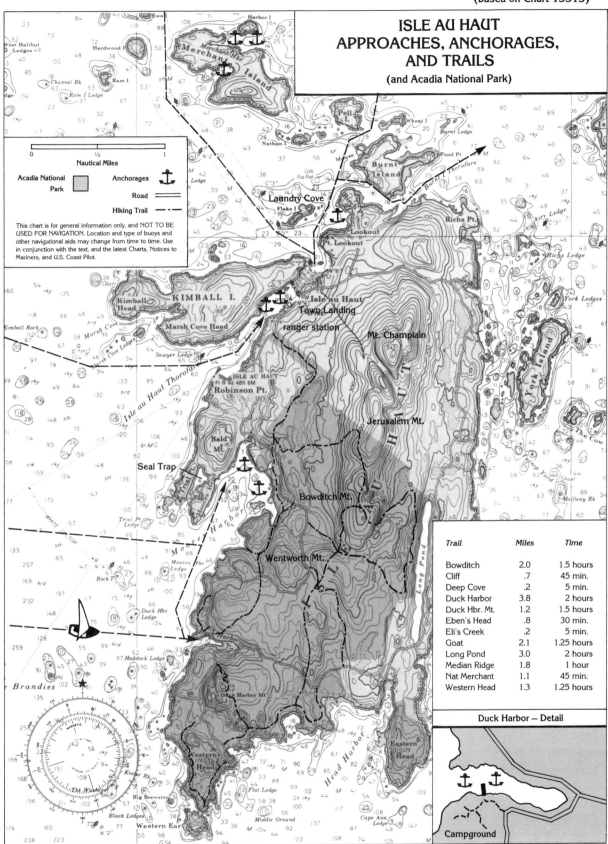

ISLE AU HAUT
APPROACHES, ANCHORAGES, AND TRAILS
(and Acadia National Park)

Nautical Miles

Acadia National Park

Anchorages ⚓

Road ══════

Hiking Trail ─ ∙ ─ ∙ ─

This chart is for general information only, and NOT TO BE USED FOR NAVIGATION. Location and type of buoys and other navigational aids may change from time to time. Use in conjunction with the text, and the latest Charts, Notices to Mariners, and U.S. Coast Pilot.

Trail	Miles	Time
Bowditch	2.0	1.5 hours
Cliff	.7	45 min.
Deep Cove	.2	5 min.
Duck Harbor	3.8	2 hours
Duck Hbr. Mt.	1.2	1.5 hours
Eben's Head	.8	30 min.
Eli's Creek	.2	5 min.
Goat	2.1	1.25 hours
Long Pond	3.0	2 hours
Median Ridge	1.8	1 hour
Nat Merchant	1.1	45 min.
Western Head	1.3	1.25 hours

Duck Harbor — Detail

Campground

lage, outside the moored boats on the Kimball Island side, in 15 to 21 feet at low. Right across from the town dock, there is an open space among the moored boats, enticing you to anchor. Don't.

The rock shown on the chart is really there. You may find a rental mooring on the north side of the Thorofare.

The current through the Thorofare is not very

strong (it floods northeast and ebbs southwest), but the combination of wind and current is likely to swing you around in every direction during the night.

If there is no room to anchor in the Thorofare, consider Laundry Cove, nearby to the north.

Getting Ashore. Take your dinghy in to the float at the Isle au Haut town landing, the westernmost dock on the south side of the Thorofare. Do not take trash ashore; there is no place to leave it. Kimball Island is private.

For the Crew. Walk left along the road a short distance to the combination market-and-post-of-fice.

Things to Do. Walk past the market until you reach a boardwalk on the right, leading up to the simple and beautiful Union Congregational Church (1857).

It is possible to explore trails of Acadia National Park from the village. Continue along the road for another quarter of a mile; on the right, immediately beyond the Point Lookout road, you'll see the trail leading to Mount Champlain. It's a fairly gentle half-hour hike to the summit, with fine views east over Jericho Bay to Swan's Island.

MOORES HARBOR★★★ No facilities
Charts: **13303, 13305, 13313**

Moores Harbor, on the west side of Isle au Haut, is large and wide open to prevailing southwesterlies, and therefore not generally appealing for an anchorage. It does provide good protection, however, when the wind is from other quarters. In settled summer weather it would offer an alternative if Duck Harbor is full.

Approaches. Approaching from the west, pass north of the nun at Rock T; continuing past Moores Harbor Ledge (visible except at the highest tide), run into Moores Harbor on either side of the large ledge in midharbor. This ledge is awash nine feet at low and visible except at dead high tide. Watch for dories and nets, and the weir at the northwest corner.

Coming from Duck Harbor, run fairly close along the shore, inside Moores Harbor Ledge.

Anchorages, Moorings. Anchor north and east of the ledge in 20 to 25 feet, mud bottom. Note the three-foot spot.

Getting Ashore. Pull your dinghy up on the pebble beach southeast of the three-foot spot.

Things to Do. Musseling here is great. Acadia National Park trails run close to the shore (see map p. 233).

DUCK HARBOR ★★★★ No facilities
Charts: 13302, **13303, 13305, 13313**

Duck Harbor is a peaceful little paradise at the southwestern end of Isle au Haut, and the best place for access to the trails of Acadia National Park. This is where the ferry from Stonington drops off and picks up campers and hikers. There is room here for only a few boats, so arrive early.

Approaches. It's hard to see Duck Harbor from a distance. Head in the general direction of Duck Harbor Mountain, the highest bump near the southern end of the island. It is just south of the harbor. As you get closer, look for a bare, conical rock at the north side of the entrance.

From 200 or 300 yards north of The Brandies (usually visible), run a straight line into the entrance of Duck Harbor, leaving to port Duck Harbor Ledge, which can be identified by the lobster buoys floating over it (see sketch map). Check out Haddock Ledge to starboard for an extended family of basking seals.

Another, and perhaps easier, approach is to pass north of the nun at Rock T, heading toward Moores Harbor. From the entrance of Moores Harbor, turn south inside Moores Harbor Ledge (visible except at the highest tide) and run fairly close along the shoreline until you reach Duck Harbor.

Anchorages, Moorings. Anchor in midchannel just before or just past the dock where the ferry lands on the south side of the harbor. Do not go as far as the large, sloping ledge that leads up into the trees on the south side.

Anchor in 10 to 15 feet at low. The bottom is rocky, so you may have to try a couple of times to get the hook in. The anchorage is exposed to the west, but otherwise it offers good protection.

Getting Ashore. Row in to the float, leaving the outer face clear for the ferry.

Things to Do. This is the least-known part of Acadia National Park, and one of the most beautiful. Walk along the south shore until you find the park bulletin board, with a trail map and other information. It is a short walk to the top of Duck Harbor Mountain (314 feet), from which there are great views of Penobscot Bay.

A much longer walk will take you around Western Head and eventually back to the main trail. Another possibility is to cut straight across the island for a swim in Long Pond. The trails are likely to be rough and wet, but they are well worth the effort.

HEAD HARBOR★★★ No facilities

Charts: 13302, **13303**, 13312, **13313**

Tucked inside Eastern Head at the south end of Isle au Haut, this pretty little harbor is exposed to ocean swells and prevailing southwest winds, but useful if the wind is from the north or east. It might also provide a good stop if you are making an off-shore passage.

Approaches. After identifying Western Ear Ledge and Roaring Bull Ledge (both of which break, even on a calm day), run in for Head Harbor, staying well clear of the ledges making out a long way from Eastern Head. The entrance is wide and easy.

Anchorages, Moorings. Anchor in the middle of the harbor before reaching the meadow on the eastern side, in 15 to 20 feet at low. The holding ground, in sand, is good. A big, heavy mooring used by fishing boats may be available.

Getting Ashore. Land on the beach at the head of the harbor, where there are a half dozen houses.

Things to Do. A paved road leading west toward Duck Harbor intersects the trails of Acadia National Park (see map p. 233), and another road leads a half mile north to Long Pond.

LAUNDRY COVE ★★★ No facilities

Chart: 13313

Between Point Lookout and Birch Point, north of the Isle au Haut Thorofare, Laundry Cove has splendid views over the islands of Penobscot Bay, west to the Camden Hills and north to Merchant Row. Ashore are a few handsome cottages, some from the island's era as an exclusive Bostonian summer colony. The beauty of this spot attests to the appreciative eyes of nineteenth-century summer people.

Approaches. From the dredged channel of Isle au Haut Thorofare, round Point Lookout, noting the rocks that make out a long way from Flake Island. From north or west, pass south of Flake Island.

Anchorages, Moorings. Work your way in midway between Birch Point and Point Lookout, anchoring in 10 to 14 feet at low. Holding ground is good. The anchorage is exposed to north and west but fine for summer weather. The stone wharf on Point Lookout is private.

BURNT–PELL PASSAGE

Chart: 13313

Heading east from Isle au Haut, the clearest and best marked passage is between Merchant Island and Hardwood Island, then eastward through Merchant Row, leaving can "9" to starboard.

A more direct route, requiring careful piloting, runs between Burnt Island and Pell Island. The western tip of Burnt has long, sloping shelves of bare rock, behind which hides little Mouse Island. Leaving Burnt and Mouse islands close aboard to starboard, head for the western end of Wheat Island, to avoid the rocks that make out a long way from the southern end of Pell. Wheat Island is low and grassy, with trees on the eastern end. It has a beach near the western tip.

When you are reasonably close to Wheat, turn north and pass between Wheat and Pell into Jericho Bay. Dangerous Channel Rock, close by to the northeast, is covered at high tide and breaks only occasionally, but it is awash eight feet at low.

BURNT ISLAND THOROFARE

Chart: 13313

Burnt Island Thorofare is a rock-strewn passage between Isle au Haut and Burnt Island to the north. While it can be threaded by strangers with care for an hour or two before and after low tide, it would be difficult when the rocks are covered. It is possible to anchor halfway through the Thorofare, but the location is not particularly attractive and the bottom is rocky.

Region 5 / Isle Au Haut to Schoodic
Mount Desert

Kent's Wharf, in Burnt Coat Harbor. (Neal A. Parent photo)

Point

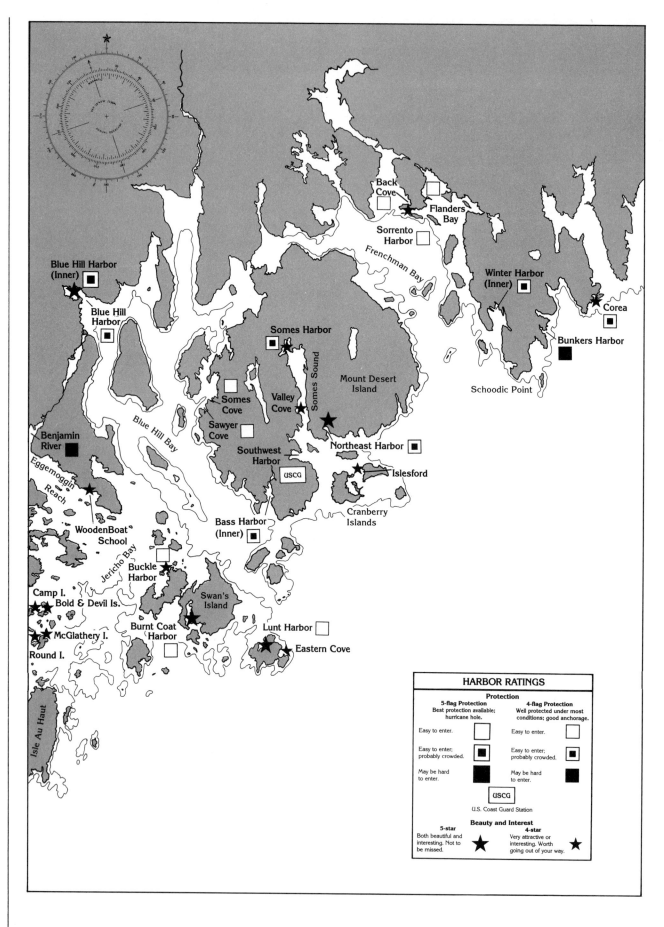

Back Cove

Flanders Bay

Sorrento Harbor

Frenchman Bay

Winter Harbor (Inner)

Corea

Bunkers Harbor

Blue Hill Harbor (Inner)

Blue Hill Harbor

Somes Harbor

Schoodic Point

Somes Cove

Valley Cove

Somes Sound

Mount Desert Island

Sawyer Cove

Southwest Harbor

Northeast Harbor

Benjamin River

Eggemoggin Reach

Blue Hill Bay

USCG

Islesford

Bass Harbor (Inner)

Cranberry Islands

WoodenBoat School

Jericho Bay

Buckle Harbor

Camp I.

Bold & Devil Is.

Swan's Island

Lunt Harbor

McGlathery I.

Round I.

Burnt Coat Harbor

Eastern Cove

Isle Au Haut

HARBOR RATINGS

Protection

5-flag Protection
Best protection available; hurricane hole.

4-flag Protection
Well protected under most conditions; good anchorage.

Easy to enter.

Easy to enter.

Easy to enter; probably crowded.

Easy to enter; probably crowded.

May be hard to enter.

May be hard to enter.

USCG

U.S. Coast Guard Station

Beauty and Interest

5-star
Both beautiful and interesting. Not to be missed.

4-star
Very attractive or interesting. Worth going out of your way.

Here are some of the great cruising grounds of the coast of Maine. The sailor bound east from Penobscot Bay has a variety of routes for entering Jericho Bay on his way to Blue Hill and Mount Desert. Farthest north is the wide, open passage of Eggemoggin Reach. South of Deer Isle, the Thorofare takes you past the fishing town of Stonington and some of the most beautiful islands of the coast. The broader passage of Merchant Row leads south of these same islands. Some sailors pass offshore, south of Isle au Haut; they avoid all complications, but they also miss the best of cruising.

Large, wide open, and mostly deep, Jericho Bay provides a lovely sail. Mount Desert looms high to the northeast, Isle au Haut to the southwest, and Blue Hill to the north, with the Camden Hills still visible to the northwest. In the foreground are the myriad granite-shored islands of Merchants Row.

Swan's Island and Long Island are special among the outlying islands, with delightful harbors, thriving communities, and distinct personalities. Fifteen miles to sea lies lonely Mount Desert Rock, where the adventurous cruising boat may find the great humpback and finback whales.

Through York Narrows, Casco Passage, or Pond Island Passage the route leads to beautiful Blue Hill Bay, with its miles of open waters and snug little coves. At the head of the bay lies the charming town of Blue Hill.

Set like a jewel between Blue Hill Bay and Frenchman Bay is the spectacular island of Mount Desert, whose mountains and dramatic headlands forge the character of the entire region. The most scenic portions of Mount Desert Island have been preserved as part of Acadia National Park, enjoyed each year by millions. There are miles of hiking trails, cliffs and beaches, views from mountain tops, lakes, glacial formations, gardens, museums, and carriage roads. Much of the park can be visited from a cruising boat. Here to be visited as well are the great sailing centers of Southwest Harbor and Northeast Harbor, bustling with boats and boating activity.

On the eastern side of Mount Desert Island, bold granite islands—the Porcupines and Ironbound—rise from the deep waters of Frenchman Bay to guard the gilded town of Bar Harbor, once the playground of the wealthy, whose fabled "cottages" still line the shores. To the east lies the last outpost of fashionable civilization at Winter Harbor, and beyond stands lonely, rugged Schoodic.

MERCHANTS ROW and Deer Island Thorofare, Eastern Coast of Deer Isle, and Eggemoggin Reach

DEER ISLAND THOROFARE

Charts: 13305, 13313, **13315**

Deer Island Thorofare and Merchant Row, running to the north and south respectively of the splendid Merchants Row archipelago, are two of the three major passages from East Penobscot Bay to Jericho Bay. The third major passage, Eggemoggin Reach, will be discussed later in this chapter.

The Thorofare is a narrow, well-marked channel no wider than 100 yards in several places. On the north side is the busy fishing village of Stonington. On the south side are the granite quarries of Crotch Island. Farther south lie some three dozen

spruce-clad islands, largely uninhabited, with the shelving white granite shores characteristic of this area.

The current through Deer Island Thorofare is not very strong, and it is influenced by the wind. With no wind, the tide floods eastward and ebbs westward. With westerly winds, both flood and ebb set eastward. With strong easterlies, both set westward.

Approaches from the West. Emerging from Fox Islands Thorofare in clear weather, you will

The lighthouse on Mark Island, at the western entrance to Deer Island Thorofare and Merchant Row. In the background, Billings Marine is the large building to the left; beyond is Stonington. (Hylander photo)

often find the east side of the bay in fog. Assuming good visibility, however, look for the standpipe north of Stonington and the tall crane, derricks, and granite tailings on Crotch Island. As you cross East Penobscot Bay, Mount Desert will be visible in the distance directly ahead, Blue Hill to the north-northeast, and high Isle au Haut to the southeast.

Approaching the Thorofare, check to make sure you are clear of the Brown Cow, an isolated ledge barely visible at high. At the entrance to the Thorofare is Mark Island, high and wooded, with white granite shores. The lighthouse on Mark Island may be hard to find at first, since it is below the trees.

After passing Mark Island, find green can "23," critical for passage between the outer ledges. Green marks are left to starboard, red marks to port. Thereafter, the passage is easy and well marked.

Approaches from the East. Coming from Casco Passage (north of Swan's Island), the easiest route is north or south of Egg Rock and then between Long Ledge and Potato Ledge, all of which are well marked. The Lazygut Islands, northward of your path, are distinctive—one large wooded island and two small ones to the west, like a dash and two dots. Deer Island Thorofare starts at the green can north of Eastern Mark Island, easily recognizable by the bold, shelving shores on its eastern side. In this direction, green marks are left to port, red marks to starboard.

Anchorages, Moorings. If you are overtaken by fog or darkness on your way through Deer Island Thorofare, there are several alternatives to consider. Anchor in Webb Cove, or among the islands of Merchants Row, or on the north side of the Thorofare. You may also be able to get a mooring or tie up at Billings Marine, on the north side, west of Stonington.

MERCHANT ROW

Charts: 13305, **13313**, 13315

Merchant Row is the southern passage linking East Penobscot Bay and Jericho Bay. Perhaps a little bit longer than Deer Island Thorofare, it is far wider and less obstructed, passing north of Merchant Island and south of most of the islands off Stonington.

The only unmarked danger in the passage is Channel Rock, at the eastern end, awash eight feet at low, but completely submerged at high.

STONINGTON ★★★★

Charts: 13305, 13313, **13315**

Stonington, at the southern tip of Deer Isle, is a working harbor and wants to stay that way. A town ordinance gives commercial fishing boats first choice for moorings; passenger vessels are next in line, and pleasure boats last. It is all very colorful and interesting here: a busy fishing harbor on one side of Deer Island Thorofare, the derricks and granite quarries of Crotch Island operating across the way, and the islands of Merchants Row stretching south toward the blue heights of Isle au Haut.

Although fishing has been part of Stonington's heritage for several hundred years, it was the late-nineteenth-century granite industry that saw the community flourish. Between 1870 and 1925, enormous quantities of granite were produced from quarries here and on Crotch Island. Stone was supplied for several New York City bridges, including the George Washington and the Triboro; for Rockefeller Center; for the Smithsonian Institution; for Boston's Museum of Fine Arts. But just when permanent prosperity seemed to have come to Stonington, the granite industry declined and the quarries closed, returning the town to the fishermen. In the early 1980s, however, new technology spurred the reopening of Crotch Island to quarrying, and granite has once again become competitive as a building material.

Approaches. The approach to Stonington is straightforward from east or west. See the Deer Island Thorofare writeup, above.

Anchorages, Moorings. Consider two possible places to lie for the night. Moorings and dockage are available from Billings Marine, on Moose Island, but here you will be some distance west of the center of town. Usually no moorings are avail-

Aerial view of Stonington Harbor. The opera house, a local landmark, sits on the promontory in the center of the harbor; jutting beyond it is the large, stone commercial fish pier. On the eastern shore of the same cove, next to Atlantic Avenue Hardware, are the floats of the town landing. (Hylander photo)

241

PASSAGES THROUGH DEER ISLAND
THOROFARE AND MERCHANT ROW

(based on Chart 13315)

This chart is for general information only, and NOT TO BE USED FOR NAVIGATION. Location and type of buoys and other navigational aids may change from time to time. Use in conjunction with the text, and the latest Charts, Notices to Mariners, and U.S. Coast Pilot.

Nautical Miles

0   1/2   1

⚓ Anchorages

■ Moorings

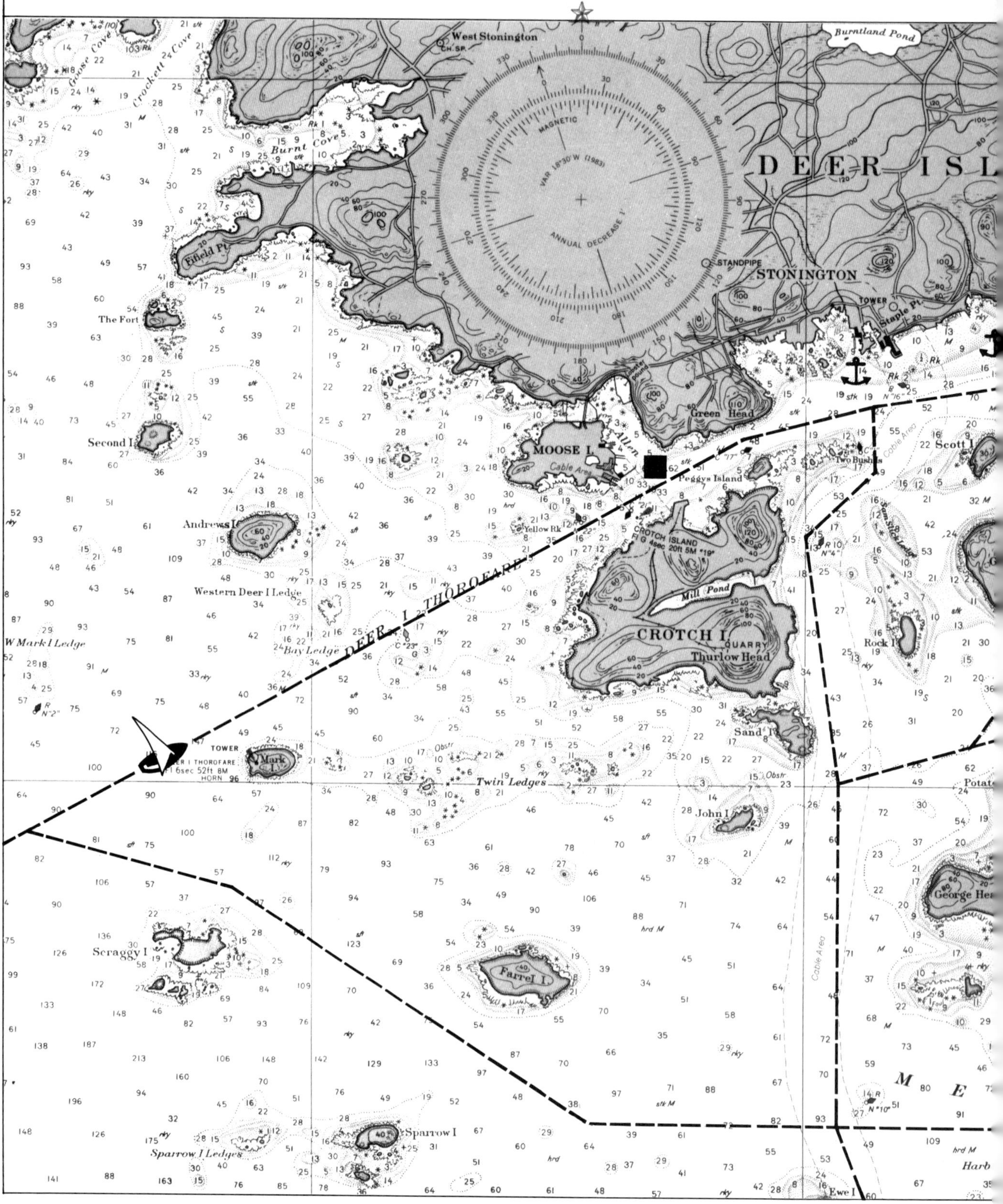

West Stonington

Burntland Pond

D E E R   I S L

STONINGTON

STANDPIPE

TOWER

Staple Pt.

Green Head

MOOSE I.

Peggys Island

Two Bushes

Scott I.

Yellow Rk

CROTCH ISLAND
4 sec 20ft 5M "19"

CROTCH I.

QUARRY
Thurlow Head

Mill Pond

Rock I.

Second I.

Andrews I.

Western Deer I Ledge

W Mark I Ledge

Bay Ledge

DEER I. THOROFARE

Sand I.

TOWER
DEER I THOROFARE
6sec 52ft 8M
HORN

Mark I.

Twin Ledges

Obstr

John I.

George Hea

Scraggy I.

Farrel I.

M E

Sparrow I.

Sparrow I Ledges

Ewe I.

The Fort

Burnt Cove

Fifield Pt

Crockett's Cove

Ghost Cove

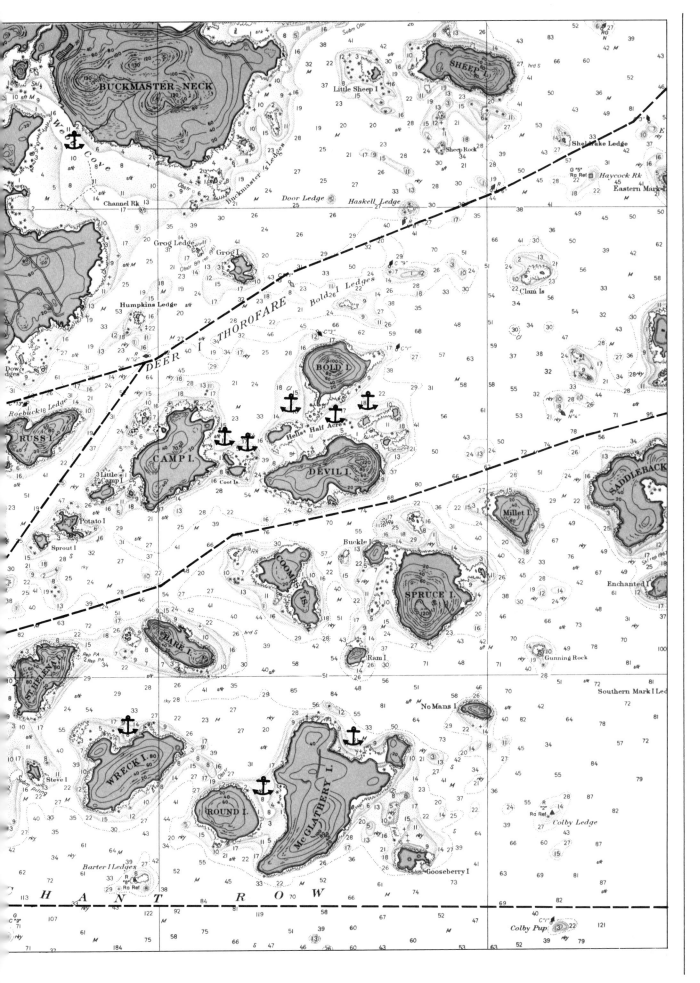

243

able off the town itself, but there is good anchorage on the north side of the Thorofare, west of nun "16" at Staple Point, in 15 to 20 feet of water. This is where the windjammers often lie, and it provides the best access to the public landing and the rest of town.

The waterfront can be confusing. Look for the two little islets with rickety lobster piers, and beyond them the huge sign on the opera house. Below the opera house is a large, stone, commercial fish pier. On the eastern shore of the same cove are the floats of the public landing, and next to it is the red front of Atlantic Avenue Hardware.

Getting Ashore. Take the dinghy in to a float at Billings or to the public landing floats north of the Atlantic Avenue Hardware building.

For the Boat. *Atlantic Avenue Hardware (tel. 367-2369).* The store has ice and marine supplies, including charts.

Billings Diesel & Marine Service (Ch. 16; tel. 367-2328, or 348-6980 nights). Billings is a very large yard with four marine railways capable of handling up to 425 tons, a 35-ton boatlift, and a 20-ton mobile crane. They can make hull and engine repairs of all kinds for wood, fiberglass, steel, and aluminum vessels. There is a large chandlery and an electronics shop.

The fuel float is located north of the large finger pier. At low tide, give the end of the pier a good berth as you enter. Gas, diesel, and ice are available, with five or six feet alongside at low. Stonington water is not good, so plan to fill your tanks elsewhere.

Conary's. At the southeast corner of Green Head, Conary's caters primarily to lobsterboats. It has a fuel float with gas and diesel, and 4½ feet of water off the end at low. Some marine supplies are available.

For the Crew. Next to the fuel dock at Billings are phones, showers, and a laundromat. From the yard, it is a mile in to town, where you will find a bookstore, galleries, post office, pharmacy, and liquor store. About .2 mile farther on is Bartlett's Market. There are several restaurants in town, two of them straight up the road past the opera house, and the Bayview Restaurant farther east. Another good place for dinner (by reservation) is Pilgrim's Inn in Deer Isle (tel. 346-6615). They may be able to pick you up, or you can call a taxi.

At the public landing, you are right in town and next door to Bartlett's Market. There are pay phones, and private parking can be arranged by the day, making it possible for yachtsmen to join a boat here and leave their cars. For a cab, call A-Z Taxi (tel. 348-6186).

Things to Do. Boats leave several times daily for Isle au Haut (tel. 367-5193) from the docks next to Atlantic Avenue Hardware. They take you to Duck Harbor, inside the park, where there are lean-tos and shelters for camping (by reservation only) or great hiking if you just want to spend a few hours. Get in touch with Acadia National Park, Box 177, Bar Harbor, Maine 04609 (tel. 288-3338) for information or reservations.

Daily sightseeing excursions run out of Stonington among the islands and along the coast of Isle au Haut.

To stretch your legs, walk east out of town on Indian Point Road to visit the Lily Pond, about three quarters of a mile each way. Go early, before the lilies close for the day.

MERCHANTS ROW

Charts: 13313, **13315**

Between Deer Isle and Isle au Haut lies an archipelago known as Merchants Row, unsurpassed for beauty anywhere in Maine. There are 30 or 40 of these islands, all darkly wooded and fringed with white and pink sloping granite shores. This is a wonderland of passages and ever-changing vistas through which the yachtsman wanders with delight. Even the names of the islands are evocative: from Sprout and Potato to Enchanted and Grog, from Devil and Hells Half Acre to St. Helena, from Wreck and Round to Bare and Green.

There are old quarries here, and stone wharves. Crotch Island is once again a working quarry, and one of the few places where this fascinating operation can be observed. Most of the islands in Merchants Row are privately owned, but four belong to environmental groups (Wreck, Round, McGlathery, and Russ.)

The most frequently used anchorages are at McGlathery, between Round and McGlathery, between Camp and Bold, between Bold and Devil, and Merchant Harbor. There are many other places to drop the hook for a short time or for the night. The major anchorages are described here; the pleasure of finding the gunkholes is left for you.

You can be dazzled by these islands, wandering among them and distracted by their beauty. The distances are small, and there are lots of hard spots, so keep the chart in hand and keep track of where you are. Save this magnificent cruising ground for a sparkling day; it may be the most beautiful place in the world.

Sidewheeler *Mount Desert* of the Boston-Bangor Steamship Company steaming through Deer Island Thorofare. (Frank Claes Collection)

CROTCH ISLAND

Charts: 13313, **13315**

Ever since the first quarry opened in 1870, Crotch Island has been renowned for the color and workability of its granite. It was Crotch Island's "Sherwood Pink" that Jacqueline Kennedy chose for the president's memorial in Arlington National Cemetery. Now Crotch Island granite is again being shipped from one of the Maine coast's few active quarries to build museums and office buildings in Boston, Washington, and New York.

The original Goss Quarry drew workers to Crotch Island from Scandinavia, Italy, and the British Isles, including skilled workmen who finished and polished the stones right on the island. It was a rough bunch who lived in the barracks of Crotch Island and Stonington. The company store was run by the *padrone*, and even during Prohibition, he imported wine directly from Italy.

In 1983, New England Stone Industries of Smithfield, Rhode Island, reopened the quarries, although the rough stone is shipped away to be cut and polished. There are plans to use the old cutting

shed again, so that granite quarried on Crotch will once more be finished there as well.

Approaches. There are two stone wharves on Crotch Island—one on Deer Island Thorofare and the second on the eastern side at the entrance to the tidal Mill Pond. Granite is shipped from both sites, but the Mill Pond wharf is closer to the active quarry on Thurlow Head.

Coming from the Thorofare, pass east of can "1" off the Two Bush Islands. Then head for Mill Pond, leaving nun "4" to port.

Anchorages, Moorings. There is good anchorage off the entrance to Mill Pond in seven feet of water at low, mud bottom. It is also possible to tie up at the stone wharf itself or alongside the scow used to transport the granite.

Things to Do. The manager of the quarrying operations welcomes visitors but asks that you come only during working hours, when someone is there to show you around.

It is fun to row a dinghy all the way up Mill

Three-masted schooner loading granite at the John L. Goss quarry on Crotch Island in 1908. (Frank Claes Collection)

Think of Maine and you think of granite: pink and white granite from Penobscot Bay, shades of gray from Somes Sound, bright red from Jonesport, rose from Deer Isle.

Granite from Maine built the Library of Congress in Washington, the House of Representatives, and the Treasury Building; it went into the Museum of Fine Arts and Jordan Marsh in Boston, the Customs House in Atlanta, the St. Louis Post Office, Union Station in Chicago, and the Cape Cod Canal. Maine granite was used for the Central Park Reservoir in New York, the Metropolitan Museum, the Brooklyn Bridge, the George Washington Bridge, and Grant's Tomb. Recently, it helped rebuild the Statue of Liberty.

There was soaring granite for the great cathedrals; humble granite for the curbstones and horse troughs of a nation; granite headstones to mark graves and granite blocks to moor boats; granite stones by the millions to pave muddy city streets; granite slabs to sheathe the office buildings of corporate America.

A wonderful substance, this—hard and lasting and beautiful. There may be flecks of shiny mica in it, crystals of quartz, chunks of rosy feldspar, and perhaps black specks of biotite. Granite of different colors and textures can be cut and polished to show an endless variety of patterns.

The largest pieces of granite ever cut in Maine were the huge shafts quarried on Vinalhaven for eight columns at the Cathedral of Saint John the Divine in New York City. In the rough, these shafts were 64 feet long and 8 feet thick, each weighing about 120 tons when put on the lathe. (The heavy columns broke while being finished, and eventually each was made in two separate pieces.)

In most quarries, the granite lies in horizontal sheets several feet thick, with a natural seam called the lift between the layers. The vertical cleavage plane along the grain of the rock is the rift, usually running east and west; the cut across the grain is the hardway. Granite was quarried by drilling a series of vertical holes a few inches apart down to a horizontal seam, packing the

holes with black powder or dynamite, and exploding off large chunks of rock.

The pieces of granite were swung from the quarry face by great derricks and booms. In some quarries, they could be rolled downhill by gravity on rail cars, or they were slung under the eight-foot wheels of galamanders, carriages drawn by teams of horses or oxen, and transported to the cutting sheds for carving and polishing. At the water's edge, the granite was loaded on granite schooners or barges for transportation to the project site.

The glamorous part of the industry supplied stone for famous monuments and buildings, but the tonnage came from paving blocks, hundreds of thousands of them, cut by hand from larger stones. Starting with a block four feet by four feet wide, and perhaps three feet thick, the stonecutter used a 32-pound hammer and chisel to split the stone to a thickness of 18 inches, then 9 inches, then 4½ inches. The final paving block was 4½ by 4 by 12 inches. A good man could cut 500 or more paving blocks in a working day, with clean, straight edges. The record was 786.

Accidents in the quarries were frequent. Sometimes a charge of powder failed to ignite, and a new charge was tamped down right on top of the smouldering embers—a good way to lose a leg or a life. Stonecutters wore no goggles, so stone chips frequently got in their eyes.

Quarrymen working outdoors were not much troubled by granite dust, which blew away with the wind. But it was different for the cutters and polishers, who labored inside sheds choked with deadly granite dust. Silicosis clogged their lungs, and many died young of "consumption," long before the days of workers' compensation.

Sometimes accidents were caused by the inability to communicate. A quarry was a Tower of Babel: Quarrymen and stonecutters and polishers came from everywhere in Europe. They bunked in company barracks (the Shamrock and the Aberdeen on Dix Island could house 500 men apiece) and they bought whatever they needed in the company store. If they had cash left over, they spent it in hard living in Rockland or Stonington. They were a tough and rowdy bunch, these quarrymen, and there was a Wild West atmosphere wherever they were on Saturday nights.

If the workmen in this rough-and-tumble industry were colorful, so were their bosses. One of the pioneers was General Davis Tillson, who returned from the Civil War with only one leg, but with his other faculties intact. He became the dictator of Hurricane Island, and woe to anyone rash enough to cross him. The Italians called him the "Bombasto Furioso."

The granite industry was organized in the decade after the Civil War, starting about 1867. Government contracts for post offices and public buildings were the lifeblood of the industry, with a guaranteed 15 percent profit. By 1877 (when they were declared illegal), the "Granite Ring" had established a monopoly on these lucrative contracts: Bodwell of Vinalhaven, Tillson of Hurricane Island, St. John of Clark Island, and Dixon of Dix Island.

But even during its palmy days, the industry was never a consistent one, dependent as it was on the uncertainties of bidding for each job, and the political pressures involved in the awarding of contracts. No two jobs were alike, so it was impossible to standardize the product or build an inventory between contracts. Granite was susceptible to the periodic booms and busts of the building market. The industry reached its peak quickly and faded out within 50 years, the victim of new materials, competition from other states, and the high cost of shipping.

In recent years, the natural beauty and durability of Maine granite have sparked a new appreciation, after a generation or two of aluminum and glass buildings. New techniques allow granite to be sliced in sheets as thin as a pane of glass—almost a new architectural material. Granite today is moved by large front-load tractors and loaded on barges for shipment. Drilling and dynamite blasting have been replaced by a high-temperature gas torch used to cut a groove in the stone. That's the way it is done these days on Crotch Island, off Stonington. It is a noisy business, and the roar is audible a long way downwind—not very popular with the summer folk who live nearby.

Crotch Island is about the only place you can see a working quarry today on the coast of Maine, but there are lots of old quarries worth visiting. They usually are recognizable by the piles of grout and tailings, and sometimes by great abandoned derricks and booms still in place. A number of old quarries have wonderful freshwater pools where you can swim—for example, Wildcat near Tenants Harbor, Hall Quarry in Somes Sound, several quarries on Vinalhaven near Carvers Harbor, and the quarry in Burnt Coat Harbor on Swan's Island. Let a visit to one of these spots serve as a reminder of an industry that marked the face of Maine yet lasted only one working lifetime.

Pond, passing huge piles of granite blocks near the entrance. The whole north shore of the inlet is strewn with granite rubble, while the south shore remains in its natural state. The current may run strong at mid-tide.

From the eastern anchorage, you can see the tops of the giant derricks and watch the heavy-duty front-loaders piling granite blocks on the wharf for shipment. The dimensions are marked in red on each stone, and it's interesting to speculate on their weights.

RUSS ISLAND

Charts: 13313, **13315**

Just east of Stonington, beautiful Russ Island rises to a height of 100 feet, offering dramatic views of the surrounding islands and shores. The uninhabited island is covered by a mature spruce forest, except for a low saddle across the central portion, which has been cleared as pasture for a small flock of sheep. Russ was quarried for granite, and the remains of two stone wharves may still be seen on the north side.

Russ was acquired by the Island Institute from well-known painter and architect Emily Muir, whose family had owned it for half a century.

The island is open to the public for day use only; this is a lovely place for picnicking and hiking. Don't bring dogs ashore because they are likely to worry the sheep.

There is a small protected cove on the north side, but the usual anchorage is off the sandy beach on the south shore. The anchorage is exposed and recommended only as a day stop.

CAMP ISLAND ★★★★   No facilities
Charts: 13313, **13315**

One of the most pleasant anchorages in Merchants Row is just east of Camp Island, about 1.5 miles east of Stonington. The anchorage is encircled by high, wooded Bold and Devil islands. To the east, Hells Half Acre and the two little Coot Islands add beauty and protection.

Approaches. The easiest approach is from Deer Island Thorofare from the north, between Camp and Bold islands. There is also a nice little backdoor between Devil Island and the Coots that is fun to sail through, favoring the eastern side.

Anchorages, Moorings. The best place to anchor is north of the Coot Islands, which provide protection from the prevailing southwesterlies (about where the 11-foot spot is shown on the chart), or eastward in depths of 17 to 24 feet at low. The bottom is excellent mud holding ground. In choosing your spot, stay well clear of the ledge extending north and east from the Coot Islands.

Boats anchored on the eastern side (toward Hells Half Acre) do not have the full protection of the Coot Islands. You will be perfectly comfortable under normal conditions, but in a strong southwesterly you will be exposed to the wind through the slot between Devil and the Coot Islands, and you may drag.

Things to Do. It's fun to explore the bold, ledgy shores of beautiful Hells Half Acre, which is state-owned. Camp and Devil islands are private.

BOLD and DEVIL ISLANDS ★★★★   No facilities
Charts: 13313, **13315**

About two miles east of Stonington, the tongue of deep water between Bold and Devil islands offers a fine anchorage. Eastward is the distant skyline of Mount Desert and all around are the beautiful spruce and granite islands of Merchants Row.

Approaches. From Deer Island Thorofare, the approach is close northward of Bold Island, leaving cans "3" and "1" to starboard and leaving to port Bold Island Ledges, a spot favored by seals. After rounding can "1" off the eastern tip of Bold, head into the slot between Bold and Devil. Note the two islets to port, the easternmost of which is smooth ledge with a clump of conifers; the westerly one is

grassy on top. To starboard, note the ledges coming down from Bold Island, tiny scraps of which are visible at all tides.

Anchorages, Moorings. Protection and the views are better in the eastern end of the anchorage, and the holding ground is good, in mud. A strong southwesterly will funnel through between Devil and Hells Half Acre.

Things to Do. Explore the islets east of Devil Island and state-owned Hells Half Acre. The smooth granite ledges are beautiful, and the clamming reputedly is good.

McGLATHERY ISLAND ★★★★   No facilities
Charts: 13313, **13315**

Probably the best-known anchorage in Merchants Row is at McGlathery Island, one of the largest in the group. Windjammers use it often, as do cruising yachtsmen. The island is owned by a conservation group called Friends of Nature. There are beautiful granite ledges and a sandy bar leading to a small offlying island. Ashore you might meet the woolliest of wild sheep.

Approaches. The anchorage is at the northern end of McGlathery. Approach from the north. The

little, wooded, unnamed island at the northeastern tip of McGlathery is conspicuous by a sloping ledge at its northern end on which rests a large boulder. No Mans Island to the east is small and wooded, with a long, sloping ledge at the western end.

Anchorages, Moorings. A large, conical rock at the edge of the trees, with a sandy, boulder-strewn beach below it, marks the eastern end of the anchorage. Come just inside the northern knob of McGlathery and anchor west of the conical rock in

248

21 feet at low, mud bottom. Protection is good except from the northeast.

Things to Do. Take a swim off the beach on sun-warmed ledges. Go across the sandbar to the adjoining little island and walk around it on the high ledges overlooking the sea (mostly easy going, with just an occasional leap across a chasm). On McGlathery, trails lead inland to where you may meet the sheep, which are likely to be just as startled as you are.

Because so many people use this lovely island, driftwood is scarce, and someone always seems to have found the raspberries first. Show your appreciation for the efforts of the Friends of Nature by leaving McGlathery cleaner than you found it.

ROUND ISLAND ★★★★
Charts: 13313, **13315**

No facilities

Between McGlathery Island and its neighbor to the west, Round Island, a Nature Conservancy preserve, is a delightful anchorage. There are views past the island to Stonington and a glimpse southward of high Isle au Haut.

Approaches. Coast down the western shore of McGlathery Island until you come to the bump of land that extends westward.

Anchorages, Moorings. Opposite the bump of land, anchor halfway between Round Island and McGlathery, in 10 feet at low, mud bottom. Protection is reasonably good, although a strong southwester will funnel through.

Things to Do. From the anchorage, you can land conveniently on the beach at McGlathery or on the beach on the eastern tip of Round Island to explore these preserves, both open to the public. Because Round Island is so heavily wooded, you probably will want to stick to the shoreline. No fires or camping are permitted.

WRECK ISLAND ★★★★
Charts: 13313, **13315**

No facilities

Just west of Round Island, Wreck also is a Nature Conservancy preserve. It has the great advantage, however, of being partially open. Much of the interior is grassy fields with patches of raspberries.

Approaches. The easiest approach is from the east, south of distinctive Bare Island, its western end marked by sloping granite outcroppings interspersed with tufts of grass. At its eastern end are a house and dock. Neighboring St. Helena Island has large, open spaces with granite monoliths and an unobtrusive house and stone dock on the south shore.

Anchorages, Moorings. While it is possible to anchor off the eastern end of Wreck and land on the nearby beaches, the best protection is on the north side. Drop the hook where Chart 13315 shows 9 to 14 feet of water, east of the large knob of land on the north side of the island. The anchorage is small, but the holding ground is good mud.

Things to Do. The eastern half of Wreck Island was kept open by a century of grazing, and sheep were reintroduced by the U.S. Forest Service in 1980 to maintain this open quality. As you explore, be careful of the old fencing and cellar holes, which are the only remaining evidence of the several farm families who lived on Wreck. You may meet some timid sheep. No dogs, camping, or fires are allowed.

Aerial view over Merchants Row, looking east toward Swan's Island. With its darkly wooded islands and shelving granite shores, this archipelago is unsurpassed for beauty anywhere in Maine. Moving clockwise from Green Island (left foreground), the large islands are Sprout, Potato, Camp, Devil, Saddleback and Millet (appearing to merge), Spruce, the two Coombs (appearing to merge), and Bare. (Hylander photo)

MERCHANT HARBOR ★★★★

 No facilities

Charts: 13305, 13313

One of the best and most attractive anchorages in the area is Merchant Harbor, on the north side of Merchant Island. Harbor Island, with beautiful, open meadows and conifers, protects the anchorage from the north and adds a sense of serenity and security. A private dock and float are at the head of the harbor, along with a few small craft on moorings.

Approaches. The approach is easy from east or west, following the marked channel of Merchant Row. As you enter, stay reasonably close to the Harbor Island side to avoid the 4½-foot spot shown on the chart.

Anchorages, Moorings. In good weather, anchor past Harbor Island toward the head of the harbor in 16 feet at low. If winds from the north are expected, anchor in the lee of Harbor Island in 27 feet at low. Protection is excellent from west to south. The bottom apparently is rocky.

Things to Do. State-owned Harbor Island has a pleasing combination of trees and raspberry thickets, open meadows and ledges.

SOUTHWEST COVE ★★★

 No facilities

Charts: 13305, 13313

On the southwest side of Merchant Island is a lovely little cove exposed to prevailing southwesterly winds but offering excellent protection if the wind is in the north or east. There is a gravel beach at the head of the cove, and a house or two set well back into the trees. A couple of decades ago, fire swept the forest on the southern shore, but the new growth is coming nicely. The cove is private, and visitors are not welcome ashore.

Approaches. From the north, run along the cable area shown on the chart, starting west of nun "10" and leaving Ewe and Hardwood islands to starboard. Both of these islands are heavily wooded, with sloping granite ledges. Find can "1" at the eight-foot spot off Merchant Island and enter the cove north of the can. Favor the south side of the entrance, which is all sloping ledge, to avoid the rocks on the north side of the entrance, visible two hours before low.

Anchorages, Moorings. Anchor all the way up in the pool at the head of the cove, in 12 to 13 feet at low. The bottom is mud and grass.

EASTERN COAST OF DEER ISLE

WEBB COVE ★★★

3 (outer cove)   4 (inner cove)   No facilities

Charts: 13305, 13313, **13315**

On the southeastern side of Deer Isle, Webb Cove is a sizable bay protected to the north by Buckmaster Neck. Anchorage is good and protection reasonable in the outer portion of the cove. Protection is better in the inner section, although this is a bit ticklish to enter. The smooth dome of granite that forms the southwest height of Buckmaster Neck was named Settlement Quarry.

Approaches. From Deer Island Thorofare, pass west of Humpkins Ledge, or between Humpkins Ledge and Grog Island. Identify Channel Rock in the middle of the entrance (two separate rocks), passing to either side. Then head straight for the quarry derricks and dock.

Anchorages, Moorings. Anchor south or west of the granite quarry dock in 10 to 11 feet at low, mud bottom. Exposure here is only to the southeast.

To enter the inner harbor, stay close to the quarry dock and make a gradual turn to port, running about halfway between the peninsula of Deer Isle to the south and the little island to the north, using the mooring stakes as your guide. The deep water is narrow and the rocks shown on the chart hard to locate. Enter cautiously.

Anchor in 9 to 10 feet at low in soft mud bottom. A stern anchor may be advisable. Here you will be landlocked in all directions except for a very small opening to the southeast.

Getting Ashore. Take your dinghy in to the float off the quarry dock.

Things to Do. Settlement Quarry is interesting to explore. Equipment and great, smooth slabs of stone were left behind when the quarry closed.

PICKERING COVE ★★★

 No facilities

Charts: **13313**, 13316

On the east side of Deer Isle, south of Stinson Neck, lie several coves that offer pleasant sailing in a little-used area. There are some interesting gunkholes in the deeper recesses. Just east of the entrance to Southeast Harbor, Pickering Cove is formed by Freese Island and a smaller peninsula of Deer Isle. The anchorage is peaceful and attractive, easy to enter, and provides good protection except to the southeast.

Approaches. As you approach from Deer Island Thorofare, you will pass the internationally known Haystack Mountain School of Crafts in Western Cove on Stinson Neck. Billings Cove and the bay west of Stinson Neck offer good anchorages and a pleasing shoreline, but they are too wide open for overnight protection. Pickering Cove, to the west, is more secure.

The rocks outside the southwestern corner of the entrance are visible two or three feet above water at high tide. Run up the middle of the cove toward the hunk of rock crowned by trees at the head of the deep water. On the mainland behind this little island are several houses.

Anchorages, Moorings. Anchor anywhere up to the island itself in 14 to 15 feet at low, good mud holding ground.

SOUTHEAST HARBOR ★★★

 No facilities

Charts: **13313**, 13316

On the east side of Deer Isle, tucked deep inside Stinson Neck and Whitmore Neck, Southeast Harbor provides excellent protection in an attractive setting.

Approaches. The entrance to Southeast Harbor, north of Whitmore Neck, is easier than it appears on the chart. Pass north of the rocks in midchannel, favoring the north side, through a channel that is roughly 75 yards wide and 40 feet deep at low water. Part of the midchannel rock is visible at all tides.

Anchorages, Moorings. Continue heading westward and anchor in the basin northeast of Warren Point, in 22 to 30 feet at low.

INNER HARBOR (Southeast Harbor) ★★★

 No facilities

Charts: 13313, 13316

West of Whitmore Neck on Deer Isle and south of Warren Point, Inner Harbor is a challenging gunkhole that offers good protection but not much swinging room.

Approaches. Because of the narrow channel and generous supply of rocks, Inner Harbor is easiest to enter near low tide.

First observe the line of rocks running north from Whitmore Neck, which should be left to port. The second important guidepost is the tiny island with a cluster of spruces (next to the "H" in "Inner Harbor" on chart 13313), also left to port. Some of the shoal areas are marked by stakes.

Anchorages, Moorings. Anchor outside the moored lobsterboats in 16 to 18 feet at low.

DEEP HOLE ★★

No facilities

Charts: 13313, 13316

North of Warren Point on Deer Isle is a small, wooded island on the west side of the arm of water leading to Deep Hole. Tucked in behind the island is a cluster of sailboats used by the Deer Isle Sailing Center, whose dock and float are on the opposite shore.

Approaches. Stay in midchannel, leaving a ledge to starboard and rounding the little island to port.

Anchorages, Moorings. Anchor north and west of the island in midchannel, in 15 to 20 feet at low. Protection is good, but there is usually one or two knots of current.

Things to Do. Use your dinghy to explore northward into intriguing Deep Hole. Author-sailor Roger Taylor reports that he once lowered a leadline here, and it really is 102 feet deep.

GREENLAW COVE

Charts: 13313, 13316

The long arm of Greenlaw Cove, at the northeastern corner of Deer Isle, looks intriguing on the chart, but has little to offer by way of scenic beauty or interest.

You can find good protection and anchorage in nine feet of water, mud bottom, between Oak Point and Campbell Island.

EGGEMOGGIN REACH

Charts: **13309**, 13313, **13316**

Eggemoggin Reach is a great body of water connecting East Penobscot Bay with Jericho Bay, between Deer Isle and the mainland. It is about 10 miles long and averages a mile in width. With summer winds, it can provide an exhilarating sail in either direction. As Robert Carter wrote in 1858, "There cannot be a finer sheet of water in the world than this Reach, which is bounded on every side by superb views."

While there are a number of ledges in the Reach, these are all well buoyed. The fixed suspension bridge connecting Little Deer Isle to the mainland is a graceful green structure with a vertical clearance of 85 feet at the center. Current floods northwest in the Reach and ebbs southeast, but it is not very strong.

Winds sometimes funnel unexpectedly down the Reach, so be cautious on gusty days. In September 1984, the 65-foot schooner *Isaac H. Evans* was knocked down by squally winds just south of Grays Point near Bucks Harbor, at the western end of the Reach. She sank in 60 feet of water, showing only the tip of her mainmast and the peak of her gaff. Most of the passengers and crew swam ashore and the rest were saved by local rescue groups.

The western end of the Reach is marked by red-and-white bell "EG," and by the handsome abandoned lighthouse on Pumpkin Island, now privately owned.

The banks of Eggemoggin Reach are wooded, with mostly deciduous trees. There is a definite feeling of arrival in some new and mysterious place as you approach the islands at the eastern end, crowned with dark conifers. Here the channel passes south of the Torrey Islands. The ledge at Torrey Castle is marked with red beacon "10" and with a distinctive metal tripod. At the eastern end of Eggemoggin Reach is red-and-white bell "EE."

There are a few good harbors along the Reach. By far the best and easiest to enter is Bucks Harbor, at the western end (described earlier, in Region 4). Another good refuge is Center Harbor, near the Torrey Islands, although it is small and crowded. The Benjamin River, east of the bridge, offers extremely good protection. *WoodenBoat* magazine and the WoodenBoat School, at the eastern end of the Reach, welcome visitors and provide guest moorings.

BILLINGS COVE ★★ No facilities

Charts: 13309, 13316

On the north side of Eggemoggin Reach, just east of the bridge, Billings Cove is easy to find, easy to enter, and protected except from the south and southeast. Other nearby harbors, however, have more to offer.

Approaches. Nun "20" marks the western edge of the entrance and nun "18" the eastern end. Go down the middle of the cove.

Anchorages, Moorings. Anchor in 10 to 20 feet at low on the midline of the cove.

BENJAMIN RIVER ★★

Chart: 13316

Benjamin River is a remarkable, 50-foot deep hole surrounded by mussel flats and guarded by an awesome ledge. Once inside, there is excellent anchorage and protection.

Approaches. The key to entering Benjamin River is the long, low ledge making out from the east shore almost all the way across the channel, leaving an entrance about 100 yards wide. Two

The suspension bridge over Eggemoggin Reach, looking south toward Little Deer Isle. (Hylander photo)

nuns and a can placed in recent years make the entrance relatively easy, but don't cut sharply around the last red nun. Even at dead low, you can't see the end of the ledge, which extends under water an additional 40 feet or so.

Here is the old rule of thumb used by local sailors when the channel was unbuoyed. Just as you enter from the Reach, you will see on your right a whitish rock slab climbing up into the trees on shore. Run a straight line from the slab of rock to the landward end of the town dock, and it will clear the ledge that obstructs the entrance. The town dock is shown on the chart on the west side of the cove.

Anchorages, Moorings. Benjamin River Marine has moorings available. There usually is plenty of room to anchor in 7 to 18 feet at low along the eastern side of the cove. Holding ground is excellent, in mud. The cove provides protection in every direction except SSW, and the ledge at the entrance prevents most seas from entering.

Getting Ashore. Land at the Sedgwick town dock, on the west side of the harbor, or—except at the lowest tides—at the Benjamin River Marine float.

For the Boat. *Benjamin River Marine (tel. 359-2244).* This small, serious repair yard has expanded its facilities on the east side of the cove. The yard hauls boats on a marine railway, and provides storage and limited marine supplies. No fuel is available. There is water and electricity at the float, which dries out at extreme low tides.

For the Crew. The nearest provisions are in Sedgwick, about 1.5 miles from either the town dock or the boatyard. You probably can hitch a ride. There you will find the post office and the Sedgwick General Store, with groceries, deli sandwiches, beer, and a good wine selection. When the tide is reasonably high, it's possible to reach the store (light brown house, with a dormer) by rowing up the river and landing in the backyard.

CENTER HARBOR ★★★

Chart: 13316

Near the eastern end of Eggemoggin Reach, north of the Torrey Islands, Center Harbor is an idyllic little place full of boats, with room for just one boatyard and a yacht club. The harbor is bounded on the south by Chatto Island, with its rock ledges. There is a fleet of lovely gaff-rigged Beetle Cats at the entrance; the bigger boats are moored inside.

Approaches. Leave to starboard nun "2," off the rocky shore of Chatto Island (it's hard to see), and leave to port green daybeacon "3," which stands on a rock in the harbor.

Anchorages, Moorings. You can anchor outside the moored boats in about 16 feet at low, but there is probably no room for anchoring inside the harbor. The Center Harbor Yacht Club has a mooring for overnight visitors, and the Brooklin Boatyard has a number of rental moorings. Protection in the harbor is good except from the northwest.

Getting Ashore. Row in to the dinghy dock at the Brooklin Boatyard or at the Center Harbor Yacht Club. The yard is closer to the market.

For the Boat. *Brooklin Boatyard (tel. 359-2236).* Located at the eastern end of the harbor, the yard is owned by Joel and Steve White who design and build wooden boats ranging from a 50-foot power yacht to the 7½-foot Nutshell pram, made for *WoodenBoat* magazine in kit form. The yard has two marine railways and a 25-ton boatlift and can handle most repairs. There is water at the float, with four to five feet alongside at low, but no fuel.

Center Harbor Yacht Club (tel. 359-8868—pay phone). Near the entrance to the harbor on the north shore, you will see the dark red building with a gray roof, flagpole, dock, and floats of the CHYC. Water can be obtained at the floats, with four feet alongside at low.

For the Crew. From the boatyard, walk up to the main road and turn right. It's .7 mile to the Brooklin General Store (which will give you a ride with the groceries), the Morning Moon Cafe, and the post office.

WOODENBOAT SCHOOL ★★★★

Chart: 13316

Near the eastern end of Eggemoggin Reach, on the north side, is the rambling, whitewashed-brick estate that serves as the headquarters of *WoodenBoat* magazine. On the grounds nearby are the large, red-brick stables housing the WoodenBoat School of Boatbuilding. There are some moorings out front, and visitors are welcome.

WoodenBoat magazine was founded on a shoestring in 1974 by Jon Wilson. Against all odds, including a disastrous fire, this seductive magazine became the bellwether of a resurgent interest in wooden boats. In 1985, it passed the astonishing circulation of 100,000—almost as high as the large yachting publications—and has continued to grow.

The associated summer school provides short courses in boatbuilding skills of all kinds, bringing in as instructors master boatbuilders, surveyors, and sailmakers. The atmosphere in the school is a wonderful blend of woodshavings, modern epoxy glues, practical work, and fun. Stop here for a visit if you want to learn about wooden boats or simply watch how these beautiful objects are built. The school also offers courses on the water, teaching seamanship in a variety of traditional craft, from schooners to Friendship sloops and small open boats. For more information about the school, call 359-4651.

Approaches. The WoodenBoat dock is located north of Babson Island. There is an old green and gray boathouse with a fieldstone base at the head of the dock. The approach may be made either west or east of the two Babson Islands. Note small Shoofly Ledge between the Babsons, to the north. This ledge is just about covered at high tide, and seals like to haul out here.

Anchorages, Moorings. Come in to the float and check with the school to see whether a suitable mooring is available, or you can anchor nearby in 10 to 12 feet at low, in good mud holding ground. When it blows hard from the south or southeast the anchorage will be very lumpy.

Getting Ashore. Row in to the dinghy float and walk up the dock past the green boathouse.

For the Boat. *Center Harbor Sails (tel. 359-2003).* This sailmaker is in the loft of the brick school building.

For the Crew. There is a pay phone at the school and a small store displaying publications. It's a 1.5-mile walk to Brooklin, which has a post office, general store, and the Morning Moon Cafe.

NASKEAG HARBOR ★★ 3️⃣

No facilities

Chart: 13316

At the very eastern end of Eggemoggin Reach, Naskeag Harbor shelters a small fleet of fishing boats but is not very useful for cruising yachts. A bar running most of the way from the mainland to Harbor Island separates Naskeag into eastern and western parts. The fishing boats are moored in the eastern part; there is room to anchor outside the moored boats in 15 to 20 feet at low, but the bottom is rocky and holding ground uncertain.

The portion of Naskeag Harbor west of the bar is difficult to enter because of the unmarked Triangles, which block the center of the harbor and are invisible even at low tide.

CASCO PASSAGE
and YORK NARROWS

Charts: 13313, **13315** (Inset), 13316

Casco Passage joins Jericho Bay and Blue Hill Bay north of Swan's Island. From Jericho Bay, the islands north of the passage (Johns, Opechee, and Black) are low and dark against the background of Mount Desert. The opening between Swan's and Black is visible a long way.

The northern channel of Casco Passage is almost a straight shot, and a bit easier than the southern fork, called York Narrows. Running from west to east, leave red marks to port, green marks to starboard. The current through the passage ebbs west and floods east with considerable force.

Starting at red bell "8," the York Narrows passage is deep but narrow and turns sharply north at Orono Island. Be sure to find green beacon "1A," marking a separate little treeless island and ledge north of Orono. York Narrows is one of the approaches to Buckle Harbor and to Mackerel Cove on Swan's Island.

OPECHEE ISLAND ★★★ 2️⃣

No facilities

Charts: 13312, **13313**, **13316**

At the southwest corner of Blue Hill Bay, north of Casco Passage, there is a small archipelago whose principal islands are Black, Pond, and Opechee. East of Opechee lies a very pretty little anchorage surrounded by wooded islands, with views of Mount Desert and Isle au Haut.

Approaches. Approaching from Blue Hill Bay, Pond Island is clearly separated from the others of the group, while Black and Opechee merge at a distance. There is a rocky promontory near the north tip of Black. Enter the anchorage north of Black Island, leaving Eagle and Sheep to starboard. Small Eagle Island is entirely wooded, while Sheep Island beyond it has been cleared. Head for a sloping granite shelf on the eastern shore of Opechee.

Anchorages, Moorings. Anchor in the large nine-foot area shown on the chart, about equidistant from Black, Sheep, and Opechee islands. The ledges between Black and Opechee break the seas even at high tide, but the anchorage is exposed to winds from several directions.

SWAN'S ISLAND

Charts: 13312, **13313**, 13315 (Inset)

Although served by several daily ferry trips from the mainland at Bass Harbor, Swan's Island is still remote, with few of the mainland amenities normally taken for granted. There are only one or two stores, no liquor sales, and no amusements except those the islanders make for themselves. The pace is slow—and Swan's Islanders like it that way. The year-round population is about 350 people; it triples in the summertime. Fishing, however, is still the main occupation. In recent years, several real estate developments on Swan's Island have brought controversy; change may be coming to the island.

Swan's, a large island of some 7,000 acres, has a highly irregular shoreline that provides secure and interesting anchorages. It is hilly, but not particularly high. There is a quarry for swimming, and places to visit on foot or bicycle. The island has three little villages: Atlantic in Mackerel Cove on the north coast, where the ferry comes in; Minturn and Swan's Island, on the shores of Burnt Coat Harbor in the south. Burnt Coat is the best harbor and has the most facilities; Mackerel Cove is also a good harbor but has fewer facilities; Buckle Harbor, on the northwest coast, is an attractive and secure little anchorage.

It must have been a dry year in 1603; perhaps lightning started a fire in the forests of Swan's Is-

SALMON AQUACULTURE

The first 10,000 salmon being transferred from a truck aboard the ferry *Everett Libby* to a fish pen off Swan's Island. The pens are now moored in Toothacher Cove. (Peter Ralston photo)

Salmon have always been prized as a delicacy. Returning from the ocean and fighting their way up ancestral rivers to spawn, they are hunted by eagles and bears and fishermen.

Salmon raised in pens taste wonderful, too.

For decades now, salmon have been raised all over the world, from Chile to Japan, from Ireland to Iceland. Norway is the world's leading exporter. Canadian researchers successfully raised salmon off Deer Island in 1974, and salmon aquaculture rapidly became a major enterprise. By 1988, the industry in New Brunswick was producing more dollars than the province's traditional fisheries.

To encourage the development of aquaculture, Maine passed a law in 1973 providing for the exclusive leasing of bottom acreage. Oysters, mussels, coho salmon, and rainbow trout were among the early aquaculture crops. Yet there was strong resistance among fishermen, and still is. As one of them puts it, "Most fishermen I know don't want to be farmers."

Lobstermen complain that good lobstering bottom is being taken away. Others worry about the spread of disease from the farmed fish to salmon in the wild, and about genetic intermingling. The introduction of antibiotics in fish feed is hotly debated for its effect on other species. There is fear of the build-up of feces and feed under the cages, and of the degradation of water quality. There are complaints by summer people about fish pens spoiling the view and reducing land values, and concerns about interference with navigation.

So Maine joined very late in the game. The overtures of a Norwegian company were rejected by Vinalhaven in 1987, but the following year Swan's Island fishermen entered a joint venture with an American company to raise salmon in Toothacher Cove. Now fish pens have appeared in a number of other Maine locations, including Cobscook Bay, Eastport, Cutler, and Cross Island.

Fry raised in freshwater hatcheries undergo changes that prepare them to enter salt water, a process known as "smoltification." The smolt, or juvenile salmon, are about five inches long when they are introduced to their saltwater pens, where they swim around endlessly, occasionally breaking the surface in a flash of spray.

Growing salmon is an art. Mussels may be encouraged to grow in the cages to filter the water. Antibiotics may be added to the feed, innoculated directly, or avoided altogether. The feed may be various mixtures of fish meal, krill to provide pinkness, plus vitamins and other additives. For the 18 to 24 months it takes to grow the fish to market size (four to 12 pounds), it's all expense and risk for the fishermen. The salmon are fed two or three times a day, tons of fish meal daily for large operations. The rule of thumb says that two pounds of feed produces one pound of fish and one pound of waste.

Small, individually owned fish farms typically include one or two round pens, 30 feet in diameter, each containing a few thousand salmon. Large corporate operations might consist of 16 to 64 pens, great rectangular rafts moored to the bottom, with 100,000 or more fish.

Divers keep careful watch of the bottom under salmon pens, monitoring any build-up of wastes and checking for "morts," fish that have died from natural causes or been killed by predators such as seals. Water temperatures in winter are critically important. When it falls just below 32 degrees Fahrenheit— "super-chill" conditions—ice crystals form in the tissues of the salmon and they die in great numbers. Swan's Island lost 30 percent of its crop the first winter.

Finally, when the fishermen judge that it is time to bring the fish to market, the salmon are bled in the water, chilled, eviscerated, and packed in ice for shipment.

Maine already grows three million pounds of salmon a year, worth $10 million. This is a tiny share of the world's total catch, and small compared with annual lobster landings in Maine of $60 million. It may be a while before a salmon replaces the lobster on Maine's license plates, but that day is coming. With its clean waters, protected coves, and great tides, the coast of Maine is an ideal place for salmon aquaculture.

land. When French explorer Samuel de Champlain visited the area in 1604, the story goes, he named it "Brûle Côte," meaning "burnt coast." This later was anglicized to Burnt Coat.

Thomas Kench, the first white settler, came to Burnt Coat in 1786 and lived as a hermit for 14 years, followed by "King David" Smith, who built his cabin on the same islet in Burnt Coat Harbor. Smith was not of hermit stock; he and his three wives produced and raised some two dozen children, practically populating Swan's by themselves.

The same year that Thomas Kench took up residence, a colorful land speculator named Colonel James Swan bought the island from the Commonwealth of Massachusetts, together with a group of other nearby islands. Swan had participated in the Boston Tea Party and was wounded at Bunker Hill. This bright and energetic young man was noticed early by those in power, and he moved easily among the leaders of the day. George Washington was a friend, and so was Lafayette. Swan's portrait was painted by Gilbert Stuart. With inherited money, Swan became a speculator on a grand

scale, buying up land confiscated from the Tories and also commissioning privateers. The "Burnt Coat Group" of islands, which included Swan's was to become "an island empire," and indeed, an enormous mansion was built on the island as his headquarters. To populate his empire, Swan offered 100 acres to any homesteader who stayed seven years.

In 1788, Swan's speculations turned sour. He escaped his creditors by moving to France, where his fortunes rose again until he was charged with embezzlement and thrown into debtor's prison. Although he could have paid his debts and regained his freedom, Swan chose to protest his innocence and spent 22 years in a Paris jail, where he died in 1830. Swan never lived in the mansion built for him on the island.

Since 1986, honoring their island's bicentennial, Swan's Islanders have made a deliberate effort—in defiance of the nautical charts and the U.S. Postal Service—to restore the grammatically and historically correct apostrophe to the name Swans—a fitting tribute to their colorful founding father.

BUCKLE HARBOR ★★★★   No facilities

Charts: 13312, 13313, **13315** (Inset)

An easy place to stop on your way east or west, Buckle Harbor, at the northwest corner of Swan's Island, is lovely and unspoiled. Not far away is the spectacular skyline of Mount Desert, and a procession of boats on their way through York Narrows passes the harbor entrance.

Approaches. Enter Buckle Harbor between cans "7" and "5" of York Narrows, turning southward along the eastern shore of Buckle Island. Al-

low for the current, which floods east and ebbs west through the narrows.

Anchorages, Moorings. Anchor off the east shore of Buckle Island in seven to nine feet at low. Holding ground is good, in mud. The harbor provides protection all around except from the north and northeast.

Getting Ashore. Take your dinghy in to any of the little beaches on Buckle Island.

MACKEREL COVE ★★★

Charts: 13312, **13313**, 13315 (Inset)

Mackerel Cove is a large bay in the north side of Swan's Island. The ferry from Bass Harbor docks here just east of can "3," and the tiny fishing community of Atlantic is in the southeast corner. The cove is large enough to handle the New York Yacht Club cruise fleet with space left over, and it offers good protection, particularly in the anchorages east and west of Roderick Head.

Approaches. From the north, the approach is wide and easy, starting at the gong at North Point, left to port, and observing the nun off the ledge at Crow Island.

Mackerel Cove may also be entered from the west. From York Narrows (inset on chart 13315), turn sharply to starboard after passing Buckle Har-

bor and green can "5." There is ample room between Swan's Island and Orono Island, which is marked by a granite wharf at the southern end. This is a remarkably pretty passage through which the current floods eastward and ebbs westward. After passing Orono Island and the two islets to starboard, continue along the shore of Swan's, with its sloping granite slabs, and leave nun "4" close aboard to port. The outermost of the two islets south of nun "4" is low and bare; the inner one is wooded.

The key to Mackerel Cove is the enormous ledge off Roderick Head. At high tide, only a tiny portion is visible. This ledge extends a long way east and southwest of this visible rock, as you will observe at low. Boats frequently underestimate the extent of the ledge and anchor too close for comfortable swinging, or actually find it with their keels. Anchor a long way from the ledge, just to be sure. There is room to pass between the ledge and Roderick Head; however, a nasty rock is reported about 250 feet offshore on a line between Roderick Head and the ledge. Proceed with caution about midway between the two, but avoid the passage altogether within two hours either side of low.

Anchorages, Moorings. There are several places to anchor in Mackerel Cove, all with good holding ground and beautiful views of Mount Desert Island. When a large fleet is in, they usually cluster west and south of can "3," but the protection is better farther south, on either side of Roderick Head. The anchorage east of Roderick Head is small and unobstructed. Anchor in 7 to 10 feet at low.

West of Roderick Head, the first small ledge on the east side is visible until about halftide. Deep water extends southward to a tiny islet that has two tanks on top of it, and there are small craft moored in the shoal cove beyond. Anchor in 15 feet at low.

It is also possible to anchor east of can "3," along the shoreline south of the ferry landing, in 10 to 13 feet at low, but the protection is not as good.

Getting Ashore. The public landing and float are on the south side of the ferry terminal, with good water alongside. Yachts often make crew changes here.

For the Crew. There is a pay phone at the ferry terminal and a modicum of civilization in the village of Atlantic—about a 20-minute walk. Follow the ferry road to its intersection with the main road: Left and left again will put you on the Atlantic loop road, where you will find a laundromat, takeout, the island's biweekly clinic at Atlantic Apartments (clinic schedule is posted at the ferry terminal), and the Atlantic post office. Right at the intersection will bring you to the village center and Seaside Hall (see below). The nearest groceries are in the village of Minturn, at Burnt Coat Harbor, a three-mile walk. (At high tide, from an anchorage east of Roderick Head, there's a shortcut. Take your

LOBSTERS AND LOBSTERING

Lobsterboat in the fog. (Neal A. Parent photo)

The history of Maine lobsters starts with James Rosier, who chronicled the Waymouth expedition of 1605. Near Burnt Island in Muscongus Bay, Rosier reports, "With a small net . . . very nigh the shore, we got about thirty very good and great Lobsters." It was child's play, in the old days. Haul a net, or lean over the side of the boat and gaff the lobsters in shallow water. Or wade along the shore and catch them with your hands, as the Indians did.

Four-foot lobsters were not at all uncommon, and they came larger. Robert Carter in 1858 dropped a hook over the side in Pulpit Harbor, got it tangled in the tail of a lobster, and pulled in a 12-pounder. In some places storms would drive ashore windrows of lobsters, which were used to fertilize the fields.

For a long time there was no lobster industry, because anyone could catch all he wanted for himself. After 1750, city folk in Boston and New York created a small market, but

simple methods of catching them still sufficed. A century later the French invention of canning changed the world of lobsters forever. The first lobster cannery was established in Eastport around 1843, and by 1880 there were 23 lobster canneries in the state of Maine. Lobsters were shipped everywhere in the United States, and even overseas.

As demand increased, so did the sophistication of the lobster fishery. The simple hoopnet trap was replaced by the wooden lobster pot, with a net funnel and a stone to hold it down. These were dumped over the side from rowing boats and hauled by hand. Sailing boats evolved for lobstering, such as the Muscongus Bay sloops, and fishermen could range farther afield to their traps. Then engines were developed, providing power to go long distances and to haul traps in deep water.

In recent years, high-tech lobstering has arrived. The rounded wood-slat lobster pot is rapidly being replaced by rectangular wire traps. They stack better, are less susceptible to rot and worm, and last longer. Because so many wire traps are lost each year, but continue to attract and kill lobsters (the "ghost trap" problem), disintegrating panels that release their catch after a period of time have been invented.

In a parallel development, wooden lobsterboats have been replaced, in part, by fiberglass. Loran and radar make it easier for the lobsterman to locate his traps and find his way home.

The surge in demand which began in 1850 had another result. The average size of lobsters started to drop immediately, and lobsters became scarcer. The problem has been getting worse for a long time, and some observers believe we may be close to an irreversible decline in lobster stocks, a disaster which has occurred in other fisheries.

Maine issues about 10,000 lobstering licenses a year, but most of these lobstermen set only a few traps. Perhaps 3,000 are fulltime fishermen, and many of these switch to other fisheries for part of the year. One lobsterman working alone may set about 300 traps, and with a sternman (assistant) he can handle perhaps 450; some highliners set 1,000 or more.

In 1887 there were about 2,000 lobstermen, hauling 109,000 traps by hand for a total catch of almost 22 million pounds. A century later, lobstermen fished 2 million traps, and caught the same poundage. There is a tendency to set more traps each year, but the total number of lobsters landed has not in-

creased as a result. In fact, it seems to be declining.

All this has led to regulation. Sometimes it is self-regulation; in Monhegan waters Trap Day is January 1, and by agreement the lobstermen close the season at the end of June. More often it is government regulation; every lobsterman carries a brass gauge, which he calls a "measure," to check the minimum carapace length for "keepers." Any lobster which measures less than $3^5/_{16}$ inches is a "short," and the maximum is 5 inches. Woe to any lobsterman who has shorts in the barrel when the warden comes aboard to inspect; the fines are heavy. Any female with eggs (berried) must be "V-notched" on the tail flipper and tossed back in; it is illegal to take one so marked. Lobstering is prohibited on Sundays in summertime, and is limited to daylight hours. Proposals to limit the number of traps are endlessly debated, and a six-year pilot project is now being evaluated in Swan's Island waters.

The lobsterman himself hasn't changed much. Still fiercely independent, he goes out when he wants to and wrests a living from the sea, winter and summer. He takes great pride in his boat, his self-reliance, and his ability to feed his family. He complains about the price of lobsters at the co-op, and the cost of fuel. He worries about over-fishing and declining lobster stocks, and too many part-timers getting lobster licenses. He gets angry about mussel-draggers and scallopers spoiling good lobster grounds. Needless to say, he doesn't much like all the regulations, and the "Gummint Fishcrats," as Captain Perc Sane calls them. He hopes maybe it will work out all right.

Lobsters hatch from eggs and start life as tiny larvae floating near the surface of the ocean. After several days they molt—a process of shedding the old shell and developing a new and larger one. After another few weeks, they molt again, getting a little larger and more complex each time. A lobster may molt seven times in its first year. By the time it has reached a one-pound size, the lobster will molt only once a

year. Rather astonishingly, when it molts, a lobster leaves its shell intact, claws and all.

Adult lobsters molt, or "shed," at times partly determined by seawater temperatures. In Long Island and Massachusetts, shedders are common in June; in Maine you'll find shedders in July along the southern coast and in August further east. The price for shedders is less than for hard-shell lobsters because the taste is different and they are considered somewhat less desirable.

When a lobsterman hauls his traps, you'll see him throw out seaweed, shorts, berried females, crabs, and miscellaneous objects (some keep the larger crabs to be picked by their wives). Legal lobsters are banded and go into a barrel or the well.

You thought those nice yellow rubber bands were put over the lobster claws to protect the customers? That's only incidental. Lobsters are notoriously nasty to one another and when thrown together will kill each other unless the crusher claws are banded (or plugged with little whittled wooden pegs).

When a lobsterman is through for the day, he heads back in and unloads his catch at a lobster car moored in the harbor, or at the floats of the co-op. The catch is weighed, and he is given credit at the going rate. The lobsters are sorted by size into the compartments of the float filled with seawater, waiting for retail customers, or for shipment to wholesale customers such as restaurants. When prices are low, lobsters are often kept in lobster pounds (large enclosures), waiting for a better time for shipment to market.

There are several places along the coast of Maine where you can visit displays about different aspects of lobstering, including the Maine Maritime Museum in Bath, the Department of Marine Resources Aquarium in Boothbay, the Ira C. Darling Center on the Damariscotta River, and the Mount Desert Oceanarium in Southwest Harbor. And in many harbors there are lobstermen who will take you out to observe how traps are hauled.

dinghy to the road at the head of the cove; from there, it's only a mile to Minturn.)

Things to Do. The Swan's Island Museum and

Library are at the ferry landing. Seaside Hall, in Atlantic, is a small museum with displays of local memorabilia.

BURNT COAT HARBOR ★★★★

Charts: 13312, **13313**

Burnt Coat Harbor, on the south shore of Swan's Island, is an attractive, well-protected harbor with one of the island's largest communities. It remains a serious fishing town; lobsterboats still leave the harbor at first light, rocking you gently in your bunk.

Approaches from the West. Burnt Coat Harbor is approached from the west through well-marked Toothacher Bay. You'll glimpse salmon aquaculture pens moored up in Toothacher Cove. The barren rock of High Sheriff merges at first with grassy Gooseberry Island behind it. Red-and-white bell "HI" marks the center of the fairway. Run down the middle of the entrance, between green can "3" to port and wooded Harbor Island to starboard. The square white tower and white building of the lighthouse on Hockamock Head are conspicuous. Enter the harbor between red beacon "4" off Harbor Island and gong "5." There is plenty of room to drop your sails after entering.

Approaches from the East. The "back door" to Burnt Coat Harbor is a neat little tickle between Stanley Point and Harbor Island, marked by two green cans left to port. From red gong "2," run inside the Baker Islands, leaving well to port the first can, which marks the western end of a very mean ledge, visible only at dead low. Curving right around Stanley Point, leave to port the inner can, marking the southern end of a ledge visible at mid-tide. Pass between this ledge and the two little wooded islands to starboard. Beyond, note the ledges off Long Cove and the little island (Potato), left to starboard. This entrance is an exhilarating experience under sail.

Anchorages, Moorings. The Swan's Island Boat Shop, on the west side of the harbor, has a number of heavy rental moorings marked with letter pennants (A, B, C, D, etc.). There is also plenty of room to anchor along the western side of the harbor outside the moorings and northward, in 17 to 25 feet at low. Holding ground is good, in mud bottom. It is also possible to anchor north of Harbor Island, but the swells may give you an uncomfortable night.

Getting Ashore. Land at the dinghy float at the Swan's Island Boat Shop, or at the first long wharf to the north, which is the Fishermen's Co-op.

For the Boat. *Swan's Island Boatshop (tel. 526-4368).* Except for rental moorings and a landing

float, Swan's Island Boatshop no longer provides any facilities.

Fishermen's Co-op (tel. 526-4327). The Fishermen's Co-op has gas and diesel at the southern float (four feet at low) and some marine supplies. The Co-op is strictly a "fishermen first" operation, and the manager requests that visiting yachtsmen not buy fuel after 1 P.M., when wharf space is needed for returning lobsterboats.

For the Crew. Lobsters are available at the Fishermen's Co-op. Walking north, turn right to the post office. A little farther along the main road is the fire station, with a pay phone in front.

The nearest market is The General Store in Minturn, with groceries, ice, and *The New York Times*, about a two-mile walk around the head of the harbor. You probably can get a lift. The Olde Salt Restaurant, in Minturn, was founded by an island sea captain and is a favorite local gathering spot. For dinner reservations (three days a week), or to reserve a lobster, call 526-4171.

Things to Do. There are no taxis on Swan's, but many islanders offer lifts to walkers as a courtesy. It is a short walk south down the road to the lighthouse at Hockamock Head, with great views of the harbor and bay. The highly visible, square white tower was built in 1872 and served as a useful mark for fishermen in setting their traps and finding their way home. In a late-1970s cost-cutting move, the Coast Guard closed the lighthouse and replaced it with a 20-foot beacon whose light could be seen only half as far. Under pressure from Swan's Islanders, the light in the tower was restored. In 1982, the Coast Guard stripped the white paint off the brick tower to reduce repainting costs. This made the tower almost invisible against the background. The islanders again protested, and the tower finally was restored to its brilliant white.

For a long walk, go past the narrow "Carrying Place" to Fine Sand Beach. This is a lovely pocket beach reached by a trail through the woods from the parking area. Do not be surprised if you see deer along the way; there are many on the island.

To swim at the Quarry Pond, take your dinghy eastward from the anchorage, passing inside Potato Island. Go beyond the old stone wharf and tie up at a public landing float. Then walk a short distance to the quarry.

SAND COVE and POPPLESTONE COVE
(MARSHALL ISLAND)
Charts: 13312, **13313**

Southwest of Swan's Island, Marshall Island is high, wooded, and sparsely inhabited. Sand Cove, at the southeast side of Marshall, has a beautiful little white sand beach in the western corner. On a sunny summer day, you are likely to find several boats anchored and people ashore enjoying the beach. The rest of the cove has rocky shores, and the pink granite of Devils Head is striped with black basaltic dikes. When the wind is from the southwest, it is hard to get far enough in for full protection, and there's an entering swell, but at other times, Sand Cove makes a fine day stop.

With good visibility, the approach is simple. Stay well clear of Yellow Ledge, the southern part of which is always visible. In poor visibility, this is a difficult area to navigate, with lots of unmarked dangers.

Popplestone Cove, north of Devils Head, looks good on the chart, but try it only if you have a yachtsman or fisherman anchor. It is aptly named for the smooth, round stones that cover the bottom and make for very poor holding ground.

FRENCHBORO (LONG ISLAND) ★★★★★
Charts: 13312, **13313**

Frenchboro is remote, very remote, and a wonderful place to visit. Here a few dozen islanders in a lobstering community cling to their century-old way of life with great determination and considerable ingenuity (see sidebar).

Long Island is largely owned by the Rockefeller family, and Frenchboro, on Lunt Harbor, is the only community. The rest of the island's 2,500 acres is undeveloped, with only a few cellar holes to tell the story of former settlers. Well-maintained trails allow visitors to enjoy the island's considerable natural beauty.

Frenchboro draws visitors from all over for its annual lobster festival the second Saturday in August. The islanders cook up 500 lobsters, prepare untold quantities of chicken salad, and bake a wide variety of pies. Simple pleasures and local color.

Approaches. Long Island is easily approached from any direction. Its shores are bold and the outlying dangers well marked. Lunt Harbor may be entered from the west by passing south of bell "1" and Harbor Island, or from the northeast from red-and-white gong "LI," passing east of Crow and Harbor islands. Watch out for the occasional ferry that plies this route to and from Bass Harbor.

The first large stone wharf on the eastern side of the harbor, with a green steel ramp, is the ferry terminal. Southward, the first large wharf on the western side of the harbor is Lunt & Lunt.

Anchorages, Moorings. Lunt & Lunt puts down a number of large granite-block moorings in 10 feet of water north of their wharf. Pick one up and row in to pay. Protection inside the harbor is extremely good except for northeasters, which occasionally wreak havoc here.

You can also anchor outside the moorings in 25 to 35 feet, although you will be more exposed.

Another possibility is to anchor on the 15-foot bar east of Harbor Island. While the inner harbor to the south is dredged to six or seven feet along the western shore, there is no room to anchor.

Getting Ashore. Row in to the dinghy float at Lunt & Lunt.

For the Boat. *Lunt & Lunt (tel. 334-2922).* Lunt & Lunt has gas, diesel, ice, and water at their wharf, with three or four feet alongside at low.

For the Crew. Lobsters are available at Lunt & Lunt, and "Lunt's Dockside Deli" is open for lunch, dinner and Sunday breakfast. The shed behind their dock is where Frenchboro Island Seafood used to pack mason jars of lobster delicacies for the Bloomingdale's gourmet market in New York City. Bambi's General Store, near the head of the harbor on the west side, carries groceries and meats; the selection is best after the twice-weekly ferry arrives.

The post office is on the eastern side of the harbor. Check with Lunt & Lunt if you need to make a phone call.

Things to Do. Frenchboro is an island of simple pleasures. Beautiful trails lead in all directions to the various coves and beaches. For example, walk to the head of the harbor and continue south along the dirt road. Then branch off on a footpath through the woods to Little Beach—about 10 or 15 minutes' walk. There you can gather beach peas, look for orchids in the nearby bog, or sit on a driftwood log while you picnic, watching lobsterboats work offshore.

For a longer walk (about 1½ hours), take the footpath from the ferry landing around Northeast Point to Eastern Beach and back on the dirt road—past green mosses, pink and green crab carapaces, and bleached skeletons of sea urchins. If you are

Aerial view of Lunt Harbor, Frenchboro, Long Island. Mount Desert in the background. (Hylander photo)

feeling energetic, walk from the ferry landing or Eastern Beach to Richs Head and the double-crescent beach at Eastern Cove.

Walking down the western side of the harbor from Lunt's, you will pass family graveyards set in the steep slopes between houses. At the head of the harbor is the fire pond, with an extended family of ducks. Several deer may come wandering up for a handout. The deer are loved and protected by the islanders, and almost tame. They stand on their hind legs to pick apples off the trees right in town. There is no hunting season here, but off-islanders have been known to shoot these trusting creatures at close range.

Where the road heads east up the hill from the fire pond is the little building of the Frenchboro Historical Museum, open afternoons, with an interesting display of island memorabilia.

EASTERN COVE ★★★★ No facilities
Charts: 13312, **13313**

Remote, unspoiled, and beautiful Eastern Cove lies between Richs Head and the main part of Long Island. The double-crescent beach (tombolo) here is piled high with driftwood.

Richs Head was settled by farmer William Rich in the early 1820s, and by 1850 the population had grown enough to warrant a school. All that remains today are seven cellar holes and stone walls.

Approaches. Easily identified by Richs Head, the cove is wide open, with no obstructions.

Anchorages, Moorings. Run in toward the center of the beach and anchor in 24 to 30 feet at low. The chart shows the bottom as rocky, but a plow anchor holds well here. Protection is good except from north to east, with little swell.

Getting Ashore. Row in to the cobble beach.

Things to Do. The southern shore of Eastern Cove has open meadows with blueberry plants everywhere, but not too many blueberries—probably because the white-tailed deer get there first. There are cranberries, too. Delightful!

It's a one-hour walk each way to Lunt Harbor, through mossy woods. From the western end of the southern beach, work your way into the trees to find the trail. Another trail leads along the shore from the beach to the cliffs on the eastern side of Richs Head.

THOSE ENTREPRENEURIAL LONG ISLANDERS

It was Massachusetts land speculator Colonel James Swan who first acquired Long Island in 1786, together with Swan's Island and 23 others. From debtor's prison in Paris (see Swan's Island writeup), Swan continued to wheel and deal, eventually losing Long Island to Michael O'Maley in 1812. O'Maley offered land to settlers, and by 1820 the census showed three households and a population of 19. In 1835, Israel B. Lunt bought 1,132 acres for $600. Lunt was truly the progenitor of Frenchboro: A third or more of today's residents have his surname, and his descendants still live in the Israel B. Lunt homestead.

Showing early signs of the opportunism that exists today, the islanders agreed to name part of Long Island Plantation for lawyer Webster French if he would arrange for a post office on the island. French used his political connections successfully; thus Frenchboro.

Fishing provided the livelihood of the early settlers, who went after groundfish such as haddock and cod. Today the fishing centers on lobstering, seining for herring, and dragging for scallops. For a while, pulpwood was harvested on Long Island and shipped by barge and coaster to St. Regis Paper in Bucksport.

The island population reached a peak of 197 in 1910 and then started a steady decline. A schoolhouse built in 1907 to hold 60 students was serving half that number by 1930, and only two children attended school in 1964. Threatened by the loss of the school, the islanders rose to the occasion by inviting 14 foster children to live in Frenchboro. The school was saved, and most of the children stayed on the island until it was time to leave for high school on Mount Desert.

Two have returned to live in Frenchboro.

Modern times have come slowly to Frenchboro. A cable brought electricity in the 1950s; telephone service arrived in 1982. As the population continued to decline, it became obvious to some that Frenchboro was in danger of extinction, like many islands before it. With impetus from the women—"a matriarchal society," as Town Manager James Haskell notes —Frenchboro obtained a $360,000 block grant from the state. Some of the money was used to build a new community hall and dump, and to upgrade housing. Perhaps most important, it has also been used to allow Frenchboro to offer inexpensive land parcels to attract young residents and increase the population. Fifty-five acres were donated by the Rockefeller family toward this goal.

MOUNT DESERT ROCK

Charts: 13312, **13313**

One of the best places along the coast to see whales is off Mount Desert Rock, where the great, gentle creatures come to feed in the upwelling waters. This is a lonely place indeed, almost 15 miles from the nearest land. The lighthouse here stands on three acres of low-lying rock, often shrouded in fog. The light is now automated, but you will still find human inhabitants here: researchers and volunteers of Allied Whale Watch, a project of College of the Atlantic in Bar Harbor. A heavy Coast Guard mooring, labeled "CG," makes it possible to tie up and go ashore, landing your dinghy on the ways.

Pick a day with good visibility and a reasonable weather forecast. Any of the harbors on Mount Desert Island are good jumping off spots. It's a shorter run, however, from Burnt Coat Harbor or from Frenchboro, Long Island.

Frenchboro drops astern and you set out to the empty horizon with the feeling of having left the world and other boats behind. As you ride the ocean swells, it won't be long before all land has disappeared. On a typical hazy day, you may be within 3 miles of Mount Desert Rock before you glimpse the lighthouse.

Prepare to be disappointed; after all, whales are not sighted every day. But also be prepared to see a great, black glistening shape rise suddenly from the water close aboard and pass down your side without a sound. Even pilot whales are impressive enough, and the great whales may dwarf your boat.

There is likely to be a whale watching vessel near the rock, and perhaps some smaller boats. Listen for the chatter about whales on various VHF channels. Watch for a sudden plume of mist shooting skyward, and a great humpback or finback whale rising majestically to the surface. Followed by a little fleet of observers, the whale will swim in leisurely pursuit of food—sounding occasionally and showing the white undersides of its flukes— then blowing again. It's thrilling.

The behavior of whales is not always predictable, and they can be dangerous. Read the whale-watching guidelines in the sidebar on page 264.

Largest mammals that have ever lived, the great whales are land creatures that returned to the sea eons ago. Their brains are larger than man's, and one species sings a song whose eerie notes may be channeled for thousands of miles along the deep acoustic passages of the sea.

Cetaceans (from the Greek word meaning "sea monster") include whales, dolphins, and porpoises. Of more than 85 species, six are often seen in the Gulf of Maine, including three of the great whales—the finback, the humpback, and the minke. The smaller pilot whales are also common, as are harbor porpoises and white-sided dolphins.

Occasionally seen are four other species: the rare right whale, the killer whale (orca), and common and white-beaked dolphins.

The great whales are usually seen near the fishing banks, where upwelling waters bring food in the form of tiny crustaceans, krill, squid, and small fish. These are filtered from enormous gulps of seawater by baleen sieves that hang from the upper jaws of most large whales. (Of the great whales, only the sperm whale has teeth).

Not unlike the human species, some whales go south in winter, to breed in Florida and the Antilles. They come north again in the spring to their feeding grounds in the Gulf of Maine.

Man has hunted whales for thousands of years, eaten its blubber, and used the oil to light his lamps. For a long time, it was a fair fight, and men in their small boats risked their lives to catch a few of the great leviathans. Then the demand for whale oil, the growth of fishing fleets, and technological developments such as engines and explosive harpoons, turned the game into a quickening slaughter. Many species of whales were hunted to the edge of extinction (including the right whale, whose numberless ranks have dwindled to 300 or 400 individuals in the entire world).

Finally, the discovery of petroleum sources and the advent of the electric light reduced the market for whale oil. And a growing awareness of the intelligence, gentleness, and beauty of these great creatures brought environmentalists and finally the public to the defense of the whale. The major countries involved in hunting whales agreed to establish quotas, and whaling came under regulation by the International Whaling Commission in 1946. Progress has been slow and frustrating, but today the factory ships of Russia and the United States are gone, and only Japan, Norway and Korea still resist the growing strength of public opinion. In the powerful words of Chief Seattle, spoken in 1884; "What happens to the beasts will happen to man. All things are connected. If the great beasts are gone, man would surely die of a great loneliness of spirit."

In Maine, you are most likely to spot whales off Matinicus Rock, Seal

Six whales that may be sighted in the Gulf of Maine, shown in the same scale as a 43-foot cruising ketch to illustrate relative size. Waterlines indicate the part of the whale usually seen above water. From left to right: humpback, killer (orca), minke, finback, right, and pilot whales.

264

Island (southeast of Isle au Haut), and Mount Desert Rock. Canada's Grand Manan also is a likely whale-watching site. From the shore, whales can be sighted from lighthouses such as Bass Harbor (on Mount Desert Island) and West Quoddy Head.

There are lots of clues to use in identifying whales. Size is important, of course, as is silhouette. The shape of the spout may give you positive identification, or if you get close enough, distinctive behavior may be conclusive. Experienced whale-watchers can recognize individuals by details such as the color pattern, shape of a fluke, or even the arrangement of callosities on a right whale's head.

In his *Field Guide to the Whales, Porpoises and Seals,* Steven Katona notes that whales sometimes sleep on the surface, but there is little likelihood of hitting one at night or in the fog. Whales occasionally approach boats, but according to Katona, "We have never heard of a case where an undisturbed whale approached and damaged a vessel in our waters." On the other hand, he points out, "Vessels coming too close to a feeding or jumping whale have been struck, resulting in narrow escapes. Give the animals a wide berth."

Whale-Watching Guidelines. Because of the growing interest in whale-watching and the increasing number of boats following whales, guidelines have been developed by the National Marine Fisheries Service (NMFS) and others to prevent harassment and damage to whales and danger to the boating public. Those pertinent to the cruising sailor are summarized below.

• When operating within a quarter of a mile of whales, avoid excessive speed or sudden changes in speed or direction. Don't rev your engines.

• When close to whales (within 300 feet):

—don't approach stationary whales at more than idle speed;

—don't approach moving or resting whales head-on;

—don't get between a mother and her calf;

—parallel the course and speed of moving whales.

• Do not intentionally approach within 100 feet of whales. If they come within 100 feet of your vessel, put engines in neutral and don't reengage props until whales are observed at the surface, clear of the vessel.

• Active whales require ample space. Breaching, lobtailing, and flipper-slapping may endanger a vessel. Feeding whales often emit subsurface bubbles to concentrate their prey before rising to feed at the surface. Stand clear of light-green bubble patches.

• Diving in the vicinity of whales is not advised because of their active and unpredictable behavior. Divers should not approach within 100 feet of whales.

• In all cases, do not restrict the normal movement or behavior of whales, or take action that may evoke a reaction from them or result in physical contact.

SOME WHALE-WATCHING
EXPEDITIONS

If you don't plan to cruise where the great whales are normally seen, consider going out for a day on a whale-watching expedition (see below). It's a fascinating experience seeing whales close up this way, including great humpbacks playing lazily around the boat, splashing, diving, rolling, and generally hamming it up, perhaps no more than 10 feet away.

Portsmouth, NH	Isles of Shoals Steamship Company Barker Wharf, 315 Market St. Portsmouth, NH 03801 603-431-5500 or 800-441-4620
Kennebunkport	Cape Arundel Cruises P.O. Box 2777 Kennebunkport, ME 04046 207-967-0707
Bangor	Seafarers Expeditions 96 Harlow St., Suite D Bangor, ME 04401 207-942-7942
Northeast Harbor	Maine Whale Watch P.O. Box 78 Northeast Harbor, ME 04662 207-276-5803
Bar Harbor	Bar Harbor Whale Watch *Acadia Whale Watch* West St. Bar Harbor, ME 04609 207-288-9794
Lubec	Captain Butch Huntley *M/V Seafarer* 9 High St. Lubec, ME 04652 207-733-5584

Whale off lonely Mount Desert Rock. (Keary Nichols photo, MPBN)

BLUE HILL BAY and Mount Desert Island

BLUE HILL BAY

Charts: 13312, 13313, **13316**

On the west side of Mount Desert Island, Blue Hill Bay has long stretches of sparkling, wide-open waters. Although less dramatic than neighboring Frenchman Bay, it offers great sailing, with alluring Blue Hill ahead and the hills of Mount Desert to the east. The bay is protected from ocean swells by the many islands at its southern entrance.

This magnificent sailing territory has relatively few good harbors. Blue Hill Harbor, at the northwest corner, is the jewel of the bay and home to the Kollegewidgwok Yacht Club. At the southeastern end, Bass Harbor on Mount Desert is the base for a substantial fishing fleet and also offers complete services for yachtsmen. Pretty Marsh Harbor and

several little coves lie along the west coast of Mount Desert Island and the eastern shore of Bartlett Island.

Much of the beauty of Blue Hill Bay will be forever preserved. The string of islands dividing the southern end of the bay—Bar, Trumpet, Ship, and the Barges—have important nesting colonies of eiders and are owned in part by The Nature Conservancy. Bartlett Island, off the west shore of Mount Desert, was bought by the Rockefeller family to preserve it from development. The Penobscot Indian word "kollegewidgwok" says it all. It means "blue hill on shining green water."

ALLEN COVE ★★ No facilities

Charts: 13312, **13316**

Allen Cove is on the west side of Blue Hill Bay between Tinker and Long islands. It is a large, open bay offering good protection from prevailing winds.

Approaches. There are no obstructions except the ledges at Harriman Point.

Anchorages, Moorings. The cove shoals gradually; find a comfortable depth in the middle. Holding ground is good, with mud and some grass.

BLUE HILL ★★★★★ (outer harbor)  (inner harbor) HARBOR

Charts: 13312, **13316** (Inset)

Year-round residents and summer people have cared about Blue Hill for a long time. The old clapboard houses are freshly painted, the lawns are tended, the market and the hardware stores and the realtors are housed in handsome old buildings, the imposing town hall rises high on a grassy slope, and the public library stands on a quiet block. There are attractive little shops offering quilts and antiques, and a pleasing selection of restaurants.

There are many things to do here, including a number of special cultural events.

Forming the background for this little town is an impressive collection of elm trees—many of them enormous, all of them healthy. They were saved by the efforts of a dedicated warden, and a community united in its determination to preserve these magnificent trees.

In summertime, Blue Hill is jammed with people, threatening the very tranquility and charm they seek, but it remains a most delightful town to visit. For the yachtsman, this requires a little doing. The center of town is at the very western end of the inner harbor, which dries out at low. You can bring your boat in to the town wharf at high tide, or anchor some distance away and arrive by dinghy, or find land transportation at the Kollegewidgwok Yacht Club.

Approaches—Inner Harbor East. Once past the ledges of Closson Point, run along the northern shore and north of the large ledge near the entrance, leaving cans "1" and "3" well to port. Then pass through the narrow entrance at Sculpin Point to the inner harbor, between can "5" and nun "6." There is a substantial current here at midtide.

The Kollegewidgwok Yacht Club is on the eastern shore, opposite Peters Point. After leaving nun "6" to starboard, head for the moored boats and the gray, flat-roofed clubhouse.

Anchorages, Moorings—Inner Harbor East. Check at the yacht club dock for a guest mooring. If none is available, there may be room to anchor south of the moored boats in 17 to 24 feet, or try the western part of the inner harbor.

Approaches—Inner Harbor West. Beyond Peters Point, the western part of the inner harbor provides even better protection and gets you considerably closer to the town of Blue Hill. There are a number of small craft and fishing boats moored here, but possibly room to anchor. Enter for the first time at midtide or below, when all the dangers are visible. It looks a bit daunting, but it's easy if you trust the buoys. Leaving can "7" close aboard to port and watching for crosscurrents, head for nun "8." Turn sharply around nun "8," leaving it to starboard, and head for the northernmost spire in Blue Hill.

Anchorages, Moorings—Inner Harbor West. Continue until you reach the moored boats, then turn westward among them. Anchor in 14 to 20 feet at low, good mud bottom. This part of the inner harbor is completely landlocked and makes a good hurricane hole. You are surrounded by rocky islets, with the masts of the yacht club to the east and the steeples of Blue Hill to the northwest—a lovely spot. Seals bask here undisturbed by your approach, and there are ospreys.

Getting Ashore. If you are at the yacht club, row in to the dinghy floats. If you take the dinghy in to town, land at the ramp next to the town wharf.

For the Boat. *Kollegewidgwok Yacht Club (Ch. 16 or 68; tel. 374-5581).* Gas, diesel, water, and electricity may be obtained at the floats, with 10 feet alongside at low. There is an ice machine.

Raynes Marine Works (tel. 374-2877). Located in a cove that dries out, just west of Peters Point, this small yard can haul boats up to 32 feet for storage and for hull, rigging, and engine repairs. Call from the yacht club.

McVay's Hardware (tel. 374-5645). Located on Main Street in town, McVay's carries a line of charts.

For the Crew. The Kollegewidgwok Yacht Club

has a pay phone. To get into Blue Hill, walk up the yacht club road and turn left. It's 1.7 miles from the club into town, but you probably can arrange for a ride.

Merrill & Hinckley (groceries and fresh fish; tel. 374-2821) is close to the town wharf, at the southern end of town, up the hill on Route 177. They will deliver to the yacht club. The liquor store is also here. Turn right from the town wharf to find McVay's Hardware, Partridge Drugs, the post office, and several restaurants. Among them is the well-known Firepond, serving superb dinners in a remodeled basement of a blacksmith shop overlooking Mill Stream. (Call ahead—374-2135—for reservations.)

Directly across from the town wharf is the Blue Hill Memorial Hospital (tel. 374-2836).

Things to Do. Right next to the town wharf is a pleasant little grassy park on the water, with picnic tables and a beach.

The hill for which the town and harbor are named is 940 feet high, with open blueberry fields, spruces, and granite ledges. The climb is well worth the effort for its magnificent views. The distance from the post office to the base of the trail is 1.25 miles. Walk up Route 15 (north) about .75 mile, turn right on Mountain Rd. (you'll see the watchtower from the intersection), and continue .5 mile to a sign that says, "Trail to Tower." It's a steep woodland trail, often masquerading as a stream bed. Allow 1¼ hours to get to the top and back to the base of the trail.

As you near the summit, a clearing provides wonderful vistas west toward the northern end of Penobscot Bay and the Penobscot River, and southwest to the Camden Hills. There are also clearings on top, from which you can see south to Isle au Haut, southeast down Blue Hill Bay, and

east to Mount Desert. If you are feeling venturesome, climb the stairway of the watchtower ("Visitors Welcome—At Your Own Risk").

The Blue Hill Fair has been an annual event for a century or so, and it draws people from all over the state. This is a real country fair, with oxen straining to pull the heaviest loads, harness racing, sheep trials, and many other traditional events. The fairground is 1.3 miles east of the post office, on Route 172.

The famed Kneisel Hall School for String and Ensemble Music, based here each summer, presents twice-weekly concerts on its campus at the edge of town. Call 374-2811 for the schedule.

The Jonathan Fisher Memorial, a lovely early-nineteenth-century home built by one of the town's most illustrious residents, is worth a visit. Among the building's attractions are fascinating inventions attributed to the multitalented Fisher.

The unique Bagaduce Music Lending Library is a short walk out of town on Main Street. Its mission is to preserve and lend vocal and instrumental music to music lovers worldwide.

In the brick Blue Hill Public Library, a couple of blocks south of the middle of town, is an extraordinary relic—a chain-and-plate vest reputedly worn by Ferdinand Magellan when he was killed in the Philippines in 1521 during the first circumnavigation of the world. The exhibit card in the library reports that a General Rumbough, with the U.S. force that conquered the Philippines in the Spanish-American War, searched the beach where Magellan was killed and found numerous artifacts. Most were given to the Metropolitan Museum, but the fanciest piece of armor was given by General Rumbough to the Blue Hill Public Library. It hangs on a wooden stand by the fireplace.

McHEARD COVE ★★★   3

Charts: 13312, **13316**

About two miles east of Blue Hill, McHeard Cove runs north to the village of East Blue Hill. The cove flats out at low tide halfway in.

Approaches. After passing east of Darling Island, enter McHeard Cove, staying on the western side. The ledges and islands on the east side generally are obvious and easy to avoid.

Anchorages, Moorings. Webber's Cove Boatyard maintains several moorings near the nine-foot spot on the chart next to a little white granite island. There is exposure to the south and southeast.

Getting Ashore. Land your dinghy at the boatyard floats if there is enough water. Otherwise, land at the ramp at the playground just before you reach the yard.

For the Boat. *Webber's Cove Boatyard (tel. 374-2841).* At the head of McHeard Cove, the floats of the boatyard are dry at low water. There is a 15-ton boatlift, and repairs can be made. Limited marine supplies are available, but no fuel or water.

Longfield Dory Co. (tel. 374-5656). Just west of the boatyard, Longfield builds dinghies and can also handle wood and fiberglass repairs.

For the Crew. Webber's Cove Boatyard can supply lobsters. The post office and public library in this peaceful village are at the entrance to the boatyard. The nearest groceries and shops are in Blue Hill, about three miles away.

MORGAN BAY

Charts: 13312, **13316**

At the northern end of Blue Hill Bay, Morgan Bay lies west of Newbury Neck. There is a confusion of islands and ledges at the entrance, but then the bay becomes wide and open all the way to the head. To enter Morgan Bay, leave Conary Nub to starboard.

Newbury Neck, to the east, is largely wooded and undeveloped, and there are attractive houses and meadows along the western shore. At least one bald eagle makes its home here.

UNION RIVER BAY

Charts: 13312, **13316**

Above Bartlett Island, Union River Bay runs six miles northward toward the large town of Ellsworth. More than a mile wide and unobstructed, the bay is a pleasant diversion if you like to sail with no particular destination in mind. Along Newbury Neck, attractive saltwater farms line the shores, and farther north are the two radio towers shown on the chart.

Although generally peaceful, Union River Bay can get rough in a strong southwester and an ebb tide. At the northern end of the bay, the Union River, leading to Ellsworth, is narrow, shoal, and not recommended. There is a reasonable anchorage in Patten Bay.

PATTEN BAY ★★   No facilities

Charts: 13312, **13316**

Patten Bay, at the northwestern corner of Union River Bay, leads to the town of Surry. The handsome south shore is steep and wooded; there are a number of houses along the north shore.

Approaches. Leaving the starboard nun "2," at the northern end of Union River Bay, favor the deeper water along the north shore of Patten Bay,

heading for the spire in Surry. Feel your way as far west as is comfortable.

Anchorages, Moorings. Anchor in 9 to 14 feet at low along the north shore. Although a southwest wind may curl around the corner, protection is good and the bottom is mud.

CONTENTION COVE

Charts: 13312, **13316**

On the northern side of the entrance to Patten Bay, little Contention Cove makes a nice day stop and provides access to the Surry Inn for dinner. Anchor outside the moored boats in mud bottom. The Surry Inn, built in 1834, (tel. 667-5091) is the second white house back from the road on the east side of the cove, with a large expanse of lawn in front.

The cove earned its name from an incident of typical Yankee stubbornness. It seems the farmers wanted the road to follow the most direct route from Blue Hill to Ellsworth, while the fishermen, naturally, wanted it to run along the head of the cove; hence, Contention Cove.

MOUNT DESERT ISLAND

Charts: 13312, 13313, 13316, 13318, 13321, 13323

The Abenaki Indians called it "Pemetic," "the sloping land." In 1524, Giovanni da Verrazzano, a Florentine working for French and Italian bankers, was the first European to record the sighting of Mount Desert Island. Eighty years later, it was visited by Samuel de Champlain, representing Pierre du Guast, Sieur de Monts, who had been designated lieutenant-general of New France by King Henry IV and granted a 10-year fur monopoly. Coasting down from a French settlement in Nova

269

Scotia, Champlain named it "l'Isle des Monts-deserts," or "Island of the barren mounts." He struck a shoal off Otter Point and landed September 5, 1604, to repair his ship and to explore.

With the assassination of Henry IV, de Monts lost royal favor, and his patent was bought by Antoinette de Pons, Marquise de Guercheville. This rich and virtuous lady founded the short-lived Jesuit mission on Fernald Point in Somes Sound in 1613. It was destroyed by Captain Samuel Argall, under British orders to clear the coast of Frenchmen.

In 1688, Antoine Laumet successfully petitioned Louis XIV for an enormous grant of land in New France, including Mount Desert Island. Adopting the title of Sieur Antoine de la Mothe Cadillac, he brought his bride to Mount Desert to establish a feudal estate. This romantic scheme failed for unknown reasons, and Cadillac went on to found Detroit, but his name lives on here.

With the conquest of Quebec by General James Wolfe in 1759, the British finally won their long struggle with the French, and the lands of New France were up for grabs. Governor Francis Bernard of Massachusetts coveted Mount Desert and persuaded Abraham Somes and other families to colonize the island in 1761, but the Revolution nullified Bernard's claims. After the Revolution, the General Court of Massachusetts split the island between two claimants. The western half went to Bernard's son, the eastern half to Marie Theresa de Gregoire, granddaughter of Cadillac.

Next came the artists and the rusticators, (as the summer people were labeled). In the mid-nineteenth century, Mount Desert became fashionable. Hotels sprang up as bases for campers, naturalists, and artists. Then the wealthy started to build imposing "cottages." "The Briars" was built in 1881 for J. Montgomery Sears of Boston, "Stanwood" in 1885 for James G. Blaine of Maine, "Casa Far Niente" for S. Weir Mitchell of Philadelphia, "Chatwold" in 1894 for publisher Joseph Pulitzer of New York, and so on, each trying to outdo the others. The roster of people who summered in Mount Desert included Vanderbilts and Fords, Carnegies and Astors, Rockefellers and Morgans. But by the time E.J. Stotesbury built his 80-room mansion in 1925, the Great Depression was just over the horizon, the automobile was opening up Mount Desert to the public, and an era was coming to a close.

The coup de grâce came less than two decades later. A sign in Acadia National Park relates the sad tale: "In October 1947, a series of fires lasting 26 days ravaged more than 25 square miles of Mount Desert Island. Bar Harbor was severely threatened, and most of the landscape in front of you was transformed into an apparent wasteland. The fire consumed 170 homes of year-round residents. Over 60 summer mansions burned, leaving only chimneys and garden statues standing. One third of the park woodlands burned before the flames died at the ocean's edge."

View of Mount Desert from the Cranberry Islands. (Christopher Ayres photo)

ACADIA—FOR THE ENJOYMENT OF ALL PEOPLE

In an old photograph, George B. Dorr stands on the shore of Jordan Pond, dressed in baggy tweeds with three-button jacket, bow tie, and cap. A canoe is drawn up, and Dorr is talking to Charles W. Eliot, former president of Harvard. These men and others like them—wealthy, educated, and public-spirited—had the vision of preserving this grand island from woodsman and developer, for the enjoyment of all people. Dorr was a doer as well as dreamer, and he persuaded others to donate land and money and to share his dream. He was also a politician, able to facilitate the sticky process of donating private lands for public use. The first association was Hancock County Trustees of Public Reservations. When its tax-free status was challenged, Dorr decided to aim for a national park. At a time when too many such proposals were overwhelming Congress, the first 6,000 acres in 1916 became Sieur de Monts National Monument, requiring only the president's approval.

With further pressure from Dorr, it finally became Lafayette National Park in 1919. When much of Schoodic Peninisula was added 10 years later, potential donors of land objected to the name, and in 1929 Congress was persuaded to change it to Acadia National Park.

One of the major land donors was John D. Rockefeller, Jr., who gave almost one-third of the park's present acreage. He is also remembered as the man who conceived the network of carriage roads criss-crossing the island, so that horses and carriages and hikers might be insulated from the automobiles that threatened to invade the island. (They were not allowed until 1913.) He did it right, inviting Frederick Olmstead (son of the designer of New York City's Central Park) to lay out the roads and design the rustic stone bridges. The roads are still here today for the enjoyment of hikers, skiers, bicyclists, carriages, and horseback riders.

ACADIA NATIONAL PARK

Second most popular national park in the whole country, Acadia National Park is visited each year by five million people or more, several times the population of Maine. Occupying large areas of Mount Desert Island, the park also includes parts of Schoodic Peninsula, Isle au Haut, and the Cranberry Islands.

Thanks to the efforts and foresight of some determined individuals, the 35,000 acres of the park cover the most spectacular scenery on the island, and probably on the whole Atlantic coast. The rays of the morning sun touch the summit of Mount Cadillac first in the United States; there are coastal drives, sheer cliffs, calm lakes for canoeists between wooded hills, natural springs, wild and formal gardens—and even a tea house at Jordan Pond. In addition to a museum of stone age arti-

facts, there are natural walks, woods and wildlife, sea birds and ocean beaches, roads leading to the mountaintops, and 57 miles of carriage roads winding everywhere for hiker, bicyclist, horse-drawn carriage, and rider.

People come from everywhere to see this most beautiful of islands, this granite-hard, fog-softened, primeval meeting place of land and sea.

The park's Visitors Center, located near the village of Hulls Cove, in the northeastern corner of Mount Desert Island, has maps, information on naturalist-guided tours, and a short film about the park. Sightseeing buses depart regularly for park tours from downtown Bar Harbor (see writeup). To plan ahead for visiting the park from your boat, write to Park Headquarters (see sidebar).

WESTERN BAY

Charts: 13312, **13316**

Western Bay forms the approach to Mount Desert Narrows. The shores are relatively low-lying and developed. Ahead lies the stream of traffic crossing the bridge to the mainland and northward the un-marked shoals surrounding Alley Island. There is

very little here to attract the cruising boat, but if you happen to need a refuge, Northwest Cove is easy to enter and offers mud bottom and reasonable protection.

BARTLETT ISLAND and BARTLETT NARROWS

Charts: 13312, **13316**

Second largest of the islands in Blue Hill Bay, 2,500-acre Bartlett Island lies close to Mount Desert. In 1973, David and Peggy Rockefeller

bought the island to preserve it from resort development.

Three of the existing homes have been remod-

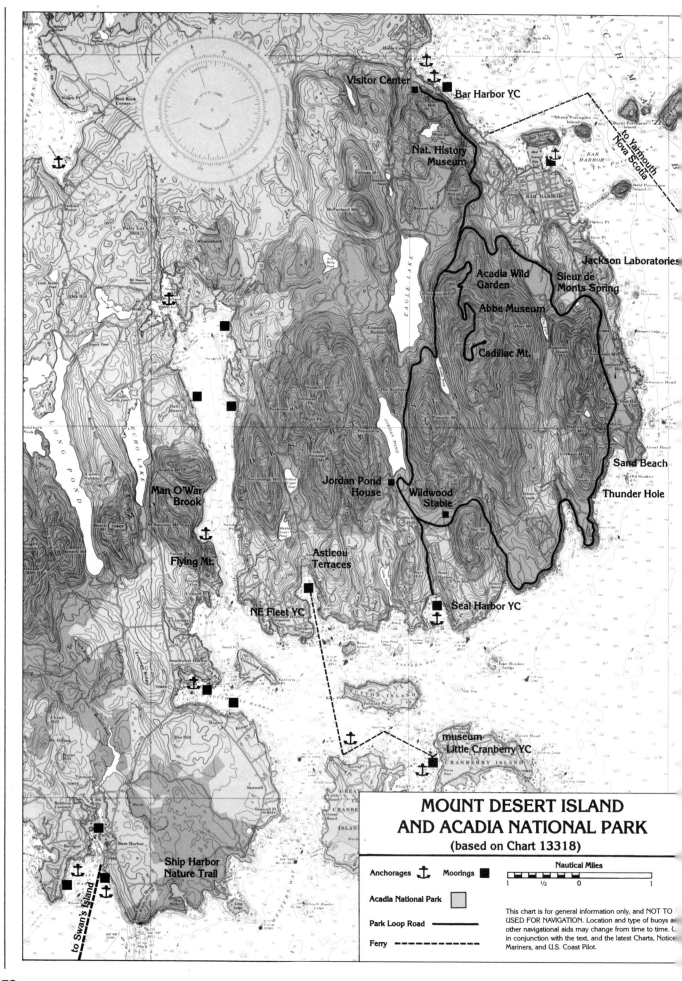

Visitor Center

Bar Harbor YC

Nat. History Museum

Jackson Laboratories

Acadia Wild Garden

Sieur de Monts Spring

Abbe Museum

Cadillac Mt.

Man O'War Brook

Jordan Pond House

Wildwood Stable

Sand Beach

Thunder Hole

Flying Mt.

Asticou Terraces

NE Fleet YC

Seal Harbor YC

museum
Little Cranberry YC

Ship Harbor Nature Trail

to Swan's Island

to Yarmouth Nova Scotia

MOUNT DESERT ISLAND
AND ACADIA NATIONAL PARK
(based on Chart 13318)

Anchorages ⚓   Moorings ■

Nautical Miles
1   ½   0   1

Acadia National Park

Park Loop Road ———

Ferry – – – – –

This chart is for general information only, and NOT TO
BE USED FOR NAVIGATION. Location and type of buoys and
other navigational aids may change from time to time. Use
in conjunction with the text, and the latest Charts, Notice to
Mariners, and U.S. Coast Pilot.

272

SEEING THE PARK FROM YOUR BOAT

With imagination and a willingness to hike a reasonable distance, the cruising family can visit all the best places in and around Acadia National Park from their floating base.

Before you start your cruise, contact Acadia National Park for maps and general information, which will make it much easier to plan your forays ashore. Write: Superintendent, Acadia National Park, Bar Harbor, Maine 04609. Or call 207-288-3338.

Below is a list of the major sightseeing attractions and the harbor from which they can be reached most easily. See the individual harbor descriptions for more details.

HARBOR	ATTRACTION
Mount Desert	
Bass Harbor	Bass Harbor Head Lighthouse Ship Harbor Nature Trail
Valley Cove	Flying Mountain Man o'War Brook St. Sauveur Mountain
Northeast Harbor	Asticou Terraces, Thuya Lodge and Gardens, Eliot Mountain
Seal Harbor	Jordan Pond House Jordan Pond trails: Sargent Mountain Pemetic Mountain The Bubbles Carriage Roads
Bar Harbor	Cadillac Mountain Sieur de Monts Spring The Abbé Museum Wild Gardens of Acadia Thunder Hole Park Loop Road Natural History Museum Jackson Laboratory Bar Island Sand Beach Otter Cliffs
Cranberry Islands	
Islesford	Islesford Historical Museum
Baker Island	Walks, Lighthouse
Schoodic Peninsula	
Pond Island	Schoodic Head Schoodic Point
Isle au Haut	
Duck Harbor	Trails

eled and two new ones built. A herd of Simmental cattle grazes on the pastures coming down to the water near Birch Cove. Bartlett is one of many examples of the efforts of the Rockefellers to preserve the beauties of the Maine coast and to restore traditional island occupations. There is no camping on Bartlett without permission, and no fires are allowed above the high tide mark. The Hub at the northern tip of Bartlett is state owned.

It's a lovely passage through Bartlett Narrows, and not difficult, although the current is quite strong. Entering from the north, note the shoal off Goose Marsh Point. A gray house with two large white chimneys marks the eastern side of the entrance.

From the south, run west of Folly and John islands, past West Point, into the Narrows. The rocks make out a long way from Ledges Point, so get well over to the Mount Desert shore as you approach Great Cove. The ledges are partially visible at all tides.

A number of boats are moored north of West Point, and the dock and float here serve Bartlett Island. The water, however, is too deep for anchoring.

GALLEY COVE ★★★

 No facilities

Charts: 13312, **13316**

This is a beautiful little cove on the eastern shore of Bartlett Island, just south of Galley Point, with views of the hills on Mount Desert and a gravel beach.

Approaches. Run up the eastern shore of Bartlett Island toward Galley Point, which is mostly wooded with some clearings at the end. Enter the middle of the tiny cove.

Anchorages, Moorings. There are private moorings in the cove close to shore. Anchor in the middle of the cove in 18 to 20 feet at low, mud bottom. There is protection here except from the east and northeast.

GREAT COVE ★★★

 No facilities

Charts: 13312, **13316**

Great Cove is on the eastern side of Bartlett Island, halfway through the Narrows. It's a good anchorage and easy to enter, with views of the hills across the way on Mount Desert.

Approaches. Staying well clear of the ledges off Ledges Point, run up the middle of the cove, which is wide and unobstructed.

Anchorages, Moorings. Anchor wherever you find swinging room in 15 to 20 feet at low. Holding ground is excellent, in mud, and exposure is only to the south and southeast.

PRETTY MARSH HARBOR ★★★

 No facilities

Charts: 13312, **13316**

On the west side of Mount Desert Island, inside Bartlett Island, Pretty Marsh Harbor provides good anchorage in a tranquil setting, far from the madding crowd. To the southwest there are islands beyond islands, with handsome buildings and meadows on Hardwood Island in view.

Approaches. Approaching from the south, run inside Hardwood Island (113 feet high and wooded) and leave Folly Island well to port (low, bushy, with a few trees). Note the ledge about 250 yards east of Folly, covered three feet at low. Entering Pretty Marsh Harbor, favor the eastern side to avoid the shoal extending 350 yards southeast of West Point.

Anchorages, Moorings. Anchor in the middle of the harbor in 8 to 21 feet at low. Holding ground varies—good mud in some places, but hard in others. Make sure the hook is in. Protection is good all around, except in a heavy southwester.

Things to Do. On the east shore of the entrance to the harbor, opposite the end of West Point, there is a rustic gazebo, and stairs leading down to the water. Land there and walk through a stately grove of spruce and cedar, a national park picnic area.

Take your dinghy and explore the little tickle of water leading off to the northeast, opening to a small pond.

SOMES COVE ★★★

 No facilities

Charts: 13312, **13316**

Somes is a tiny cove on the west side of Mount Desert Island, opposite the southern tip of Bartlett Island. Anchorage and protection are good.

Approaches. There are two islets at the southern corner of the entrance, the outer one low and rocky, the inner one bushy. Enter north of the islets, down the middle of the cove.

Anchorages, Moorings. Anchor just west of a line between the dock on the north shore and the dock on the south shore, in 12 to 20 feet at low. The only exposure is to the north. The bottom is mud and grass, with good holding.

SAWYER COVE ★★★ No facilities

Charts: 13312, **13316**

Opposite the northern tip of Hardwood Island, Sawyer Cove is an attractive small anchorage with excellent protection from prevailing winds. A bald eagle may sometimes be seen soaring above the 100-foot bluff that forms the southern entrance.

Approaches. The large ledge in the mouth of the entrance is visible almost until high water, and some kind soul has built a small rock cairn on the eastern part of the ledge. The approach south of the ledge is wider, but you can pass safely on either side.

Anchorages, Moorings. Anchor in 8 to 21 feet at low, with good mud holding ground. The only exposure is to the north.

SEAL COVE ★★★ No facilities

Charts: 13312, **13316**

The farther into Seal Cove you get, the prettier it becomes. Flanked by Murphy Hill and Robbins Hill, with Bernard Mountain in the background, the innermost section is a delight.

Approaches. Dodge Point can be identified by the conspicuous white boulder on shore just south of the point. Moose Island is wooded in the middle with meadow around the southern shore. Run up the middle of Seal Cove, staying well clear of the ledges east of Dodge Point, toward the estuary at the head of the cove.

Anchorages, Moorings. Anchor in 6½ to 14 feet at low among the moored boats. Holding ground is good, in mud. The cove is exposed to the west and southwest, but it would offer excellent protection from north around to east and south.

Getting Ashore. Land at the public launching ramp on the north shore.

Things to Do. Explore the estuary with your dinghy toward Seal Cove Pond, or walk along Seal Cove Road, which skirts the harbor.

GOOSE COVE ★★ No facilities

Charts: 13312, **13316**

A couple of miles north of Bass Harbor, on the west shore of Mount Desert, Goose Cove is open and easy to enter but exposed to the prevailing southwesterlies.

Approaches. The best way to identify Goose Cove is by the spire in West Tremont. The cove is south of Goose Cove Rock (whitish and grassy) and between Dix Point and Nutter Point (both are wooded and extend a long way). Run up the middle.

Anchorages, Moorings. Anchor outside the private moorings on the south side in 10 to 15 feet at low. Despite the "Rky" designation shown on the chart, there is mud bottom with good holding.

BASS HARBOR ★★ (outer harbor) (inner harbor) All facilities

Charts: 13312, 13313, **13316**, 13318

At the southwestern corner of Mount Desert Island, Bass Harbor is home port for Mount Desert's largest lobstering fleet. It is also a growing yachting center. The outer harbor is open to the south, but there is better protection inside. The ferry to Swan's Island and Frenchboro leaves from Bass Harbor. This is where Ruth Moore lived for 40 years and wrote most of her novels of life on the Maine coast, now popular once more. Among the best known are *Speak to the Winds* and *The Weir*.

Approaches. The entrance to Bass Harbor is marked by Bass Harbor Head Light, on the eastern shore, with a small white tower and connected building.

Coming from the west, there are no problems entering Bass Harbor. Weaver Ledge at the entrance is marked by a nun and a can at either end. From the east, the usual approach is across Bass Harbor Bar.

Bass Harbor Bar. A channel with 13 feet of depth has been dredged near the Mount Desert end of the bar, close to Bass Harbor Head Light. The east end is marked by red-and-white bell "EB" and the west end by red-and-white gong "WB." Run a

Windjammer *Adventure*, with a crewmember climbing the ratlines, beating her way up Blue Hill Bay. (Neal A. Parent photo)

straight line the short distance between them.

The current floods west and ebbs east across the bar, at an angle to the channel. It normally is an easy passage, but when the wind is against the current, a nasty chop can build up. With conditions quite benign just a short distance away, even 50-footers can pitch violently and dip their bowsprits as they cross the bar. Be prepared.

Anchorages, Moorings. Bass Harbor Marine maintains a number of moorings south of their dock on the eastern shore, which is just south of the ferry terminal and across the way on the western shore. You can anchor in about 23 feet near the moorings on either shore. In both cases, the holding ground is good, but it is likely to be rolly.

Bass Harbor Marine also manages slips and moorings way up inside the harbor near nun "6," at Bass Harbor Boat. The dredged channel shown on the chart is deep enough but narrow, and full of moored lobsterboats. Stay in the channel and wind your way among the boats.

Getting Ashore. In Bass Harbor, take the

dinghy to the Bass Harbor Marine floats or to the Tremont public landing. In Bernard, land at the Bass Harbor Boat floats.

For the Boat. *Bass Harbor Marine (Ch. 9 or 16; tel. 244-5066).* Bass Harbor Marine can provide almost anything you need. Gas, diesel, water, and electricity are available at the floats, with 15 feet alongside at low. This is a full-service yard, with a 35-ton boatlift and hydraulic trailer; hull and engine repairs can be made. Bass Harbor Marine is under the same ownership as Henry R. Hinckley & Co. in Southwest Harbor, and BHM manages the Hinckley charter fleet.

Bass Harbor Boat (tel. 244-3514). The yard's gray-and-white buildings occupy the last dock and floats northward, on the Bernard side near nun "6." Gas, water, electricity, and ice are available at the floats, with eight feet alongside at low. The yard builds wood and fiberglass boats and can do hull repairs. There are several marine railways, and a trailer that can transport boats up to 50 feet. The slips and moorings here are managed by Bass Harbor Marine.

C.H. Rich Co. (tel. 244-3485). North of the ferry landing is the red brick cannery, and just north of that is the blue shingled building of C.H. Rich. Gas and diesel are available alongside.

Little Island Marine (Ch. 6; tel. 244-3466). Billing itself as "the fisherman's boatyard," Little Island is north of C.H. Rich. With two marine railways and a 15-ton boatlift, powerboats up to 45 feet can be hauled. The yard specializes in work on engines, shafts, and propellers, and offers 24-hour emergency service.

F.W. Thurston Co. (Ch. 16; tel. 244-3320). The green-and-gray buildings of F.W. Thurston are on the Bernard side, partway along the dredged channel and just south of the big red fish plant. Catering primarily to commercial fishermen, they sell gas and diesel at their float, with seven feet alongside at low.

Tremont Public Landing. The floats at the public landing are on the east side, just north of the ferry dock, with six to seven feet alongside at low and a two-hour maximum tie-up.

For the Crew. Bass Harbor Marine has showers, a laundromat, and a pay phone.

The Maine-ly Delights takeout is right next to the ferry terminal. Up the hill from the boatyard is the Deck House Restaurant and Cabaret Theatre, where college students put on enthusiastic performances of Broadway shows (tel. 244-5044).

Walking north from the boatyard about a quarter of a mile, you will arrive at the Bass Harbor Country Store and the Seafood Ketch restaurant. Bear right at the restaurant and you will come shortly to Reed's General Store, with ice, groceries, pizza, and sandwiches, and the post office.

You can buy lobsters at F.W. Thurston in Bernard across the harbor, and there is a fish market a short distance south of Bass Harbor Boat.

Things to Do. There are several antique shops in Bernard, across the harbor. The easiest way to get there is to row.

To visit the Bass Harbor Head Light, turn right at Reed's General Store onto Route 102A and continue until you see signs to Bass Harbor Head Light. The round trip is three miles, a delightful walk.

A short trail to the left takes you down to the pink granite ledges and provides a good view of the lighthouse (now privately owned). A paved path to the right goes to the lighthouse itself, with a great bronze bell mounted next to it, marked "U.S. Lighthouse Establishment 1891."

East of Bass Harbor is Ship Harbor, which has an interesting nature trail (part of Acadia National Park). Walk out Route 102A toward the lighthouse, but continue on 102A instead of turning off. After .7 mile, you will find the beginning of this self-guiding trail, which is easy walking and delightful, with insectivorous pitcher plants in the bogs and shoreline paths among the spruce, a total of 1.3 miles.

SOUTHWEST HARBOR ★★★

Charts: 13312, 13313, 13318, **13321**

 All facilities

The great boating centers of Mount Desert—Southwest Harbor and Northeast Harbor—flank the entrance to Somes Sound. Both are working harbors, with an interesting mixture of fishing boats and handsome yachts.

There are two concentrations of boats in Southwest Harbor. Along the southern shore, in Manset, the well-known Hinckley yard provides a multitude of services for yachtsmen. On this side of the harbor, however, you will be a long way from town. Manset will be considered separately, in the following writeup.

The Coast Guard, the town dock, and many other facilities are based along the north shore of Southwest Harbor on Clark Point, a mile or less from the center of town. The working fleet is concentrated here.

Except for a channel along the northern shore, the harbor is full of moorings, but there usually is room left to anchor. Southwest offers good protection except for winds out of the east.

Although Hinckley is probably the best-known name around here, there are half a dozen other builders based in Southwest Harbor, including

Jarvis Newman and Ralph Stanley, producing everything from small boats to oceangoing trawlers. To serve the working and boating community, a broad range of marine service organizations are also based here, so you can probably find any help you need, from supplies and repairs to charters—and even that new cruising boat you've been looking for.

Approaches. Southwest Harbor is easy to approach by either the Eastern Way or the Western Way. Coming from the west, run up through Western Way, between Great Cranberry Island and Mount Desert Island, starting at gong "1" off Long Ledge. The start of the narrower portion is marked by red-and-white bell "WW," followed by a nun and can marking shoal areas on either side. Thereafter, the passage is clear to the nun on Cow Ledge, which you leave to starboard, and the red-and-white gong "SP," marking the end of Western Way.

Coming from the east, pass north or south of East Bunker Ledge. Then run through Eastern Way, along the north shore of Sutton Island, leaving to starboard several red marks and the lighthouse on Bear Island.

Anchorages, Moorings. The big, yellow mushrooms are 500-pound guest moorings put out by the town of Southwest Harbor. You will need your own pendant. A few rental moorings are available from Beal's Lobster Pier (red buildings next to the Coast Guard station) and from Morris Yachts. Next to Beal's Lobster Pier is the Southwest Harbor town dock, with temporary tie-up.

There is also room to anchor among the moorings and north of them, along the channel, in about 10 feet at low. Holding ground is good. This is a busy part of the harbor, however, with lots of lobsterboats going by in the early morning, lots of wake, and in the background two loudspeakers at the Coast Guard station and Beal's.

Getting Ashore. Go in with your dinghy to the town dock float. If you want to land closer to town, use the upper town dock, near the head of the harbor, next to Ralph W. Stanley's boatshop.

For the Boat. The Coast Guard station is at the end of Clark Point if you need help (tel. 244-5517); in an emergency use channel 16 or call 244-5121.

Beal's Lobster Pier (Ch. 16; tel. 244-3202). Next to the Coast Guard, Beal's has water, gas, and diesel at their floats (12 feet alongside at low), plus ice and marine hardware.

Downeast Diesel & Marine (tel. 244-5145). They handle engine repairs and have floats for repair work only.

McEachern & Hutchins (tel. 244-7243). This hardware store, at the main intersection in Southwest Harbor, carries a variety of marine items.

Morris Yachts (tel. 244-5509). On Clark Point Road, near town, Morris is a builder of sailboats

but also does complete hull repairs. Their marine railway can handle boats up to seven tons.

Shore Sails (tel. 244-5722). Located above Morris Yachts, Shore Sails is a service loft, providing new sails, sail repair, and canvas work.

Ralph W. Stanley (tel. 244-3795). Stanley, a well-known builder of wooden boats, is located near the head of the harbor. He has three marine railways that can handle boats to 15 tons; the yard can perform complete hull repairs.

Village Electronics (Ch. 16; tel. 244-7227). Located next to the town dock, Village Electronics sells and repairs electric and electronic gear.

For the Crew. You can eat outside on the deck at Beal's Lobster Pier, next to the town dock, or at Kay and John's Lobster Pier behind the Oceanarium. Walk up Clark Point Road toward the town of Southwest Harbor and you will pass several inns that serve meals. There are restaurants in town, within a mile or so from the town dock.

It is also possible to sail around the peninsula that forms Southwest Harbor and anchor off the docks and floats of the Claremont Hotel, opposite Greening Island. The hotel maintains guest moorings, and there is eight feet alongside the floats. Lunch and cocktails are served in the informal waterfront Boathouse, and dinner in the formal dining room (coats and ties). For reservations, call 244-5036.

Lobster and fresh fish are available at Beal's. Sawyer's Market in the center of town will deliver to the waterfront (tel. 244-3315).

About .2 mile north of the center of town, on Route 102, you will find The Village Washtub, a full-service laundromat (tel. 244-7228). Half a mile farther north is a little shopping center, with a liquor store, fish market, and beauty parlor.

The Southwest Harbor Medical Center, a division of Ellsworth's Maine Coast Memorial Hospital, provides emergency care at all hours. Walk up Clark Point Road and turn right on Herrick Road at the Medical Center sign. Distance from the town dock is .8 mile (tel. 244-5513).

Things to Do. To rent a car and explore Acadia National Park, try Hertz (tel. 667-5017) or U-Save (tel. 667-6130) at the Bar Harbor airport, or Hopkins Taxi in Bass Harbor (tel. 244-7725). Bikes can be rented at Southwest Cycle, on Main Street (tel. 244-5856).

The Mount Desert Oceanarium is right on the waterfront, west of the town dock, marked by a blue lobsterboat. Its building once was a "coal and vittlin' station" for coastal schooners. It's well worth a visit, especially for the children. In addition to fish tanks and exhibits on commercial fishing, lobstering, and the causes of tides, there is a touch tank where you can pick up sea cucumbers, clams, and other shellfish. The lectures on lobstering and lobsters by David Mills, founder of the

Oceanarium, are particularly interesting.

Another superb experience is offered by the Wendell Gilley Museum, north of town on Route 102, about 1.3 miles from the town dock. The late Wendell Gilley earned his living as a plumber, but while fixing oil burners and thawing pipes, he started carving birds. Completely self-taught, he carved barn owls and ospreys, ducks and herons. Samples sent to Abercrombie and Fitch in New York were well received, and Gilley put his son through college with the proceeds. After 27 years in the plumbing business, he turned to carving full time. The handsome museum has an extensive collection of his work, and a complete set of Audubon prints. There are also some good films and frequent classes in bird-carving. Even if you aren't a dedicated bird-lover, this is a fascinating place.

MANSET (SOUTHWEST HARBOR)

(For Charts, Harbor Ratings, and Approaches, see under Southwest Harbor, above.)

Manset is on the southern shore of Southwest Harbor. On this side of the harbor, the well-known Hinckley yard provides a multitude of services for yachtsmen, although you will be a long way from the activities centered across the way.

Call it a cult, or call it a group of sailors who *know* they own the best boats in the world, Hinckley owners are a race apart. Now well into its second half-century, the company was started by Henry Hinckley in 1932, building wooden boats including Sou'westers and Pilots. By the late 1940s Hinckley had become the nation's largest builder of cruising sailboats. Then came fiberglass. Hinckley was one of the first to learn how to use the new material. Their first glass model, starting in 1959, was the classic Bermuda 40. Well over 200 of these comfortable, beamy centerboarders have been built, and the B-40 is still in production.

Henry Hinckley sold the company to Canadians in the late 1970s, but in 1983 it was purchased by Shep McKenney and Bob Hinckley, Henry's son. So the family tradition continues. The yard today limits production to 10 or 15 boats a year, including the B-40, the popular Sou'wester series, and, more recently, Talaria powerboats. In addition to molding hulls, Hinckley fabricates all its own spars, electrical panels, and metal parts—everything except the engine—and the emphasis is still on quality.

Anchorages, Moorings. Hinckley has the first very long dock on the south side of the harbor, marked with a little gray building at the end. The yard maintains a large number of moorings, and dockage for 100-footers. There is also plenty of room to anchor off the moored boats in 20 to 30 feet of water at low. The Manset town dock is a few hundred yards west of Hinckley and provides temporary tie-ups for boats to 45 feet, plus water and electricity.

Getting Ashore. Take your dinghy in to the floats at Hinckley, or the Manset town dock. Hinckley has a launch service that responds to channel 9 or three toots.

For the Boat. *The Hinckley Company. (Ch. 9 or 16; tel. 244-5531).* This major boatyard provides diesel, water, ice, and electricity at the floats with 10 feet alongside at low. Hinckley has a marine railway that can handle boats to 65 feet, a 20-ton crane, and a 70-ton lift, and continues to expand its service facilities. Hull, rigging, electronics, and engine repairs of all kinds can be made. There is a well-stocked ship's store.

For the Crew. Showers and laundry facilities are provided by Hinckley right at the head of the dock; there is also a pay phone. The Moorings Restaurant is right next door (tel. 244-7070).

Walk south about a quarter of a mile from Hinckley to the Double J Grocery & Deli, at the intersection of Route 102. From Hinckley to the center of Southwest Harbor, via the shore road (Route 102A and then 102), it is 1.7 miles. Hinckley may be able to arrange transportation. It is possible, of course, to row directly across the harbor.

NORTHEAST HARBOR ★★★★★   All facilities

Charts: 13312, 13318, **13321**

At the eastern side of the entrance to Somes Sound, in a setting of great natural beauty, Northeast Harbor is one of Maine's major yachting centers. Still reflecting its history as the playground of affluent society, the harbor has the elegant Asticou Inn and a wonderful armada of pleasure craft, with a working fleet of lobsterboats mixed in. The best large harbor in the Mount Desert area, Northeast makes it very easy for the yachtsman: services are concentrated on the waterfront, stores deliver, and the town is water-oriented.

This is home port for *Sunbeam IV*, the missionary boat that brings religious services and practical help to many of the isolated islands of the coast.

The 65-foot steel vessel is recognizable by the prominent white crosses on her bows. It is also the home of Maine Whalewatch, which will take you out to see finbacks and humpbacks, and perhaps even a rare right whale. The ferry to the Cranberry Islands operates from here as well.

One of the treasures of Northeast Harbor is Asticou Terraces, gardens that are easy to reach by dinghy and not to be missed.

Approaches. Coming from west and south, approach through Western Way, between Great Cranberry Island and Mount Desert Island, starting at gong "1" off Long Ledge. The beginning of the narrower portion is marked by red-and-white bell "WW," followed by a nun and a can marking shoal areas on each side. Thereafter, the passage is clear to the nun on Cow Ledge, which you leave to starboard, and red-and-white gong "SP," marking the end of Western Way. From there, it is open water to red bell "2," left to starboard, and a wide, clear entrance to the harbor. A buoyed channel leads among the boats.

Coming from the east, pass north or south of East Bunker Ledge. Then run through Eastern Way, along the north shore of Sutton Island, leaving to starboard several red marks, the lighthouse on Bear Island, and red bell "2" at the entrance.

Anchorages, Moorings. On the west side of the harbor, near the southern end, is the large town dock and marina (also called the municipal pier). The inner portion is reserved for commercial use, but the outer finger floats are available to yachts, with 10 feet alongside at low. For dockage, check with the harbormaster on channel 16 or 68, or look for him in his gray office at the head of the pier.

A large number of town-owned rental moorings are available, identified by bright green pickup buoys. They vary in weight; call the MDI water taxi or the harbormaster on Ch. 16 or Ch. 68 to have a mooring assigned. The town mooring agent will come by to collect the fee.

All of the deep water in the inner harbor is full of moorings, and anchoring is not allowed. There appears to be space on the east side of the entrance, but the bottom is hard clay; neither Danforths nor plows will hold there.

Keep your eyes open. There is a lot of traffic around the town dock, including cruise boats and the Cranberry Islands ferry.

Getting Ashore. Yachtsmen should come in to the dinghy floats farthest north and parallel to the shore. (The public float south of the town pier is intended for fishermen's dinghies.) Another possibility is the MDI water taxi cruising around the harbor; it answers on channel 16 or channel 68, or call 244-7312.

For the Boat. *F.T. Brown (tel. 276-3329).* On Main Street, Brown has hardware, propane, charts, and marine supplies.

Clifton Dock Corp. (tel. 276-5308). On the west side of the entrance to Northeast Harbor, Clifton Dock is a convenient spot to take on gas, diesel, and water, with 22 feet alongside the fuel float. Also available are ice and trash disposal.

Curved Tree Communications (tel. 276-5090). Located on Tracy Road, a few blocks from the waterfront, Curved Tree sells and services marine electronics.

Mount Desert Yacht Yard (tel. 276-5114). At the northwestern end of the harbor, the yard has moorings and dockage for its customers, but occasionally available to others. There is six or seven feet alongside at low, with water and electricity, but no fuel. There are two boatlifts (one for 35 tons) and a crane, and the yard can perform hull and engine repairs.

Northeast Harbor Fleet. The club is located in Gilpatrick Cove, to the west. See ahead.

Northeast Harbor Marina (Ch. 16 or 68; tel. 276-5737 for harbormaster). The town dock here is one of the largest facilities of its kind, with many floats, parking spaces, open greens, and tennis courts. The dock is used by tour boats, ferries, fishing boats, and yachts, so traffic is heavy. Water and electricity are available at the public float (farthest south), where you can tie up for two hours, with eight or nine feet at low.

For the Crew. Pay phones are right at the town dock. The Chamber of Commerce has a shingled building at Sea Street and Harbor Drive, close to the waterfront. It includes the "Yachtsman's Building," with showers, reading room, and recent copies of the *New York Times*. The Chamber of Commerce (tel. 276-5040) handles reservations for the public tennis courts at the marina.

There are takeouts close to the waterfront on the road into town, and two restaurants at the edge of the green opposite the waterfront.

Walk a short way into town, turn right on Main Street, and you will find Provisions, a market that monitors channel 16, or call 276-5163. They will deliver quality meats, cheeses, wines, and fresh produce to your boat. There is an ice machine.

The Shirt Off Your Back Laundry, next door to Provisions, offers full service. Laundry brought in in the morning is ready that afternoon. The post office is also to the right on Main Street.

To the left on Main Street is Pine Tree Market, which sells fresh produce, prime meats, and groceries, and will deliver to the dock (tel. 276-3335). Stanley's Fish Market is nearby (tel. 276-3660). Right behind Pine Tree Market, facing on Tracy Road, is Pine Tree Liquors (tel. 276-3303), which also will deliver.

In the same direction are a convenience store,

drugstore, wine and cheese shop, deli, bakery, cafe, bookstore, and newsstand.

For day trips, island tours, or transportation to the Hancock County Airport, 15 miles away, call Island Rent-A-Car (tel. 276-3383) in town, or Hertz (tel. 667-5017) or U-Save (tel. 667-6130) at the Bar Harbor airport. For Airport Taxi call 667-5995.

Mount Desert Medical Center (tel. 276-3331) is on Kimball Road at the south end of town.

Things to Do. Beal & Bunker, Inc., offers a variety of sightseeing cruises starting from the waterfront, including one with an Acadia Park naturalist aboard, and an evening cocktail cruise. Sign up at the waterfront booth (tel. 244-3575). They also run the mailboat trips to the Cranberry Islands. The *Delight,* a 32-foot antique open launch, provides water-taxi service to the outlying islands (tel. 244-5724). The *Islesford Ferry* offers nature cruises to the Cranberry Islands (tel. 276-3717).

Maine Whalewatch (tel. 276-5803) makes a full-day trip out to Mount Desert Rock, looking for finback and humpback whales, porpoises, and many species of seabirds. A naturalist is aboard.

One of the most rewarding experiences is to visit Thuya Lodge and Gardens in Asticou Terraces. Climbing the hill at the northeast side of the harbor, the terraces and gazebos were designed by Joseph Henry Curtis (1841–1928) "for the quiet recreation of the people of this town and their summer guests." The rustic paths lead upward to the Thuya Lodge and Gardens. The small formal garden is a delight for botanist and gardener alike, and there is a rare botanical book collection in the lodge. From the gardens, a leisurely trail leads to Eliot Mountain, or you could follow the park trails east a couple of miles to Jordan Pond House. Take your dinghy in to the float of Asticou Landing, at the northeastern part of the harbor, built with pink granite. Follow the path to the main road and cross on the crosswalk to Asticou Terraces.

In town, to your left on Main Street, is the Old Fire House Museum, with its "Great Harbor Collection." If you are socked in by weather, make a visit to the charming public library; the Milliken Room devoted to books about Maine is especially interesting.

GILPATRICK COVE (NORTHEAST HARBOR FLEET)

Charts: 13312, 13318, **13321**

Gilpatrick Cove, around the corner to the west from Northeast Harbor, is home to the Northeast Harbor Fleet (tel. 276-5101). There is a handsome little clubhouse on the east shore, plus a launch, water, and 4½ feet at the floats at low. The rare visiting yachtsman is well received, but there are no guest moorings or other facilities. The club exists primarily for racing and has a fleet of Internationals and J-24's.

SOMES SOUND

Charts: 13312, **13318**, 13321

Somes Sound is a glacial river valley drowned by the ocean, and there's nothing like it our side of the Atlantic. It would be worth coming to Maine just to sail in this majestic fjord, mountains ahead, islands astern and towering cliffs on either side.

The splendid harbors of Southwest and Northeast flank the entrances to Somes Sound, and the Northeast Harbor Fleet is based in Gilpatrick Cove. There are several boatyards in the Sound.

Sailing in Somes Sound is variable and challenging. The wind usually funnels straight up or straight down the sound, and it is likely to shift rapidly. Downdrafts come off the mountains, cat's-paws spread in all directions, and the current runs strong in the Narrows. With the cliffs in many places falling straight off into the sea, you can hold your course till the last minute and tack under the loom of the rocks. In one or two spots, you can lay your boat right up against the cliffs. Porpoises are often seen here.

Valley Cove is a wonderful spot to anchor, under Eagle Cliffs, and around the next headland, Man o'War Brook still tumbles into the sound as it did when English ships filled their water casks here. If you venture close to the western shore you'll find a bronze plaque set in the vertical stone in memory of the Reverend Cornelius Smith and his wife, Mary Wheeler, who were pioneers of the summer colony of Northeast Harbor (1886–1913), and who gave Acadia Mountain to the public. Just beyond are the silent granite faces of Hall Quarry. Five miles up at the head of the sound is the narrow entrance to Somes Harbor and the peaceful village of Somesville. There are a number of places along the sound to spend the night, including Valley Cove, Somes Harbor, and several of the yards mentioned below.

For the Boat. *John M. Williams Co. (tel. 244-7854).* At the old Hall Quarry on the western side of Somes Sound, Williams is a custom boatbuilder.

Gilpatrick Cove, home for the Northeast Harbor Fleet. In the background is Somes Sound. (Hylander photo)

ATLANTIC NEPTUNE

Cruising the coast of Maine is challenging enough with today's excellent and detailed charts. Think what it must have been like with no charts—or, perhaps worse, with inaccurate charts. When Joseph F.W. DesBarres began his survey of the eastern coast of Canada and the United States in 1764, the English charts (even those of the British Isles) were full of mistakes. The Hydrographer in Ordinary to Charles II referred to "the common scandal of their badness."

When DesBarres published the first of the *Atlantic Neptune* series, in 1774, they showed a marked advance in accuracy and detail over what had been available previously

to mariners. Called "the most splendid collection of charts, plans and views ever published," the *Atlantic Neptune* charts remain fascinating to this day. Strikingly colored, they are works of art in themselves.

The foreword to the 1781 edition, kept in the Map Room of the British Museum, says this about the utility of the *Atlantic Neptune:* "The Northern Coast and Harbours of His American dominion were unexplored, and very partially and imperfectly known, and that only to a few fishermen. The Isle of Sable itself was a terror to all Navigators at large going to America, or returning thence to Europe, and shipwrecks were innumerable. In the progres-

sive execution of the Royal Commands, every master of a vessel became himself a Pilot of the district exhibited in the part of the work which fell into his hands, and no shipwrecks are heard of, excepting from insurmountable stress of weather or negligence. In the safety, abridgement, confidence, and frequency of Voyages, the notion has saved millions . . . . "

The *Atlantic Neptune* became the standard charts for almost a century, and they were still the best when DesBarres died in Halifax, aged 102. The chart of Mount Desert is reproduced in this book.

The *Atlantic Neptune* shows a number of intriguing and amusing

282

He also has rental moorings. There is a 30-ton boatlift, and the yard can make engine, hull and rigging repairs or allows you to do it yourself. Water is available at the floats, with plenty of depth alongside.

From the Williams yard, walk up the tarred road until you are even with the top of the quarry, then walk left on the dirt road to the shack once used by the crane operator, whose gears and levers have rusted there in place. There is a dizzy view

differences in nomenclature from our present charts. Rockport is "Goose River," Rockland is "Owls Head Bay," Camden is "Meguanticook Harbor," the Camden Hills are the "Penobscot Mountains." Going east, you pass through "Edgemogin River" and reach "Mount Desert Island," beyond which is "Moose a Becky's Beach," leading to "Great Island" [Roque].

There is a fascinating footnote. For the *Atlantic Neptune* series, British surveyor Samuel Holland made a detailed chart of Mount Desert, reproduced here. Compare it with your own chart and you may notice a strange omission. This meticulous cartographer, known for the accuracy of his charts, has somehow missed Northeast Harbor and Seal Harbor altogether. The southeast coast of Mount Desert is devoid of harbors. Historian Samuel Eliot Morison surmises that "fog must have concealed the harbor entrance" on the day the surveyor sailed by. More likely, this was where the British fleet was based, and the chart was an early example of "disinformation."

DesBarres's methods are interesting to those of us who wonder how such a thing can be done. In one of his reports he explains that he measured a base of 350 fathoms along the shore of a harbor, then sighted the angles from the end of the base line to objects placed on the opposite shore, calculated the other sides of the triangles by trigonometry, and drew the results on paper fixed on a plain table.

Then, he said, "from points as were most commodiously situated on those islands, and head lands, I observed the distant head lands, bays, islands, points, and other remarkable objects, as far as they could be distinguished. Next I went along shore, and reexamined the accuracy of every intersected object, delineated the true shape of every head land, island, point, bay, rock

above water, etc and every winding and irregularity of the coast; and, with boats sent around the shoals, rocks and breakers, determined from observations on shore, their positions and extent, as perfectly as I could.

"When the map of any part of the coast was completed in this manner, I provided immediately each craft with copys of it: the sloop was employed in beating off and on, upon the coast, to the distance of ten and twelve miles in the offing,

laying down the soundings in their proper bearings and distance, remarking every where the quality of the bottom. The shallop was, in the meantime, kept busy in sounding, and remarking around the headlands, islands, and rocks in the offing; and the boats within the indraught, upwards, to the heads of bays, harbors etc."

The *Atlantic Neptune* charts the coast in detail from the St. Lawrence to the Mississippi—quite an accomplishment.

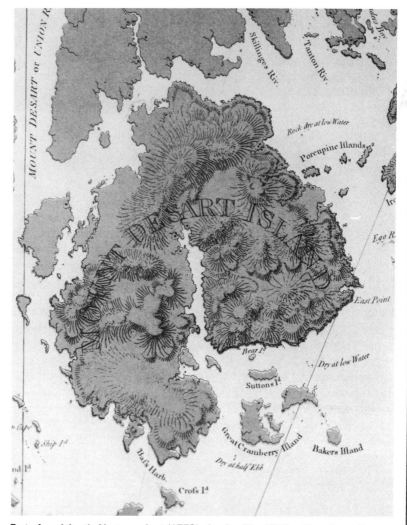

Part of an *Atlantic Neptune* chart (1772) showing Blue Hill Bay, Frenchman Bay, and Mount Desert. This chart, prepared by British surveyor Samuel Holland, omits Northeast Harbor, where the British fleet lay—perhaps an early example of "disinformation." (Courtesy Maine Historical Society)

down a vertical face of stone into the quarry pool. From the yard, walk up to the paved road and turn left, continuing to Route 102. Turn left again about 100 yards to the sign for Ike's Point. There you will discover a tiny beach on beautiful Echo Lake. The swimming is great. Total distance is 1.3 miles one way.

Bar Harbor Boating (Ch. 9 or 10. tel. 276-5838). This yard, with a big red shed and gray doors, has several moorings in a little cove on the east side, directly opposite Hall Quarry. They have a dock, floats (six feet alongside), and a 20-ton marine railway, and can make hull and engine repairs. Water, ice, and propane are available, but no fuel.

Henry R. Abel Yacht Yard (tel. 276-5837). The Abel yard is located on the northeast side of Somes Sound, just beyond nun "10." There a number of

granite-block moorings inside the ledge marked by the nun. Take care, however. The yard reports that each year boats cut the nun and end up on the ledge. The yard has several floats, with seven feet reported alongside. Water, electricity, and ice are available, but no fuel. This expanding yard handles hull repairs and painting in its large sheds, including one for spray-painting. It has two boatlifts, of 35 and 50 tons. Engine repairs can be arranged. Abel's Lobster Pound restaurant, next to the yard, has tables outside in a pine grove. Very attractive.

It's about 2 miles to Somesville by road for groceries, or you can get there, of course, by water.

To enter the national park trails, walk up from the yard to the main road and turn right. About three-quarters of a mile south you will find a sign for Giant Slide Trail, leading to Sargent Mountain.

VALLEY COVE ★★★★   No facilities
Charts: 13312, **13318**

Just inside the entrance to Somes Sound, on the western shore, Valley Cove is one of the grandest spots on Mount Desert for the cruising sailor. Below the great cliffs and spruce forest, where French and British and perhaps even Vikings have moored before, a boat seems small against the backdrop of nature and history.

A short but vigorous hike from Valley Cove will take you to the top of Flying Mountain, with marvelous views.

Approaches. The only dangers at the entrance to Somes Sound are marked by can "7," which is left to port, just before The Narrows. Thereafter, the channel is deep to Valley Cove.

Anchorages, Moorings. Feel your way in toward the southern shore and anchor in 25 to 35 feet at low. Although the wind can funnel up or down Somes Sound, and gusts blow down from the mountains, protection here is good.

Getting Ashore. Land on the pebble beach on the southern shore, near a small footbridge.

Things to Do. To the left, the trail leads southward to the summit of Flying Mountain, through a spruce forest. The Appalachian Mountain Club calls this trail, "the greatest reward on the island for a small effort." It is rough and steep in places, but well blazed with orange marks on the rocks. There are two lookouts from which you can gaze up and down Somes Sound, but don't stop. Con-

tinue southward along the crest of the mountain until the trail leads you to the bare rocks on top, with U.S. Coast and Geodetic Survey marks that call it "Fernald Hill."

From there, look south to the historic meadows of Jesuit Spring, past Greening and Sutton islands to the Cranberry Islands and the great Atlantic. The distance is .3 mile to the crest, and about an equal distance along the crest to the southern summit. Allow three-quarters of an hour to go up and back, or take a picnic and linger on top.

If you walk north for a mile on the trail instead, you will reach Man o'War Brook. This is a difficult hike. The first part leads over the tumbled rock scree just under the cliff face, and the footing is tricky. When you round the headland at the north end of Valley Cove, the path is much easier through the cedar, pine, and spruce forest. After one mile, turn right at the signpost and take the path down toward the sound of rushing waters and the overlook. Man o'War Brook tumbles down steep ledges and finally vertically into Somes Sound. The brook runs into the tiny indentation just north of Valley Cove, and it is easier to reach by water than by land. British ships found the stream to be a perfect place to take on drinking water. It served naval vessels as late as 1878, when *Cimbria* of the Imperial Russian Navy topped off here.

SOMES HARBOR ★★★★
Charts: 13312, **13318**

At the northwest end of Somes Sound, the little village of Somesville is a quiet backwater that seems to have changed little since a cooper, Abra-

ham Somes, brought his family here from Gloucester in 1761. There are some attractive old white clapboard homes, a market, a gas station, the Masonic Hall, and suddenly there's the blinking light and you're out of town.

Somes Harbor is snug and well protected, open only through the narrow entrance to the south. There is no commercial activity in the harbor, and it is thoroughly restful and charming.

Approaches. There are no problems in the approach. Somes Sound is deep and clear almost until you reach the end. Leave nun "8," marking Myrtle Ledge, to starboard, then pass through the narrow entrance west of Bar Island, leaving cans "9" and "11" to port.

Anchorages, Moorings. Anchor north and east of can "11," in 15 to 20 feet of water at low. Holding ground is good. Local sailors report that Bar Island breaks the wind and Somes Harbor offers the best protection anywhere around.

Getting Ashore. Take your dinghy in to the float and dock maintained by the Somesville Landing Association, off the meadows at the west side of the harbor.

For the Boat. There are no facilities in Somes Harbor itself. If you are in need of repairs, try one of the Somes Sound boatyards listed earlier.

For the Crew. Walk up the gravel road a short distance to Route 102, and turn left. It is .3 mile

from the landing to A.V. Higgins Market, a pleasantly old-fashioned general store where you can buy fish, meat, groceries, and ice, and find homemade bread and great blueberry pies. There is also a pay phone.

If you turn right on Route 102 instead, the road will take you a bit farther to A.C. Fernald & Sons, with groceries, hardware, pay phone, a takeout, and the post office nearby.

Things to Do. People looking for something to do on a rainy day have been known to pack the little library in Somesville, if it happens to be Wednesday or Saturday, or the even tinier Mount Desert Museum next to the millpond.

In the Masonic Hall at the south end of town, the Acadia Repertory Theatre offers professional productions—thrillers, drama, and farce—during July and August (tel. 244-7260). Bring a flashlight. Arcady Music Festival plays a regular concert series at the Union Meeting Hall, generally on Monday evenings, during July and August.

Bar Island, in the entrance to Somes Harbor, is owned by the state and awaits your exploration. A halftide gravel bar connects the wooded island to the mainland. Land on the bar or scramble up the slippery rocks along the shore.

CRANBERRY ISLANDS

Charts: 13312, 13318, **13321**

The Cranberries are beautiful and peaceful islands, with miles of walks and spectacular views of sea and mountains. Named for their extensive cranberry bogs and known for their mosquitoes, the islands undertook a program of drainage in the 1920s. As islander Wilfred Bunker says, "The mosquitoes came back, but the cranberries didn't."

The Cranberry Islands are in transition. Fishing islands for two centuries, their small population now includes more summer people than fishermen. Of the five islands considered part of the Cranberries, the two closest to the mainland, Bear

and Sutton, are now private. Baker Island is uninhabited, half of it belonging to Acadia National Park. Only Great and Little Cranberry still have the schools, post offices, and stores that make them viable year-round communities. Perhaps 55 families live on Great Cranberry year round, and fewer on Little Cranberry.

A private ferry service connects the Cranberries to Northeast Harbor. The Beal & Bunker vessels take islanders to the mainland for supplies and transport tourists to enjoy the simple pleasures of the islands.

GREAT CRANBERRY ISLAND ★★★

Charts: 13312, 13318, **13321**

Larger but seemingly more remote than the other islands in the group, Great Cranberry lies due south of Northeast Harbor, only two miles away. The lobstermen share the island with summer people, many of whom have come here for generations. This is a delightful place to enjoy peaceful walks, island beauty, friendly people, and almost-tame deer.

Approaches. The approach to Spurling Cove, on the north shore, is open and unobstructed.

Anchorages, Moorings. Moorings are available from Island Woodworking, which also has some space alongside the floats at the eastern dock. You can anchor outside the moored boats, in 16 to 25 feet at low. There is considerable exposure from northwest to northeast.

Getting Ashore. Land at the dinghy float of the public dock, to the west.

For the Boat. *Island Woodworking (Ch. 68; tel. 244-7225).* At the eastern dock Island Woodworking offers gas, diesel, and water at their floats, with 9 to 10 feet alongside at low. The yard hauls boats on 30-ton ways; it can handle electrical and minor mechanical repairs and arrange for repairs of all kinds.

For the Crew. The post office and a pay phone are at the head of the Island Woodworking dock. Ferries and water taxis use the public dock. A short way up the road is the Pine Tree Market, with groceries, beer, and wine. A 15-minute walk will bring you to the Granite Napkin, in an old house just past the church. It serves elegant light lunches with garden produce and home-baked specialties (also Thursday suppers by reservation, tel. 244-7758). Not far beyond is the Whale's Rib gift shop, which offers a selection of seeds of island plants and flowers—lupine, beach pea, beach rose, and wild iris.

Things to Do. A single paved road runs two miles or so, the length of the island. There are flower-filled meadows, well-kept cottages, and side roads to explore. One of these leads eastward to "The Pool," where the Cranberry Island Boatyard builds custom boats. The main road leads you to beautiful rocks on the southern shore. The many high fences around the gardens are to protect them from the deer.

LITTLE CRANBERRY ISLAND ★★★★ (ISLESFORD)

Charts: 13312, 13318, **13321**

Less than two miles to seaward of Mount Desert, the town of Islesford on Little Cranberry Island enjoys spectacular views of the mountains to the north and the lights of Southwest Harbor twinkling to the west. This is a small, quiet island, with pleasant walks, an interesting little museum, and a waterfront restaurant. Transportation is furnished by Beal & Bunker ferry from Northeast Harbor. There is a constant coming and going of water taxis, fishing boats, and yachts in the anchorage.

Approaches. The harbor in Hadlock Cove can be approached from the west or north. From red bell "2" in Gilley Thorofare marking Spurling Rock, leave cans "1" and "3" to port.

As you look toward land from the harbor, there are three docks: The one to the left is Islesford Dock, in the center is the Fishermen's Co-op, and to the right is the town dock. Be careful of the granite remains of a former pier (shown on the chart), just left of the Islesford Dock.

Anchorages, Moorings. All of Cranberry Harbor can be used as an anchorage, with depths of 14 to 23 feet at low, but the best protection is found in Hadlock Cove. The Little Cranberry Yacht Club, whose one-room clubhouse is on Islesford Dock, has guest moorings (marked "LCYC"). Puddles Restaurant maintains several rental moorings on the western edge of the anchorage.

If no mooring is available, there is plenty of room to anchor outside the moored boats. Some people have reported difficulty with kelp on the bottom, but you should have no trouble if you have a heavy plow anchor. The anchorage is quite exposed in several directions.

Getting Ashore. Land your dinghy at the town dock or the Islesford Dock.

Island transportation: a load of lumber being delivered by barge and lobsterboat to Islesford (Little Cranberry Island). (Christopher Ayres photo)

For the Boat. Limited amounts of gas and diesel are available at the floats of the Fisherman's Co-op, with nine feet at low. Not far up the road is a lumberyard that carries marine hardware.

Hill's Boat Yard (Ch. 16; tel. 244-7150). On Sand Beach, near the south end of the moored boats, Hill's Boat Yard has a marine railway and can arrange for repairs of all kinds.

For the Crew. There is a pay phone on the Islesford Dock, and public restrooms in the "Blue Duck," ashore. Overlooking the harbor is Puddles Restaurant (tel. 244-3177), serving meals in pleasant surroundings. A short walk eastward on the main road will bring you to the Pine Tree Market and a post office in the same building. Lobsters can be bought at the Fisherman's Co-op.

Things to Do. Be sure to visit the Islesford Historic Museum, in the handsome Georgian Revival brick-and-granite building close to the docks. It houses a collection of nautical memorabilia, old documents, tools, charts, photos, and domestic furnishings depicting the history of the Cranberry Islands.

The women of Islesford display and sell their "winter work" in a shop on Islesford Dock.

It's a half-hour walk from the waterfront to the old Coast Guard station at Bar Point (now private). To visit Heirloom Weavers, turn north before the Pine Tree Market. Across the street from Heirloom Weavers is Island Artists, displaying paintings and watercolors by local artists.

A short walk leads down Sand Beach to the Maypole, site of the island's eighteenth-century celebrations of spring. According to Ted Spurling, "this custom was brought by a beautiful Frenchwoman, Margarite La Croix Stanley, wife of John Stanley, the first permanent settler."

BAKER ISLAND
Charts: 13312, 13318, **13321**

In 1899 Charles W. Eliot, president of Harvard, wrote a well-known history about pioneer life on Baker Island. In *John Gilley of Baker's Island*, he related the story of William Gilley and his wife, Hannah, who arrived in 1806 on Baker Island, most remote of the Cranberries. "There it lay in the sea, unoccupied and unclaimed," wrote Eliot, "and they simply took possession of it." The island is still beautiful today, and probably not very different from the way it was back then. Half of Baker Island is privately owned, and the other half is a part of Acadia National Park. In the middle of the island is an automated lighthouse maintained by the Coast Guard. Sightseeing boats come to Baker Island from Northeast Harbor with a park ranger aboard, but it is easy for a yachtsman to make a day stop here.

A sign in the park portion of the island summarizes Eliot's history of the Gilleys: "William and Hannah Gilley raised 12 children to maturity. Forest and sea shaped their world; farming, fishing and hunting sustained them. They worked hard. Calloused hands wielded an ax, guided a plow, trimmed a sail, treadled a spinning wheel or held a child. To their skilled labor, the land produced vegetables, forage for stock and a little wheat. They caught herring and mackerel and picked up lobsters in the shallows. Like us they knew joy and sorrow, labor and rest, adversity and success."

Approaches. As shown on chart 13318, a line of cans and a whistle guard the eastern shores of Little Cranberry and Baker islands. Run outside this line until you reach can "3," at Baker Island. Using chart 13321, coast along the north shore of Baker toward the bight in the ledge south of Gravel Nobble.

Anchorages, Moorings. Anchor off the north shore of Baker where you have swinging room, in 10 to 17 feet at low.

Getting Ashore. Row in to the rock beach where the path hits the shore, as shown on the chart.

Things to Do. Walk right along the beach to where the path leads through a thick growth of beach roses, then follow it past the red and white houses to the lighthouse. Just before the lighthouse, the path makes a sharp right through the woods and leads to the storm beach and "Dance Hall Floor," an aptly named spot. Cranberry Islanders used to pack up food, spirits, and wind-up Victrolas and while away time on these beautiful flat ledges.

SEAL HARBOR ★★★   2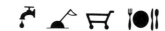
Charts: 13312, 13318, **13321**

The first home in Seal Harbor was built by John Clement in 1809, but Rockefeller is the name more commonly associated with this harbor. Peggy and David Rockefeller, who summer in Seal Harbor, helped found the Maine Coast Heritage Trust, which has been influential in preserving and protecting many of the state's islands and shores that yachtsmen enjoy today.

The harbor itself is exposed to the south. During normal summer weather, you will be safe here, but there is likely to be a roll even when it's calm. During strong southerlies or southeasterlies, the harbor would be unpleasant.

Other than the town wharf and the Seal Harbor Yacht Club, there are no boat facilities. The big gray shed at the western end of the harbor is the Rockefeller boathouse.

An entrance to Acadia National Park is nearby, with access to Jordan Pond House and to Wildwood Stables.

Approaches. The approach to Seal Harbor is easy. Note Bowden Ledge off the entrance, marked by nun "6," and the ledge uncovering six feet at the left-hand side of the entrance. Leave can "1" to port coming in. From the east, the white pyramid on East Bunker Ledge is a good landmark.

Anchorages, Moorings. The Seal Harbor Yacht Club has some guest moorings, marked "SHYC"; pick one up and check at the club. Otherwise, anchor anywhere convenient, in 9 to 18 feet at low. Holding ground is good.

Getting Ashore. Tie up your dinghy behind the float at the town wharf or at the yacht club dinghy float.

For the Boat. *Seal Harbor Yacht Club (tel. 276-5888).* The Seal Harbor Yacht Club is perched on the rocks on the east side of the harbor, with an elevator leading down from the road above. Water and electricity are available at the floats, with about six feet alongside at low, but no facilities other than a simple clubhouse.

Town Wharf. The town wharf is a substantial granite dock on the east side of the harbor, just south of the yacht club. Depth is 10 to 13 feet alongside the floats at low, and there is water.

For the Crew. Walk half a mile from the town wharf into town where you will find the Seal Harbor General Store, supplying groceries, fresh fruit and vegetables, gourmet foods, ice, and wine. Nearby are a pay phone, the post office, and the Lighthouse restaurant. Farther up the street is a gas station with beer, wine, soda, ice, and ice cream.

Things to Do. A highlight for many visitors to Acadia National Park is Jordan Pond House, a unique restaurant that serves luncheon, tea, and dinner (tel. 276-3316). It is about a two-mile walk from the Stanley Brook entrance to the park, at the head of Seal Harbor. (You probably can hitch a ride.) A sign at the restaurant reveals something of its history: "In the late 1800's and early 1900's fashionable cottage dwellers and wealthy visitors dined in rustic style at the Jordan Pond House. Built as a simple farmhouse in 1847, it later expanded into a restaurant with several wings. Fire ravaged the entire structure on June 21, 1979. Rising from the ashes a new tea house/restaurant has replaced the old, continuing a tradition of gracious dining in an atmosphere of genial surroundings. Luncheon on the porch, tea on the lawn, dinner by the fireside. Now, as then, specialties include chicken, lobster, home-made ice cream, fresh popovers, big brown and featherweight." Tea on the lawn has been a special event for generations of patrons. Be ready to wait, however; Jordan Pond House is not a secret. Reservations are recommended.

Just north of the restaurant, a number of lovely trails lead off around Jordan Pond (1.8 miles), to the Bubbles, Asticou, Sargent Mountain, and Pemetic Mountain.

One of the most delightful ways to see Acadia National Park, including Jordan Pond House, is in a horse-drawn carriage, on the 57 miles of carriage roads that wander through the eastern part of the park. Wildwood Stables (tel. 276-3622) will pick you up for one of their scheduled tours.

FRENCHMAN BAY
and Western Schoodic Peninsula

Charts: 13312, 13318, 13322, 13323

The name of Frenchman Bay commemorates Samuel de Champlain, that early French explorer who visited Mount Desert in 1604 and named so many of the islands. It is the most dramatic of the bays along the Maine coast, dominated by the pink granite of Cadillac Mountain, highest point on the eastern seaboard. Below Cadillac, Champlain Mountain rises from the ocean, then Schooner Head, Great Head, and Otter Cliffs. To the east, the rolling, wooded Schoodic Peninsula frames the bay.

The smooth ledges of Egg Rock and its welcoming lighthouse mark the middle of the entrance to Frenchman Bay. Northward lies a procession of bold and cliffy islands and peninsulas—the Porcupines to Ironbound and Grindstone Neck. There are caves in the seaward cliffs of these islands, and narrow passages: Halibut Hole between Ironbound and Jordan, the slot between Rum Key and Long Porcupine, the passage west of Sheep Porcupine—a pleasure to thread under sail.

Frenchman Bay can claim only a few good harbors: Bar Harbor, Winter Harbor, and Sorrento. But what glorious sailing territory it is. Below the

Porcupines, the bay is open to the ocean swells; north of the Porcupines, the bay is calmer and the shores not quite as dramatic.

Much of the natural beauty of Frenchman Bay is protected by Acadia National Park, which includes the mountains of Mount Desert and most of Schoodic Peninsula to the east. There are Nature Conservancy preserves on Turtle Island in the south, Long Porcupine, and Dram and Preble islands near Sorrento.

BAR HARBOR ★★★

Charts: 13312, 13318, **13323**

Once the summer playground of the very wealthy, Bar Harbor still has many of its great mansions. The awesome mass of Cadillac Mountain remains the backdrop to the town, and the bold profiles of the offshore islands still lead the eye across the sparkling waters of Frenchman Bay to Schoodic Peninsula. The beauty endures.

But today the great "cottages" have been converted to other uses—a college, a museum, an inn, a nursing home—and the quiet elegance of Bar Harbor has been replaced by the bustle of a tourist town.

As a yachting center, Bar Harbor is small compared to Southwest Harbor and Northeast Harbor, but the town has a variety of attractions. There is a constant coming-and-going of boats of every size and description—from the Nova Scotia ferry to traditional schooners and numerous excursion vessels. The QE2 and other cruise liners make Bar Harbor a regular port of call. Every move is scrutinized by people lining the docks in the harbor and the rails of the day-trippers.

Approaches. All of the moorings and shore facilities of Bar Harbor are east of the bar connecting Bar Island to Mount Desert, and the approach is without dangers. The usual path from the south is east of Bald Porcupine Island—very bold, with high cliffs at the southern end. It is also possible to run between the breakwater west of Bald Porcupine and the Mount Desert shore. The breakwater is covered at high, but its western end is marked by a white beacon.

Anchorages, Moorings. East of the large town pier, Bar Harbor maintains a number of rental moorings, separated by an approach channel from the private moorings to the north. A mooring can be reserved by calling the harbormaster on channel 16 or at 288-5571. Or pick up a vacant mooring and check at the harbormaster's office near the head of the town pier. There is also overnight dockage at the floats east of the town wharf, with eight to nine feet at low. Harbor Place, next to the town pier, has some space alongside their floats with eight feet at low, and several moorings.

You can anchor outside the moorings in 15 to 30 feet at low. Holding ground is good, and the harbor is reasonably protected by the surrounding islands and the breakwater to the south.

A mile north of town, just beyond the ferry terminal, the Bar Harbor Regency Hotel marina can accommodate yachts up to 120 feet, with deep water along the outer floats.

Getting Ashore. Land your dinghy at the floats on the east side of the town wharf or at the Harbor Place floats.

For the Boat. *Bar Harbor Yacht Club.* The BHYC is not in Bar Harbor, but close by in Hulls Cove (see ahead).

Harbor Place (Ch. 16; tel. 288-3346). The floats of Harbor Place are just west of the town pier. Gas, diesel, water, ice, and electricity are available alongside.

Town Pier (Municipal Pier) (tel. 288-5571, harbormaster). Floats for pleasure craft are on the east side of the large pier; floats on the west side are for fishermen. Water is available at the floats in limited quantities.

Fisherman's Landing. Just west of Harbor Place, Fisherman's Landing is mostly commercial but sells diesel at the float (dry at low water).

Bar Harbor Regency Hotel (tel. 288-9723). Water and electricity are available, but there is no fuel. Visitors may enjoy meals in the hotel or request food service at the floats.

For the Crew. The big buildings at Harbor Place house a restaurant, ship's store, chandlery, laundromat, and showers. There are pay phones and restrooms on the town pier. From there, a walk up Main Street (with all the lampposts) and a right turn on Cottage Street will take you to most of the useful places in town. On Cottage you will find Don's Shop 'N Save and the post office. The state liquor store is a couple of blocks south of Cottage.

There are many restaurants to choose from, the one with the best view being on a pier next to the Golden Anchor Inn. Right next door, Fisherman's Landing offers lobster lunches and a waterfront bar.

To reach the Bar Harbor Laundromat, walk up Main Street, turn right on Cottage Street, and continue to Holland Avenue, about half a mile from the waterfront.

Bikes can be rented from Acadia Bike and Canoe on Cottage Street (.3 mile from the waterfront) or from Bar Harbor Bicycle Shop, at the far end of Cottage Street, which will deliver to the waterfront (tel. 288-3886). The YMCA on Mt. Desert Street has showers, a swimming pool, and a

Nautilus room open to the public. For Acadia Taxi and Tours call 288-4020. To rent a car call Hertz (667-5017) or U-Save (667-6130) at the airport. For Airport Taxi call 667-5995.

Things to Do. From the little park near the town pier, tour buses depart several times a day and circle the Loop Road of Acadia National Park, including a run to the top of Cadillac Mountain, with its spectacular views. This is a great way to see the park if you don't have a car. For reservations call National Park Tours at 288-3327 or Oli's Trolley at 288-9899.

Frenchman Bay Company at Harbor Place runs sight-seeing cruises of the bay, fishing and whale-watching cruises, charters, and park naturalist cruises. Several windjammers and power vessels offer day trips into the bay, and the three-masted schooner *Natalie Todd* takes passengers for longer cruises as well. The *Acadian Whale Watcher* (tel. 288-9794) leaves from the Golden Anchor pier and cruises to Mt. Desert Rock with a naturalist aboard. At Harbor Place you can visit the lobster hatchery of the Mount Desert Oceanarium.

The Natural History Museum at the College of the Atlantic is great for kids and adults alike. Less than a mile north of the town pier, the waterfront campus can be reached by land or sea. There are several large guest moorings (call on Ch. 16 to check availability) and 11 feet of water at low at the end of the float; you can also anchor off in 15 to 30 feet. By land, walk out West Street to Route 3. The campus features a former summer estate cottage appropriately named "The Turrets." You can enjoy the lovely, historic terraced gardens, waterfront landscape, and pebble beach for a quiet stroll or a picnic.

There are displays of birds and mammals, including a realistic diorama of a snapping turtle about to seize the leg of an unsuspecting duck and drag it down. The skull of a finback whale is propped against a building; next door is the Naugahyde Whale, which unzips to reveal his Naugahyde innards. Whales-on-Wheels challenges you to assemble the backbone of a Minke whale, like a 20-foot jigsaw puzzle. There are interpretive programs and a natural history speaker series. Call

288-5016 for the schedule.

Jackson Laboratory is the largest center in the world for mammalian genetics research. More than 700 pure mouse strains have been bred for decades, and two million mice are shipped annually to labs all over the world for research on cell biology, immunology, genetics, various diseases, and drugs. The lab offers a fascinating hour-long presentation for visitors several afternoons a week (call 288-3371 for the schedule). It's 1.7 miles from the waterfront, south on Main Street (Route 3), and there is a bicycle path.

In the basement of Jesup Memorial Library on Mount Desert Street, the Bar Harbor Historical Museum has a large collection of early photos—summer cottages and visitors, hotels, steamers, and the Green Mountain Railway—and memorabilia of all kinds, including a large scrapbook of the disastrous 1947 fire.

Bar Harbor was named for the gravel bar that connects Bar Island to the mainland. At halftide or below, you can walk across the bar and explore the western half of Bar Island, part of Acadia National Park. To get there from the town pier, walk along West Street, past the Golden Anchor Pier, then turn right down Bridge Street to the water. Another pleasant walk starts in front of the Bar Harbor Inn, east of the town pier, and leads south along the shore for half a mile to Grant Park, with its balancing rock.

Visit the Ledgelawn Inn on Mt. Desert Street. One of the last great "cottages," it was built in 1904 for a wealthy Bostonian. The sweeping staircase, grand fireplace, and original furnishings will help you to appreciate the elegance of old Bar Harbor.

Another option is a little side trip to Canada aboard the *Bluenose*, a well-appointed car ferry that leaves for Yarmouth, Nova Scotia, each morning and returns late the same day. There is live entertainment aboard, plus duty-free shopping, friendly bars, good birdwatching, and an ocean cruise with someone else worrying about the navigation. The Marine Atlantic ferry terminal is a mile north of town. For information, call 1-800-341-7981 (in Maine, call 1-800-432-7344; in Bar Harbor call 288-3395).

HULLS COVE ★★

Charts: 13312, 13318, **13323**

Hulls Cove is an open cove a couple of miles north of Bar Harbor. Its most inviting feature for cruising yachtsmen is that this is home base for the Bar Harbor Yacht Club.

Approaches. From Bar Harbor, round the bell off Sheep Porcupine Island and run alongshore past the dock from which the *Bluenose* ferry departs for Yarmouth, Nova Scotia. The Bar Harbor Yacht

Club is near Canoe Point, inside nun "4."

Anchorages, Moorings. The BHYC has a guest mooring, or you could anchor off in 24 feet at low.

For the Boat. *Bar Harbor Yacht Club (tel. 288-3275).* There is water at the floats, with 12 feet alongside at low.

Bar Harbor Boating (tel. 288-5797). On the north side of Hulls Cove, Bar Harbor Boating has gas, water, electricity, and ice at the floats, with six feet alongside at low. The yard has a marine railway and can handle hull repairs.

For the Crew. At the yacht club are a shower and a pay phone. There is a restaurant and fish market in Hulls Cove Village, about .7 mile away. The Hulls Cove General Store sells groceries, beer, and ice and has a fresh fruit and vegetable stand.

EASTERN BAY and MOUNT DESERT NARROWS ★

Charts: 13312, 13316, **13318**

Mount Desert once was truly an island and could be circumnavigated, from Eastern Bay into Western Bay through Mount Desert Narrows. While this is still possible for smaller boats, the narrows is shoal and unmarked, and the fixed bridge has a vertical clearance of only 35 feet.

West of Sorrento and Back Cove, there are few anchorages or facilities, but pleasant sailing in open waters, against the magnificent backdrop of Mount Desert.

Sullivan Harbor leads to Taunton Bay, but do not plan to go above the reversing falls at Falls Point, which are turbulent and dangerous (see the *Coast Pilot*). The swing bridge just above the falls is normally closed.

The Skillings River degenerates rapidly into a narrow, crooked passage with many unmarked dangers, as does the Jordan River, farther west.

Past Old Point, just beyond the entrance to the Jordan River, you will see the large sheds of Able Marine on the mainland. Note the rocks and shoals west of the yard.

Anchorages, Moorings. Able Marine has several moorings off the yard, with 10 feet of water at low. The depths here are greater than shown on the chart.

For the Boat. *Able Marine (tel. 667-6235).* Adjacent to Bar Harbor Airport, Able Marine is a builder of very large fiberglass boats, and a service yard as well. Hull, engine, and rigging repairs can be accomplished. Because of the 1,500-foot seaplane ramp nearby, the yard can haul boats up to 50 feet by hydraulic trailer at almost any tide. The airport next door makes this a convenient place to change crews.

For the Crew. A short walk from the yard will take you west to Route 3 and a selection of restaurants. Rent a car at the neighboring airport to explore Mount Desert and Acadia National Park.

SORRENTO HARBOR ★★★★

Charts: 13312, **13318**

On the mainland facing Mount Desert, this is a beautiful spot—a reasonably well-protected harbor with spectacular vistas of Cadillac Mountain on the horizon. Many of today's summer folk here are fourth- and fifth-generation descendants of the people who founded Sorrento as a resort in the 1880s. "Waukeag Neck" lacked the romantic touch envisioned by Frank Jones, enthusiastic promoter of a new, exclusive resort, so it became Sorrento instead. Sorrento was never a rival to Bar Harbor in social pretensions. Although it attracted many distinguished families, the emphasis was on sailing, and the atmosphere was one of low-key elegance. In the early days, a steamship sailed from Bar Harbor to the docks of the great hotel at Sorrento.

Fifteen-foot Wee Scots were the first one-design class raced by the Sorrento Yacht Club in 1926. Despite the later introduction of S-boats and Mercurys, a number of the stable little Wee Scots still exist, some owned by their original families.

Part of Sorrento's beauty is the view of Mount Desert between unspoiled Preble and Dram islands. In the mid-1960s, when it appeared that Dram Island might be clear-cut for pulpwood, summer resident Bayard Ewing made an extensive search to locate the owner, who turned out to be a minister living in Wyoming. The minister needed an organ for his church. Ewing swapped an organ for the island and then donated the island to The Nature Conservancy. The protection of the harbor is now complete with the donation of Preble Island as well to The Nature Conservancy by the Ewing family.

Approaches. Run up Frenchman Bay for red-and-white bell "SH," which marks the entrance, and enter halfway between Dram and Preble islands, both high and wooded. Ledges make out from both sides. From the west, it is also possible to enter between Dram Island and Bean Point. Since ledges extend almost halfway across from the north, favor the Dram Island side.

Anchorages, Moorings. The Sorrento Yacht Club puts out three guest moorings at the west end of the harbor. Two are memorial moorings with

wooden pickup floats. One is marked, "Robert M. Lewis, 1886–1958. He cruised." The other is for Robert E. Montgomery. What a unique way to be remembered.

Anchor anywhere you can find room, in 6 to 15 feet at low, outside the moored boats. Holding ground is good, in mud. Do not approach the two little islands (each with a clump of trees) marking the ledge that separates Sorrento Harbor from Eastern Point Harbor.

One pays a price for the view. It's likely to be a bit rolly, and there is considerable exposure to the west, and southeast or southwest, depending on where you are in the harbor. If there is no room, or strong southerlies are expected, go around to Back Cove.

Getting Ashore. Land your dinghy at the town wharf.

For the Boat. *Town Wharf.* Water and electricity are available at the town wharf, with four feet alongside at low. There are rocks lying off the west end, so at low tide, approach the floats from the east.

Sorrento Yacht Club. The yacht club uses the town wharf and has no facilities except guest moorings. Their office is in the Sorrento Public Library.

For the Crew. There is a pay phone at the town wharf. It is three miles to the nearest grocery store, but if you look like a visiting sailor in despair, someone is likely to give you a ride. To find the post office, take a left from the town wharf, then the next right. This road also takes you to West Cove Boat Yard, in Back Cove.

An unusual treat awaits you at Le Domaine, a French haute cuisine restaurant and auberge in Hancock (tel. 422-3395). If you reserve for dinner, the restaurant will pick you up in Sorrento, or send a taxi. Expensive but superb.

Things to Do. The walk is beautiful westward along the harbor, then back through the streets of this serene and appealing community. Visit the Sorrento Public Library, in an 1892 shingled building.

BACK COVE ★★
Charts: 13312, **13318**

What you gain on the swings, you lose on the roundabouts. Just around Bean Point from Sorrento, Back Cove is much better protected but you lose the spectacular view.

Approaches. Approach around Bean Point. There is a long halftide ledge running north from the southern side of the entrance of Back Cove. A rock in the middle of the entrance is barely visible at low tide. To avoid these dangers, come in near the northern side of the entrance and down the eastern shore.

Anchorages, Moorings. The West Cove Boat Yard has several moorings. Anchorage is good in the middle of the cove in seven to nine feet at low, mud bottom.

For the Boat. *West Cove Boat Yard (tel. 422-3137).* The yard is a custom builder of wooden boats. It has a 20-ton marine railway plus a 15-ton crane, and can do hull and engine repairs.

EASTERN POINT HARBOR ★★ No facilities
Charts: 13312, **13318**

Eastern Point is primarily a working harbor. There is a lobster pound in the northwest corner (wholesale only), and many lobsterboats are on mooring stakes here.

Approaches. The entrance between Calf and Preble islands is open and easy. Head for the small, wooded island on the bar that separates Sorrento from Eastern Point.

Anchorages, Moorings. Anchor outside the moored boats wherever you can find room in 8 to 15 feet at low, mud bottom. Protection is not as good as it appears on the chart, since southerly winds are funneled in by Calf Island.

FLANDERS BAY ★★★ No facilities
Charts: 13312, **13318**

In the northeastern corner of Frenchman Bay, Flanders is a large, round bay big enough to hold a whole cruising club. Reached by a zigzag route, it is almost entirely landlocked and would be an excellent hurricane hole if it were not so large. There are seals on Halftide Ledge and sometimes a bald eagle soars overhead.

Approaches. There are two possible approaches—east or west of Calf Island. The most direct route is east of Calf, leaving can "1" close to port, continuing around can "3" at Halftide Ledge and northwest again past Schieffelin Point (with several houses, trees, and large meadows) into Flanders Bay. The route west of Calf Island is more open but longer.

Anchorages, Moorings. The bay shoals gradually. Anchor in whatever section provides the best protection from the wind, in 8 to 20 feet of water at low. The bottom is mud and good holding ground.

STAVE ISLAND HARBOR

Charts: 13312, **13318**

Stave and Jordan islands, on the east side of Frenchman Bay, form Stave Island Harbor. While this would be a good harbor for small ships, it is much too large and open to provide a comfortable anchorage for cruising boats. Reasonable protection can be found in Myrick Cove, east of Jordan Island.

WINTER HARBOR ★★★

Charts: 13312, 13318, **13322**

(For Protection and Facility Ratings, see under individual harbor areas below.)

Between spectacular Schoodic Peninsula and equally handsome Grindstone Neck, Winter Harbor has three distinct populations: fishermen, summer people, and the Navy. Here, in the space of less than half a mile, are the vastly different ways of life that make Maine so interesting.

In 1935, John D. Rockefeller, feeling that the Navy installation on Otter Cliffs on Mount Desert was unsightly, paid out of his own pocket to have it moved to nearby Big Moose Island, at the end of Schoodic Peninsula. Ever since, Navy families have been part of Winter Harbor.

Every August, the Winter Harbor Lobster Festival draws a large crowd of spectators, especially for the main event, the annual lobsterboat races, with 13 classes rated by size and power. Speed is the objective. Not only do the races generate intense rivalries and devoted fans, but they teach fishermen and boatbuilders how to improve hull design and engines.

The harbor provides varying degrees of protection, depending on which part you choose. There are three coves: to the west is Sand Cove and the Winter Harbor Yacht Club, quite deep and wide open, province of the summer people. The fishermen, who were here first, sensibly chose Inner Winter Harbor, a tight, almost landlocked hole in the middle. Henry Cove, to the east, is exposed to south and southwest winds and the least used. The anchorages and facilities of these three coves will be considered separately.

Approaches. There are several good landmarks as you approach Winter Harbor: the big, white lighthouse building on Egg Rock to the west; the white abandoned lighthouse on Mark Island at the entrance to the harbor (visible a long way); and a green water tank on Big Moose Island, at the end of Schoodic Peninsula.

Starting with red-and-green bell "MI" off Mark Island, the approach to Winter Harbor is wide and easy. Follow Grindstone Neck around into Sand Cove, or follow the buoys to Inner Winter Harbor and Henry Cove.

SAND COVE (WINTER HARBOR)

No more than five miles by water east of Bar Harbor, Grindstone Neck was bought by a group of New Yorkers and Philadelphians in 1889, "for development into a cottage colony of the character, for instance, of Tuxedo, of Llewellyn Park, or of North East Harbor." The great cottages of Bar Harbor have been recycled as nursing homes, museums and motels, but the summer colony on Grindstone Neck has maintained its character. Though socially exclusive, the people of Grindstone Neck have always felt that the beauties of the land should be open to everyone, so there is access to the shoreline, and "the rocks are free." Centerpiece of the community is the handsome Winter Harbor Yacht Club, on the west side of Sand Cove.

On occasion, when herring are running, fisher-

Guillemots never seem to get much press. They are not as dramatic as bald eagles, as raucous as seagulls, or as endearing as puffins. And the name is hard to pronounce ("gill-a-mot," like "tot"). But it is fun to watch them swimming near a boat, then suddenly disappearing underwater with a tiny plop.

These handsome little diving birds seem to have become more common along the coast in recent years. They have little fear of man and paddle around in many harbors among the boats, as well as offshore. Guillemots are not gregarious, so you usually will see only one or two at a time, or at most a few pairs.

The black guillemot is velvety jet black, with a distinctive oval white patch on each wing, short tail, and red legs. Sometimes called "sea doves" or "sea pigeons," guillemots are members of the auk family. Like their cousins, the razorbills and puffins, they have a rapid wingbeat and swim expertly underwater with their wings, in pursuit of bottom-dwelling fish and crustaceans.

Guillemots are tough, breeding all over the Arctic as well as in Iceland, Finland, and Ireland. They are just barely able to tolerate the warmth of Maine, at the southern end of their range. Those born in the Arctic feed all winter under the ice—provided they have a few breathing holes. These little birds form strong attachments to their feeding places; if disturbed by your boat, they will simply circle around to the same spot after you pass. And when it comes to laying eggs, guillemots are not fussy about fancy contraptions like nests. They simply deposit the eggs on bare rock, in any crevice that offers a little protection from the wind.

There is a small mystery about guillemots that seems to defy explanation. The inside of its mouth is bright scarlet—exactly the same color as its favorite food, the red rock eel. No one seems to know why.

Great Duck Island, south of Mount Desert, now owned and protected by The Nature Conservancy, has the largest colony of black guillemots on the east coast (as well as the largest colony of Leach's storm petrels). In 1900, there were only 80 pairs of guillemots left in all of Maine; now there are more than 400 pairs on Great Duck Island alone.

men may shut off the cove by running a net from the yacht club across to Harbor Point.

Approaches. From red-and-green bell "MI" off Mark Island, follow Grindstone Neck around into the cove, staying clear of Grindstone Ledge to port.

Anchorages, Moorings. For a mooring rental, inquire of the launch or at the floats of the Winter Harbor Yacht Club, the large, gray-shingled building on the west side of the cove whose cupola is shown on the chart. The mooring floats are mostly white lobster buoys, marked "Guest." You can anchor off to the north or outside the moored boats, as many yachts do. It is rather deep here for anchoring (27 to 32 feet at low), but the holding ground is good, in mud. The anchorage is open and exposed to the south, and likely to be quite rolly.

Getting Ashore. Land at the yacht club floats.

For the Boat. *Winter Harbor Yacht Cub (Ch. 16 or 71; tel. 963-2275).* Water and electricity may be found at the yacht club floats, with 20 feet alongside. Stay clear of the southern floats, which are private.

For the Crew. The yacht club is hospitable to visiting yachtsmen, offering launch service and showers. Lunch is served in the comfortable clubhouse, where there is a fire burning on cold days. Look for the grindstone set in the fieldstone chimney and an old print of the original land division on Grindstone Neck. There is a pay phone.

Walk north on the shore road, past the golf course, just over a mile to the town of Winter Harbor. There you will find restaurants, a gallery, the post office, 5¢ & 10¢ store, drugstore, library, and a good market (with ice) called the Winter Harbor Food Service. Often a yacht club member will spot you lugging groceries and offer a ride back to the clubhouse.

Things to Do. It is a pleasant walk of about a mile from the yacht club to the end of Grindstone Point, with its great smooth whalebacks of pink granite intruded by dikes of black basalt, and spectacular views of Mount Desert and the islands scattered in the bay.

INNER HARBOR (WINNER HARBOR)

This tight little harbor is home to a fleet of lobsterboats. There is a purposeful bustle, starting early in the morning, and much to observe. It's an interesting place to spend the night if you can find a mooring.

Approaches. The entrance is marked by a can left to port and a nun left to starboard. Note the red daybeacon marking the ledges to starboard.

Anchorages, Moorings. The inner harbor is jammed with lobsterboats, floats, and dinghies, and there is no room to anchor. On a given night, there may be two or three moorings available. Ask a lobsterman. Sometimes eight or nine yachts will be here, nested three on a mooring. This little harbor is extremely well protected.

Getting Ashore. Land at the dinghy float of the town wharf.

For the Boat. *Town Wharf.* The first dock on the east side as you enter, just past the daybeacon, is the town wharf, with 15 feet or more alongside the floats. Water is available.

Winter Harbor Co-op (Ch. 6; tel. 963-5857). The Co-op has a dock and a float near the head of the harbor on the east side, with water, electricity, gas, and diesel.

For the Crew. The town of Winter Harbor is near the head of the cove.

HENRY COVE (WINTER HARBOR)

Though somewhat exposed to south and southwest winds, Henry Cove is convenient to town and to the Winter Harbor Marina.

Approaches. Leave to starboard the nun marking the ledge off Sargents Point. Leaving to port the entrance buoys of the Inner Harbor, run up the middle into Henry Cove.

Anchorages, Moorings. Winter Harbor Marina, on the eastern shore, has a number of rental moorings, and dockage at their floats, with six to eight feet alongside. The cove is exposed to the south, and likely to be rolly.

Getting Ashore. Land at the marina floats.

For the Boat. *Winter Harbor Marina (tel. 963-7449).* You will find water and electricity at the floats, gas, diesel, and ice. The yard has a small chandlery, with charts, and can handle hull and engine repairs. There is a boatlift and a 22-ton hydraulic trailer.

For the Crew. There are showers at the marina, and a pay phone. From there, it is half a mile into the town of Winter Harbor; the marina may be able to provide transportation.

You will find them lying in the grass of upland meadows, or on coastal paths, their delicate domed shells mossy green, with meridians of white dots. Their shattered carapaces line the margin of the sea, where seagulls swoop and drop them to be broken on the rocks below. Sea urchins. Spiny sea urchins.

Until recently no one in Maine gave them a second thought, except perhaps the lobsterman cursing his fouled traps. "The trap," wrote Ruth Moore, in *Speak to the Winds,* "looked like nothing so much as a trap-shaped mound of sea-urchins, piled one on top of another. 'Whore's eggs,' Liseo said, eyeing them glumly. 'Wouldn't we get rich, Elbridge, if whore's eggs was worth a cent apiece.' "

Today the lowly sea urchin has become another cash crop, not yet in the same league as lobsters, but a growing alternative for Maine fishermen. Much as the roe of Russian and Iranian salmon is appreciated around the world as caviar, the roe of the sea urchin is prized as "uni," served in the sushi bars of Japan and wherever there are populations of Japanese. Rumored to be an aphrodisiac, uni is also served on the French Riviera, nothing unusual in a culture that savors snails, tripe, and sea cucumbers.

"Roe" is a euphemism. Uni, which resembles sections of tangerine, is actually the reproductive organs of the urchin.

How does it taste? Suffice it to say that sea urchins have not yet achieved great popularity in the United States, even among fishermen. Descriptions vary from "salty melon with a hint of iodine in the after-taste" to "not unlike cold Cream of Wheat bathed in salt water."

All uni is not created equal. Color and texture and general appearance are crucial. The red sea urchin found on the West Coast of the U.S. does not produce prime uni. The green sea urchin of the East Coast, however, looks and tastes like the native Japanese product, with the orange and yellow roe favored by the Japanese.

Traditionally, fishermen in the U.S. have paid little attention to quality control. As a result they have lost out to foreign fisheries that deliver the product to market fresher and undamaged. With uni, quality is everything. Roe that is off-color, streaked, or broken commands a much lower price, or is rejected by buyers and dumped at sea.

Though urchins are found in deep water as far south as New Jersey, the rocky shores of Maine are their favorite grounds. For reasons both of urchin biology and market conditions, the best time to collect them is winter, from November through February. This is precisely opposite the season for Japanese urchins, a fact that provides a ready-made market for Maine fishermen.

Dragging for sea urchins damages the delicate creatures, not to mention what it does to the urchin beds and other valuable fishing bottom. Equipment to suck up urchins like a giant vacuum cleaner has been developed. Mostly, though, urchins are harvested by hand, one at a time. Gathering them is no picnic. It's cold down there in winter, perhaps 30 degrees Fahrenheit; wet suits and scuba gear are standard equipment. The diver picks up the urchins, avoiding painful punctures from the sharp spines, and puts them in a basket for hauling to the surface. He chooses carefully, leaving most of them to feed and grow for the next time.

Then most of the urchins are flown, alive and whole, 7,000 miles to Japan. There they are processed, with 90% of the animal discarded, and the precious roe packaged for market.

"Wouldn't we get rich, Elbridge, if whore's eggs was worth a cent apiece." Now they are worth 50 times that, and good quality uni commands a price of $100 a pound in the Tokyo market. Elbridge would be surprised.

SCHOODIC POINT

Charts: 13312, **13318**, 13322, 13324

Schoodic is a very special place. Once it belonged to one man, John Moore, who loved it well enough to open it to the public in 1897, and now it is a part of Acadia National Park.

Here the waves roll unchecked across the Atlantic and crash in dazzling spray upon the pink granite ledges. Here you can stand at the end of the world and sense the great forces that have formed the coast of Maine: upwellings of granite eons ago; then the intrusion of dramatic black basaltic dikes into the pink granite; the glaciers carving and grinding down the rocks, and the ceaseless working of the wind and sea.

Normally approached by land, Schoodic is difficult for the cruising boat to visit. One way is to leave your boat in Winter Harbor and hitch a ride, or find a garage there willing to rent you a car.

It is also possible to find reasonable temporary anchorage north of Pond Island on the west side of Schoodic Peninsula, and explore from there.

POND ISLAND (SCHOODIC PENINSULA)

Charts: 13312, 13318, **13322**

The anchorage north of wooded Pond Island is a great gunkhole and provides access for the cruising boat to the beauties of Schoodic Peninsula, most of which is part of Acadia National Park. Although the cove is reasonably easy to enter, the bottom is rocky and there is some exposure to the ocean, so it is not recommended for overnight.

Big Moose Island at the end of Schoodic Peninsula is easily identified by the high, green water tank. Wooded Pond Island lies close by to the north, and 440-foot-high Schoodic Head is prominent to the eastward. Enter north of Pond Island, favoring the northern side of the cove to avoid the ledges along the southern shore; the westernmost of these ledges is just visible at low tide.

Anchor beyond the ledges in 11 to 16 feet at low, north of the eastern tip of Pond Island. The bottom is rocky and holding ground doubtful. Consider leaving someone aboard while you explore.

Land near the causeway that crosses the head of the road, which will put you right next to the gravel road leading up to Schoodic Head. It is a half-hour hike to the top of Schoodic Head, and well worth it. From the turnaround, the view is west across Frenchman Bay to Mount Desert, the lighthouse on Egg Rock, and your own boat riding at anchor below.

A short trail continues to the granite ledges on top of Schoodic Head, from which you look east along the coast to the lighthouse of Petit Manan. Another vantage point overlooks Schoodic Island.

From your landing opposite Pond Island, it is a 1.3-mile walk to the end of Schoodic Peninsula, where great Atlantic swells break on the pink granite ledges.

For a less strenuous outing, explore West Pond with your dinghy.

Region 6 / Schoodic Point to West

Down East

The 123-foot lighthouse on 'tit Manan Island, one of the foggiest places on the coast of Maine.
(Christopher Ayres photo)

Quoddy Head

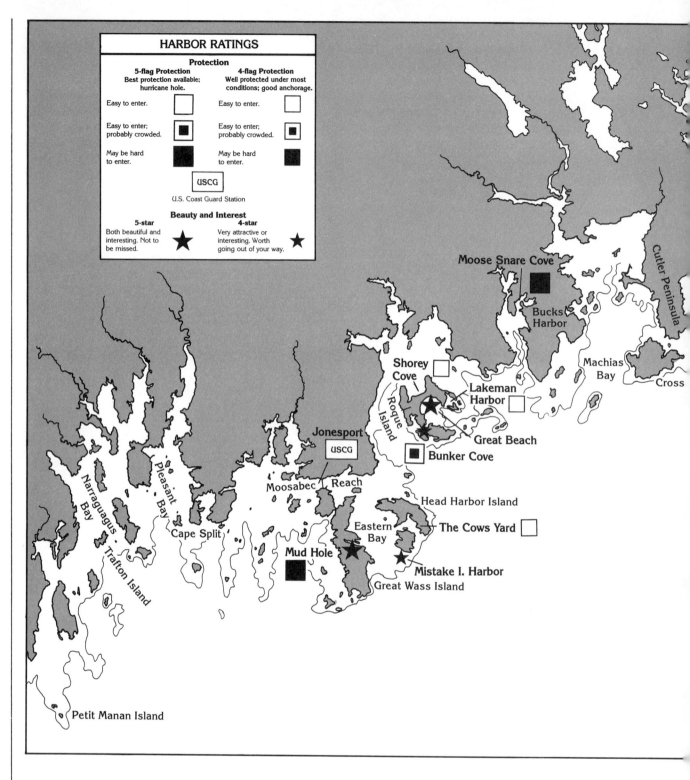

As you pass Schoodic Point, heading east, civilization drops behind and you have entered a more primitive world, one where fishing and lobstering command attention and the affairs of Boston and New York seem far away and insignificant. All the coves are working harbors, yachts are rare, and facilities for yachts are almost nonexistent. The last big marina (until Eastport) lies astern, and you must now depend on your own resources more than ever before.

This is a land of weirs and blueberry barrens, of uninhabited islands, narrow bays, and countless estuaries. Wildlife is abundant here, including seals and ospreys and bald eagles. You can see puffins and razor-billed auks at close range on Machias Seal Island. There are lovely white granite and spruce islands in

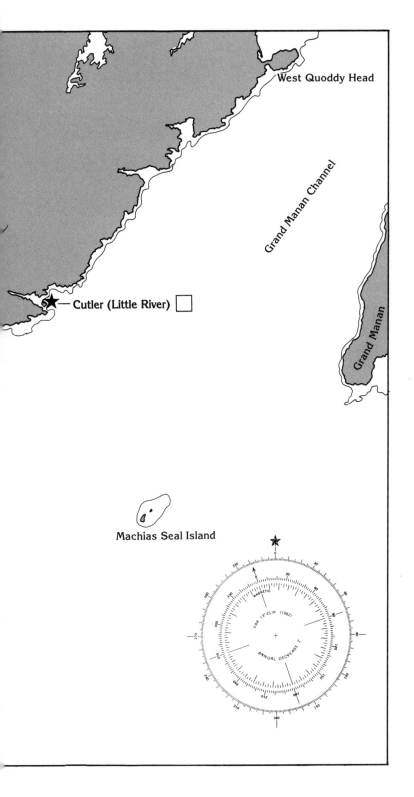

West Quoddy Head

Grand Manan Channel

Grand Manan

Cutler (Little River)

Machias Seal Island

Eastern Bay and Western Bay, unusual harbors in the area of Great Wass, and a remarkable Nature Conservancy preserve. Just beyond is fabled Roque Island, with its mile-long white-sand beach, goal for generations of cruising sailors.

This is also a region of dense fogs, strong currents, and steadily higher tides as you approach Canada and the Bay of Fundy. Anchoring and tying up in an area with tidal ranges of 20 feet or more require different techniques from those used with smaller tides. Starting with Cutler, the mean tidal range is given for every anchorage, including average (mean) tides and large (spring) tides. Time your passage to take advantage of the current, which floods east along the coast and ebbs west.

This stretch of the coast is very exposed and also subject to heavy fog, most prevalent in July and August. Before starting, it would be wise to identify on the chart a number of possible harbors of refuge along the way, including Winter Harbor, Prospect Harbor, Trafton Island, Eastern Harbor, Mistake Island Harbor, and The Cows Yard—all of which are easy to enter and close to your path.

Running east from Schoodic, you will go progressively farther out of VHF range, both for communication with marine operators and for receiving U.S. weather forecasts. There is a dead spot from Roque Island eastward until you enter Canadian waters. Because of powerful radio transmitters on the Cutler Peninsula, Loran reception may be intermittent or completely blanked out in the region from Great Wass Island eastward to Cutler and Grand Manan Channel.

Sailing down east is very different from the typical cruising experience. When you have spent a week or two in this special part of the world, it becomes familiar—and, after a while, normal. Be prepared for a bit of culture shock when you return to more populated cruising grounds.

EASTERN SCHOODIC PENINSULA
to Petit Manan and Cape Split

WONSQUEAK HARBOR

Charts: 13312, 13318, **13324**

At the northern end of Schoodic Harbor, Wonsqueak is a crack in the rocks, a narrow estuary with just room for half a dozen lobsterboats, moored fore-and-aft. The harbor is shoal, exposed to the south, and, despite its appealing name, of no value to cruising boats.

BUNKERS HARBOR ★★

Charts: 13312, **13324**

On the east side of Schoodic Peninsula, Bunkers is a snug harbor for a dozen or more lobsterboats, but tricky to enter. Unmarked ledges obstruct the entrance, making it dangerous except within two hours of low tide.

Approaches. Enter from the south. From the whistle buoy off Spruce Point, run north along the shoreline at a comfortable distance. Dangerous Bunkers Ledge is marked by can "1" at the eastern end. Pass inside the ledge, coming close along the shore, between the large reddish rock near the southern tip of the harbor and a ledge to starboard (visible two or three hours after low), through the seven-foot spot shown on the chart. Once past the southern point, turn to port down the midline of the harbor.

Anchorages, Moorings. Anchor in the outer harbor in 23 to 25 feet at low. Protection is reasonably good, although some swells enter. The fleet of lobsterboats is moored in the inner harbor, leading northward, with depths of six to seven feet at low. You are not likely to find room to anchor, but there might be an unoccupied mooring.

Getting Ashore. Row in to the floats near the head of the harbor.

For the Boat. Gas, diesel, water, and some marine supplies are available at a pier and float near the head of the harbor, next to the lobster pounds and a tiny fishing village.

For the Crew. Ask where to buy lobsters. It is about a mile walk northward to the intersection at Birch Harbor, where you will find a variety of stores.

BIRCH HARBOR

Charts: 13312, **13324**

Largely shoal, unmarked, and exposed to ocean swells, Birch Harbor is difficult to enter and would be an uncomfortable anchorage. Roaring Bull, in the entrance, breaks at low water and can be avoided by entering along the southwestern shore.

The complex of stores at the head of the harbor includes a market, laundromat, liquor store, post office, and takeout.

PROSPECT HARBOR ★   No facilities

Charts: 13312, **13324**

The westerly bight of Prospect Harbor is a good anchorage—easy to enter and offering reasonable protection in summer weather, although exposed to the south and southeast. A dozen lobsterboats moor in the inner harbor. There are no facilities for visitors.

The harbor is dominated by the Stinson Canning factory on the west side, and there are houses all around the head of the cove. The radio antenna on Cranberry Point and the white dome on Prospect Harbor Point further detract from the scenery.

Approaches. Gong "3" and green daybeacon "5" are both left to port. The lighthouse on Prospect Harbor Point marks the eastern shore.

Anchorages, Moorings. Anchor past the cannery, outside the moored boats, in 14 to 18 feet at low. The holding ground is good mud.

COREA ★★★★

Charts: 13312, **13324**

Remote, well-protected, and charming, Corea is the quintessential lobstering port, with room, perhaps, for one or two visiting yachts. It is home for a fleet of 40 or so lobsterboats, and the surrounding docks are piled high with traps. The summer community is relatively small, and there is no doubt that the fishermen are in charge. This is the home of Young Brothers, well-known builders of hundreds of lobsterboats.

Approaches. From a distance, you can see a white church steeple at the head of the harbor, and a huge circular antenna west of Corea on the same peninsula. (It sinks below the trees as you enter the harbor.) On radar, lobstermen say, it looks just like a miniature doughnut.

Western Island is higher and far more wooded than Outer Bar Island. Western Island has a red-roofed cottage on the south side, and smooth, sloping reddish rocks.

Because of unmarked rocks and ledges covered at high tide, this is not an easy harbor to enter. Start at red-and-white whistle buoy "CE." Pass west of Western Island, fairly close aboard, curving eastward around the northern tip of the island. Then head for the sloping white granite ledges on the eastern side of the entrance to Corea Harbor. When you have almost reached these ledges, turn to port and head up into the harbor, staying toward the right-hand side of the channel as you pass the red buildings of the Corea Lobster Co-op.

This will keep you clear of the nasty rock ("REP" on the chart) and the two ledges in the mouth of the entrance. At high tide, the inner and higher of these two ledges may show a slight ripple on the surface, or it may not. These ledges are shown on the chart, but they are very deceiving, and many boats have found them with their keels. They are on a line from the middle of Western Island to the center of the harbor entrance, and you must be east of this line while approaching the entrance (see sketch map).

Avoid coming in at dead high, dead low, or in poor visibility.

Anchorages, Moorings. The *Coast Pilot* says that in May 1984, a depth of 7$^1/2$ feet could be carried to the anchorage, where 6 feet is available, except for shoaling along the edges.

There is one guest mooring right at the entrance, off the Co-op floats—a wonderful place for observing all the action. The whole fishing population of Corea will motor past you in the early morning, leaving a sea of punts in the harbor. Young Brothers (second pier on the left, tel. 963-7467) can usually find you an unoccupied mooring. Or ask a lobsterman.

There appears to be room to anchor opposite the Co-op, but there are hidden rocks. Elsewhere, the harbor is too full to anchor.

Getting Ashore. Land at the Co-op floats. Be sure to pull your dinghy up on the floats, out of the way.

For the Boat. *Corea Lobster Co-op (tel. 963-7936).* Gas, diesel, and lobsters can be bought at the floats below the red buildings of the Co-op, at the right side of the entrance, with 8 to 10 feet alongside.

For the Crew. The post office is at the head of the harbor; from there, a short walk north on Route 195 will bring you to Harborside Bakery (tel. 963-2311), which sells pies and cakes and serves breakfast.

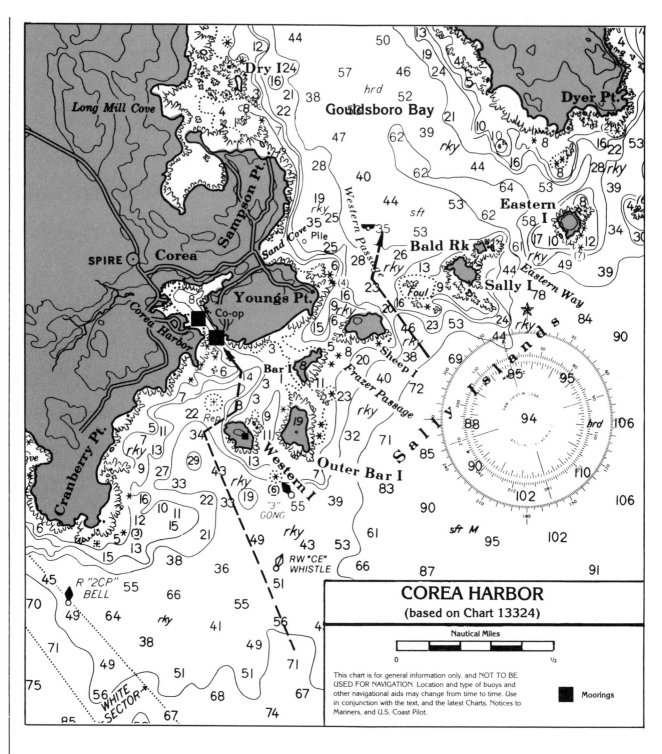

COREA HARBOR
(based on Chart 13324)

Nautical Miles

0   ¹⁄₂

This chart is for general information only, and NOT TO BE
USED FOR NAVIGATION. Location and type of buoys and
other navigational aids may change from time to time. Use
in conjunction with the text, and the latest Charts, Notices to
Mariners, and U.S. Coast Pilot.

Moorings

GOULDSBORO and DYER BAYS

Charts: 13312, **13324**

From the point of view of the cruising sailor,
Gouldsboro and Dyer bays have relatively little to
offer. Both are five or six miles long, but there are
no harbors of consequence and several unmarked
and narrow estuaries at their northern ends.

Gouldsboro Bay is probably the more attractive.
Across the entrance lie the handsome Sally Islands,
and the bay itself is wide and open for several
miles, with a miniature range of beautiful hills at

the head. West Bay is choked with unmarked
ledges and shoal areas, as is Joy Bay, leading to
Steuben.

Of the several entrances to Gouldsboro Bay, the
easiest is Western Passage, since the strong current
of two or three knots runs straight through the
channel, and Sheep Island is bold on the eastern
side. Be sure to identify the Sally Islands correctly
so you are in the right place. Outer Bar Island and

Bar Island are both low, with just a few trees. Sheep Island is heavily wooded. Leave Sheep Island close to port. The channel is about 100 yards wide. There is at least one active weir on the west side of the bay near Newman Cove, but otherwise few obstructions.

In the early 1980s, Gouldsboro Bay was selected for detailed study by the Smithsonian Institution as a representative water body of the Maine coast. The resulting Washington exhibit includes mudflat, rocky shore, and salt marsh, complete with rockweed, crabs, and lobsters, and a three-foot tide. (The Maine diorama is contrasted with the shoreline of St. Croix in the Virgin Islands.)

Dyer Bay, next door to Gouldsboro, flanks the west side of low-lying Petit Manan Point. It is marked by sandy bluffs at Yellow Birch Head and by Eagle Hill near the head of the bay.

PETIT MANAN ISLAND
Chart: 13324

Petit Manan Island (known familiarly and universally as 'tit Manan) is an important landmark on the direct passage from Mount Desert cruising waters to Roque Island. Part way across Frenchman Bay, the tall (123 feet), slim pencil of the lighthouse on Petit Manan beckons enticingly over Schoodic.

The stretch from Schoodic to Head Harbor Island is one of the foggiest areas on the coast of Maine. At 'tit Manan there is an average of 250 hours of fog a month during July and August. Unless you're prepared to depend on radar and Loran, you may be holed up in a harbor here for days, waiting to head east.

Green Island and neighboring 'tit Manan are low-lying, treeless, and surrounded by ledges, and in thick fog you could easily be up on the rocks before seeing the light. In a southwesterly breeze the foghorn to leeward is often inaudible until you have left it astern.

Waves coming in from the Gulf of Maine encounter relatively shoal water as they approach 'tit Manan, and often a very rough sea builds up. The current floods east along the coast and ebbs west; it also floods north into the bays and ebbs south, resulting in turbulent waters off 'tit Manan where the currents meet, especially with a southwest wind and an ebb tide. To avoid this area of rough water, pass outside red-and-white bell "PM," about a mile offshore. In thick fog or heavy weather you would do well to run even farther offshore, outside red whistle "6A" off Southeast Rock.

Petit Manan Bar. A long bar runs between 'tit Manan Point and Green Island. There is a marked channel about midway along the bar, with 13 feet of water at low. Unless you are proceeding toward Pigeon Hill Bay, however, there is little point in using this channel.

The western end of the short passage is marked by red-and-white bell "WB," and the eastern end by an unusual red-and-white nun "EB." Run a straight line between the buoys, leaving them close aboard on either side. The shoaler water is to the north.

A very ugly chop can build up on this bar, particularly with the wind against the current. In poor visibility the small buoys are very hard to find; in heavy weather the passage will certainly be unpleasant and dangerous. It's usually easier and safer to take the longer route outside 'tit Manan. On occasion, however, the passage over the bar is clear when it's thick-a-fog outside.

PIGEON HILL BAY
and BOIS BUBERT ISLAND
Charts: 13312, **13324**, 13325

Pigeon Hill Bay lies between Bois Bubert Island and the eastern low-lying shore of Petit Manan Point. The bay is open and relatively unobstructed and makes a pleasant sail south of Pigeon Hill, a local landmark. The entrance north of Pigeon Hill and Bois Bubert is a rock garden.

Bois Bubert is a large island of 1,000 acres paralleling Petit Manan Peninsula. The island preserves for history the name of a Frenchman otherwise unknown and locally pronounced "Bo-Bare." Monsieur Bubert's woods now shelter ruffed grouse, woodcock, and white-tailed deer.

Most of the island has been acquired by The Nature Conservancy for transfer to the U.S. Fish and Wildlife Service, complementing the refuge on 'tit Manan Point. If you are attracted to the seven-acre freshwater pond at the northern end of Bois Bubert, you should know that it is surrounded by a quaking bog.

Shoal draft boats can use Little Bois Bubert Harbor, at the south end, to get ashore, but for deep keel boats the best bet is Seal Cove, on the east coast. A pleasant day stop, it is sufficiently exposed to ocean swells to make it an uncomfortable anchorage for the night.

There is an old weir leading from Bois Bubert, opposite the north end of Seal Cove Ledge, so the easiest entrance is from the south. Favor the southern shore, since Seal Cove Ledge extends a long way southward. There is reasonable anchorage near the beach at the southwest corner, but the bottom is rocky. There are views of the handsome Douglas Islands and usually an audience of curious seals on the ledge.

NARRAGUAGUS, HARRINGTON, and PLEASANT BAYS

Charts: 13324, 13325

The complex and sparsely settled coastline between Petit Manan and Cape Split has been formed by four small rivers and many more creeks and brooks, which in turn broaden out to Narraguagus, Harrington, and Pleasant bays.

Pleasant Bay is by far the most open of these bodies of water, and it offers delightful sailing among spectacular islands. These bays are often free of fog when it is thick farther out. Many islands in this region have distinctive shapes or formations, including Ladle Ledges and Pot Rock, Shipstern Island, Jordans Delight, and the Douglas Islands. Weirs have always been important here, and it remains one of the few areas of the Maine coast where they still are in active use.

Secure harbors are few and far between. Eastern Harbor, between Cape Split and Moose Neck, is the best in heavy weather, although it is exposed to the southwest. With winds from south to east, the anchorage north of Trafton Island is comfortable.

This part of the coast is far more important to ospreys and bald eagles, fishermen and blueberry growers, than it is to cruising sailors. Enormous numbers of fish run up the estuaries to spawn, among them alewives, herring, small striped bass, and shad. At certain high tides in the spring, every local resident who can walk and who owns a net or a scoop is standing up to his knees in alewives, feverishly collecting fish for the larder.

Two of the rivers are buoyed, the Narraguagus and the Pleasant, so it is possible to reach the towns of Milbridge and Addison. However, both routes are difficult, should be undertaken only on a rising tide, and are more suited to a salmon than a cruising boat.

The Narraguagus River, in particular, is famous for its Atlantic salmon runs, and fly fishermen flock here in June from all over Canada and the United States. Fifteen- to 20-pound salmon are common. Herons based in the Douglas Islands and ospreys on Trafton Island also appreciate the fishing, and there are more bald eagles in Pleasant Bay than anywhere else on the Maine coast, for the same reason.

The 1806 edition of *The American Coast Pilot* dismisses Pleasant River as "too difficult to describe." Almost two centuries later, the *Coast Pilot* has progressed somewhat, commenting that "the river is seldom used except by fishermen and the once-extensive trade in lumber ceased many years ago. Passage up the river is suitable for small craft only, except with local knowledge, as the river is reported to have shoaled in many places."

Along the shores of Washington County, from Cherryfield to Machias Bay, lie the blueberry barrens—open slopes and heaths often dotted with boulders left by glaciers. In June, the blueberry fields are covered with delicate white blossoms; by late July or early August, the harvesters are raking the blueberries. With the first frost, the fields take on an extraordinary reddish hue. Each year, some 30 to 40 million pounds of blueberries are shipped fresh or frozen from the fields of Maine.

TRAFTON ISLAND ★★★   No facilities

Charts: **13324**, 13325

Just east of Petit Manan and northward, at the mouth of Narraguagus Bay, Trafton Island has been a favorite of yachtsmen for generations. One of the few harbors in the area, the anchorage at the northern end of the island provides good protection from east around to south and southwest, and a base from which to explore the nearby bays or take departure for Great Wass and Roque islands. There might be half a dozen yachts anchored here on a summer afternoon; on occasion, you might have it all to yourself.

This is a lovely anchorage, and one of the best places in Maine to watch ospreys—perhaps because of the enormous numbers of alewives, bass, and smelt that run up the nearby rivers to spawn. At least two osprey families live near the anchorage. The adults stand by the nest, white-breasted and alert, or fly home chirping with fish in their talons or with branches to make repairs. The young birds in the nest tentatively lift their wings and are carried aloft on the breeze. Sometimes there are six or seven ospreys soaring over the island.

Trafton has been privately owned by one family for decades, and the owners are in residence much of the summer. Because so many people have come ashore uninvited in recent years, the owners now request that you *not* land unless invited.

Approaches. From the west, the steep little Douglas Islands are easy to identify, then the abandoned lighthouse on the east coast of large Pond Island. As you leave to starboard the cliffs of Jordans Delight, admire the unusual sea arch in a sloping buttress.

Having identified dramatic Shipstern Island, with its rocky southern point like the stern of a galleon, run west of Western Reef, marked by a nun, and west of Tommy Island (partially wooded with multicolored bands of rock—reddish, gray, black, and white), then along the bold eastern shore of Trafton Island. You will see the red beacon on Trafton Halftide Ledge half a mile to the north. Round the northern tip of Trafton and head back into the anchorage.

When Trafton is familiar to you, it is also easy to approach around the west side of the island, focusing on the outlying ledge on the west side of the anchorage.

Anchorages, Moorings. Anchor in 8 to 10 feet at low, eastward of the little wooded island and the outlying ledge (visible at all tides). The water shoals on a line that runs from the northern tip of the little island to another ledge 100 yards eastward making out from the south shore, to a big, white rock with dark lichen on the eastern shore of the anchorage. Anchor well northward of this line in good mud.

DYER ISLAND (NORTHEAST COVE) ★★★ No facilities
Charts: **13324**, 13325

Dyer is a long, wooded island that separates Narraguagus and Pleasant bays. Of the several coves on the island, only Northeast offers a good overnight anchorage. Southwest Cove has an active lobster pound and a fishing camp at its head. It is exposed to the southwest, with doubtful holding ground. Northwest Cove is lined with the rustic cottages and buildings of a boy's camp. There are docks and floats and several small sailboats on moorings.

Northeast Cove is a charmer, with two little islands on the north side and a secret little inlet in the corner to explore. There once was a lobster pound here, but today there is no sign of civilization.

Approaches. Run up the east side of Dyer Island and enter south of Otter Island.

Anchorages, Moorings. Do not go westward of the smaller island. Anchor in nine feet at low. The cove has good holding ground and is well protected for prevailing summer winds, although exposed to the north and southeast.

EASTERN HARBOR (CAPE SPLIT) ★★★
Charts: **13324**, 13325

Eastern Harbor, between Moose Neck and Cape Split, is one of the best harbors between Schoodic Point and Head Harbor Island, and one of the easiest to enter. It can be bouncy in a strong southwesterly, but it offers excellent protection in every other direction. Out the harbor entrance there is a beautiful view of the bright-green, rounded forms of Ladle Ledges. South Addision is a small fishing community that has considerable atmosphere but not much to offer in the way of facilities.

Approaches. Enter halfway between the nun and the can off Eastern Pitch and Marsh Island, and continue between the next pair of red and green buoys. A large weir (visible at all tides) is at the western side of the entrance to the inner harbor.

Anchorages, Moorings. Your choice is to anchor in Otter Cove, which has lots of room, or farther north in the inner harbor, where the lobsterboats lie at their moorings. Both anchorages have about the same amount of exposure to the southwest.

In Otter Cove, anchor in about eight to nine feet at low, outside the few moored boats. It is hard to get in far enough to avoid the current, so you will skate around a bit between wind and tide. Holding ground is good in mud. Mooseneck General Store maintains a mooring here.

In the inner harbor, the lobsterboats are

moored between the small dock on the eastern side and the ledge at the northern end of the harbor. There may be room to anchor outside the moored boats in seven to eight feet at low, but be sure you know where the ledge starts.

Getting Ashore. Row in to the dinghy floats east of the small dock.

For the Boat. *Eastern Harbor Lobster Sales (tel. 483-4475).* Gas and diesel are available at this lobster dock in the inner harbor, but there is only about four feet alongside at low. Water can be ob-

tained from a nearby spring if you are willing to lug it. There is chipped ice at the ice plant on the dock.

For the Crew. Lobsters are certainly available, and there is a pay phone on the dock. The Mooseneck General Store (tel. 483-2223) is .4 mile north of the harbor, and has a nice variety of groceries, plus wine, beer, sandwiches, and pizza. The store is owned by cruising couple Mary and Bob Lappeus, who will deliver to the docks and hold mail for cruising boats.

MOOSABEC REACH, Western and Eastern Bays

Charts: 13325, **13326**

Separated by Moosabec Reach and protected by the complex of islands to seaward, Jonesport and Beals Island are busy fishing communities, with the largest fleet of lobsterboats in eastern Maine. Passage all the way through the Reach is barred to many cruising sailboats by the Beals Island bridge, built in 1959, with a vertical clearance of only 39 feet. The voyage from West Jonesport around Great Wass Island, Head Harbor Island, and back up to Jonesport covers some 25 miles, including a sea passage.

Moosabec Reach was known as "Moose a' Becky's Beach" in the 1770s British charts of the area. By 1896 the *American Coast Pilot* was referring to it as "Moosepeek Reach."

Great Wass, Steele Harbor, and Head Harbor islands stand boldly out in the Gulf of Maine, taking the brunt of the ocean attack. Both on the chart and in the appearance of their weathered cliffs, these great rock bastions show ample evidence of the ceaseless pounding of the waves. This is one of the foggiest parts of Maine. The combination of

fog, swift currents, complicated channels, and ledges command the respect of the cruising sailor.

There are, however, two excellent harbors in the area, both easy to enter under most conditions. First is the Cows Yard in Head Harbor Island, and the second is Mistake Island Harbor. A third anchorage—the Mud Hole on the east side of Great Wass Island—offers absolute security but is much harder to enter.

The islands of Eastern and Western Bays are spectacular, with sloping shores of white and pink granite, contrasting with dark spruce and fir above, and countless ledges on which the ocean swells break with dramatic force.

There are seabirds of every kind here, great blue herons flapping along the shores, and bald eagles. In recent years razor-billed auks have returned, and even an occasional puffin. Much of Great Wass Island has been preserved by The Nature Conservancy as a treasury of rare, endangered species.

WESTERN BAY

Charts: 13324, 13325, **13326**

Western Bay is easily approached through the wide southern entrances, or from the west through Tibbett Narrows. This is a well-marked passage between Tibbett Island (low, partially wooded, gravel beaches) and higher Ram Island, with shores of shelving white granite.

There is pleasant sailing in the open stretches of Western Bay, particularly around the beautiful western islands like Drisko and Toms. The bay has no good harbors, but you will find some temporary anchorages in settled weather.

WEST JONESPORT ★★ No facilities

Charts: 13325, **13326**

Ashore, West Jonesport and Jonesport are part of the same community. However, since the bridge was built across Moosabec Reach to Beals Island,

West Jonesport has been completely separated from Jonesport as far as the cruising sailor is concerned (unless your mast can fit under the bridge).

West Jonesport and Moosabec Reach, looking north from Beals Island. The Coast Guard pier is the large facility just west of the bridge. (Hylander photo)

The U.S. Coast Guard has a major installation just west of the bridge (the last one until you reach Eastport), but most services are in Jonesport, east of the bridge.

Approaches. The western part of Moosabec Reach is deeper and wider than the eastern section, and well buoyed. Since the current floods eastward and ebbs westward, your approach will be a lot faster if you time your visit accordingly. With a southwest wind and ebb tide, the Reach is choppy.

After passing Shabbit Island, be alert for cross-currents from Western Bay that may push you out of the channel. The shoreline along the north side, from Wohoa Bay to Jonesport, is low and dark in color, with gravel beaches—in startling contrast to the white granite islands of Western and Eastern bays. One striking landmark on privately owned Hardwood Island is the rusting red sheds, stone wharf, tailings, and machinery of a former granite quarry.

There are a number of lobster docks along the north shore as you approach West Jonesport, and the Coast Guard station with its long pier and large boatshed will be clearly visible at the northern end of the bridge causeway.

This causeway has narrowed the Reach and greatly increased the current at that point. Sometimes it reaches six to eight knots. If your mast is too high to fit under the bridge (vertical clearance is 39 feet; mean tidal range is 11.5 feet), stay away from the swift current at the bridge, particularly at midtide, and allow for strong eddies near the north side.

Anchorages, Moorings. You can anchor in 16 to 24 feet at low off the northern shore, near the end of the Coast Guard pier. Holding ground is good, and you will be out of most of the current.

It's possible to come alongside the Coast Guard pier, except near low tide. You must call in advance on channel 16 or 497-2200 to ask permission; otherwise you risk interfering with operations. Tie up on either side of the east-west finger (there is a float-

Small, quick-winged and graceful, terns are a pleasure to watch. Often called sea swallows, they hover above the sea, then dive straight down into the water with a delicate splash to seize a tiny fish, returning effortlessly to the air with a beat or two of their strong wings. Their bodies are white, with a long, white forked tail. The tops of their swept-back wings are gray, and their heads wear a black cap.

Terns and seagulls are natural enemies. In the places where puffins and auks thrive, such as Matinicus Rock and Machias Seal Island, there usually is a large population of scrappy terns, which make a lot of fuss and chase off intruders, including gulls. But given a good opportunity, the gulls eat tern eggs and chicks and sometimes will drive terns from a nesting site.

The resident naturalist on Machias Seal Island tells this story. Being in mortal competition with gulls, terns react with fury to the orange spot under the bill of a herring gull. One day a cruising sloop arrived at the island with a white mainsail and orange spinnaker. As they dropped the spinnaker, it made a crescent of orange under the white mainsail, forming the world's most enormous seagull. The whole tern population went wild.

Near the end of the nineteenth century, terns were hunted for their feathers to grace milady's hat, and almost were exterminated on the coast of Maine by 1900. One group of feather hunters reported a kill of 1,200 birds in a single day, and as many as 100,000 were killed in a season. Although long since protected from such deliberate slaughter, terns have come back slowly.

Terns and gulls and people are involved in a story with confusing moral issues. Part of the proliferation of the herring gull and consequent pressure on terns is due to the free food found in open dumps and fish wastes thrown over the side from fishing boats. Not long ago, gulls took over Maine's largest nesting sites for arctic and common terns, on Petit Manan Island and neighboring Green Island. Feeling responsible for redressing the original balance, the U.S. Fish and Wildlife Service, with the reluctant support of the Maine Audubon Society and other wildlife groups, poisoned the gulls on those two islands. The experiment worked, and the terns have come back.

In addition to the least tern, found in southern Maine, three other species of terns are found in Maine during the summer. The arctic tern, aside from its grace and beauty, is extraordinary for its annual migration of some 22,000 miles—almost a complete circumnavigation of the earth. Breeding in the Arctic and down the U.S. east coast as far as Massachusetts, these terns cross the Atlantic and then fly down the coasts of Europe and Africa.

The tern most frequently seen on the coast of Maine (they are hard to distinguish) is the common tern, which breeds from Labrador to the Caribbean. Rarest, and probably endangered, is the roseate tern.

ing camel along each side to keep you clear of the pilings), or to the west side of the pier itself. There is about four feet at low along the inside of the east-west finger, and less along the pier.

For the Crew. There is a pay phone inside the Coast Guard building. The IGA supermarket and the post office are a mile eastward, and you usually can get a ride back with your groceries. (For other facilities, see Jonesport writeup.)

Things to Do. Walk across the bridge to explore Beals Island.

BEALS ISLAND

Charts: 13325, **13326**

Beals Island is connected to the mainland by the bridge over Moosabec Reach (39-foot vertical clearance). It is an island of fishermen, lobstermen, and boatbuilders, and lobsterboats are everywhere. The boats built here are famous for their speed and durability.

The first Beals Island settler in 1764 was an unusual man in many ways. Manwarren Beal was enormous, smart, a poet, tough, and certainly prolific.

Other unusual people came to Beals, among them George Washington Adams, an itinerant preacher. In 1865, he launched the Palestine Emigration Association and persuaded 156 presumably sensible citizens of Beals and Jonesport to emigrate to Jaffa (now Israel), to establish a colony to carry on the work of the Lord. They sailed from Jonesport and arrived in the Holy Land, but funds ran out, most of the colonists fell ill, and many died. Most never got back to Maine. "One old lady," Maine author Louise Rich reports, "stayed in order to spite herself for having been such a fool as to come in the first place."

Before the bridge was built in 1959, Beals was an isolated community that even had its own peculiarities of speech—a quaint Elizabethan English that now has disappeared.

To visit Beals Island, walk across the bridge from Jonesport, or anchor in the first cove west of the bridge, outside the moored boats, and row ashore to a convenient float.

EASTERN BAY

Charts: 13325, **13326**

The bay is filled with ledges. Its northern portion should be navigated by strangers only with good visibility and near low tide, when most of the dangers are visible.

The usual approach to Eastern Bay is from the south, through the deep and clear passages of Mud Hole Channel or Main Channel Way. It is also possible, but considerably more difficult, to approach from the north from Moosabec Reach, through the winding buoyed passage just west of Head Harbor Island.

In addition to Mistake Island Harbor and the Mud Hole, Eastern Bay offers other anchorages to the adventurous sailor, including Sand Cove North on the east shore of Great Wass Island, and the cove north of Middle Hardwood (known as Sealand). In good years, naturalist Philip Conkling reports, Middle Hardwood has an enormous crop of blueberries and huckleberries. "The island looks like a sea of blue."

MUD HOLE

(GREAT WASS ISLAND) ★★★★★

[5]   No facilities

Charts: 13325, **13326**

Mud Hole is a wonderfully private and well-protected anchorage on the east coast of Great Wass Island. It is difficult to enter, but once inside, you are in a completely natural little fjord lined with granite and spruce, with herons, seagulls, and bald eagles for company. Best of all, Mud Hole gives you easy access to The Nature Conservancy's Great Wass Island Preserve and some wonderful trails through mossy forests, stands of rare, gnarled jack pines, across sunny granite ledges, and out along the cliffs of Eastern Bay.

Don't be surprised to find yourself sharing Mud Hole with several million clamlets growing in incubator cars. They are part of an experiment with the University of Maine at Machias underwritten by a group of nearby towns and shellfish dealers. The plan is to raise clams from spawn at the Beals Island hatchery, and distribute millions of juvenile clams to participating towns for seeding on local clam flats.

Approaches. Approach through Mud Hole Channel, paralleling the line of islands and ledges south and west of Mistake Island. Black Ledges to port are usually breaking. Green Island is the first little island with trees to starboard; Mink Island is the second. Well before reaching Mink Island, bear westward and head in north of Mud Hole Point, giving it a wide berth.

Enter and leave Mud Hole between halftide and high tide, preferably about 1¹/₂ or two hours before high, when there is enough water in the entrance channel but the ledges are still detectable. The ledges cover at about halftide, but they are discernible for some time thereafter by their dark color and rockweed.

There is an old rotting weir along the south shore not visible at high. It's just north of the word "Hole" in "Mud Hole Pt." on the chart. To avoid it, approach near the northern entrance point, where the chart shows 14 feet (see sketch map).

After approaching the northern entrance point to avoid the weir, turn sharply to port and head directly over to the south shore. Run along this shore until you have passed the midchannel ledge. The lobster buoys usually will give you an indication of deep water.

The midchannel ledge in the entrance extends almost all the way across at low tide, leaving only a 20-foot channel northward and a 50-foot channel southward. While it is possible to go to either side of this ledge near high tide, the southern channel is deeper and wider.

After passing the entrance ledge, continue to favor the south shore until you have passed the second ledge, which extends to midchannel from the north shore. There may be a stake beyond this

ledge. Aim south of this stake. Here the anchorage starts to widen.

Anchorages, Moorings. The deep water runs a relatively short distance west of the second ledge. Anchor in 12 to 20 feet at low. You may find it useful to put out a stern anchor to keep from swinging with the tide into shallower water. Not surprisingly, the bottom is mud.

Getting Ashore. Row to the south shore of the anchorage and tie up to a convenient tree.

Things to Do. The Mud Hole Trail runs along the south shore of the harbor. Scramble up the hill 50 yards or so until you reach the well-defined trail. For a long walk (three or four hours), head west to the parking lot and then back via the Little Cape Cove Trail, closing the loop by walking along the cliffs and beaches and northward to Mud Hole Point.

For a shorter walk, head east from the anchorage on Mud Hole Trail until it emerges on the cliffs at Mud Hole Point. Then walk south along the shore to Little Cape Point.

Just south of Mud Hole Point, after a good rain, a gurgling stream runs out of the woods and over the shelving granite to form Taft's Bath—a delightful series of little pools, basins, and cascades of fresh water just right for sitting and splashing. Dry off in the sun on the warm rocks.

MISTAKE ISLAND HARBOR ★★★★ No facilities
Charts: 13325, **13326**

One of the most beautiful harbors in Maine is hidden away among the ledges behind Mistake and Knight islands. This is not the "Mistake Harbor" shown on the chart. Once inside, you are surrounded by pink and white granite shoreline, protected from the ocean swells that crash on the rocks only a few hundred yards away. Over this tranquil scene of natural beauty stands Moose Peak Light. You may be lulled to sleep by its sonorous double note.

Approaches. There are at least two possible approaches. Most boats enter through Main Channel Way, leaving Moose Peak Light to port and the sloping granite cliffs of Steele Harbor Island to starboard. As you pass the lighthouse, there is a glimpse of open water at high tide between treeless Mistake Island and heavily wooded Knight Island. Do not be tempted, however. Continue past Knight Island, turning to port around the end of the island and southward back into the harbor.

A line between the northern tips of Knight and Mistake crosses a tiny and dangerous ledge that should be left to port. The rockweed on this ledge is just barely visible at high tide, and some kind

Moose Peak Light on Mistake Island. (Peter Ralston photo)

soul has placed a short metal pipe on it. The ledge is just opposite a small green cottage on privately owned Knight Island. The larger ledge to the west is left to starboard. It is visible at all tides (see sketch map).

If you are coming from Mud Hole or elsewhere in Eastern Bay, Mistake Island Harbor is easily approached from the north. Pass south of can "1" marking a rock, then head for the northern end of Knight Island.

Anchorages, Moorings. Anchor in 10 feet at low off the northern end of Mistake Island, inside the ledge. Best protection is up in the corner between Mistake and Knight, although this is a cable area.

Mistake Island Harbor is well protected from ocean swells by the outlying ledges, although a strong southwesterly would blow into the anchorage. It is exposed to the north and northwest, and boats may drag if a strong front comes through.

Getting Ashore. Row into the ways of the old boathouse at the northern end of Mistake Island.

Things to Do. A convenient boardwalk maintained by the Coast Guard leads to Moose Peak Light, automated in 1970. Stay on the boardwalk or granite outcroppings to avoid damage to the rare and delicate plants found on Mistake Island. These are mostly members of one plant family notable for their ability to survive in the cold, moist, and salty air and poor soil. They include lush blueberry, crowberry, leatherleaf, lambkill, and Labrador tea. You will also find abundant raspberries and the beautiful beachhead iris. Underlying these plants are several feet of peat.

Most of Mistake Island was acquired by The Nature Conservancy from a grandson of the man who was lighthouse keeper from 1890 to 1910. The remaining six acres is still owned by the Coast Guard.

THE COWS YARD and HEAD HARBOR ★★★ No facilities
Charts: 13325, **13326**

The Cows Yard is a secure anchorage, attractive and easy to enter under any conditions from the south through Head Harbor. It's one of the best harbors between Mount Desert and Roque Island. If you are caught out in fog or bad weather, this is a good refuge. The anchorage is largely undeveloped, with only a few summer cottages

Approaches. From Crumple Island, past Great Wass, Mistake Island, and Head Harbor, the coast is steep-to. Even in thick fog, you can approach within visual range without getting into trouble and run along the 150-foot curve with your fathometer, paralleling the coast. Or you can tack in toward the cliffs, seeing and hearing the breaking surf in plenty of time to come about for the next outward leg.

There are two excellent clues to help you find the entrance as you coast along toward Head Harbor and The Cows Yard. First is the lonely lighthouse at Moose Peak, whose foghorn has warned mariners since 1827. The second is a dramatic difference between the light-colored rocks on the west side of the entrance and the dark rocks of Head Harbor Island and Man Island on the east side of the entrance.

Approaches. The ledge at the west entrance of Head Harbor normally breaks. The first ledge to starboard, off the little point with trees, is visible above halftide. Run up the middle of Head Harbor, aiming for the rock that forms the eastern entrance of The Cows Yard, to the right of which is a long, gray-shingled cottage. Enter The Cows Yard halfway between the rock to starboard, which shows at all tides, and the island to port.

Anchorages, Moorings. The Cows Yard is big enough to provide anchorage for several boats but much shallower than shown on the chart. Where the chart shows 20 feet, the actual depth is only 9 or 10 feet at low. Do not go past the second island to port. Best protection is found toward the east side of the deep water, behind the big rock that forms the eastern entrance. There is considerable kelp on the bottom, so make sure your anchor is set.

Even with a strong southwest wind, hardly any ocean swell penetrates into The Cows Yard. This is generally a serene anchorage, often with the reassuring double note of the Moose Peak foghorn.

The same cannot be said of the outer Head Harbor, which has a rocky bottom and is exposed to ocean swells.

JONESPORT ★★★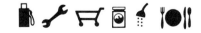
Charts: 13325, **13326**

Jonesport, like Beals Island across Moosabec Reach, is a fishing town. The shores are lined with docks piled with lobster pots, and lobsterboats are moored in every cove. Each year, the Fourth of July Races are held here on Moosabec Reach to pick "the world's fastest lobsterboat." The races began

MUD HOLE, MISTAKE ISLAND
HARBOR, AND THE COWS YARD (based on Chart 13326)

This chart is for general information only, and NOT TO BE USED FOR NAVIGATION. Location and type of buoys and other navigational aids may change from time to time. Use in conjunction with the text, and the latest Charts, Notices to Mariners, and U.S. Coast Pilot.

Nautical Miles

0   1/2   1

⚓ Anchorages

around the time of the Civil War, with dory rowing. Dories were succeeded by Friendship sloops, then by boats powered with naphtha engines, then make-and-break gasoline engines, and finally by the handsome, powerful, and seaworthy Jonesport lobsterboats of today.

This is the best place in the area to pick up supplies, most of which are found east of the bridge in town. The Coast Guard station, with search-and-rescue capabilities, is in West Jonesport, just west of the bridge (channel 16; tel. 497-2200).

Approaches. Moosabec Reach is a busy thoroughfare, with lots of traffic. The narrow eastern entrance is well marked, starting with green bell "1" north of Mark Island, but the passage is not easy in low visibility. If caught in the fog, anchor anywhere along the channel in mud bottom. There is considerable current in the Reach, flooding eastward and ebbing westward.

Anchorages, Moorings. The town is on the west side of Sawyer Cove, which is now partially protected by a 1,200-foot steel and stone breakwater. Enter the anchorage from the west, and anchor off the town marina (the easternmost of the docks) in six to eight feet at low, good holding ground. The breakwater provides shelter from southeast winds, but less protection from prevailing southwesterlies.

Dockage may be arranged at the town marina floats, with four feet alongside at low, or Jonesport Shipyard may have a mooring available.

Getting Ashore. Row in to the dinghy floats of the town marina.

For the Boat. *Town Marina (tel. 497-5929).* The town marina has a launching ramp and floats.

Jonesport Shipyard (Ch. 16; tel. 497-2701). East of the town marina, this yard provides hauling, storage, and repairs. It may be identified by the "Shipyard" sign on the roof of a gray building. Boats up to 17 tons or 45 feet can be hauled, and showers, laundry facilities, and ice are available.

O.W. & B.S. Look Co. (Ch. 77; tel. 497-2353). Look's floats and blue buildings are opposite the western end of the breakwater. Gas is available at the floats, and diesel is available halfway up the dock. Come at halftide or better; there is only a foot of water off the floats at low, and a ledge lurks a couple of boatlengths eastward of the floats. Ice and frozen crabmeat can be found at Look's.

For the Crew. There is a hardware store (with marine supplies) right up from the landing, along with the Win-Place-Show lunch counter and convenience store. Walking left into town, you will find the post office, another convenience store and takeout, a bank, and pay phone. Church's Hardware carries marine supplies, including propane and charts. The IGA market is just beyond.

Things to Do. Captain Barna Norton, champion of United States ownership of Machias Seal Island, lives in West Jonesport. He will take you out on sightseeing trips (tel. 497-5933) to any of the surrounding islands, and, in season, to Machias Seal Island, home of arctic terns, puffins, and razor-billed auks.

It's an interesting walk across the bridge to Beals Island.

ROQUE ISLAND ARCHIPELAGO

Charts: 13325, **13326**

For a long time, Roque Island has been the ultimate goal of sailors cruising down east—perhaps because of the beautiful, mile-long white sand beach, perhaps because of the sense of something special about this island, perhaps because it takes determination to sail east of Schoodic and Petit Manan.

Roque is the centerpiece of an archipelago that includes Great and Little Spruce, Lakeman, Marsh and Bar, Double Shot, Anguilla, and Halifax islands—all set in a body of water called Chandler Bay to the west and Englishman Bay to the east. Shaped roughly like an H, the Roque archipelago offers a delightful variety of anchorages. Most familiar is the great southern beach on Roque Harbor. Lakeman Harbor to the east, surrounded by Lakeman, Marsh, and Bar islands, provides a secure anchorage. To the west is tiny, landlocked Bunker Cove. On the north side of the island is another long sand beach on Shorey Cove.

Indians were the earliest-known summer inhabitants of Roque, and numerous shell heaps have been studied by archaeologists. Joseph Peabody acquired Roque in 1806, and for almost two centuries, the island has served as a resort and retreat for his descendants, the Gardner and Monks families. The old family buildings and farmhouses, red and yellow, are on the eastern side of Squire Point, overlooking Shorey Cove. There is a private boatyard, with a dock, metal and woodworking shops, and a small fleet at the moorings. Boats are hauled by attaching a farm tractor to a great old anchor half-buried in the ground, and winching them up the ways.

Roque is a working farm, and almost self-sufficient, with cattle, sheep, pigs, geese, chickens, pigeons, and other animals. Products of the island include milk, butter, eggs, wool, beef, pork, squabs, raspberries, rhubarb, herbs, and vegetables. The caretaker and the owners take pride in both frugality and ingenuity, and the island has

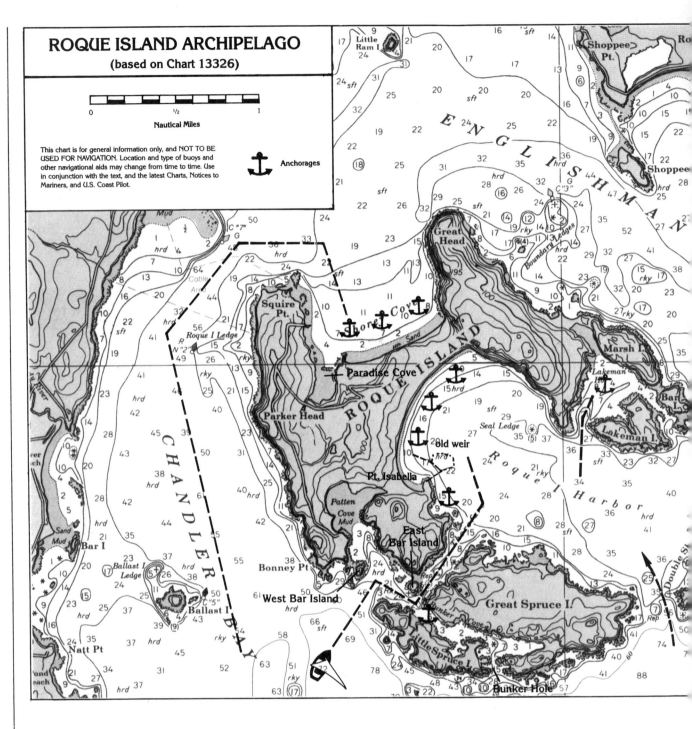

ROQUE ISLAND ARCHIPELAGO
(based on Chart 13326)

Nautical Miles

This chart is for general information only, and NOT TO BE USED FOR NAVIGATION. Location and type of buoys and other navigational aids may change from time to time. Use in conjunction with the text, and the latest Charts, Notices to Mariners, and U.S. Coast Pilot.

⚓ Anchorages

some marvelous Rube Goldberg contraptions, including a continuous conveyor belt to cut and split firewood, built from scrap material.

In summertime it is not unusual to see family members traveling in a horse-drawn carriage; during the winter, the resident Clydesdales haul guests on old blue sledges. As John Peabody Monks said in his book *Roque Island, Maine—A History:* "The visitor to Roque forgets the urgencies of time and place."

"Perroquet" is the French word for parrot, and it seems plausible that, as Samuel Eliot Morison suggests, Roque was named by the French explor-

ers for the puffin, or sea parrot. Or perhaps the origin was "rogue," considering the pirates who were based nearby.

When Joseph Peabody bought Roque, he made good use of it. First he built a tidal dam across Paradise Cove to power a gristmill and a sawmill. Several large vessels were built for him at a shipyard in the little bight at the mouth of Paradise Cove, just west of Point Olga. Peabody owned 63 ships, and at one time employed more than 3,000 men in his various shipping and trading enterprises.

In 1868, John and Catharine Gardner sold

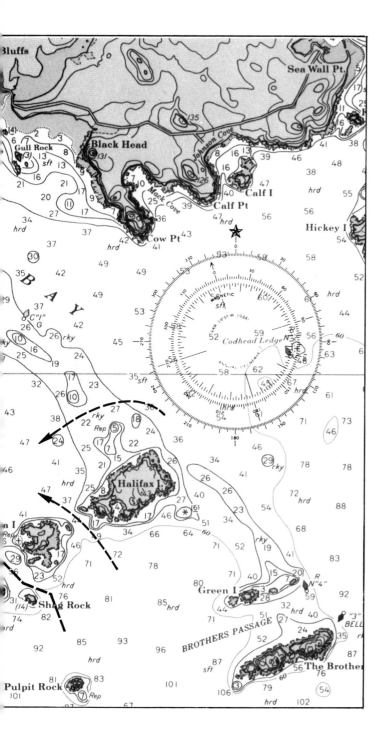

Roque Island for reasons unknown. Ten years later, two of their sons bought it back for double the price, and the island has been in the family ever since. Shortly thereafter, the Gardners bought Great and Little Spruce, Lakeman, Anguilla, and Little Bar islands. Double Shot was acquired in the 1930s.

A lumber mill once stood at the head of Patten Cove from which laths were shipped on coastal steamers to New York, about three million of them between 1926 and 1928.

There are lots of stories of life on Roque, both human and animal. Pigs were once allowed to roam free on the island, and it is reported that a particularly bright pig learned how to dig clams on the shore. Then there is the story of lobsterman Horace Dunbar, who enjoyed a party ashore with some visiting yachtsmen and had his share of liquor. Finally it was time to go, so Horace got in his skiff and started to row home. "Two hours later, he was found by more sober members of the party still rowing steadily, with his boat's painter attached to the wharf."

THE THOROFARE

Charts: 13325, **13326**

The Thorofare is a narrow, winding, hidden, and altogether delightful passage from Chandler Bay to Roque Island Harbor. From the west, it is hard to find. One good way is to run a compass course from the eastern end of the Jonesport channel until the Thorofare starts to open up. At first, there appears to be no entrance, but have faith. You will see the small, wooded island (Westerly Bar Island) southeast of Bonney Point. Passing halfway between this island and the western end of Little Spruce Island, turn southeast toward the slot between Little and Great Spruce islands. Then, leaving Easterly Bar Island to port, turn eastward through the Thorofare.

With a southwesterly wind, it's a pleasure to sail the Thorofare. You will be blanketed by Little Spruce but probably get enough puffs to tiptoe through the passage. There is not much current.

Right next to Easterly Bar Island, the chart shows a rock ("REP"), but many people have sailed through the Thorofare over the years without finding a trace of it. Perhaps the prudent thing to do is to avoid the passage near dead low. The shallowest portions of the Thorofare are farther east, where you may find seven or eight feet or less near mid-channel.

BUNKER COVE ★★★★   No facilities

Charts: 13325, **13326**

Where the Thorofare meets The Gut between Great and Little Spruce islands is a splendid little anchorage, secluded and secure, known as Bunker Cove. In his history of Roque Island, Monks calls it "an almost landlocked small anchorage, considered by some yachtsmen the most beautiful on the Atlantic Coast."

It is named for Jack Bunker of Somes Sound. During the Revolution, he heard about a British ship on the Sheepscot River collecting food, so he and a friend canoed down the coast and found the ship at anchor in Wiscasset, unguarded and full of provisions. They cut her cable, hoisted sail, and headed east to Somes Sound, where they distributed the provisions to their starving neighbors. Then, chased by another British vessel, they fled with their prize toward Roque and ran her into Bunker Hole, east of Little Spruce Island. Without local knowledge, the British were afraid to follow,

and by the time they rowed past Little Spruce, the ship's masts had been cut away and she was camouflaged with branches and trees. They never saw a thing.

Approaches. From the west, enter the Thorofare between Little Spruce Island and Westerly Bar Island, which guards Patten Cove. Swing southward, leaving Easterly Bar Island to port, and enter Bunker Cove, in the narrow slot between Great and Little Spruce. The water shoals rapidly after you pass the cliffs on Great Spruce.

Anchorages, Moorings. Boats drawing six feet or more should not go past the indentation on Little Spruce. Boats of lesser draft can go farther, to the headland on Little Spruce. Anchor in six to eight feet at low. The bottom is mud, with some weed. One effective way to anchor here is to drop the hook in the middle and take a stern line to a tree on the cliffs of Great Spruce.

TWIN BEACH ★★★   No facilities

Charts: 13325, **13326**

Near the southern end of Great Beach, south of Point Isabella, is a little cove between rocky headlands with a tiny beach of its own (see sketch map). There is room for one boat to lie here in relative privacy, with good protection from prevailing winds.

Approaches. There are no dangers. Head straight into the cove.

Anchorages, Moorings. Anchor in 10 to 11 feet at low, just inside the headlands. The bottom is mud but there is also some kelp.

GREAT BEACH ★★★★★   No facilities

Charts: 13325, **13326**

There is no civilization here on the great southern beach of Roque—just the sweeping, mile-long arc of white-sand beach flanked by a meadow, and

behind it the dark spruce of fabled Roque Island.

Signs posted on the beach explain the owners' wishes—all visiting yachtsmen should respect them. In particular, avoid the south end of Great Beach, reserved for the family, and refrain from walking inland beyond the beach.

Approaches. Great Beach usually is approached from the west through the Thorofare (see above writeup). From the east, the approach is wide and easy, north of Halifax Island into Roque Island Harbor. It is also possible, with care, to run through the slots between Halifax, Anguilla, Double Shot, and Great Spruce. The only danger in Roque Island Harbor is Seal Ledge, visible for about two hours after low tide.

There is an old weir extending 350 feet from the rocky point at the south end of the beach, and visible till about halftide. The weir is more of a nuisance than a real danger, but the sketch map will help you stay clear of it.

Anchorages, Moorings. Anchor anywhere along the beach in a comfortable depth. Best protection from prevailing winds is toward the south end. The holding ground is fine, but a slight swell coming in from the sea makes this a rolly anchorage, and you may be happier for the night somewhere else.

Most days during July and August, you will find six or eight boats anchored here, and occasionally a yacht club cruise will make it seem downright congested. In September, Great Beach returns to its natural state.

LAKEMAN HARBOR ★★★ No facilities
Charts: 13325, **13326**

Lakeman is an excellent harbor formed by Marsh Island, Lakeman Island, and the southeastern tip of Roque Island. Ocean swells do not enter and there is good protection in every direction except southwest. The islands have remained in their natural state except for a fishing camp or two, and you will be lulled by the chirps of ospreys, the chuckles of eiders, and the baas of sheep on the islands.

Great Beach at Roque Island Harbor, a mile-long crescent of white sand. (Peter Ralston photo)

319

Approaches. Coming from Great Beach, be cautious of Seal Ledge, which is visible for a couple of hours after low tide. Otherwise, the approach is obvious between Roque and Lakeman islands. Favor the Lakeman side to avoid the ledge that makes out from Roque. From the entrance, head toward the southern end of the cliffs on Marsh Island. The deep water ends about 300 yards from Marsh.

Anchorages, Moorings. Anchor in seven to eight feet at low. Holding ground is good, in mud, although there is some kelp. Lakeman is open to the southwest, and the afternoon breeze comes in across Roque Harbor. This usually calms down in the evening, and the anchorage otherwise is entirely secure.

Things to Do. Row up between Marsh Island and Roque at high tide, or out between Bar and Lakeman.

SHOREY COVE ★★★ No facilities
Charts: 13325, **13326**

On the north side of Roque Island, the beach at Shorey Cove is not as long as Great Beach on the south side, nor as beautiful. Nevertheless, it runs almost three-quarters of a mile—from Paradise Cove on the west to the high cliffs of Great Head on the east. The red and yellow buildings of the Monks and Gardner clan, plus their dock, boathouses, and barns, grace the eastern shore of Squire Point. Shorey Cove provides good, secure anchorage anywhere along the beach.

John Shorey, shipwright and onetime owner of Roque Island, lived here, and Paradise Cove is where nineteenth-century owner Joseph Peabody built the tidal dam for his sawmill and shipyard. Several ships of his extensive fleet were built here.

Approaches. Coming up Chandler Bay against the current is a slow proposition. Look for small nun "2" at Roque Island Ledge and green can "7," marking Great Bar. You will see open green meadows on Squire Point and horses, sheep, and cattle grazing. Give Squire Point a good berth because of the ledge at the northeastern end.

Approaching through Englishman Bay, note in particular can "3" at Boundary Ledges, left to port.

Anchorages, Moorings. There is a small fleet of boats moored in the western part of the cove. The owners prefer that you do not anchor "right out in front." Anchor south of the dock and well outside the moored boats, or anywhere along the sand beach, in 7 to 10 feet at low. If winds from the east are expected, Great Head provides excellent protection.

Things to Do. You are welcome to walk on the beach. No fires; no camping.

SPAR ISLAND
Charts: 13325, **13326**

Spar Island is at the mouth of Mason Bay, north of Roque Island. There is an interesting little nine-foot hole north of Spar Island and west of Dunn Island. The approach is through the deep but narrow passage between Flake Point Bar and Dunn Island. Fishermen from the area use Flake Point Bar as though it were a pier—landing gear and loading supplies from the bows of their boats up on the hard gravel spit.

HALIFAX ISLAND
Charts: 13325, **13326**

Halifax Island lies at the eastern tip of the Roque archipelago, next to Anguilla and half a mile from the beach at Roque. The island is uninhabited, with gently rolling meadows rising to a 60-foot cliff at the western end, where guillemots nest. At one time, Halifax probably was cleared by fire or logging for use as a sheep pasture.

The island is privately owned and protected by a Nature Conservancy easement because of its freshwater bog and several uncommon plants, including the beachhead iris and roseroot stonecrop. Blueberries, raspberries, and cranberries abound. Beware of the fierce, insectivorous sundew.

There is a partially protected anchorage at the

northwestern tip, toward Roque, and landing is easy on the cobble beaches. Most interesting is the miniature harbor on the southwest corner, its mouth partially blocked by a ledge in the middle. The best entrance is to the east of these rocks, diffi- cult if a swell is running. This is a great place to explore with the dinghy. A shoal-draft boat can lie in four feet in this tiny bay with good protection for the night, but it is not big enough or deep enough for larger craft.

LITTLE KENNEBEC BAY
Charts: 13325, **13326**

Extending northward from Englishman Bay, Little Kennebec Bay invites exploration. With a summer southwesterly, you can sail gently up the sparsely settled shores of the bay. It's eyeball navigation all the way, with flats on either side of the channel—a gunkholer's dream. The shores are low-lying, and in places the bay widens to a mile or more.

The western entrance is easy to distinguish with its high, wooded heads, east of sandy Roque Bluffs. Point of Main, at the eastern entrance, is also high and rocky, and northward are the two white domes on Howard Mountain. Hickey Island is barren at the southern end and marked by scraggly trees at its northern end. Fan Island is easy to identify—high, rocky, and wooded.

After leaving Fan Island to port, head for Grays Beach to avoid the ledge making out from Sea Wall Point. Turn northward after passing Sea Wall Point, noting the rock that lies off Grays Beach (visible for two hours after low). Give Yoho Head ample clearance. The ledges off Yoho are visible at halftide. From there on, finding the deep channel between the flats is a matter of informed guess-work—easiest at low tide with the sun behind you. Caution and a rising tide are the key elements. It's possible to work your way up Collins Branch into Moose Snare Cove, or up the West Branch past Marston Point.

JOHNSON COVE ★★★ No facilities
Charts: 13325, **13326**

Near the western entrance to Little Kennebec Bay, Johnson Cove offers good shelter behind Calf Island, with a gravel beach and vistas out to sea. There are several cottages and homes at the head of the cove. Calf Island is rocky, wooded, and beautiful, with eiders feeding all along its shores.

Approaches. Approach Johnson Cove on either side of Calf Island. If you use the western ap- proach, favor the Calf Point side as you enter. The ledge north of Calf Island is very large, and visible until high tide. You should have no trouble with the eastern entrance, which is wider.

Anchorages, Moorings. Anchor where Calf Island will provide the best protection from the wind, in 16 feet at low. Holding ground is good, in mud.

MOOSE SNARE COVE ★★★ No facilities
Charts: 13325, **13326**

At the very end of the Collins Branch of Little Kennebec Bay lies intriguing Moose Snare Cove. How do you snare a moose? The cove provides the perfect gunkhole, hidden way up around and beyond Hog Island. The north shore is high and partially cleared, with a cabin or two, and a number of clamming skiffs are moored here.

Approaches. Tiny, wooded Porcupine Island lies off the grassy meadows of Johnson Point. Work your way slowly past Hog Island, and there-after stay close to the northern shore of the cove. At low tide, you may ground out, but no harm will come to you in the mud. The cove continues around into Mill Pond, where there is a cluster of yurts, but the entrance is too shoal except for small craft.

Anchorages, Moorings. Anchor along the north shore of Moose Snare Cove in five to eight feet at low, with mud bottom. A stern anchor will keep you lined up in the narrow channel and off the mudflats to the south. This would be a perfect spot to hide during a hurricane, and it is unlikely you will find other boats here.

MACHIAS BAY to Cutler and West Quoddy Head

Machias Bay

Charts: 13325, **13326**, 13327

Machias Bay is neither grand nor extensive, but it is blessed with wonderful scenery, wildlife sanctuaries, and relative anonymity. Guarding the entrance are the barren Libby Islands, with the lighthouse at the southern end, now automated.

To the east is Cross, one of the largest undeveloped islands on the coast—home for deer, bear, seals, eiders, bald eagles, and razor-billed auks. The western shore of Machias Bay is particularly beautiful; dramatic Yellow Head Island lies like a dragon in the water, with handsome, high, wooded Bare and Bar islands behind. Part of Salt Island is a preserve of The Nature Conservancy and the home of bald eagles.

At the entrance to Machias Bay, the 90-foot cliffs of Stone Island drop straight into deep water, and there were plans in the 1960s to offload supertankers here. After a decade of public debate, these plans were abandoned. Stone Island was bought by the Landguard Trust, and sold at cost to The Nature Conservancy. Great blue herons, ospreys, and bald eagles nest on these forbidding shores.

There is a rare jasper beach in Howard Cove, and a gravel bar over which the residents of Starboard Island drive at low tide to reach their homes. Looming over Howard Cove—and hard to miss anywhere in Machias Bay—are the huge, white radomes on Howard Mountain. The Machias River empties into the northwestern corner of the bay, passing on its way the home of the best strawberry pie in Maine, served at Helen's Restaurant in Machias. Bucks Harbor, on the west side, offers excellent anchorage and protection. Downeast Hospital is in Machias (tel. 255-3356).

"Machias" is the Indian word for "bad little falls." There were lumber mills here in the early days, plus shipyards and extensive fisheries based in Machiasport. In the early eighteenth century, pirates such as John Rhoades and Captain Bellamy kept their ships in this remote area.

The southern portions of Machias Bay are open and generally free of obstacles. High Avery Rock, with its beacon and adjacent red bell, makes a good mark. Go as far as Round Island and Salt Island. Beyond that start the flats and shoals of Holmes Bay. A good chop can build up in Machias Bay, especially with the southwest wind against the ebb tide, but generally it provides a lovely sail. Do not count on your Loran in this area; it's likely to be put out of commission by the complex of radio towers on the Cutler Peninsula.

The Machias area is full of historical footnotes, most connected with the American Revolution. At Burnham's Tavern in Machias patriots met to discuss the British demand for lumber for barracks. The discussion continued on June 11, 1775, near a little stream now known as "Foster's Rubicon." Calling for resistance to the British, Colonel Benjamin Foster leapt across, followed by the men of Machias. The next day saw the first naval battle of the Revolution and the capture of the armed British schooner *Margaretta* by the patriots' sloop *Unity*, under the command of Captain Jeremiah O'Brien.

STARBOARD COVE ★★★

Charts: 13325, **13326**

Starboard Cove is formed between the mainland and Starboard Island, to the south. Residents of Starboard Island are served neither by bridge nor ferry; they reach home by pickup truck across the gravel bar at low tide.

Approaches. Enter the cove north of Starboard Island.

Anchorages, Moorings. Anchor anywhere in the cove, in 13 to 20 feet at low, mud bottom. A line between the northern ends of Stone and Starboard islands marks the start of shoaling near the gravel bar, and an old weir; anchor north of this line. Check Pettegrow Boat Yard if you want a mooring.

Getting Ashore. Row the dinghy in to the beach.

For the Boat. *Pettegrow Boat Yard (Tel. 255-8740).* This unpretentious yard has rental moorings, limited marine supplies (including charts), and a 90-ton marine railway, but no fuel. Hull and engine repairs can be made. This is the last boatyard until you reach Eastport, and one of the least expensive on the whole coast.

Things to Do. Walk across the bar to Starboard Island at low tide, or walk north to Jasper Beach in Howard Cove.

HOWARD COVE
Charts: 13325, **13326**

In the southwestern corner of Machias Bay, Howard Cove is easy to enter but exposed to south and southeast winds. Holding ground is poor, and there are no facilities.

Jasper Beach, at the head of the cove, is a half-mile crescent gravel beach, backed by a marsh, with a tidal inlet at the eastern end. The beach pebbles are a mixture of jasper quartz of many colors and smooth, dark, volcanic rhyolites. The town of Machiasport, with help from The Nature Conservancy, has preserved public access to this unique beach, which has been registered by the state as a Critical Area. To visit the beach, anchor off and row your dinghy in.

BUCKS HARBOR ★★★
Charts: 13325, **13326**

The most useful harbor in Machias Bay is Bucks Harbor, on the western side. It offers a well-protected anchorage and fuel in the attractive setting of a small fishing village. Forty or more lobsterboats, some scallopers, and many lobster cars are moored in the harbor.

Approaches. Enter halfway between Bar Island and Bucks Head.

Anchorages, Moorings. Anchor west or southwest of Bar Island, outside the moored boats, in 8 to 15 feet at low. The holding ground is good, in mud bottom.

It may be possible to get a mooring (stake) if a fisherman is away for the night. Inquire at the fishermen's Co-op or at Eastern Atlantic Lobster. The Port and Starboard Yacht Club maintains a guest mooring but has no other facilities.

Getting Ashore. Row in to the floats at the Co-op or at Eastern Atlantic Lobster, or to the beach south of the lobster pound.

For the Boat. *Bucks Harbor Fishermen's Co-op (tel. 255-8888).* At the long dock and floats of the Co-op, at Bucks Neck, you can obtain gas and diesel. There is four to six feet alongside at low.

Eastern Atlantic Lobster Company (tel. 255-4792). Under Mt. Aetna, on the southwest side of Bucks Harbor, is the lobster pound and dock of Eastern Atlantic Lobster Company. This is primarily a service for commercial lobstermen, but gas and diesel are available.

For the Crew. Lobsters may be bought at either lobster dock. There is a pay phone above Eastern Atlantic.

MACHIASPORT and MACHIAS RIVER
Charts: 13325, 13326

Two miles up the Machias River, in the northwestern corner of Machias Bay, Machiasport has little to offer the cruising sailor. The channel through the mudflats is deep but very narrow, and the buoys quite far apart. The only remaining wharf belongs to Machiasport Packing. If none of their boats are in, you may be able to get permission to tie up to the wharf. The river above Machiasport is unbuoyed, and there is a fixed bridge at Crocker Point with a vertical clearance of 25 feet.

On a ledge close to shore near Birch Point, south of Machiasport, are carved some eroding Indian petroglyphs more than 3,000 years old, depicting deer and moose, human figures, and images from an Indian legend. More recently, there were sawmills on the Machias River, and ships were built here in the nineteenth century. Way upstream from Machias is Whitneyville, where great booms of logs were collected before being floated downriver for shipment from Machiasport. This was the site of the last long river drive on the eastern seaboard.

In modern times, little Machiasport became known for its valiant and successful fight against the oil refineries that tried to locate here and in Eastport, attracted by deep water and easy access. Today the big economic news in the area is blueberries.

CROSS ISLAND (NORTHWEST HARBOR)

Charts: 13325, 13326, **13327**

At the northwestern corner of Cross Island, Northwest Harbor is easy to enter, in spite of the major fish pen operation on the western side. The sparkling outlet of a saltwater pond runs across the beach, and there are deer browsing in the early morning. This makes a fine day stop; even Cutler's imposing radio towers are almost out of sight.

However, the holding ground is very doubtful. There are impressive quantities of rockweed and kelp, with sandy patches between. Anchoring is difficult unless you can get the hook in one of those sandy patches.

CROSS ISLAND

(NORTHEAST HARBOR) ★★★

 No facilities

Charts: 13325, 13326, **13327**

Looking inland to Cross Island, Northeast Harbor's shores are in a natural state. Looking northward, however, your vision is assaulted by Cutler Peninsula's cluster of enormous towers, used for worldwide radio transmission by the U.S. Navy. At night, each tower is garnished with six blinking red lights, and sometimes low-lying mists drift across—both eerie and beautiful.

There are signs of bear on Cross Island, and certainly deer. Bald eagles have nested on Mink Island.

Cross Island is uninhabited except for the Hurricane Island Outward Bound School (HIOBS) base at the old Coast Guard station, just east of the harbor. The island formerly was owned by Tom Cabot of Boston, who gave the Coast Guard buildings to HIOBS and the rest of the island to The Nature Conservancy, which passed it on to the U.S. Fish and Wildlife Service.

Approaches. Coming from the east, you pass green, rocky Old Man Island. In a cleft in the middle are 140 nesting pairs of razorbills—one of the few nesting sites on the east coast of the United States. Seals bask on the ledges east of Mink Island.

Find green bell "1A," close to the end of Cutler Peninsula, and leave it to port. Follow the narrow buoyed channel, leaving red beacon "2" to starboard and green can "1" to port. Turn sharply to port around can "1," heading south to Northeast Harbor, leaving Mink Island to port.

From the west, leaving green can "3" to starboard, run through Cross Island Narrows, almost to green can "1" before turning south toward Northeast Harbor, leaving Mink Island to port.

Anchorages, Moorings. Anchor where the chart shows 14 feet at low. This should be far enough in to get you out of the current of Cross Island Narrows. HIOBS has several moorings here, but they are small, 100-pound mushrooms.

Things to Do. There are trails leading all around this spectacular island. Row in to the south shore and walk around the shoreline to the HIOBS base.

LITTLE MACHIAS BAY

Charts: 13325, **13327**

As the *Coast Pilot* says, Little Machias Bay "is not used for an anchorage as it is exposed to southerly and southeasterly winds and is close to Little River and Machias Bay, both excellent anchorages." Another good reason not to anchor here is the overwhelming presence of the radio towers on Cutler Peninsula at the western side of the bay, creating the most powerful radio station in the world. These towers, some almost 1000 feet tall, form an important communication link with U.S. Navy units around the world, particularly submerged submarines.

Perhaps the only redeeming feature—other than the importance to our worldwide defense system—is the pleasure of trying to count the towers as you sail by. Sometimes it's 21, sometimes 25, sometimes 26—you try it.

MACHIAS SEAL ISLAND

Charts: 13325, **13327**; Canadian Chart 4340

Remote, fascinating Machias Seal Island has been disputed territory between the United States and Canada since the lighthouse was built here by the Canadians in 1832. It is hard to imagine why the sovereignty of this 15-acre scrap of land is in contention, but in dispute it is, and the outcome probably will be decided at the International Court of Justice in The Hague, several thousand miles to the east. If the issue were simply a question of which flag should fly at the lighthouse, it would be faintly ludicrous, but nowadays, with the 200-mile limit and fishing rights at stake, the issues are more serious.

As noted in the Canadian *Sailing Directions*, "Machias Seal Island is home to 5 species of breeding seabirds: Puffins, Razorbills, Petrels, Arctic and Common Terns. It is one of the largest known colonies of Arctic Terns on the east coast of North America and the largest Razorbill and Puffin colony south of Newfoundland." If you want to see the spectacular bird population, come early in the summer, because they will have migrated by mid-August.

Machias Seal Island is 10 miles due south of Cutler, almost equidistant from Grand Manan Island, off to the northeast. Several commercial operators make runs to Machias Seal from mainland ports. Perhaps the best known is Captain Barna Norton, who operates out of Jonesport (tel. 497-5933). Captain Norton has long been a champion of American ownership of the island. Once, when he rowed ashore brandishing the stars and stripes, a Royal Canadian Mounted Police helicopter swooped down on the island in retaliation. Captain Butch Huntley operates out of Lubec (tel. 733-5584), and Preston Wilcox operates out of Seal Cove on Grand Manan Island (tel. 506-662-8296). The Maine Audubon Society also sponsors occasional trips.

You can also get to Machias Seal Island in your own boat, Cutler being the most convenient point of departure. Set your course directly for Machias Seal, whose 82-foot lighthouse is visible for 14 miles. There is a horn at the lighthouse. Be sure to pick up the flashing red bell, two miles north of Machias Seal Island, which guards North Shoal and North Rock. On the way out, you will occasionally see buoys marking bottom trawls, sometimes with a radar reflector at one end. You may also see fluorescent floats marking the nets beneath. All of these things are to be avoided.

Be aware of the strong tidal current of three to four knots that ebbs from the direction of Lubec Narrows and floods toward it. The direction and amount of current will be very evident as you pass the fishing buoys.

If a heavy swell is running, anchoring will be difficult and landing dangerous. Even if you can't

Lonely Machias Seal Island, 10 miles at sea, due south of Cutler. Cruising sailors can land here to observe puffins, razorbill auks, and terns at close range. The island is managed by Canadian naturalists and the Canadian Coast Guard, but ownership is disputed by the United States. (Christopher Ayres photo)

RAZOR-BILLED AUKS

Razor-billed auks, or razorbills, are the rarest nesting bird on the coast of Maine. In contrast to the gaudy colors of their smaller cousins, the puffins, auks are as elegant as Victorian dandies, jet black with modish white piping on back and bill, and snowy white shirtfronts.

About 100 pairs of razorbills nest on Machias Seal Island, coexisting comfortably with puffins and terns. There is a smaller nesting colony of about 40 pairs on Matinicus Rock (also with terns and puffins) and two even smaller sites on Old Man Island and Freeman Rock. Although rare in Maine, and seldom seen from the shore, auks breed in Greenland, Iceland, and northeastern Russia, wintering on Long Island and in the Mediterranean.

If you take your boat to Machias Seal Island or Matinicus Rock, it's not hard to spot these handsome birds. They have little fear of man, and in fact are curious enough to be attracted by loud noises or arm-waving.

Like the puffin, the auk dives below the surface for fish and crustaceans, propelling itself underwater with short, stubby wings. Its nest is often on an inaccessible cliff or in a crevice. Auk eggs, resting precariously on tiny ledges high above the sea, would be vulnerable to the slightest misstep were it not for an ingenious solution of nature. The eggs are radically tapered at one end, so when disturbed they merely roll around in a small circle. The Razorbill produces only a single egg per year.

Until well into the nineteenth century, the razorbill had a larger relative in the North Atlantic, the great auk. Standing 30 inches high, this ungainly fowl was flightless.

Having adapted to conditions similar to those in Antarctica, and occupying the same ecological niche, the great auk resembled the penguin in general structure and appearance, even though it was unrelated—an example of convergent evolution.

Naturalist Phil Conkling in *Islands in Time* says the Great Auks were "the fastest and most powerful diving bird in the evolutionary record of life. They used their short, tapered wings to propel themselves down to 40 fathoms in pursuit of schools of smelt, herring or capelin. The few observations of their fishing techniques made by naturalists be-

fore the auks disappeared described rafts of 20 to 50 birds that would dive to surround a large school of herring, actually driving the fish to the surface."

Early European explorers and fishermen found enormous concentrations of great auks on this side of the Atlantic, in colonies of hundreds of thousands. The birds were easy prey for a man on foot, providing badly needed meat and oil, and later a European market developed for these products. For a few seasons, commercial hunters prospered, wiping out whole populations at a time. By 1844, the great auk was extinct.

get ashore, however, you'll see lots of puffins, auks, and terns flying and fishing all around. Don't be tempted to pick up the moorings, which are private and lightweight. Anchor due east of the lighthouse, in the lee of the island, in 9 to 16 feet. The bottom is rocky and holding uncertain, so leave someone aboard. Take your dinghy ashore

to the seaweed-covered rocks and work your way cautiously to the wooden plank leading to the ways. As the sign says, *"Debarcadere Dangereux."*

The Canadian authorities feel strongly that human intrusion is damaging to the nesting birds, so there is a strict limit of 30 visitors per day. If you are number 31, you are not allowed to land. The com-

PUFFINS

Surely the puffin is one of the world's most endearing creatures. Seen up close, this is a small, chunky bird that walks as though wearing galoshes. Its cheeks are puffy and its eyes marked like the tuft of a sofa; it flies like a buzz bomb, with rapidly beating wings. Part of a puffin's charm is the contrast between its sober black morning coat and earnest expression with its orange feet and brilliantly colored beak. It looks rather like a clergyman on a binge.

Puffins and razor-billed auks are both members of the alcid family, whose characteristics include black-and-white plumage and short, stubby wings that propel them underwater for fishing. Puffins and auks usually are found in the same nesting area, as are terns, whose noisy and aggressive tactics help drive off potential predators—primarily gulls.

A century ago, puffins nested on six of the outlying islands of the coast of Maine, as far west as Muscongus Bay. But harvesting of eggs by farmers and fishermen, and the killing of adult birds for their feathers, destroyed their populations, and by 1900 they were gone from all the islands except Matinicus Rock.

Then, in the mid-1970s, Steven Kress, director of Audubon's Ecology Camp on Hog Island, launched an imaginative program to reintroduce the puffins to their old nesting sites. Burrows were dug by hand in the tuff of Eastern Egg Rock, in Muscongus Bay, and young birds were brought from Newfoundland (home of hundreds of thousands of puffins).

Naturalists became foster-parents, hand-feeding puffin chicks for months. The chicks were grown and allowed to fledge naturally and then the waiting began. Puffin decoys stood on the rocks; seductive mating calls wafted out over Muscongus Bay. Would they return to nest? After years of effort, the puffins reared on Eastern Egg did, indeed, return to mate and nest, and the colony has been successfuly reestablished.

Today you can see puffins in three places along the coast of Maine if you arrive before August 15: Eastern Egg Rock, in Muscongus Bay; Matinicus Rock, at the entrance to Penobscot Bay; and Machias Seal Island, way down east. At Eastern Egg and Matinicus Rock, you can see them from your boat, but it is extremely difficult to land, and you would be likely to disturb the birds. At Machias Seal Island, you can land and watch the birds from blinds, only a few feet away.

Maine is at the southern end of the puffin breeding range, which extends north to Iceland and south to the British Isles. The puffins arrive at Machias Seal in late March but remain in the water around the island for some time. In the shelter and concealment of the large granite boulders, they make simple nests from plant materials—seaweed and grasses. The single egg is incubated by both parents. The boulders also serve as convenient launching pads

for these short-winged birds, which frequently have difficulty achieving flight.

The peak hatching time is mid-June, and for the next month-and-a-half, the demands of the offspring totally occupy the parents. Often one parent will spend all day away from the island diving for small herring, their principal food. Finally the young refuse food and the parents leave them to fend for themselves. For three days to a week, they fast in their burrows before leaving their nests in the middle of the night for the surrounding waters. The young become expert swimmers and divers before learning how to fly. By mid-August, all the puffins have left the island to spend the fall and winter in the North Atlantic.

mercial skippers schedule predawn departures to be sure of being included in the quota. They note with wry satisfaction that yachts tend to arrive in the afternoon.

Remember to carry your binoculars. You may take a picnic ashore, and there are toilet facilities.

You will be greeted by a resident naturalist who will give you an orientation. By all means take your turn in one or more of the blinds, which allow you to observe and photograph the puffins and auks at close range. Even if you are not an avid bird-watcher, this is a fascinating experience.

CUTLER (LITTLE RIVER) ★★★★

Charts: 13325, **13327**

Tidal Range: *Mean* 13.5 feet; *Spring* 15.4 feet

Cutler is a working harbor with a small fleet of lobsterboats and a pleasant little town of 400 residents, but it is more than that. The island at the entrance provides a warm and prehistoric feeling of security, like the rock at the mouth of your cave.

This is the last good harbor in Maine before Eastport—easy to enter and offering excellent protection under almost all conditions. The southern tip of Canada's Grand Manan Island is visible out the entrance, and Cutler is the best place from which to sail for Machias Seal Island or Grand Manan, six miles offshore.

On a return trip from Canada, you can check in here with U.S. Customs by phoning their Lubec office (tel. 733-4331).

Like many other Maine coastal towns, the history of Cutler includes a golden era of shipbuilding, from 1845 to 1855. Excursion vessels docked here in the 1880s, but it has been pretty quiet since then.

Elsewhere in the world, Cutler is, unfortunately, better known. Because of the VLF radio towers on Cutler Peninsula, used to communicate with submerged U.S. subs, Cutler has been grouped with the Pentagon, the White House and SAC headquarters in Omaha as likely first targets in a nuclear war.

Approaches. Approaching from the west, the enormous Cutler Peninsula radio towers, near Little River, are visible a long way up the coast, popping in and out behind headlands. Then Western Head appears around the corner, looking at first like a little wooded island.

First find the whistle, then the bell. Red whistle "2LR" stands quite a distance off the coast opposite the entrance; red-and-white bell "LR" is close by the entrance to the east.

The harbor is not immediately obvious. There are three weirs inside, two on the south side and one on the north, which from a distance appear to block the whole entrance. As you approach the nun, the entrance opens up, comfortably wide.

Enter north of Little River Island, with its 56-foot lighttower, observing nun "2," which marks the ledge just beyond. Be careful of the weir that extends a long way from the right shore, past the nun. Salmon pens are moored along the southwest shore, well out of the channel.

Anchorages, Moorings. Lobsterboats are moored in two groups, opposite the two working docks. The first group is in the little indentation to the right, and the second farther into the harbor. There is room to anchor on the south side of the harbor between the two groups of moorings, with good mud bottom, in 14 to 16 feet at low. Protection is excellent, with only slight exposure to the southeast.

Be sure to put out enough scope. Lobstermen report that yachts drag and go aground here every year. You may be offered a vacant mooring stake.

Getting Ashore. Both lobster docks have vertical ladders from their floats. Land your dinghy on the beach in the middle of town, where fishermen careen and paint their boats.

For the Boat. Gas and diesel may be obtained at the two lobster docks.

A. M. Look Canning Co. (tel. 259-7712). Look's dock and red shack is closest to the entrance, in the indentation to the right. There is three to four feet at low alongside the small float.

Deano's Wharf, Little River Loster (tel. 259-7704). Deano's dock is about 300 yards farther into the harbor, with seven to eight feet alongside the float.

For the Crew. Close to Look's dock are the post office and the Village Market, with groceries, wine, ice, and a luncheonette. There's a pay phone outside.

Little River Lodge (tel. 259-4437). Walk up the hill on the main street to the Town Hall, which has a fish hatchery in the basement. Opposite is Little River Lodge, which serves dinner (by reservation), and provides showers and a phone.

Things to Do. This is a fascinating place to observe the workings of a down east fishing community. Watch the twice daily ritual of hauling feed out to the salmon pens, check out the boats bringing in their catch, and visit with local residents.

There is a peaceful back road east along the coast past Money Cove, about a 20-minute walk.

Both of the beautiful headlands at the entrance

to Little River are now open to the public. To explore more than three miles of wild and unspoiled coastline, from Western Head to neighboring Great Head, owned by Maine Coast Heritage Trust, land your dinghy somewhere convenient on the western shore, and follow the road and path toward the sea.

SANDY COVE
Charts: 13325, **13327**

Between the bright green hill of Eastern Head and Haycock Harbor is a delightful and altogether unspoiled little cove, separated from Haycock by a spine of rocks. Eastern Head is owned by Maine's Bureau of Parks and Recreation. On the eastern horizon stretch the romantic cliffs of Grand Manan.

A weir projects from the north shore of the cove, and a line of rocks extends from the west

To reach Eastern Knubble, protected by a conservation easement, walk eastward along the road toward Money Cove (see chart 13327). Just after the last house on the right before Money Cove, look for a tiny path to the right with a "Money Cove" sign. One branch of this woodland path leads to the headland, another to the cove itself.

side. There is just room to pass between these hazards and anchor off the pretty sand beach in 15 to 22 feet at low. Holding ground is uncertain, sand and rock.

Sandy Cove provides protection from the southwest, but it is open to ocean swells and not sheltered enough for safe overnight anchorage. This is recommended only as a day stop.

HAYCOCK HARBOR
Charts: 13325, **13327**

This is not a harbor for deep-draft boats. Small craft can enter The Pool at high water.

BAILEYS MISTAKE
Charts: 13325, **13327**

Baileys Mistake is a beautiful spot with an evocative name. There are grassy shores and a gravel beach at the head, a few houses around the cove, and little boating activity. The harbor is exposed from southwest to southeast, and the holding ground is poor, so this is not a good overnight anchorage.

The harbor is easily entered from red whistle "2BM," favoring high, wooded Jims Head to avoid the ledges at the entrance, which are marked with a green-and-red can. Look for the old weir close to the eastern shore.

One foggy day Captain Bailey sailed his four-masted schooner with a load of lumber into Quoddy Narrows, headed toward Lubec—or so he thought. His dead reckoning was about six miles off, and the ship ran hard aground. Rather than face the music with the ship's Boston owners, so the story goes, Bailey and his crew unloaded the lumber and used it to build a settlement on the shores of this lovely little harbor.

Region 7/ West Quoddy Head to
Passamaquod

An old weir near Eastport, Maine.
(Christopher Ayres photo)

Calais

dy Bay

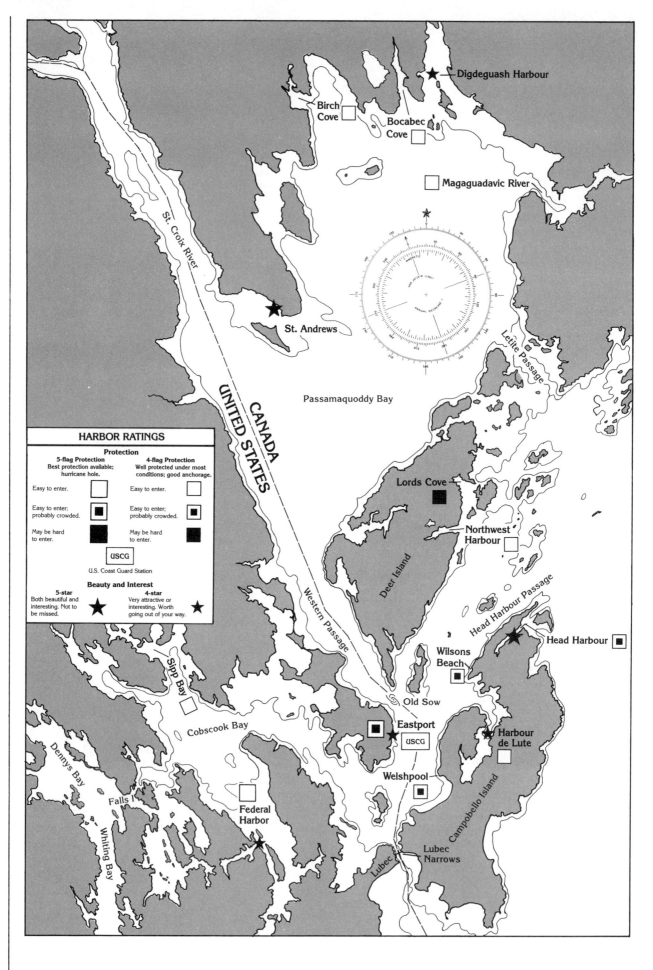

Canada lies before you. Just a few miles off rugged West Quoddy Head loom the foggy cliffs of Grand Manan Island, with snug harbors, brightly colored fishing boats, and friendly people. Due north are the beauties of Passamaquoddy Bay, teeming with fish and birds, guarded by swift currents and whirlpools.

In this part of the world lies Franklin Delano Roosevelt's beloved Campobello, his summer cottage now an international park. Across the bay, the resort of St. Andrews still cherishes Loyalist houses moved by barge from Castine after the American Revolution. As the St. Croix River passes St. Croix Island, where Samuel de Champlain established the first European settlement in 1604, it marks the border between the United States and Canada.

This is where Maine and the United States trickle to an end—in the struggling towns of Lubec and Eastport, once bustling fishing communities, now fighting to regain their economic health. Both communities guard the entrance to isolated Cobscook Bay, haunt of eagles, with its reversing falls.

NAVIGATION

Navigation is more difficult in this region, with its huge tides, strong currents, and heavy fogs. Average tidal ranges run from 18 to 20 feet, and up to 27 feet during the spring tides, which occur each month.

Loran works fine in this part of the world, with better results usually obtained by shifting to the Canadian East Coast Chain (GRI 5930). However, you are well out of range of VHF Marine Operators in the United States, and on the fringes of Yarmouth Radio in Nova Scotia.

The Canadian Coast Guard operates a Vessel Traffic Service (call name "Fundy Traffic") based in Saint John, New Brunswick. Fundy Traffic can be of great assistance to you, especially in fog or heavy weather. After you call them on channel 16, they will ask you to switch to channel 12 or 14. By radar or triangulation on your VHF transmissions, they can pinpoint your location and warn you of nearby ship traffic. Fundy Traffic will also inform you of weather conditions, times of high and low slack tides, and other useful information. You should have no trouble reaching them from Grand Manan or Campobello.

Although based on the same general principle as in the United States (red, right, returning), Canadian buoys differ in size and shape, coloring, and numbering. Spar buoys are much in use. Before arriving, study the Canadian charts and the buoyage system described in the Canadian *Sailing Directions*. (For information on obtaining Canadian charts and publications, see Introduction.)

Weirs are still common throughout the area. If you remember that they normally extend out from the land to trap herring swimming alongshore, they won't cause you much trouble.

Lobstering season ends the last Friday in June in this part of the world, so the risk of fouling your prop in lobster buoys is greatly reduced.

ANCHORING AND TYING UP

If this is your first visit, you probably are worried about how to deal with the large tides, how to anchor, and how to tie up to the high bulkheads of the many man-made harbors. These imposing structures have been built by the Canadian Government at many locations to provide convenient shelter for the fishing fleets. They are large wharves designed with one or more right-angle turns, and once through the narrow entrance, boats find almost perfect protection.

With a tidal range of 20 feet, a depth of 16 feet at low becomes 36 feet at high, and a ratio of 6:1 means 216 feet of scope. That requires a lot of swinging room, and translates to a ratio of 13:1 at low tide. If the anchorages here were as crowded as they are near Martha's Vineyard, this amount of swinging room would be unavailable. Fortunately, however, they are not. In the many unfrequented harbors, there is plenty of room to swing, with all the scope you need.

In the crowded man-made harbors, there are other solutions. Here the answer is to tie up to something afloat—another boat, a mooring, a lobster car, a floating pile driver. It is unlikely that you ever will be the inside boat, right next to the wharf. Probably your boat will be rafted outside five or six assorted fishing vessels. Only the inner boat has to worry very much about the rise and fall of the tide. When the boats inside leave at 4:30 A.M., you won't even be disturbed. The fishermen will shift your lines and slip out while you sleep. Nice people.

If you do happen to be the inside boat, next to the wharf, your bow and stern lines should be at least 100 feet long, and you'll be glad you remembered to bring a couple of fenderboards. You will need some way to hold yourself close to the wharf as the tide rises (to keep the whole line of boats from drifting out, and so you can reach the ladder on the wharf). The usual solution is a breastline looped around a vertical rope or wire on the wharf itself. The local fishermen are pros; watch how they do it.

When 5 or 10 boats are nested, wind and current will bend the line of boats, like crack-the-whip. To counteract this problem, the inner three or four boats often run bow and stern lines to the wharf.

CURRENTS AND WHIRLPOOLS

The strong currents in the area are a major consideration. Plan your departures to spend a maximum amount of time with the current and the least possible time bucking it, especially on long passages like Grand Manan Channel. Study the approaches to Passamaquoddy Bay—Head Harbour, Letite, and Lubec Narrows—and time your passages for the best conditions of tide and visibility.

The eddies, boils, and whirlpools in the approaches to Passamaquoddy Bay are unlike anything encountered elsewhere on the coast of Maine. At full strength, they may make your boat yaw violently, or even spin you around in a circle. These conditions are definitely dangerous to small craft, but merely disconcerting for a well-found cruising boat. Avoid the whirlpool off Eastport (Old Sow) at maximum turbulence (see Western Passage, page 356).

MONEY, TIME ZONES, BOATYARDS, AND SUPPLIES

You do not have to worry about getting Canadian currency; U.S. dollars are accepted everywhere in the region, and most stores give an appropriate discount. Nova Scotia and New Brunswick are in the Atlantic Time Zone, so the time is one hour later than in the U.S. However, dates for switching to Daylight Savings may vary between the two countries.

This is an area of small towns, so most of the harbors offer no supplies and services. Plan to stock up in Eastport, Lubec, or St. Andrews. The only boatyard in the area is in Eastport, which is also the base for the easternmost station of the U.S. Coast Guard.

The much-photographed, red-and-white candy-striped lighthouse at West Quoddy Head, easternmost point in the continental United States. The original light was built in 1808 at the order of President Thomas Jefferson. (Boutilier photo)

ENTERING THE UNITED STATES AND CANADA

The once-easygoing border-crossing formalities between these two friendly countries have become a lot more serious in recent years, with the increase in drug-running (especially by boat) and the growth of terrorism. Canadian and American Customs officials still are friendly and courteous to cruising sailors, but in border-crossing matters, you'd be wise to go by the book. Penalties for customs violations are severe, including possible seizure of your boat. Canadian and U.S. Customs regulations and information on ports of entry are discussed below.

Entering Canada. As you enter Canadian waters you should be flying a Canadian courtesy flag (ensign) at the starboard spreader. The yellow "Q" flag (requesting free pratique) is not in general use. Canadian officials advise: "When a vessel arrives in Canadian waters, it should call ship to shore to the Canada Customs office and state its docking location and time in order for the Customs Inspector to be present on its arrival. This expedites the clearance of the vessel so visitors are free to enjoy their stay. If, however, a vessel does not wish to use its radio, it may dock and allow one member of the crew (preferably the Captain) to go ashore and use the nearest telephone to contact Customs. The crew member must then return to the vessel to await the arrival of the Customs Inspector."

"Please note that until Customs clearance has been completed, no visitors are allowed to board the vessel, and no crew or passengers aboard are permitted to leave with the exception of tying up and in the case of an emergency."

"When due to weather conditions or other unforeseen emergencies, a vessel lands at a place not designated as a place for Customs report, the circumstances must be reported to the *nearest* Customs office or the Royal Canadian Mounted Police (who may also be contacted after Customs office hours)."

Documents you may be asked to produce include:

- the boat's documentation or papers

- crew list

- identification papers showing citizenship for each member of the crew, such as driver's license or passport, birth, baptismal, or voter's certificate.

- for dogs and cats, a certificate from a licensed vet showing vaccination against rabies during the preceding 36-month period.

Convenient ports of entry in New Brunswick are listed in the accompanying chart.

Customs offices are also located at St. Stephen, at the head of the St. Croix River, and on Deer Island, but these are more difficult to reach.

Plan your arrival at a port of entry during business hours; otherwise, there may be a stiff surcharge. Remember that New Brunswick is in the Atlantic Time Zone, one hour later than the United States.

When you report to Canadian Customs, apply for a Cruising License for the time you expect to be in Canada. This license is issued without charge and allows you to cruise for up to 90 days in Canadian waters, arriving and departing at Canadian ports without entering or clearing again at Customs.

For information on duties, exemptions, and entry by a private boat into Canada (including regulations on firearms, alcohol, and tobacco) write: Canada Customs, 6169 Quinpool Road, Halifax, Nova Scotia, Canada B3J 3G6. Or call 902-426-2911.

Entering or Reentering the United States. When a pleasure boat or yacht arrives in the United States, the first landing must be at a Customs port or designated place where Customs service is available. It is often useful to call ahead and tell Customs your estimated time of arrival. All U.S. and foreign pleasure boats, upon entering the United States, must report to U.S. Customs within 24 hours. No person or baggage may leave a vessel until it has been cleared by U.S. Customs, except that the captain may leave the vessel to call Customs. It is best to avoid arriving on Sundays or holidays or outside of business hours, because an extra fee will be charged.

All non-U.S. pleasure boats entering the United

PORTS OF ENTRY: NEW BRUNSWICK

Area	Ports of Entry	Hours	Phone Number
		(Mon.–Fri.)	(area code 506)
Grand Manan*	North Head Seal Cove	9 A.M.–5 P.M.	662-3232
Campobello Island**	Wilsons Beach	8 A.M.–6 P.M.	752-2091
Passamaquoddy Bay	St. Andrews	9 A.M.–5 P.M.***	529-3198

*Customs office is in North Head.
**Customs office is at the International Bridge, but there is nowhere to land nearby.
***On weekends or after business hours, call 466-2363 (St. Stephen).

States must pay a navigation fee of $9 and should request a Cruising Permit good till the end of the year. Various forms must be filled out. All U.S. and non-U.S. pleasure boats 30 feet or longer will be assessed a yearly $25 for a Customs User Fee. A decal is issued upon payment.

Be prepared to show documentation for boat and crew. Dogs must have a rabies certificate at least 30 days old, and cats must appear healthy.

Convenient ports of entry in Maine are listed in the accompanying chart.

Calais and Bangor are also ports of entry, but they are more difficult to reach.

For information on duties, exemptions, and entry by a private boat into the United States (including regulations on firearms, alcohol, and tobacco), write: U.S. Customs, P.O. Box 7407, Washington, DC 20044. Or call 202-566-8195.

PORTS OF ENTRY: MAINE

Area	Ports of Entry	Hours	Phone Number
		(Mon.–Sat.)	(area code 207)
Passamaquoddy Bay	Eastport	8 A.M.–5 P.M.	853-4313
Passamaquoddy Bay	Lubec	24 hours	733-4331
Cutler	Cutler	24 hours	733-4331 (Lubec)
Mount Desert	*	8 A.M.–5 P.M.	947-7861
Tenants Harbor to Mount Desert	Belfast	8 A.M.–5 P.M.	338-3954
Kittery to Tenants Harbor	Portland	8 A.M.–5 P.M.	780-3328

*Enter any major harbor on Mount Desert and call Customs at the number shown (in Bangor). A local Customs representative will visit your boat.

GRAND MANAN

Canadian Charts: 4011, **4340, 4342**; U.S. Charts: **13325, 13327**

Sailing to Grand Manan is a grand adventure for cruising boats. There is a definite feeling of setting out to sea toward a foreign land, and the sunlit cliffs of the western shore are infinitely alluring on a clear day. When the fog shuts in, the voyage is an anxious one, but the bold shores of the island make it reasonably easy to approach in safety.

Because U.S. maps and charts usually eliminate Grand Manan, a great many Americans are unaware that it exists, only six miles off our shores. Simple and old-world in feeling, Grand Manan is absorbed with fishing and the sea. Tides are more important than the clock, a man's boat more sacred than his car. Since you have cruised this far, take time to visit Grand Manan, and allow yourself a few days on this special island.

There is charter plane service to an airstrip on the island, but most of the inhabitants are linked to the outside world by ferry service north to Blacks Harbour on the New Brunswick mainland, a 20-mile trip. There are several lodgings and a few restaurants on Grand Manan, but otherwise the island is not geared for tourism. People come here to enjoy the simple pleasures.

The colder and harsher the environment, it seems, the warmer and more hospitable its inhabi-

tants. And so it is here. The people of Grand Manan are extremely friendly and courteous. "If you need help," they say, "just stop anyone and ask." The population of the island is only about 2,500, and after a couple of days, a lot of faces start to seem familiar.

The large draggers and seiners of Grand Manan are freshly painted in brilliant greens and reds and blues, almost as though the paint salesman had just come through town—typical of islands where the predominant color is fog gray. The fishing fleet appears remarkably sturdy, new, and well maintained. The big trawlers head north to fish off Nova Scotia, and their catch is sold to factory ships at sea. Cod and halibut, scallops and lobsters are taken in the waters off Grand Manan. Herring are seined from the weirs and smoked in shingled smokehouses with red doors, although this picturesque industry is on the decline. Dulse, a kind of edible seaweed raked from the rocks of Dark Harbour, on the west side of the island, is used to make emulsifiers for ice cream and other products. It was also valued in the past century as a source of iodine, to prevent goiter.

More than 300 species of birds have been identified on Grand Manan, where walking trails are a paradise for hikers, birders, and photographers. Particularly spectacular are the trails along the rugged shoreline, and the cliffs of the northern and western side, providing views of interesting geological formations like "Hole in the Wall." Near the south end of the island is the aptly named cluster of white glacial erratics called "Flock of Sheep."

Lobstering season in this part of Canada ends the last Friday in June, so the waters around Grand Manan are pleasantly free of lobster buoys during the summer. In late June, you will see the fishermen dragging loads of lobster pots ashore on homemade sledges, and storing them in colorful piles. On July 1, Canada Day, there are water sports and other events, including a greased-pole contest.

Weirs are still very active along the shores of Grand Manan, and each weir has a name, like a boat: *Admiral, Jubilee, Hard Luck, Grit,* and *Try Again.* The enormous Bay of Fundy tides require that the weirs have very long poles, driven into the bottom with floating pile drivers.

The two best man-made harbors for boats drawing six feet or more, and the two easiest harbors to reach, are North Head and Seal Cove, at either end of the island.

Most of the east coast of Grand Manan is strewn with islands, ledges, and shoals, among which the strong tidal currents swirl and tumble. The passages between Ross, Cheney, and White Head islands dry out at low. Local fishermen use these passages, knowing the signs that indicate when time is running out; leave them to the locals. More dangerous are the shoals that stretch southeastward from White Head Island—Bulkhead Rip, Clarks Ground, and Old Proprietor Shoal. Here the current runs four to six knots, and heavy rips build up on the ebb. Heading north with a flooding tide and good visibility, you might have a lovely sail. In the fog, or with the ebb tide among the shoals, it could be a nightmare. Better to avoid the east coast of Grand Manan altogether, or stay outside the 50-fathom curve.

There are various ways to get around Grand Manan and see the sights. The island is 14 miles long, so walking the whole way is impractical. Motor scooters and bikes can be rented, and taxis are available (see North Head writeup). There are no formal car-rental outfits, but inquire; you might find a local resident who wants to strike a deal. Hitchhiking is also an option.

PASSAGES TO GRAND MANAN

If conditions are right, you can reach Grand Manan comfortably on your third day out of Penobscot Bay, spending the first night near Mount Desert and the second at Roque Island. It would be wise to allow at least one more day for the trip, to provide for the usual surprises.

Logical places from which to begin the last leg of the voyage are Roque Island, Cutler, and Head Harbour (Campobello Island). Roque is probably as far away as you want to start, some 40 miles from Grand Manan's North Head. If the weather turns bad, Cutler can be a fallback.

The trick is to pick a day with reasonable visibility, and to maximize the hours of riding the flood current up Grand Manan Channel. The current runs 1.5 to 2.5 knots, flooding northeast and ebbing southwest. Along the west coast of Grand Manan, the current reaches three knots. Grand Manan Channel can be extremely rough when the

wind is against the current, creating short, steep waves.

Only little bits of Grand Manan show on U.S. charts, so you will have to do some switching back and forth between U.S. and Canadian charts as you run up Grand Manan Channel. Remember that the network of radio communication towers on Cutler Peninsula may interfere with Loran reception in this area.

Approach the island along the bold western shore, rounding the southern tip of the island to reach Seal Cove or the northern tip to reach North Head.

To avoid a substantial fee, it is desirable to arrive at Customs during business hours Monday through Friday. That takes a bit of planning. If you have to make a choice, opt for visibility and favorable current and let Customs fall where it may.

NORTH HEAD ★★★★★ 　5　

Canadian Charts: **4340, 4342**

Tidal Range: *Mean* 17.9 feet; *Large* 24 feet

On the northeast corner of Grand Manan, North Head is a fishing village, home to a fleet of brightly painted seiners and trawlers. The harbor is always

bustling with activity, a fascinating place to spend a few days and meet the friendly residents.

The village and man-made harbor are on the

A weir (pronounced "ware") is a large trap for herring, widely esteemed as bait. Slice the head off a small herring and it becomes a sardine, and sardines used to be big business in Maine and Canada. A century ago, there were more than 50 canneries along the coast of Maine, and annual shipments of 500 million cans of sardines.

Herring are caught by surrounding a school of fish with nets (purse-seining), or by closing off a cove when the fish are inside (stop-seining). One of the oldest methods of catching herring is by building weirs.

The farther east you go, the more weirs you see. Most of the ones west of Schoodic Peninsula are abandoned, the netting and brush long gone, with only the rotting poles sticking forlornly above the surface. One vigorous exception

is in the Isle au Haut Thorofare. In Narraguagus Bay and Cutler, however, the weirs are actively maintained and still in use. When you cross over into Canada, in Passamaquoddy Bay and around Grand Manan, weirs are everywhere.

Fortunately, they are not a great danger to alert yachtsmen. Remember that weirs usually extend from the shoreline, and do not try to pass inside them. Active weirs generally

Fishermen hauling nets in a weir, 1910. (Frank Claes Collection)

south side of the peninsula of North Head. This is a port of entry for Canadian Customs, an excellent refuge, and the best place to start your exploration of the island.

Approaches. Coming from the coast of Maine, by far the safest approach is along the western

coast of Grand Manan. If you are using Loran, you probably will want to shift from the U.S. chain (GRI 9960) to the Canadian chain (GRI 5930), which gives better results in this area. Another important consideration is the current in Grand Manan Channel, which averages 1.5 to 2.5 knots, flooding

are visible at high tide, or are marked by a high pole at the outside. Old weirs may lurk under the surface until midtide or below. Even so, hitting an old weir pole is not like hitting a rock.

Weirs have been around for a long time, and their heart-shaped design hasn't changed much. They usually are made from materials found locally, and repaired each spring after the ravages of winter.

Herring come inshore at night, usually with the flooding tide. A long "leader" of poles, driven close together, leads out from the shore, diverting schools of fish swimming alongshore into the "pocket," where they become disoriented and swim around in circles, unable to find the exit. When the fishermen become aware that there are herring playing in the weir (often by the dark of the moon), they bring in a dory or two and drop a purse seine beneath the herring. Drawing the fish together as they close the seine, the fishermen then dip or pump their catch into the hold of a lobsterboat or herring carrier.

A weir is a semipermanent installation, and very valuable. "My father fished it before me, and my grandfather before him," a fisherman may tell you. In Canada, weirs have names, and there are weirs such as *King George,* and *Victoria, Gamble* and *Ruin, Bread 'n' Butter, Last Ditch, Iron Maiden,* and *Cora Belle.*

In the Bay of Fundy, enormous stakes are required because of the huge tides. You may see 75-foot Douglas fir stakes piled in Grand Manan waiting to be driven. Homemade, floating pile drivers are a common sight way down east, and small cruising boats often moor

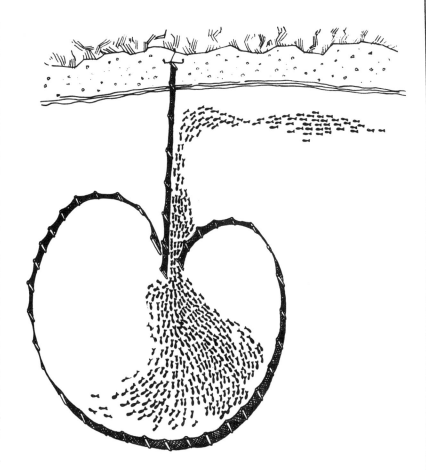

A school of herring moving along the shore at night is diverted by the leader into the pocket of the weir, where the fish are trapped, unable to find the exit. Fishermen in dories draw up a purse seine around the herring, which are then transferred by dipnet into a lobsterboat or pumped aboard a sardine carrier.

alongside one of them for the night.

After the long weir stakes are driven, shorter top poles are attached. The structure is tied together with a rope rib, lashed horizontally. In earlier days, the space between the poles was filled by brush, until this was replaced by the more effective netting ("twine"). The "top twine" is hung on the rib around the pocket and reaches to

high water level; divers secure the "bottom twine" on the sea floor.

Weir fishing is passive, and weir fishermen become experts on the habits, needs, and whims of the elusive silvery fish, analyzing their cyclical behavior and debating how their movements are affected by tides, moon, and weather. As one old-timer says, "You got to think like a herring."

northeast and ebbing southwest. Near the west coast of Grand Manan, the rate is about three knots, parallel to the shore.

In clear weather, the high cliffs of the west side of Grand Manan will be visible a long way. The west coast of the island is wooded, with steep cliffs

300 feet high; north of Dark Harbour, they rise to 400 feet. Head for a point off the northwestern tip of Grand Manan, keeping good DR and Loran fixes against the possibility that fog may shut down. The coast is bold, with no outlying dangers. Even in thick weather, you would probably be

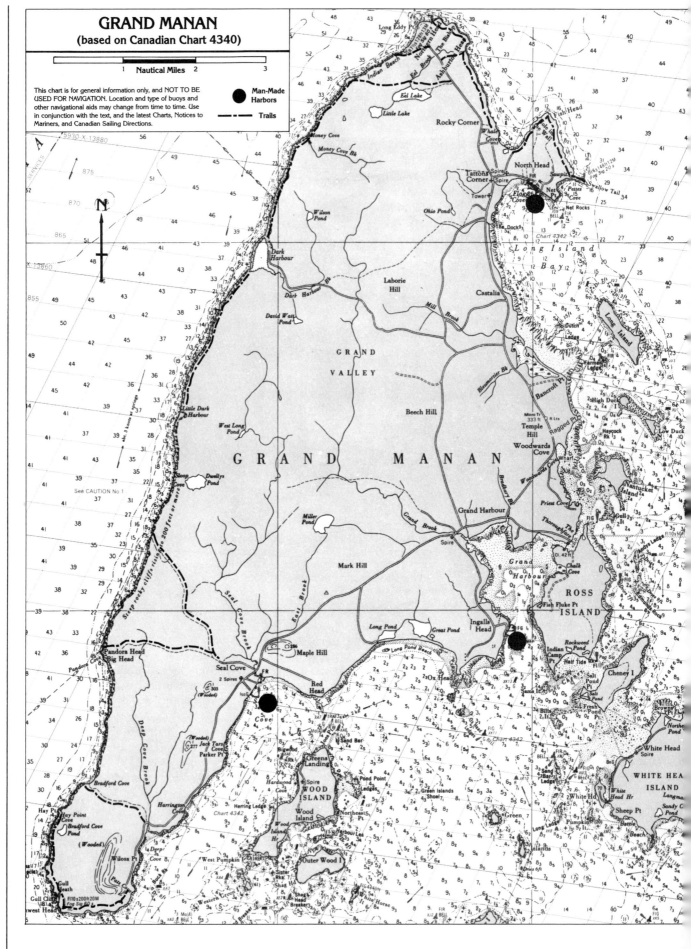

GRAND MANAN
(based on Canadian Chart 4340)

|——————————|——————————|——————————|
1　　Nautical Miles　　2　　　　　　3

This chart is for general information only, and NOT TO BE USED FOR NAVIGATION. Location and type of buoys and other navigational aids may change from time to time. Use in conjunction with the text, and the latest Charts, Notices to Mariners, and Canadian Sailing Directions.

● Man-Made Harbors

–·–·– Trails

aware of the crash of the surf and loom of the cliffs before getting into trouble.

As you near the northern tip of the island, you will see the lighthouse at Northern Head on a plateau halfway up the cliffs: a square white tower and several separate houses with red roofs. Rounding the northern point, with its dramatic scalloped cliffs, note the multiple layers at Ashburton Head known as "Seven Days Work." There may be turbulence and tide rips here, and you are likely to be blanketed for a while by the island. Keep a lookout for the ferry, which runs several times a day between North Head and Blacks Harbour to the north. (In thick weather, you might want to call the ferry on channel 16 and find out where they are.) At this point, there is still some distance to go to reach the harbor, especially if the tide is flooding and the current against you.

As you round Fish Head, the distinctive Swallow Tail lighthouse will appear (white octagonal tower with a red top, guyed all around). Continuing south past Swallow Tail, leave the red bell off Net Point to starboard as you make the turn westward toward the harbor. Note the weirs close to shore; they are typical of those found all around Grand Manan.

The Canadian courtesy flag should now be flying at the starboard spreader, and you are in the Atlantic Time Zone. The time here is one hour later than in the eastern United States.

Anchorages, Moorings. There are two large wharves in Flagg Cove, off North Head. More easterly is the ferry wharf, marked with a fixed red light at the outer corner. Just west of the ferry wharf is Fisherman's Wharf, in the shape of a bent T, with a flashing red light at the outer corner (see inset, Canadian chart 4342). Fish pens moored in the western part of the cove are far enough from the wharves to present little danger, although they may not be lit at night.

There is deep water at both ends of Fisherman's Wharf, and you can tie up inside either end of the crosspiece of the T. The most convenient place to be is inside the westerly part, where there is more room as well as access to a float for landing. The inner corner is reserved for large herring seiners. Along the western portion of the wharf, you probably can find a boat about your size to tie alongside. Boats here usually moor heading westward. If there are fishermen around, they will help you tend the lines.

Getting Ashore. If this is your port of entry, report to Customs in the brick house just west of the wharf (see section on "Entering Canada"). Row into the "pontoon" and ramp near land. Another possibility is to clamber across the neighboring boats and climb a vertical ladder to the wharf.

For the Boat. Fuel can be obtained by truck from Irving, located near the ferry landing. For ice, check the gray fish plant near the ferry landing.

Water is hard to come by. Use a five-gallon container and ask for water at a nearby store. Trash cans are few and far between; the closest ones are in the ferry parking lot. Charts and publications are sold by Herbert Macaulay in Castalia (two miles away) at the Oar and Anchor. Call him at 662-3245, and he will deliver them or pick you up.

For the Crew. There are takeouts and dairy bars near the ferry, and several restaurants within walking distance west of the wharf. The Compass Rose, on the harbor, serves three meals a day, plus tea.

A short walk east of the wharf will bring you to McCulley's Market. The Grandisle grocery and drug store is about a mile west of the docks, where the main road turns south; there is a bakery and the Grand Manan Hospital just beyond. Pay phones can be found near the ferry dock and at the Customs House, where the post office is also located.

Bikes can be rented at the Irving garage, to the west, or check Capt. Look's in Grand Harbour (tel. 662-3330) for bikes and scooters. For a taxi, call Avis Green (tel. 662-8212), who lives in Grand Harbour and has lots of interesting comments about the island.

The only liquor store is in Castalia, more than two miles away, and the only bank is eight miles away in Grand Harbour.

Things to Do. Tourist pamphlets and maps of the walking trails are available at markets and stores.

One nearby walk is a must. Turn right from the wharf and follow the road and signs .7 mile out to Swallow Tail Light. The path leads down and across a bridge over a chasm to the spectacular little peninsula on which the white-shingled, octagonal tower stands, firmly anchored against the winter winds by guywires. The former keeper's house is still there, and a boathouse; notice the angle of the ways down which the boat was launched.

For a much longer, spectacular hike, take the trail along the cliffs starting near the Swallow Tail parking lot out to Fish Point and back, along Whale Cove and "Hole in the Wall." The trail through the woods is rough, often emerging on high cliffs. Wear long pants, take insect repellent, and allow 2½ hours.

The main road runs down the eastern shore of Grand Manan, past several small coves. At Woodwards Cove, take a look at the shingled smokehouses with their red doors, still used to smoke herring. A ferry runs from the man-made harbor at Ingalls Head to White Head Island.

At Grand Harbour, southward via the main road, there is a wonderful little museum with an impressive Fresnel lens from a lighthouse, marine and geological exhibits, and a large collection of island birds.

The Marathon Inn in North Head offers nature

expeditions "in search of whales, porpoise, seals and pelagic birds" (tel. 662-8144). Almost as interesting is the social phenomenon of loading the ferry, lifeline of all islands: cars line up on the main street hours before departure time, large trucks inch down the ramp into the ferry's maw, families walk aboard for the long ride to the mainland.

SEAL COVE ★★★★

Canadian Charts: 4011, **4340, 4342**

Tidal Range: *Mean* 14.3 feet; *Large* 19.6 feet

Seal Cove is a small and pleasant fishing community near the southern end of Grand Manan, on the eastern side, and a possible port of entry into Canada. The approach from the south is easy, and a man-made harbor provides excellent protection. Like most Grand Mananers, the people of Seal Cove are extremely friendly and helpful.

This is a harbor used mostly by lobsterboats, which turn to other fisheries when the lobster season officially ends in June, to allow lobsters to shed their shells unmolested and breed. At other seasons, nets are laid out in the fields to dry, among the neat little houses. In the spring, Douglas-fir poles 60 to 80 feet long are piled on the docks. They are sharpened at one end and ready to be driven by floating pile drivers to build or repair the island's weirs.

The old harbor at the head of the cove, which dries out, is lined with handsome, shingled, red-trimmed smokehouses, some still in use.

Lying secure in Seal Cove on a foggy day, there is a great feeling of peace, occasional raucous seagull cries, sometimes the rumble of a lobsterboat diesel starting up, and the rise and fall of voices on the wharf as fishermen discuss the catch, the market, and weather.

With prevailing summer winds, there will be fog at Grand Manan if the mainland is warm. "It can be desperate foggy in Seal Cove," the fishermen say, "but burned off by the time you reach North Head."

Approaches. From the south or west, make for high Southwest Head and the lighthouse (with two radio towers nearby). Then pick up red-and-white whistle "XA," near the head, or red-and-white bell "XAD," southeast of the head. From the bell, coast up between Wood Island (low and partially wooded) and the east shore of Grand Manan.

Note green can "XA3" off Buck Rock, left to port, and look for the "Flock of Sheep" near Pat's Cove—glacial erratics left browsing 10,000 years ago. Stay in midchannel to clear the weirs along the Grand Manan shoreline. Otherwise, this channel is wide and open with the few dangers all marked. Ahead you will see the dark bulk of the wharves and the cluster of houses in Seal Cove. Fish pens moored south of the harbor are clearly visible, but may not be lit at night.

Anchorages, Moorings. There are two man-made harbors in Seal Cove. The northern one dries out at low water.

The southern harbor, which you come to first, has good, deep water and excellent protection. Not shown on the charts is a breakwater and wharf extending from the north and perpendicular to the main wharf, forming a narrow entrance. Be careful entering; someone may be coming out.

Tie up to a boat along the main wharf, or (after June 30) to a lobster car in midharbor. Before deciding on a lobster car, however, get permission to stay alongside and check how well it is moored. On an average low tide, you will find about 12 to 14 feet of depth along the inner wall of the south wharf, and 9 to 10 feet at the southern edge of both rows of lobster cars and along the inner edge of the north wharf.

Lobster cars float around quite a lot. If you are tied to one, don't be surprised to find yourself bumping one of the boats nested at the wharf. Fenders are good insurance.

Getting Ashore. Take the dinghy in to the float near the land end of the south wharf. If you are entering Canada here, call the Customs office at North Head (tel. 662-3232). There are pay phones at the head of the dock and in the markets. Customs would prefer to have you arrange your own transportation to North Head, but will drive down to Seal Cove if necessary.

For the Boat. Fuel can be obtained at several lobster cars in midharbor. There is no fresh water piped to the wharf; if you need it, ask around. Someone will be glad to give you water at his home, but you will have to lug it in containers. There is a trash can on the dock. Small amounts of ice are sold at the markets.

For the Crew. The nearest groceries are at the big pink building of Helshiron Fisheries, Ltd., just up the road from the wharf. Continue on half a mile into town to find High Tide Market and the Waters Edge family restaurant.

Things to Do. Preston Wilcox makes trips in *Senorita* to Machias Seal Island out of Seal Cove (tel. 662-8296).

Visit the handsome, shingled smokehouses around the inner harbor nearby. For a long hike, walk about 4½ miles down the road to Southwest Head, where you will be rewarded by wonderful views southward to Machias Seal Island and southwestward to the mainland.

INGALLS HEAD ★

Canadian Charts: 4011, **4340, 4342**

Tidal Range: *Mean* 14.3 feet; *Large* 19.6 feet

Ingalls Head is a man-made harbor at the southeast corner of Grand Manan serving a substantial fishing fleet, which unloads the catch here for processing in shoreside plants. The harbor provides excellent protection, and has been dredged to a depth of about 10 feet. The ferry to White Head Island leaves from here.

Approaches. From Seal Cove, follow the buoyed channel north of Wood Island, leave the green bell off Ox Head to port, then head north for Ingalls, leaving to port the two green spar buoys.

Anchorages, Moorings. The man-made harbor is heart-shaped, divided by a central pier. The southern section is more convenient because it has a float for landing. Tie up in any free space along the sides of the harbor, or, preferably, alongside another boat. The finger piers in the northern section are used by the boatlift.

For the Boat. Gas and diesel are available from lobster cars in the harbor.

Fundy Marine Service Center (Ch. 69; tel. 662-8314). Just north of the harbor is the two-story, shingled building of this storage and hauling facility, owned by the province and managed by the Grand Manan Fishermen's Association. This do-it-yourself yard, available to transients, has an enormous 150-ton boatlift and electricity, but no other facilities.

Getting Ashore. Row in to the float in the southern section of the harbor.

For the Crew. The nearest amenities are in Grand Harbour, a walk of about .75 mile. There you will find a bank, groceries, hardware, and restaurants.

Things to Do. For a pleasant outing to a remote island, take the free ferry from the concrete ramp in the southern section of the harbor to White Head Island. A small number of fishing families have lived on White Head for two hundred years. It is a haven for wildlife, and a friendly and hospitable place. The main preoccupations of the island are fishing, tending weirs, raking dulse, and the sea. Stroll along Battle Beach to the lighthouse on Long Point, past ponds full of ducks and other birds. For a long walk, take the main road along the northwest coast and around to Gull Cove on the eastern side of the island. There's a grocery store at the docks. Don't miss the last ferry back to Ingalls Head.

CAMPOBELLO AND DEER ISLANDS, Cobscook Bay, and Approaches to Passamaquoddy Bay

Campobello Island, Deer Island, and a chain of smaller islands overlap to guard the entrances of Passamaquoddy Bay, tucked away to the north. Campobello also protects the struggling industrial towns of Eastport and Lubec, which flank the entrance to the wild and empty waters of Cobscook Bay.

As the enormous Bay of Fundy tides pour through these complex passages, they form strong and turbulent currents, which, together with the frequent fogs, make navigation difficult in the area. The three major approaches to Passamaquoddy Bay are Lubec Narrows, Head Harbour Passage and Letite Passage, all three with very strong currents. Head Harbour Passage is the main channel and by far the easiest (see sketch map on page 332 and tidal diagrams, following).

U.S. chart 13396 is particularly useful in this area. Based on Canadian charts, it includes details such as the location of fish weirs; depths are in meters.

Lubec Narrows. The International Bridge joining Lubec and Campobello Island over Lubec Narrows has a vertical clearance of 47 feet (at high tide). This passage should be used by strangers only at high slack, if they can pass under the bridge. Currents at strength run seven or eight knots, with substantial eddies and turbulence, and there is danger of collision with one of the bridge piers. At low tide the approach channel is narrow and crooked. It's far better and safer to make the longer trip around Campobello Island and through Head Harbour Passage.

Head Harbour Passage. Between Campobello Island and Deer Island, Head Harbour Passage is several hundred yards wide and clear of obstructions. Although you may encounter tide rips and boils, the passage is basically safe and easy.

Letite Passage. North of Deer and McMaster Islands, Letite Passage is wider and deeper than

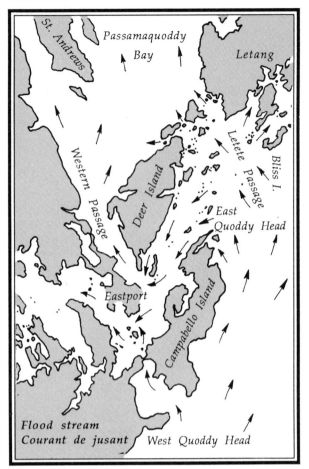

Direction of tidal streams in approaches to Passamaquoddy Bay. (Reproduced with permission of the Canadian Hydrographic Service—not to be used for navigation.)

Lubec Narrows, but the maximum current here also runs some eight knots, and there are numerous obstructions and buoys. Passing through with the flood, you will have the sensation of being swept along at an enormous pace, although with care and in good visibility you should have no trouble. The best time to make the passage is within a short period on either side of slack water, either high or low. Unless you know it well, avoid Letite

Passage in poor visibility.

Western Passage. From Eastport the usual approach to St. Andrews and Passamaquoddy Bay is through Western Passage. Time your passage in either direction to avoid maximum turbulence in Old Sow, one of the world's largest whirlpools, between Eastport and Deer Island (see Western Passage on page 356).

CAMPOBELLO ISLAND

Canadian Charts: 4011, 4340, 4343, **4373**; U.S. Charts: **13328, 13396**

Campobello is a large Canadian island that protects the entrances to Cobscook and Passamaquoddy bays. Seven and a half miles long and 2½ miles wide, Campobello is joined to the mainland by the International Bridge, over Lubec Narrows. A lovely island, with hard-working fishing communities, Campobello is famous as the summer home of President Franklin D. Roosevelt, and his cottage on Friars Bay has now become part of Roosevelt-Campobello Island International Park, maintained by both the United States and Canada. Welshpool has a man-made harbor from which you can pay a visit

to this charming old home.

Along the northern and western shores of Campobello runs Head Harbour Passage, with depths of 200 and 300 feet. On the island are two excellent natural harbors: Head Harbour at the northern end and Harbour de Lute on the western side. There are also a number of small man-made harbors which will provide refuge in a pinch.

There is a Canadian Customs port of entry at the bridge but no place for a boat to stop. The easiest place to clear Customs is at Wilsons Beach.

Aerial view of the entrance to Head Harbour, at the northern end of Campobello Island. Head Harbour Passage and Deer Island are in the background. (Christopher Ayres photo)

HEAD HARBOUR ★★★★★

Canadian Chart: 4373; U.S. Charts: **13328, 13396**

Tidal Range: *Mean* 18.1 feet; *Large* 25.2 feet

A picturesque lighthouse at the end of a series of bold, rocky islets gives the mariner a dramatic welcome to Head Harbour, at the northeastern end of Campobello Island. On early French charts, this was "Port aux Coquilles." Less euphoniously named nowadays, it is still one of the best harbors in the Passamaquoddy region, a good place to spend the night or to wait out the tide before entering Head Harbour or Letite Passage. The entrance is easy, and there is always a fascinating bustle of fishing activity.

Approaches. Nancy Head, on the east coast of Campobello Island, is high and prominent. The distinctive lighthouse at East Quoddy Head, with its white buildings and red roofs, is visible a long way. The white tower sports an enormous red cross, as though wrapped in red ribbon. Islands and headlands range away to the northeast along this beautiful coast.

There are two entrances to Head Harbour, one on each side of Head Harbour Island. The northern entrance is better. Run down the middle of the northern entrance, noting weirs on both sides. Moorings and a long private dock are near the western end of Head Harbour Island.

After passing the island, you will see three green buoys close together. Run north of these buoys, leaving them to port. Favor the north shore at Cubs Point, then proceed down the middle of the channel. From just past Cubs Point to the L-shaped public wharf, the water in the channel is more than 30 feet deep at low. Salmon pens are moored along the edges of the channel and vessels lie off a large cannery to port.

Anchorages, Moorings. Fishing boats are tied up along every wall of the public wharf, the largest nested along the outer edges of the L. There is good depth inside as well (15 feet or so at low). Pick the most convenient boat to come alongside.

If there is no room alongside, inquire about a vacant mooring, or find a spot to anchor west of the wharf. There is a line of stake moorings extending west to shoal water, and usually room to anchor. The rocky southern shore west of the wharf is steep-to, with depths nearby of 12 to 15 feet at low and good mud holding ground. Small yachts often tie up to the resident pile driver.

Getting Ashore. Clamber over the adjoining boats and climb a ladder to the top of the wharf, or take your dinghy around to the float on the inside of the L.

For the Crew. From the dock, turn left and walk 1.3 miles to the small market and post office at Wilsons Beach.

Things to Do. East Quoddy Head Light stands on the most seaward of a number of small islets. It's a challenging walk—up and down steel ladders, across treacherous seaweed and sharp rocks —until you reach the sign that says, "Danger— Rising Tides can get you stranded on this island." The lighthouse can be reached only near low tide. The walk from the public wharf to the parking lot at the lighthouse is 1.6 miles.

During July and August, you may be able to spot whales from East Quoddy Head Light; often a pod will come in on the flood, spouting frequently.

345

HEAD HARBOUR PASSAGE

Canadian Charts: 4011, **4373**; U.S. Charts: **13328, 13396**

The main approach to Eastport, Passamaquoddy Bay, Cobscook Bay, and the St. Croix River is Head Harbour Passage. With its distinctive white tower and large red cross, East Quoddy Head Light, at the northern end of Campobello Island, marks the entrance.

This deep and unobstructed passage follows the steep north shore of Campobello Island for about four miles, until it meets Friar Roads and Western Passage south of Deer Island, a spot marked by the lighthouse on Cherry Island.

The best time to come through Head Harbour Passage is with the current, which floods southwest and ebbs northeast at maximum strength of perhaps five knots. At the entrance, strong east or northeast winds against an ebb tide may create a heavy breaking sea off East Quoddy Head. The flood tide will set you hard toward Spruce Island and Black Rock. In the passage, you may encounter boils, eddies, and turbulence strong enough to make your boat yaw—unsettling, but not dangerous except for small craft.

WILSONS BEACH ★★★

Canadian Charts: 4340, **4343**, 4373; U.S. Charts: **13328, 13396**

Tidal Range: *Mean* 18.1 feet; *Large* 25.2 feet

Just north of Windmill Point on Head Harbour Passage, Wilsons Beach is a small but active fishing community with a man-made harbor. It can be identified on the chart by the light shown at the end of the wharf.

Approaches. The approach from Head Harbour Passage is straightforward. The long wharf is angled toward the land to provide a protective pocket. Several boats probably will be rafted inside the face of the wharf, with barely room to squeeze by between them and the land.

Anchorages, Moorings. There is about six feet of depth at low along the inner face of the long

wharf. Tie up to one of the resident boats.

Getting Ashore. There are no floats in the harbor, so you will have to climb a vertical ladder to get ashore.

You can enter Canada at Wilsons Beach by calling Canadian Customs at the International Bridge (tel. 506-752-2091).

For the Boat. Water may be obtained at the wharf adjacent to the long wharf. It dries out at low tide.

For the Crew. Near the docks you will find a small grocery store and a post office. A mile or so south is Phinney's takeout and fish market.

HARBOUR DE LUTE ★★★★   No facilities

Canadian Charts: 4340, **4343, 4373**; U.S. Charts: **13328, 13396**

Tidal Range: *Mean* 18.1 feet; *Large* 25.2 feet

On the northwest side of Campobello Island, opposite Eastport, this excellent and seldom-used refuge was called "Harbour de L'Outre" on early charts. Several man-made harbors have been built

on either side of the entrance, and presumably the fishermen find these more convenient. For a cruising yacht, however, Harbour de Lute provides a serene and private anchorage.

Because of the many decaying weirs in the harbor, it is preferable to enter below midtide, when most of the stakes are visible. Be prepared for mosquitoes.

Approaches. The entrance to Harbour de Lute, between Windmill Point and Man of War Head, is wide and open, except for salmon pens on either side. Favor Man of War Head to stay clear of the nine-foot spot, and head for green spar "UX1." Two weirs extend from the western shore, one before the green spar and one beyond it. The second of these weirs has lost its top poles and is not visible after halftide.

Leaving the spar fairly close to port to clear the weirs, make a wide turn to starboard toward Bunker Hill, favoring the eastern shore. There are several more weirs in the inner portion of the harbor. Continue to the 20-foot mark on the chart. A ledge west of this spot is visible except at very high tides.

Anchorages, Moorings. Anchor in 11 to 20 feet at low in midharbor. The holding ground is good, in mud, and there should be ample swinging room. Protection is good from every direction, although a strong northerly may funnel into the harbor.

After anchoring, pick out a range on the northeast shore that will take you clear of the weir on the western shore, in case you leave at high tide.

Getting Ashore. Row in to the beach at a convenient spot on the eastern shore.

Things to Do. If you land at the meadow north of Bunker Hill, a brief struggle through the bushes will bring you to a dirt road shown on the chart. There are lots of wildflowers, and you may see a resident bald eagle.

WELSHPOOL ★★★

Canadian Charts: 4340, **4343**, 4373; U.S. Charts: **13328, 13396**

Tidal Range: *Mean* 18.4 feet; *Large* 24.7 feet

On the west side of Campobello, the man-made harbor of Welshpool offers a way for the cruising vessel to visit President Franklin Roosevelt's summer cottage, the 2,600-acre Roosevelt-Campobello Island International Park, and other parts of the island.

Approaches. The harbor is at the north end of Friars Bay, which is wide open with no dangers except two large fish weirs and some fish pens.

Anchorages, Moorings. As shown on the chart, the man-made harbor at Welshpool has the shape of an L, with the arm pointing southeast. There is 9 or 10 feet at low along the inner face of the wharf, but there probably will be two rows of boats nested there. If no more than three or four boats are nested, there should be room to squeeze through between the outer boat and the land, with five or six feet of water at low.

Tie up to one of the fishing boats, checking the depth. Depending on the tide, you can probably lie over here for a few hours.

You can also anchor in the northeast corner of Friars Bay in 25 to 30 feet of water; check the locations of the weirs and fish pens.

Getting Ashore. Land at the float at the inner corner of the harbor.

For the Boat. There is electricity at the wharf, but no water or fuel.

For the Crew. A restaurant and a gift shop are half a mile along the road to the south. The post office is .2 mile away, up the road to the right.

Things to Do. FDR's cottage is about three-quarters of the way down Friars Bay, a walk of 1.5 miles from the wharf. The building is unmistakable—red with a green roof—and signs point the way. At the Reception Centre are films about FDR and Campobello, and furnishings used by the Roosevelt family are on display. A plaque at the home commemorates the former president: "In happy memory of Franklin Delano Roosevelt (1882–1945) who, during many years of his eventful life, found, in this tranquil island, rest, refreshment, and freedom from care. To him it was always the 'Beloved Island.'"

A bit beyond FDR's house is Friars Head, where there are nature trails and a lookout station with a spectacular view of Cobscook Bay, Lubec, Eastport, and the islands. You may also get a look at "Old Sow," the largest whirlpool in the world, which forms between Eastport and Deer Island. It is best viewed about three hours before high tide.

For a longer walk, go 1.8 miles from the wharf at Welshpool to Herring Cove Provincial Park, on Campobello's east coast. Here there is a lovely, mile-long crescent beach, with dark sand, grassy borders, driftwood, and a great view of Grand Manan.

Take a pleasant ride on the scow-ferry, which makes several trips a day to Deer Island, departing from the beach just north of Welshpool. Another ferry makes hourly roundtrips between Deer Island and Eastport.

LUBEC ★★

Canadian Charts: 4340, 4373; U.S. Charts: **13328, 13396**

Tidal Range: *Mean* 17.5 feet; *Spring* 20 feet

Lubec is a small town on the west side of Lubec Narrows through which pour the great tides of Cobscook and Passamaquoddy bays. This is a Customs port of entry for the United States. The International Bridge, spanning Lubec Narrows, leads to Canada's Campobello Island. The fixed bridge has a vertical clearance of 47 feet at high tide.

Lubec Narrows is one of the three approaches to Passamaquoddy Bay, Cobscook Bay, and the St. Croix River, but certainly not the easiest or safest. The main difficulty is the extremely strong current, which runs six knots on the flood and eight knots at maximum ebb.

If you can fit comfortably under the fixed bridge, the time to make the passage in either direction is high slack. (The period of slack water in the Narrows is only 5 to 15 minutes.) If your mast is too tall to pass under the bridge at high slack, use Head Harbour Passage instead.

It would be difficult to fight your way under the bridge against an ebb current. Even going through with the flood is likely to be uncomfortable and dangerous because of the risk of yawing into the bridge piers.

It is possible to come through at low slack water, but the dredged channel south of the bridge is narrow and crooked. As Canadian sailors have warned, "The passage is dicey at low water." Remember that high water will be higher than normal during spring tides and low water will be lower.

Approaches—From the South. Leave flashing green whistle "1" off West Quoddy Head to port, giving it a good berth to avoid the swirls that form near Sail Rock. Then run to red-and-white fairway bell "WQ." If you are waiting for the tide, anchor in Quoddy Narrows, in 12 to 25 feet, north of West Quoddy Head.

When the tide is favorable, follow buoyed Lubec Channel, running between three sets of red buoys and green buoys. After leaving green can "5" to port, head for the center span of the bridge, sheathed in riprap. (The line on the chart consisting of small crosses marks the international boundary, not the route.)

After passing under the bridge, look for the breakwater to port at the northern end of the Narrows. (Normally easy to see, the breakwater is covered at extreme high water, but it is marked by a white pyramid midway along its length.)

Approaches—From the North. Waiting for the tide at the northern end of the Narrows, anchor in Johnson Bay or tie up to the public landing floats at Lubec, west of the breakwater. When the tide is favorable, start the passage near green can "7" and head for the center span of the bridge. The current is at its strongest near Mulholland Point.

Anchorages, Moorings. At the northern end of town, just past the breakwater and around to the west, is the public landing (town marina), with floats and a launching ramp but no other facilities. There is about eight feet of water alongside the floats at low. This is out of the current and a convenient place to stop, but it can be very uncomfortable here when a north or northwest wind bangs you into floats or nested boats. The youth of Lubec meet in the parking lot above the landing, so it can be a bit noisy at night.

You can also anchor to the west in Johnson Bay while waiting for the tide, in 15 to 25 feet at low, but this is not convenient to the town of Lubec.

Getting Ashore. Land at the public landing floats at the northern end of town.

To check in with U.S. Customs, walk a few blocks to the brick Customs building (tel 733-4331) at the International Bridge.

For the Boat. There is a hardware store in town.

For the Crew. It's about a half mile from the public landing to a group of three small markets. Turn right up the hill (Main Street), past the bandstand, and down the other side to the traffic light, which will take you past Wasson's Market to a Quik-Stop convenience store (ice and pay phone) and to a Red and White Market, open every day. Along the waterfront in town, you will find a bank, pizza shops, a takeout, and a barbershop.

Things to Do. Lubec once was the sardine-packing capital of the world. Today it is like a ghost town, with many homes for sale. Only occasionally does the whistle blow in the early morning to signal the packers to go to work. A sardine plant and a smoked herring plant are still operating on the waterfront, remnants of the 20 or more canneries that once were here.

Although there is no pedestrian path on the International Bridge, it is easy enough to walk across to Canada. American and Canadian Customs officials guard the road at either end.

Captain Butch Huntley of Lubec leads bird- and whale-watching trips on *Seafarer* (tel. 733-5584).

To get to the lighthouse at West Quoddy Head and Quoddy Head State Park, call the Lubec town manager at 733-2202. He knows several local residents who (for a fee) are willing to drive you there. The candy-striped lighthouse was built in 1791 on the easternmost point of land in the United States. There are trails all along the cliffs, picnicking sites, and wonderful views of Grand Manan.

Herring on racks ready for smoking; Eastport, 1920. (Frank Claes Collection)

JOHNSON BAY ★★ No facilities

Canadian Charts: 4340, 4373; U.S. Charts: **13328, 13396**

Tidal Range: *Mean* 17.5 feet; *Spring* 20 feet

West of Lubec, Johnson Bay is more useful than attractive. It is easy to enter and provides good anchorage and protection for boats waiting out the tide at Lubec Narrows. It is also a more comfortable place than the town marina at Lubec if the wind is from the north.

Johnson Bay itself offers a gravel pit, a trailer park, and considerable development. Once you are anchored, however, the views north and east are most attractive—Lubec transformed into a quaint little town, its white houses clustered on the hill and topped with two steeples. There is handsome little Popes Folly Island, and beyond it Friars Head and Campobello.

Approaches. The approach is wide and straightforward on either side of Dudley and Treat islands. A large group of fish pens is centered in the bay, marked by privately maintained buoys.

Anchorages, Moorings. Continue in until you reach depths of 13 to 14 feet at low, between the little peninsulas on either side of the bay. Favor the south or the north side, depending on the wind. Holding ground is good, in mud.

RODGERS ISLAND ★★★ No facilities

U.S. Charts: **13328, 13396**

Tidal Range: *Mean* 17.5 feet; *Spring* 20 feet

Rodgers is a small, wooded island with rocky headlands and attractive little beaches at the northwest corner of Johnson Bay. There is a pleasant anchorage between it and the mainland.

Approaches. From Johnson Bay, aim halfway between the end of Rodgers Island to starboard and the mainland peninsula to port.

Anchorages, Moorings. The passage between Rodgers Island and the mainland is narrow and unmarked. The safest place to anchor is halfway between the eastern tip of Rodgers Island and the eastern tip of the mainland peninsula, before reaching the long ledge extending from the mainland (partially visible at halftide). Note also the ledge extending south from the tip of Rodgers. Anchor in 9 to 15 feet at low, mud bottom; there is ample swinging room.

EASTPORT ★★★★   5   All facilities

U.S. Charts: 13328, 13396 (Insets) (Note that depths are shown in meters on Chart 13396)

Tidal Range: *Mean* 18.4 feet; *Spring* 20.9 feet

Called the "Island City," Eastport is the easternmost deepwater port in the United States and one of the most isolated. Built on Moose Island and connected to the mainland by causeways, it forms the northern entrance to Cobscook Bay and looks out across the border to Deer Island and Campobello.

This is a particularly interesting fishing town. Since the mid-1970s, Eastport has attracted millions of dollars in state and federal funds to rebuild its waterfront area. This has resulted in a magnificent cargo pier from which freighters load lumber and paper for shipment overseas. Another promising new industry is aquaculture: salmon smolt are raised here in pens until they reach market size.

But it's still a toss-up whether the process of decay will win, or the periodic renovation efforts. The town remains in a depressed state, with little industry and high unemployment. Eastporters look to Calais, 28 miles away, for entertainment.

Water Street is the main street of Eastport, where everything happens. The old stone post office is here, and the Customs House. The huge breakwater wharf was built here to give Eastport a man-made harbor as good as those in Canada. Water Street is where the big ships tie up to be loaded —a result of Eastport's most recent rehabilitation scheme.

Twice every day, 70 billion cubic feet of water enters and leaves Passamaquoddy Bay. Underlying the causeway that links Eastport to the mainland is part of the dam built in the 1930s as the first step in harnessing this enormous source of free power. The project languished during the Depression and was finally killed, but the concept of tidal power on a huge scale is still intriguing, and schemes for reviving the project surface periodically.

From a beach just north of town, a ferry-scow leaves for Deer Island, in Canada. Another ferry runs from Deer Island to Campobello.

The most easterly U.S. Coast Guard station is in Eastport (a division of the USCG facility in Jonesport), with search-and-rescue capability (channel 16; tel. 853-2845). The Border Patrol also operates out of here.

Approaches. Eastport is easily approached through the deepwater entrances of Head Harbour Passage and Western Passage, which converge into Friar Roads. Aim for the south end of the L-shaped breakwater, which dominates the town (see sketch map). The pink granite seawall lining the shore behind the breakwater is visible a long way.

To enter the harbor, go between the southern tip of the breakwater and the Fish Pier, which extends eastward from the shore to form the southern end of the anchorage.

This entrance is wide enough, but there is a large dolphin with a bollard standing in the middle. Go to either side of the dolphin and turn northward into the anchorage. There is often a tugboat tied up at the southern tip of the breakwater, and someone may be coming out, so enter cautiously.

To come alongside the floats reserved for pleasure craft, just outside the breakwater, head in toward the north, outer face of the breakwater where you will see floats and another large dolphin, with ample room to turn around.

When leaving Eastport for St. Andrews through Western Passage, time your departure to avoid maximum turbulence in Old Sow, the world's largest whirlpool, between Eastport and

EASTPORT
(based on Chart 13328 — inset)

This chart is for general information only and NOT TO BE USED FOR NAVIGATION. Location and type of buoys and other navigational aids may change from time to time. Use in conjunction with the text, and the latest Charts, Notices to Mariners, and U.S. Coast Pilot.

the southern tip of Deer Island. Old Sow is most active during flood tide, about three hours before high (see Western Passage, page 356).

Anchorages, Moorings. *(Inside the Breakwater).* Although space inside the breakwater is reserved primarily for commercial fishing boats, transient cruising boats may still be able to find space. There are three possibilities. You can tie up alongside a large fishing boat or dragger on the inside face of the breakwater, remembering that the fishermen may well be getting underway at dawn. A second possibility is to find room at the floats along the landward side of the harbor; these are likely to be occupied, however, by small craft used in the salmon aquaculture business. The third option is to tie up to the town float at the north end, with permission from the harbormaster. Next to the town float is the Coast Guard float. There is 13 feet of water in the southern end of the harbor and 9 feet in the northern end, but no room to anchor.

(Outside the Breakwater). Pleasure craft are requested to come alongside the floats lining the northern, outer face of the breakwater, where protection is excellent from prevailing winds. In case of severe weather from the north or east, of course, you would have to move inside the breakwater.

Another possibility is to lie along the north side of the Fish Pier, although there are no floats, and you will have to use long mooring lines. The outer, eastern face of the breakwater is reserved for big commercial ships.

Slips and heavy moorings are also available at Northeast Marina, although these are exposed.

Getting Ashore. There is access by ramp from all floats in the harbor to the top of the breakwater. For yachts returning from Canada, Eastport is the most convenient port of entry. U.S. Customs is in the post office, right next to the breakwater (tel. 853-4313).

For the Boat. Water is available at the pleasure craft floats on the northern, outer face of the breakwater. Ice can be purchased in town.

Northeast Marina and Fuel Depot (Ch. 16 and 69; tel. 853-4295). About one-quarter mile south of the harbor, just south of the inlet shown on the chart, is the fuel dock of Northeast Marina, providing gas, diesel, water, and ice. There is 14 feet of water at low along the outside of the floats. Approach into the current, which normally runs south both on the flood and ebb.

Moose Island Marine, Inc. (Ch. 16; tel. 853-6058). At the head of the breakwater, Moose Island Marine handles all sorts of dockside service, particularly mechanical repairs. The chandlery offers a good selection of marine supplies, including charts and courtesy flags.

Eastport Boat Yard & Supply. See Deep Cove, ahead.

For the Crew. Northeast Marina has showers

A freighter loading at the pier in Eastport, while small fishing boats nest inside the man-made harbor. The tidal range here is more than 20 feet. (Christopher Ayres photo)

for yachtsmen and sells groceries, beer, and wine. A pay phone is next to Rosie's hot dog stand on the wharf. A supermarket is one block away. Fishermen land their catches at the little wharf on the west side of the harbor, and fresh fish and lobsters are for sale at the red shed (Flood Tide Seafood). There are a number of restaurants, take-outs, and diners along Water Street, as well as a liquor store, hardware, drug store, galleries, and bookstores. There is a laundromat in town two blocks up the hill from Newberry's.

Things to Do. Stroll one way along Water Street and back along the attractive waterfront path. It's interesting to watch the loading and unloading of fishing boats and freighters—quite an operation, especially when the tide is down.

The office of the *Quoddy Tides* newspaper, next to the wharf, also houses a little marine library, shop, and aquarium.

Fourth of July has been a big deal in Eastport for a century, and it is lots of fun. Lasting for several days, it involves everything from beauty contests and parades to water sports and a codfish relay. Events may include the Caledonian Bag Pipe Band, in kilts, a torchlight parade, and a blueberry pie–eating contest. Parachutists come floating down out of the sky to land at the wharf, and sometimes a U.S. Navy ship makes an appearance. The festivities are officially completed with a grand display of fireworks over the bay, watched by half of the population of Washington County and New Brunswick. Unofficially, firecrackers continue to go off until 2 A.M., and sleep is scarce.

COBSCOOK BAY

U.S. Charts: **13328, 13396**

The most northerly bay on the east coast of the United States, Cobscook remains isolated and undeveloped. Here there are bald eagles and a wide variety of wildlife, scattered saltwater farms and tremendous currents. Hardly a boat is to be seen. Areas attractive to most cruising sailors are limited. There are pleasant anchorages in South Bay and the Pennamaquan River, but the bays beyond Falls Island—Dennys and Whiting—are inaccessible except through narrow passages with extremely strong currents. "Cobscook" is an Abenaki word meaning "boiling tides," and the Abenakis had it right.

Approaches. After passing Broad Cove and Deep Cove, leaving Cooper Island Ledge and green can "7" to port, leave red nun "8" marking Birch Point Ledge to starboard. This nun is known for towing under; if you cannot find it, stay close to the end of Gove Point to avoid this dangerous ledge.

Now head for little Red Island (which really is red), leaving it to starboard.

BROAD COVE

U.S. Charts: **13328, 13396**

Broad Cove is a large commercial bay on the south shore of Moose Island, next to Eastport. Although anchorage here is good, the bay is wide open to the south, obstructed by a very large salmon aquaculture operation, and home to lumber mills and two large fish-reduction plants. (Fish reduction produces the pearlescence derived from fish scales and is used to add luster to eye shadows and nail polishes. It also produces fish meal and fertilizer.) Find another place to spend the night.

DEEP COVE ★★

U.S. Charts: **13328, 13396**

Tidal Range: *Mean* 18.7 feet; *Spring* 21.3 feet

On the west side of Moose Island, next to the Eastport airport, Deep Cove has a long dock and harbors an aquaculture operation. The big blue building is home for the Washington County Marine Trades Center, which offers courses in commercial fisheries, marine mechanics, painting, and boatbuilding.

Approaches. The approach is through the entrance to Cobscook Bay, with currents of four to five knots. Favor the Shackford Head side of the channel to avoid Cooper Island Ledge. The entrance to Deep Cove is wide and unobstructed, except for a large flotilla of fish pens.

Anchorages, Moorings. Tie up near the end of the long dock, which has 12 feet at low along the outer face, or pick up a rental mooring from Eastport Boat Yard. The cove is much exposed from northwest to southwest.

Getting Ashore. There are a float and ladder at the south side of the dock.

For the Boat. *Eastport Boat Yard & Supply (tel. 853-6049).* Just inland from the Marine Trades Center, Eastport Boat will haul and store, provide mechanical maintenance and repairs, and hull repairs for wood and fiberglass boats. Rates are among the lowest in the northeast. Normal capacity is 15 tons, but the 60-ton boatlift of the Marine Trades Center is available. The MacNaughtons of Eastport Boat are also designers and builders, specializing in wooden boats.

Washington County Marine Trades Center (tel. 853-2518). The marine center has a 60-ton boatlift for emergencies. You can also make below-waterline repairs by tying up to the specially reinforced dock and letting your keel settle with the tide on the granite ramp along the northern side of the dock.

For the Crew. A walk of 1.5 miles takes you to the stores and waterfront of Eastport.

SIPP BAY ★★ No facilities

U.S. Chart: **13328**

Tidal Range: *Mean* 19.1 feet; *Spring* 21.8 feet

At the northern end of Cobscook Bay, East Bay has two branches, with Sipp Bay stretching to the northwest. At the head of Sipp Bay is a trailer park.

Approaches. After leaving Red Island to starboard, bear northward into East Bay, favoring the east side until Leach Point, past the two-foot spot,

BALD EAGLES

The bald eagle is a magnificent wild creature with a wingspan as much as six or eight feet, awesome talons and beak, and the fierce, independent gaze that made it the national emblem of the United States. The adults are easily recognizable by their white feathered heads, white tails, and enormous size. More eagles are found near Pleasant Bay, east of Petit Manan, than any other place on the coast of Maine because of the ample supply of fish nearby. Cobscook Bay is another favorite eagle haunt.

Not surprisingly, eagles are at the top of the pecking order as far as birds are concerned (with the exception of the great horned owl). They frequently steal fish from ospreys, and smaller birds cease their chatter and seem to melt into the trees when an eagle is near. For a bird with such an intimidating reputation, eagles are indifferent fishermen, subsisting largely on dead or dying fish at the surface, and the occasional live fish stolen from another bird. They also sometimes prey on ducks and other seabirds.

In Indian and Colonial times, eagles were common along the coast of Maine—witness the numerous Eagle Islands and Eagle Points still on the chart. "Swango" was the Indian name for "eagle island," and Swan Island in the Kennebec River is now the site of Maine's westernmost eagle nest.

Eagle nests (or aeries) are impressive structures of sticks and branches, floored by grasses, moss, and feathers, and held together by a rich layer of guano. The nests are used year after year by the same pair (which mate for life), with repairs and additions each spring, so that the nest may reach an enormous size. One record nest (described in a National Audubon Society Publication) was 10 feet across and 20 feet deep.

Eagle pairs usually maintain alternate nesting sites, and during a given year will abandon one nest for another nearby. This almost-human desire for change of scenery apparently is related to survival of the young, which are thus protected from the parasites that thrive in the nest guano.

There is an active eagle nest on wonderfully inaccessible Shipstern Island (a Nature Conservancy preserve), off Pleasant Bay. A decade ago, the owners of this nest moved over to neighboring Flint Island (also protected by The Nature Conservancy) because their large nest

became so heavy that it broke the branch on which it rested and fell to the ground. Apparently this is the only eagle pair in Maine to claim two islands for their nesting sites.

Eagles are not tolerant of human disturbance; as the human population grew, their range shrank. Far worse was the genocidal effect of pesticides such as DDT, which accumulated in the food chain and interfered with the reproduction of eagles, ospreys, and other birds. By 1965, only four nesting pairs of eagles in Maine succeeded in producing eaglets.

With the banning of DDT and the conservation of islands and other areas suitable for eagle nests, this trend has gradually been reversed. The Nature Conservancy, the University of Maine, the Maine Department of Inland Fisheries and Wildlife, and the U.S. Fish and Wildlife Service have all been instrumental in assisting the recovery of eagles. Today they can be seen again in several coastal locations, although they are far less common than they once were, and still are very much an endangered species. It is always a thrill to spot one of these great creatures.

then turn west into Sipp Bay. Stop short of the little island on the north shore.

Anchorages, Moorings. Anchor in the middle of Sipp Bay, southeast of the little island, in 8 to 12 feet at low, mud bottom. There is some exposure to the south, but otherwise good protection all around.

PENNAMAQUAN RIVER ★★★

   No facilities

U.S. Chart: 13328

Tidal Range: *Mean* 19.1 feet; *Spring* 21.8 feet

Pennamaquan River flows into the northwest corner of Cobscook Bay, between Leighton Neck and Hersey Neck. This pleasant river is rich in wildlife, including seals, loons, and bald eagles.

Approaches. After leaving Red Island to starboard, head for green can "11" at Gangway Ledge, south of Hersey Neck. The river is comfortably wide. Follow the buoyed channel, leaving green cans to port. As you pass the oil tanks to starboard,

check the wharf to see whether ospreys are still nesting at the end of it.

Anchorages, Moorings. Anchor southwest of Hersey Point, where the chart shows 13 feet at low. The holding ground is adequate, with a mixture of mud and weed. Protection is reasonably good, although there is some exposure to the southeast and considerable fetch northwestward.

FEDERAL HARBOR ★★★★

   No facilities

U.S. Chart: 13328

Tidal Range: *Mean* 19.2 feet; *Spring* 21.9 feet

The best and most attractive harbor in Cobscook Bay, snug little Federal Harbor lies amid four rocky headlands in South Bay. Bald eagles nest nearby, and traces of civilization can be detected only with binoculars.

Approaches. Leaving Red Island to starboard, make your turn down into South Bay. Stay well clear of Razor Island, whose underlying ledge extends a long way east and west. Favor the Denbow Neck side of the bay. Horan Head is conspicuously high, while Hog Island nearby is an even higher bump. Enter the anchorage between Hog Island and Long Island.

Anchorages, Moorings. Anchor dead center among Hog Island, Long Island, Black Head, and Horan Head, in 8 to 12 feet at low. There is ample swinging room for one boat. The rocky islet between Hog Island and Horan Head provides

considerable protection to the north, and you are landlocked in every other direction. Holding ground is good, in mud.

For an even more secure spot, continue westward between Black and Horan Heads, anchoring in eight feet at low. It's narrow enough that you may want to set a stern anchor. The inner part of Federal Harbor dries out at low.

A third possibility is the long, narrow slot between Long Island and the mainland, where you can anchor in 10 feet at low.

Things to Do. Eagle-watching from your boat is good sport. Long Island, donated to The Nature Conservancy by Robert Rimoldi, is the largest undeveloped island in Cobscook Bay and a sanctuary for bald eagles. Tiny Federal Island, southwest of Horan Head, is owned by the state, and you are welcome to explore.

FALLS ISLAND PASSAGE

U.S. Chart: 13328

West of Cobscook Bay is a narrow entrance, between Leighton Point and Denbow Point, leading westward to Dennys Bay and Whiting Bay. In the middle of this entrance, like a cork in a bottle, Falls

Island obstructs the great flow of water that rushes by on either side.

Between Falls Island and Leighton Neck are the well-known reversing Cobscook Falls. The current

Things to Do. Farther up in the bay to the north lie two small, state-owned islands that are accessible by dinghy. The smaller island to the south is Cedar; larger Virgin Island, to the north, appears untouched by man.

ebbing from the inner bays, after passing the ledge south of Mahar Point, turns sharply north, then plunges southeastward around the ledge at the northwest corner of Falls Island, forming an S-pattern. At full strength the current is probably eight knots or more, and this is a whitewater river. The ledges are covered at high tide.

Although the passage south of Falls Island is far easier, the tidal stream is still extremely strong, and there are dangerous unmarked ledges. Entering between Fox Island and Falls Island, stay east of the ledge northeast of Ruth Point (near the 23-foot spot). After making your turn westward between Race Point and Ruth Point, favor the Crow Neck side of the passage to avoid the dangerous ledge southwest of Falls Island (near the 21-foot spot). This ledge shows about 5 feet at midtide and is covered at high.

It is probably impossible for a low-powered auxiliary yacht to fight its way in against the current. The best time to make the passage south of Falls Island is with the last of the flood or at high slack, which lasts only a short time.

The current around Falls Island is strongest during periods of Spring Tides, when the area becomes very turbulent. A wind against the current can produce large standing waves in the passages.

Cruising yachts are at substantial risk here. Intrepid yachtsmen take their boats through south of Falls Island, and some have run Cobscook Falls to the north, but unless you have a great need for white-knuckle adventure, leave Whiting and Dennys bays for the eagles—or make the passage in someone else's boat. (See photo on page 363.)

DEER ISLAND

Canadian Charts: 4011, 4331, 4343, 4373; U.S. Charts: **13328, 13396**

More remote and harder to reach than Campobello, beautiful Deer Island forms the southern end of Passamaquoddy Bay. Ferries run to Deer Island from Eastport and Campobello, and from New Brunswick to the north. A number of small fishing villages are scattered along its wooded shores, and the island is bounded by the turbulent currents of Western, Head Harbour, and Letite Passages.

The east coast of Deer Island is quite delightful, with sparsely settled rocky shores, weirs, jutting promontories, and handsome farmhouses. Starting at the southern end, keep your eyes open for the ferry-scow from Eastport and Campobello, which lands on the eastern side of Deer Island Point. The sailing is great between Indian Island and Deer Island, especially on the flood. The current here is strong, with some tide rips, boils, and

eddies (not too troublesome) that weaken as you go farther north. You pass the tiny hole of Chocolate Cove and then the busy fishing community of Leonardville. Casco Bay Island, Popes, and many other lovely islands dot the eastern horizon. Northwest Harbour presents a possible refuge, and north of it is intriguing Lords Cove, whose entrance channel is barely wider than your boat.

Great Chief Glooscap was paddling his canoe one day along the shores of Passamaquoddy, so Indian legend tells, when he saw a deer and a moose pursued by a pack of wolves. With a wave of his hand Glooscap changed them all to islands. The Wolves still slaver north of Grand Manan, but Deer and Moose lie safe in Passamaquoddy Bay.

NORTHWEST HARBOUR ★★★ No facilities

Canadian Charts: **4331**, 4373; U.S. Charts: **13328, 13396**

Tidal Range: *Mean* 18.1 feet; *Large* 25.2 feet

Midway along the east coast of Deer Island, Northwest Harbour is a delightful surprise. Attractive and well protected, this tiny fjord has banks that are high and wooded, few houses, and good anchorage.

Approaches. Approach north of Dinner Island, staying well clear of Net Ledges, marked by green spar "UP3." Continue northeast outside Net Ledges until you can see well inside the harbor

before turning westward. To avoid the weir extending north of Dinner Island, leave red spar "UP4" fairly close aboard to starboard and run up the centerline of the harbor. As you come to the cove on the north side of the harbor, favor the southern shore. Do not go past the point at the western end of the cove.

Anchorages, Moorings. Anchor in midchannel at the eastern end of the cove in 21 feet at low.

LORDS COVE ★★★

Canadian Chart: **4331**; U.S. Chart: **13328**

Tidal Range: *Mean* 18.1 feet; *Large* 25.2 feet

A tight little working harbor with excellent protection, Lords Cove is nestled inside Beans Island and St. Helena, at the northeastern corner of Deer Island. The approach channel is extremely narrow but well marked with ranges.

Approaches. Lords Cove may be approached from the north or south. The buoyed channel west of St. Helena Island is easier, since the northern approach requires some eyeball navigation. Leaving to starboard red spars "UP4" and "UP6," favor the St. Helena side until you are past the green beacon and light at Richardson and the following green spar, left to port.

Look for two white range boards with red stripes on shore at the head of Lords Cove. Each board has a fixed green light clearly visible in the daytime. Run this range carefully. It will take you past the green beacon standing in the water, left close aboard to port. There are fish pens on either side of the narrow channel and a sunken vessel to starboard.

Anchorages, Moorings. There are several moorings in the small turning basin, but no room to anchor. Tie up to the western end of the U-shaped wharf, with 12 to 15 feet at low, or to a boat already alongside. There is three to four feet at low off the eastern end. Do not enter the little cove on the west side of the wharf, which is shoal.

For the Boat. There is an ice plant at the head of the harbor.

For the Crew. A short distance to the right up the coastal road are a small grocery store and the post office.

WESTERN PASSAGE and OLD SOW

Canadian Chart: 4373; U.S. Charts: **13328, 13396**

Western Passage runs west of Deer Island between Friar Roads to the south and the St. Croix River and Passamaquoddy Bay to the north. This is the usual route between Eastport and St. Andrews. Be alert for the ferry-scows, which make frequent crossings from Eastport to the eastern tip of Deer Island and return. Currents are strong in the passage, averaging three knots for both flood and ebb. A rate of seven knots has been measured off Deer Island Point, diminishing northward. Strong eddies and countercurrents form near the shores.

Old Sow. The flood stream coming down through Head Harbour Passage and passing either side of Indian Island turns sharply north into Western Passage, producing "Old Sow," the world's largest whirlpool, between Deer Island Point and Dog Island. Time your passage to avoid Old Sow at its most turbulent, about three hours before high, when it is a dangerous place for small craft. It may be extremely difficult even for substantial vessels, causing them to lose control, yaw back and forth, lose headway, or even spin around. While this is not the Edgar Allan Poe kind of maelstrom that sucks you down into the depths, it is awesome enough to produce white knuckles and high anxiety. At other times the passage may be quite benign.

The lighthouse on Deer Island Point is a small white tower. The lighthouse on Cherry Island is also a small, round white tower, but with a red top.

On the west side of the passage, opposite Clam Cove, is the large Passamaquoddy Indian Reservation at Pleasant Point, established on a promontory surrounded on three sides by the ocean. A monument in the cemetery, dedicated by the D.A.R. in 1916, honors 200 members of the tribe who assisted the early colonists during the American Revolution. Pleasant Point administers Passamaquoddy lands and holdings throughout eastern Maine, acquired as a result of the historic Indian Land Claims Settlement of 1981.

NORTHERN HARBOUR

Canadian Charts: 4331, 4373; U.S. Charts, **13328, 13396**

On the western side of Deer Island, north of Clam Cove Head, is the intriguing gunkhole of Northern Harbour. It is a pretty spot with a rocky shoreline all around and only two or three houses visible.

However, the holding ground is poor, a mixture of soft mud and sticks. This and the northwest exposure suggest Northern Harbour only as a day stop.

A group of fish pens is moored in the entrance, and one of the world's largest lobster pounds occupies the northern branches of the harbor.

356

PENDLETON ISLAND

Canadian Chart: 4331; U.S. Chart: **13328**

North of Deer Island lies high, wooded Pendleton Island. In the bight on the north shore of Pendleton is a nice beach that is a favorite day stop of local yachtsmen. They report that you can put your bow right up on the sand.

LETITE PASSAGE

Canadian Charts: **4111**; 4313, 4331; U.S. Chart: **13328**

Letite Passage is the entrance to Passamaquoddy Bay north of Deer Island between McMaster Island and the mainland to the north. Canadian chart 4111 is much larger in scale than the U.S. chart and more likely to show the latest changes in buoyage. Overhead power cables across the passage have a vertical clearance of 128 feet.

Currents in Letite are extremely strong, with a maximum at midtide of six to eight knots, with eddies and boils. The passage is obstructed by many rocks and ledges, and although the most dangerous of these are buoyed, the combination of swift current and many buoys can be confusing, especially when tacking back and forth. Blue ferries cross Letite Passage between Butler Point on Deer Island and Matthews Cove. They can be contacted on channel 69.

Good visibility is extremely important here, so you should avoid this passage in foggy conditions. Sailing through Letite with a strong flood current is an exhilarating experience, with the shore moving by at an alarming rate and quick decisions required. It is less exciting but more comfortable to make the passage near high slack; the best time is 45 minutes before or after high water. Fighting your way through against the ebb is a losing proposition.

Letite Passage can be identified at a distance by the three high towers carrying overhead power lines; these are very useful in orienting yourself during the passage. The middle tower stands on Dry Ledge, and you can go to either side. In addition to the towers, the most helpful landmarks are wooded Mohawk Island and the cluster of buildings and lights at Greens Point. There is a white, octagonal lighthouse with a radio tower behind it, and a light on a skeleton tower on Morgan Ledge.

By far the easiest route from the south is to pass between Greens Point and Mohawk Island, leaving to starboard the series of red buoys along the eastern shore and passing to either side of Dry Ledge. (Note Little Dry Ledge to the south.) Then exit south of Thumb Island, which is grassy with some scraggly trees (see sketch map).

Another route takes you between Parker Island and Black Ledge, thence west of Mohawk Island, but the passage is much narrower, with a confusion of buoys and more effect from the current.

As you emerge from the passage, you will see the great red roof of the Algonquin Hotel in St. Andrews and the circling mountains of Passamaquoddy Bay.

Coming from the north, reverse the route described above, entering Letite Passage between the high northern tip of McMaster Island and scruffy little Thumb Island. Use the center tower on Dry Ledge to guide you, passing to either side, then go over to the eastern shore, leaving to port the line of red marks and exiting between Mohawk Island and Greens Point.

PASSAMAQUODDY BAY and St. Croix River

Canadian Charts: 4011, 4331; U.S. Chart: **13328**

There is magic in the name of Passamaquoddy Bay—perhaps because it is so remote from the areas where most sailors usually cruise; perhaps because it shares with the Bay of Fundy the image of enormous tides, swift currents, and impenetrable fogs; perhaps because of the lingering memory of the gigantic tidal dam project of Franklin Roosevelt's era.

The deep, cold, upwelling waters bringing nu-trients to the surface make this an immensely rich feeding area for birds and fish. Millions of phalaropes, Bonaparte's gulls, and birds of other species congregate in Passamaquoddy Bay during the late summer. "Passamaquoddy" itself means "pollock plenty place."

This is a beautiful open bay of no great extent—some five miles across and a bit more north and south. Well protected by the islands across the en-

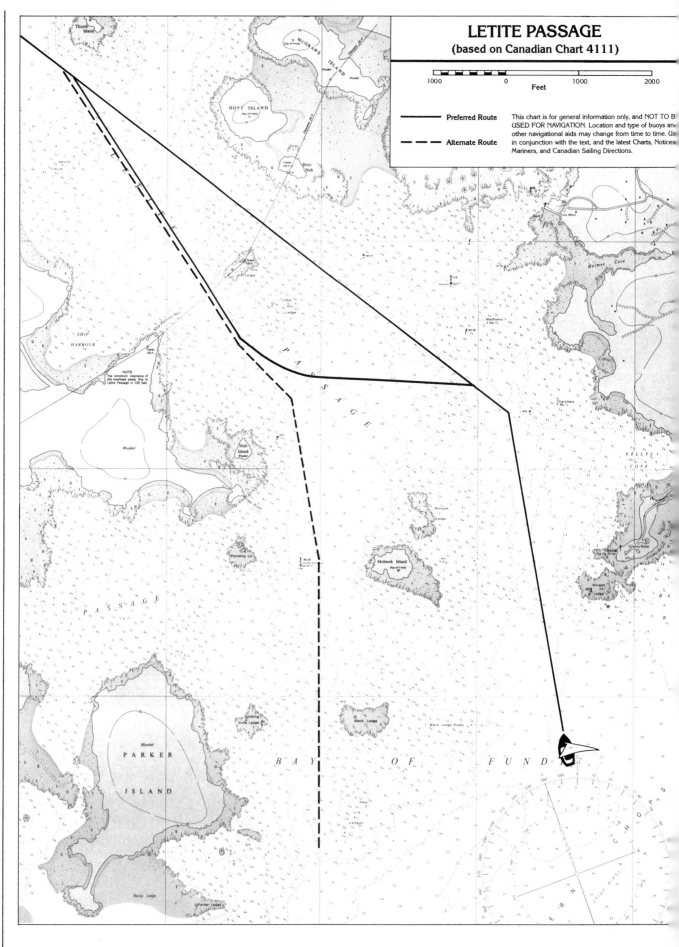

LETITE PASSAGE
(based on Canadian Chart 4111)

1000   0   1000   2000
Feet

———————— Preferred Route

– – – – – – – Alternate Route

This chart is for general information only, and NOT TO BE USED FOR NAVIGATION. Location and type of buoys and other navigational aids may change from time to time. Use in conjunction with the text, and the latest Charts, Notices Mariners, and Canadian Sailing Directions.

trance, the bay is ringed by a bold shoreline of bays and promontories. There are hardly any dangers except a few islands; Hardwood Island, in the middle, provides a convenient reference point.

The northern and eastern parts of Passamaquoddy are prettier than the western, much less developed and almost in a natural state, with circling hills. Because of the protecting islands, ocean swells do not penetrate the bay, making for calm anchorages. Air temperatures here are warmer than elsewhere on the coast, and often it is clear in the bay when the fog lies in thick banks outside.

In the small area of Passamaquoddy Bay there are several good harbors, but no facilities except in

St. Andrews at the southern end. Good protection may be found in Chamcook Harbour, Birch Cove, the Bocabec River, the Digdeguash River, and the Magaguadavic River. Of these, the three river anchorages are the most pleasing for their isolation and beauty. Cruising sailboats are still a rarity here.

At the northwest corner of Passamaquoddy Bay, the St. Croix River marks the boundary between the United States and Canada. It offers good sailing in the lower section and a good deal of wildlife to enjoy along the entire length. Head of navigation are the twin border towns of Calais (U.S.) and St. Stephen (Canada).

MAGAGUADAVIC RIVER ★★★

Canadian Chart: 4331; U.S. Chart: **13328**

Tidal Range: *Mean* 19.6 feet; *Large* 27.2 feet

 No facilities

Fed by the waters of Lake Utopia, the Magaguadavic River, on the east side of Passamaquoddy Bay, offers very good protection in a peaceful setting. This is one of the nicest harbors on the bay.

Shoal-draft boats can follow the buoyed channel upriver, preferably on a rising tide, to the little town of St. George.

Approaches. Use high Midjik Bluff as your landmark, rounding its steep cliffs into the wide entrance of the river. Favor the red buoys on the starboard side of the channel to avoid the flats that extend from the low point to the north. Fish pens

are moored in midharbor.

Anchorages, Moorings. Anchor just south of a line between red buoys "SM4" and "SM6," in 6 to 12 feet at low. Protection is good except from the north.

Harder to reach but better protected is a spot northwest of red buoy "SM8," just west of a brown rock bluff with a house above it. There is 7 to 12 feet at low, and the bottom is partly rock, partly mud. There are shoal spots nearby, so feel your way cautiously.

DIGDEGUASH HARBOUR ★★★★

 No facilities

Canadian Chart: 4331; U.S. Chart: 13328

Tidal Range: *Mean* 19.6 feet; *Large* 27.2 feet

At the northern end of Passamaquoddy Bay, the mouth of the Digdeguash River is protected by a little group of beautiful islands whose rocky shores are tinged with orange lichen. The banks of the river are forested, with only one or two houses visible. Well up at the head of the harbor, a highway bridge betrays one of the few signs of civilization.

This is a lovely harbor with good protection. The cries of loons echo across the water during the night.

Approaches. The eastern side of the entrance to the Digdeguash River can be identified at a distance by distinctive Oven Head on the mainland, with its rounded brown bluffs and meadow.

Run up the tongue of deep water between Long

Island, to starboard, and a group of three smaller islands (including Hog), to port. Having passed the western tip of Long Island, turn gradually to starboard, favoring the western side of the channel to avoid the ledges shown on the chart, and continue northward between two small islands. The buoys shown on the charts may or may not be in place.

Anchorages, Moorings. Anchor to either side of the deep tongue of water north of the two small islands, in 9 to 10 feet at low. Under most conditions, the western part of the anchorage offers the best protection. At high tide, there is some exposure through the islands to the south or southwest; at low tide, you will be entirely landlocked. The holding ground is good, in mud.

Things to Do. The three parts of Hog Island are connected at low tide and pleasant to explore. There are small meadows filled with ferns and abundant raspberries in July. The islands at the mouth of the Digdeguash are nesting areas for herring gulls.

BOCABEC COVE AND RIVER ★★★   No facilities

Canadian Chart: 4331; U.S. Chart: 13328

Tidal Range: *Mean* 19.6 feet; *Large* 27.2 feet

Attractive Bocabec Cove (as identified on Canadian chart 4331) is the entrance to the Bocabec River, just west of the Digdeguash River. A small fleet of fishing boats is based here, and there is anchorage with good protection except in a southerly gale.

West of Bocabec Cove, Dick Island was taken over by cormorants a couple of decades ago. The deciduous trees have all been killed by shag droppings, and the remaining skeletons are full of cormorant nests—sometimes six or more on a branch. The whole island is a shag tenement, with seagulls occupying the basement.

Approaches. Starting west of Hog Island, run up the middle of the entrance to Bocabec Cove. Stay in the deep water just off the ends of the two weirs extending from the western shore. This will keep you clear of a rock near the eastern shore. A third weir extends from the squarish promontory on the eastern shore.

Anchorages, Moorings. Just beyond the promontory on the eastern shore, the water deepens. Anchor west of the moored boats, in 15 to 20 feet at low. Do not go north of the moorings, where it dries out.

Getting Ashore. Land near the public road on the eastern shore, next to the white house.

BIRCH COVE ★★   No facilities

Canadian Chart: 4331; U.S. Chart: 13328

Tidal Range: *Mean* 19.6 feet; *Large* 27.2 feet

At the northwestern corner of Passamaquoddy Bay, Birch Cove extends west of Bocabec Bay. It offers good protection except from the southeast, but the western shore is crowded with camps.

Approaches. The approach from Bocabec Bay is wide open, except for a large weir at the entrance extending from the south shore of the harbor.

Anchorages, Moorings. Anchor near the western shore in 9 to 14 feet at low. Holding ground is good.

CHAMCOOK HARBOUR ★★★

Canadian Chart: 4331; U.S. Chart: 13328

Tidal Range: *Mean* 19.6 feet; *Large* 27.2 feet

Although good protection can be found in both sections of Chamcook Harbour, the view is marred by the ruins of a cannery and wharf on the western shore. In contrast is a magnificent barn near the western shore of Minister Island.

Approaches. Minister Island can be identified from a distance by the round stone tower (with white conical roof) at its southern end. Enter through the narrow buoyed channel north of Minister. The current in the channel is moderately strong, but not bothersome inside.

Anchorages, Moorings. Anchor in the northern portion of the harbor, west of Craig Point, in 18 to 21 feet at low, or in the center of the bay, where the anchor is shown on the charts, in 33 feet or more. There is a campground on the north shore.

The inlet over the bar leading to the southern portion of the harbor has 6 to 12 feet at low, but it is hard to locate. Cross on a rising tide. Once across the bar, anchor in 24 to 30 feet at low. Some of the available space is taken up by fish pens and aquaculture. The harbor is partially protected to the south by a bar between Minister Island and the mainland (cars drive over it at low tide), but this protection disappears at high tide.

Things to Do. Near low tide, walk across the gravel bar to Minister Island (now owned by the province), to Covenhoven, the magnificent estate of Sir William Van Horne, builder of the Canadian Pacific railway from Montreal to Vancouver. **Caution:** The bar is exposed about two hours before low tide, but don't cut it close. People have lost their lives here in the rapidly rising Passamaquoddy tides.

ST. ANDREWS ★★★★★ ☐3

Canadian Charts: 4331, **4332**; U.S. Chart: 13328

Tidal Range: *Mean* 19.6 feet; *Large* 27.2 feet

St. Andrews-by-the-Sea is a pleasant resort town at the southern end of the peninsula between Passamaquoddy Bay and the entrance to the St. Croix River. It is the largest Canadian settlement in Passamaquoddy Bay, and a convenient port of entry.

Port St. Andrews is relatively easy to enter, and partially protected by Navy Island. The enormous town wharf provides access to the heart of the town, with a variety of restaurants and other services. On top of the hill looms the great old Algonquin Hotel.

The wide streets and handsome houses of St. Andrews may remind you of the Maine town of Castine—not surprising since it was founded in 1783 by British loyalists from Castine who moved their houses here by barge.

Approaches. *From the South.* Leaving Eastport for St. Andrews through Western Passage, time your departure to avoid maximum turbulence in Old Sow, the world's largest whirlpool, at the southern tip of Deer Island. Old Sow is most active during flood tide, about three hours before high (see Western Passage, page 356). As you approach St. Andrews, some of the buildings can be seen, partially obscured by Navy Island, and the long red roof of the Algonquin Hotel emerges above the trees. Although the port can be entered from either side of Navy Island, the eastern approach is deeper and preferable.

The southeastern tip of Navy Island is a sand bluff off which the dangers are marked by spar buoy "SX1." Pick up green bell "SX3" off the eastern entrance, then follow the series of channel buoys through the flats into the harbor. It is almost a straight channel.

The CPR wharf at North Point no longer exists. Leave to starboard the flashing red light on a skeleton tower (between buoys "SX10" and "SX11") marking the end of the former wharf. Government Wharf, shown on the chart, is also called Market Wharf.

Western Channel is well marked but narrow. Avoid it near low tide.

From the North. Approaching St. Andrews from the north, or leaving St. Andrews for Passamaquoddy Bay, be sure to identify the two red marks at the end of Tongue Shoal, which extends for an improbable distance from the mainland. Pass east of Tongue Shoal.

Anchorages, Moorings. Most convenient is the float moored in deep water near the St. Andrews Yacht Club, southeast of Government Wharf. The float will normally handle four boats. Another possibility is to anchor in 8 to 14 feet at low, south of the end of the wharf. The current runs strong through the harbor, flooding west and ebbing east; you will need lots of scope.

Boats often lie alongside the floats on the east side of Government Wharf, although this is intended to be for short-term use only.

You can also tie up to the face of the wharf or the side, or perhaps to a boat already secured alongside. You may see small yachts moor to an anchored pile driver, and other imaginative solutions. The mooring area on the Navy Island side, opposite the wharf, is quite shoal.

The harbor is well protected by the flats surrounding Navy Island. These are covered, however, as the tide rises, and within 1½ hours of high, most of the protection is under water.

Getting Ashore. Row around the eastern end of Government Wharf to the landing floats and ramp.

St. Andrews is a port of entry, and Customs is right at the head of Government Wharf, through a side entry to the post office building. Office hours are 9 A.M. to 5 P.M. weekdays (tel. 529-3198). If you come in after hours or on a weekend, call St. Stephen (466-2363). (See "Entering Canada" for more details.)

For the Boat. There is a pay phone on Government Wharf, and water is available at the floats. Ice can be bought at the Save-Easy supermarket, a block away. Walk left from the head of the Wharf to Blue Peter Books, which sells charts (529-4466).

St. Andrews Yacht Club. The club has a small house not far east of Government Wharf, a hundred yards from the water at low tide. There are no facilities for visiting yachtsmen, but you will find some kindred spirits there. They graciously provide the guest mooring float.

For the Crew. The Tourist Bureau (with restrooms) is at the head of the wharf. Pick up a town map. Everything you need is within a short walk. The Save-Easy supermarket is only a block away to the right. A beauty shop and laundromat are in the same direction. Across the street is a drugstore, and walking left will bring you to the liquor store, and bike rentals.

There are several places to eat in town, including a takeout at the end of Government Wharf. For a good dinner try L'Europe (tel. 529-3818), and for a fabulous Sunday brunch, walk up the hill to the Algonquin Hotel (tel. 529-8823). Robicheau's Fish Market is .7 mile east, near North Point.

For a taxi, call 529-3371.

Things to Do. Browse through the town's china and woolen stores and craft shops. Of special quality are the woolens, tweeds, and hand-knit sweaters at Cottage Craft, in the red building opposite the Tourist Bureau. It's an invigorating walk to the great five-story pile of the Algonquin Hotel, at the top of the hill. Historical plaques show where the Loyalists landed, and the old Loyalists Cemetery still guards their graves.

Walk half a mile west along the waterfront to the Blockhouse, with a pleasant little park and three 18-pounders still commanding the harbor. This is the sole survivor of the 12 blockhouses built to defend New Brunswick during the War of 1812 between the United States and Britain. Don't forget to check the machicolations.

St. Andrews is unique in Canada because of the high proportion of buildings more than 100 years old. Most of these attractive old structures are well maintained, and many are listed in the *Walking Guide for Historic St. Andrews*, available at the Tourist Bureau.

A walk of 1.8 miles to the west, or a short cab ride, will take you to Huntsman Marine Centre in Brandy Cove (tel. 529-8895), where you can watch seals being fed twice a day, or dabble in a touch-tank to pick up starfish, sea cucumbers, and other marine creatures in your own hands.

ST. CROIX RIVER, CALAIS, and ST. STEPHEN

Canadian Chart: 4331; U.S. Chart: **13328** and **Inset**

Tidal Range: *Mean* 20 feet; *Spring* 22.8 feet

The St. Croix River, at the northwest corner of Passamaquoddy Bay, marks the boundary between the United States and Canada. The lower section of the river, from St. Andrews northward, is deep and almost a mile wide, more like a bay than a river, and with good sailing. Currents in this part of the river run about two knots.

The shores of the river are relatively low and mostly wooded, with occasional houses and large meadows. Hills and mountains inland frame the peaceful scene. Visible in the distance upriver is the big, dark pyramid of Devils Head, where the river narrows and turns westward, forming part of the cross for which it was named.

Don't be lulled by this broad and peaceful river and forget the shoals south of St. Croix Island. The first European settlement in the New World was on this island, where Sieur de Monts, Samuel de Champlain, and 79 other Frenchmen landed in 1604. It was an unusually severe winter, and by the time the supply ship arrived in June, two months late, 35 of the Frenchmen had died of scurvy. The settlement was abandoned, and the French retreated to Port Royal, Nova Scotia. The five-acre island is now an international park.

Among its attractions are an inviting beach on the southeastern end, a freshwater spring, and clumps of trees. On top of a sandy bluff is a grassy plateau and room for an acre or two of farm. Right in the middle of the river, the island was relatively safe from Indians, and a cannon at the south end commanded the approaches. It was more extensive in Champlain's day. His men cut trees to build their fort and houses, and subsequent erosion washed away much of the original island, creating today's shoals.

Opposite Devils Head, you may see a large freighter tied up at the Sand Point Marine Terminal loading lumber and potatoes. Devils Head is high and wooded and sometimes creates downdrafts dangerous to small craft.

From Devils Head, the river runs west about six miles to the International Bridge linking Calais (United States) and St. Stephen (Canada). Both towns are ports of entry. This section of the river should be navigated on a rising tide. Above Spruce Point the river is narrow and winding, entering a channel that was dredged but is not maintained. The current runs three to four knots. At The Narrows, near Whitlocks Mill, the buoys on the north side of the channel may be towed under at the strength of the tide.

It is possible to anchor on the west side of the channel, just above Whitlocks Mill Light, in 14 feet at low, with excellent protection.

The river west of Devils Head is for the most part lined with small camps, with occasional stretches of pristine riverbank. There remains a great deal of wildlife to enjoy, including herons, seals, loons, an occasional eagle, and a constant procession of ospreys carrying fish back to their nests.

The scene suddenly becomes suburban and then urban as you arrive at the head of navigation, Calais and St. Stephen. There are wharves and floats on both sides of the river. The wharves dry out at low tide, but it is possible to anchor in midriver during average tides if you draw no more than four feet. The mean tidal range in Calais is 20 feet, more than any other town in the continental U.S.

For most cruising boats there is not enough water to spend the night at Calais/St. Stephen, but it's possible to make a brief visit by powering upriver on a rising tide and coming down with the ebb. Allow an hour or so each way from Devils Head.

Calais and St. Stephen were once prosperous ports and lumber towns, their banks lined with wharves and sailing ships. Many of the handsome old houses and churches are still there for the finding.

Calais (rhymes with Alice). Calais is a small city, with supermarkets, drugstores, restaurants, a bank, and a movie theater, but no facilities for boats. There's a tourist information center above the landing, a duty-free shop next to the bridge, and the Calais Regional Hospital is in town (tel. 454-7521).

St. Stephen. St. Stephen is also convenient, with nearby restaurants, liquor store, and shops, a laundromat, supermarket, and pay phone.

Visit the Ganong Chocolate store (with a brown awning); they sell sinfully delicious chocolate by the piece or the pound. Ganong has been in business since 1809, and there are interesting displays of early candy making and equipment.

OAK BAY ★★★ No facilities
Canadian Chart: 4331; U.S. Chart: **13328**

Tidal Range: *Mean* 19.6 feet; *Large* 27.2 feet

Oak Bay lies north of the entrance to the narrow portion of the St. Croix River. The wide, encircling shore of this attractive bay has a number of small summer camps, and St. Croix Mountain forms a backdrop across the way.

Anchorage is good in much of the shallow bay, and this would be a convenient spot to wait out the tide in the St. Croix River.

Approaches. The approach from the southern portion of the St. Croix River is wide open and without dangers, except for possible strong downdrafts off Devils Head.

Anchorages, Moorings. Anchor in 9 to 12 feet along the western shore, south of the pointed little island that lies near the head of the bay. Holding ground is good, in mud bottom. You will be comfortable here in settled summer weather, but the bay is too wide to offer protection if it blows.

The reversing Cobscook Falls at the western entrance of Cobscook Bay. The ebb current forms an S-curve as it seethes northward around Mahar Point, then plunges southeastward around a nasty ledge. Falls Island is at the left. For a description of the Falls Island Passage, see page 354. (Christopher Ayres photo)

APPENDIX A Tidal Current Charts

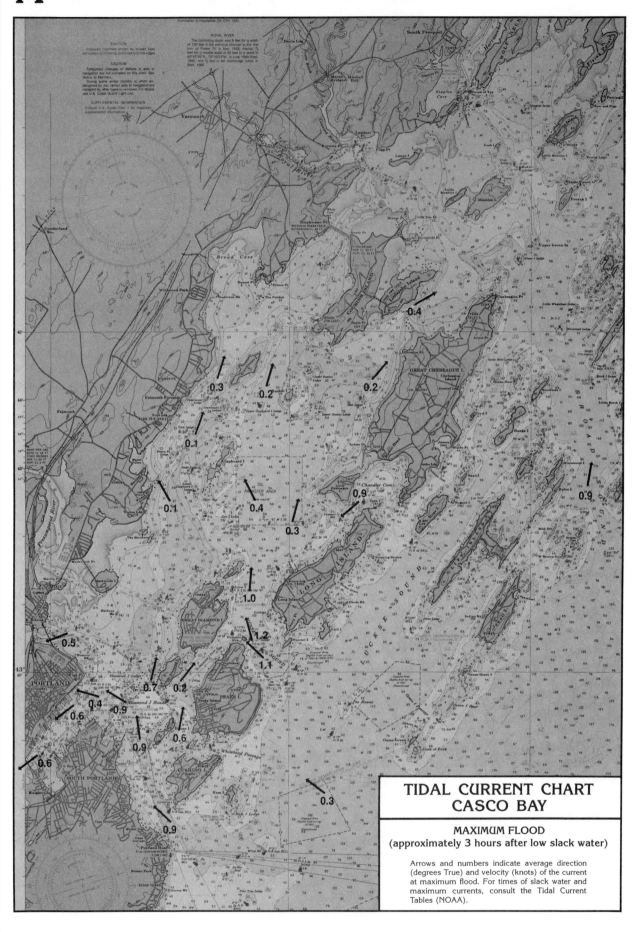

TIDAL CURRENT CHART
CASCO BAY

MAXIMUM FLOOD
(approximately 3 hours after low slack water)

Arrows and numbers indicate average direction (degrees True) and velocity (knots) of the current at maximum flood. For times of slack water and maximum currents, consult the Tidal Current Tables (NOAA).

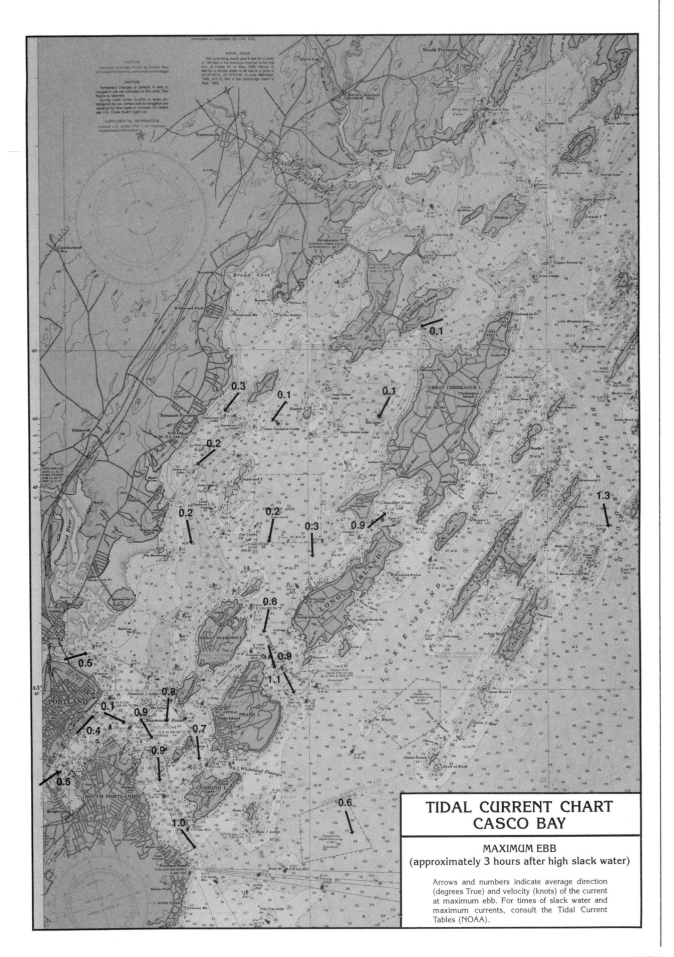

**TIDAL CURRENT CHART
CASCO BAY**

MAXIMUM EBB
(approximately 3 hours after high slack water)

Arrows and numbers indicate average direction
(degrees True) and velocity (knots) of the current
at maximum ebb. For times of slack water and
maximum currents, consult the Tidal Current
Tables (NOAA).

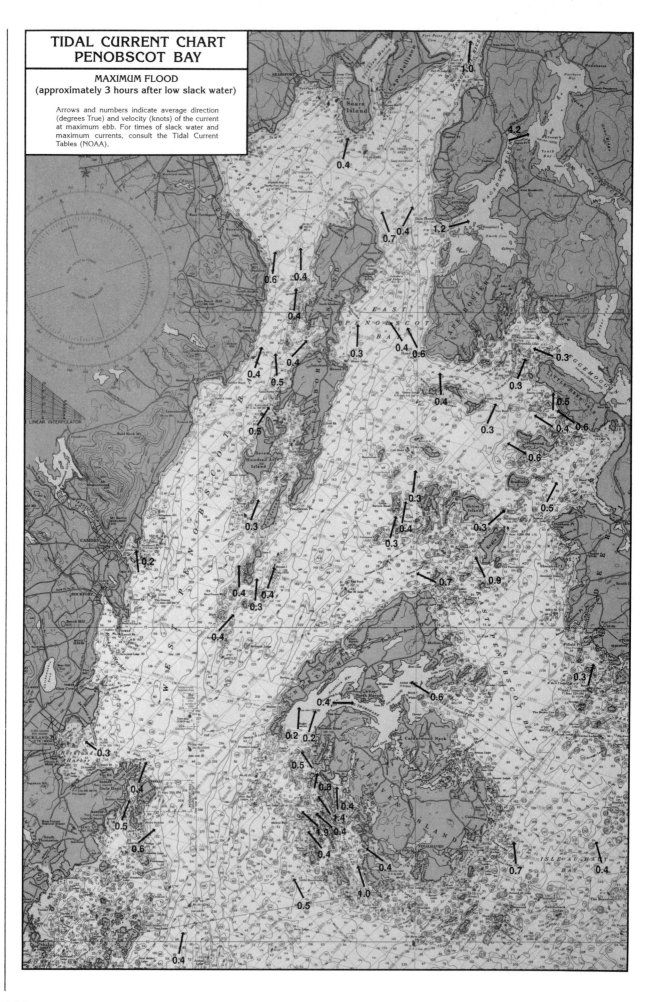

TIDAL CURRENT CHART
PENOBSCOT BAY

MAXIMUM FLOOD
(approximately 3 hours after low slack water)

Arrows and numbers indicate average direction (degrees True) and velocity (knots) of the current at maximum ebb. For times of slack water and maximum currents, consult the Tidal Current Tables (NOAA).

TIDAL CURRENT CHART
PENOBSCOT BAY

MAXIMUM EBB
(approximately 3 hours after high slack water)

Arrows and numbers indicate average direction (degrees True) and velocity (knots) of the current at maximum flood. For times of slack water and maximum currents, consult the Tidal Current Tables (NOAA).

APPENDIX B Ferries (Public and Private)

Islands Served	Terminal	Phone
Isles of Shoals (Star)	Portsmouth, NH	Isles of Shoals Steamship Company 603-431-5500
Peaks, Little Diamond, Great Diamond, Long, Cliff, Chebeague, Bailey	Portland	Casco Bay Lines 207-774-7871
Chebeague	Cousins Island, (Yarmouth)	Chebeague Transportation Company 207-846-3700
Monhegan	Boothbay Harbor New Harbor Port Clyde	*Balmy Days* 207-633-2284 *Hardy* 207-677-2026 *Laura B.* (Monhegan Boat) 207-372-8848
North Haven	Rockland	Maine State Ferry Service 1-800-521-3939 (Maine) 207-596-2202 (outside Maine)
Vinalhaven	Rockland	Maine State Ferry Service (see North Haven)
Matinicus	Rockland (once a month) Rockland	Maine State Ferry Service (see North Haven) Offshore Freight and Passenger Company (*Mary and Donna*) 207-366-3700 (days) 207-366-3926 (nights)
Islesboro	Lincolnville Beach	Maine State Ferry Service (see North Haven)
Isle au Haut	Stonington	Isle au Haut Company 207-367-5193
Swan's, Frenchboro (Long Island)	Bass Harbor	Maine State Ferry Service (see North Haven)
Cranberry Islands	Northeast Harbor	Beal and Bunker 207-244-3575 MDI Water Taxi 207-244-7312 Water Taxi (*Delight*) 207-244-5724

Canadian Ferries

Grand Manan	Blacks Harbour (New Brunswick)	Coastal Transport Ltd. 506-662-3606
Campobello-Deer Island		East Coast Ferries, Ltd. 1-800-561-0123*

International Ferries

Eastport-Deer Island		East Coast Ferries, Ltd. 1-800-561-0123*
Yarmouth, Nova Scotia	Portland	Prince of Fundy Cruises, Ltd. (*Scotia Prince*) 207-775-5616 (local) 1-800-482-0955 (within Maine) 1-800-341-7540 (U.S.A.)
Yarmouth, Nova Scotia	Bar Harbor	Marine Atlantic (*Bluenose*) 207-288-3395 (local) 1-800-432-7344 (within Maine) 1-800-341-7981 (U.S.A.)

*New Brunswick Tourist Information   1-800-561-0123 (United States and Canada)
1-800-442-4442 (within New Brunswick)

INDEX

(Principal entries are indicated in **bold type**)

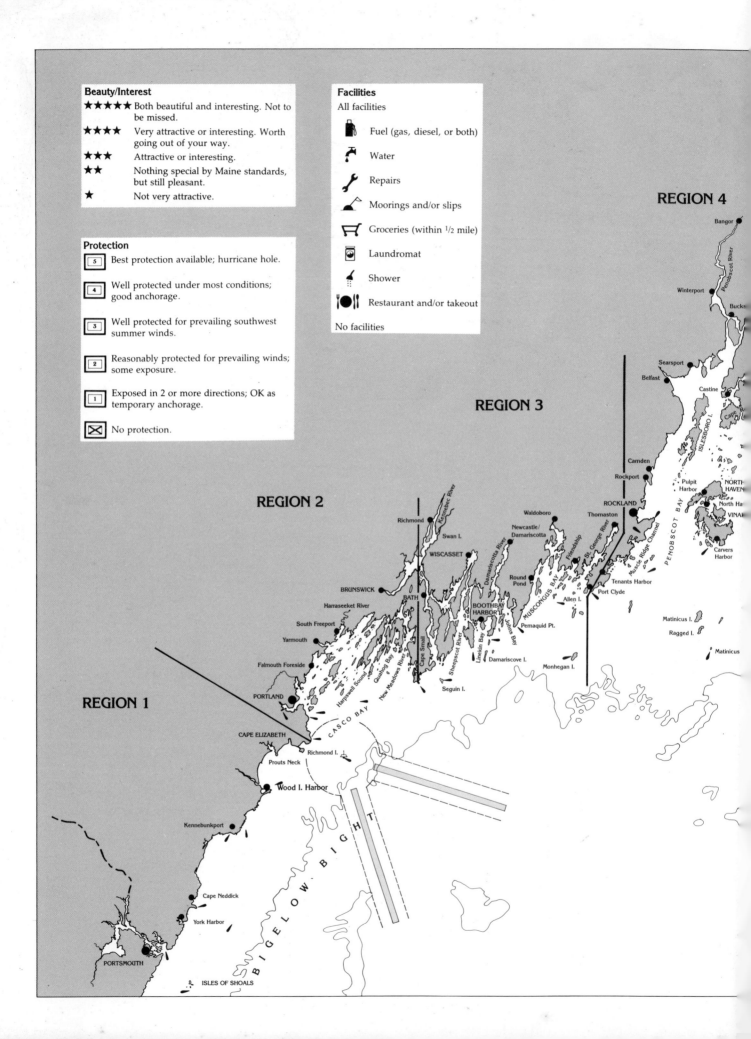

Beauty/Interest

★★★★★ Both beautiful and interesting. Not to be missed.

★★★★ Very attractive or interesting. Worth going out of your way.

★★★ Attractive or interesting.

★★ Nothing special by Maine standards, but still pleasant.

★ Not very attractive.

Protection

[5] Best protection available; hurricane hole.

[4] Well protected under most conditions; good anchorage.

[3] Well protected for prevailing southwest summer winds.

[2] Reasonably protected for prevailing winds; some exposure.

[1] Exposed in 2 or more directions; OK as temporary anchorage.

[⊠] No protection.

Facilities

All facilities

Fuel (gas, diesel, or both)

Water

Repairs

Moorings and/or slips

Groceries (within ½ mile)

Laundromat

Shower

Restaurant and/or takeout

No facilities

REGION 4

REGION 3

REGION 2

REGION 1

Bangor

Winterport

Bucks

Searsport

Belfast

Castine

ISLESBORO I.

Camden

Rockport

Pulpit
Harbor

NORTH
HAVEN

ROCKLAND

North Ha

VINAL

Waldoboro

Thomaston

Richmond

Kennebec River

Swan I.

WISCASSET

Newcastle/
Damariscotta

Damariscotta River

Friendship

St. George River

Muscle Ridge Channel

PENOBSCOT BAY

Carvers
Harbor

BRUNSWICK

Harraseeket River

BATH

Round
Pond

MUSCONGUS BAY

Tenants Harbor

Matinicus I.

South Freeport

BOOTHBAY
HARBOR

John Bay

Allen I.

Port Clyde

Ragged I.

Yarmouth

Sheepscot River

Linekin Bay

Pemaquid Pt.

Matinicus

Falmouth Foreside

Cape Small

Seguin I.

Damariscove I.

Monhegan I.

PORTLAND

Quahog Bay

New Meadows River

Harpswell Sound

CASCO BAY

CAPE ELIZABETH

Richmond I.

Prouts Neck

Wood I. Harbor

Kennebunkport

BIGELOW BIGHT

Cape Neddick

York Harbor

PORTSMOUTH

ISLES OF SHOALS